Benedetto Croce's

POETRY
AND
LITERATURE

*An Introduction to
Its Criticism and History*

*Translated with an Introduction and Notes
By Giovanni Gullace*

SOUTHERN ILLINOIS UNIVERSITY PRESS
Carbondale and Edwardsville

Benedetto Croce's Poetry and Literature was originally published as *La Poesia* (Bari: Giuseppe Laterza and Sons, 1936). The present translation is based on the 6th edition (1963).

Library of Congress Cataloging in Publication Data

Croce, Benedetto, 1866–1952.
   Benedetto Croce's Poetry and literature.

   Translation of La poesia.
   Bibliography: p.
   Includes index.
   1. Poetry. 2. Literature. I. Gullace, Giovanni.
II. Title.
PN1035.C713 1981   801'.951   80–19511
ISBN 0–8093–0982–3

Contents

Translator's Preface

Although the impact of Benedetto Croce's esthetic theory on the Anglo-Saxon world has been pervasive and of long standing, translations of his works on the subject still remain astonishingly skimpy. The only major book to appear in English was his *Aesthetic*, which, in its somewhat inaccurate translation, has been widely circulating since 1909. And it seems that all of the knowledge about Croce's esthetics in the English-speaking countries is generally based solely on that work, which represents no more than the first sketch of a thought that developed, clarified, and corrected itself through new literary experiences and more mature reflection. Croce, in fact, considered his *Aesthetic* "as a sort of program or outline to be completed . . . by means of a series of books, theoretical and historical, which should serve to define my philosophical position more precisely."[1]

If the *Aesthetic* (1902) marks the first major step in Croce's career as a philosopher of art, *La poesia* (1936) represents his full thought on the problem of man's creative activity. It condenses the basic theoretical discoveries of his previous speculation and, at the same time, opens up a broader perspective which sheds new light on the whole of Croce's work on esthetics, literature, and criticism. But of his numerous writings in these areas, which appeared after the *Aesthetic*, only a few pieces were published in English;[2] and most of them, for one reason or another, passed almost unnoticed or at best attracted the attention of very few specialists and are now completely forgotten. The knowledge of Croce's esthetics in the English-speaking world remains, therefore, regrettably incomplete, and in most cases is derived from second-hand sources which have often corrupted its real meaning. By and large, the most genuine judgments or misjudgments of the doctrine have been based on the pronouncements contained in that early work: the sympathy from the New Critics, the attacks by the New Humanists, and the many remarks about Croce's esthetics found in books and articles had no other point of reference.

The lack of a full and direct familiarity with Croce's thought has caused general misunderstanding which still persists.[3] A major case in point is that of John Dewey, who, despite the many ideas he had in common with Croce, especially in the field of esthetics, showed a knowledge of Croce's philosophical position far removed from the true one. Croce's philosophy is not a philosophy of the abstract; it is not meant to go beyond the sphere of the activity of man: human action does not aim at something beyond the human. Croce felt no need to conduct any inquiry into the problem of *being*, to examine ontological questions. For him metaphysical speculation would result in a "theologizing philosophy." Yet Dewey mistook him for one of those abstract Hegelians having no touch with human reality.[4]

In the hope of filling a part of the gap concerning Croce's theory of art and literature, I have undertaken

1. *An Autobiography*, trans. R. G. Collingwood (Oxford: The Clarendon Press, 1927), p. 67.

2. See Gian N. G. Orsini, *Benedetto Croce: Philosopher of Art and Literary Critic* (Carbondale: Southern Illinois University Press, 1961), pp. 304–06; and Benedetto Croce, *Philosophy, Poetry, History: An Anthology of Essays*, trans. Cecil Sprigge (London: Oxford University Press, 1966), pp. 215–494.

3. See Frederic S. Simoni, "Benedetto Croce: A Case of International Misunderstanding," *Journal of Aesthetic and Art Criticism* 11 (1952):7–14.

4. See Croce, *Indagini su Hegel e schiarimenti filosofici*, pp. 291–92.

the difficult task of translating *La poesia* (in the words of G. N. G. Orsini, "Croce's work most urgently needed in English"),[5] so that a total and perhaps more precise view of the author can be offered to English-speaking readers. Those who approach this work (especially if they have never gone beyond the *Aesthetic*) will find in it a new Croce, with a fresher and broader vision of the problems on which he toiled most of his life, even if some of the principles enunciated at the beginning of his intellectual career stand substantially unchanged: *La poesia* represents a rigorous rethinking of his whole esthetic doctrine. Moreover, the perceptible tendency of modern criticism to go back to fundamental concepts of esthetics has been for me a concomitant reason for my endeavor.

This translation has been conducted on the sixth edition of *La poesia*, published in 1963. The original title of the work was altered in English in order to make it more suitable to, and more inclusive of, the subject matter. Since the subtitle of the original—"Introduction to the Criticism and History of Poetry and Literature"—indicates that the author's discussion is not limited to poetry, I have felt that the title *Poetry and Literature* better reflects the content of the work. Luigi Russo, in fact, correctly hinted that the book should have been entitled *La letteratura* rather than *La poesia*.[6]

The rendering of Croce into English is, indeed, a great challenge even for the most highly skilled translator. In the course of my enterprise (the second of this kind) I came to realize more and more that, in order to appreciate fully the style of a writer, one must undergo the experience of rendering his work into another language! The problem of translation is a problem of linguistic and conceptual equivalence between two cultures, of equivalence between two different habits of thinking and of expressing ideas and images. Where this equivalence does not exist, it must be created. Such a procedure requires complete mastery of the subject matter and of the two languages with which the translator must deal. Since the latter condition is not always present, the problem of the *belles infidèles* or of the *traduttore traditore* can seldom be entirely avoided, especially in works in which every nuance is important. There is, in fact, no translation which is fully satisfactory in all respects, for the possibilities of rendering an idea or an image into another language are so numerous that the choice is invariably difficult. The problem of "fidelity" raises two main questions for the translator: fidelity to the author's

thought and style, or fidelity to the particular nature of the new medium? Which should take precedence? Finding the point where the exigencies of the text and the peculiar character of the host language are respected and satisfied is sometimes as hard a task as that of the author himself; and the successful outcome of the work depends almost entirely on taste.

Croce's style, while discursive or explanatory in tone and lacking in lyrical flights, is complex, rich, full of asides, and sometimes a bit wordy. This makes it impossible to translate without a partial or total reconstruction of his circumlocutory sentences. A literal translation would be beyond understanding in English; it would be tortuous, twisted, almost painful. Some redundancies had to be partially removed in order to bring his thought to terms with the English language. I would have liked, in translating, to capture not only the meaning of his sentences but also the quality and even the idiosyncrasies of his style. To do so, however, was seldom possible without serious damage to the intelligibility of the text. Many rough spots had to be smoothed over in order to achieve the necessary clarity in English.

Croce is a philosopher and, at the same time, a man of letters. He loves the well constructed, complex, and nuanced sentence, although his expression always has a plain and unpretentious tone. As a result, it is difficult, in a translation, to do full justice to Croce the philosopher and writer, and to the English language as well. He himself wrote: "Literary prose, like any other form of literature, is elaborated so as to give it an esthetic character. And this presents an insurmountable obstacle to translation, similar to that of translating poetry. Plato and Augustine, Herodotus and Tacitus, Giordano Bruno and Montaigne are not, strictly speaking, translatable, for no language can render the color and the harmony, the sound and rhythm of the original."[7] The same can be said of Croce, who belongs to that category of thinkers and historians possessing a pronounced literary taste. And because of this literary taste, he cannot be fully rendered into another language. While most of his works (philosophical, historical, and critical) read smoothly in the English translation, they do not always reflect the style of the original. In this, no fault can be justly placed on the translators who, faced with long, involved, and cumbersome sentences (however well constructed in Italian), had to reshape the text by pruning it radically.

I have been aware that in this game one of the parties is unavoidably going to be hurt. Most translators

5. *Bulletin of Croce Studies in the U.S.*, no. 2 (1960):7.

6. See *La critica letteraria contemporanea*, new ed. (Florence: Sansoni, 1967), p. 225.

7. P. 115 below.

have tended to hurt Croce more than their own language; I have endeavored to do the opposite, because what matters here is the author's thought, not the stylistic elegance of the new medium. The foreign trace can never be totally obliterated from any faithful translation. To do so, one would have to rethink and rewrite the work; but in such an instance, it would, to a large extent, become the translator's work. No translation can be a national literary momument unless it becomes one of the *belles infidèles*.

The volume *La poesia*, though classified as a philosophical essay, is in many respects also a literary essay, imaginatively written and not entirely free of rhetorical embellishments (strangely enough Croce, who for so long scorned what he called "literature," was one of its best practitioners!). What I have tried to do in this case is to translate Croce the philosopher of art, not the man of letters. Wherever I had to sacrifice one of them, I sacrificed the man of letters. Between the letter and the spirit, I chose to be faithful to the spirit, and to remain as close to the letter as possible, or as close as the English language would allow without excessive strain. Too many decisions had to be made concerning words and expressions which have no equivalent whatever in English; for these I shall take full responsibility. I hope, however, that I have not betrayed the text. Treason is a voluntary act, whereas any infidelity here should be simply considered the result of bad judgment, for which I apologize.

Croce's book is divided into two parts: the *text* and the *postscripts* (or critical notes). The latter are a bit longer than the text itself; they must be considered, as Croce indicated in the foreword of the book, "as a relaxed conversation after the tension of the theoretical exposition"; such an extensive conversation dwells "on some particular points in an effort to document, specify, and exemplify them." Croce felt that "this part may be useful to scholars" and, therefore, he decided to add it. And I may say that it is useful, indeed, and almost an integral part of the book. The author, in fact, insisted that the postscripts not be separated from the text or eliminated even in part. The added elucidations and illustrative material they contain are of great interest to all students of literary theory and criticism.

In the original Italian each postscript refers to a page of the text where a particular idea was mentioned or dealt with. Since in this translation both text and postscripts are run together in double column, the subheadings of the postscripts and the page numbers referring to the text were no longer necessary and were, therefore, eliminated. As an assist to the bilingual reader or those already familiar with the original

text, I have maintained the order of the postscripts established by the sixth edition of *La poesia* rather than effecting a strict correlation of the postscripts to the text in my translation. Both text and postscripts have been annotated in order to make them thoroughly intelligible to those English-speaking readers who may not be familiar with Italian culture. In my notes I generally took little or nothing for granted, and I may have gone beyond the limits; but I felt that in these cases the word is *melius abundare quam deficere*. One of my major concerns was to trace sources of quotations (which Croce not always discloses) and identify lesser-known writers and book titles, especially Italian, recurring in the book.

Quotations in Latin have been translated into English and follow in brackets the original in both text and postscripts. The translations in brackets following modern-language phrases or passages were made directly from the original; the few following in parentheses, however, were made from Croce's own rendition into Italian. Quotations in French have not been translated since it is assumed that most readers are able to understand the original. As for English authors, whom Croce quotes in his own translation, I used the original, disregarding his translation. The English version of verses from modern languages is simply meant to give the literal meaning and makes no pretense of accurately rendering the quality of the original.

It must be further noted that all words or phrases in brackets, when not my translations, are my own additions, throughout the text and the postscripts. Moreover, the titles of Croce's works occurring in this book are given in English whenever an English translation exists, and the page numbers refer to the English edition. The Italian title is, of course, given only for works which have never been translated into English. In my Introduction, however, *Poesia e non poesia* was consistently cited in its original title, since its infelicitous English title (*European Literature of the Nineteenth Century*) does not properly reflect the intent and the substance of the book. I must point out, finally, that all of Croce's books cited in Italian throughout the present work, unless otherwise indicated, are published by Giuseppe Laterza and Sons of Bari. There was, therefore, no need to repeat this information in every instance.

Quod potui, feci, faciant meliora valentes!

GIOVANNI GULLACE

Binghamton, New York
6 June 1980

Translator's Acknowledgments

Without the assistance of my wife, who read and reread the manuscript and took care of the proofs, and of my daughter, Gina, who went over the work in its final stage, this project would have never been carried out. Thanks are due to my colleague and friend, Carrol Coates, for reading part of the proofs. For any errors (except typographical) I take full responsibility. A word of gratitude must also be extended to Professor Raffaello Franchini, of the University of Naples, for suggesting the present translation, and to Dr. Alda Croce, daughter of the philosopher, for authorization to undertake the work.

Translator's Introduction

1. One or Four Crocean Esthetics?

Readers who did not follow closely Croce's intellectual career would perhaps find it difficult to appreciate fully the importance of *La poesia*, unless they are brought up to date concerning the author's thought as it evolved up to the time of the publication of the work. This introduction, addressed mainly to such readers, is meant to provide a broad outline of the major steps through which Croce's esthetic theory unfolded, of the problems it raised, and of the contribution *La poesia* represents in the total picture of the theory.

No serious system of ideas or theoretical doctrine in any field of intellectual endeavor has ever come into being fully developed in all its parts and in all its possibilities. Every conception, however illuminating and well founded, must always struggle its way through to maturity. Croce's theory of art is no exception. Students of his philosophy speak of a first, a second, a third, and even a fourth Crocean esthetics (or phases of it). "The first esthetics," wrote Luigi Russo, "is that of 1900, the *Tesi fondamentali;*[1] the second is that of the *Breviary of Aesthetics* of 1912,[2] to which the *Nuovi saggi*

d'estetica of 1920 must be attached;[3] the third is the *Aesthetica in nuce* written in 1928,[4] to which various pieces of research collected in *Ultimi saggi* (1935) are related;[5] the fourth is the one having as its central volume *La poesia*, to which essays of these last years and the years to come are probably associated."[6] Croce himself, in a note added to the end of his essay "Pure Intuition and the Lyrical Character of Art," stated: "This is the first integration of my *Aesthetic* of 1900; a second integration is found in my essay of 1918, 'The Character of Totality of Artistic Expression' (now in *Nuovi saggi d'estetica*), a third in the book *La poesia* (1936), in which the distinction between art and literature is more precisely indicated. I use the term "integration" because in none of these further developments have I ever felt the need to abandon or change the principles which I had already set forth; I needed only to go deeper and expand them."[7] And years later,

---

1. *Fundamental Propositions of an Esthetics as Science of Expression and General Linguistic.* This work, as Croce states in the preface to his *Aesthetic,* "was read at the Accademia Pontaniana of Naples during the sessions of February 18 and May 6, 1900, and printed in vol. 30 of its *Proceedings.*" The author, then, reworked the text, amplifying it and rearranging the sequence to make the exposition plainer and easier. In this second version it constitutes the theoretical part of his *Aesthetic* (pt. 1), published in 1902. As for the historical part of the volume (pt. 2), only five chapters appeared in the Neapolitan review *Flegrea* (April 1901), under the title "Giambattista Vico: First Discoverer of Esthetic Science," and were then reworked and "brought into harmony with the rest" in the final arrangement of the 1902 work, *Aesthetic as Science of Expression and General Linguistic.*

2. *Breviario d'estetica,* written for the Rice Institute. The English

translation by D. Ainslie was published in *The Book of the Opening of the Rice Institute* (Houston, Texas, 1912), vol. 2, pp. 450–517; republished as *The Essence of Aesthetic* (London: Heinemann, 1921).

3. *New Essays of Esthetics,* which contains major developments of Croce's theory.

4. This constitutes, in the translation of R. G. Collingwood, the entry "Aesthetics" in the fourteenth edition of the *Encyclopaedia Britannica* (1929). The original was collected in *Ultimi saggi* (1935).

5. *Last Essays,* containing an entire section (pp. 3–209) devoted to esthetic problems from the theoretical and historical point of view. It includes the "Difesa della poesia," a lecture given at Oxford on October 17, 1933.

6. *La critica letteraria contemporanea,* nuova edizione (Florence: Sansoni, 1967), p. 212.

7. "Pure Intuition and the Lyrical Character of Art," a lecture given at Heidelberg in 1908; see *Problemi d'estetica e contributi alla storia dell'estetica italiana* (3d ed., 1939, pp. 3–30), originally published in 1910 as a 500-page volume containing a large number of writings complementing his *Aesthetic,* with particular reference to the problem of literary criticism; some additions were made in subsequent editions, but several questions dealt with in the volume received, as the author indi-

aware that critics had spoken of a second and third form of his esthetics, he emphasized that in reality all this amounted simply to a constant progression and enrichment of his thought, "which would be impossible to divide into sections, designated as first, second, and third Esthetics."[8]

Despite these explicit statements, seemingly defensive in character, students of Croce's thought have not been altogether convinced that he did not deviate from the path taken in the first formulation of his theory. The problem raised at each step in the unfolding of his thought had been whether he retained or reversed his previous positions. The question still hanging in the mind of some interpreters is whether there are four *different* Crocean esthetics or four *phases* of the same esthetics in its logical process of growth. Giovanni Gentile, commenting in 1918 on two new essays by Croce, "The Character of Totality of Artistic Expression" and "L'arte come creazione e la creazione come fare," (Art as creation and creation as spiritual activity), both collected in *Nuovi saggi d'estetica*, pointed out "a new attitude of his [Croce's] esthetic theory, of his criticism, and of the whole of his philosophical doctrine."[9] Adriano Tilgher spoke of three different esthetic doctrines in Croce, observing that with the theory of *totality* "we are a long way from the conception of art as knowledge of the individual";[10] G. A. Borgese stated, in reference to Croce's concept of totality, that "the new wine has burst the old bottle";[11] Alfredo Gargiulo found *La poesia* to be in contradiction with what Croce had maintained in the past.[12]

Other students of Croce, however, took an opposite view, closely in line with Croce's own assessment of his work. Luigi Russo, though distinguishing four Crocean esthetics, saw in the author's earliest essays the theorist and the literary critic of the mature years, and for that matter of Croce's entire intellectual career: "for one must admit," Russo wrote, "that in the infancy of our mind is traced first in mysterious lines and later in ever clearer letters what the course of our destiny will be, what the logical history of our mental life."[13] In

emphasizing that Croce's first writings contain the whole of Croce, Russo was probably aiming at dispelling the frequent claims concerning Gentile's influence on the author of the "Philosophy of the Spirit." All these conflicting statements are by no means unfounded or totally contrary to fact. In some respects Croce indeed remained faithful, throughout his life, to certain principles enunciated at the very beginning of his intellectual career; such is, for example, the notion of identity between intuition and expression. But, on the other hand, there is no doubt that, along the way, he found it necessary to correct himself; and this process of "correction" caused his unfolding thought to deviate from its original course, so much so that he appeared to be reversing himself. Even if Croce's thought developed, expanded, and modified itself within the perimeter of his earliest assumptions, at times the departures are too sharp not to be noticed. Croce's philosophical vocation revealed itself a bit late in his life. He made the full discovery of Hegel after he had written his *Aesthetic*, and the impact of the discovery led him to revise his views. He strove to get as close as possible to an idealistic conception of philosophy as absolute subjectivism, in which everything is resolved into the indivisible unity of the Ego. His philosophy of art underwent profound changes, too, under the influence of a more mature philosophical reflection and a wider literary experience. His *Aesthetic* has the defects of the first step in a philosophical career. John Dewey wrote his *Art as Experience* toward the end of his career, after he had settled all other philosophical issues. Croce, having treated the problem of art at the beginning, was bound to modify his views according to his ever-new findings. Thus, his final doctrine generally appears extensively altered. The significance of *La poesia* lies in the fact that it shows the long distance traveled from the *Aesthetic*. While this first book is more controversial than systematic, and the *Breviary of Aesthetics* a romantic-idealistic systematization, *La poesia*, which summarizes Croce's mature thought, is a restatement broader in scope and extremely close to the classical and cathartic ideal of art.

Whatever the case, the following pages make no pretense of solving any controversial problem; they are meant simply to point out the main questions raised by critics as Croce's theory advanced to its final stage and to provide the context in which those questions were raised. In speaking of Croce's esthetics, it is impossible to avoid frequent references to Gentile, since the respective philosophical doctrines of the two men grew in friendly polemics with each other. Gentile's views may, therefore, throw some light on Croce's

cated in 1939, "a better development and a more complete form in my *Nuovi saggi d'estetica* (2d ed., 1926) and, particularly, in the book *La poesia* (2d ed., 1937)." The date given for "The Character of Totality of Artistic Expression" in *Nuovi saggi d'estetica* is 1917; an English translation of this essay was published in the *English Review* (June 1918).

8. *Indagini su Hegel e schiarimenti filosofici* (1952), p. 225: "Stato degli studi estetici in Italia."

9. *Frammenti d'estetica e letteratura* (Lanciano: Carabba, 1921), p. 173.

10. *Estetica: teoria generale dell'attività artistica* (Rome: Libreria di scienze e lettere, 1931), pp. 18–19.

11. *Poetica dell'unità* (Milan, 1934), p. xxiv.

12. "Crisi di un'estetica," in *Scritti di estetica* (Florence: Le Monnier, 1952), pp. 302–16 (first published in *Nuova antologia*, 1 May 1936).

13. *La critica letteraria contemporanea*, p. 95.

strong points and on his weak ones as well. The comparison of ideas and any reference to the relationship between Croce and Gentile, which are occasionally made in the course of this presentation, should in no way be interpreted as attempts to establish who of the two was greater or who was the leading light in their efforts to renovate Italian culture and free it completely of the prevalent positivistic tendencies of the time, but should be viewed merely as devices for a better understanding of their respective positions, particularly the problems arising from Croce's esthetic theory.

2. *Croce's Early Life and Works*

Benedetto Croce's external biography offers little of interest for the general reader; like most philosophers he lived mainly an inward existence whose major events were simply the publications of his books. Born in 1866 at Pescasseroli in the province of Aquila (Abruzzi) of a well-to-do family, Croce was educated in Naples at a private Catholic school. His education in a Catholic atmosphere, however, failed to develop in him any particular religious vocation or interest. From his early age he showed a great love for books and an inexhaustible desire for learning. What he cherished most were literature and history, and his attachment to these disciplines prevailed throughout his life, surviving the speculative interests which arose in him during his mature years. Young Croce's love for books showed him to be more of a potential scholar and bibliophile than a philosopher. As a student at the *liceo* he proved to be laborious, methodical, well disciplined, and tenacious in all of his intellectual endeavors. He read and reread the works of De Sanctis and Carducci;[14] but, although he drew from the former some guiding principles for literary criticism, he remained for the time almost indifferent to De Sanctis' "well-balanced and exquisite moral character," preferring "the violent and combative attitude of Carducci."[15]

In 1883 a family tragedy deeply upset his adolescent years. While the Croces were vacationing on the island of Ischia, his parents and his only sister were killed in an earthquake, and he himself remained buried under the ruins for several hours. Following this tragic event he and his brother Alfonso (who was absent at the time of the tragedy) were taken to Rome, to the house of a close relative, Silvio Spaventa, a prominent patriot and politician and the brother of the Hegelian philosopher Bertrando Spaventa. The

change did not lessen the shattering effects of the domestic disaster; for some time, in fact, it exacerbated Croce's distress, the more so since the new social and intellectual environment was so far removed from the one in which he had grown up that it was difficult for him to adjust easily. His family had been conservative, faithful to the Bourbons, alien to political meddling (his father had been a landowner concerned only with the good administration of the family property), and cool or even hostile to the figures of the Risorgimento; in addition, they had been very much attached to the church. The home of Silvio Spaventa was, on the contrary, frequented by outstanding politicians, professors, and journalists, all public-minded people and staunch defenders of the newly constituted state of Italy, in whose affairs they took an active part. But all their exciting debates concerning politics, science, law, did not pull young Croce out of his depressed mental state. He described these years in his *Autobiography* as the darkest and most bitter.[16] Silvio Spaventa envisioned for him a diplomatic career and had him enroll at the University of Rome to study law; but Croce felt no interest in the subject, and in fact seldom attended classes and never sat for the examination.[17] He preferred to shut himself up in libraries and pursue research on subjects of his own choice, with no definite goal and in a rather disorderly way, in an attempt to improve his mind.

The second year he decided to attend Antonio Labriola's lectures on the moral philosophy of Herbart at the university. He had already met Labriola at the home of the Spaventas and had developed a great admiration for his sparkling conversation, full of wit and "overflowing with original ideas."[18] Labriola's lectures gave Croce a new view of life. Having lost the guidance of religious doctrine, he had felt a danger of falling into materialistic, sensationalistic, and associationist theories which, in his estimation, were the negation of morality; Herbartian ethics "achieved for me," he wrote, "the restoration of the majesty of the ideal, the *ought to be* as opposed to the *is*."[19]

In 1886, without finishing his university studies, Croce left Rome and returned to Naples to establish himself permanently. The Neapolitan cultural atmosphere seemed to be more agreeable to his taste and he found himself almost happy in the new environment: "I had left behind me the bitterness and passion of the Rome political circles and entered a society of librarians, keepers of archives, scholars, antiquarians, and

---

14. Croce, *An Autobiography*, trans. R. G. Collingwood (Oxford: The Clarendon Press, 1927), p. 37.
   15. Ibid., p. 37.

16. Ibid., p. 39.
17. Ibid., p. 40.
18. Ibid., p. 41.
19. Ibid., p. 42.

such-like good, worthy, gentle souls . . . not much given to thinking."[20] No philosophical calling was yet in sight. Though he had worked in philosophy and read philosophical books, it had never occurred to him "that this spontaneous mental impulse might be pointing out the road on which I should put forth my best efforts and enjoy my purest pleasures and highest consolations."[21] He had been attracted to philosophy by the longing to assuage his misery and to give an orientation to his moral and intellectual life.[22] But once in Naples, he adapted himself to that erudite society, and his life was "wholly given up to antiquarian studies."[23] The philosophical questionings of his youth "had been driven into the dark recess of my spirit."[24] Occasional meetings with Labriola in Naples or in Rome would arouse in him momentary enthusiasm for Labriola's ideas; but nothing prevailed over his own scholarly vocation, and he spent several years in archival research concerning civic history and in publishing scholarly essays. He devoted himself almost entirely to his research, remaining completely indifferent to the burning social questions of the time. For a while he attended directly to the affairs related to his property, but he did so in a manner that would cause him the fewest headaches. Later he entrusted his affairs to somebody else so that he could devote himself more freely to his studies and research.

In order to move away from the narrowness of local history, which he soon began to feel, he decided to broaden his studies; he planned a national history since the Renaissance—a history conceived not as a chronicle of political events, but as a moral history, the history of sentiment and spiritual life. This would have required a thorough knowledge of the reciprocal influence between Italy and the other nations of Europe. Thus, as a first step, he undertook to study the influence of Spain on Italy through unknown literary documents that he began to unearth for the purpose. He soon realized, however, that he was filling his mind "with lifeless and disconnected facts at the expense of much toil and with no constructive result."[25]

His doubt as to the method to follow led him to the problem of the nature of history and knowledge. He read many Italian and German books on the philosophy and methodology of history, including Giambattista Vico's *New Science*. Since he had read De Sanctis during his *liceo* years and some German works on es-

thetics while attending Labriola's lectures in Rome, he had never altogether ceased to think about questions of esthetics; he therefore found it easy now "to connect the problem of history with the problem of art."[26]

In 1893, after much hesitation, he finally sketched out, under the influence of De Sanctis and Vico, his first speculative work, *La storia ridotta sotto il concetto generale dell'arte* (History subsumed under the general concept of art).[27] Although this marks the first step toward the construction of his esthetic theory, there is no indication that Croce would pursue further the ideas he set forth in his essay. Satisfied that he had clarified certain concepts to himself and thrown light on common misconceptions about the problem, "I plunged," he writes, "once more into working for my projected history,"[28] having now more or less set in order his logical and methodological principles. But even now, he remarks, "I did not regard philosophical speculation as a path opening before me."[29] In 1894, while working on the Spanish-Italian relations, by "another of these unforseen and irresistible impulses, or involuntary blazings-up of the mind,"[30] he wrote in a couple of weeks a short polemical essay, *La critica letteraria* (Literary criticism), following a friendly discussion he had with a professor of philology. The essay aroused several controversies which lasted for months. It was iconoclastic in character, showing the inconsistencies of the various approaches to literary criticism: "it was an act of personal liberation, not the first step in the career of a professional philosopher,"[31] for it did not arrive at a definition of criticism. Although in his previous work, *La storia ridotta sotto il concetto generale dell'arte*, Croce had for the moment established the relation between art and history, in *La critica letteraria* he was unable to make up his mind concerning the true method of literary criticism, limiting himself mainly to pointing out the confusion existing in that field.

As soon as the controversies had quieted down and Croce had taken up the thread of his historical research, Labriola suddenly came again to disrupt his mental habits and to give his thought a new direction. Labriola was now a Marxist neophyte who had devoted himself to the interpretation and spreading of Marx-

---

20. Ibid., p. 45.
21. Ibid., p. 44.
22. Ibid.
23. Ibid., p. 45.
24. Ibid., p. 46.
25. Ibid., p. 52.

26. Ibid., p. 53.
27. The work is now collected in *Primi saggi*.
28. *An Autobiography*, p. 54. Croce's erudite studies of the time were collected in *Primo passo*, *Iuvenilia*, *La rivoluzione napoletana del 1799*, *Aneddoti e profili settecenteschi*, *Curiosità storiche*, *I teatri di Napoli dal Rinascimento alla fine del secolo decimottavo*, *Saggi sulla letteratura italiana del Seicento*, *La Spagna nella vita italiana durante la Rinascenza*, *Storie e leggende napoletane*, and *Pagine sparse*.
29. Ibid.
30. Ibid., p. 55.
31. Ibid., p. 56.

ism. In April 1895 he sent Croce the first of his essays on the Marxist conception of history (more specifically the essay on the *Communist Manifesto*), urging him to devise some way of printing it. "I read and reread it," wrote Croce, "and again I felt my whole mind burst into flame."[32] He stopped his historical research and turned to the study of economics, completely new to him. His dormant interest in philosophy was thus revived, and through the author of *Das Kapital* he was brought back to philosophical problems, "especially to those of ethics and logic, but also to the general conception of the spirit and its various modes of operating."[33] His new thoughts and his studies of economics, however, were still directed toward history as their ultimate goal, for Croce did intend to return to his historical work, armed now with his knowledge of economics and historical materialism. The interest in Marxism awakened him to the so-called social question, and for a while "in the socialistic vision of the rebirth and redemption of mankind through labor and in labor, I seemed to breathe a new air of faith and hope."[34] An important factor in Croce's philosophical orientation was probably his relation with Gentile, which began a year later, and his gradual breaking away from Labriola, who had disapproved of some of the conclusions Croce was drawing from Marxism.

3. *Croce's Studies on Marxism and His Early Relation with Gentile*

Croce's relation with Giovanni Gentile began in 1896, when the latter was only twenty-one and still a student at the University of Pisa. At that time Croce, under the inspiration of Labriola, was already engaged in his Marxist studies.[35] The dialogue between the two men started with a friendly exchange of notes. Although still at the beginning of his intellectual career, Gentile (who was nine years Croce's junior) showed such an unusual philosophical perspicacity that he easily won Croce's friendship. Thus their first epistolary contacts soon developed into a true intellectual partnership which was to last about thirty years and to have a strong impact on Italian culture.

Their close association often raised the question of which of the two philosophers led the way in their common speculative efforts. Had Gentile more influence on Croce than Croce on Gentile? Claims and counterclaims have been made by students from both sides, especially after the bitter rift between the two men following the advent of Fascism. But, whatever the answer, no real purpose can be served by trying to determine what was given or taken by each man. The fact is that the contact with Gentile gave Croce a new and more philosophical outlook concerning intellectual problems. Gentile's deep philosophical interests contributed greatly to drawing Croce from literary and historical problems to more strictly philosophical ones and, most particularly, to the study of Hegel, whose thought helped him discover his own vocation. Croce, in fact, quickly realized that he was now "in far better intellectual company"[36] than he had been during his early Neapolitan days and that he had a new impulse to work on an idea he had entertained since his school years—that of writing an esthetics. Gentile's influence on Croce, while it often facilitated and enriched the latter's philosophical development, in no way altered the originality of his thought or changed its general direction. Despite the reciprocal mental stimulation, the two men stand as two distinct philosophical personalities, each so deeply rooted in his own individuality that no influence could change or modify his intellectual mold. "In our association" wrote Croce, "he neither yielded to me, nor I to him, the one thing that cannot be given up—one's temperament and mind."[37]

Edmondo Cione, in his book on Croce, sketches an interesting contrast between the two philosophers.[38] Croce, in his estimation, is a commonsense thinker who brings to a logical and lucid form all of his intellectual and practical experiences; he is not attracted to the heights; he treads on level ground slowly, method-

32. Ibid., pp. 56–57. Why and how Croce became suddenly interested in Marxism and historical materialism is told by himself in detail not only in his *Autobiography* (pp. 56–61) but also in "Come nacque e come morì il marxismo teorico in Italia (1895–1900)," an article written in 1937 and added to the sixth edition of Croce's *Materialismo storico ed economia marxistica* (1941), pp. 253–94.

33. Ibid., p. 58.

34. Ibid., pp. 59–60.

35. Antonio Labriola (1843–1904) systematized Marxist doctrine in Italy and became the leading authority on Marx's works. A pupil of the Hegelian Bertrando Spaventa, he soon turned against both Hegelian idealism and Spencerian positivism, the two philosophical deities dominant in his time. He became a Herbartian, holding to the belief that philosophy is not just abstract metaphysics nor the study of facts in their objective materiality. Later, impatient with the corruption of Italian politics, he moved from conservativism to radicalism and began to give courses at the University of Rome (where he taught from 1874 to the end of his life) on historical materialism and Marxism, expounding Marx's orthodox doctrine. He was a brilliant and influential teacher and made a great impact on Croce until the end of the century, when the increasing disagreement between them concerning Marxism turned Croce away from him. Labriola's major works on Marxism are *In memoria del Manifesto dei Comunisti*

(Rome: Loescher, 1895), *Del materialismo storico, delucidazione* preliminare (Rome: Loescher, 1896), *Discorrendo di socialismo e di filosofia, lettere a Georges Sorel* (Rome: Loescher, 1897).

36. *An Autobiography*, p. 62.

37. *Terze pagine sparse*, vol. 2, p. 88, from Croce's indirect answer to Ugo Spirito who, in an open letter to Benedetto Croce (*Giornale critico della filosofia italiana* 29 [1950]), pointed out Croce's debt to Gentile.

38. *Benedetto Croce ed il pensiero contemporaneo* (Milan: Longanesi, 1963), pp. 92–93.

ically, and untiringly. He is a thinking machine which produces clear and perfect thoughts, proceeding relentlessly with ready mind and unfaltering heart. Gentile, on the contrary, is genial and passionate, always aiming for the untouched peaks. In his thought breathes a powerful inspiration which is often lacking in Croce. But, while Croce's ideas mark advances in the history of culture, Gentile's ideas are fascinating paradoxes, unacceptable as definitive conclusions. They exercise a strong suggestion, they stimulate further research, they give the feeling of depth, but they are ultimately deceptive.

Despite these differences in temperament and intellectual inclinations, which often render fruitful collaboration impossible, Croce felt immediately a certain kinship with Gentile:

I was drawn to Gentile both by certain resemblances in our practical attitude and by a similarity of education and mental development; for he also had first tried himself in literary studies as a pupil of D'Ancona, and had trained himself in philological investigations. Like myself, he took and still takes great pleasure in work of this kind, which calls the mind to a determinate and concrete object—a task which cannot be entrusted to "hacks," but must be done by every competent scholar through his own efforts and for his own needs and purposes.[39]

The first influence on Croce was De Sanctis, whose books he had read at an early age; the second was Vico. Although by reading De Sanctis he had absorbed a great deal of Hegelian idealism, he turned against Hegel as soon as he tried to study the German philosopher in the works of Bertrando Spaventa, during the three years in Rome. Spaventa had come to philosophy from the church and from theology; his interpretation of Hegel was theological and abstract, centering mainly on the relation between being and knowing. Croce felt, in fact, that Hegel was too abstract, the exact opposite of De Sanctis, who was so full of concreteness and reality.[40] Consequently, he preferred the anti-Hegelian Labriola, who was a Herbartian and later a Marxist. Croce's state of mind, as reflected in his writings of the time, was that of "an idealist of De Sanctis' school in esthetics, a Herbartian in ethics and the general conception of values, an anti-Hegelian and antimetaphysician in the theory of history and the general conception of the world, a naturalist or intellectualist in the theory of knowledge."[41] But the growing rift with Labriola brought Croce closer and closer to Gentile, whose philosophical mind was now a sort of testing ground for Croce's own ideas. And his

dialogue with Gentile greatly contributed to orienting Croce toward the basic concepts of idealism.

From 1895 to about 1899, Croce devoted most of his attention to Marxism and historical materialism. His concern with these problems immediately attracted the young Gentile, from the very beginning of their friendship, to the debate aroused by Labriola's works. In 1896 Croce wrote his first two essays on the subject, "Sulla concezione materialistica della storia" (On the materialistic conception of history) and "Le teorie storiche del professor Loria" (The historical theories of Professor Loria), which he sent to Gentile for comments.[42] Gentile's perspicacious remarks did not fail to impress Croce, who wrote "[Your letter] aroused in me a sincere admiration; it showed me that you are fully possessed of the problem concerning historical materialism, that you have digested and absorbed Labriola's books, and that you formulate objections with a limpidity and exactness of expression really remarkable."[43] Gentile, in fact, had lost no time in studying the problem, and by the summer of 1897 had completed a solid essay, "Una critica del materialismo storico" (A criticism of historical materialism), which was published the following fall.[44]

Their interest in Marxism and historical materialism, however, was short-lived, and ended for both at about the same time, that is, in 1899, when their studies and discussions were collected and published, respectively, in Gentile's *La filosofia di Marx* and Croce's *Historical Materialism and the Economics of Karl Marx*.[45] Gentile's interest in Marxism at that time did not develop into a political faith; it remained as a purely speculative effort, its primary aim being simply to penetrate the system critically. In fact, he studied the metaphysical origins and implications of the Marxist doctrine with no particular interest in the socialist theory derived from it. Croce, on the contrary, more attentive to the socialist movement, studied with particular care the economic doctrine of Marx-

---

39. *An Autobiography*, p. 61.
40. See ibid., p. 87.
41. Ibid., p. 91.

42. "Sulla concezione materialistica della storia," paper read at the Accademia Pontaniana and then published in the *Proceedings* 26 (1896). See "Lettere di Benedetto Croce a Giovanni Gentile," *Giornale critico della filosofia italiana* 23 (1969):4–5. "Le teorie storiche del professor Loria" had appeared in French in *Le Devenir social* (November, 1896); see also *Giornale critico della filosofia italiana* 23 (1969):5–6. Achille Loria was a Marxist economist who enjoyed a considerable reputation and whose interpretation of Marxism was widely discussed.
43. See *Giovanni Gentile: lettere a Benedetto Croce* (Florence: Sansoni, 1972), vol. 1, pp. 17–28 (letter of January 17, 1897); and "Lettere di B. Croce a G. Gentile," *Giornale critico della filosofia italiana* 23 (1969):7.
44. *Studi storici* 6 (1897):372–423.
45. Gentile, *La filosofia di Marx* (Pisa: Spoerri, 1899); the work contains two studies: "Una critica del materialismo storico" and "La filosofia della prassi." Croce, *Materialismo storico ed economia marxistica* (Palermo: Sandron, 1900); the book contains seven essays, but others were added in subsequent editions.

ism, in an attempt to understand better history and the part economics plays in it (in his *Aesthetic* economics appears as one of the four categories of the Spirit). His work, like Gentile's, was colored by his preoccupation with the nature of history rather than with the practical problems of party politics. He saw Marxism from the point of view of its philosophical or scientific value, rather than its practical application. "To me," he wrote, "it was important above all for what it could contribute to a live and full conception of philosophy and to a better understanding of history."[46] But he added, "Historical materialism appeared to me doubly fallacious both as materialism and as a conception of the course of history according to a pre-established design, that is, as a variation of the Hegelian philosophy of history."[47] These ideas, expressed in his first piece on the subject, aroused a polemics between Croce and his former teacher Labriola, whose interests were mainly to adapt Marx's theories to the aims and needs of political action.

As a result, the political faith and passion with which Croce engaged in the study of Marxism could not last. It was undermined, he wrote, "by my own criticism of Marxism—a criticism the more damaging that it was meant for a defense and a restatement; . . . the passion burnt itself out because *natura tamen usque recurrit*, and mine was at bottom the nature of a student and thinker."[48] In a letter to Gentile (November 23, 1898), he had already written: "As for historical materialism, I must inform you that I no longer intend to concern myself with it. . . . From Marxism I have drawn what I needed. If I were oriented toward a political life, I would interest myself in the proletarian movement; but this would be perhaps premature in Italy."[49] The Marxist experience, however, was of great importance for him, since it gave him a more definite outlook on philosophical problems: "The excitement of those years bore good fruit in the form of a widened experience of human problems and a quickening of philosophical activity. From that time on, philosophy played an increasing part in my studies."[50] His gradual estrangement from Labriola and his correspondence with Gentile contributed to redirecting his studies. Gentile's strong philosophical orientation made Croce increasingly aware of some of his own philosophical deficiencies. In a letter of November 1898 he wrote to Gentile:

I told you that I was studying philosophy. Here is what it is all about. Up to now I concerned myself with philosophical questions only to satisfy an irresistible intellectual need, but somehow occasionally; *sicut canes ad Nili fontes bibentes et fugientes*. Now I would like to drink with ease. Therefore, I have worked till now so that I may have the necessary leisure for it. I will be able for one or more years to devote myself to philosophy only. I confess that I would like, among other things, to bring to completion a treatise on esthetics, and consequently I must delve more deeply into all philosophical questions which are related to esthetics, that is, into the whole of philosophy. I am doing this now, and perhaps in a few months we may talk about the results.[51]

His study of historical materialism and Marxist economics not only allowed him to gain a better insight into the nature of history, but it also helped him define the economic moment, so important in the development of his budding "Philosophy of the Spirit."

Croce's criticism of Marxism bears upon both its conception of history and its economic theories. Marx, in Croce's view, was neither an economist nor a philosopher, but was instead a vigorous revolutionary genius. His socialism did not spring from a philosophical or scientific concept, for he lacked an a priori theory to guide his action. His scientific theses concerning economics and history are completely invalid; they were an a posteriori attempt to justify his revolutionary movement. Historical materialism, conceived as a philosophy of history, that is, as a set of laws governing human events, was for Croce quite absurd, for in history there are no predetermined laws, but simply intuitions and facts whose connections can only be established a posteriori. He had already theorized in the previously mentioned *La storia ridotta sotto il concetto generale dell'arte* that history is related to art, not to science, for it represents the particular, individual fact, rather than general laws. From the philosophical point of view, historical materialism, as a law of history allowing us to predict the future course of events, would aggravate the errors of the old theological or metaphysical conceptions of history.

Croce shows that, according to Engels, dialectic is the rhythm of the development of things, that is, the inner law by which they evolve, and that this rhythm cannot be determined a priori by a metaphysical deduction; it can only be grasped a posteriori through repeated observations and verifications in the various fields of reality. As a result, it is impossible to give historical materialism a scientific character, for it lacks

46. *Materialismo storico ed economia marxistica*, 6th ed. (1968), p. 274.
47. Ibid., p. 275.
48. *An Autobiography*, p. 60. Latin quote is from Horace (*Epistles* 1. 10. 24): "Naturam expelles furca, tamen usque recurret" (You drive out nature with a fork, it will always come back running).
49. "Lettere di B. Croce a G. Gentile," *Giornale critico della filosofia italiana* 23 (1969):48–49.
50. *An Autobiography*, p. 60.

51. "Lettere di B. Croce a G. Gentile," *Giornale critico della filosofia italiana* 23 (1969):52.

the capacity to foresee the course of history. Therefore, it can lend no theoretical or scientific support to socialism. The only positive aspect of the so-called historical materialism was a practical one which concerned the field of historiography. It called the attention of historians, exclusively interested in ideological and philological interpretations, to the importance of economic factors in human affairs. While Labriola considered historical materialism to be a definitive philosophy of history, Croce saw it as a practical canon for the historiographer. To accept historical materialism as a philosophy of history would have meant for him to reduce history to the economic factors and to say with Marx that "it is not the consciousness of men that determines their being, but, on the contrary, it is their social being that determines their consciousness."[52]

As for Marxist economics, Croce denies it a scientific character, holding it to be a simple device (such as the theory equating the value of things to the amount of work required to produce them) to dramatize the conditions of the working class in a society dominated by private capital. Marx's theory was not the foundation of a new science of economics, for its concept of value was logically erroneous and even absurd. It was the result of a comparison between an abstract working class, taken as typical, and a capitalistic society. Furthermore, the fall of the rate of profits (as posited in the third volume of *Das Kapital*)—the great historical law which implied the automatic and imminent end of capitalism—rested, according to Croce, on a gross error by Marx concerning technical and economic phenomena, for it was neither a historical nor an abstract economic law. The value of Marxism was purely pragmatic, not scientific; from the scientific point of view it offered only a pseudoeconomics, a pseudophilosophy, and a pseudohistory.[53]

4. *Toward the Formulation of an Esthetics*

With the publication of the book on Marxism, the interest of Croce and Gentile in the subject came to an end. Croce said that he had put together all of his

articles on Marx as though "in a coffin." His attention had already shifted to the problem of esthetics, which was now his first priority. On January 15, 1899, in a letter to Gentile, he wrote: "My mind is now very far removed from our discussion on Marxism."[54] Their correspondence since the end of 1898 revolved in fact around the esthetic problem, which had been in Croce's thought since as far back as 1893, when he wrote his *La storia ridotta sotto il concetto generale dell'arte*. It is difficult, at this point, to determine which of the two fields of studies—Marxism and esthetics—had more sway on the further development of his thought. Was the "Philosophy of the Spirit" motivated by his aversion to historical materialism or by his interest in esthetics?

By all indications Croce's concern with the problem of art and history was not momentary or accidental; it continued to grow with his philosophy, thereby acquiring an increasing importance. It is thus impossible to separate in his thought the problem of art from that of history. With the triumph of positivism and naturalism and the consequent discredit of the theological and metaphysical conceptions of history, as well as the elimination of all absolutes from the empirical domain of facts, the old debate about the nature of history had been revived and had assumed a lasting interest in Croce's mind. What is history? Is it an art or a science? In his *La storia ridotta sotto il concetto generale dell'arte*, as Croce explained in a note added to the second edition of his *Logic* (1909), the main drive of his first "philosophical study" (1893) was, primarily, "to combat the attempt of the natural sciences to resolve history into their scheme"; then, "to assert the theoretical character and seriousness of art, which positivism, dominant at that time, considered as an object of pleasure"; finally, "to deny that historicity was a third form of the theoretical spirit, different from the esthetic form and the intellective form."[55] In short, Croce's aim was to subtract history from the domain of science into which positivism had drawn it, to affirm the theoretical character of art which positivism held to be simply a means for pleasure, and to fight the idea of a third level of mental activity (the historical level) different from the two recognized levels—the esthetic, productive of art, and the intellective, productive of science. Croce stresses that art is a form of knowledge, but that the knowledge obtained through art differs from the knowledge obtained through science. While art represents objects in their

52. See Erich Fromm, *Marx's Concept of Man* (New York: F. Ungar Publishing Co., 1969), p. 17.

53. For the strictly philosophical part, for the relationship of Marxism to Hegelianism, and for the metaphysical formation of Marx, Croce refers the reader to Gentile's *La filosofia di Marx* (Pisa: Spoerri, 1899): ". . . the subject has now been treated by Professor Giovanni Gentile, . . . and I refer the reader to his excellent work" (*Materialismo storico ed economia marxistica*, p. x). Gentile's book is aimed at examining Marx's philosophy of history, and dealing with Marx's metaphysics and its relation to Hegel's.

54. "Lettere di Benedetto Croce a Giovanni Gentile," *Giornale critico della filosofia italiana* 23 (1969):60.

55. *Logic as the Science of the Pure Concept*, trans. D. Ainslie, London: Macmillan 1917, p. 327.

concreteness and individuality, science reduces objects to their concepts. The former represents human experiences, the latter conceptualizes them; art is concerned with individual realities; science with abstract universals. Since history is not the elaboration of concepts or categories, but the representation of the real in its particularity, it is akin to art and not to science. Both art and history deal with the passions and destinies of men, with what appears and disappears in space and time, and not with the universal concept of man. In the world of art and history there are no general laws, but individual realities. The difference between art and history is that art produces a *possible* reality, while history produces a *factual* reality; the former represents what is imagined as possible, the latter what really happened. This implies the rejection of historical laws as well as the rejection of theological and metaphysical principles governing history. Like art, history aims at the individual; both are *conoscenza* and not *scienza*.

But the most acute assessment of the work was made by Gentile in a review-article appearing in 1897.[56] Although Gentile fully agrees with Croce's ideas, he finds the relation between the *factual* and the *possible*, which constitutes the difference between history and art, not to be rigorously treated by Croce. To bring the concept of history under the general concept of art within the relation of the *part* to the *whole* presented a series of difficulties that Croce had not foreseen. If the object of history is what *really happened* and the object of art is *what may possibly happen* and the relation between *factuality* and *possibility* is identical with the relation between the *part* and the *whole*, it may concern only the content of history and art. But Croce had emphasized that, in the study of the relation of history to art, the important thing is the kind of elaboration (form) that each gives to its object. And since he assumes that the elaboration is identical in both, it follows that their relation is one of identity. In this case, it is no longer necessary, Gentile maintains, to bring history under the general concept of art, for the inverse is also possible. Why should the concept of art be more general than that of history? Why should the former encompass the latter? It is clear, then, that the element of differentiation between history and art is not to be sought in the *form* (which leads to identity), but in the *content*. What history and art have in common is the *particular*, which may be *factual* or *possible*, and these two concepts are coordinate rather than subordinate to each other. Thus nei-

ther can be brought within the other. Gentile concludes that history and art cannot be identical, for both have elements in common and elements which vary; they are like different parts of the same whole. Their relation consists in the coordination of one part to another.

Croce recognized the validity of Gentile's friendly criticism and in a letter to him (May 23, 1897) he declared the review to be "the most serious and keenest" his work had thus far received. Croce agreed with Gentile's objections ("I declare myself touché"), admitting that the points of criticism were well taken. Gentile's remarks concerning the possibility of a philosophy of history, which Croce had denied (if history is the representation of the individual, its course cannot be conceptualized), made him recognize the necessity for further study on the problem. "I shall say nothing," wrote Croce, "on the remarks you made concerning the philosophy of history. The problem is difficult and I now realize that I was not yet *mature* enough for it."[57]

Croce's major effort had been to demonstrate solidly the essential difference between science on the one hand and art and history on the other, as two distinct forms of mental activity, and to assert the basic kinship between art and history. However, the specific differences between art and history were left somewhat unclear. Gentile was quick to spot the deficiencies of the work; but in his review he confined himself to pointing them out without elaborating on ways to remedy them. He returned to the subject with a long article, "Il concetto della storia," published in 1899.[58] Always within the framework of his agreement with Croce's position, Gentile in this article subjects the concepts of science, art, and history to a most rigorous and penetrating analysis in order to arrive at the specific nature of history and its particular relation to art. He brings in Croce and his opponents in an effort to clarify the difficult points of the problem, and the result of his analysis is a thorough and enlightening restatement of the whole matter in a logical and coherent manner. In the end he fully agrees with Croce that the mind operates on only two levels—the artistic and the scientific—with the first producing images and the second producing concepts; that the object of the second level is the universal (concepts and laws); that there is no third level of activity which might be

56. "I primi scritti di B. Croce sul concetto della storia," *Studi storici* 6 (1897):137–52. Now in *Frammenti d'estetica e letteratura*, pp. 379–93.

57. "Lettere di B. Croce a G. Gentile," *Giornale critico della filosofia italiana* 23 (1969):11–12 (letter of May 23, 1897).

58. *Studi storici* 8 (1899):103–33, 169–201. Now in *Frammenti d'estetica e letteratura*, pp. 1–60. The article, to a large extent, discusses the work and, in general, the ideas of one of Croce's critics; see F. R. Trojano's *La storia come scienza sociale* (Naples: Pierro, 1898), vol. 1.

called "historical" as distinct from the esthetic and the logical; that history partakes of the nature of art and not of science. But his main effort was aimed at determining the nexus between art and history through the analysis of the specific characteristics of each. Croce had not gone beyond a general identity between them, submerging the particular differences into this general identity. If art and history aim at the production of the particular, so do geography and geology; yet geography is not geology, and history is not geography. Gentile concludes that art and history have the same nature and indeed the same aim, that is, "the beautiful representation of the individual,"[59] but that they distinguish themselves from each other, for, while the beautiful in art does not necessarily have to coincide with truth, the beautiful in history *must* do so. The conception that history aims at the representation of the *datum* in its immediacy while art constructs its object through the mediation of the esthetic form is for Gentile absolutely false. History, like art, does work through the esthetic form. The *datum* of history, in order to come to life, must be elaborated by the historian's mind, must be esthetically constructed. But while the representations of art are limited by factual reality, the representations of history must preserve factual reality through the esthetic elaboration of it.

Gentile's fresh insights into the problem were greatly appreciated by Croce, who was seeking new stimulation for his own thought. In a letter (April 22, 1899) to Gentile, Croce wrote: "I like what you said about the regulatory and constitutive aims of history. Since your essay does not have the paradoxical tone of my writings and it comes as a comprehensive study after the many discussions aroused by them, it should have a better fate, just as it has a better persuasive form."[60] And in another letter (July 31, 1899): "These days I have reread your work on *History*, which gave me a great deal to think about. I will go back to it again and I will write you."[61] And again, a few days later (August 10): "I have reread your work on Marx and I have in my hands the one on history. I ought to write you at length on many things, not to fight what you have maintained in your work on history, but to tell you about some ideas which came to my mind in regard to it. But I am now deeply immersed in building the structure of my book on Esthetics, and my mind is not free."[62]

This was the period in which Croce was toiling on the first sketch of his *Tesi fondamentali* (Fundamental propositions) and his correspondence with Gentile shows clearly the fruitfulness of their exchange of views in the clarification of ideas and in the test of new conceptions. In the first two essays on esthetics, *La storia ridotta sotto il concetto generale dell'arte* and *La critica letteraria*, Croce had more or less retained traditional positions echoing De Sanctis and Hegel; he had accepted the distinction between the various arts, based on the different physical means of expression which characterize "a special field of representations."[63] Furthermore, he had viewed art as an activity aiming at the production of the beautiful, which was defined as the sensible representation of the Idea.[64] He had distinguished natural beauty from artistic beauty, the former representing particular realities, the latter reality in general.[65] The representation through sensible means of expression had been conceived as language: "For what is the form of art if not language: marvelous language of sounds, colors, words, and fancies?"[66]

Some of these points are rejected in his *Aesthetic*; others represent an anticipation of basic concepts treated in it or in subsequent developments. Such are the identification of art with language, of esthetics with linguistics, and the lyrical character of art which is foreshadowed by the necessity of the artist's personal involvement in order to transform a content into art. From the first two essays to the *Tesi fondamentali*, the contribution of Gentile to Croce's doctrine is very significant. During this period of gestation and actual composition of the work, Croce kept his friend abreast of his progress, discussed with him new discoveries and difficult problems, and, most of all, constantly defended his position against Gentile's objections, though always seeking Gentile's consensus.

A first generous acknowledgment of his debt to Gentile is found in an essay of 1899 in which Croce, in discussing the problem of content and form in relation to seventeenth-century literature, admits that previously he had accepted the distinction between the two elements, but that he immediately had realized his mistake, for "in no case is it possible to separate content from form or to grasp the content outside the form."[67] He explicitly states that it was Gentile who showed him the error into which he had fallen, and points for this purpose to Gentile's "important ar-

59. *Frammenti d'estetica e letteratura*, p. 59.
60. "Lettere di B. Croce a G. Gentile," *Giornale critico della filosofia italiana* 23 (1969):67.
61. Ibid., p. 80.
62. Ibid., p. 81.

63. *Primi saggi*, p. 28.
64. Ibid., p. 8.
65. Ibid., p. 15.
66. Ibid., p. 107.
67. "I trattatisti italiani del concettismo e Baltasar Gracián," in *Problemi d'estetica*, 4th ed., 1949, p. 343.

ticle," "Il concetto della storia," which had appeared that year (1899).[68] Gentile had convinced him that content and form are two abstractions acquiring reality only in their unity in the work of art.[69] For Croce the solution of the problem concerning content and form meant a decisive step toward an idealistic esthetics and the elimination of the "naturalism and Herbartianism" to which he was still shackled.[70] (In 1913, in fact, Gentile reminded him of "the rich and systematic series of corollaries" that he [Croce] had drawn for his esthetics from the concept of the abstractness of content and form, each considered in itself).[71] Moreover, Croce's concept of esthetic "re-creation" (see *Aesthetic*, Part I, chap. 16), which remained one of the cornerstones of his theory, was also anticipated by Gentile in his "Concetto della storia."[72]

Most of their epistolary exchanges during the three or four years prior to the publication of the *Tesi fondamentali* revolve around the identity of esthetics with linguistics, the relationship between esthetics and logic and between economics and ethics, the nature of language, expression and thought, action and will, content and form, and a number of other topics connected with the esthetic problems. "When I write about these things," confides Croce, "I always have the feeling that I am talking nonsense. These questions are very subtle and in them it is easy to mistake a cow for a bull."[73] Croce has a great respect for Gentile's judgment, which he constantly solicits: "I want you to read the manuscript of my work on Esthetics when it is completed"; "what you tell me on the necessity of rigorously developing the concept of *form* is very right. This past winter I thought much about it, and I noticed many aspects of which I was not aware earlier"; "when I draft the first part in September, I will send it to you to have your views on it."[74]

Gentile's comments on an article by Croce about the linguistic theory of G. Gröber are thus received by Croce:

The question is of such importance for me, who am writing on esthetics and am used to putting so much weight to your observations, that you will allow me to answer immediately and to beg you to reply immediately, too. I have thought again about what I meant by the word *intellectual* and by my *quid* which is neither intellectual nor affective. Try to see whether we may now agree. I used intellectual for conceptual, and I spoke of a *quid* which is expressed and which is neither conceptual nor affective, but is the unqualifiable content of expression. You now say: but if this content stands before the mind, it means that it is already intellective and therefore already expression. Agreed: but intellective in this second sense is not *intellectual*, that is, conceptual, the meaning in which I used it. In short, if I take a theorem exposed by Euclid and a sonnet by Petrarch, can I say that the former has a conceptual fact as its *antecedent* and the latter has *none*? But both, to your mind, would be intellective and therefore expressive facts (thought and expression being inseparable). Help me, for I am afraid that I may go astray.[75]

Gentile's answer immediately prompted another letter from Croce: "I hope to be able to develop these things in writing and to submit them for your examination."[76]

Despite the constant expression of agreement, a certain conflict is clearly perceptible. Croce's tendency to distinguish and somehow to unify after distinguishing, and Gentile's tendency toward a priori unity and resistance to distinction cannot escape the attention of the alert reader of the correspondence. "I assure you that I am very happy in finding myself so much in agreement with you not only in the ideas but also, which counts more, in the method of seeking them, and in their presuppositions. The agreement of ideas is often a *dead* agreement; the agreement of method and presuppositions is a *live* agreement. It sometimes results in the pleasure of being corrected by a friend and of being put on the right track."[77] So writes Croce. But it would be an underestimation of the extent of their basic differences to believe in a total harmony between them. Sometimes Croce entrenched himself in his positions and tried to fight Gentile's objections: "Here are the gates from behind which I cannot get out. I have tried to point them out to you in all their solidity. If you help me break them, I will happily get out and see the stars. But I beg you to mind that my problem is to find the distinction between the *logical form* and the *esthetic form*, and not between the *esthetic form* and the *content*."[78]

All this reveals the laborious process, the hesita-

68. Ibid., p. 343, fn. Gentile's article had appeared in *Studi storici* 8:103–33, 169–201; now in *Frammenti d'estetica e letteratura*, pp. 1–60. The idea of the identity of content and form, however, had already been discussed by Gentile in a previous essay, "Arte sociale," *Helios*, no. 3 (1896), pp. 17–21, praised by Croce (see "Lettere di B. Croce a G. Gentile," *Giornale critico della filosofia italiana* 23 (1969):5.

69. See letter from Gentile to Croce, October 16, 1898, and Croce's answer of November 6, in *Giornale critico della filosofia italiana* 23 (1969):37–43, 45–47.

70. *An Autobiography*, p. 93.

71. "Intorno all'idealismo attuale. Ricordi e confessioni," *La Voce*, 11 December 1913. See now the reprint of *La Voce*, ed. Angelo Romanò (Turin: Einaudi, 1960), p. 610.

72. See *Frammenti d'estetica e letteratura*, pp. 43–44.

73. "Lettere di B. Croce a G. Gentile," *Giornale critico della filosofia italiana* 23 (1969):97.

74. Ibid., p. 81; ibid., p. 73; ibid., p. 83.

75. See *Problemi d'estetica*, 4th ed., 1949, pp. 141–51; and "Lettere di B. Croce a G. Gentile," *Giornale critico della filosofia italiana* 23 (1969): 94–95.

76. See Gentile, *Lettere a B. Croce*, vol. 1, pp. 222–23; and "Lettere di B. Croce a G. Gentile," *Giornale critico della filosofia italiana* 23 (1969):96.

77. "Lettere di B. Croce a G. Gentile," p. 73.

78. Ibid., p. 99.

tions, and the uncertainties through which the first sketch of Croce's esthetic doctrine was achieved and the part Gentile played in it.

5. *The First Esthetics and the Shaping of the "Philosophy of the Spirit"*

In 1900 Croce's *Tesi fondamentali d'una estetica come scienza dell'expressione e linguistica generale* was finally published, after much travail due to his as yet inadequate philosophical knowledge.[79] The work contained the essential points of his theory, which was subsequently developed and reorganized in a more suitable logical sequence, thus constituting, with the addition of part two (History of esthetic), the volume *Aesthetic as Science of Expression and General Linguistic*, published in 1902. In 1902 Gentile hailed *Tesi fondamentali* as the work which in a period of triumphant positivism presented the right solution to the problem of art by asserting its subjectivity;[80] the same year he also called attention to the importance of Croce's article, "Giambattista Vico scopritore della scienza estetica" (G. V. discoverer of esthetic science), pointing out that Vico's novelty lay in the fact that he not only discovered the autonomy of imagination, but that he also introduced the concept of mind as development, without which the concept of a new esthetics would have been impossible.[81] Following Croce's activity closely, Gentile could not refrain a year later, however, from criticizing the antimetaphysical character of the first edition of the *Aesthetic*, feeling that Croce's repudiation of metaphysics would leave his theory with no roots in the life of the Spirit:

Croce, coherent with his antimetaphysical attitude in general, excludes metaphysics from every corner of his esthetics and calls mystic every metaphysical esthetician, regardless of the school. And this is all right. But, then, what is the meaning of the spirit as the only reality which is the object of science?—that spirit whose expression is form, the first form? If it is a reality, what can it be if not a metaphysical reality? Consequently, what can the expression be if not a metaphysical form? Furthermore, if the spirit is the only activity, and the esthetic and logical activities are moments or degrees of this activity, how can we say that between the esthetic and the logical fact, between intuition and concept, there is the abyss by which Croce meant to separate them? Don't we have to consider them as fundamentally the very same reality which is the spirit, though in two different forms? And if this is true, since from intuition the spirit

rises to the concept, which is a higher degree of knowledge, how can we imagine that in the form called intuition there is no trace of what we call concept? Let us admit that, in the particular as such, intuition is unable to perceive any trace of the universal; but is it possible that the mind of the philosopher is also unable to perceive it?[82]

Croce's doctrine was meant to be an idealistic one in reaction to the dominant positivistic tendencies of the time; but he was not fully aware that this implied the resolving of all reality into subjective activity and the suppression of all traces of objectivism. Despite the gigantic effort he had made to overcome naturalism and Herbartianism and to establish a true "Philosophy of the Spirit" in a strict idealistic sense, without dualisms, Croce came to recognize that both the *Tesi fondamentali* and the first edition of the *Aesthetic* "retain traces of a certain naturalism, or Kantism, which here and there conjures up once more the ghost of nature, and states distinctions . . . somewhat abstractly."[83]

Croce's work certainly does not arrive at a total and all-encompassing formulation of his theory of art. His main concern being at that time to clear the field of weeds, he seems to insist on demonstrating more what art *is not* than what art *is*. He is thus led to a vast refutation of all the "false esthetics" of the past, especially "naturalistic esthetics," which considers beauty as a quality of physical objects existing outside the sphere of the Spirit, and "intellectualistic esthetics," which presents art as the intellective activity of the mind and confuses poetry with literary prose. The historical part of the work is, in fact, polemical and iconoclastic in character. Against naturalistic tendencies Croce affirms the "spiritualistic" nature of art, and against intellectualistic tendencies its "alogical" character.

The *Aesthetic*, into which Croce imagined that he had emptied all of his philosophy, had instead, he wrote, "filled my head with fresh philosophy, with doubts and problems concerning especially the other forms of the spirit, the theories of which I had outlined in their relation to aesthetic, and the general conception of reality."[84] The work in fact turned out to be the formulation of a problem rather than its solution. The solution was now to be achieved through other works which would offer a complete picture of the philosophical issues involved in the esthetic problem. In writing the *Aesthetic*, Croce had become aware of the close relations between the basic forms or activ-

---

79. The work was read at the Accademia Pontaniana of Naples at the sessions of February 18, March 18, and May 6, 1900, and was published in the *Proceedings*, vol. 30.

80. See *Frammenti d'estetica e letteratura*, pp. 117–20.

81. See ibid., pp. 121–35. Croce's article had been published in the journal *Flegrea*, in the issues of April 5 and 20, 1901.

82. "La prima edizione dell'*Estetica*," *Giornale storico della letteratura italiana* 41 (1902):89–99; now in *Frammenti d'estetica e letteratura*, pp. 149–50.

83. *An Autobiography*, p. 95.

84. Ibid., p. 67.

ities of the Spirit, and from the field of esthetics he had now to move to that of logic, and from there to that of economics and ethics. He felt that esthetics, being a part of philosophy, had to be treated within the framework of a philosophical system which would give a full account of man's theoretical and practical processes.[85]

In 1905 he published the first sketch of his *Logic as the Science of Pure Concept* (completely rewritten for the second edition, 1909), in 1907 the *Philosophy of the Practical: Economics and Ethics*, and in 1912–1913 the *Theory and History of Historiography*, which complete the "Philosophy of the Spirit." These developments deepened and clarified further his esthetic theory, which found a strong support in the other forms of spiritual activity. In constructing his philosophical doctrine, Croce had realized that he had to delve more deeply into idealistic philosophy in order to be able to proceed in his work. "When I had published the *Aesthetic* and sketched a logic," he wrote, "I felt that the time had come for a closer acquaintance with the Hegel whose doctrines I had hitherto sampled rather than studied in their entirety."[86] In a brief article of 1904, "Siamo noi hegeliani?" (Are we Hegelians?), he conceded that "philosophy cannot come back to life and progress unless it somehow links itself to Hegel," and added that "after him the world was once more divided into appearance and hidden reality, matter and God, crude facts and transcendental value. Philosophy (not metaphysics in a questionable sense) was dispossessed."[87]

The fragmentary knowledge Croce had of Hegel at that time came from his study of De Sanctis and from his research on Marxism and historical materialism. Although he perceived vaguely the hidden richness of Hegelian philosophy, he continued to regard Hegel with a suspicious and critical eye. This is shown by his essays on historical materialism—*Historical Materialism and the Economics of Karl Marx*—in which, as he wrote in *An Autobiography*, "I set myself to purge that doctrine of every trace of abstract a priori thought, whether in the form of 'philosophy of history' or in that of the later 'evolutionism,' and to defend the value of the Kantian ethics and reject the mystery of a substructure of Economy—the Idea in disguise—operat-

ing beneath the level of consciousness, and a superstructure or consciousness described as a superficial phenomenon."[88]

The passage from anti-Hegelianism to Hegelianism (accepted critically and only partially) was made under the influence of Gentile, who followed Croce's intense activity with discussions of the various difficulties arising from Croce's thought. That Gentile acted as his mentor is evident from the following passage of *An Autobiography*: "I came into a more direct touch with Hegel through the friendship and collaboration of Gentile, in whom the tradition of Spaventa came to life again more flexible, more modern, more open to criticism and self-criticism, richer in spiritual interest; and in this way, in spite of occasional differences between the paths which we respectively followed, Gentile and I came to influence each other and to correct each other's faults."[89] The results of Croce's Hegelian studies, undertaken around 1905, are contained in his book *What Is Living and What Is Dead in Hegel's Philosophy* (1906), which gives a critical assessment of Hegel's doctrine and serves to clarify Croce's own position in relation to Hegelian idealism. Croce's criticism of Hegel focuses mainly on the dialectic of opposites constituting the essential part of the system. Monistic systems conceived of only one of the terms of the opposition as being real, declaring its opposite to be illusory; dualistic systems, on the contrary, considered both terms to be real and their unity to be illusory. The first sacrificed the opposition to the unity, the second the unity to the opposition. Hegel recognized that neither the opposites nor the unity is illusory. The concrete unity is but a unity of opposites; it is, therefore, not immobility but movement, a dialectical process accomplished through the fundamental triad: thesis, antithesis, synthesis. Without the negative term, there would be no development. Reality is, in fact, development, history.

But, according to Croce, the first error committed by Hegel was in confusing the dialectic of opposites with the dialectic of "distincts." Two distinct concepts are conjoined while preserving their distinction; two opposite concepts exclude each other. A distinct concept is presupposed and comprised by the subsequent concept. For Croce unity can be meaningful only if there is something *there* to be unified, that is, distinct and autonomous concepts. And since Hegelian opposites are merely abstract outside the synthesis, any unity of opposites is but a specious one. Apart from Becoming, for example, Being and Nonbeing are not

---

85. Croce wrote: "The first treatise, published in its complete form in 1902, remains as an outline of what later was to become the *Aesthetic*, enriched with all the elements added subsequently. These elements must be sought in the other volumes by the author, not in those of esthetics alone, but in the special works in practical criticism and history, and in controversial notes" (*Indagini su Hegel e schiarimenti filosofici* [1952], p. 224).

86. *An Autobiography*, p. 95.

87. *La critica*, 2, p. 262.

88. P. 92.

89. P. 93.

two concepts but two abstractions, Croce argues, and consequently Becoming cannot possibly represent a genuine synthesis; it can neither "suppress" nor "conserve" what does not exist to begin with. Examples of distinct concepts are imagination, intellect, economics, ethics; examples of opposites are good and evil, true and false, and so on. What makes possible the unity of philosophical concepts is, precisely, their distinct and autonomous existence. In the unity of the Spirit we distinguish the sphere of theoretical activity from the sphere of practical activity. Every distinct form preserves, in its relation to other distinct forms, its own autonomy. The artistic and the logical, the economic and the ethical forms are the stages through which the Spirit develops its unity. Unlike the opposites, which outside their synthesis are mere abstractions, each distinct form is concrete and real. The distinct forms are the Spirit in its particularizations, not the universal concept in its intrinsic constitution as a synthesis of opposites. Hegel's error was, therefore, to conceive the nexus of the "distincts" in the same manner in which he conceived the dialectic of opposites. His failure to understand the autonomy and concreteness of the distinct forms of spiritual activity prevented him from understanding the autonomy of history. Furthermore, Hegel conceived of a philosophy of history as a "reflective contemplation of history," thus falling into a dualism between concept and fact, rationality outside reality, and reality outside rationality. The same position is found in his treatment of the philosophy of nature, which becomes an abstract and hollow science outside the reality of the Spirit.

It is evident that Croce, while trying to bring everything within the Spirit, including nature, insists on the reality of the distinct forms of spiritual activity. His philosophy rejects the Hegelian triad of Logos, Nature, and Spirit, and asserts "the sole reality of Spirit itself."[90] He moved in the direction of Gentile, but he never renounced the concept of the reality of the "distincts." In fact, his progress from the *Aesthetic* to the *Logic* to *The Philosophy of the Practical* and to the *Theory and History of Historiography* (also published in English as *History, Its Theory and Practice*) was characterized by "the gradual elimination of naturalism, the growing emphasis laid upon spiritual unity, and the deepening of the meaning attached to the conception of intuition in aesthetics, now elaborated into that of lyricism."[91] A significant testimony to his striving for spiritual unity is his rewriting of his *Logic*, which he describes as an "affirmation of the concrete universal"

and, at the same time, "of the concrete individual," the harmonization of the Aristotelian *scientia est de universalibus* with the Campanellian *scientia est de singularibus*.[92] In a long note he indicates that, when he wrote his monograph *La storia ridotta sotto il concetto generale dell'arte* in 1893, he maintained that "history is to be subsumed under the general concept of art," as the title suggests; after sixteen years, he adds, "I maintain, on the contrary, that history is philosophy, or rather that history and philosophy are the very same thing."[93] In explaining his effort to overcome the difficulties encountered before reaching this conclusion, he states: "I was greatly helped not only by my own studies in the 'philosophy of the practical' and the identity I found between intention and action, but also, and above all, by the studies of my dear friend, Giovanni Gentile (to whom my intellectual life owes a lot more in the way of help and stimulation), on the relation between philosophy and the history of philosophy, which I have extended to the relation of philosophy to history in general."[94]

From the emphasis on the character of concreteness of history and the abstractness of science, Croce moved gradually to the demonstration of the concrete nature of philosophy, and, he said, "the two concretenesses [that of philosophy and that of history] proved finally to be one."[95] Croce's conception of the unity of the Spirit is clearly expressed in his *Autobiography* in reference to *The Philosophy of the Practical*; such a unity is not a unity of opposites, but a process of "distincts":

As I worked at my *Philosophy of the Practical* and inquired into the relation between intention and action, my denial of any such dualism and of the conceivability of an intention without action led me to think once more of the dualism which I had left standing in the first *Logic* between the concept and the singular judgment, that is, between philosophy as antecedent and history as consequent; and I realized that a concept which was not at the same time a judgment of the particular was as unreal as an intention that was not at the same time an action. Then I remembered the long discussions between Gentile and myself, a few years before, concerning the Hegelian formula which identifies philosophy with the history of philosophy. I had rejected it, and Gentile had defended it, but his defence had not convinced me; now I was disposed to agree with Gentile, but on condition that I might interpret the formula freely in my own way, in other words, conformably to my notion of Spirit, in which philosophy is one "moment," and thus convert it into a formula identifying philosophy with history, which I worked out in the second edition of the *Logic*.[96]

90. *An Autobiography*, p. 100.
91. Ibid., p. 102.

92. *Logic*, p. xii.
93. Ibid., p. 210.
94. Ibid., p. 211.
95. Ibid., p. 211.
96. *An Autobiography*, pp. 104–05.

The various particular problems arising from Croce's *Aesthetic* are, directly or indirectly, reflected in *Problemi d'estetica* (1910), in which is collected a large variety of writings clarifying, defending, and complementing the theory set forth in his first major work. After the publication of the *Aesthetic*, Croce planned, with the collaboration of Gentile, the founding of *La critica*, a bimonthly journal devoted to literature, history, and philosophy. The appearance of the first issue of the periodical in January, 1903, marked an important step not only in the career of the two men, but also in the history of culture in twentieth-century Italy. Gentile took responsibility mainly for the philosophical part, and Croce devoted himself mostly to problems of esthetics and literary criticism; but often their contributions overlapped. "The founding of *La critica*," wrote Croce, ". . . marked the beginning of a new period in my life, the period of maturity or harmony between myself and reality."[97] All hesitations, indecisions, and self-searching activities came to an end. Croce now felt that he was on the right path, having found his vocation and his philosophy; and as he continued to work on *La critica* he became ever more convinced that, after years of disharmony between his studies and his actions, he had reached the coherence between the theoretical and the practical man that he had been looking for.

La critica immediately became a most powerful vehicle for the dissemination of neo-idealistic philosophy and for the total obliteration of positivism. Along with the theoretical development of his esthetics and the other parts of his philosophy, Croce engaged in literary criticism in order to give concrete illustrations of his theory, thus linking theory and practice. The first period of his activity as a literary critic produced the first four volumes of *La letteratura della nuova Italia* (The literature of modern Italy), which contain a number of monographs appearing in *La critica* during the period 1903–1913 (published in volumes in 1914–1915).[98]

6. *Art, Beauty, Expression, Language*

Croce's *Aesthetic* is, as we have seen, the true starting point of his philosophical thought. When he wrote it, however, he was unaware that the problems he dealt with were capable of further development; he thought

at first that he was writing a self-sufficient work which in no way implied a philosophical system, for at the time Croce had not yet conceived or outlined his "Philosophy of the Spirit." His study of esthetics was carried out simply within the domain of human experience; the work is therefore not speculative, but, so to speak, phenomenological in character.

Its highlights are summarized by Croce in the last chapter of Part I, but they can be further reduced to the following propositions: beauty is expression, and expression is identical with intuition; intuition-expression is alogical knowledge, clearly distinct from the logical activity of the Spirit; art, being intuition-expression, is one and the same thing with language; art is independent of the other forms of the Spirit (these, on the contrary, depend on the artistic activity) and is knowledge of the individual (logic being the knowledge of the universal); taste is the only criterion for the judgment of art; taste is a faculty common in all men and its judgments are universally valid.

All this means that art is a human creation, spiritual in character, and that whatever is considered to be beautiful in nature is not so in its own right, but because subjective esthetic experience confers beauty upon natural objects. Thus, everything is resolved into the subjectivity of man: so-called physical beauty becomes a reflection of that subjectivity. The Spirit confers beauty upon the objects within its grasp, just as the economist confers value upon objects in accordance with the inner desires men project toward these objects. Esthetic expression is distinguished from "natural" expression, the latter being equated to the utterance of emotion in men and animals. Emotion, which is a chaotic perturbation, constitutes the matter to which the artist gives form in his esthetic expression. Matter is formless and receives form through the expressive process, which imparts life and individuality to something which was formerly indeterminate. The formative activity is the first stage of knowledge, for the Spirit knows only what it does. As a result, the idea of art as imitation is eliminated and that of art as creation (which had already been asserted by Kant) is firmly upheld. For art is a synthetic process which unifies the varied; art is nothing but form, and any content can be transformed into art. Content and form, however, can be distinguished only in abstract; in actuality they are inseparably united, for there is no content without form—form always being the form of a content.

But form only gives intuitive knowledge—representations, pictures, images. It does not distinguish between real and unreal; it presents the object in its concreteness without asking what the object is. Art

---

97. Ibid., p. 70.

98. The journal *La critica* was published for forty-two years, appearing punctually on the twentieth of every other month. Continued by *Quaderni della critica* (1945–1951), the publication covers nearly half a century of intellectual life.

therefore represents the particular as such. It is pure contemplation and is the necessary step to logical knowledge which subsumes the particular under the universal. There are two forms of knowledge: esthetic and logical, that is, individual and universal; there is the truth of the imagination and the truth of the intellect. Croce echoes here Vico's thought: "By the very nature of poetry it is impossible for anyone to be at the same time a sublime poet and a sublime metaphysician, for metaphysics abstracts the mind from the senses, and the poetic faculty must submerge the whole mind in the senses; metaphysics soars up to universals, and the poetic faculty must plunge deep into particulars."[99] The two forms of knowledge are not coordinate, but subordinate; they are degrees of a process. The first degree (the artistic form), which is autonomous, constitutes the necessary antecedent of the second degree (the logic form): logic presupposes intuition, imagination, that is, art, which is the expression of the *concrete individual*.

If art is expression, it follows that esthetics and language coincide. Art is in fact language, and language marks the passage from animal sensibility to human activity. Moreover, the content of expression cannot be an external object, for external objects have a form, whereas the content of expression is formless; it is something which can only be grasped through expression. To conceive of content as external would mean to make of art a mechanical reproduction or an imitation.

But, despite these assertions concerning the subjectivity of art, Croce is still far from the idealistic position totally resolving the outer into the inner world. He could not succeed in avoiding the suggestion that there is an external content, which becomes the true content of expression when it is received by consciousness through impression, that is, when it is humanized. But this does not eliminate the object by thoroughly resolving it into a state of mind. When Croce wrote his *Aesthetic* he did not yet have a speculative philosophy, and most of his observations were based on psychological considerations. His main effort was to liberate esthetic intuition (intuitive knowledge), from its dependence on intellectualistic elements on the one hand and from the brutal animalistic emotions on the other. Having discarded logic from esthetic intuition, he turned his attention to the physico-psychic

activity of man, which is a perpetual and indistinct flowing of chaotic sensations, characteristic of animal life. Expression throws light on the formless flux of obscure impressions, giving them eyes, so to speak. Art as language represents the birth of the human grafted on the animal which still persists in man. Art is passage from the formless to the formed, from passivity to activity, from multiplicity to unity, from becoming to being.

Intuition and expression are one and the same thing in the reality of the Spirit. The Spirit intuits only insofar as it makes, forms, expresses; and whoever separates intuition from expression never succeeds in reuniting them, since intuitive activity intuits to the extent that it expresses.[100] The identity of intuition and expression remains one of the basic foundations of Croce's doctrine. Intuition is the activity by which the Spirit gives the material of art the expressive form, that is, language; it is, as we said, a knowledge of the individual obtained through the mediation of emotion, but never subsumed under any universal concept: intuition is pure contemplation *(teoresi)*.[101] Form is nothing but the actual identity of language and image, that is, intuition and expression. This form of knowledge is mere vision, which escapes the distinction between real and unreal. The process goes from impression to intuition and from there to perception, which is judgment (perception indicates something that has happened). The first designates formless matter, the second and the third designate degrees of theoretical activity. The formless matter cannot be grasped except in the form. And "it is impossible to distinguish intuition from expression in the cognitive process: the one appears with the other at the same instant, because they are not two, but one."[102]

The conception of "expression," however, has in Croce a peculiar meaning which requires some clarification. The term "expression" is not to be taken as a means of communication, but as an "inner language" which gives expressive form to an obscure content, bringing it to the level of conscious life. But such an expression is all internal; it communicates the content of consciousness, and has nothing to do with externalization or communication in a social sense. Hence the

---

99. *The New Science*, bk. 3, chap. 5, sec. 11 (p. 314). See also bk. 1, "Elements," sec. 53 (pp. 75–76): "Men at first feel without perceiving, then they perceive with a troubled and agitated spirit, finally they reflect with a clear mind. . . . This axiom is the principle of poetic sentences, which are formed by feelings of passion and emotion, whereas philosophic sentences are formed by reflection and reasoning. The more the latter rise toward universals, the closer they approach the truth; the more the former descend to particulars, the more certain they become."

100. See *Aesthetic*, trans. D. Ainlie (New York: The Noonday Press, 1970), p. 8.

101. Croce often employs "intuition" and "contemplation" almost interchangeably (see, for example, *Problemi d'estetica*, pp. 11, 29, 34; *Nuovi saggi d'estetica*, p. 9; p. 25 below; *Discorsi di varia filosofia*, vol. 2 [1959], p. 120: "Poetry is knowledge, but knowledge as intuition and contemplation"). Those who are not aware of this may find it puzzling since the concept of intuition as creative, that is, as a form of making, and contemplation as a passive vision (if taken in this sense) may be contradictory terms.

102. *Aesthetic*, p. 9.

peculiarity of Croce's conception of language and the problems arising from it.

There is no methodical and exhaustive treatment of the problem of language in Croce's works. But the indications given in his *Aesthetic* and in other pieces preceding and following this work are sufficient for a general view of his linguistic theory.[103] The term "linguistics" is taken by Croce to mean not "science of language" in the positivistic sense, but "philosophy of language" in the speculative and theoretical sense and within the framework of idealistic philosophy. Resuming Vico's thought, he seeks the essence of language which is closely related to the subjective activity of the Spirit. Thus, he remains far removed from positivistic linguists who study language as a phenomenon governed by certain laws independent of the creative activity of man, that is, as a fact which can be analyzed and reduced to scientific principles. As conceived by Croce, language is an act in ever-changing creativity; it is not the language of the grammars and dictionaries, that is, an objective mechanism for the purpose of communication. In short, language does not exist per se, as a system of signs, outside the expressive activity of man, the individual utterance, the spoken sentence spontaneously formed by man's state of mind—without mechanical rules. The parts of speech have no expressive value in isolation; they become language in the synthetic utterance which is always new and which never repeats itself. The uniqueness and individuality of the expressive act makes translation impossible, for every translation is a new linguistic act, a new work of art. The linguistic act is, moveover, not the expression of thought or logical activity, but of fancy, of passion elevated and transfigured into images.[104]

Language is therefore a free creation of the Spirit never conditioned by grammatical schemes; it is identical with artistic creation. This implies that poetry is language; hence the concept of the *poeticality* of language, which is form (the form shaping a certain content). This view certainly appeared to critics more controversial than the conception of language as *free spiritual creation*, for it was difficult to imagine true linguistic activity confined only to the esthetic form. In fact, after the *Aesthetic*, Croce seems to have tried gradually to modify the theory of the intrinsic poeticality of language in order to attune it to a broader concept of poetry developing from the initial, incomplete formulation of his doctrine. The character of *to-*

tality later attributed to art implied the same character in language, for the two had been declared identical. The linguistic act, which was first the expression of individual feeling, must now be the expression of the totality and universality of man (see below, sec. 10). But whether language reflects the individuality or the universality of man, the question still remains: are all linguistic acts equally poetic acts? It did not appear to be so to Croce's critics. Croce himself, upon returning to the problem, had to realize that there are nonpoetic expressions which are language and that therefore only *certain* linguistic acts can be considered poetic. When, in fact, he writes that language in its purity can be employed by thought and logic "as the sign for the concept,"[105] one may conclude that in the expression of ideas there is something esthetic in character.

In the book *La poesia* Croce points out four forms of expression: the immediate or natural (which is a chaotic utterance below the level of intuition and which is the symptom of emotion in men and animals), the poetic (which is the only one to be considered as language), the prosaic (which is the sign of ideas and concepts), the practical (which consists of articulated sounds aimed at persuading or entertaining, at arousing feelings or volitions); to these he adds "literary expression," which is a quality associated with the other expressions. The practical form of language is the one which particularly concerns the linguists, for it serves as a means of social communication. This form of expression is conventional; it is a system of signs which one must learn and practice. But here again Croce maintains that language, whether conventional or poetic, is *praxis* and not an independent organism, as the linguists believe.

Croce's error, in the eyes of some linguists, was to overlook the semantic aspect of language and to reduce language to a creative act and poeticality. Words have meanings which condition the speaker. This fact makes language autonomous and independent of praxis, but it would mean falling back to positivistic positions. If language is a body of rules and a list of words with fixed meanings, independent of poetic, logical, and practical activities, it becomes an abstraction rather than living language, for living language is an act, not a fact. In short, Croce denies the objectivity of language defended by positivists; for him language is the utterance, the sentence, and the phrase as they are spontaneously used. The dictionary contains dead words; when the words are spoken, they become alive and acquire new meanings in accordance with the state of mind of the speaker. Grammars and rules are

103. See (besides *Aesthetic*, pp. 140–52) *Problemi d'estetica*, 4th ed. (1949), pp. 141–230; *Conversazioni critiche*, vol. 1 pp. 87–113; *Philosophy, Poetry, History*, trans. Cecil Sprigge (London: Oxford University Press, 1966), pp. 248–60; *Letture di poeti*, pp. 247–58.

104. *Philosophy, Poetry, History*, p. 249.

105. Ibid., p. 249.

a posteriori theorizations with limited practical value. Authentic expression always remains a free and creative act, obeying only the state of mind of the individual speaker. It is, therefore, always mutable, instable, and approximate.

Although Croce concerns himself only with esthetic language, that is, an agrammatical language governed by the individual disposition and feeling of the artist, and thus impossible to reduce to general rules, he does not undermine the function and importance of the language of dictionaries and grammars. It certainly must not serve as a pattern to be followed, as an imperative to be obeyed, but only as a reminder of tradition. The poet passes through it, but does not stop there; he goes beyond it and creates his own. There is no true poet or writer who does not pay some attention to it or who is not affected by the abstract forms of the dictionaries and the patterns of grammars. The most original and creative among them cannot completely conceal the fact that they had their "course in rhetoric." Those who are unable to supersede the "historically existent" and copy and repeat it do not contribute to the living history of art; only the unfaithful disciple, the "unfaithful-faithful," who brings in something new, can be considered worthy of his master.[106]

To understand Croce's position, one must keep in mind the two main activities attributed to the Spirit—the theoretical and the practical. In the first case, the Spirit contemplates and thinks; in the second, it acts to satisfy its individual or universal needs. True language (or expression in the esthetic sense) belongs to the contemplative moment of the Spirit, that is, the moment of art, which is, as we have seen, "inner language"; the other forms of language are simply *signs*, not expressive in character. In the first instance, the word is the full expression of a psychic content which becomes one and the same with the word; in the second instance, the word is detached from its content and becomes a mere "label." The "inner language" coincides with the living experience and changes from one moment to another, being ever new, diverse, and strictly personal. It is the expression in which life acquires consciousness of itself and, fixing itself in a series of syntheses, forms language. (The life of animals, on the contrary, develops in the darkness of instinctual drives.) All this amounts to the identity of intuition and expression as knowledge of the individual.

The major problem in Croce's doctrine, however, arises from the clear-cut distinction he maintains between "expression" and "externalization" or "communication." For Croce these terms mean two different things: "expression" is the inner form given to feeling, that is to say, the constitution of the image; "externalization" is the physical production of the image on paper or on a canvas. This physical production is not language in its pure sense, for its purpose is the communication of the image already formed, and it belongs to the sphere of *signs*. Language is an inner process. Croce completely disregards the social aspect of language, which is communication. The fixation of the "inner expression" in something concrete, such as color, sound, writing, is not a theoretical act; it is carried out for practical purposes, one of which is the preservation of the expression in order to make its recreation and judgment possible.

Croce's doctrine must be viewed within the framework of idealistic philosophy for which language represents the moment in which the Spirit acquires consciousness of itself and utters words within itself. What men use, instead, to communicate among themselves is a system of signs, which the listener translates into a psychic content.

True language is an act of knowledge or self-awareness belonging to the theoretical Spirit which is art. Linguists, on the contrary, conceive of language as communication, because they view the individual as a real entity and distinguish him from society; language is thus a social, not an individual, product because it springs from societal needs. They consider *speech* (living utterance) and *language* (the objective system of signs) to be interrelated, with *language* existing prior to *speech*. Croce, on the contrary, maintains the priority of *speech* over *language*, a priority ideal and chronological. *Speech*, of course, falls to the level of *language*: from a live state it becomes dead, from Spirit it becomes nature, from an expressive act it becomes a fact, the fact which grammarians analyze to abstract their rules and schemes. In summary, there is for Croce the expression-image (poetry) and the expression-concept (logic); before the expression-image there is the natural expression; after the expression-concept there is the oratorical expression. Thus, to the four forms of spiritual activity, there correspond four forms of expression, with only one being, in the theoretical sense, true language.

7. *The Lyrical Character of Art*

In the third edition (1907) of the *Aesthetic*, Croce made some revisions (especially in pt. 1, chaps. 10,

---

106. See pp. 182–187 below, "The Precepts."

12) which were, he says, the result of "further reflection and self-criticism." He points out in the preface that the minor problems of esthetics and the objections brought against his theory had been and would continue to be dealt with in "special essays" and that he would "shortly publish a first collection which will form a kind of explanatory and polemical appendix to the present volume." [107] The collection alluded to was *Problemi d'estetica*, appearing in 1910. Gentile was very pleased with the new edition of the *Aesthetic*, and in reviewing it he emphasized the progress Croce had made toward a more definite idealistic affirmation—the fruit of his study of Hegel and logic. The corrections in the new edition seemed to be aimed at a complete abolition of nature as a reality existing outside the Spirit. The research and reflection necessary for the composition of his *Logic* and his *Philosophy of the Practical* had clarified for Croce some of the problems, still hazy in his *Aesthetic*; and the corrections or modifications made in the third edition reflect a clearer and more cogent view of the esthetic problem within the framework of a general philosophy of the Spirit. In fact, most of the corrections concern his general philosophical doctrine. Gentile noticed that Croce's negation, in the first edition of his *Aesthetic*, of a general metaphysical conception or a total vision of reality (of which esthetics is an integral part) was jeopardizing the philosophical character of his theory, but that this negation now applied only to "certain arbitrary and fantastic metaphysics." [108] The correction was, to Gentile's mind, very significant because it gave Croce's work a more rigorous idealistic character. Furthermore, in the new form, Croce's theory reflected the distinction between history and art, elaborated in his *Logic*. Unlike art, history implies an intellectual element, a philolosophical concept; as a result, history can no longer be subsumed under the general concept of art, for there is a deep variance between the function of taste and the function of historicity.

But one of the problems which awaited further development and clarification was that concerning the content of the intuition-expression characterizing art. In the *Tesi fondamentali* and in the *Aesthetic* Croce vaguely identifies such content as "sensations" and "impressions," formless psychic material which does not exclude external stimulation. In 1908, developing some earlier hints, [109] Croce introduced a new element into his theory—an element worked out in the paper

"L'intuizione pura e il carattere lirico dell'arte" (Pure intuition and the lyrical character of art), [110] presented at an international conference in Heidelberg. Art is "pure" intuition because it is free of any intellectual element; its content is feeling, radically different from impression or sensation. While the latter are passive and remain below the spiritual level in the sphere of mechanical drives, feeling is placed in the sphere of the *practical* and identified with the economic moment. Feeling gives art its lyrical character, and "lyricity" is, in Gentile's comments, "the form of the spirit shorn of every intellectual element and thus reduced to pure feeling." [111] This new development, although it was not reflected in the third edition of his *Aesthetic*, permeated Croce's esthetic theory thereafter, offering a better understanding of the individuality of intuition in relation to the universality of the concept and showing the presence of the subject in every act in the life of the Spirit and the transcendental character of art: "Since pure intuition does not produce concepts, it can only represent the mainfestations of the will, that is, the states of mind. And the states of mind are passionality, feeling, personality, which are found in every art and which determine its lyrical character. Whenever this lyrical character is lacking, art is absent, because pure intuition is lacking." [112] Outside the logical activity in its various forms, there is no other psychic content except what we call appetitions, tendencies, feelings, will—all manifestations of the practical form of the Spirit in its infinite gradations and in its dialectic of pleasure and suffering. By assigning the content of art to the practical Spirit, Croce closes the circle of human activity, for the beginning and the end of such activity come together.

The concept of lyrical intuition pervades the *Breviary of Aesthetics* (1912), in which Croce summarizes his doctrine in a tight and coherent manner. The work of art must not only be formally perfect; it must also be warm and moving. The classical and the romantic exigencies seem to find in Croce's conception a perfect harmony. Great works of art are neither classic nor romantic; they express "a vigorous feeling transformed into a lucid representation." [113] The new conception of art is opposed to every kind of false art—imitative or realistic, [114] for it eliminates every object outside the Spirit; art becomes a process entirely within the Spirit.

107. P. xxx.

108. *Frammenti d'estetica e letteratura*, p. 165.

109. See "Intuizione, sentimento, liricità," *La critica* 5 (1907):248–50 (now in *Pagine sparse* [Naples: Ricciardi, 1919], vol. 1, p. 152).

110. Published in *La critica* 6 (1908):321–340 (now in *Problemi d'estetica*, pp. 3–30).

111. *Frammenti d'estetica e letteratura*, p. 171.

112. *Problemi d'estetica*, 4th ed., p. 23.

113. *Nuovi saggi d'estetica*, 4th ed. (1958), p. 26.

114. *Aesthetic*, 5th ed. (1921), p. xii.

Furthermore, the assertion of the lyrical character attached to art in general implied the rejection of the literary genres; the designation of "epic," "dramatic," "comic," and so on, as distinctive characteristics of works of art, would be replaced by the concept of "lyricalness," the only criterion for determining what is art and what is not art. The term "lyric" no longer applies to a particular genre, but to all forms of art.

The *Breviary of Aesthetics*, however, in addition to incorporating the concept of feeling in its formulation of art, introduces still another element which marks one more step forward in Croce's doctrine. In the essay of 1908, the relation between content and form does not appear adequately explained in the light of the newly found concept of feeling:

If the essence of art is merely theoretical and consists in intuition, it is difficult to see how such essence can be practical, that is, feeling, personality, and passionality; and, if it is practical, it is difficult to see how it can be theoretical. One may say that feeling is the content and intuition the form; but content and form do not constitute duality, as do water and the container, for content is form and form is content. Here, however, content and form appear to be different from each other: content has one quality, form another; and art appears as the sum of two qualities, or . . . of two values.[115]

The solution of the problem is found in the *Breviary of Aesthetics*, where the seeming identity between content and form becomes an a priori synthesis. "Art," writes Croce, "is a true a priori esthetic synthesis of feeling and image in intuition; we repeat that feeling, without the image, is blind; and that the image, without feeling, is empty. Feeling and image do not exist for the artistic spirit outside the esthetic synthesis."[116] The relation between intuition and expression is not one of identity, but one of dialectical unity.[117] This development marks a return to Kant. The identification of feeling with practical life will lead Croce to a further step in which feeling becomes a true category designating not a particular content, but the whole universe *sub specie intuitionis*.[118] In so doing he raised the content of art from the mechanical world of nature to the spiritual life of man, giving to the circular movement of the Spirit the form of a spiral.

But some difficulties could not be entirely avoided in the reshaping of the doctrine. The a priori synthesis is a union of two elements which were merely abstractions before the union. Feeling is not the content of art existing without form, but a content resolved into

form, for content in itself cannot be grasped. If feeling, as postulated by Croce, has a form in practical life—economics and ethics—how can it be the formless content of art? The question is amply explained by Croce through his conception of the Spirit as development, process, historical movement: "As soon as we have pronounced the quality of a reality, such quality is no longer valid, because it has already produced a new reality which awaits a new qualification."[119] In the circular process of the Spirit there is a series of syntheses springing from one another—the esthetic synthesis (the only one which is independent), the logic synthesis, and the practical synthesis. The passage from the practical to the theoretical, that is, from feeling as economic and ethical activity to feeling as the content of art, occurs through a transformation of the practical synthesis into a new reality: from form it reverts to content and this becomes the content of a new synthesis (artistic synthesis), for the content of art is nothing but the suffering and joy which constitute the fabric of practical life. Thus art becomes a real creation which transfigures practical form into content, giving the latter theoretical form. Art raises the passivity of matter to the activity of form.

8. *Intuition, Externalization, the Arts*

As originally formulated, Croce's doctrine met with a great deal of criticism from different directions. He answered most of it in *Problemi d'estetica*, in which he collected, together with new developments and explanations of his original thought, the writings directly or indirectly connected with the controversial points of his theory. One of these points concerns the concept of intuition. Critics contended, in contradiction to Croce, that there are ordinary intuitions and artistic intuitions and that, therefore, if art is intuition, not all intuitions are art. Croce had made no distinction; and his objectors felt that even if the identity of intuition and expression were valid for artistic intuition it was not valid for the other intuitions. Following in the footsteps of Vico, who considered poetry to be the first form of spiritual activity, appearing prior to man's logical reasoning, Croce held all intuitions to be artistic. Antonio Aliotta remarked that, if all individual facts or events revealing themselves to our consciousness are the product of esthetic intuition, one must conclude that "sensations, emotions, and hallucinations, no less than perceptions and representations, are artistic facts; but this is disproved by our esthetic ex-

---

115. *Problemi d'estetica*, p. 20.
116. *Nuovi saggi d'estetica*, p. 33.
117. See "Unità dialettica ed espressione," in *Indagini su Hegel*, pp. 51–53.
118. *Nuovi saggi d'estetica*, p. 34.

119. Ibid., p. 60.

perience." If we must exclude emotions and hallucinations, which, while we are experiencing them, give us the immediate consciousness of themselves or of external objects as concrete individuals, we must assume that the knowledge of the individual can be achieved without the esthetic intuition. This implies, Aliotta concluded, that "Croce's theory is false."[120] Croce refuted the argument by pointing out the distinction between matter and form and by stressing that the differentiation between intuitions concerns solely matter (which in itself does not exist) and not form (which is inalterable and in which matter acquires existence). Nonesthetic intuitions are sensations and emotions, and so on, a chaotic mixture of intuitive, intellective, and practical elements; they are at the same time intuitions, reflections, and impulses toward a goal; they are, in other words, always accompanied by rapid reflections on the reality and unreality of what had been intuited. Esthetic intuition is free from these elements which are foreign to esthetic experience. The difference between artists and other men lies in this: "Great artists have the power to remain much longer then ordinary men in the state of pure intuition and to help others to persist in that state."[121] They are able to fight for a longer period the intrusion of judgment and practical considerations into their state of contemplation; they are like children for a longer time than the common man—completely unconcerned with practical matters.[122] These statements imply two things: (1) that between esthetic and nonesthetic intuition there is a quantitative difference; (2) that artistic intuition must be free of considerations which might adulterate its purity (intellective or practical elements). But when Croce brings feeling (the content of intuition) within the sphere of the practical Spirit (economics and ethics), this purity can no longer be retained, because the transition from the practical to the theoretical is not like the crossing of the Acheron in a state of deep sleep to be broken by a thunderclap upon reaching the other bank. It is impossible to be a child again, once one has been an adult, and to live again in the purity of childhood.

Strong reservations concerning Croce's indistinction between esthetic intuition and other intuitions were voiced by Alfredo Gargiulo; Croce had argued that the conversion of a quantitative to a qualitative difference between artistic and ordinary intuitions had led to the objectionable conception of genius as something descended from heaven—a conception which was exag-

gerated to ridiculous proportions during the romantic period. By separating the artists from ordinary men, "art is no longer conceived of as an elementary, essential, and necessary function of the spirit, but as a final ballet which closes the opera or the play, and which the spectators would gladly renounce."[123] Linking himself to Vico, Croce rejects the aristocratic concept of art, viewing the artistic function as a spiritual process common (in different "quantitative" degrees) to all men.

Gargiulo's refutation of Croce's argument is contained in a perceptive and lucid essay, tightly constructed and cogently supported by appropriate quotations from Croce's own pronouncements.[124] He discards Croce's assumption that the distinction between *ordinary* intuition and *artistic* intuition derives from the general superstition concerning genius, and maintains that this distinction has more profound origins. The two intuitions are for Gargiulo qualitatively different, ordinary intuition being something passive, a given object resisting the activity of the subject. It implies the existence of a content not conquered by the creative activity of the Spirit through the expressive process—form. Therefore, not all intuitions reach the expressive stage. Artistic intuition, on the contrary, is the victory of spiritual activity over the passivity of the content, which becomes one and the same thing with form. The identity of intuition and expression is true only with reference to artistic creation, for here the activity of the Spirit possesses the object, which emerges through expression (form).

Unfortunately, Croce extends this identity to all intuitions—ordinary and artistic—implicitly arriving at the conclusion that even the datum, which the Spirit suffers, is nothing but a product of the Spirit. In Gargiulo's criticism there is a fundamental disagreement which concerns the nature of idealistic philosophy. He views the problem in light of nineteenth-century German idealism and particularly Hegelian doctrine, which retains the idea of a nature facing the ego. This disagreement led to a criticism whose validity rests on the assumption that no spiritual process is possible without an object on which the activity of the subject exercises itself. Some hints in Croce's *Aesthetic* regarding the existence of something that "the spirit of man suffers, but does not produce"[125]—something mechanical, passive—gives Gargiulo the elements to build up his argument pointing out a contradiction in Croce's theory. The object, Gargiulo believes, is un-

---

120. See *Problemi d'estetica*, p. 478. Croce quotes and refutes Aliotta's essay, *La conoscenza intuitive nell'Estetica del Croce* (Piacenza, 1904).
121. *Problemi d'estetica*, p. 482.
122. See ibid., p. 482.

123. Ibid., p. 486.
124. "Per la distinzione d'intuizione ordinaria e intuizione estetica" (1908–1909), in *Scritti d'estetica*, pp. 271–98.
125. P. 6.

conscious and passive, as opposed to spiritual activity which seeks to conquer and possess it. But objects exist in their own right and cannot appear simultaneously with the intuition: the object of intuition must be something before intuition conquers it and resolves it into the unity of art. What characterizes esthetic intuition is its formative activity, not the subjection to the object. I may describe an object which imposes itself upon me; this, however, is mechanical reproduction, not artistic production. When one assigns the character of expression to every intuition, one admits that the Spirit is equally active in its subjection to an object and in its artistic creation. The truth is that there is a passive intuition which does not lead to expression.

The reason that Croce extended the character of activity to every intuition, Gargiulo argues, was to conform to the idealistic exigency of suppressing the object facing the mind, that being the main intent of Italian neo-idealism. Gargiulo, however, sees no philosophical necessity for this extreme development. While recognizing that "the absolute spirituality of the datum has constituted the problem confronting absolute idealism after Kant,"[126] he points out that the absolute idealists "did not deny the passive and immediate character of the datum; they accepted it, they confirmed it fully," finding in it the otherness of mind. In fact, they recognize that there are *ordinary* intuitions (the passive) and *artistic* intuition (the active). Croce himself seems to admit the *active* and the *passive* when he writes:

How often we strive to understand clearly what is passing within us! We do catch a glimpse of something, but this does not appear to the mind as objectified and formed. It is in such moments as these that we best perceive the profound difference between matter and form. These are not two acts of ours, opposed to one another; but the one is outside us and assaults and sweeps us off our feet, while the other inside us tends to absorb and identify itself with that which is outside. Matter, clothed and conquered by form, produces concrete form. It is the matter, the content, which differentiates one of our intuitions from another: the form is constant; it is spiritual activity, while matter is changeable. Without matter spiritual activity would not forsake its abstractness to become concrete and real activity, this or that spiritual content, this or that definite intuition. . . . Some confound the spiritual activity of man with the metaphorical and mythological activity of what is called nature, which is mechanism and has no resemblance to human activity, save when we imagine, with Aesop, that "arbores loquuntur non tantum ferae." Some affirm that they have never observed in themselves this "miraculous" activity, as though there were no difference, or only one of quantity, between sweating and thinking, feeling cold and the energy

of the will. Others, certainly with greater reason, would unify activity and mechanism in a more general concept, though they are specifically distinct.[127]

Although Croce acknowledges in his *Aesthetic* the existence of ordinary intuitions, that is, psychic contents outside the formative activity of the Spirit, he goes as far as to consider, for the sake of the coherence of the system, all intuitions as expressions. If the character of spiritual form is given to all intuitions, including the passive intuitions which the Spirit suffers, one falls into the contradiction of intuitions that are *active* and *passive* at the same time. If, on the other hand, one rejects the existence of a datum present in consciousness, the consequences would be equally contradictory, for it would be impossible even to explain the subject matter, the content of art. The activity of the Spirit would be, in this case, an empty activity: "Even the contemplation of art would become unexplainable, since in the contemplative act the passive moment comes first. Before a work of art, before the activity of the contemplator is awakened, so to speak, to form the synthesis which was already in the artist, one is subjected to the passive parts, as they are given in the physical means of expression."[128] The character of activity and the identity of expression and intuition, maintained by Croce in his *Aesthetic*, apply only to artistic intuition. The additional element which characterizes artistic intuition and distinguishes it from ordinary intuition is not an addition, but a differential element—the character of *activity*. Gargiulo insists on the independent existence of *sensible objects*, which explains for him why art does not give a copy of nature, but does not operate, on the other hand, outside *natural objects;* this also explains the idealization of nature by art, which consists in the penetration of the datum by the Spirit. In art the Spirit isolates, through form, the contemplative moment; art is also liberation from the datum which kept the Spirit under subjection.

Gargiulo questions, furthermore, Croce's identification of art with language. He holds that "one can speak when subjected to something, just as one speaks when creating poetry."[129] One speaks, describes, without achieving a work of art; when dominated by the datum, one speaks, but speech is not art; language, therefore, is not always art. Gargiulo views Croce's position in general as that of an ultra-idealist tending to resolve every form of objectivity into the creative activity of the Spirit. This leads to the most serious

---

126. *Scritti d'estetica*, pp. 289–90.

127. *Aesthetic*, p. 6.
128. *Scritti d'estetica*, p. 295.
129. Ibid., p. 296.

problem in Croce's esthetics—that of externalization and the existence of the various arts.

As I have said, poetic language (which is true language) is for Croce all inward; it is an inner dialogue which only the poet hears; it has nothing to do with communication, for the outsider cannot hear it. The externalization of artistic creation shaped by this inner language does not belong to the esthetic process. It is a practical act aimed at a practical purpose. The distinction among the various arts and the theory on the nature and limits of each of them are based merely on the technique of externalization which Croce considers to be extrinsic to the esthetic process. Externalization, he holds, is the process of physical production of the work of art, and it begins when the esthetic creation ends. Esthetic intuition is one and the same for the poet, the painter, the musician, and so on; only the instruments of material realization vary. The difference in the means of externalization created the distinction among the various arts—a distinction which is to be considered purely empirical, just as one must consider as empirical the precepts and rules constantly formulated for each art. The distinction between the arts, therefore, has no meaning from the purely esthetic point of view.

One may agree with Croce that intuition and expression are one and the same thing, that they are born by the same act, that the seeming priority of intuition in relation to expression is logical rather than chronological; but this may be true of poetry, which the poet may sing within himself; when we deal with figurative arts, however, the problem becomes much more difficult: Croce's conception of language as an inner experience, unrelated to communication or externalization, becomes harder to accept. The unpainted painting does not exist because the process of its creation is one and the same with that of its physical production (externalization). From intuition to expression there is a temporal dimension. Time and effort are required before the artist can portray or paint on the canvas the image he has in his mind.

Croce's theory in fact could not satisfy critics in general, particularly art critics, fine arts lovers, and the artists themselves, who considered the expressive means as an integral part of the creative process. Certainly, putting a poem on paper is not the same thing as painting a picture. While Croce's position, however difficult, might be valid for poetry, it raises a great deal of legitimate objections when applied to the figurative arts. Croce, nevertheless, is adamant in remaining firmly entrenched in his position. The disagreement with his critics is one of basic philosophical principles on which his theory is founded. Even the

Hegelians (with the exception of Gentile) view the spiritual process in the opposition of an *inner* to an *outer*, the former striving to find expression in the latter. Art is for them the outward reality of something within. Croce keeps everything within. The technique of externalization is declared to be extrinsic to the creative process, for such a process ends with the intuition-expression, which is internal. When the poet or the artist has molded the image or the psychic content lying within himself, the esthetic act is concluded. He now needs skill and tools such as ability to write, ink, pens, colors, chisels, brushes, and so on, to externalize his work, to put his poem on paper or to sculpt his image in marble; but externalization, for which a technique is required, belongs to the world of practical things and acts. Technique is, therefore, a body of knowledge and skills absolutely foreign to the esthetic process. Since technique is a conscious activity in which every word, every line, every touch of color is weighed and controlled, it could find no appropriate place within the esthetic sphere, which is one of innocence similar to that of a child's. But one is puzzled by reading the following passage from the *Aesthetic*:

The individual A is seeking the expression of an impression which he feels or anticipates, but has not yet expressed. See him trying various words or phrases which may give the sought-for expression, the expression which must exist, but which he does not possess. He tries the combination *m*, but rejects it as unsuitable, inexpressive, incomplete, ugly: he tries the combination *n*, with a like result. *He does not see at all, or does not see clearly*. The expression still eludes him. After other vain attempts, during which he sometimes retreats from the mark at which he aims, all of a sudden (almost as though formed spontaneously of itself) he forms the sought-for expression, and *lux facta est*. [130]

Can all this labor be performed in a dream state? It seems that the choice of expression requires a wide-awake taste, one in full possession of its power of evaluation.

The theory of externalization has been a focal point in the criticism against Croce. Can one conceive a work without the capacity to externalize it? The idea of an internal expression which completes the esthetic process is like conceiving without necessarily giving birth. Croce would say that the work of art is a personal affair, and we need not know whether it exists in reality. But how can we re-create it if it is not externalized? Without the material expression of the work, criticism would be impossible, for criticism begins from the complete work as a material object. To imagine is not a work of art until one succeeds in molding, from within, the outside matter according to the inner

130. P. 118.

image. The work, in order to be such, must come forth; it cannot remain within. It cannot be complete while it is still within, eluding externalization. Consider the variants of works of art, the corrections made in successive writings, from the first draft to the final product: how much toil to reach perfection! But nothing could have been done without externalizing the work. The painter, while trying to represent the image on the canvas, steps back to take a better look at his work, to see where it needs more color or a correction in the design. It is through the process of externalization that he achieves the perfection of the image. No artist could complete and perfect the image internally; he may see it vaguely, but until he gives birth to it he does not know whether he has brought forth a monster or a thing of beauty.

In trying to dispel the idea that there is a distinct faculty for each art (which would not have fitted into his scheme), perhaps Croce went too far, thus destroying the arts by bringing them under the all-encompassing concept of Art. And he persisted in his stand to the end, with no concessions.[131] Most of the objections to Croce's theory on this matter are based on historical rather than logical considerations. If esthetic concepts are derived from the concrete existence of the works, history suggests that the difference among the arts has been constantly felt by critics and theorists. No logical systematization should be allowed to destroy the truth of history for the sake of systematic coherence. And history offers no definite proofs that the concept of the unity of the arts was originally perceived and then lost in the meandering course of man's reflections on art. Although the unity has been vaguely felt at a germinal level throughout the history of esthetics, the arts have always been treated in view of their specific individual problems. But Croce's main concern in this instance seems to be not so much the distinction of the arts, but the physical means of expression from which that distinction derives. The physical means of expression, being practical in nature, would invalidate the alogical character of esthetic creation. It seems that Croce, who identifies philosophy with history and who considers all theoretical problems as constantly emerging from history, is taking a stand against it; for the arts, which developed together with their own expressive means, are also history, and their historical value cannot be denied in favor of the logical coherence of the system.

The negation of the arts is certainly one of the most disconcerting problems. It springs from the tendency to unify, to reach the common ground of all arts, while preserving the clear distinction of the four forms of the Spirit. The elimination of the arts stems more specifically from an ultra-idealistic conception which rejects the existence of a material reality and reduces everything to the essential unity of the Spirit. The arts must be considered in their basic unity and not in their material externalization. If the "internal language" (which may be a musical motif, a figure, the form of a statue) is the true esthetic expression, the separation of language from communication makes impossible the existence of the arts as such, and reduces poetry to a *silent creation*. If "writing" and "painting" are simply "physical facts," only useful for the re-creation of works of art (which must begin from the material object), one is led to the absurd conclusion that printing a book and painting a picture or sculpting a statue are more or less the same thing. Since the esthetic creation occurs in the interiority of consciousness, there is an "inner painting or statue" and an "external painting or statue"; and the same can be said of poetry: there is the work conceived and the work communicated. The separation between creation and communication or externalization may raise the question: why the identity of feeling and expression and not the identity of expression and communication? For Croce every work is pictorial, musical, poetic—all these terms coinciding with esthetic expression.

But while Croce denies the different arts (based on the technique of externalization), he considers externalization as being inseparable from the work. He writes in the *Breviary of Aesthetics*: "If one takes away from a poem its meter, its rhythm, and its words, there does not remain the poetic thought, as some surmise: there remains nothing. The poem was born as those words, that rhythm, and that meter."[132] And there seems to be an apparent contradiction when a few pages further on he writes: "Painting and poetry do not draw their value from the sounds which strike the air, the colors which refract the light, but from what they can say to the spirit as they interiorize themselves in it."[133] But for Croce evidently sounds and colors exist as physical facts and spiritual acts. The work of art is a spiritual act as well as a piece of material in which a feeling was fixed. In the passage from the spiritual act (intuition-expression) to the material fact (externalization), there must be a chronological succession. The problem, however, becomes particu-

131. See "Critica e storia delle arti figurative" (1919) in *Nuovi saggi d'estetica*, 4th ed. (1958), pp. 261–85. See also *Aesthetica in nuce* (1928), in *Ultimi saggi*, 2d ed., pp. 16–21; *La poesia*, pt. 4, chap. 4: "Poetry and the other arts."

132. See *Nuovi saggi d'estetica*, pp. 37–38.
133. Ibid., pp. 47–48.

larly complicated when Croce admits the possibility of simultaneity: "The point of separation between expression and communication is certainly very delicate to grasp in actuality, because in actuality the two processes habitually alternate so rapidly that they seem to merge."[134] From the continuation of the passage quoted, one may be led to suspect that the distinction is simply an abstraction. The work of art seems to be an esthetic creation which incorporates, within the creative process, the communication as well. The point of separation between the inner elaboration and the material externalization is so uncertain as to seem to disappear, thus leaving the whole process unbroken. Technique in this case not only is the inner capacity to elaborate the psychic content artistically; it encompasses the means of expression and the necessary discipline to acquire them.[135]

The problem of literary genres is treated by Croce on the basis of his avowed theory of externalization and technique. The concept of genre becomes for him completely arbitrary, for esthetic creation does not yield to generalization. The genre is a pseudoconcept, not an act of knowledge; it is a construction of the practical spirit. In esthetics there are individual works, and they cannot be subjected to general rules such as those of the genre. Every work of art, in its

concreteness, is a genre in itself, an expression which cannot be repeated. Works cannot be compared to one another. The uniqueness of the work of art makes even translation impossible, for the poetic translation is a re-creation; it is the work of the translator, expressed in his own words and rhythms. Each work of art is a new and original expression of its author, who obeys no external precepts of any sort, except his own inner creative impulses: "Since every work of art expresses a state of mind, and the state of mind is individual and always new, intuition implies infinite intuitions which cannot be brought into a narrow classification by genres."[136] The classification of works of art in "tragedy," "comedy," "epic," "novel," and so on, is again based on extrinsic elements—the technique of their physical production. While denying the literary genres any theoretical justification and while pointing out the deleterious effects they had in literary criticism, Croce nevertheless recognized their practical usefulness especially for didactic purposes. They offer the student of literature groups of works under general labels which help in the memorization and identification of single works. They are useful to the librarian who must classify books and shelve them according to subject or other designation.

All this amounts to saying that the genres are a posteriori classifications having no part whatever in the creative process. And if we accept the notion that the classification of works by literary genres is based on *extrinsic* considerations, nothing can impugn Croce's position. One may argue, however, that the techniques of the various genres are definitely intrinsic and not extrinsic to artistic creation and that the idea of genre, possessed by the artist, conditions his creation spontaneously, operating from within. Those who set about to compose a work of art are always aware of the genre in which they will shape their image; they are not going to give artistic expression to a feeling in a form which only by accident happened to be a tragedy or an epic poem. The notion of genre serves as a silent guide in the structuring of their esthetic experience.

It is agreed that each work of art bears the mark of the unique personality of its author, but no one can deny that a given work is a tragedy sharing with other tragedies the structure of experience. The consciousness of genres and their rules helps the self-realization of the expressive process: it is not a passive force in the artist's mind; it is a creative power which contributes to the fashioning of an emotional content into a particular artistic form.

Historically (and here again history seems to dis-

---

134. *Ultimi saggi*, p. 17.

135. A reader of this work in manuscript made the following observation concerning externalization: "It would help make Croce seem less arbitrary to discuss how his concept of externalization has its origin in the *Estetica*, where he is still thinking of intuition as identical with a single, static *image*. As a result of this argument, all the multiplicity implied by externalization is of course something extrinsic. By the *Breviario*, however, intuition is conceived as a synthesis of feeling and image, and 'image' itself is now said to mean a 'nexus of images (insofar as what is called image is always a nexus of images, there existing no images in isolation any more than thoughts in isolation).' Once having admitted this much complexity into his concept of intuition, the prejudice against externalization because of its multiplicity should, logically, have been abandoned. It was not. . . . In any case, I feel it would be worthwhile to indicate that, in the *Breviario* and in *Nuovi saggi d'estetica*, there is not the same logical necessity to continue his tirades against externalization as there is in the *Estetica*." I doubt that these remarks are absolutely correct. The complexity of the concept of intuition does not seem to be connected to the problem of externalization. The view that intuition is a synthesis of feeling and image has little significance in this matter: the synthesis is a spiritual act within the sphere of the creative process and unrelated to externalization. Croce's position in this regard did not change much in the *Breviary*; to remain coherent with his doctrine, he could not depart from the pronouncements made in his *Aesthetic* concerning the extrinsic character of externalization. Had he done so, he would have undermined the very foundation of his idealism. Art is for him a spiritual process resulting in an ideal product; externalization is, on the contrary, a physical process bringing about a physical object and, therefore, incompatible with spiritual activity. Allowing a practical act to be part of a spiritual process would have created serious difficulties. Moreover, once he had declared the identity of intuition with expression, there was no room for externalization within the creative activity. The coherence of the system would not have permitted any other solution. Whether his position is defensible outside the domain of logical reasoning is another matter.

136. *Nuovi saggi d'estetica*, p. 47.

agree with Croce's logical reasoning) the genres must have answered some psychological needs of writers and readers; they cannot have been invented by some madman for the simple purpose of memorization and classification. After Croce's devastating onslaught, they continue in fact to live and be widely used in literary history and criticism. Everyone seems to be aware of a distinction between a tragedy and a novel, a comedy and an epic poem. These are felt as the conceptualization of historical experiences which have become part of the personality of the artist and which operate as inner elements, ideal forms illuminating the concrete act of creation. Every new acquisition enriches and enhances his artistic personality. Categories are functions of the subject in his thinking; they do not exist a priori: they are the result of experience; but once formed they become part of the constitution of the subject. In short, the genres must have had a psychological justification throughout history, which cannot be dismissed on the basis of logical deductions. Nor are they entirely extrinsic categories tyrannizing artistic creation; they are, on the contrary, intrinsic modes of experience. If this were not so, one would wonder why so many people fashioned their artistic experience in the form of a tragedy or an epic poem. The genres are spontaneous ways of perceiving reality or conceiving and expressing it through images; they are not artificial plants: they are exigencies deeply rooted in human nature. The Aristotelian classification was based on extrinsic elements, that is, the manner of telling a story by narrative or by dialogue, or both. It was a posteriori and did not take into account the psychological aspect of the problem, the aspect which would have shown those forms of art to be the result of archetypal exigencies of the human mind. The genres express the diversity of our esthetic enjoyment, for the pleasure derived from an epic poem is not necessarily the same as that derived from a comedy.

Certainly, if they were the outcome of extrinsic and accidental classification, Croce's position would be definitely unchallengeable. But there are serious doubts as to the correctness of his analysis which, to some extent, was prompted by the demand for coherence within the system and by his adverse attitude toward the superficial use and abuse of genres in literary criticism over the centuries. In our times everyone agrees that it is foolish to judge works according to the rules of the genres: the uniqueness of each work of art does not allow reduction to a common pattern. But the genres are not inflexible forms which reject individuality and uniqueness. On the other hand, to qualify a tragedy by the generic (though fundamental) distinction of poetry and nonpoetry is not enough.

There are artistic differences between tragedies as tragedies and epic poems as epic poems which cannot be ignored.

For Croce the universal qualities of a work of art are its sincerity of emotion, its unity and expressivity, and its ideality; and the basic question for the critic is whether a given work, in the light of these elements, is or is not art. Strangely enough, both the merits and the shortcomings of Croce's literary criticism lie in his stopping at the fundamental question. Asking and trying to answer this question without dwelling in "trifles" is certainly his major achievement; however, not to proceed further is a sign of narrowness. Poetic expression is achieved through the devices offered by a particular genre. How can one do real justice to works of art without taking into account these devices through which its concreteness was realized? Apart from them the work eludes us completely. One may argue that, when the fundamental mood of a poem has been re-created and characterized, the critical process has not yet come to an end. The integration of the means of externalization to the fundamental feeling is still to be considered, before a final judgment is formulated. By stopping at the most general question as to whether a work is poetry or nonpoetry, Croce leaves completely unexplored the vast and rich field of craftsmanship, which cannot be entirely detached from the esthetic domain. To determine whether a work is or is not art is an important part of the critical process, but it is not all. There should be the possibility to evaluate it as a tragedy or an epic poem. Croce's refusal to proceed beyond the general character of a work prevents him from formulating a thorough and complete judgment. The poem sings only in the form of a genre. Can we now judge the spirit while disregarding the body in which it is incarnated?

Croce's intransigence against the literary genres, though coherent with his system, inevitably led him to a narrow evaluation especially of theatrical works. Let us confine ourselves to the case of Corneille. Judging a play on the basis of its fundamental character—the lyrical expression—does not do justice to a theatrical work as such. The structure or the elements in which the poetic pearl is set have no esthetic value for Croce. While admitting that the structural elements are a part of the whole, he never allows them equality with lyrical expression. Thus he cannot be said to assess the total value of a theatrical work, which is a complex organism exceeding the restricted sphere of esthetics as he defines it. There is no question about the exactness of his observations concerning the lyrical character of certain parts in Corneille's plays; but the crux of the matter is whether one judges a work for what it is (in this case, tragedy) or for what it is not (a series of lyrical passages). Croce's theoretical premise is that from the esthetic point of view tragedy does not exist and that, esthetically speaking, there is only poetry (or nonpoetry) with no specifications; tragedy is simply an empirical classification outside the esthetic domain, genres not being based on esthetic differences. This clearly means that all literary forms are brought to a common principle—lyricism—and that anything else has no esthetic importance. If, on the contrary, one believes that the theater has its particular exigencies, the critical problem begins to appear under a different light from that envisioned by Croce—which is rather unilateral. Have we said all there is to say about a theatrical work when we have grasped the lyricism of some passages? Croce, of course, is convinced that we have. But one may object that the reduction of all arts to a common denominator is actually disregarding the special exigencies of each art for the full expression of its object. The epic poem, the drama, the novel are, in their concrete and total reality, more than pure lyricism. They require particular techniques, sometimes so intimately connected with the creative process that it is impossible to separate them from such a process when a total judgment is to be expressed.

It is common knowledge that poetry completes itself when read aloud; otherwise, why write it in meter and rhyme? If this is true, a dramatic work completes itself in the stage presentation; otherwise, why stage it at all? If it could express all of its meaning in the written form, there would be no real need for theatrical presentation. But if it is brought to the stage, it is because the work (or the expression) is incomplete in its written form; it needs the stage setting, the decorations, and living beings as expressive devices in order to render the author's vision in its fullness and totality. Unfortunately, all the technical invention which enters into the construction of a dramatic work—the organization of episodes, the conflict between characters, the scenery that the author imagined in conceiving the play, and, above all, the tone and the accent of phrases and words through which he tried to bring forth the image—are in Croce's criticism reduced to nothing. His method stops at the distinction between poetry and nonpoetry. It is useless to speak of drama criticism, art criticism, music criticism; for criticism is one (as is art), and its purpose is to recapture the lyrical source and to characterize it by distinguishing the structural elements as something alien to poetry. Whether it be a dramatic work, a symphony, or a painting, the aim of criticism is always the same. But how can one conceive of a painting without

knowing the means of expression by which the artist gives concrete reality to his work? Croce's criticism of theatrical works is, therefore, fragmentary, for in a tragedy the lyrical parts do not encompass the whole of the work. A tragedy is a living organism in which the parts (lyrical and nonlyrical) are in such close relation with each other that it is impossible to detach one part without damaging the whole. Two eyes are not beautiful or ugly when detached from the face; or the face, from the general structure of the body. In the case of Corneille, it seems that the dramatist must be read in an anthology of lyrical pieces, for Croce judges him on the basis of these pieces detached from the whole of the play. But this would not give the full dramatic value of a tragedy as such.[137]

9. *The First Phase of Croce's Literary Criticism*

Croce's concept and methodology of literary criticism developed alongside his activity as a critic, which began immediately after the publication of his *Aesthetic*. It has been rightly suggested that his theoretical advances went hand in hand with his experience with works of literature. Both theory and practice seem to have grown through mutual support. In fact, his *Aesthetic* does not offer much on the methology of literary criticism; his views on the matter (see pt. 1, chaps. 16, 17) do not go beyond the romantic formula: the critic re-creates the work of art by reliving and re-expressing it *(artifex additus artifici)*. "When the entire aesthetic and externalizing process has been completed," he says, "when a beautiful expression has been produced and it has been fixed in a definite physical material, what is meant by *judging it?* To *reproduce it* in oneself."[138] And he adds further: "The activity of judging which criticizes and recognizes the beautiful is identical with the faculty producing it. The only difference lies in the diversity of circumstances, since in the one case it is a question of aesthetic production, in the other of reproduction. The activity which judges is called *taste;* the productive activity is called *genius:* genius and taste are therefore substantially identical."[139] Without this identity, communication and judgment

137. The conception of the theater and the actor as instruments for externalization was abandoned in his later years; and so was his theory of the stage presentation as a "translation" and, therefore, as a creation of new works of art by the actors (see *Nuove pagine sparse*, [Naples: Ricciardi, 1948], vol. 1, p. 200). In *Terze pagine sparse* (1955), vol. 2, pp. 267–68, there is evidence that Croce had recognized diction and mimicry and scenery to be "a single act of artistic creation, in which they cannot be distinguished."
138. *Aesthetic*, p. 118.
139. Ibid., p. 120.

would be impossible. The critic must possess artistic genius in order to create a work of beauty. Taste is active in the artist because it is a part of the creative process (it is the discerning eye of genius); it is passive in the critic because it receives and judges the completed work. But taste is universal and absolute in character because it is substantially the same in all men. Croce rejects the judgment founded on metaphysical and objective models or on individualistic relativism. To judge means to look at things from the author's point of view, to penetrate the situation which inspired the work; and in this, all judgments, whether in morality or in science, present a certain analogy, for the critic must enter the point of view of the author.

The critic, therefore, transforms himself into an artist. While the man of taste stops at the re-creation, the critic goes further: he tells in his own words what the artist said. The reproduction, however, is always a new expression, because artistic expression cannot be repeated. Even translations result in works which are different from the original. The reproduction, thus qualified, is possible only if we succeed in creating in ourselves the state of mind which produced in the artist the creative impulse. Unless this is done, the communication within ourselves and with others would be impossible. In the *Aesthetic*, criticism seems to follow three steps (see pt. 1, chap. 17): first the historical reconstruction of the text, which consists in the philological and exegetical work and the reconstruction of the conditions of life in which the work of art was produced; the second consists in the re-creation by taste; the third in the judgment of the work. The scholar, the man of taste, and the historian designate "three successive stages of work, each independent of the one that follows, but not of the one which precedes. . . . But the true and complete historian, while containing in himself both the scholar and the man of taste as necessary prerequisties, must add to their qualities the gift of historical comprehension and representation." [140]

It seems that criticism is concluded with this "historical comprehension and representation," amounting to redoing what the artist had done. And artistic and literary history becomes "a historical work of art founded upon one or more works of art." [141] All this did not go far beyond what Croce had said in his essay *La critica letteraria* about eight years earlier. But these views were soon abandoned and critical activity transferred to the sphere of logic. The practical criticism in which he engaged after the *Aesthetic*, the writing of his

Logic (see pt. 2, chap. 3), and his *Philosophy of the Practical* (see part 1, sec. 2, chap. 6) threw more light on the matter and better clarified the problem of criticism. This appears particularly clear in some writings collected in *Problemi d'estetica* and in the fourth chapter of the *Breviary of Aesthetics*. Criticism is no longer simply re-creation; it is a logical operation in which one applies a category (the concept of art) to a fact (artistic intuition). In his *Logic* Croce had postulated the identity between the judgment of fact (or individual) and the judgment of value: "True judgments of fact—individual judgments—are nothing but judgments of value, determinations of the particular quality and, therefore, of the meaning and value of the fact; nor is there any other criterion of value except the concept itself. Consequently, the distinction between the history of the fact and criticism (evaluation of the fact itself) must be rejected. All history is at the same time criticism, and all criticism is history: to ask what is that fact called the *Divine Comedy* is to ask what is its value, that is, to express a critical judgment." [142] This pronouncement leads to the identification of esthetic judgment with historical judgment, that is, of criticism with history, which remained the cornerstone of his critical methodology. Such identity implies an immanentistic vision of reality that does not admit any value transcending historical facts, for Croce's philosophy does not arise as a solution to the ultimate problems of "being," but as an elucidation of the character of the categories of the Spirit and as research on the canons for the interpretation of the world of history. It is not a metaphysics, but a philosophy of culture. Croce, in fact, consistently condemns metaphysics as a "theologizing philosophy," and defines philosophy as a methodology of history. All reality is reduced to historical reality conceived as the activity of man, independent of metaphysical, theological, or realistic objectivity conditioning this activity. As a result, judging is no more than *qualifying* the nature of a fact; it is *qualifying* and *distinguishing*, since no values above the fact are conceivable.

In a short essay of 1909, after refuting the two dominant critical tendencies of the time—estheticism and historicism—Croce clearly expounds his own new formulation of criticism. [143] The esthetes, though gifted with artistic sensibility, seek art in its abstractness without ever grasping a concrete work; the his-

---

140. Ibid., p. 131.
141. Ibid.

142. *Logic*, p. 294.
143. "Critica e storia letteraria," in *Problemi d'estetica*, pp. 51–55. "Historicism" refers here to the *positivistic* school (whose tendencies were expounded by *Giornale storico della letteratura italiana*) and must not be confused with Croce's own *idealistic* doctrine, which he defined as "absolute historicism" (see *Philosophy, Poetry, History*, pp. 13–31).

toricists, insensible to art, fragment the work of art through their analyses and through comparison to other artistic facts without ever entering into a relation with art. Historical criticism aimed at explaining the work historically and paid little heed to esthetic considerations; the so-called esthetic interpretation, by reaction, went to the opposite extreme, declaring historical knowledge and erudition to be dangerous for criticism. Croce's conclusion is that historical information is useful insofar as it helps the critic to re-create the impression or emotion which entered into the composition of the work. The antinomy between "historicism" and "estheticism" is resolved by Croce into a unity. Art can be understood only in light of the historical factors which produced it; art can be judged only in itself. The right position lies in the synthesis, which considers the work of art as an organism composed of parts (to be evaluated in order to understand the whole) and as a whole (which must be understood in relation to the parts): "The true historical interpretation of art and true esthetic criticism are not two, but one—two in one and one in two."[144]

The first step of the critical process is philological and historical in character, furnishing all the textual elucidations and the historical information necessary for a full understanding of the work of art; the second step is that of *taste*, which re-creates and enjoys the work; but this is not yet criticism:

When . . . history and art are joined together so that art may be seen in its historical reality and history is considered from the exclusive point of view of the history of art . . . we have the fusion of taste and erudition . . . the true and concrete taste, but not yet art criticism or literary criticism. We relive the work of art, but we are not yet in a position to judge it. . . . It is necessary that the esthetic object, which has been reproduced by our imagination, be qualified, that is, thought as esthetic; that contemplation is followed by a logical art (subject, predicate, copula). Criticism (as such, and not as a mere hermeneutic preparation) consists in this very simple act of adding a predicate to the subject of contemplation.[145]

To judge, then, implies the possession of a concept of art, which, if it is not a presupposition for taste, is a presupposition for criticism, since criticism without a concept of esthetics would be inconceivable. Criticism is judgment which distinguishes between real and unreal; it is a logical operation determining the nature (logical, esthetic, moral) of a fact; and historiography means simply distinguishing and qualifying a series of facts. This operation cannot be performed by taste, which can only relive the work without judging it. The criticism of art is a logical formation implying

judgment, distinction, discrimination. It distinguishes art from the other forms of the Spirit. Those who do not like logic may create or enjoy art, but they cannot sufficiently reason about their enjoyment. The judgment of art is a synthesis of subject and predicate, esthetic contemplation and concept. The synthesis is the conscious reflection on art; it does not decompose in order to reconstruct logically the work of art, for in this case we would fall into the logicist's conception of art based on the degree of clarity between art and logic, and since art was supposed not to be clear enough, critics would give its logical equivalent. The difference here is, on the contrary, qualitative and not quantitative:

The criticism of a work of art gives neither the logical nor the intuitive equivalent of the work. It does not give the first because art is not logical thinking; it does not give the second because art cannot be translated. Criticism gives only the knowledge that what stands before us is, or is not, a product of art. Its problem is formulated in these terms: "*A* is art"; or "*A* is not art"; or "*A* is art in parts *a*, *b*, *c*; it is not art in parts *d*, *e*, *f*." In other words, criticism enunciates: "There is a fact, *A*, which is a work of art"; or "it is mistakenly believed that there is a fact *A*, which is a work of art." The judgment, which is called evaluation judgment, is resolved into historical judgment. For this reason, every art criticism is art history; and, conversely, every history of art is art criticism. To judge a work means to understand its nature (that particular nature), and thus to place it in its historical series. In this way the identity between art criticism and art history, between literary criticism and literary history is demonstrated.[146]

This conception of criticism, however flexible in its practical application, is re-emphasized in the *Breviary of Aesthetics* (chap. 4) where it receives a wider and more detailed treatment. Criticism is not a partial or unilateral act, but a comprehensive one, encompassing all the particular forms of literary analysis and historical information. The critic cannot be a preceptor giving orders, assigning themes, prescribing or prohibiting formulae: no one can tell the artist what to do. The critic is not merely a judge, either: discerning the beautiful and separating it from the ugly is a function accomplished by the genius and taste of the artists in their creative activity. This criticism would break through an open door. Nor can the critic be a simple interpreter and commentator. No one questions the usefulness of a learned guide, of someone who teaches how to read a work of art; but this is not criticism proper; it is no more than exegesis. True criticism is all these things together. Philological and historical exegesis is necessary for the re-creation of the work by taste, and both are preconditions of the true esthetic-historical judgment.

144. "Critica e storia letteraria," p. 43.
145. Ibid., p. 52.

146. Ibid., p. 54.

The main problem here appears to be whether the re-creation is possible or not, whether it is possible to reproduce the *individuum ineffabile*. Croce asserts that it is possible, because the beautiful is universal in character as is taste, which recognizes it. Spiritual unity makes possible the reproduction of art, since what the poet feels is what all the readers feel or can feel by virtue of the unity and universality of the Spirit. In principle only the universal can be reproduced; but the universal cannot be separated from the individual, for the true universal is the *concrete universal*. Artistic creation, historical and philological exegesis, the reproduction and enjoyment through taste are the antecedents of criticism. The *artifex additus artifici* is no more than a translator giving a variation of the work of art: in short, another work inspired by the first. Criticism begins when the *artifex additus artifici* becomes *philosophus additus artifici*, since criticism belongs to thought, which throws new light on reality and transforms intuition into perception, thus distinguishing the real from the unreal.[147] The criticism of art arises with the question, "Whether and to what extent this fact before us is intuition, that is, is real as such, and whether and to what extent it is not real."[148] Reality and unreality are, in esthetics, the beautiful and the ugly, respectively; just as they are, in ethics, good and evil; in logic, truth and error; in economics, the useful and the harmful. Criticism can be condensed in this formula: "There is a work of art *A*"; or "there is no work of art *A*." The formula implies, like any judgment, a subject and a predicate; the subject (the fact before us) presupposes all the exegetical and historical work, the re-creation with the accompanying discernment by taste; the predicate presupposes the esthetic category. But the determination of the subject, as well as the category, present numerous difficulties: the first, because of the complicated work it involves; the second, because the philosophy of art is always subject to changes due to philosophical developments in general. Since criticism depends on the concept of art, which changes constantly, there arose as many forms of false criticism as there are of false philosophies of art. There is a criticism that, rather than re-creating and characterizing, breaks up and classifies; there is a moralistic criticism which judges the works according to the ends that the artist proposes or should propose; there is a hedonistic criticism which presents art as a means of enjoyment; there is an intellectualistic criticism which is only interested in the intellectual content of art; there is a psychological criticism which separates content and form, and there is one which separates form from content as if form were completely abstract; there is rhetorical criticism which sees beauty only in stylistic ornaments; there is one founded on the literary genres and the distinction among the various arts, establishing laws for each genre and art and judging accordingly.

But the two principal enemies are esthetic criticism and historical criticism (which in reality are pseudoesthetic and pseudohistorical): one aims at the enjoyment of art in itself and rejects historical exegesis; the other believes that historical exegesis is the only *positive* criticism. Both have common enemies: philosophy in general and the philosophy of art in particular. For the esthetes criticism is the function of the artist; for the others criticism is the domain of scholars; the former reduce criticism merely to the activity of taste, the latter to exegetical research. But taste without concept is impossible, and history as disconnected erudition is not history because it lacks the concept. True criticism is esthetic in nature, but it does not reject philosophy. On the contrary, it operates as philosophy, that is, as a conception of art; it is historical criticism, but does not dwell on elements alien to art: it uses historical elements for the re-creation of art, but it becomes *history* by determining, after the re-creation, the *fact* reproduced by the imagination, that is to say, by *characterizing the fact* through the concept of art and by establishing exactly what the fact is.

It is evident that the two critical tendencies (the esthetic and the historical), though in conflict on a superficial level of criticism, coincide perfectly upon reaching the true critical stage: one evokes the comprehension of art; the other, the historical objectivity of such a comprehension. History, as a synthesis and not as a complex of erudite elements, is the end of criticism. As a result, true criticism of art cannot remain within the limits of the contemplation of the beautiful; it must rise to the level of explanation. And since, in the world of history there are no negative facts, whatever might appear ugly to the taste is not so in the historical consideration: history knows that whatever is not artistic is still something which has the right to exist, for it is a positive fact and cannot be condemned. The criticism of art, when truly es-

---

147. Croce established a clear-cut distinction between *intuition* and *perception* (see *Aesthetic*, pp. 304); intuition does not distinguish the real from the unreal: "In our intuitions we do not oppose ourselves as empirical beings to external reality, but we simply objectify our impressions." Whereas perception is the apprehension of "something as real": "What is perception if not a historical intuition, that is, the intuition of something which has really happened, and is judged as such? At the very instant in which we perceive it, the fact perceived has already become a historical fact" (*Problemi d'estetica*, p. 481, n.). Perception, that is, acting on a formed reality, is akin to reflection and judgment.

148. *Nuovi saggi d'estetica*, p. 79.

thetic or historical (the two terms then become synonymous), is thus broadened to a criticism of life, for one cannot judge a work of art without at the same time judging the works of life by assigning to them their own character. Since the forms of the Spirit are distinct in their unity, the judgment on one involves the others. It is clear that in literary criticism one speaks about a writer who is an inseparable aspect of the whole. De Sanctis serves here as a model for Croce: a model because he was a man profound in art, in philosophy, in ethics—profound in each one because profound in all. Croce concludes: "True and accomplished criticism is the serene historical narration of what has happened; and history is the only true criticism which can be exercised on the facts of humanity, which cannot be nonfacts, because they have happened, and cannot be dominated by the Spirit in any other way except by understanding them."[149] Since the criticism of art is inseparable from other criticisms, the history of art similarly cannot be separated from the history of human civilization, which is the whole Spirit and not one form detached from the rest. If the history of art seems to be separated from the rest of history, it is merely for the purpose of giving relief to its artistic aspect within the whole movement of history.

The *Breviary of Aesthetics* concludes, more or less, the first phase of Croce's esthetics and methodology of criticism. Croce's position as a literary critic, which has accompanied the development of his esthetics, is based on the absolute unity and indivisibility of the category of the beautiful: there are no degrees of beauty. The beautiful does not admit qualitative or quantitative differences; art either is or it is not: there is no other alternative. The ugly is the nonbeautiful, that is, the true, the good, the useful, posing as the beautiful. And of the beautiful one can say only that it *is beautiful*; of the ugly, on the contrary, one can give specifications, saying exactly what it is, indicating whatever reality it may contain. Criticism ends with the qualification of the work of art, which implies the thinking of the category. The statement that judgment is also the history of poetry contains two elements coinciding with each other: *fact* and *value*, historical research (which establishes the existence of the fact) and judgment (which attributes value to the fact). Judgment implies the universal and the particular in their a priori synthesis, which is the truth of the concrete universal in Hegel's dialectic—the unity of history and philosophy. The predicate in the judgment is the power which converts pure intuition into indi-

vidual judgment and poetry into history. The full understanding of a work is achieved by placing it in the proper historical succession of the works of the same author, for each poem contains his previous poems. To write a history means to distinguish and qualify a series of facts. It follows that the most appropriate form of literary historiography is the monograph.

The first phase of Croce's literary criticism is concerned with the individualistic nature of art. It aims at defining the distinctive character of art in relation to the other forms of the Spirit and at showing the original individuality of each writer. The object is the single personality historically determined. This canon governs, in an ever-clearer manner, the essays collected in the first four volumes of *La letteratura della nuova Italia* (1914–1915). One may say that this phase is dominated by lyrical intuition and the conception of art as the representation of the *individual*. Croce seeks the purity and distinctness of a work of art and considers that such a work contains more art when there is in it less of anything else. He strives at isolating the purely intuitive moments from those nonintuitive in character. The esthetic judgment follows the principle of any other historical judgment; it requires a particular subject and a universal predicate. The subject is the work to be judged; such a work, however, must not be considered in its objective existence, but in its re-creation in the mind of the critic—not as a fact, but as an act or process. Croce uses the term "taste" to indicate the act of re-creation as well as the inner consciousness governing creation. Since sometimes between the author and the reader there is a chronological distance, the re-creation demands the preparatory work of interpretation; this is achieved by the philologist, who reconstructs the cultural situation in which the work was born. The first step of criticism is, therefore, philological. The predicate of the judgment implies the category of the beautiful, which requires in the critic the knowledge of the philosophy of art; and since the philosophy of art or esthetics is related to the other parts of philosophy, he must know the whole of philosophy. In short, the critic must have the sensibility of the poet (in order to re-create poetry) and the mind of the philosopher (in order to possess the complete system of the categories). Criticism resolves intuition into judgment through the connection of the subject with the predicate, of the particular with the universal. Only in the judgment can one determine whether the emotion experienced is or is not artistic in character. In criticism the judgment alone (the intermediate phase) has an esthetic-logical value; the other two (the philological phase and the characterization) are subsidiary.

---

149. Ibid., p. 87.

Croce rejects stylistic criticism and the determination of artistic techniques, which deal with externalization. Art is all internal, and the physical means by which it is externalized do not belong to the esthetic sphere. To speak of the new technique of a novel means simply to speak of a new novel, for the new technique is nothing but the new novel. The use of literary genres for the analysis of entire groups of works is also rejected on the basis of the uniqueness of each artistic intuition. Croce, in addition, makes a complete separation between biography and poetry, and discards research on the life of an artist as not being necessarily a help for the understanding of his work. When the exegetical moment is over, the critic must immerse himself in the work and remain in it. Formalistic criticism and the criticism addressing itself to content (whether psychological or sociological) has for Croce nothing to do with true criticism, which is a synthesis. Starting from the work the critic must move backward and redo the process of creation, dwelling on the moment when the matter of life is superseded and resolved into form, in which the emotion has taken on a private character. *Character* means the reference of the feeling expressed by poetry to a class (or genus and species), so that it may be defined by a formula. By performing the same operation with the other works or parts of works of a poet, one may build his poetic personality, by indicating the fundamental state of mind and by arranging around it his whole production from the very beginning. But the psychological classes (genera and species) are not those derived from scièntific psychology; they must be found through a delicate study of the poetic works and a profound experience about the human mind. Characterization has simply an empirical value and is always an approximation, for its formulae are never definitive: they must be corrected, improved, refined constantly. The critical discourse, however, can never be a substitute for the work of art; it must refer to it repeatedly, the function of criticism being only subsidiary in character.

Croce's practical criticism, though flexible, follows in general a certain pattern. It does not shun polemical points aimed at dismantling, on concrete grounds, what he had condemned in theory and at proving the truth of what he had maintained. The first step is often the criticism of criticisms, that is, the refutation of erroneous characterizations; then, the delineation of the essential characteristics of the artistic personality in its development: this comprises the psychological definition, the principle of individuality and creativity (in opposition to literary genres), the theme of sincerity, and finally the general characterization. Within this framework Croce misses no opportunity to refute whatever in criticism is foreign to the true judgment of art—stylistic criticism, the concept and relevance of technique, the impersonality in art, the sociological, psychological, intellectualistic tendencies in the consideration of works of art; classicism, romanticism, naturalism as esthetic concepts; erudition, grammatical analysis, pure poetry, science and poetry, dialectal literature; the writer as a social reformer; and a number of other problems which, in his opinion, have no relation to the esthetic problem. These discussions, which are prompted by the particular nature of each writer studied, serve as a foil for the portrayal of individual authors and for the articulation of the main points of Croce's doctrine on the level of practical criticism. The distinction of "the poetic from the unpoetic, the beautiful from the ugly," which becomes more apparent and conscious in *La letteratura della nuova Italia*, remains the basic canon of his literary criticism throughout his career.[150]

The essays (which began to appear in *La critica* in 1903) contained in the four volumes of *La letteratura della nuova Italia* certainly lack homogeneity. Being to a large extent an illustration of Croce's theoretical positions, they follow the evolution of his doctrine on art. The theoretical digressions, which were to serve as clarifications of such a doctrine and as a refutation of other critical methodologies, amply attest to this. Since these essays occupy about twelve years of critical activity (encompassing over fifty years of literary history, 1860–1914), one might vaguely distinguish three periods of his criticism, in each of which a dominant theme seems to obtain. The series opens with an essay on Carducci (which was completely rewritten seven years later), who among the moderns remained Croce's favorite poet for the moral health of his poetry. But in this first period Croce shares some ideas with the "verists": having defined art as an expression of impressions, he admits tacitly the external stimulation for artistic creation. He does not, however, share the "veristic" idea of art as "document." "The artist," writes Croce in reference to Capuana, "does not examine documents, which is the function of the investigator of ultimate reality; he does not describe typical examples, for this is the function of the naturalist; he does not proceed . . . from the outer to the inner, but from the inner to the outer: this makes him an artist."[151] In the essays on Verga and on Capuana he combats "verism" and the doctrine of the impersonality in art, defended by Capuana: "Impersonal art

150. *La letteratura della nuova Italia*, vol. 5, p. 5.
151. Ibid., vol. 3, p. 107.

should be an art which neither laughs nor weeps, which shows neither sympathy nor antipathy, which does not color its representations with passion and feeling. Such an art never existed and can never exist. Man, in the presence of a scene that moves him, cannot remain indifferent, and he impregnates his representation with his feeling and his judgment, whatever these may be." [152] The program of "verism" to join poetry and science was not only an impossibility, but a gross theoretical mistake. Its doctrine contained a unilateral view of things, that of man lowered to the level of an animal. Some "verists," however, saved themselves through their artistic talent which led them beyond the doctrine. Verga is the most important of them. Croce's admiration for Verga is, in fact, prompted by the feeling of human sympathy by which the writer's representations are pervaded: "The impersonal Verga reveals his personality made up of goodheartedness and melancholy." [153] In Verga subjectivity prevails over objectivity. Between Verga, who felt, and Capuana, who judged (without feeling) "human documents," the contrast is evident and shows that for Croce the work of art is nothing more than a state of mind.

The criticism of verism brings about the theory of the lyrical character of art and of art as the expression of personality. Croce abandons the objective elements of artistic representation and develops the new concept thoroughly: "What the characters have that is real is the feeling of the artist, which manifests itself in his narration." [154] Croce views art only as stimulation from within, from the spirit to the body, from the unity of feeling to the variety of its incarnations. Art is imagination, pure intuition, formal perfection, regardless of the quality of its content. This view in Croce's doctrine (theoretically elaborated in his "L'intuizione pura e il carattere lirico dell'arte") allows him to appreciate D'Annunzio, the "dilettante of sensations," and to defend him from the accusation of immorality and lack of thought. He asserts the autonomy of artistic form and he brings to light, with admiration, the formal perfection of D'Annunzio's poetry, the Poet's art being entirely imagination, never troubled by reflection. [155] D'Annunzio represents his psychic dilettantism *perfectly*, and that is what concerns us, for art is the *perfect* expression of a state of mind. Poetry does not arise if passion is absent: "We do not ask the artist to teach us about real facts and thoughts, or to startle us with his rich imagination, but to have a personality capable of

firing the soul of the listener or spectator." [156]

With the maturation of his "Philosophy of the Spirit," Croce's criticism begins to involve the totality of the Spirit, its ethical-political content, the value of thought and moral life. This development led him to his attacks against decadentism, which appeared to him to be completely empty as compared to the previous period represented by Carducci. Croce finds positivistic philosophy, rhetoric, and irrelevant erudition in literary criticism to be somewhat justified by certain exigencies of the time: they had an object, a faith in an ideal which, unfortunately, was false. But decandentism lacked everything; it was "the great industry of emptiness." The triad representing decandentism consisted of D'Annunzio, Fogazzaro, and Pascoli, of whom Croce denounces the falsity and vacuity. The causes of this situation are, according to him, the declining faith in thought, the false idealism called mysticism: "This factory of emptiness, this emptiness which pretends to be something, this non-thing which appears among things and wants to take their place or to dominate them, is *insincerity*." [157] And this insincerity is characterized as "lack of inner clarity," resulting from the lack of thought. In an essay entitled "Il carattere della più recente letteratura italiana" (written in 1907), [158] Croce remarks that in this literature " . . . blows a wind of insincerity," which was exemplified by the three most important writers of the time—D'Annunzio, Fogazzaro, Pascoli:

My readers know my great esteem of a part of their works, particularly of the first [D'Annunzio], who is the most vigorous and the richest artistic temperament of the three, and how indignant I am when I see them ignored or despised. Some malicious people would say that I am indignant and that I defend them so that I may speak ill of them in my own way. . . . But in the maliciousness of these people one thing is true, namely, that I dislike in the three writers exactly what other people admire: the heroic morality and the civil and patriotic lyricism in D'Annunzio, the neo-Catholicism and the heroic morality in Fogazzaro, the magnification of Pascoli to the level of professional poet and *vates* assuming a pacifistic and humanitarian mission. This is a triple lie, which brings about the rhetoric of emptiness in their works—truly artistic only when the real strings of their hearts resound. In passing from Carducci to these three it seems sometimes like passing from a healthy man to three nervous wrecks. Doubtless they are artists whose names are written in our literary history; but I am afraid they are written in a less glorious manner in our civil history, which soon must remember them as a document of today's spiritual vacuity. [159]

Croce's ethical-political orientation is evident. His

---

152. Ibid., vol. 3, pp. 106–107.
153. Ibid., vol. 3, p. 29.
154. Ibid., vol. 3, p. 113.
155. Ibid., vol. 4, pp. 10ff.

156. *Problemi d'estetica*, p. 18.
157. *La letteratura della nuova Italia*, vol. 4, p. 196.
158. Ibid., vol. 4, pp. 188–206.
159. Ibid., vol. 4, p. 200.

criticism becomes more and more encompassing as his literary experience grows. His model poet is Carducci, whose mature poetry "springs from those feelings which could be called elementary in humanity—heroism, struggle, fatherland, love, glory, death, the past, virile melancholy. Carducci's ideal is not transitory, but an ideal which sings in the depths of every strong and sensitive, complex and serene soul: he is thus within the tradition of great poetry." [160] Art expresses the fullness of life; and criticism, by judging art, becomes a judgment of life.

In light of this more advanced concept of art, the essay on Carducci was rewritten and enlarged in 1910 with the new perspective which had matured in the course of the years. Here Croce takes a decisive anti-romantic and anti-irrationalistic attitude, reiterating his attacks against decadentism. Carducci's ethical ideal was the opposite of D'Annunzio's sensuality, which Croce had praised a few years earlier because of its perfect expression. Croce began to feel perhaps a certain uneasiness toward D'Annunzio as a result of the development of his esthetic in the direction of the ethical-political concept of art. Art is the synthesis of the whole of spiritual life which, having reached the ethical form, reverts to matter of artistic intuition by virtue of the circularity of the Spirit: "The *matter* of poetry is action or the desire for action; the matter of action is what one has poetically dreamed of and rationally known. . . . Thus, to understand a poet critically means to understand the dialectic of his soul, the practical and passional no less than the contemplative and poetic forces which agitate him, and to show how from the conflict of these forces his poetry is sometimes facilitated and sometimes hindered." [161] D'Annunzio, the pure *dilettante of sensations*, no longer fits the new poetic formula.

Croce's practical criticism follows a general pattern, which seems to be almost constant throughout his career. He approaches each of his writers through a refutation of erroneous characterizations. Once he has weeded the field, he enters into the heart of the matter, trying to reach and define the fundamental feeling that animates the writer's creative impulses and to study their development, and, finally, to characterize him by a comprehensive formula. This is done by keeping the eyes constantly fixed on the writer's work and by distinguishing art from nonart. Other problems are irrelevant to the critical judgment. The essay on Carducci, with which Croce begins, serves as a model for the essays which followed. The false defini-

tions of Carducci as the "political poet," the "pagan poet," the "antiromantic poet" are all dismissed as misleading. Carducci is the "poet of history, of the history of civilization and culture: the poet of philology in the Vichean sense"; he is the poet of the heroic, the strong, and the human. After reaching this characterization, Croce outlines the inner conflicts from which Carducci's poetry springs and its growth toward the maturity of his art. Criticism does not limit itself to the distinction of the beautiful from the ugly, but it aims at reconstructing the spiritual process which generates the artistic expression.

The first four volumes of *La letteratura della nuova Italia* are practically concluded with an essay on De Sanctis, which celebrates the thinker and the critic, the teacher of moral life and the writer. De Sanctis and Carducci, with the richness of their ideals and their ethical-political aspirations, represent the exemplary critic and the poet, respectively. Despite the changing perspectives which are noticed in *La letteratura della nuova Italia*, there is a persistent point dominating the work, the creative subjectivity of art, a subjectivity which reverses positivistic criticism and any other critical methodology which departs from the creative personality of the artist and which loses itself in matters alien to artistic intuition. The purpose of criticism is the identification and definition of this subjectivity.

10. *The Polemics against Actual Idealism, and the Cosmic Character of Art*

The first important development in Croce's *Aesthetic* of 1902 was, as we have seen, the "lyrical character of art," theorized in 1908. The *Breviary of Aesthetics* (1912), which condenses with more firmness and coherence his entire theory, was written with this new concept in mind. But a major step forward was made in two essays published a few years later—"The Character of Totality of Artistic Expression" (1917) and "L'arte come creazione e la creazione come fare" (1918)—both collected in *Nuovi saggi d'estetica* (1920). In the first of these essays, Croce gives art a broader meaning and a more comprehensive humanism; in the second, he seeks to eliminate completely the "receptive" character of art and therefore its objectivism, for art, being the self-creative activity of the Spirit, becomes totally idealistic in nature through the suppression of everything outside spiritual activity, every object standing as something other than the Spirit itself. "Art . . . ," says Croce, "does not reproduce anything already existing; it always produces something new; it forms a new spiritual situation and, therefore, is not

160. Ibid., vol. 4, p. 189.
161. Ibid., vol. 2, p. 35.

imitation, but creation." [162] This essay definitely improves upon the concept of "lyrical intuition," in which feeling seemed to stand outside intuition itself as its content. In fact, Croce wrote in the preface to the fifth edition of his *Aesthetic* (1921) that the two developments given to his doctrine—the lyrical character of pure intuition and its universal or cosmic character—were respectively "an attack directed at every sort of false art, imitational or realistic," and an attack "at the no less false art made of unrestrained or *romantic* passional effusion." [163]

As previously postulated by the author, art is the first form of knowledge, that is, esthetic knowledge, which is alogical and is, therefore, knowledge of the individual, logical thinking being the knowledge of the universal. [164] To obviate the narrowness of art, Croce broadened the concept of lyrical intuition to encompass not merely the individual but the universal, the totality of spiritual reality; thus art becomes the intuition of the universal in the individual, that is, the individualization of the universal—the expression of the concrete universal. Art expresses the feeling of the individual, but, since the individual bears the mark of the human condition, it expresses at the same time the universally human. Concurrently, Croce sets forth the principle of art as creation against the still persistent traditional theory of imitation, and he defines creation as spiritual activity—the self-creative activity of the Spirit. With these two essays Croce arrives at a sort of integral classicism, for the idea of totality represents the overcoming of the romantic conception of art as purely lyrical effusion: totality or universality or "cosmic character" means synthesis of pathos and ethos.

These developments appeared to bring Croce close to the positions of "Actual Idealism" and to justify Gentile's claims that Croce's esthetics, in order to become idealistic, had to move in that direction. If, in fact, the esthetic moment is the beginning of the circular movement of the Spirit and if the ethical moment, which contains all the others, is the end and is at the same time the beginning of a new circle, it follows that the content of art is the ethical world of the poet, that art draws its substance from the totality of spiritual life, which includes intellectual elements. But Croce categorically rejects any intellectual element, declaring that to attribute the universal character to art he does not need to depart from the conception of intuition or to correct it. He interprets the

totality of art as a totality *sub specie intuitionis*: in the dialectical movement of the Spirit, the ethical world reverts to the subject matter of art, to a new content of intuition. Totality would appear similar to adulthood falling, by virtue of the dialetic process, to infancy's state of contemplation and dream.

If at first Croce aimed at defining the distinctive character of art in relation to the other activities of the Spirit, he now concentrates on the total human rhythm of art, which offers an integral vision of man. In the first instance the object is the individuality of art; now it is the universality which the individual image expresses. Poetry is the perennial voice of humanity in its complexity and totality, in its conflicts and harmonies. Croce emphasizes at this point the principle of *intensity* and *unity* rather than that of singleness: the image of the poet is artistic when the life of the cosmos vibrates in it intensely and when the moral conscience from which it springs is highly rich and profound. To achieve this cosmic character art must stress, alongside "romantic" spontaneity, the discipline which constitutes its humanistic moment. The category of *literature*, which Croce will introduce later, with a positive meaning, confirms this attitude, for in literature precepts, rhetoric, imitaion, and so on, have a definite importance.

His universalistic conception of art matured, significantly enough, during the tragic years of the First World War and was in harmony with his internationalistic tendencies and his opposition to a narrow inhuman nationalism. Art transcends nationalism. But the concept of universality in Croce's doctrine must also be viewed in the light of Gentile's "Actual Idealism," which had received its first formulation in 1908 with the essay "Le forme assolute dello spirito," followed in 1912 by "L'atto del pensare come atto puro," the two together containing the substance of one of his major theoretical works, *General Theory of Spirit as Pure Act* (1916). [165]

Croce's collaboration with Gentile, while friendly, did not always reflect complete agreement on philosophical grounds. Their lack of consensus, latent at the beginning, increased in fact slowly and came into the open through an "amicable" public exchange during the years 1913–1914. Gentile did not fail to notice in Croce the persistence of Herbartianism, which hampered the attempted unification of spiritual life. As a result, the dualism of subject and object in Croce's philosophy was still present. But the philoso-

162. *Nuovi saggi d'estetica*, 4th ed., p. 152.
163. P. xii.
164. See *La storia ridotta sotto il concetto generale dell'arte*; *Aesthetic*, p. 1; *Problemi d'estetica*, pp. 1–30; and also *Logic*.

165. See "Le forme assolute dello spirito," in *Il modernismo, Opere complete* (Florence: Sansoni, 1962), vol. 35; and "L'atto del pensare come atto puro," in *La riforma della dialettica hegeliana*, *Opere complete* (Florence: Sansoni, 1954), vol. 27.

unify; Gentile, on the other hand, rejected the *thereness* of distincts as an empirical and naturalistic remnant of Croce's thought. He insists that the Spirit is unity only to the extent that it is *becoming*, development, which implies distinction, but *within* the developed unity, as its motor force. But the pure relationality of such ceaseless becoming was considered by Croce as mystical. Although Croce's negative attitude toward "Actual Idealism" continued unabated, the friendly confrontation with Gentile did not leave him indifferent to the latter's philosophical position. The two developments of his esthetics, "The Character of Totality of Artistic Expression" and "L'arte come creazione e la creazione come fare," seem to reflect a movement of his thought toward Gentile's views. Gentile, in fact, received the two essays favorably, seeing in them a new attitude, not only in Croce's esthetics, but in his philosophical doctrine as well.[170] The first essay postulates a conception of art as an expression of the universal in the particular (previously Croce had identified intuition with the knowledge of the particular). This need for giving unity and totality to the act of the mind had been formulated by Gentile several years earlier in discussing Croce's distinction between art and thought in connection with the third edition of the *Aesthetic*. Since from intuition Croce goes to the concept, which is a higher degree of knowledge, it seems to Gentile arbitrary to deny that in intuition there can be the seed of the concept, if the life of the Spirit is to be considered as development. Poetry cannot be separated from logic, one being contained in the other. Contrarily, if the ethical moment, which comprises the other three moments of activity of the Spirit, is the end of the process and coincides with the beginning of a new process, it is clear that art encompasses the whole experience of the Spirit, both theoretical and practical, and that poetry and philosophy are not completely separated. In "The Character of Totality of Artistic Expression," Croce had taken a considerable step toward the unity and totality of the spirit through conceiving of the finite, the individual, as nothing outside the infinite or the total: "To give artistic form to a particular feeling is to give it altogether the character of totality, the cosmic afflatus; and, in this sense, universality and artistic form are not two things, but one."[171] In the accent of the poet, in every creature of his imagination, there is the whole human drama, the hopes and illusions, the suffering and joys, the miseries and greatness of the whole reality.

The other essay, "L'arte come creazione e la creazione come fare," is considered by Gentile as another attempt to unify a persistent duality in Croce's philosophy. Since Croce distinguishes theoretical activity from practical activity, each conditioning, and irreducible to, the other, it seems that both were bound to chase each other around in a circle without ever coinciding. In this case, intuition would presuppose a situation (feeling or life in its instinctual immediacy) which would be brought to light by art. This would mean, under a different form, a return to the old theory of art as imitation, even if the object to imitate is no longer an external nature but an inner state of mind. The new proposition of art as creation eliminates any object outside the creative process of the Spirit, for art does not reproduce anything already existing, but forms a new spiritual situation. In Croce's philosophy the concept of *knowing* considered as *doing* is not the identification of knowing with doing, thought with will (which would be a mystical unity): knowing is a theoretical doing, a perpetual creation of problems and production of solutions which are all spiritual acts never directed to external objects. Art knows its object by creating it within the Spirit. If the object were outside its creative activity, art could not know it. The problem that art solves is the problem that art itself posits: "Life and feeling," Croce writes, "must be transformed, through artistic expression, into truth; and truth means transcending the immediacy of life in the mediation of imagination, that is, in the creation of an image which is that feeling situated within its relations, that particular life situated within universal life, and thus elevated to a new life no longer passional, no longer finite, but infinite."[172] Art intuits the particular within the universal, the part within the whole, the finite within the infinite. This, according to Gentile, indicates a sort of "intrinsic relation between art and philosophy" (art being the knowledge of the particular and philosophy the knowledge of the universal), a relation that Croce had always denied.

With these remarks Gentile's critical contribution to Croce's esthetics came to an end. Unquestionably, Croce was not insensitive to the need for absolute unity in the spiritual act. The growth of his esthetics from the concept of intuition and then of lyrical intuition of the individual to the broader and more comprehensive notion of the universality and totality of lyrical intuition, to art as spiritual activity, and, finally, to art as morality, seems to obey the general preoccupation concerning the unity and totality of

---

170. See "Nuove idee estetiche," in *Frammenti d'estetica e letteratura*, pp. 173–78.

171. *Nuovi saggi d'estetica*, p. 124.

172. *Ibid.*, p. 150.

every act of the Spirit. Art thus comes surprisingly close to philosophy (the totality of knowledge); it is no longer alogical knowledge, the dawn of spiritual activity, but ethical life embracing the whole human drama.

The closeness of art to philosophy, however, is here simply a logical deduction which does not correspond to fact. Croce's background and concrete literary experience prevented him from accepting the identity of art and philosophy advocated by "Actual Idealism." Although he was attracted by the inner logic of a system of absolute immanence which guarantees the unity of the Spirit, he certainly saw the danger of suppressing all distinctions. The direct outcome of such a suppression was, in his opinion, mysticism and the ineffable character of reality. While Gentile fought vigorously the specter of dualism, Croce tried to avoid that of mysticism. As a result, Gentile did not budge from his extreme subjectivism submerging everything in the *mare magnum* of indistinction (which, in the opinion of his critics, renders impossible every value judgment of the particular); Croce, on the other hand, was unable to free himself completely of an objectivistic conception of art: his definition of art as intuition implied the existence of something to be intuited (feeling, nature) outside the self-creative activity of the Spirit. In the main, Croce remained attached to the particular as real, and he accepted the unity as the necessary relation which the particular entertains with the whole: "I confess," he writes, "that what always interested me is the moment of particularity, whereas unity appeared to me as something to be taken for granted, understood (how can one think that the universe is two or more rather than one?), offering no other difficulty than those arising from a misunderstanding of its nature."[173] A few years later (1922) Croce summed up the philosophical difference between himself and Gentile in these terms:

Our general conception of philosophy of the Spirit (of the subject, and never of nature, or the object) has developed a peculiar stress in Gentile, for whom philosophy is above all that point in which every abstraction is overcome and submerged in the concreteness of the act of thinking; whereas for me philosophy is essentially methodology of the one real and concrete thinking—historical thinking. So that while he strongly emphasizes unity, I no less energetically insist on the distinction and dialectic of the forms of the Spirit as a necessary formation of the methodology of historical judgment.[174]

Croce's essay on the "character of totality . . . ," though surprising in its pronouncements, was wel-

comed by some of his followers who felt the lack of universality in his esthetic theory. His opponents, however, saw in this development the reversal of positions Croce had previously held. Within the framework of his theory, the essay expounding the "character of totality" is a baffling piece in which Croce seems to be at pains trying to reconcile all the conflicting elements without contradicting the doctrine he had thus far professed. From the concept of art as totality there followed the idea that art is a logical process (which Croce firmly denies) and most importantly that the source of art is the totality of spiritual life, that is, the all-inclusive ethical world. Since totality and morality seem to mean the very same thing, the new concept was viewed as a deviation from Croce's earlier theory which asserted that art is "knowledge of the individual." Gentile wrote in this regard: "Here we are faced by a new aspect of the Crocean doctrine . . . a concept which comes unexpectedly to anyone who has followed the development of Croce's thought."[175] Certainly, as Adriano Tilgher observed, "we are a long way from the conception of art as knowledge of the individual," and it is also true that "the new wine" had burst "the old bottle";[176] this development, however, was already anticipated in previous works. In the essay on the "lyrical character of art" we read: "The esthetic image is loosened from the limitations of space and time . . . and belongs not to the world but to the supraworld, not to the passing moment but to eternity."[177] And in *The Philosophy of the Practical*, a similar idea is suggested: "The characteristic that Schelling and Schopenhauer noted in music, of reproducing, not indeed the ideas, but the ideal rhythm of the universe, and of objectifying the will itself, belongs equally to all other forms of art."[178] But a more definite anticipation is found in the *Breviary of Aesthetics*: "The emotion or state of mind is not a particular content, but the whole universe viewed *sub specie intuitionis*."[179]

If art is the whole universe *sub specie intuitionis*, what is logic? Let us go back for a moment. There is in Croce a naturalistic conception of art (*Aesthetic*), a humanistic conception of art (art as lyricism), and the conception of art as total truth (the cosmic character). But if art is a totality, autonomous and complete in itself, there is no room for logic. The first formulation that art is the knowledge of the particular and logic that of the universal seems to be more coherent than

---

173. *Conversazioni critiche*, vol. 2, p. 72.

174. Introduction to Gentile's *Reform of Education*, trans. Bigongiari, p. x.

175. *Frammenti d'estetica e letteratura*, p. 175.

176. Tilgher, *Estetica: teoria generale dell'attività artistica*, pp. 18–19; Borgese, *Poetica dell'unità*, p. xxiv.

177. *Problemi d'estetica*, p. 27.

178. *The Philosophy of the Practical*, trans. D. Ainslie (London: Macmillan, 1913), p. 269.

179. *Nuovi saggi d'estetica*, 4th ed., p. 34.

the new expansion of the theory, which eliminates the degrees of knowledge and blurs the distinction between intuition and logic. That the individual is inseparable from the universal is a truth which can only be perceived by *reflective thought*; the individual as known by the intuition is the individual per se, completely unrelated. To affirm (as Croce did in later pronouncements) that "in art the universal is *indistinctly* united with the particular,"[180] constitutes a negation of the distinctness of art.

It seems (and this is a view shared by some Croce students) that what changes here is not the nature of intuition but the content of it, which is immensely broadened in comparision with that of the *Aesthetic*. The content is no longer the physical sensation, or the subhuman impulse; it is not the individual feeling, or the whim of the moment, but feeling in its plenitude—sin and redemption, suffering and joy, egoism and altruism. The totality is attributed to feeling, not to the image. Images supposedly continue to be individual, that is, determined. Therefore, artistic knowledge is intuition, not logical discourse. In this sense and within these limits the knowledge of the individual prevails. It is feeling which is transfigured and from particular (tied to determinate situations and characterized by a definite emotional tonality) becomes total, universal. Feeling loses its narrowness and individuality and becomes cosmic in its passage from practical life to its condition as object of contemplation—a passage accomplished through art. The "character of totality" emphasizes the theoretical nature of art as contemplation. But intuition now encompassed the whole of reality, not just the particular, as previously theorized.

All this, however, is not entirely supported by Croce's text, which postulates that content and form are both individual and universal or total—individual because the dominant element in art is the individual feeling realized as image; universal or total because in the image is reflected the whole human condition: "Particularity, finiteness . . . does not characterize feeling—which is both individual and universal, as is every form or act of reality, and does not characterize intuition—equally individual and universal at the same time—but it characterizes feeling which is no longer simply feeling, and representation which is not yet pure intuition."[181] This means that the individual

acquires totality and universality when it transcends its immediacy through the artistic image: thus every artistic expression is the transformation of the individual into the universal through a purely intuitive process.

The "character of totality" is in line with Croce's attacks against decadentism, the essence of which is a lack of ideals and affections. The synthetic unity of content and form implies on the part of the poet a moral soul without which the synthesis cannot be achieved. A soul lacking balance, one which is fragmentary, dehumanized, cannot rise to the level of synthesis. The pure poetry of decadentism reflects a tendency toward animality, irrationality, lack of faith and of humanity; it is the expression of brutal and turbulent impulses, instincts of blood and sexuality, or ecstatic contemplation of refined beauty from an ivory tower, with no other concern. This attitude led to the bloody orgy of the Second World War. Croce writes: "Poetry, as life in its whole, has no other theme than the dialectic of the relation between the *high* and the *low* in man, between his moral ideal and his sensuality."[182] Man is an integral entity, not a pure poet, and this integrality is morality. Art must reflect the whole man, his total experience—feeling, logic, practical activity, the whole drama of life, providing, of course, that all this reverts to feeling and thus becomes the material of art. Personality means a complete man who feels and understands the fundamental exigencies of life—the desire for truth, for the beauty of action, for morality which comprises all and causes the individual to live in the humanity of the world. Art thus appears as a sort of intuitive metaphysics. In the individual motif the poet expresses the whole. He cannot consider or express the fragment without enlightening it by means of the universal. Art is the expression of the eternal structure of reality. The Spirit always remains the same, with its categories and the

---

180. See Gian N. G. Orsini, *Benedetto Croce: Philosopher of Art and Literary Critic* (Carbondale: Southern Illinois University Press, 1961), pp. 224–25.

181. *Nuovi saggi d'estetica*, p. 123. A reader (see above, n. 135) made the following suggestion: "Maybe the best way to explain 'the character of totality' is by comparison to the argument in the *Breviario*, where the

poem is said to begin in an immediate feeling, an *aspirazione*, a longing which is realized as images. Now, however, Croce wants to recognize still another element of the artist's activity, this 'love of cosmic harmony' or 'character of totality' which turns the immediate feeling with which the poem begins into a kind of problem, a source of dissatisfaction as well as satisfaction. Thus throughout his expressive act, the poet must be asking himself what his entire cosmos, all the images he is in the act of creating, would be like if they were dominated and unified by his immediate feeling. This drive toward 'harmony' and 'totality' is itself a feeling; it involves not concept or predicate affixed ex post facto to the immediacy of intuition. But it is also a form of judgment, a specifically poetic judgment, what Croce calls an 'auroral' form of knowing, operating as a 'self-correction,' a 'self-limitation'; it is the artist's way of criticizing himself, or refusing to exclude other feelings and actions from the immediate and dominant feeling of his creation. The 'totality' or universality comes from this inclusiveness; the particularity from the immediate feeling with which the poem began."

182. *Letture di poeti*, p. 141.

dialectical relations among them; the Spirit is the substratum of the ever-new creations of history, for art is the expression of the eternal through the historical. However, the question arising from these ideas is whether they constitute a philosophy which would exactly fit the description of "absolute historicism," as Croce later defined his philosophy.

The concept of "totality" implies, as we have seen, the problem of art as morality. But the latter was fully recognized in Croce's *Aesthetica in nuce* (1928). [183] While in the *Breviary of Aesthetics* he had made a clear separation between art and morality, he now brings in morality in order to give unity to the various forms of spiritual life—a unity which he always fought to preserve. He posits, as the foundation of art, human personality unfolding in the light of moral laws: "The basis of all poetry is human personality, and, since human personality finds its completion in morality, the basis of poetry is moral consciousness." [184] By this Croce does not mean that the artist as a man must be morally exemplary, but that he must take part in the world of thought and action and live through direct experience the "full human drama." [185] He must have a clear consciousness of good and evil. To be *vir bonus*, however, is not enough for being a poet, for the poet must possess the gift of poetry without which all else would be like a pile of firewood without kindling.

Croce's attacks against contemporary tendencies defending "pure art" is the direct outcome of this broader concept of art. The poet must nourish himself through the events of his times; he must be a complete personality, involved in political life, facing moral toil, searching for truth. In fact, the idea of the "complete personality" required for the poet prompted Croce to reject decadent literature. His critics retorted that his distaste for modern poetry was mainly due to ethical exigencies; but their argument was not well founded for it misconstrued the true relation between art and morality. The problem was not one of moralism, that is, whether art should preach virtue or piety rather than portray reality; morality must be taken as viewed by Croce in the dialectic of spiritual forms. Morality is the highest form of spiritual life, and it contains art within itself; and since the totality represented by morality reverts to material for poetry, poetry is this totality *sub specie intuitionis*. Thus the moral world is within the world of art. There is no question of boundaries between the two domains, for one lies within the other.

The whole fabric of life (with no exception) can become the object of a work of art when this fabric is elaborated by the intuition-expression, that is, when its narrowness as living experience is transcended. It appears then in its truth, which may be good or evil, for these are the essential elements of reality. Morality is not asceticism, which suppresses one of the terms of the dialectical process intrinsic in ethical life; art is moral because it springs from this dialectical polarity, resolving it into the artistic form: "The dialectics of poetry corresponds in this, through its own law, to the dialectics of the moral conscience." [186] Poetry cannot be conceived outside the moral conflict which is the essence of life. By suppressing moral conscience and the clash between the moral will and the forces of evil, one suppresses poetry, which transcends and harmonizes their polarity in the contemplation of life.

Decadentism contains a moral and an esthetic fault and, therefore, lacks art. From the moral point of view, it is the opposite of asceticism, since it suppresses everything except sensuality and egoism (which Croce qualifies as the "libidinous"—not only eros, but the actual desire for blood and war); from the esthetic point of view, it lacks catharsis as a result of its suppression of the moral conflict. It confuses art with the tumult of the senses—the tumult that is not art, but the matter of art. [187] Decadentism remains at the level of animal brutality, below the artistic level.

Croce's negative evaluation of decadentism (he had already expressed the same negative judgment about baroque literature) reflects his taste for the classical tradition which, according to his critics, prevented him from understanding contemporary art. In Croce's eyes the contemporary period was one of decadence. But one might raise the question: had not Croce always maintained that esthetic theory must proceed hand in hand with artistic production and that no theory could be held definitive? New esthetic experiences must create new problems requiring new solutions. Should we say, in this regard, that his doctrine was out of tune with the artistic and literary developments of his times?

11. *Poetry and Literature*

In its process of development, Croce's esthetics tended to accept within its domain cultural elements which he had rejected at the time of the first formulation. In *The Poetry of Dante* (1921), for instance,

---

183. See the entry "Aesthetic" of the *Encyclopaedia Britannica*, 14th ed.

184. *Ultimi saggi*, 2d ed., p. 10.

185. Ibid., p. 11.

186. *Poesia antica e moderna*, 3rd ed., p. 182.

187. See *Ultimi saggi*, p. 28.

Croce recognizes the positive role of structure in the *Divine Comedy*, that is, the "theological-political romance" within which poetry flourishes; and in *Poesia popolare e poesia d'arte* (1929) he gives positive value to all the cultural elements dissolved into poetry, fostering and enhancing it.[188] The romantic concept of poetry as an expression of uncultivated and barbaric ingenuousness in the Vichean sense is transcended in this recognition of the function of culture in poetic creation. The book *La poesia* (1936) brings Croce's speculation on the problem of esthetics to a final conclusion and offers a complete theory and justification of nonpoetry, that is, "literature."

In fact, the most important novelty here is precisely the category of "literature" as distinct from that of poetry. This development is, as I mentioned earlier, the logical outcome of Croce's concept of art as totality. If art encompasses everything, it must comprise also what is not art. In summary, one may say that in the first phase of his esthetics Croce's main concern was that of the emotional content of art; thereafter its theoretical character takes a primary position. At first art is the expression of the individual; then it becomes the expression of a cosmic image, of the whole. At the beginning the theory of art is conceived as a theory of poetry, but this concept was gradually broadened and finally included a theory of literature as well. It must be noted that poetry and literature do not designate two *genres*, in the general sense of the word, but two *qualities* found in creative works. Whereas previously Croce had qualified the nonbeautiful as *ugly* and *esthetically indifferent*, in *La poesia* he distinguishes the beautiful as *poetical beautiful* and *literary beautiful*, always remaining anchored to the concept of poetry and nonpoetry.

In the ancient world poetry and literature were governed by two distinct disciplines—poetics and rhetoric—which denoted two fields of composition, two habits of conceiving and ordering.[189] Poetics was viewed as the art of expanding man's vision, its method being primarily imaginative (a progress from image to image determined emotionally); rhetoric was considered as the art of instructing and persuading, its method being intellectual (a progress from well-dressed ideas to well-dressed ideas determined logically and emphasized through their attractive appearance). Poetics, in other words, dealt with the composition of images; rhetoric with the composition of ideas.

Although Aristotle maintained a clear-cut distinction between the two disciplines, they were gradually drawn toward each other. Rhetoric, overwhelmingly favored in the schools, tended to absorb poetics within its sphere.[190] As a result, the two distinctive forms of composition were blended and confused to the disadvantage of poetics, which assumed a dependent role. Many concepts belonging to rhetoric, such as the distinction between content and form, between "bare" and ornate, proper and metaphorical expressions, and, in general, all precepts concerning the use of figures of speech were transferred into poetics and from there (in modern times) into esthetics. Needless to say, ideas on the theory of art were profoundly affected. The persistent confusion between poetics and rhetoric generated confusion between poetry and literature, with serious misunderstanding especially in the field of criticism, where works are often praised or condemned for what intrinsically they *are not*.

When Croce undertook to formulate his own theory of poetry, he immediately noticed the confusion of esthetics and rhetoric, and the common practice of applying the principles of the latter to the judgments or appraisals of poetic works. In his determination to clear the field of esthetics of erroneous principles, he showed a particular aversion to rhetoric, in the precepts of which he sensed a complete disregard for po-

---

188. See *Poesia popolare e poesia d'arte*, pp. 21–36.

189. The term "literature" was first used by the Latins to denote the art of reading and writing, the knowledge of letters. Literature had therefore a subjective meaning, being the state of a person's literacy or literary education. It was not an object of knowledge, a number of works that one can study, but a skill that one possesses. To speak of the "literature" of a person meant to speak of his learning in the field of letters. Critics and theorists, referring to what one may today call "literary works," would use the word "poetry" or, in the case of prose, "oratory." This earlier meaning of the term "literature" persisted until the second half of the eighteenth century, when its denotation gradually shifted from men to works, thus taking on an objective and all-inclusive meaning, that of literary production. Literature denotes now, in its general acceptation, all the writings of imaginative nature or in which the imaginative movement is present. However, while the term has, on the one hand, tended toward a concrete, material meaning, on the other it has tended to assume an abstract meaning, that of an intellectual category. In the latter sense, literature loses its various specifications such as "French" or "English" to become a science, a body of knowledge—"literature" in the singular form. Croce employs the term in this unqualified sense. Literature is for him the art of ornate expression, and it can be identified with rhetoric. There is, then, literature (stylistic ornaments, formal elaboration) and the *works* of literature (those possessing formal beauty, bestowed by the appropriate use of rhetorical embellishments). Scientific, philosophical, historical works, when expressed in elaborate and elegant form, become literary works as well, literature being the adornment of content.

190. Originally rhetoric was a large and varied *corpus* of disparate precepts—literary, ethical, psychological, political, and so forth—meant for lawyers, politicians, and others in public life. With the disintegration of ancient civilization, a good part of the compound body of rhetoric decayed while the rest of it grew as the art of literary composition and ornate expression. In the modern sense rhetoric contains, on the one hand, a little more, on the other, much less than it contained for the ancients. It deals no longer with the *quid dicendum*, but exclusively with the *quemadmodum*.

etry. Croce's keen concern with the theory of poetry led him, at the time, to scorn non-poetry (literature) and the principles governing its production. He later admitted that in his youthful radicalism he had failed to consider whether that which was not compatible with poetry might find a useful place in another area of human activity.[191] After all, how could he reject literature forever, without damaging his own work as a writer? Was he not also a man of letters par excellence?

The problem of literature is adumbrated in the third chapter of his *Aesthetic* when he speaks of *poetry* and *prose*: "Poetry is the language of feeling, prose of the intellect; but since the intellect is also feeling, in its concreteness and reality, all prose has its poetical side."[192] But in his *Conversazioni critiche*, under the title of "Poesia, prosa ed oratoria, e valore di questa tripartizione per la critica letteraria," he speaks of a threefold spiritual attitude—poetry, prose, oratory; imagination, intellect, practical activity; authentic language, language-sign, language-instrument—which extends to all arts (painting-poetry, painting-prose, painting-excitement) and which is difficult to distinguish in concrete cases.[193] After the theorization of the cathartic and cosmic characters of art, it followed that further distinctions were in order. This led to the question of what relation these nonpoetic expressive forms can have to art. Under what conditions can they aspire to the dignity of art? Hence the problem of literature. Already in *La letteratura della nuova Italia* there are references to "literary" qualities, as distinct from poetry. But no step was taken to rehabilitate literature. Only in *Poesia popolare e poesia d'arte* was the value of literature underlined for the first time.

After about thirty years of study on the origin, character, and criticism of poetry, the author returned, with a definitely changed attitude, to the long-neglected problem of literature in *La poesia*, finding at last a place for literary expression and its theory (rhetoric) in the sphere of the mind. He subsequently articulated in a clearer manner the theory of literature and its relation to that of poetry in an article published in 1949 in *Quaderni della critica*, "Poesia, opera di verità; letteratura, opera di civiltà."[194] Croce's analysis of the diverse nature of poetic and literary expressions, and the various particular elucidations he gave through many examples are worthy of serious consideration, since they contain excellent points of orientation in the dark forest of literary theories and critical methods.

While Croce seems to give great importance to spontaneity in artistic creation, he is always concerned with the formal elaboration which subdues passion. The value of romanticism and that of classicism, passion and discipline, must constitute the poetic synthesis. But, though he emphasizes the formal elaboration in poetry, he rejects attempts to establish rules and norms, the whole of the rhetorical tradition. Rhetoric is an old error, but the source of it must be investigated. What exigency made rhetoric so important throughout the ages? In the error of rhetoric there must be some truth. This problem led the author to theorize on literature. What is literature? His *Aesthetic* begins with the question, "what is art or poetry?" *La poesia* (which gives the conclusive formulation of his esthetic theory) on the first page raises the question, "what is literature?" In order to determine the origin, nature, and purpose of literature and to study the nucleus from which the complicated organism called "literary work" developed, Croce proceeded with an accurate analysis of the four fundamental forms of expression (which correspond to the universal forms of the Spirit), namely, the "expression of feeling in its immediacy," "poetic expression," "prose expression," and the "oratorical or practical expression." "Literature" cannot be identified with any one of them. Three of these forms of expression belong to either the intellectual or the practical spheres of the mind and, although serving legitimate purposes in life, result in non-poetic works.[195]

Since art is identified with language, the true expression is the poetic expression. The expression of feeling in its immediacy is an explosion of uncontrolled emotions such as joy, fear, sorrow, and surprise, the simplest form of which is the interjection. These natural utterances emitted through vocal articulations, gestures, mimicry, contortions of the facial muscles are, of course, not art; they are "symptoms." The romantics made the mistake of confusing these

---

191. P. 43 below.
192. *Aesthetic*, p. 26.
193. *Conversazioni critiche*, vol. 1, p. 62.
194. See now *Philosophy, Poetry, History*; "Poetry, the Work of Truth; Literature the Work of Civilization," pp. 296–308.

195. The three spheres are those of logic, economics, and ethics. The activity of the Spirit begins with art and ends with ethics. But the beginning and the end coincide. Since feeling belongs to the world of man's action, the life of the Spirit begins, ends, and begins again with feeling: ". . . beginning with feeling and its natural expression, then passing to intuition or fancy, which transforms feeling into image and relative expression and gives it poetic form; and from there to thought, which existentializes and judges the world of images; and from thought to action, which from the world thus apprehended goes further to create a new world of reality. . . . The movement of spiritual activity, upon reaching its completion, begins afresh as though returning to its point of departure; it becomes feeling again and thus a new cycle begins" (*La poesia*, pp. 28–29). This circularity, however, seems to jeopardize the absolute independence of art, which Croce had maintained (see *Aesthetic*, chap. 2).

crude emotions with poetic expression; they rebelled against any poetic temperance and smoothness, giving free vent to the violent impetus of their inner tumult. But a torrent of disorderly phrases is not artistic beauty; Baudelaire and Flaubert in France and Carducci in Italy reacted against the precipitous effusions of romanticism. The domain of natural and uncontrolled feelings is part of the world of human action. Emotions spring from man's practical activity; they are life itself in its joy, suffering, enthusiasm, fear, hate, and love.

"Poetic expression" (expression in the theoretical sense, that is, a form of knowledge) is transcendence of the obscure emotional state; it appeases the violent outburst of feeling, transforming it into images. Poetry is not joy or suffering in its natural manifestations; it is joy or suffering transfigured by poetic expression into sweet remembrance. It is the contemplation of joy or suffering in the melancholic serenity of recollection. While feeling "remains . . . within the narrowness of passion, the antinomy of good and evil, the excitement of joy and suffering, poetry, on the contrary, ties the particular to the universal; it embraces suffering and pleasure, transcending them and, rising above the clash between the parts, it reveals the place of each part in the whole, the harmony over the conflict, the sweep of the infinite over the narrowness of the finite."[196] Feeling is the content which poetic expression molds and converts into images—images in which the emotion, still trembling, achieves that catharsis which is the joy of poetic beauty. Poetry is alogical knowledge and is, therefore, characterized by indistinction. This form of knowledge is not, however, merely passive or receptive in character; it is creative. Poetry is, in fact, creation, since it never reproduces anything already existing, but always produces something new, always creates a new psychological situation by placing feeling, that is, individual life, in relationship to universal life. Poetic expression is viewed as universality or totality, since it contains the drama of the individual in its universal dimension: "Every genuine artistic representation is both itself and the universe, the universe in that individual form, and that individual form as the universe. In every accent of a poet, in every creature of his imagination, there is all of human destiny, every human hope, illusion, suffering and joy, greatness and misery, the entire drama of reality."[197] The humblest folk song, if brightened by a ray of humanity, is poetry and can compare even with sublime poetry. The impression

which poetry leaves in the heart and mind of men was spontaneously felt as "melancholy." Poetry was compared to love, but it is rather the waning of love if all its reality burns in passion—the waning of love into the serene vision of a transfigured reality.[198]

"Prose expression" belongs to a higher sphere of mental life. While "poetic expression" moves in the realm of indistinction between reality and unreality, "prose expression" converts the imaginative world into the world of reality; it consists in the determinations of thought, symbols, and or signs for concepts. "Poetic expression" distinguishes itself from "prose expression" as imagination does from thought and as poetry does from philosophy. "Prose expression" is logical reasoning in which language is a symbol for concepts; it transcends the alogical world of poetry, elevating it to a conceptual form. Hence the profound meaning of the saying that poetry is "the maternal language of mankind," that poets precede prose writers. Poetry is language itself in its purity and originality.

"Oratorical expression" belongs to the world of practical activity, that is, the world of economics and ethics, and is meant to arouse particular emotions and states of mind, to bring about persuasion, or to provide entertainment. If the simplest forms of the expression of feeling in its immediacy are interjections, those of oratorical expressions are imperatives: "Hurry!" "Come now!" "Well, then!" and so on, which are used as sounds and as meaning. Under the category of oratorical expression one may group a variety of practical forms of expression, represented by political and forensic allocutions, didactic and moral works, books for entertainment, and so on, the main purpose of which is to move or to persuade in view of practical ends. Language here is simply in function of practical activity. Croce does not distinguish the *economic* from the *ethical*, seeing no difference between the *useful* and the *good*, from the point of view of expression.

"Literature" cannot be identified with any of the above-mentioned expressions, since it does not belong to the same domain of spiritual activity. Literary expression, theorizes Croce, "is a part of civilization and education like courtesy and politeness, and it consists in the harmony attained between nonpoetic expressions (such as the passional, the prose expression, the oratorical or exciting) and the poetic, so that the former, while remaining essentially what they are, do not offend esthetic sensibility." Thus, Croce continues, "if poetry is the maternal language of man, literature is his preceptor, or at least one of his preceptors,

---

196. Pp. 15–16 below.
197. *Nuovi saggi d' estetica*, p. 122.

198. See p. 21 below.

in civilization. The song of the poet springs forth spontaneously in times of uncouthness and rusticity, and there are those who exaggeratedly maintained that poetry has no more propitious social conditions than barbarity. But no literature can flourish under such conditions, because if it could, those times would have reached the civilized state."[199] "Literary expression" is, one may say, an expression of the expression. It arises when the fundamental expressive process (of whatever nature) is completed, when the activity of the Spirit has taken one of its forms. This means that "literature" does not belong either to the sphere of the beautiful or to that of the true, the useful, the good. At this point one might think that, since the beautiful, the true, the useful, and the good exhaust reality, literature, not being identified with any of them, has logically a dubious existence. But this is not the case. Literary expression, as we have seen, is not an essential function of the mind, a categorial form of it, but is a historical product related to the progress of civilization. It is possible to know and to act without passing through literature, without seeking harmony between nonpoetic expressions—a harmony which is reached by giving esthetic adornments to nonpoetic expressions, so that, though basically different from poetry, they may acquire the flavor of poetic beauty. Literature is then ornament, decorum, civilized restraint, the sense of refinement and courtesy, the appropriateness of language, the beauty of external form, which are, in a word, the expression of civilization. It does not operate on formless matter, but on spiritual expressions already formed; it is, therefore, something added; it is dress. As a result, the duality of content and form, which is rejected in poetry (where only the synthesis is real) must be accepted in literature. This duality, alien to esthetics, thus becomes characteristic of the theory of literature,[200] provided that for content one means a spiritual form already realized and that for form one means nothing but an ornament, that is, something not essential. By this theory Croce aims to do justice to the old rhetoric, but, by accepting the principle concerning the ornate form, he makes a point of breaking the union of rhetoric with the esthetic form, which had existed for centuries.

Literature, in short, is the esthetic form given to nonesthetic expressions, which constitute its content. It applies to the three forms of nonpoetic expressions as dress whose purpose is to bring them close to the esthetic expression—poetry. It is, therefore, the work of refinement and coherence, rhythm, articulation,

tone, decorum, which these expressions acquire through the finishing touch of literary adornment. These qualities are added to nonpoetic expressions through the application of literary skill and through the proper use of a pertinent technique guided by sound literary taste. In a civilized society nonpoetic expressions nearly always assume this external decorum required by good taste; therefore, a certain dose of literature is found in all these expressions, since civilized persons wish to express themselves in an effective and elegant manner in all manifestations of life, lest they be considered uncouth and rude: "Poetry is the expression of truth; literature the expression of civilization."[201]

The literary form is not an autonomous form in addition to the other four. Its function is to satisfy the esthetic exigencies of nonpoetic expressions; therefore, its existence is conditioned by this function. The literary form is not really one, but many, according to the needs of the expressions demanding its help. Literature is not necessary: it only represents an attempt to give a poetic flavor to the expressions which do not possess it in their own right. The human soul is poetic and feels the power of harmony and beauty; as a result, it seeks to extend more and more its domain in order to modify or change whatever might disturb it. Literature tries to bring beauty where none exists; it smooths the violence of immediate expressions; it embellishes whatever is ugly, though substantial. To say something in any field (philosophy, science, history, and so on) is not enough; it must be said well, and this is literature. It gives rhythm, coherence, beauty, proper emphasis, melody. The faculty which governs literature is "tact," "practical ingeniousness." The nature of nonpoetic expression is not transformed by literature; such nature remains fundamentally the same. Literature does not transcend practical tactfulness and skill; it dresses them. Literature carries a moral justification for itself, even when it improves its content, for the content remains as it is and is never redeemed. There is in literature, however, an esthetic element, but it is not clear in what this esthetic element consists: does it consist in the character of sociability and urbanity? Croce delineates here an expressive sphere which is placed next to poetry, rather than opposite it;

---

199. P. 41 below.
200. See *Discorsi di varia filosofia*, vol. 1, p. 251–60.

201. A historical view of the concept of art as truth is given by Francesco Flora's "La rivolta romantica e la poesia come verità" (*Letterature moderne* 7 [1957]:5–33). The ancients conceived of poetry as a beautiful lie, a sweet fancy, and this conception persisted up to the time of romanticism. Perhaps one of the most significant achievements of romanticism is the introduction of the concept of poetry as truth, a notion which gradually replaced the old doctrine. Croce's esthetics developed further this concept of poetry as truth, defining its character as intuitive truth and, therefore, the first form of knowledge. Poetry coincides with language, which is the first form of consciousness of the world in its mere existence or presence and consequently the first possession of truth.

and this sphere is endowed with positive characteristics: even style has a meaning, since there are as many styles as there are authors, whereas in poetry there is only one style, which is always the same, the eternal accent of beauty.

This conception of literature justifies and rehabilitates the existence and the teaching of the *ars rhetorica* governing literary expression, against which Croce had directed his onslaughts in his *Aesthetic*.[202] Rhetoric is the theory of *belles lettres*, of ornate form, and the schools teaching it perform a legitimate historical and social function. At the beginning of his research into the field of esthetics, Croce radically and scornfully expelled from the domain of poetry the concept of form as "dress," of beauty as ornament added to the "bare" expression—elements which rhetoricians, estheticians, and critics had erroneously associated with poetic expression. In *La poesia* the severe critic of rhetoric, the scorner of literary form, finally recognizes fully the positive value of literature and the discipline governing it. He rehabilitated literature and rhetoric, giving them their rightful place in the civilized world of which they are an integral part. Croce had slowly come to realize that the contempt of the romantics for rhetoric and the disparaging undertones attached to literature when compared to poetry (*et le reste est littérature!*) had no theoretical justification. Literature is not to be despised, for it fulfills an important task; it has only to be distinguished from poetry. The recognition that literature is not poetry should not lead to a negative judgment as it often does among those who, because of an exaggerated love for poetry, show little respect for so noble a part of human culture as literature. This prejudice created the belief that, when criticism has proved a work to be, in its theme and execution, oratorical and didactic and not fundamentally poetic, it deserves only condemnation. The concept of beauty in literature differs from that same concept in poetry. In the literary sense beauty is not the mysterious goddess who infuses a sweet and melancholy feeling into the hearts of men, but a gentle and dignified presence which, with a calm and harmonious voice, appeases and refines their impetuousity.[203]

The concept of art is also modified in literature. Croce had previously identified the term "art" with that of "poetry," and he had constantly used the two synonymously. In *La poesia* art no longer seems to be the poetic elaboration of feeling, but it is distinguished from poetry, as the elaboration of literary expression which belongs to the domain of practical activity and is governed by reason. Art is then literary skill, technique, founded on a body of knowledge; it is not pure and authentic expression springing from the heart of man. At times art and poetry seem to be opposite concepts, the term "art" being applied to that which requires a certain skill or technique and used synonymously with literature.

Consequently, the concept of taste is also modified. Taste is no longer the awareness of the poet in his creative moment (in which case taste and genius are identical), but something practical supported by rationality, which governs all practical activities. Good writers, in their elaboration of literary expression, are always guided by the principle of appropriateness or aptness. When ornaments are immoderately used, expression degenerates into affectation, pedantry, bombast; when ornaments are disregarded, expression falls into primitive crudeness. By using literary embellishments according to the principle of "aptness," one obtains the result of rendering nonpoetic expressions agreeable to the esthetic sensibility. In this sense taste can, Croce suggests, be more appropriately called "tact"; and "genius" will take another meaning contained in the etymology of the word "ingenium" (*ingegno*), namely, skill, which suggests practical contrivance.

One cannot expect from literature the complete abandon which characterizes poetry, since the main concern of literature is to express its purpose clearly, in full awareness of the public to which it is directed.[204] The "sacred furor," the "divine mania," the "inspiration of genius" are foreign to literary expression, which needs a different source of inspiration,

---

202. See *Aesthetic*, pt. 2 ("Rhetoric or the Theory of Ornate Form") pp. 422–36; see also *Problemi d'estetica* ("Poeti, letterati e produttori di letteratura") pp. 103–11.

203. See p. 43 below.

204. A distinction between poetry and literature somewhat similar to Croce's was pointed out by Sartre in his book *What Is Literature?* (New York: Philosophical Library, 1949). Sartre also indicates that poetry belongs to a purely imaginative and contemplative sphere, whereas prose (literature) belongs to practical activity and must always be directed to practical purposes. Hence the impossibility for the poet to be *engagé* and the impossibility for the writer not to espouse a cause. "Doubtless, emotion, even passion—and why not anger, social indignation, and political hatred?—are at the origin of the poem. But they are not expressed there, as in a pamphlet or in a confession. Insofar as the writer of prose exhibits feelings, he illustrates them, whereas, if the poet injects his feelings into his poem, he ceases to recognize them" (pp. 18–19). And further on, Sartre adds: "Prose is, in essence, utilitarian. I would readily define the prose-writer as a man who makes use of words. . . . The writer is a speaker; he designates, demonstrates, orders, refutes, interpolates, begs, insults, persuades, insinuates. . . . Prose is never anything but the privileged instrument of a certain undertaking. . . . It is only the poet's business to contemplate words in a disinterested fashion. It is reasonable to ask the prose-writer what his aim is in writing, since he cannot have pure contemplation as an end. For intuition is silence, and the end of language is to communicate" (pp. 20–21).

namely, a deep interest in the social and cultural world, a love for thought and action. Although literature belongs to the sphere of practical activity, it must never be a trade, for, if it lacks conviction and sincerity, it becomes completely vacuous, colorless, and awkward. Convictions enliven style, which is a purely literary element. In fact, there exist in literature as many styles as there are people and things; whereas in poetry, however varied it may be, the style is one— the eternal accent of poetry which resounds magically through all times and places regardless of the diversity of the subjects. Poetry is a *repraesentatio perfecta*, for it encompasses the universality in which life throbs; literature is a *repraesentatio imperfecta*, for it is always confined to the realistic motive which inspires it. Thus it is impossible to read a literary work and enjoy it as poetry, because it reveals in every word and in every accent its narrow, realistic aim.

Despite its important role in the civilized world, literature, Croce points out, has many enemies: some of them are practical men aiming straight at their practical purposes, feeling no esthetic need and having no taste for literary beauty; others are extremely sensitive souls who, unable to get out of their passional world, consider the search for the beautiful and polished expression as a profanation of sincerity; still others are scientists who, in their concern for factual truth, become asocial and insensible to literary beauty. Among further enemies of literature are those who prefer extraliterary expressions, namely, convulsive oratory, unordered utterance, unpolished prose, finding in these forms of expression a more direct contact with reality. Literary expression is for them a hindrance to directness and clarity. Literature, however, continues to have its devotees in the civilized world. It has always been taught in the form of precepts, and the tradition of its teaching was never extinguished. The Renaissance and post-Renaissance were the great periods of literature and literati. But even the Enlightenment, which was mainly concerned with facts rather than with the ornaments of expression, cultivated literature extensively. Romanticism, delighting in screams and moans, despised the studied and dignified expression and the art of rhetoric, but practiced the virtue of literary decorum which contributes to the preservation of civilization.

This conception of literature led Croce to classify literary artifacts into four broad groups. The first embraces works of which the content is feeling—not in the crudeness of its immediacy, but smoothed and embellished through literary elaboration, pruned of any unbecoming elements offending good taste or decorum, and clothed in artistic beauty. This literary elaboration of feeling must not be confused with poetic expression, although it seems to be close to it. Poetry is alien to exterior embroidery and ornamentation, since it is beauty in a pure and genuine form. Furthermore, the main characteristic of poetry is a pervasive sentiment of humanity and universality. Effusive literary works resulting from the elaboration of feeling, even when at their best in gentleness and refinement, confine themselves to man in his individual and practical reality. They never rise above the sentiment of the individual to the sentiment of humanity; the feelings they express remain anchored to the ego of the author and to a particular situation. One may infer, then, that feeling, only when touched by that state of grace which is the inspiration of genius, results in poetry, that is, the expression of the individual transmuted into the sentiment of humanity. When poetic inspiration is lacking and replaced by literary skill aiming at a particular purpose, the elaboration of feeling will result in effusive lyricism. All literatures are rich in this form of effusive lyricism (distinguished by Croce from *liricità*, that is, poetry) which finds expression in poems, epistles, diaries, memoirs, novels, and a good part of the so-called religious poetry. Writers such as Byron, Lamartine, Musset are typical of this mode of effusive-literary expression, since they nearly always remain complacently within the close circle of their own personal feelings, incapable of extending their vision beyond their ego. Moreover, effusive-literary works must be distinguished from "biography," since biography presents man's feelings and actions with a view to moral or historical judgment, whereas the form of lyricism in question presents emotions and actions without judging them, but lending to them literary decorations and formal beauty. It must be said that the exhibiting of private affairs, personal emotions, and sentimental attachments is not a defect of effusive literature but its logical and necessary characteristic.

The second group of literary artifacts consists of a large variety of oratorical works of which the main purpose is to propagandize an idea, to demonstrate a thesis, or to air a problem. Poems, dramas, novels, and so on, with a political, social, patriotic, or moral bias belong to oratorical literature. Although some of them reach a perfection of their kind, they are by no means poetic works. If they were, the very purpose of their existence would be defeated. Thus, when Flaubert remarked that *Uncle Tom's Cabin*, which was a weapon against American slavery, should not have been conducted "au point de vue moral et religieux," but "au point de vue humain," and that the novel should have risen above "l'actuel" and transcended the passions of the time, he did not realize that a work, conceived in that manner, would have been useless.[205] It would not have been an instrument of war but a book of high and serene poetry. One might wish only for more art and style in its composition, but nothing else. Manzoni is a typical case in point. His *Betrothed* is from the beginning to the end a work of moral exhortation conducted with an exquisite sense of literary form. Its spontaneousness and stylistic perfection led critics to consider it, erroneously, as a novel of poetic character, whereas it is one of fine literature.

The third group of works in Croce's classification of literature includes writing for entertainment, from horror stories to the purest comedy. Between these two extremes is a rich gamut of literary compositions portraying bravery, gallantry, love, and so on, in the form of short stories, poems, melodramas, songs, novels, and others. These works, which fill volumes of verse and prose, occupy one's leisure time. Although some of them are moving and enjoyable for their gracefulness, decorum, and suggestive stylistic power (as, for example, some of Poe's mystery stories), they are different from poetry even when the literary elaboration of the subject matter renders them perfect as such. Poetry is individuality and universality at the same time, whereas the writings in question tend to present the "typical" of the various modes of emotion. Thus tragedies of this sort remain within the "tragic type," comedies within the "comic type," novels within the "novelistic type."

The fourth group comprises works of didactic nature. Didactic literature is, like the other forms of expression mentioned, not realized in prose alone but occasionally in verse as well. Its field extends from philosophical and scientific treatises to historical, social, scientific, philosophical novels, dramas, and poems, the purpose of which is the vulgarization of problems and ideas. The role of literature in this category is difficult to understand. Why, for instance, do science and philosophy, instead of remaining outside the literary domain, often lend themselves to the embellishments of literature? Thinkers and scientists are not abstractly such. They are men who throw all of themselves into their work—their hopes, their sufferings, their joys. Their drama as thinkers and scientists unfolds within their drama as men. In order to keep the way open for their thinking and research, they must convince others of the importance of their field

of specialization or investigation. They often need to fight prejudices, to defend their doctrines, to arouse interest in their work. They must, then, come to terms with literature. The scientist, the philosopher, the historian become also men of letters—men of letters speaking to their times and their public. Such were Plato, Cicero, and Thucydides in antiquity; and such were Petrarch and Erasmus, who put an end to scholastic jargon and who treated moral and religious problems humanistically; Galileo, who presented his great discoveries in noble prose or in witty dialogues; Voltaire, who defended the light of reason and fought superstition with his agile and maliciously graceful language. The glory of literary prose belongs unquestionably to France. Countries such as Germany suffered long from the lack of it, and when Lessing appeared he was received with enthusiasm and a sigh of relief. There are thinkers and philosophers who disregard literature and try to remain aloof from its allurements. But even Calvin, who professed antipathy for poetry, maintaining that language was not given to men "pour faire rever les auditeurs et pour les laisser en tel état," could not resist the pleasure of writing "avec rondeur et naïveté," thus becoming the father of French literary prose.

Admittedly Croce's thinking, beginning with a rather narrow concept of art, became gradually more and more comprehensive by assimilating elements at first either ignored or scornfully rejected. This observation certainly applies to literature, which was to find full recognition of its positive value and historical role in his last book on esthetics, where it is analyzed as something distinct from poetry, but equally noble and dignified in the purpose it serves. The need for revaluating the nonpoetic forms of expression was already strongly perceptible in Croce's *Aesthetica in nuce* and in his *Poesia popolare e poesia d'arte*. *La poesia*, bringing the author's esthetics to its conclusive formulation, is the rehabilitation of nonpoetry, or literature, and its apology as the expression of civilization. Literature and its theory find thus their justification. This new development was viewed by Croce's critics as a contradiction of his theory of art, or perhaps as a crisis in this thinking, brought about by some of his allegedly false premises.[206] But it would have been a terrible mistake for him to leave out of his system such a conspicuous cultural activity as literature, simply because it did not fall within the sphere of poetic creation.

Croce's theory, however, appeared somewhat uncon-

205. Flaubert, *Correspondance* (Paris: Conard, 1927), vol. 3, p. 60: letter of December 9, 1852.

206. See Alfredo Gargiulo's "Crisi di un'estetica," *Nuova Antologia* (May 1, 1936), pp. 76–82. Reprinted in *Scritti d'estetica*, pp. 303–16.

vincing, especially the practical character of literature expounded in it. Some critics gave literature a quasi-poetic meaning: it is not poetry, but is an approximation, a foreshadowing, a presentiment of poetry. Beside the eternal expression of poetry, there are in human history a series of expressions which are not devoid of esthetic values. The category of *literature* encompasses all of them which, from a certain point of view, belong to the domain of esthetics even if they do not attain the level of timeless poetry. The man of letters has a moral conscience which confers sincerity upon these works: "Even when the writers do not touch the sphere of poetry, they draw from their moral conscience the virtue of sincerity, which is highly praised and greatly pleasing, for only a moral conscience can be sincere toward itself before being so toward others."[207]

One of the questions arising from the concept of literature concerns the esthetic quality contained in literary elaboration. This esthetic quality seems to be difficult to grasp. Literature suggests a lack of poeticality; it is harmony, rhythm, melody, which belong to poetry, but are not its essential part. The lack of poeticality is accompanied by the love of poetry, or at least a bit of it. However, while representing a lack of poeticality, literature may be a sign of poetic exuberance, for poetry sometimes extends beyond its own sphere. What, then, is the relation between poetry and literature? Their relation is based on the degree of poeticality of the two. But one may object that what gives literary value to certain pages of Descartes, Hume, Voltaire is the remembrance of the poetic rhythm transferred to a different domain. There is literature which approaches poetry; but there is literature which has a figurative value of its own far removed from poetry. The character of sociability or urbanity is not always the distinctive feature of literature.

The other question bears on the problem of criticism of literature. The dualistic and practical aspect of the doctrine (the distinction between content and form) not only undermines the spontaneity implicit in idealistic philosophy, but also moves away from the concept of unity. Croce's distinction between literature and poetry, although clear enough on theoretical grounds, may present some difficulties for the practical critic. It is indeed not easy to see where poetry ends and literature begins in a given work. Many of the concepts of rhetoric have become mental habits, patterns of conceiving and ordering intrinsic to the activity of the creative talent. Furthermore, Croce's

division of literary works into categories creates other practical problems, because no work will ever correspond perfectly to the norms he established for each group. His definitions are obviously to be taken in a broad sense as orientative concepts. The difficulty of recognizing poetry becomes greater because the concept of esthetic beauty applies to both poetry and literature. How can one be distinguished from the other?

12. *The Second Phase of Croce's Literary Criticism*

The theorization of the concept of "totality" (or universality or the cosmic character of art) enhanced Croce's critical approach, broadening its perspective. His critical essays no longer centered around the individual personality of a writer, but around the moments of his artistic life which reflected the eternal life and the universality of the esthetic spirit of humanity. In fact, with this idea in mind, Croce wrote his monographs on Goethe, Ariosto, Shakespeare, and Corneille, which directly or indirectly seem to emphasize the principle that art has no limits, that there is no Latin classicism or German romanticism or any other restrictive classification, but that there is only eternal poetry, universally human.

Croce was not a philosopher of the abstract; he believed that ideas live and operate in the world of facts, that they can be grasped in their existential form only through facts. His esthetics is not, therefore, that of a pure theorist; its constant application in the field of criticism kept it, in the process of its development, in direct contact with *artistic facts*, his theory of art stemming mainly from his keen interest in literary criticism. Sound criticism must, to his mind, be based on theoretical principles if it is not to be blind and nonsensical. Such theoretical principles, however, while conferring upon his esthetics a certain philosophical solidity, do not completely account for the great influence his doctrine exerted. Its vitality lies especially in the vast series of applications accompanying its development. Every new theoretical acquisition is followed by a new exemplification testing it in the field of criticism.

The first phase of Croce's doctrine is, in fact, as I have shown earlier, reflected in the first four volumes of *La letteratura della nuova Italia*. But around 1917, he abandoned the Italian literary scene (from 1860 onward) and undertook a series of monographs on major European writers, so that he might illustrate his concept of totality or universality in artistic intuition. This endeavor led to the volumes *Goethe* (1919), *Ariosto, Shakespeare and Corneille* (1920), *The Poetry of*

207. *La letteratura italiana del Settecento*, p. 352.

Dante (1921), *Poesia e non poesia* (1923), and several others, such as *Storia dell'età barocca in Italia* (1929), *Nuovi saggi sulla letteratura italiana del Seicento* (1931), *Poesia popolare e poesia d'arte* (1933), *Poesia antica e moderna* (1941), volumes five and six of *La letteratura della nuova Italia* (1939–1940), *Poeti e scrittori del pieno e tardo Rinascimento* (vols. 1, 2, 1945; vol. 3, 1952), *Letteratura italiana del Settecento* (1949), *Letture di poeti* (1950), all of which reflect, to varying degrees, the new concept of the universality (or totality) of art. I say "to varying degrees" because Croce's practical criticism, from the first four volumes of *La letteratura della nuova Italia* to *Letture di poeti*, while broadening itself and seeking new means to distinguish the *poetic* from the *nonpoetic*, never completely abandoned its early positions. Thus the application of the concept of universality in no way obliterates that of individuality: the latter is encompassed in the former. As a result, the views held in his early criticism are always present in his later criticism, so that the change noticed in his new approach is never a very sharp departure from the old.

Within the framework of his conception of poetry, the main themes of Croce's criticism are the *artistic* personality of the poet vis-à-vis the *practical* personality, the distinctions between poetry and structure, poetry and allegory, poetry and literature; in short, the distinction between what is poetry and what is not. But these distinctions cannot dispel the impression of fragmentation, which undermines the concept of totality and universality, for these two terms would imply logical, intellectualistic, ethical, and philosophical elements as integral parts of the poetic "whole." And in his effort to reconcile the individual with the universal, Croce is faced with serious difficulties which force him sometimes to remain in the seemingly ambiguous theoretical position of two conflicting attitudes. To avoid further misunderstanding, it is necessary at this point to try to elucidate the concept of *individuality* and that of *universality* and their relationship as viewed by Croce.

These two concepts do not coincide, in his theory, with *individuality* and *universality* as conceived in philosophy. Universality in philosophy has an intellectualistic and transcendental character; Croce firmly rejects any rational or intellectualistic elements from the idea of universality in art. In his view problems arise when universality in art is given an intellectualistic and transcendental meaning "in the form of allegory or symbol, in the semireligious form of revelation of the concealed God, in the form of the judgment which, by distinguishing and unifying subject and predicate, breaks the spell of art and replaces its ide-

alism with realism, the naive fancy with the perceptive judgment and the historical consideration."[208] Artistic representation, while presupposing a universal feeling, offers a completely intuitive universality, totally different from that employed as a category of judgment. Such universality is meant as plenitude of humanity, or pure humanity, independent of the particularity of history and the empirical personality of the artist. For in genuine poetic works the character of a particular historical time vanishes, and what remains is the eternally human.

His concept of universality or totality or cosmic character of artistic intuition is, nevertheless, shrouded in ambiguity and obscurity. It can be interpreted in two ways: one which might be somewhat consistent with Croce's previous doctrine; the other which might represent the total reversal of it. The crucial point seems to be whether "universality" refers only to content or to both content and form. In some instances universality signifies "full humanity"; in others, "cosmicity." Does it comprise intellectual elements? Croce categorically denies this, and everything is made to appear as a sort of intuitive metaphysics. But some of his pronouncements lead us to believe that universality is the result of a logical process, in which case it loses its purely intuitive nature. This lack of complete elucidation makes the concept of universality a moot point in his esthetic doctrine.

In his *Logic* Croce considered the particular to be inseparable from the universal: the particular is the concrete universal. Outside their synthesis (which is a priori), the universal and the particular would be empty abstractions.[209] In *The Philosophy of the Practical*, he stated that "the individual is the historical situation of the universal spirit at every instant of time, and, therefore, the sum of habits due to the historical situation."[210] In *Nuovi saggi d'estetica*, he wrote: "Artistic representation, even in its most individual form, embraces the whole and reflects in itself the cosmos";[211] in *Pagine sparse* art becomes "the intuitive and poetic moment of the immediate union of the individual and the universal, which only thought opposes and mediates."[212] At times only content seems to be universal: a feeling universally shared by all men, or a feeling which expresses the life of the whole in its perpetual rhythm. But at other times the *form* of art is also universal: "Artistic form, by individualizing, harmonizes individuality with universality, and in so doing univ-

208. *Nuovi saggi d'estetica*, p. 125.
209. See *Logic*, pp. 218–31.
210. P. 241.
211. P. 119.
212. Vol. 3, p. 50.

ersalizes."[213] This implies a logical process which universalizes the individual; but Croce denies any logical process, insisting on a "universality completely intuitive."[214] The concept of totality, to be consistent with Croce's previous pronouncements, ought not to have gone beyond the universality of content. If content and form are both universal, the individuality of art, theorized earlier, is lost forever, and we have a radically new doctrine which reverses the previous one. Despite the ambiguity of the new development, however, most interpreters took universality to apply only to content (form being the individual mark of the single artist), though this view rests on shaky grounds.

As we have seen, the first phase of Croce's criticism centered on the *poetic personality* of the artist, the single artist in his individuality detached from external elements such as history and nature. The artist thus appears in his "uniqueness," free of antecedents such as tradition, school, and so on. Croce rejects the idea of impersonal art as conceived by the naturalists; the artist has a soul endowed with passions which permeate artistic representations with their warmth; hence the lyrical character of art. In *The Philosophy of the Practical* he had tackled the problem of individuality from a philosophical point of view, concluding that the individual is not a metaphysical entity but an empirical abstraction: what is real is not the *individual* but the *act* in which the life of the universal Spirit realizes itself.

In practice, however, Croce is not prevented from speaking about individuals as realities, for he can never treat living beings as abstractions or instruments of the universal Spirit. Each artist has a unique personality which is the real protagonist of history. But gradually the personality seems to move into the background, leaving the foreground to the *works*. We are no longer in the presence of Shakespeare or Dante, but in the presence of *Hamlet*, and the *Divine Comedy*; the real protagonists of history become the works, not the personalities. The emphasis is now on universality rather than individuality, on the classical moment rather than the romantic moment. Only that which rises above the narrowness of the individual has esthetic value.

This attitude reflects Croce's theory of the universality of art, by which he intended to purge art from romantic individualism—an individualism lacking moral purpose. Men should adore God rather than try to become gods themselves. Works of art are not the manifestation of the exceptional personality of the art-

ist, for the esthetic personality is nothing but the work. And there is no need to have the one in order to understand the other. There is no bridge between the biographical and the artistic personalities; there is no a priori set of general principles; at the most there is a relation which must be established in each individual instance. Artistic personalities are *ideal*, autonomous entities, entirely original and unrelated to biographical antecedents. A poem is something new, something which did not exist before in the world of realities. The history of art is, therefore, an infinite chain of *acts* in which the poetic spirit of humanity realizes itself. Humanity is the only authentic author of existing poems.

The first application of Croce's new critical orientation is his study on Goethe. The work was written in 1917 (published in 1919) when the Italian defeat at Caporetto seemed for a time to be jeopardizing the very existence of Italy. During those sad days Croce reread Goethe and, as he stated, found deeper consolation than he could have received from any other poet. He now saw in the German poet a general attitude which has a great affinity with his own—a contemplative disposition, a desire for harmony, the aspiration toward wisdom rising above the conflicts of life and political passions; in short, the vision of the total man belonging to *Weltliteratur*.[215]

Croce's approach does not deal with all aspects of Goethe's activities, but only with the poetic personality, leaving aside whatever is not relevant to the consideration of his poetic works. Whatever is external to poetry (the acts of the practical personality, his philosophical thought, and so on) is for him outside the sphere of criticism. Croce concentrates on the unfolding of Goethe's poetic genius.

Previous criticism on the Poet had stressed biographical, historical, and ideological elements; it had dwelt on the practical personality of the author, praised his wisdom and the ethical nature of his works, while neglecting his poetry. This approach, prevalent in Germany, is discarded by Croce, who considers the poetic personality to be the essential aim of esthetic criticism and historiography. While taking into account the extraordinary life of Goethe, which was said to have been "a work of art" in itself, he maintains that the unfolding of it from the Poet's youthful "titanism" to his serene wisdom, from rebellion to appeasement, was an ethical process, not a poetic one. According to Croce, the poems of Goethe's youth are more poetic than those dictated by mature wisdom. Intellectual and ethical evolution and bio-

213. *Nuovi saggi d'estetica*, p. 124.
214. Ibid., p. 126.

215. See *Goethe*, trans. D. Ainslie (London: Methuen, 1923), p. xviii.

graphical events do not correspond to the poetic history of Goethe's works. The practical existence of an artist is extrinsic to his poetry. Croce undermines from the onset the widespread conception of Goethe as a philosopher-poet, for the two elements of this designation have no relation; he deals separately with the intellectual and ethical world and with the poetic personality. Neither biography nor philosophy are of any value in the consideration of critical judgment. The critic must single out the poetic (which is eternal and not merely the expression of the aspiration of an age) and distinguish it from the nonpoetic, which belongs to the practical sphere.

Croce finds Goethe's genius to be fragmentary in nature. The Poet's rich vitality did not allow in him the slow maturation of a central theme. His poetry is, therefore, a series of fragments, complete in themselves, but having little to do with the artificial structure imposed on his works for the sake of unity. If there is unity it is intellectual, not poetic. Thus Croce breaks this structure and isolates the poetic from the nonpoetic, that is, the authentic pieces of poetry from the philosophical and ethical intentions of the Poet. These intentions he considers to be a posteriori acts aimed at giving a systematic form to what had sprung naturally from poetic inspiration.

Croce's attention is directed to the inner history of Goethe's artistic achievements in terms of the Poet's constant overcoming of inner conflicts, bringing them into harmony and unity in a serene vision of total life. The charm of *Werther* lies in "the perfect fusion of the directness of feeling and the mediation of reason, the union of the fullness of passion with the transparency of this tumult."[216] The words "romantic" and "classic" used to characterize Goethe's earlier and later poetry, respectively, are meaningless for Croce. There is only eternal poetry, which is the voice of the human spirit. The ethical exigency common to all men, on the one hand, and the individual egocentricity, on the other, constitute the two polarities of the dialectic of the Spirit. Classicality is their synthesis, which constitutes the universality of poetry. Goethe's art is one of harmony, balance, and common sense. Classicism and romanticism are for him the two constituting elements of an indivisible whole, the synthesis into which a positive and a negative are resolved. The harmony reached between passionality and restraint is not a characteristic of the mature Goethe. It is found in all his works, regardless of the date of composition, whenever he reaches the poetic synthesis in a superior harmony.

In the case of *Faust*, Croce dismisses the philosophical meaning of the work as being irrelevant. He looks at the poem rather than at the symbolic meaning of the main character, showing the impossibility of fusing the two. The rejection of the philosophical intention and structure of the work allows him to consider the poetic fragments per se, with disregard for their ideological meaning. What matters is the poetry, not the theme. But the poem as a whole, Croce argues, lacks poetic unity and coherence. The unity that critics have found in it is an intellectual one, artificially established: the poem has an ethical or philosophical sense, but this sense has no poetic relevance. The moral maturity of the Poet does not correspond to esthetic excellence.

Of course, the works of Goethe's mature years present a great challenge for Croce, for the ethical attitude resulting in harmony and restraint is difficult to separate from esthetic values. Although he finds the poetic greatness of Goethe in the early dramatic-lyrical fragments and in the first *Faust*, which are free of intellectual and moral admixtures, Croce also sees in the later works passages of authentic poetry. And these are the things he is interested in. In its general structure *Faust* is not a poetic work, but a work expressing the meaning of life. It deals with three themes joined together mechanically: "The Faust of poetry is the Faust we have just seen forming such a contrast to simple Wagner. The other Faust, the Faust of the whole poem, is little more than a concept of the intellect, worked out, moreover, inconsistently."[217] Goethe is not viewed as a unified whole, but as a variety of attitudes both moral and esthetic. And his *Faust*, whose unity is mechanically imposed upon it, is a monster. But this monster contains a number of poetic fragments of the highest esthetic quality; it is, in fact, a long series of poetic fragments.

This discovery of a lack of unity scandalized the critics, who were accustomed to see in *Faust* an intellectual coherence which in Croce's opinion was far removed from poetry. The task of criticism is to keep its eyes on the whole personality of the Poet, but, Croce remarks, "with the sole object of understanding how this personality prepares in the various periods the various forms of his art, or how it interferes with the latter, and sometimes disturbs and spoils it."[218]

The concept of poetry as a lyrical fragment (however esthetically perfect in itself) gives Croce's doctrine too narrow a basis for a comprehensive artistic vision which could be called universal. Poetry needed to ex-

---

216. Ibid., p. 39.

217. Ibid., p. 53.
218. Ibid., p. 16.

pand in the direction of intellectual experiences in order to encompass the totality of the Spirit in all of its articulations. But Croce, despite the avowed universality and cosmic character of art, remained to some extent persistently anchored to positions which he had outgrown in the theoretical sphere. The transition from the critical approach used in *La letteratura della nuova Italia* to the new approach was not, as I pointed out earlier, a revolutionary one. The method was expanded to include the universal within the individual, but no real, drastic departure from Croce's previous essays is noticed in his work on Goethe. He reaffirms his stand against the critical habits of his times, which revolved around external elements of the work of art; and he continued in the same vein in almost all of his subsequent essays. The concept of universality or totality of artistic expression seemed to remain for the most part inoperative in practical criticism; it was thought to be a verbal solution to appease his critics (especially the actualists) who maintained that he had divided the Spirit into compartments.

The essay on Ariosto, which followed that on Goethe, is perhaps the one which best reflects the theorization of the "cosmic" character of art. Croce views Ariosto as the poet of harmony, not the poet of irony, as De Sanctis had done. In the author of *Orlando Furioso* all conflicts of reality are resolved into harmony, into a serene and smiling vision of the universe observed by the Poet with indulgence and sympathy, with love for the life which throbs in all creatures and which is the emanation of the life of the Whole. De Sanctis had found Ariosto to be a great artist, but not a great poet—a great artist in the sense of formal perfection, as conceived by the Renaissance. In De Sanctis' mind, Ariosto lacked the depth and richness of content and the imagination of Dante. He was an artist for art's sake, not a creator of universal human types. He detached himself from his subject and looked at it with benevolent irony, without taking his poetic world too seriously. Ariosto is for De Sanctis the expression of the esthetic ideal of the Renaissance, the expression of an age.

Croce, on the contrary, does not find Ariosto to be representative of a historical period, but a moment in the eternal voice of poetry. There is in the Poet not only humor but also pathos: love is the main theme of his poem, but there are in it many other emotions and conflicting passions (not only that of pure art) which he brings into harmony. Ariosto is in fact the poet of harmony in the cosmic sense. Croce's concept of "totality" must not be understood here as the whole of the personality (which would imply the intellectual and practical elements of life), but as a universal feel-

ing. The Poet does not express his personal feelings toward life, but the feelings of man toward it; he does not offer the feeling for a particular aspect of life, but the feeling for life as the life of the whole, the love of life which pulsates in all the creatures of the universe. Poetry thus rises from the individual to the universal, from immediate expression to cathartic expression, from romanticism to true classicism. There is in Ariosto an affection and sympathy for life in itself, for the life of reality, not as truth, beauty, or something else specific in character, but simply as "vital movement," vital spectacle, as the pleasure of contemplating the living being in its eternal conflicts, in its attained harmonies, and in its new conflicts and harmonies in the eternal rhythm of universal life. The artistic emotion becomes thus an emotion for the universe.

Croce wrote in *Nuovi saggi d'estetica* that in the intuition palpitates "the life of the whole, and the whole is in the life of the individual"; and he continued, "in every poetic accent, in every creature of his [the poet's] imagination there is the whole of human destiny, all the hopes, the illusions, the sorrows and joys, the greatness and the wickedness of humanity, the entire drama of the real, which grows and develops constantly, through suffering and enjoyment. It is, therefore, unthinkable that artistic representation may ever affirm the mere particular, the abstract individual, the finite in its finiteness."[219] For artistic form implies the universal.[220]

This esthetic of the universal is supposedly the guiding principle in the essay on Ariosto, but most critics were perplexed by this unexpected development, for Croce's philosophy had been oriented toward individuality. The character of universality is given to things by logic; as a result, Croce should have admitted that art cannot be free of intellectual elements. This would have meant the rejection of his earlier views on art as the expression of the individual. The concrete universal implies a concept of the universal that only logic can offer. How can this passage to universality be carried out without creating a contradiction? Even Croce's most knowledgeable students, when faced by the difficulty presented by the essay on the "universality of artistic expression," cannot give a satisfactory explanation.

The main theme in both Ariosto and Shakespeare is life with its conflicts. But while Ariosto resolves these conflicts into harmony, Shakespeare expresses the eternal antithesis of the opposing forces, with no vision of

219. *Nuovi saggi d'estetica*, p. 122.
220. Ibid., p. 124.

catharsis; everything is left in mystery. In the essay on Shakespeare, Croce builds up the kind of ideal personality which supposedly is the only object of esthetic criticism. He applies his usual method which discards any concern for the Poet's biography or alleged philosophical intentions. The practical personality is thus separated from the poetic personality, for personal experiences had no bearing on Shakespeare's art. Poetry must be considered apart from biography and from the purposes Shakespeare might have had in writing his works. Erudite studies concerning chronology are also deemed irrelevant, since the critical judgment must always be founded on intrinsic reasons. A feeling really experienced, when elevated to the sphere of poetry, is completely removed from the sphere of practical life and transferred to the realm of contemplation.

Croce asserts here again his strong opposition to biographical criticism, which was plaguing Shakespeare studies, and to the historical research aimed at determining the extent to which the Poet reflected his own times. This positivistic criticism had reduced Shakespeare from a great poet to a supplier of works catering to cheap public taste, thus undermining his powerful poetic imagination. Croce concerns himself with poetic themes and the fundamental state of mind from which they spring, without paying heed to biographical conjectures or other extrinsic elements. His main purpose was to determine the "fundamental state of mind" and to study the single works as attempts to reach the full expression of that state of mind. Each work appears as an approximation of the goal. Croce groups Shakespeare's works by theme: the "comedy of love," the "longing for romance," the "interest in practical action," the "tragedy of good and evil," the "tragedy of the will," "justice and indulgence." But these themes follow one another ideally, not chronologically; the "ideal development" does not coincide with the "chronological sequence" because

the chronological order takes the works in the order in which they are apprehensible from without, that is to say, in the order in which they have been written, acted, or printed, and arranges them in a series that is quantitatively irregular or, in other words, chronicles them. Now this arrangement must not be opposed to or placed on a level with the other, as though it were the real opposed to the ideal development, for the ideal is the only truly real development, while the chronological is fictitious or arbitrary, and thus unreal; that is to say, in clear terms, it does not represent the development, but simply a series or succession.[221]

The tracing of the fundamental state of mind, from the first imperfect expressions to the full expression, through a series of successive attempts, constitutes the

221. *Ariosto, Shakespeare and Corneille*, trans. D. Ainslie (New York: Holt, 1920), pp. 267–68.

history of poetry (or criticism), which always deals with a single author. This history is also the construction of the *ideal* or *poetic* personality of the artist. The various motifs springing from the fundamental state of mind are particularizations of it; the characters are diverse or contrasting aspects of this fundamental state of mind, and, although they seem to have a life of their own, they all live the same life of the Poet; they are like sparks from the same fire. The central poetic vision of Shakespeare is defined by Croce as the unresolved conflicts of human life: good–evil, joy–sorrow, will–passion, virtue–vice, loyalty–deceit, decision–irresolution, and so on. The Poet feels these conflicts to be right against wrong, light against darkness. The characters incarnating these antithetical positions are not individuals but "eternal attitudes of the human spirit." Cordelia is goodness itself; Iago, evil for evil's sake; and so on. They are "types" which fit Croce's poetic of the universal rather than that of the individual.

Shakespeare, in summary, is the poet of the conflicts of life—conflicts which he cannot resolve, for they are rooted in human nature. It is always good against evil, joy against suffering, will against passion, virtue against vice, decision against hesitation, loyalty against treason. In this eternal struggle the triumph of the positive element is never certain: thus life is, in substance, nothing but a profound mystery and an incomprehensible play of light and darkness. Hence its tragic sense. But this irremediable conflict of things is not, in Shakespeare, a logically defined concept, an intellectual form of the Spirit; it is simply a feeling, a state of mind, an intuition. And it is from these elements that the situations and the characters draw their existence and shape.

In the preface to *Ariosto, Shakespeare and Corneille*, Croce indicates that the three poets (so different from one another) were collected in one volume for a definite purpose. And the purpose was to show that the same principles can be applied for the understanding and appreciation of the most diverse, and even opposite, forms of art. The principles applied here are those theorized in his *Nuovi saggi d'estetica*, particularly in the essay on the universality of art. Certainly, of the three poets studied, Corneille was the most difficult to reconcile with Croce's esthetic doctrine. Croce's approach, however, proved to be productive. He discards all problems around which most of the criticism on the Poet had resolved, namely, the problems related to the neoclassical theory of tragedy. The greatness of Corneille as an authentic poet does not lie in the intellectual or rational sphere where other critics thought to have found it; Corneille is a lyric poet, and his lyr-

icism springs from the emotion he feels in the exercise of his *deliberative will*, in the act of choosing among the various possibilities of action. His ideal of free will is a state of mind, not a philosophical concept; his fundamental themes are lyrical images, not speculative principles. And it is these lyrical images that make a poet of him, not the regularity of his tragedies or his conformity to classical tenets.

These lyrical moments of the deliberative will are found in all of Corneille's works. There is, therefore, no distinction between the early and the later Corneille, for the later plays abound in poetic passages just as the early ones do. But the myth that Croce intended to dispel was that of a Corneille as the expression of French rationalism or of the French mind. Poetry is above nationality, and the greatness of the French Poet lies in the fact that he expresses a human ideal and not a national characteristic. Between romantic criticism, which undermined Corneille as a rationalistic poet lacking feeling, and classical criticism, which exalted Corneille for his rationality, Croce takes a course which leads to the vindication of the true Corneillean genius—a genius which is above the classification of romantic or classic or national identity and which is to be found in an eternal human dimension.

Here again Croce reduced poetry to lyrical fragments which, though a complete world in themselves, are still fragments kept together by nonpoetic structures. This attitude emerges more clearly in *The Poetry of Dante*, in which the concept of "totality" seems to have found little or no application. Croce, in fact, stresses here the distinction between *structure* and *poetry*, which was to arouse a great stir among Dante scholars and critics. By structure Croce meant the system of thought which constitutes the framework of the poem. He made a similar distinction in connection with Goethe's *Faust*, in which he singles out the poetic motifs from the artificial framework of the tragedy supposedly representing an ethical ideal. But in the study of Dante's *Divine Comedy*, the distinction is applied methodically, and the work becomes, like *Faust*, a series of lyrics. The aim of the poem, which governs its construction, is completely disregarded as being alien to poetry. It is a necessary element for the construction of the poem, but it is not the poetic element. Once more the distinction between the practical and the poetic personalities is accentuated as the cornerstone of criticism. In *Faust* the design (philosophical and religious) is devised a posteriori, after the lyrical poems had been written; in the *Divine Comedy* this design is a priori: the "theological-political romance" antecedes the composition of the lyrical episodes.

Croce makes no attempt to penetrate the religious and philosophical world which motivated Dante's poetry. This was the most serious shortcoming of his essay. For Croce structure and poetry are two moments of the Spirit; but they are united in a dialectical synthesis. This does not imply that the *person* and the *work* are united and that there is a relation of dependence between the practical and the poetic personalities. This relation is restricted to the various elements of the poem: "Scheme and poetry, theological and lyrical romance, are not separable in the work of Dante, any more than the parts of his souls are separable from one another. One conditions the other and flows into it. In this dialectical sense, the *Divine Comedy* is certainly a unity."[222] But if structure and poetry are inseparable, how can one separate the practical personality (which produces the structure) from the poetic personality? Croce, in reality, asserts the structure-poetry unit more to appease the critics than to satisfy an exigency of his esthetic doctrine. The dialectical relation between structure and poetry would result in the introduction of intellectual elements into the poetic intuition, which was supposed to be free of intellectualism. But this purity would create a break between poetry and structure, and the whole enterprise would amount to making the *Divine Comedy* a series of lyrical fragments, the structure serving simply as a framework.

Dante's spirit was, according to Croce, divided between the Middle Ages and the Renaissance, between religion, transcending this world, and the passions of this world. This antithesis led him to the conception of the journey, which provides the structure of the poem, and to the portrayal of human life in all of the aspects and moods: sublime and low, tragic and grotesque, tortured and glorious, which constitute its poetry.[223] What is objectionable in Croce's interpretation is not so much that he distinguishes poetry from nonpoetry as that he presents as poetic only worldly passionality, discarding from poetry the religious fervor in the light of which Dante interprets life. If Croce could have seen in the characters and events of history, as other critics saw, a metaphor of Dante's feelings, he could have evaluated the use that the Poet made of these characters and events and shown how they enhanced his feelings and his expression.

In his later views Croce admits that the elements of the *Divine Comedy* do not fight against each other, but accompany each other or alternate, always standing together in a sort of pacific coexistence, but never losing

222. *The Poetry of Dante*, trans. D. Ainslie (New York: Holt, 1922), p. 96.
223. See *Letture di poeti*, p. 11.

their own individual qualities: they are adversaries but not repulsive to each other.[224] These views were meant to avert the misunderstanding that structure and poetry are, respectively, a negative and a positive element, and to assert that they simply are distinct elements, structure not being the opposite of poetry but something different. In this case one may ask: does the "different" give us a dialectical unity? How can one bring about the synthesis without the antithesis? If the two elements are not the positive and the negative, light and darkness, how can they be joined dialectically? On the other hand, if one can exist without the other, why is the dialectical synthesis necessary?[225]

The other major problem which aroused violent criticism against Croce's approach to the *Divine Comedy* was that of *allegory* in relation to poetry. Croce's position is that where there is allegory there is no poetry. If what we call allegory is the highest expressive form that the poet has found to shape his images, then it is no longer allegory but the poetic language itself. To add extrinsically one expression to the other is an arbitrary procedure, which can exist in intellectual expressions where the image is the symbol of a concept. In poetry there is only the poetic language, which cannot be replaced by extrinsic symbols.[226]

The study on Dante is the least affected by the concept of "totality," for the poetry of the *Divine Comedy* consists in lyrical passages throughout the work. Croce, in fact, deals with the lyrical personality of the Poet, attaching little or no importance to the critical research aimed at evaluating Dante's thought and determining Dante's significance as a philosopher, a moralist, a prophet, and a religious guide. What created the structure was Dante's "intentionality," for he meant to be a teacher of truth; but his actual world was the poetic world, the world of human feelings. Croce considers all the studies on the life of the Poet, on his political activity, and on the historical and cultural events connected with his life and work as a practical man to be heterogeneous elements having no relevance to his poetry. In the *Divine Comedy*, as in *Faust*, the unity of the poem cannot be sought in the intellectual unit. To seek poetic unity in intellectual unity is to subscribe to the esthetics of intellectualism, according to which the value of a poem depends on the ideas or concepts it expresses. This would make of a metaphysical work a great poem and of the *Iliad* a poor one.

After *The Poetry of Dante* Croce undertook the ex-

amination of some prominent nineteenth-century European writers for the purpose of refuting current prejudices and proposing new judgments, but above all for focusing the attention on poetry, which many professional critics seemed to have forgotten. His enterprise resulted in one of the most popular critical works, *Poesia e non poesia*, published in 1923 (in English as *European Literature in the Nineteenth Century*, 1924). The work consists of twenty-six concise monographs on as many well-known French, Italian, German, English, Spanish, and Scandinavian literary figures, chosen more or less at random. The criteria here are based on objective principles of judgment aimed at dispelling the arbitrariness of individualism in literary criticism. Critical judgment must be founded on a category of judgment, and this category is the concept of poetry. The title of the book (Poetry and nonpoetry) indicates the focus of Croce's essays, though he remains flexible in his method and far removed from rigidly judicial attitudes. In many cases he tends to dismantle the various judgments expressed by others, thus winding up in a sort of "criticism of criticism." But he never loses sight of his main object, which is to bring out the "poetic" and to discard the other elements—philosophical, ethical, social, biographical, and related problems raised by critics. He holds to the distinction of poetry from oratory or literature, from practical life (not transformed into pure contemplation), or from technical dexterity or rhetorical skill. By this he established certain principles which give a new perspective concerning the authors he studies. But he ends by relegating a great number of nineteenth-century writers to the domain of oratory or literature, outside the sphere of poetry, thus greatly reducing the number of real poets in one of the richest periods in the history of poetry.

The concept of the universality of art, or classicality, is the guiding principle in Croce's evaluation of writers. This leads him to divide the nineteenth century into two worlds of expression: that of poetry and that of oratory, with the first represented only by a few resplendent lights: "If we stick to the criterion of what is authentic poetry, classical poetry, and in light of it we look at the thousands of authors emerging in Europe during that century, those thousands are reduced to a few dozen free talents, each with his own personality, but all illuminated by the same ray of poetry. Only they compose, in their various groupings, the representative panorama of that literature."[227] Although Croce traces for each author an individual physiognomy, according to his early principles of criti-

---

224. See ibid., p. 12.
225. See *Conversazioni critiche*, vol. 3, p. 203.
226. See *The Poetry of Dante*, pp. 18–24; *Philosophy, Poetry, History*, pp. 375–81.

227. *Poesia e non poesia*, 328.

cism, he emphasizes the universal accent of poetry: poetry is the song of the individual insofar as it is the song of humanity—the humanity which is at the bottom of all men.

In *Storia dell'età barocca in Italia* the principle of distinction between poetry and nonpoetry continues to be the guiding light in the treatment of the subject matter. Croce's negative judgment of the baroque age is well known. Baroque is for him the artistically ugly. It represents the decadence of Italy after the splendors of the Renaissance. The last poetic voice of Italy, after the Renaissance and before Alfieri, was *Jerusalem Delivered*. The baroque age is marked by the "silence of great poetry," for baroque poetry is "pseudopoetry," a sort of artistic aberration, an expression of bad taste, the tendency toward empty words—words concealing in their brilliant combinations the emptiness of the spirit of the time. Baroque poetry is at best versified eloquence. The decadence of taste prevented the age from noticing the absence of great poetry. Such an absence was felt only when, toward the end of the eighteenth century, a new poetic consciousness emerged, which led to Foscolo, Leopardi, and Manzoni. The central part of the book, "Poetry and Literature," offers very little in the way of authentic poetry. Croce, unswervingly keeping in mind the principle of distinction, demonstrates that most of the authors of the time lacked creative imagination and that, as a result, their works were verses devoid of poetry.

Nuovi saggi sulla letteratura italiana del Seicento is an amplification of the central part of *Storia dell'età barocca in Italia*. It deals with a number of minor authors who serve as further examples to prove Croce's concept of poetry. The method of distinction remains the same; the book, therefore, complements the previous volume.

The nature of the poetry as "eternal poetry" is somehow implied in the titles given to two significant volumes of criticism, *Poesia popolare e poesia d'arte* and *Poesia antica e moderna*. The distinctions between folk poetry and the poetry born of conscious art, between ancient poetry and modern poetry lack real foundation, for there is, according to Croce, only "poetry" *tout court*—carrying no particular qualification which is the eternal voice of humanity, always the same even in different ages and forms. Poetry is above time and space; it is found in the simplest folk song, and in its essence it does not differ from one level of sophistication to another or from one age to another.

The first of these two works deals with the Italian literature of the fourteenth through the sixteenth centuries; but Croce's main intent is to emphasize the universal character of poetry and to distinguish it from literary skill and purely technical perfection. To the idea of the universality of art, however, Croce adds other considerations pertinent to the clarification of his evolving esthetic doctrine. The concept of classicism, which he had adopted in *Poesia e non poesia* and through which he excluded from the sphere of art a large number of authors, appears here more flexible. Between poetry and nonpoetry there is no sharp distinction; there is instead a gradual passage from one to the other. The pureness of poetry (in its universal character) is an ideal, while the poetic forms in their concreteness are only approximations. A clear-cut distinction between poetry and non-poetry can be made in theory; in actuality it does not exist. Poetry appears to Croce in the greater or lesser complexity of its form, in its high or low degree of intensity or purity.

Folk poetry is no less perfect than "art poetry"; only it is much simpler: the difference between the two is one of complexity and not one of intrinsic quality. From the empirical point of view there is "great poetry" and "minor poetry," and "folk poetry is, in general, minor poetry, that is, less complex, with fewer allusions and spiritual references, and it can be compared to the idyll in relation to the drama or tragedy of life."[228] This distinction between the less complex and the more complex applies to both content and form:

Folk poetry is, in the esthetic sphere, the analogue of common sense in the intellectual sphere, and candidness or innocence in the moral sphere. It expresses movements of the soul which do not have behind them, as immediate antecedents, great travails of thought and passion; it depicts simple feelings in correspondingly simple forms. High poetry stirs in us great masses of remembrances, experiences, thoughts, multiple feelings and gradations and nuances of feelings. Folk poetry does not take such ample breadth to reach its goal; it reaches it through a shorter and more rapid path.[229]

The superiority of "art poetry" is one of spiritual complexity. But the difficulty with Croce's doctrine lies in the fact that, while it abolished all scales of value among poetic works, it establishes one here based on the more or less spiritual richness of each work. Croce, for his part, gives preference to "art poetry" because of its complexity and formal elaboration, thus pointing to his antiromantic attitude. Romanticism had extolled "folk poetry" for its passionality, spontaneity, ingenuousness, elementariness, irreflection, and freedom from culture and tradition, that is, for its immediate expression of feeling. Croce emphasizes, against romanticism, the *formal* moment of poetry. The principle of passionality which dominated his mind when he formulated the theory of art as "lyr-

---

228. *Conversazioni critiche*, vol. 3, pp. 267–68.
229. *Poesia popolare e poesia d'arte*, p. 5.

ical intuition" was now reconsidered in light of the doctrine of universality, which represents the overcoming of the individual passions in a cosmic harmony; such a doctrine implies discipline and cultural formation, tradition, and literary skill in order to realize the fusion of the primitive and the cultivated, of inspiration and schooling. In his *Aesthetica in nuce* Croce had written: "The present task of esthetics is the restoration and defence of classicality against romanticism, of the synthetic and formal and theoretical moment, which is intrinsic to art, against the affective moment, which art must resolve into itself."[230] Croce recognizes literary discipline and the value of tradition more and more as he advances in his career. In fact, he sees as one of the positive aspects of the baroque "the stylistic training, the course in rhetoric, the initiation to the secret of art, that refinement of which Europe was then in need in order to escape from certain medieval practices."[231]

The purpose of *Poesia popolare e poesia d'arte* was "to illustrate the difference between folk poetry and 'art poetry' and the function of culture in the life and development and growth of poetry."[232] And Croce adds: "The direction of my thought has constantly been toward accepting the romantic anti-intellectualism and passionality; but only for the purpose of restoring in classicism its lymph and vital force, thus preventing it from perverting itself into the classicistic or academic, and not certainly for the purpose of mortifying poetry and condemning it to a sort of mental poverty or even infantilism."[233] Croce sought to harmonize the "classic" and the "romantic" in a synthesis which unites them inseparably. As a result, tradition, which for the romantics was a hindrance to free expression, becomes for him a school of formal discipline, necessary for the perfection of poetic expression. The concept of poetry as an eternal synthesis of passionality and formal elaboration implies the condemnation of the literary genres, which Croce consistently discarded from the domain of art. He recognized their didactic value (the a posteriori grouping of works externally alike), but he attributed to them no esthetic relevance. He remains firm in his belief that there are as many genres as there are individual masterpieces, and that the work of art cannot be judged by reference to a genre.

The theme of *Poesia antica e moderna* is basically not much different from that of *Poesia popolare e poesia d'arte*, for both works seem to place stress on the same

subject: the eternity of poetry, be it ancient or modern. Poetry is above distinction, above space and time. Croce examines here a number of poets from all epochs and countries, emphasizing the essence of poetry, which is neither ancient nor modern, neither Italian nor French nor Spanish, but simply poetry. "It is," he writes, "one of the intentions of this book to strengthen, through a series of examples, the idea of the intrinsic steadiness of poetry, which does not change its essence . . . according to the various ages and peoples."[234] The other intention of Croce is to remind us that, however important the delineation of the personality of the poets, poetic reality is "the single poem," on which he directs his attention. The criterion of evaluation is always the poetic and the nonpoetic; so Croce puts into relief what he considers to be "poetic," through samplings from the forty-odd authors he chose to study. What is relevant to him is the perennial voice of poetry, which he keeps on distinguishing from structure and from moralistic and intellectualistic elements which are foreign to it.

After *La poesia* no noticeable developments are perceived in Croce's theory. The concept of *literature* seems to be the last acquisition of his esthetics. Through this concept a hierarchy of esthetic values is more or less established. As a result, fewer works reach the pinnacle of poetry, for works of art which reflect the life of the "whole" and which possess the unique quality of poetry are rarely attained. Homer, Sophocles, Virgil, Dante, Petrarch, Ariosto, Tasso, Shakespeare, Goethe are the most important among those who reached the sphere of poetry. Byron, Lamartine, Musset belong to effusive literature; Boileau and Pope are stylists whose aim was to make technically perfect verses, having little or nothing to say; Schiller is a man of letters and not a poet; many others, such as Aristophanes, Horace, Rabelais, Fielding, Goldoni, Scott, Manzoni belong, in different ways, to literature.

The theorization of the concept of literature led Croce to accentuate the distinction between poetry and literature in his critical evaluation of writers. Whereas earlier the term "literature" had a negative overtone, even when it meant "beautiful literature," now the qualification of "beautiful," applied to literary expression, began to assume a less negative sense. There can be a literature which is not artificial and empty rhetoric, but may contain esthetic qualities, providing we distinguish them from those of poetry. This is apparent in *Poesia antica e moderna*, which, like *Poesia e non poesia*, reflects the application, on a large scale, of Croce's theoretical advances. "The *Odyssey*,"

---

230. *Philosophy, Poetry, History*, p. 237.
231. *Storia dell'età barocca in Italia*, p. 39.
232. *Poesia popolare e poesia d'arte*, p. x.
233. Ibid., pp. x–xi.

234. *Poesia antica e moderna*, p. vii.

Croce maintains, "is a work of art, but not intrinsically of poetry"; while the *Iliad* is "at the head of all great modern poetry, the *Odyssey* is an exquisite example . . . of the literature of travel and adventures," because of the rationality of its construction, the moral tone, the technical skill with which the work was carried out.[235] *Poesia antica e moderna* is one of the best examples of Croce's mature criticism, not only for the range of authors treated, but also for the clarity of the criterion adopted.

In volumes five and six of *La letteratura della nuova Italia* (1939–1940), Croce resumes the work interrupted in 1914, in which, he said, he had outlined the physiognomies of about one hundred writers, "distinguishing in them the poetic from the nonpoetic, the beautiful from the ugly."[236] The two volumes contain mostly whatever was left out in the first four volumes, some new figures who had emerged in the meantime (especially Pirandello), and some up-to-date essays already published in the first volumes in an incomplete form. But the critical perspective is somewhat changed particularly in regard to certain authors. Of special interest is the correction of his early judgment on D'Annunzio—very favorable in 1903 (vol. 4), now almost reversed. The Poet, previously defined as a dilettante of sensations, but an authentic artist, now lacks the full humanity, the moral strength and health of Carducci. He lacks the moral conflict between good and evil and, therefore, the superior synthesis intrinsic to poetry. D'Annunzio was one-sided, without dialectical conflict. Croce's idea of eternal poetry and its cosmic nature now dominates his judgment, and D'Annunzio no longer fits into the new scheme.

The two volumes, which collect for the most part "gleanings" and curiosities concerning a period of bad literary taste, are nevertheless animated by an attitude of moderation, smoothing in some cases the harsh judgments expressed about thirty years earlier, though reconfirming the substance of them. The clear-cut distinction between poetic and nonpoetic is attenuated in view of the new concept of literature. There is a sense of sympathy accompanying even the negative evaluations. Pirandello, however, is considered to be a "confessor" rather than a poet, which, in Croce's mind, explains the world success of the writer—a success that great poetry never attains.

The work which offers the largest number of hints concerning the function of literature, the criticism of it, and the limits of *humanistic* poetry (which most of

the time is essentially literature, even when it is technically perfect) is *Poeti e scrittori del pieno e tardo Rinascimento* (vols. 1 and 2, 1945; vol. 3, 1952). The work deals with minor figures of the period and with other cultural subjects, most of them historical in character, in an attempt to glean whatever was left behind and was worth preserving. The period is one of men of letters par excellence, and the criterion of distinction between poetry and literature becomes much more relevant than for any other period. The fact is that Croce's approach is now not to demean literature, but to recognize its value and benefits while at the same time to distinguish it from poetry. He frequently restates here his conception of poetry and reiterates his opposition to histories of poetry which tend to characterize the poetry of an age by generalizations: this, in his opinion, resulted in meaningless abstract schemes. His method is to study individual authors or works and to assess them in their concrete individuality, shunning abstractions and general schemes. Croce explains in a postscript to volume two his approach and the reasons for it, which are based on his conception of poetry: poetry which is incarnated in the individual and cannot be found in generalizations.[237] This echoes what Croce had said in his *Philosophy of the Practical*: "The universal is in concrete the universal individualized, and the individual is real insofar as he is also universal."[238]

He recognizes that alongside poetic works there are works of literature, finely composed though lacking poetic qualities. And he chooses from the abundant material of the period whatever deserved to be rescued from oblivion. Unquestionably literary art prevails in Croce's selections, for most of the authors had a consummate literary skill, but no poetic power in the Crocean sense. Between poetry and nonpoetry an intermediary world seems to exist, thus preventing an abrupt break. In this intermediary world there is room for many compositions which are beautiful though not authentically poetic.

Letteratura italiana del Settecento is of the same character as the volumes of the poets and writers of the full and the late Renaissance, and presents no distinctive feature requiring discussion. Croce's last critical work, which resembles an extension of *Poesia antica e moderna*, is *Letture di poeti e riflessioni sulla teoria e sulla critica della poesia*. The book is divided into two parts, the first containing literary criticism about authors of different times and countries from Dante on, the second a number of writings directly or indirectly linked

235. Ibid., p. 38.
236. Vol. 5, p. 5.

237. See *Poeti e scrittori del pieno e tardo Rinascimento*, vol. 2, pp. 251–58.
238. P. 445.

to the polemic against "pure poetry" and to his essays on Mallarmé (one published in *Poesia e non poesia*, two others in the first part of *Letture di poeti*). Here again Croce concerns himself mainly with works rather than with the characterization of the authors' personalities, as he had done in *Poesia e non poesia*. He acts as a reader of poetry, discriminating the poetic from the non-poetic. Whereas in his earliest criticism the nonpoetic was an unredeemable negative, it has now a positive value, for beautiful literature has esthetic qualities. The distinctive mark of poetry is melancholy; when the veil of melancholy is absent, there is no poetry. Lope de Vega is a folk poet, but an authentic poet; Calderón is a highly skilled man of letters, rich in rhetorical images, but he is not a poet.[239]

Besides the relation between poetry and literature, the universality of art, and so on, the other theme recurring frequently in the last period of Croce's literary career is the relation between poetry and structure. In chapter two (sec. 6) of *La poesia* he examines fully the function of the structural parts in poetry. Although these parts are not poetic, Croce recognizes that they cannot be avoided: they are padding necessary to the poetic expression and must be treated with indulgence in real poets. As for the universality of poetry, the point had been clarified further in *Poesia antica e moderna* ("Poesia d'amore e poesia eroica") and applied consistently:

The poetry which elevates earthly affections toward the divine is altogether the poetry of those affections, which are living and present even when they are outgrown; they are alive in the love of the divine which cannot be love unless it partakes of the earthly, unless God is made flesh. On the other hand, where can one ever find a true love poem which does not contain ethical and religious elements, the yearning for the infinite and the eternal, the sadness for that which passes and dies, the obscure sense of sin and the desire for redemption and for the elevation of oneself and one's beloved to a heaven of purity, and the vain and sorrowful striving to break down the barrier which has always separated the souls of lovers, the barrier which lies in the very nature of love for a creature, in the unconquerable finitude of that love? Is there any true love poem which does not contain conflicts and troubles and torments, joy, hope, and despair, wild desire and the restraint and modesty which veils and refrains it, a refinement and ennoblement of the mind and its education for the heroism of a renunciation for the sake of a better gain, its transcendence of the human in order to achieve a wider, fuller, deeper humanity?[240]

Poetry springs from the dialectic between feeling and moral and religious ideals: "Poetry, as the whole life, has no other theme than the dialectical relation be-tween the loftiness and baseness of men, between moral ideality and sensuality."[241]

In conclusion, Croce's critical approach remains consistent from beginning to end. Its sole objective is to distinguish poetry from nonpoetry, bringing to full light the former and thrusting into oblivion the latter (or at least assigning it to its appropriate place). He separates poetry from the biography and the practical intentions or endeavors of the poet; he distinguishes poetry from intellectualistic or philosophical or moralistic content, from structure, from literary embellishments, from rhetoric and oratorical art, so that it may shine above them all. But his concept of poetry undergoes changes: it is at first the expression of the individual, then of the universal. The change of emphasis from the one to the other marks the passage from the first to the second and final phase of Croce's criticism.

13. *The Final Development of Croce's Thought*

The final development of Croce's esthetics, which remained in a sketchy and ambiguous state, seems to be the concept of art as pure contemplation and, therefore, apractical in character. In a short piece collected in *Discorsi di varia filosofia* (1945), Croce writes: "Poetry is knowledge, but knowledge as ateleological, aconceptual, acritical intuition and contemplation."[242] He contends, however, that many philosophers were unable to understand this form of contemplation and that they considered art to be either an imperfect form of thought or the obscure world of feelings, or a particular brand of hedonism, or a sort of revelation from above. Art, on the contrary, transcends the practical world in which man lives and suffers, and offers the serenity in which beauty lies; for beauty is not the pleasure of a particular truth or good, but a vision of the cosmos, and it penetrates us with celestial joy.[243] Thus art places itself above "the living world" on a sphere of serene contemplation akin to mysticism. Passions and conflicts, joy and suffering are left with the individual, for art is the contemplation of the eternally human in its fixity. Hence the difference between poetry and history, the latter being mobility, an eternal becoming.

The apracticality of art is reiterated in another short piece, "Praticità della storia e apraticità della poesia" (1947; in *Filosofia e storiografia*, 1949), in which poetry

---

239. See *Letture di poeti*, p. 39.
240. *Poesia antica e moderna*, pp. 179–80.

241. *Letture di poeti*, p. 141.
242. "L'arte come la forma del puro conoscere," *Discorsi di varia filosofia*, vol. 2, p. 120.
243. See ibid., pp. 120–21.

is the contemplation of the eternal dialectic of the human soul, the perpetual struggle between sensual passions and the passion for our moral and religious ideals, between flesh and spirit: "This dialectic, in its infinite forms, intuited and expressed in all languages and through the customs of all peoples, confers upon poetry its apracticality, also called ideality, this being its character." Poetry, while drawing its matter from life, rises above the conflicts of life: "thus, purified of any contact with the world of action, poetry is the only form of knowledge which can be called pure."[244] While history is the expression of our individual moral and practical needs, aspirations, and interests, poetry moves away from these areas, transforming the world of practical life into a cathartic vision, which is the synthesis of the eternal dialectic of the soul rising above the antinomy of good and evil, duty and passion, to the sphere of contemplation.

These views, to some extent offshoots of the concept of universality, could still be contained within the system without perceptible disruption. The apracticality of art was already implicit in its alogical character (a state of indistinction between the real and the unreal). Since only the logical form of knowledge creates volitions and therefore practical acts, poetry, being contemplation, remains outside the world of action. Placed at the point where the spiritual circle ends and begins anew, poetry draws its substance from the world of action (seen as passion) and sets in motion the stage for new actions.

But when considered in the light of the concept of *vitality*, which Croce introduced into his philosophical system during the last years of his life, the concept of poetry may run into a web of complications. The main difficulty derives from the ambiguity of the category of the *vital*, which lends itself to conflicting interpretations. Croce explicitly identifies the *vital* with the *economic*: "By the category of *vitality* is meant the one in which the individual satisfies his own volitions and desires of individual well-being. As such it is amoral in character."[245] But the concept of the *vital*, while a verbal variation of the *economic* in a somehow amplified form, becomes at the same time a great deal more than one of the fundamental categories (or forms) of the Spirit; it becomes a force permeating all the other categories: "Vitality is a necessary integration of the different forms of the spirit, which would have neither voice nor other organs or forces, if, by some absurd hypothesis, they remained detached from *vitality*."[246]

Pleasure, which is the only aim of the *vital*, accompanies all the forms of the Spirit, for all human activities are motivated by pleasure. *Vitality*, in this case, is a sort of supercategory, the moving force of the Spirit, an untamed force which incites and revolutionizes spiritual life and is akin to the blind power of organic nature: "It offers the matter to successive categories; in such a circle, what was *form* lends itself to the function of *matter*, and so on. Nor does *vitality* only offer the *matter*, but it gives its cooperation to the successive categories, endowing them with its own power."[247]

Whether the *vital* is a category (that of the *useful* or the *economic*) among the other categories or whether it is a supercategory, a pervasive force, is a moot point, and Croce's pronouncements on the subject are of no help for a convincing elucidation of the problem. When seen in the light of Croce's system, the new development raises some basic questions concerning the solidity and stability of the system itself. Croce had, as early as 1938, begun to alter the systematization of the four fundamental categories of the Spirit by giving morality the function of a supercategory, thus placing it above the other categories.[248] "The aim of morality," he said, "is to further life."[249] But he adds that all spiritual activities further life with their works of beauty, truth, and practical usefulness; and to those who contend that morality contributes works of goodness, one may answer that "the works of goodness, in their concrete form, can be none other than the works of beauty, of truth, and of usefulness," and that morality itself, in order to realize itself in the world of practicality, "becomes passion, will, usefulness, and it thinks with the philosopher, molds with the artist, and works with the farmer and the laborer."[250] In other words, moral activity is no longer a specific category, but a force governing all the other activities. It prods these activities to accomplish their proper functions, which are to maintain spiritual unity and to oppose disunity. Since in every organism there is a tendency to disorganization (which is evil), since this negative tendency is the result of the prevailing of one category over the others, of the exigencies of the individual over the exigencies of the whole, the function of morality is to maintain order and balance in the organism. Moral activity, then, if on the one hand it does not perform "any function," on the other it performs "all of them," and "directs and corrects the work of the

244. *Filosofia e storiografia* (1949), p. 79; Ibid., p. 77.
245. *Indagini su Hegel e schiarimenti filosofici*, 1952, p. 35.
246. Ibid., p. 30.

247. *Ibid.*, pp. 35–36.
248. See *La storia come pensiero e come azione* (1938), chap. 11: "L'azione morale."
249. Ibid., p. 44.
250. Ibid.

artist, of the philosopher, of the farmer, of the industrialist," respecting their individual autonomy, but "keeping each within its limits."[251]

Morality is the struggle against evil (for without evil there would be no morality); but it disappears as the distinctive category that Croce had theorized earlier. "At the beginning of my philosophical reflection," Croce wrote, "I proposed to add to the venerable triad of values and forms of the spirit—the True, the Good, and the Beautiful—the form which I designated as that of the Useful or Economic: . . . a fourth category which extended the sacred triad to a tetrad";[252] but later he shrank the tetrad to a modified triad by elevating morality to a higher and more general function than it previously had. With the introduction of the concept of *vitality*, which some students of Croce interpret as another supercategory (rather than the equivalent of the useful), the original order of the system appears profoundly altered.[253] If *vitality* is no longer identified with the useful or economic and if it becomes a force which "stirs up all the forms of life, from the organic or physiologic or telluric form to that of knowledge and, in a larger sense, to the spiritual form,"[254] we shall have two supercategories—that of *morality* and that of *vitality*—one stirring up the categories to action, the other regulating or checking their action so that unity and balance can be maintained in spiritual life. The *vital* is a crude force, nature, which, while necessary to move the other forms of the Spirit, invariably produces imbalance by alternately favoring one form or another to the detriment of the rest of the forms. But the other supercategory, morality, intervenes to restore and maintain order, balance and harmony among the forms of the Spirit. The *vital* is the force of evil, which generates the good; and the good does not exclude evil, it transforms evil into good in a higher sphere—the synthesis. In fact, abolishing evil would mean abolishing life, for life is a dialectic movement, a constant effort to reconcile opposites. By setting itself as the opposite to the *moral*, the *vital* is therefore at the origin of dialectic. This might lead us

to think that Croce interprets dialectic in a fashion akin to Marx, who places it at the level of sensations, rather than at the level of logical thought, as Hegel did. But Croce, unlike Marx, does not remain in the *vital*; instead, he takes the *vital* out of the sphere of the individual and raises it to the level of morality, which is a superior human exigency.

The *vital* was identified with feeling in the pleasure-pain polarity. Thus at the bottom of the system there is a stimulating organic force, outside the circle of the distinct forms and, therefore, outside history; and at the top of the system there is morality (also outside the distinct forms) as a regulating force: on the one side there is the subhuman, the unconscious; on the other the superhuman, the light of intelligence and wisdom, the former agitating and the latter controlling the movement of the circle which is composed of two theoretical forms (the beautiful and the true), and one practical form (the useful). The identification of *vitality* with feeling aims at giving a more definite entity to the latter, which in Croce's system had not received a precise definition and position. Feeling is, in fact, an obscure and unqualified impulse, essential to theoretical activity and to practical activity, without being either a theoretical or a practical form of the Spirit. Now its function is broadened: it is the moving power of the world and affects all the forms of the Spirit, which it forces into action through pleasure. Without its catalytic power, the will would be paralyzed, the *amor vitae* extinguished. The *vital* is the absolute beginning of the life of the Spirit and the catalyst of its distinct activities.

Whatever the right interpretation of the concept of *vitality* might be, what concerns us here is the possible impact (positive or negative) it may have on Croce's esthetics. It seems that the introduction of the *vital* has broadened the esthetic category by giving feeling (which is the matter of art) a more extensive meaning. The esthetic category, as formulated by Croce, was in fact somewhat narrow, and it stood to benefit from a broadening of its base in the direction of the *vital* and of its top in the direction of intellectual experiences. The concept of *universality* had opened the door to the latter; the concept of *vitality* may provide a richer matter to the former. The boundaries between the distinct forms of the Spirit have as a result become more flexible and fluid, so that they may now be understood in a more dynamic sense.

---

251. Ibid., p. 46.

252. *Indagini su Hegel*, p. 133 ("Intorno alla categoria della vitalità").

253. See Alfredo Parente, "Il concetto crociano della vitalità," *Rivista di studi crociani* 7 (1963):399–409. Parente's article is a lucid exposition of the problem. However, his interpretation does not appear to be supported by Croce's pronouncements on the matter, which remain shrouded in ambiguity and could also be interpreted as a contradiction of his own system, whose logical order is now profoundly altered.

254. Ibid., p. 403.

Benedetto Croce's
Poetry and Literature

Foreword

The guiding idea of this book and its relationship to the Philosophy of Art or Esthetics is clearly explained on the last page. The second part of the volume, which contains the postscripts, may be considered as a relaxed conversation after the tension of the theoretical exposition. It dwells on some particular points in an effort to document, specify, and exemplify them. I felt that this part may be useful to scholars and, therefore, decided to add it.

In writing this book I have constantly kept in mind the teaching I received, since my earliest years, from the works of both Francesco De Sanctis and Giosuè Carducci—two masters who, in various ways, have contributed to the development of a purer and deeper consciousness of poetry in the Italians. Therefore, my dedication of this book to their memory was a spontaneous act. In the course of my work I felt that I was addressing myself to them, asking questions of them and waiting for their approval of the ideas I was expounding. I kept imagining that I would also have such approval whenever dealing with problems they had never considered or whenever departing from their own conceptions.

Meana di Susa, September 1935.

In the third edition additions were made to the postscripts which constitute the second part of the volume.

B. C.

Naples
May 1942

I

Poetry and Literature

In the esthetic experience of our times there has been a growing awareness of the profound difference between "poetry" and "literature." This difference, strongly felt during the romantic period, was scarcely perceived in previous times, including the Greco-Roman era. But it has now taken the form of a conflict in which "literature," having only a few defenders among those who are not afraid of appearing retrograde and reactionary, is regarded with some scorn. Although the conflict and the scorn cannot logically be justified and although the reasons for the distinction are not always well founded, that is, not proved to correspond to truth, the difference between "poetry" and "literature" does exist, nevertheless. The vigorous assertion of this difference in our days proves its importance and effectiveness in our effort to arrive at a sound critical judgment and to remove difficulties and dispel confusions which would otherwise continue to puzzle our mind.

But what, in fact, is literature? What is its definition, that is, its nature, its origin in the human mind, and, finally, its function? I have searched in many books, and in nearly all of those on esthetics, poetics, and rhetoric; but (perhaps because I did not search well) I found either no answers at all or only unsatisfactory answers to my question. I even came to realize that for a long time, in my studies of poetry and literature, I used the distinction without ever trying to explain it thoroughly and thus to clarify matters to myself. To have a concept and to be fully aware of it are two different things, for to be fully aware of a concept means to rediscover and redefine it satisfactorily whenever new difficulties and objections arise. This is what man is forced to do, for, being dissimilar from animals and gods, he is condemned to think.

Thus I have decided to submit the distinction between poetry and literature to a methodical examination; and in order to keep to the essential and avoid wandering into the multitude of literary works in their complexity and magnificence, I have fixed my attention mainly on the original cell—literary expression—from which these large and complex organisms develop. Everyone along the way can color such expression with easier and clearer examples of his own, without confining himself merely to the ones which I provide. On the other hand, so that my inquiry may proceed with the perceptiveness and orderliness required, I have begun by asking myself whether literary expression is to be identified with one of the four other forms of expression, generally known as emotional or immediate expression, poetic expression, prose expression, practical or oratorical expression. In the event that it is not identical with any of these, I will proceed to determine the relationships it may have with them.

1. Emotional or Immediate Expression

Emotional or immediate expression, although commonly called "expression," is not really expression in either a practical or a theoretical sense, for, being immediate, it lacks the active and creative quality which characterizes true expression. When we say that thirty-eight degrees centigrade is the "expression" of fever, that a cloudy sky is the "expression" of imminent rain, that the rise in foreign exchange is the "expression" of a lower purchasing power of a given currency, that blushing is the "expression" of decency, and flushing the "expression" of anger, we use the word in the emotional or immediate sense. In all of these cases the particulars noted, while serving to point to certain facts, are in reality constituent and inseparable parts of these facts; similarly, the emotion expressed by articulate sounds, which for an observer is the symptom of that emotion, is for the person experiencing it the emotion itself as an integral part of the expression.

The various modes of expression. It should be clear that, in undertaking here the examination of the five modes of expression, we did not mean to assert that expression has five modes, but only that the word "expression" is used in five different senses. The only genuinely true expression is, as we shall demonstrate later, language in its virginity and purity, that is, poetry. Other so-called expressions are spiritual acts and facts, diverse in quality, as will be shown in the course of this inquiry.

Immediate expressions of feelings. In addition to Darwin's book, The Expression of the Emotions in Men and Animals (1872; Ital. tr., Turin, 1878) and the works cited in it, one might refer also to an Italian book by [Paolo] Montegazza, Fisonomia e mimica (Milan, 1881).

That which we called expression in a naturalistic sense was designated by Hegel as "corporeity that the spiritual determinations assume, especially in affections," and he assigned it to a special science, "psychical physiology," still to be founded. One must try to understand, he wrote, the connection by which anger and courage are felt in the human breast, blood, and nervous system, and the reflection and spiritual preoccupations in the head, the center of the sensorial system. It would be necessary to acquire a more profound knowledge than we now have of the best-known connections through which weeping, the voice in gen-

eral (more precisely, speech, laughter, sighing), are generated in the soul; and then still many other particularizations which belong to pathognomy and physiognomy. The viscera and the organs are considered in physiology only as stages in the development of the animal organism; but together they form a system corporifying spirituality and, in this way, are also subject to a totally different interpretation (*Encyclopedia*, sec. 401).

Many treatises on the expressions of affections are owed to artists or were composed for use by artists, such as the one by Lebrun, *Conférences sur l'expression des passions* (1698; Ital. tr., Verona, 1751). But, of course, these expressions are always considered as a possible matter for art, as are books on the proportions of the human body, and the like. "Mimicry," a language among languages, is, on the other hand, a different matter. Some considerations on this can be found in my essay "Il linguaggio dei gesti" (*Varietà di storia letteraria e civile*, 2d ed., 1949, vol. 1, pp. 271–80).

Symptomatic expression and spiritual expression. The distinction between the two is so pronounced that it is encountered repeatedly even in the most common books. For instance, just to mention a novel which I happened to have at hand: "She [Julia] knew why in the spring she had acted so badly that Michael had preferred to close down; it was because she was feeling the emotions she portrayed. That was no good. You had to have had the emotions, but you could only play them when you had got over them. She remembered that Charles had once said to her that the origin of poetry was emotion recollected in tranquillity. She didn't know anything about poetry, but it was certainly true about acting" (W. S. Maugham, *Theatre*, New York, 1937, p. 290).

Interjection and language. Since the discussion of interjections is given so much space in books of science and the philosophy of language, we must refer the reader to the most intelligent of these works, namely, that by [Heymann] Steinthal and that by H. Paul, in which the interjection, being a "reflex movement" (that is, natural manifestation), is distinct from its use in "communication," becoming language only in communication (see, for instance, Paul's *Principen der Sprachgeschichte*, Halle, 1886, p. 150). This is, on the whole, an approximative and sociological way of marking the difference between immediate expression and that which is theoretical and intuitive.

The images in passion and in poetry. That feeling and passion carry with them the images of desired or abhorred things and become one and the same with these things must be admitted without question; but such images—overbearing, strident, and often con-

If we reduce emotional expression to its simplest element, we will find it to be an exclamation such as "oh!" or "ah!" or "alas!" and so on. But this is not the exclamation which has become a theoretical expression,[1] that is, speech, the exclamation resounding in poetry and which the grammarians abstractly treat as one of the "parts of speech"; it is, on the contrary, the exclamation which would be more appropriately called "natural," for it bursts from the chest or larynx of the person overcome by wonder, joy, grief, discomfort, or terror, that is, by emotions and feelings which, in agitating him, transform themselves into articulated sounds. Whenever we attempt to inhibit these vocal manifestations for the sake of prudence or good manners, we only succeed in repressing them, and the repressed emotion always finds other outlets; it changes into other more or less analogous forms which can be expressed by gestures, mimicry, the movement of facial muscles, the visible inhibitory effort. And from the lips there may burst forth not only the rapid exclamations we have already given as examples, but also torrents of words louder and more impetuous than those poured out, in a sequel of flowing stanzas, by Donna Julia in Byron's *Don Juan*, when, surprised in bed by her husband, she chose to express her feigned indignation.[2] These torrents of articulated sounds may find a place in writings and fill many volumes; however, if their source is an emotional agitation, they

1. The term "theoretical" is used by Croce in the sense of "speculative," that is, aiming at knowledge, or being an act of knowledge. In the life of the spirit he distinguishes two activities—the theoretical, aimed at knowing; the practical, aimed at doing.

2. Canto I, cxlv–clvii.

will always be exclamations, that is, feeling, and not the theoretical expression of feeling, which entails a new spiritual act and a new form of consciousness. Charles Darwin, although a naturalist, did not hesitate to assert the diversity between the two facts, mistakenly considered as being homonymous. When he set out to study the expression of feelings in men and animals, he hoped to find help in the works of painters and sculptors; but having gained nothing or almost nothing from them, he realized, as he said, "that in works of art, beauty is the chief object; and strongly contracted facial muscles destroy beauty."[3]

The confusion between emotional or natural expression (that is, nonexpression) and poetic expression was principally made by the romantics in their theories and judgments which, while not always affecting their own works, are an illustration of their illusion. Some postromantic and more recent schools repeated the same mistake, with the unfortunate difference that they were unable to offer feelings as noble and as deeply human as those often found in the pages of the romantics.[4] In Italy Giosuè Carducci reacted against these romantic tendencies, in the name of authentic poetic experience. Carducci's rejection of the widespread idolatry of the "heart" as the very source of poetry and his sarcasm and invectives against "that vile muscle harmful to great art" are well known. In France, just to mention some names and episodes of the long and difficult struggle, we may cite Baudelaire and Flaubert, the latter especially who, in reaction against romanticism, went as far as to formulate his paradoxical doctrine of the "impersonality" of art. In recalling the struggle and the men who took the side of passion, feeling, the heart—men who were far from ordinary, whose very power of sublime and delicate feelings made them forgetful or rebellious against the discipline of art, the demands of poetry and the idea of beauty—one feels ashamed and annoyed in hearing the same doctrine of poetry as feeling being mumbled once more in poor sophisms by academicians and professors insensitive to art and lacking experience in the historical development of esthetic doctrines.[5] Their argument that feeling is not formless matter but has a form expressing it breaks open an open door, for, as has already been pointed out, feeling, like any other act or fact (including poetic intuition itself, which is never without expression), is not a soul without a body, but is soul and body, internal and external, sepa-

flicting—do not belong to poetic fancy, which, even when it seems to intervene in order to purify and render them harmonious, in reality creates them anew, as images of its own.

The poetry-feeling. "Ah! frappe-toi le coeur, c'est là qu'est le génie!" (Musset).[1] But from another Frenchman I memorized, when I was a boy, certain lines which said: 'Et tout homme qui souffre et pleure est un poète/ Chaque larme est un vers, chaque poème un coeur." Of these sugary definitions of poetry one could quote hundreds from the romantic period. There was in them the hint that those who uttered them were themselves men of great feeling, sensitive and sad.

The caricature of "genius". In the seventeenth century, the baroque age, the type of would-be "genius" was already noted, that is, the type who pretends to be crazy so that he may appear to be obsessed by poetry. See the satire La poesia by Salvator Rosa, the tercets beginning: "Ché per parer filosofi e saputi, ecc." [For, in order to appear to be philosophers and learned, etc.],[2] which is, in substance, an imitation of a satirical portrait sketched out by [Giambattista] Basile in his Cunto de li cunti [The tale of tales]. But the age of the self-styled "geniuses," sometimes insane, sometimes charlatans—the geniuses "who lacked the artistic form," which, in any case, they scorned (being persuaded that they possessed something more and better, a great heart and the eye of seers)—was that of the late eighteenth century (the period of "geniuses" in Germany) and that of romanticism (spread out a little all over).

Impersonality. "Pas de sanglots humains dans le chant des poètes!" this formula says too much and too little.[3] The following, however: "Est-elle en marbre,

---

3. *The Expression of the Emotions in Man and Animals* (1872; New York: D. Appleton & Co., 1896), p. 15.

4. Croce had a marked bias against decadent literature and most of twentieth-century poetic production.

5. This stricture is directed mainly at Giovanni Gentile whose *La Filosofia dell'Arte*, critical of Croce's theory, had been published in 1931.

1. "A mon ami Edouard B.," *Premières poésies* (Paris: Charpentier, 1885), p. 220.

2. Salvator Rosa (1615–1673), painter and poet. The satire mentioned by Croce is "Satire II" *(Satire)*, against the poetic faults of the baroque age.

3. Line from Catulle Mendès, *Philoméla* (the poem entitled "Pudor").

rate in the abstract but one in reality where the word becomes flesh. This does not, however, open to them another door, that of poetic expression, which is distinctly diverse from the pseudoexpression of feeling. Even William Shakespeare, considered for a long time to be the symbol of unbridled passion in art, not only demonstrated the contrary in his works, but, whenever hinting at his own theory, also avoided dwelling on emotion and passion; he defined poetry, on the contrary, as a kind of magic by virtue of which the poet, turning his eyes from heaven to earth and from earth to heaven, gives a shape, a place, and a name to "airy nothings," and he recommended to the artist not the explosion of violent emotions, but "temperance" and "smoothness" even in the storm and turmoil of passion.

ou non, la Vénus de Milo?" which is meant to reinforce the impersonality of poetry, is completely silly.[4] But in Flaubert the formula of "impersonality," however imperfect under another aspect, had a polemical value against the "sentimentalism" and the "social mission" assumed by art. It is enough to quote some passages: *"Artistes . . . de ceux dont la vie et l'esprit étaient l'instrument aveugle de l'appétit du beau, organes de Dieu par lesquels il se prouvait à lui-même. Pour ceux-là le monde n'était pas; personne n'a rien su de leurs douleurs; chaque soir ils se couchaient tristes, et ils regardaient la vie humaine avec un regard étonné comme nous contemplons des fourmilières"* (Correspondance, vol. 1, p. 120: letter of August 9, 1846). Compare these words with the following, written a few days later: *"Je me suis toujours défendu de rien mettre de moi dans mes oeuvres, et pourtant j'en ai mis beaucoup. J'ai toujours tâché de ne pas rapetisser l'Art à la satisfaction d'une personnalité isolée. J'ai écrit des pages fort tendres sans amour, et des pages bouillantes sans aucun feu dans le sang. J'ai imaginé, je me suis souvenu et j'ai combiné"* (Correspondance, vol. 1, p. 128: letter of August 15, 1846). It is evident here that he intended to exclude, as "personalistic," the "satisfaction d'une personnalité isolée," that is, passional and practical unilaterality.

"Objectivity" of poetry. When by "objectivity" in poetry is meant something other than the "objectification" of feeling within imagination, the door is open to the confusion of poetry with history, psychology, sociology, and so on. Curiously enough the Goncourts noted: *"Le roman actuel se fait avec des documents racontés, ou relevés d'après nature, comme l'histoire se fait avec des documents écrits. Les historiens sont des raconteurs du passé, les romanciers des raconteurs du présent"* (Journal, October 24, 1864).

It is superfluous to say that the Goncourts as well as Flaubert were far from being impersonal in their works, in both the good and the bad sense; on the contrary, the defect of some of their works consists in their failure to subdue and soothe their passional impulses. For Flaubert this is shown and explained in my *European Literature in the Nineteenth Century,* pp. 297–311.[5]

The unity of intuition and expression. Objections with no critical value were raised against this unity, which is one of the first propositions established in my *Aesthetic* (1902). These objections were drawn from commonplace psychological descriptions of the expressive process and therefore are not worthy of being collected here. The unity I proposed is entirely speculative and

4. Verlaine, *Poèmes saturniens,* "Epilogue" 3.
5. Italian title: *Poesia e non poesia.*

Feeling ceases to be form and becomes matter by the very fact and at the very moment that it is superseded by poetic expression. This change is the result of the law governing the living dialectic of the spirit; and according to that law, whatever was form in a preceding stage becomes matter and receives a new form in a subsequent stage. Consequently, passion, which reaches its form in a passionate man, reverts to matter when reflection on his passion arises. Needless to say, the relationship between matter and form is not a relationship of cause to effect as in the physical world; nor is it a relationship between original and copy, as might be suggested by the metaphors of common speech which distinguish the language that "renders" or "represents" feeling, from art which is an "image" or "mimesis" or "imitation" of nature and reality. The naive theory of knowledge conceived as a copy—*Abbild*— which simply raises these metaphors to the level of logical relations, is easily refuted by gnoseology through the demonstration that such a theory unnecessarily replaces the act of knowledge with a double object of knowledge. This theory has for years been refuted in relation to art by the popular argument that statues of colored wax, while giving the illusion of reality, are neither paintings nor sculptures; nor is poetry or art the perfect imitation of barking, mewing, or roaring. Poetry cannot copy or imitate feeling, because feeling, while having a form within its own sphere, is formless in relation to poetry; it is nothing determinate, it is chaos, and chaos, being simply a negative moment, is therefore nothingness. Poetry, like every other spiritual activity, simultaneously creates the problem and the solution, the form and the content, the latter always being formed, not formless, matter. Prior to the kindling of the poetic spark there are no figures drawn in light and shade, there is only darkness; this spark alone sheds light, the light which caused the apparition of Homer to be likened to the sunrise upon the earth. And "Homeric clarity" is still the mark of all true poetry.

founded on the criticism of the abstract distinction (typical of the natural sciences) of the inner from the outer, of the spirit from the body, and the like. Goethe himself, in the face of natural science, asserted this truth by inculcating that "Nature has neither core nor skin, and is all uniform." If we were to expand on this point, we could demonstrate, historically, that the identity between inner and outer began in modern philosophy when Spinoza and Leibniz excluded every reciprocal influence between the soul and the body and that an anticipation of this identity is already in the "pre-established harmony."

Form which reverts to matter. Hegel described this relation (which made it possible to found the conception of the circular life of the spirit and the resolution of nature into spirit) by taking his starting point from a profound sentence of Goethe: "Goethe somewhere truly says, 'That which is formed ever resolves itself back into its elements.' Matter—which as developed has form—constitutes once more the material for a new form. Mind again takes as its object and applies its activity to the Notion in which in going within itself, it has comprehended itself, which it is in form and being, and which has just been separated from it anew" (*Lectures on the History of Philosophy*, tr. E. S. Haldane, vol. 1, p. 27). The concept that form reverts to the matter of a superior form goes back, moreover, to Aristotle.

The copy of reality. Plutarch (*De audiendis poëtis*, chap. 3) recalled the delight offered by Parmenon's imitation of the grunting of pigs and by Theodorus' of the screeching of machines.

Today's so-called futurists, although unaware of their ancient predecessors, take to this sort of counterfeiting. They make an effort to reproduce cries, shrieks, squeaks, and other noises, simultaneously with every kind of visual, olfactory, and tactile impressions; by this they believe themselves to be doing not only something new but something poetic; they sincerely think, at least those whose good faith deserves recognition, that such recognition applies to their "sottise," which is great. The various forms of "impressionism" tend nevertheless, in a manner certainly less gross, to retain the disintegrated and the chaotic in reality; hence their usual disagreeableness and insipidity.

Realistic prejudices. Although it is commonly admitted that poetry is not a "copy of reality," many an erroneous judgment must be attributed to an unconscious realistic presupposition, as when it is requested that a character be seen not only in profile, that is, in that unique manner in which the poet presents him, but frontways or from all sides, integrated in his entire *personal reality. This is the curious illusion, noted specifically in Shakespearean criticism, that it is possible to inquire into the nature of characters beyond the poet's words and into their life prior and subsequent to that appearing in the drama (see my essay on Shakespeare in the volume Ariosto, Shakespeare and Corneille, pp. 312–19). This criticism fails to understand or loses sight of the fact that the characters of a drama are nothing but the very parts of the poet's soul and that they have no reality outside his soul.*

In a more moderate form the same error is committed when a work of art or the personage of a work of art is characterized by reference to a psychological possibility, that in such a case may be an esthetic impossibility because it conflicts with the lyrical motif, that is, the poetic, which is (or should be) in the work. Whenever this kind of reasoning is heard, one must answer that everything would be perfectly well if we were dealing with a letter entrusted to the mailman or to some other person with whom we are acquainted, but that we are dealing here, on the contrary (and this should not be forgotten), with poetic creatures, that is, musical notes.

Art and reality. Art certainly expresses reality when by reality is meant the only reality, which is the soul, the spirit; but the same proposition makes no logical sense when by reality is meant something external to the spirit and schematized under the name of "nature" by positivisitic thought. This proposition derives from the naive belief that poetic creations reproduce a reality outside ourselves: it derives from the same naive belief that there is an "external reality," that is, one outside the mind. The development of the thought on esthetics, which from the "mimesis" of Hellenic philosophy has arrived at the modern "lyrical intuition," is the very evolution from philosophical materialism or dualism to absolute idealism.

The sign of the embarrassment resulting from the concept of artistic expression as the portrayal of reality or the "imitation of nature," is shown by the opposite theory, also prevalent in antiquity, that the domain of poetry was that of "fiction," of the "beautiful lie"—a theory which stands and falls as does its contrary.

That poetic creations and works of art in general are admired for their "liveliness of reality," for their "faithfulness to nature," and the like, is the usual and plausible metaphorical expression which cannot be forbidden to anyone, although one can legitimately request that those words be taken in their exclamatory value as an expression of admiration for poetic or artistic perfection, and not misunderstood as being definitions of poetry and art, and critical interpretations of art works.

However, darkness is not nonexistence, just as nothingness is not nothingness, but, as we have said, a negative moment originating from a positive one; and if that formless feeling had not been anteceded by a positive one, poetry would not have come into being, for the spirit is not an abstraction, nor are the forms of the spirit unrelated—"nulla ars in se tota versatur" [no art depends entirely on itself];[6] the life of each form is dependent upon the life of the other forms. The suggestion, often voiced by critics, poets, and literary experts, that poetry is the creation of beauty and consequently has no content and no meaning is to be considered an excessive defense. They do not realize that poetry is the transfiguration of feeling, in which, just as in the transfiguration described in St. Matthew's Gospel, "resplendet facies sicut sol, vestimenta facta sunt alba ut nix" [and his face shone as the sun, and his garments became white as snow].[7]

If those who are ignorant of the real nature of art and poetry were not as talkative as they are, and if the notion that knowing is copying and that spiritual creation is a creation in the abstract were not so persistent, there would be no reason to argue and demonstrate that poetry is distinct from feeling, that feeling is its necessary material, and that poetry is the transfiguration of feeling. For all these statements would then be peacefully accepted without challenge. Everyone, in fact, observes in himself the genesis of poetic expressions, noting that, however ineffective these may be, they always spring from an emotive experi-

6. Cicero, *De finibus* 5.6.16.
7. Chap. 17.2.

The darkness of feeling and the light of poetry. In the terminology of the Leibnizian school, "obscure perceptions" correspond to what we call "feeling": "Sunt in anima perceptiones obscurae. Harum complexus fundus animae dicitur." "Status animae, in quo perceptiones dominantes obscurae sunt, est Regnum tenebrarum; in quo clarae regnant, Regnum lucis est" [There are in the soul obscure perceptions. The whole of them is called the bottom of the soul. The state of the soul in which the dominating perceptions are obscure is the realm of darkness; that in which clear perceptions reign is the realm of light] (Baumgarten, *Metaphysica*, Halae Magdeb., 1743, secs. 511, 518).

False "creativity". Great tenderness, extreme jealousy, which according to a certain current philosophy foster poetic "creativity," in reality hide a lack of appreciation for poetry and for any specific spiritual act by equating everything to creation for its own sake, which is false creation, irrational and blind, for, in this case, thought loses its critical seriousness, morality its sense of duty, poetry its particular magic, leaving nothing but a sterile agitation of an organ in a vacuum adorned by the name of "actuality of the act."[6]

Poems considered to say nothing. Thus, among others, the fine poet and critic A. E. Housman writes: "Even Shakespeare, who had so much to say, would sometimes pour out his loveliest poetry in saying nothing" (*The Name and Nature of Poetry*, Cambridge, 1933, p. 39); and he quoted as an example of "nonsense" the following, which is nevertheless even for him "ravishing poetry":

> Take, o take those lips away
> That so sweetly were forsworn,
> And those eyes, the break of day,
> Lights that do mislead the morn;
> But my kisses bring again,
>   bring again,
> Seals of love, but sealed in vain,
>   sealed in vain.

But, evidently, Housman argues here that "saying something" means enlightening the mind with ideas or communicating to it factual information; otherwise, one would not understand why he considers as bereft of meaning this sweet and doleful song of lost love and of vibrating remembrance of past sweetness—a song, indeed, full of poetic meaning.

Poetic transfiguration. It is understood, then, how beauty, in which every practical interest purifies itself, suggested to Winckelmann the image of water taken from the heart of the source, that is, that the less taste it has, the purer and healthier it is (*Geschichte der Kunst*

6. Reference to Gentile and his "actual idealism."

ence which attains form and self-awareness in language. And everyone is led, by similar experiences, to assume that the same happens to those who are specifically and eminently poets, although their emotional life is unknown. Thus, it is easy to construct by imagination romances and dramas of love, heroism, misfortune, and grief, in which artists or poets are the heroes or the victims, and to fancy and embellish links between feeling and imagination. Goethe never tired of repeating that all poems are "occasional poems," for reality alone could provide the "incentive" and the "material." He even wrote that his own vast and varied production of lyric poetry, tragedies, idylls, lengthy poems, and tales was to be considered as the "fragments of a long confession," adding that he used to free and purify himself of whatever pleased or tormented him, or in some way occupied his mind, by transforming it into an "image" through that theoretical act which is designated as "catharsis," that is, the purification of passion through poetry.

des Altertums, sec. 23), and the idea of the "nonmeaning" of the beautiful. Taking the image in his own way, and not from hydrology (as Winckelmann did), but from zoology and geology, Flaubert said that "les chefs-d'oeuvre sont bêtes, ils ont la mine tranquille comme les productions mêmes de la nature, comme les grands animaux et les montagnes" (Correspondance, vol. 2, p. 122: letter of 1852).

Novels or biographical novels of poets. Sometimes these novels are presented as critically prepared stories; they are, in other words, a sequence of integrated imaginary elements and conjectures converted into verified facts—as in the book by Brandes and even more in that by Harris on Shakespeare. For the criticism of these books see my essay on Shakespeare in the volume Ariosto, Shakespeare and Corneille, pp. 122–34, and a note in Conversazioni critiche, 2d ed., vol. 3, pp. 60–62.

Poetry is always occasional. "[The world is so great and rich, and life so full of variety, that one can never want occasions for poems.] But they must all be occasional poems; that is to say, reality must give both impulse and material for their production. A particular case becomes universal and poetic by the very circumstance that it is treated by a poet. All my poems are occasional poems; that is to say, suggested by real life, and having therein a firm foundation. I attach no value to poems snatched out of the air" (Conversations with Eckermann, September 18, 1823). Goethe even felt a sort of "pietas" toward the category or the name, found in some poetics, of "occasional poetry" ("Gelegenheitsdichtung") and wrote in his autobiography, in regard to the conditions of poetry in Germany during his youth: "Occasional poems, the first and most genuine of all kinds of poetry, had become despicable to such a degree that the nation cannot even now come to a conception of the high value of these" (Poetry and Truth, bk. 10, par. 1).

Passional life in poetry. Baudelaire, speaking about Les Fleurs du mal, said: "Dans ce livre atroce, j'ai mis tout mon coeur, toute ma tendresse, toute ma religion (travestie), toute ma haine. Il est vrai que j'écrirai le contraire, que je jurerai mes grands Dieux que c'est un livre d'art pur."

Catharsis. Goethe writes in Poetry and Truth (bk. 13) in regard to Werther: ". . . for by this composition, more than by any other, I had saved myself from a stormy element, on which by my own fault and that of others, by an accidental and voluntary way of life, by design and precipitation, by obstinacy and compliance, I had been driven hither and thither in the most violent manner. I felt myself again joyful and free, as if after a general confession, and justified in a new life.

*The old remedy had this time served me admirably. But while I felt myself eased and illuminated by having changed reality into poetry, my friends were perplexed by the work." See also, in bk. 7, what he has to say about his transforming into images (*Bild*) that which tormented him.*

Heine, in his usual manner, played with Goethe's thought in order to make it witty:

> *Krankheit ist wohl der letzte Grund*
> *Des ganzen Schöpfungsdrang gewesen:*
> *Erschaffend konnte ich genesen,*
> *Erschaffend ward ich gesund.*

(Sickness is certainly the ultimate reason for the whole impulse to creation: by creating I could heal; by creating I healed.)

As for "catharsis," there is no need to collect here the copious controversial literature on the interpretation of the Aristotelian term, for we are interested solely in the modern concept that the word now signifies (be it the development of the Aristotelian concept, the correction, or even the misunderstanding of it): and that is the detachment from and elevation above passionality through the activity of poetic intuition.

Passional agitation and poetry. *We take from Goethe himself the story of the artistic repugnance preventing him from imitating Schiller's early manner: "Upon my return from Italy, where I had tried to educate myself to a greater clarity and purity in all branches of art, unconcerned about what in the meantime was happening in Germany, I found some recent and less recent poetic works which enjoyed great reputation and acclaim, but were unfortunately of the kind extraordinarily repugnant to me: I shall mention only Arding-hello by Heinse and The Robbers by Schiller. The former was hateful to me because the author sought, through the figurative arts, to ennoble and support sensuality and abstruse ways of thinking; the latter because, being a vigorous but immature talent, Schiller had begun to pour on our country, like an overpowering stream, precisely those ethical and theatrical paradoxes of which I had endeavored to purify myself. . . . The noise that those works had produced in our country, approbation generally given to those strange abortive productions by unbridled students as well as cultivated court ladies, frightened me, for I felt that all my labor was completely lost; the objectives for which I had educated myself appeared to me as thrown aside, and the very manner of my education paralyzed. And what grieved me most was the fact that all my friends, Heinrich Meyer and Moritz, as well as the artists of similar spirit, Tischbein and Bury, seemed to me to be equally leaning in that direction. I was very much as-*

tounded. If it had been possible I would willingly have abandoned altogether the study of figurative art and the practice of poetry; for what possibility was there of surpassing those productions, basically brilliant but in a disorderly form? Imagine my state of mind! I had sought to cultivate and communicate to others the purest conceptions; and there I was squeezed between Ardinghello and Franz Moor!" ([Paralipomena zu den] Annalen, on the date of 1794).

The reader will notice that these postscripts of mine refer frequently (and the frequency could have been even greater) to words by Goethe; but Goethe, although he was not a professional philosopher, is the man who best represents a situation which I consider to be essential, not only for esthetics, but for every branch of philosophy: a living experience of his own subject matter (of moral life for ethics, of political life for philosophy, of historiography for a theory of history, and so on). Professors of philosophy lack all this, for they spend their youth in concocting qualifications to compete for academic chairs, and their later years with school manuals. "Why," said Goethe in reading the esthetic theories too frequently put out by philosophers of his own time, "why don't they listen to the lover of art concerning art. . . . He who has no sense experience of art should give up theorizing. Why should he interest himself in such things? Because it is fashionable? He must consider that with his theories he shuts the door to real enjoyment, for they are the most damaging nullities" (see the book reviews of the works on esthetics by Sulzer in 1772, in Goethe's Werke, ed. Goedeke, vol. 27, pp. 13–20, 25–31). I must, however, beg the reader's pardon for the frequent references to my own writings; he will be kind enough to understand that this is dictated only by the necessity of avoiding the repetition of things I said elsewhere, and, at the same time, of pointing out that I have not neglected certain problems and certain difficulties, and that I dealt with them in other works, if someone is interested to know.

2. Poetic Expression

What, then, is the poetic expression which appeases and transfigures feeling? It is, as has been said, a cognitive process, a form of knowledge and, therefore, it differs from feeling, which, however lofty and noble its source, cleaves to the particular and remains, of necessity, within the narrowness of passion, the antinomy of good and evil, the excitement of joy and suffering. Poetry, on the contrary, ties the particular to

The cosmic meaning of poetry. "Ce qui semble à d'autres incohérent et contradictoire, n'est pour le poète qu'un contraste harmonique, un accord à distance sur la lyre universelle. Lui-même il entre bientôt dans ce grand concert, et, comme ces vases d'airain des théâtres antiques, il marie l'écho de sa voix à la musique du monde" (Sainte-Beuve, *Vie, poésies et pensées de Joseph Delorme*, [Thoughts, XX]).

the universal; it embraces suffering and pleasure, transcending them, and, rising above the clash between the parts, it reveals the place of each part in the whole, the harmony over the conflict, the sweep of the infinite over the narrowness of the finite. This mark of universality and totality is the very character of poetry. And whenever this character is weak or missing, even if there seem to be images, we say that these images lack fullness, that the "supreme imagination," the creative fancy, the true poetry are absent. Like every other form of the spirit, poetry realizes itself only through the inner struggle of the spirit, that is, through the struggle against feeling which, while providing the poetic matter, imposes at the same time the resistance and the obstacle of matter. Thus, the victory by which the reluctant matter is transformed into images is marked by a serenity in which the emotion still trembles like a tear lighted by a smile, and by a new and appeased feeling which is the joy of beauty.

The effect of poetry appeared to the ancient Greeks to be so marvelous and miraculous that they identified it with sacred inspiration, with exaltation, frenzy, divine madness; and they distinguished the bards from other mortals, honoring them as the mouthpieces of the gods, the Muse's beloved disciples, whose songs reach the vastness of the heavens.[8] The moderns have not entirely denied the poets a similar tribute; they have, in fact, surrounded them with unanimous ad-

8. See the *Odyssey* 7. 479–81; 8. 73–74; 17. 359, 385, 518–20; 12. 345–46 (Croce's note).

The following stanza by Carducci grasps this individual-universal process in action:

> Son io che il cielo abbraccio, o dall'interno
> mi riassorbe l'universo in sé?
> Ahi, fu una nota del poema eterno
> quel ch'io sentiva, e picciol verso or è!
> [Giambi ed epodi, XXX]

[Am I encompassing the heavens, or is the universe reabsorbing me from within itself? Alas, what I felt was one note of the eternal poem, and it is now just a little verse!] This harmonization in the cosmos, given as restraint or divine proportion to things which are upset by passions, was expressed in a different way in the following lines by Platen, if my memory does not fail me:

> Um den Geist emporzuheben
> von der Sinne rohen Schmaus,
> Um der Dinge Mass zu lehren,
> sandte Gott den Dichter aus.

(To lift up the spirit from the crude orgy of the sense, to teach moderation in things, God sent the poet.)

The question is amply treated in my essay "The Character of Totality of Artistic Expression," in Nuovi saggi d'estetica *(3d ed., pp. 117–34) [translated by D. Ainslie,* English Review *26 (1918):475–86.]*

The tone in poetry. Carducci *used to say, by contrast to the realistic and familiar poetry, low in tone and, all considered, prosaic, which was favored in Italy between 1860 and 1880: that poetry cannot exist unless it has "a tone heightened by a degree over prose"* (Opere, *vol. 3, p. 440).*

Wilhelm Humboldt, in his correspondence with an old friend, while agreeing with her that it is impossible to say what poetry is and that poetry must be felt, added that it was easier to clarify the matter through examples; and he cited as examples Gellert and Klopstock, both nobly pious, both exerting a wide and profound influence on the minds and hearts of their contemporaries; however, in Klopstock's poetry there was an incomparably greater imaginative impulse because he was of a poetic nature, while Gellert's poetry was rhymed prose (Briefe an eine Freundin, *letter of May 6, 1831).*

Poetic ecstasy. The raising of crude feeling and its expression to the level of poetic intuition and expression with its cosmic afflatus was always perceived and expressed through the doctrine of inspiration, the agitating god, fury, poetic mania, and the like. A curious reflection of this doctrine is shown by the interest and admiration aroused, particularly at the beginning of the nineteenth century in the eyes of foreigners, by the Italian "improvisers," held in low esteem by the Italians, but seeming to offer to others, preromantics and

miration and reverent protection, attributing to them (and to them alone) the privilege of "inspiration" and the gift of "genius." Strictly speaking, inspiration and genius, and the "quid divinum" are present in every human being and human work (otherwise, it would not be authentically human); but the importance that these attributes seem to acquire in poetic creation results precisely from the elevation of the particular to the universal, the finite to the infinite—an elevation which does not occur (or does not occur in the same way) in practical and passional life, in which the inverse process takes place, but in thought and philosophy, as a further step through the mediation of poetry. Compared to the knowing of philosophy, the knowing of poetry seemed different and, rather than knowing, it appeared as a producing, a shaping, a molding, ποιείν: hence the name it retains in modern languages. And for the first time the concept of knowing as "receiving" was abandoned, while that of knowing as creating was recognized and attributed to poetry.

romantics alike, a tangible proof of poetic rapture!

The "world" of poets. Traditionally the expression "world of poets" meant the complex of fictions, that is, unreal things, invented or adopted by poets: "Complexum et satis male cohaerens systema fictionum omnis generis, iam a pluribus elegantioribus ingeniis adoptatarum et suppositarum, synecdochice dicamus Mundum Poetarum" [We call, by synecdoche, the World of Poets, a complex and rather incoherent system of fictions of every kind, already adopted or invented by many of the most elegant talents] (Baumgarten, *Aesthetica*, sec. 513). Baumgarten satirically associated with that world many cosmologies by philosophers, not omitting that of Descartes, together with the theogonies of the ancients and every Greek and Roman and Indian and Eddaic mythology, including the *Acta sanctorum*, and so forth). But the expression later took on another meaning: the "world as seen by the poet," who makes his soul the center of it.

Imagination and fancy. This distinction presented itself persistently to the mind of estheticians, and De Sanctis himself used it. The lack of fancy, or "supreme imagination," was studied in some poets who were highly endowed with many gifts, including a vivid imagination, such as Byron. This is the reason posterity was not favorable to him, in contrast to the fervent admiration he enjoyed from his contemporaries. But among his admirers we do not find Leopardi, who wrote in his *Pensieri* (vol. 5, p. 215): "Although the fancy (that is, imagination) of Lord Byron is naturally extraordinary, nevertheless, it is quite true that it, too, is for the most part artificial, that is to say, forced; as a result, it is clearly evident that the majority of Lord Byron's poems come from his will and from a habit acquired by his talent, rather than from inspiration and fancy spontaneously moved." A collection of unanimously negative judgments from the best English criticism is found in a recent study by G. Foà, *Lord Byron, poeta e carbonaro* (Florence, 1935), first part. These judgments point out in Byron a lack of "atmosphere," of "chiaroscuro," of "images that, though permeated by the individuality of the poet, may look like a discovery and appear as having always existed," and so on.

Elevation of poetry above itself. Not taken into account here are the elevation of poetry to the rank of supreme medium of philosophy (Schelling, the philosophy of intuition and the like, not excluding the works of poets such as Keats: "Beauty is truth, truth beauty") and the broadening of the concept of poetry so as to encompass the whole of human life, as in *Defence of Poetry* by Shelley (on which see my lecture "La difesa della poesia," in *Ultimi saggi*, 2d ed., 1948, es-

But so that the universality, divinity, and cosmic character of poetry may not be misunderstood and materialized by restricting it exclusively to a particular type of poetry, or still worse, by drawing up a program of poetry or of a poetic school which should produce that poetry (attempts of this kind have been made and still are being made), it is well to repeat what was said, in words allowing no room for ambiguity. We shall say, then, that the universality, and any synonym used for it, is simply the whole and undivided humanity of the poetic vision; and whenever such a vision is formed (whatever its particular content) the universality is found in that very content, without the need for evoking the infinite, the cosmos, God through direct images as in *Coeli enarrant* or in *Laudes creaturarum*.

The distinction between poetic and nonpoetic matter, on which philosophers and authors of treatises in the past toiled fruitlessly and which, fortunately, seems abandoned nowadays, reflects the attempt to discover, in the content of poetry, the poeticalness which lies (and it could not be otherwise) in poetry itself. There is nothing exclusively poetic about a Hector, an Ajax, an Antigone, a Dido, a Francesca, a Gretchen, a Macbeth, a Lear, for Falstaff, Don Quixote, Sancho Panza are equally poetic; similarly, if a Cordelia, a Desdemona, an Andromache are poetic figures, so are a Manon Lescaut, an Emma Bovary, or the Countess and Cherubin in the world of Figaro; the feelings of a Foscolo, a Vigny, or a Keats are no more poetic than those of a Villon; poetic are not only the hexameters of Virgil, but also the macaronic hexameters of Merlin Cocai,[9] which contain beautiful traits of touching humanity; and not only the sonnets of Petrarch, but even the pedantic and the burlesque of Fidenzio Glottocrisio.[10] The humblest popular song, if permeated by a ray of humanity, is poetry which can stand up to any other poetry, however sublime. A certain presumptuousness and false gravity render some people reluctant to recognize the poetic quality, particularly in works which display gaiety and laughter, while they are ready to recognize that same quality in works heavy with solemnity, gloom, catastrophe, and terror. Yet it is not infrequent that these latter kinds of works are stiff, raw, violent, and unpoetic, whereas

pecially pp. 65–66). Poetry is already lofty enough by its own nature that it need not push itself to altitudes where, by encompassing all, it would lose itself.

The place of the poet in society. The imagined or believed hostility of society toward poets is no more than a case of romantic neurosis (see my own remarks in regard to Vigny in *European Literature in the Nineteenth Century*, pp. 131–44). The obstacles encountered in all kinds of works and the ever greater struggles endured with newer works gave origin to the imaginary persecution against genius and the alleged misfortune waiting to strike him. However, the attitude of society toward the recognized poet is the one explained in the text [p. 6 of this book]. An attempt was even made to express this homage by an official mark of distinction such as the "laurea poetica" or the wreath of which Dante dreamed: ". . . ed in sul fronte/ del mio battesmo prenderò il cappello" [. . . and I shall put on my head my baptismal cap (*Paradiso* 25. 9)]; and which Petrarch received and which Tasso was about to receive when he died. But the practice, badly conceived and practically unworkable, dragged on and ended in the scandals of the coronations on the Capitol, such as that of the improvisers Bernardino Perfetti and Corilla Olimpica.[7] It would be worthwhile to read the strange list of "poets laureate" in the book by Vincenzo Lancetti, *Memorie intorno ai poeti laureati d'ogni tempo e d'ogni nazione* [Memoirs concerning the poets laureate of all times and all nations] (Milan, 1839). Conservative England still reserves the name of "poet laureate" for those who once were called "Caesarean poets" or "court poets."

Manon Lescaut. In this short novel one can observe how a poetic masterpiece was born, without any practical intention, any conceptual design, any sensual or emotional gratification, but by just overcoming, in the clarity of the narration, the very suffering which tore the soul of the author. This is a vision of human reality, without comments and with a sense of astonishment, a vision of love in its primitive and wild force which breaks down and shatters everything, and which the force of moral law cannot restrain, force being its own and only law; and to this force everything must succumb. In the woman, a completely natural creature, there is something that is lacking in her lover—a sort of innocence not yet conscious of good and evil, not a moral conflict, but an alternation

9. Merlin Cocai, pseudonym under which the foremost Italian macaronic poet, Teofilo Folengo (1491–1545), published his main burlesque poem, *Baldus* (1517), written in macaronic hexameters.

10. Pseudonym of Camillo Scrofa (b. 1526), author of *L'Amorosa elegia d'un appassionato pedante al suo amatissimo Camillo* (ca. 1550), by which he is credited to have initiated a sort of subgenre of jocular poetry, called "fidenziana." In other compositions he treated, in a comical vein, themes taken from Petrarch, Catullus, and Horace, writing in a deliberately pedantic macaronic language.

7. Bernardino Perfetti (1681–1747), renowned extemporaneous poet, was crowned at the Capitol as poet laureate in 1725 by order of Pope Benedict XIII. Corilla Olimpica, whose real name was Maddalena Maria Morelli (1727–1800). The most celebrated improviser of the eighteenth century, she lived at the court of the Grand Duke of Tuscany and was crowned poet laureate in 1776 at the Capitol.

gaiety and laughter reveal, if considered attentively, a strain of suffering and an understanding of the human condition.

between love and desire for enjoyment and luxury. We are confronted with the perennial effort of humanity within itself and against itself, trying to free and elevate itself, but falling again painfully and desperately: "Hélas, oui, c'est mon devoir d'agir comme je raisonne! Mais l'action est-elle en mon pouvoir? De quel secours n'aurais-je pas besoin pour oublier les charmes de Manon?" And the theologian friend here recognizes with astonishment, catching it in its living concreteness, the reason which was drawing Lutherans, Calvinists, and Jansenists to their doctrine; and he is astounded rather than scandalized: "Dieu me pardonne, reprit Tiberge, je pense que voici encore un de nos jansénistes. . . . Je ne sais et je ne vois pas trop clairement ce qu'il faut être, mais je n'éprouve que trop la vérité de ce qu'ils disent." The philistines, seeking the sublimity of poetic subjects, would be scandalized to hear that Manon Lescaut *is considered to be poetry. Not so Goethe, who would have answered jokingly as he did concerning his Filines and his Cretchens when he was accused of preference for a society of questionable morality: he said that disreputable society offered him hints for poetry that good society was not able to offer.*

Villon. *Villon remains caught up in flesh and vice, but he feels his state as fate or misfortune and feels the nullity of his sensual life through the corporeal decay and death awaiting him, and he has the humility of a sinner who cannot resist sin but who at the same time recognizes a superior power, human goodness of which he begs pity, and God Whom he never denies. The circle within which he moves is a small one, but as profound as the one within himself! The motifs of rapidly passing youth, of horrifying old age, of death, of things that pass away, are not common motifs as their generic expression might suggest; but they are entirely his own, and are rendered in simple and vivid images. And these images are at times very gentle and tender, more often doleful and sad and macabre; nor does the poet turn his eyes away from the most cruel aspects of life; but he sanctifies all, so to speak, through his suffering and pity. Reread* La ballade des pendus, *in which those bodies swinging in the wind, washed by rain, dessicated and blackened by the sun, nibbled at by magpies and crows, pitted like thimbles, horrifying and ridiculous, are turned into poor human creatures to whom we are bound by a brotherly tie. One may compare, for the sake of contrast, Villon's poem with the* Bal des pendus *by Rimbaud: "Au gibet noir, manchot aimable, dansent, dansent les paladins." The stupid inhumanity of the latter arouses a salutary repulsion and is an edifying experience in relation to certain modern poetic infatuations.*

Merlin Cocai and Fidenzio. *See this short passage*

(among so many that could be taken as examples) from *Baldus*—the passage which narrates how the fugitive princess Baldovina was overtaken by the pains of childbirth in the cabin of the peasant Berto:

> Baldovina casa remanet soletta, nec imbrem
> acquetare potest oculorum, abeunte marito.
> Pensorosa manu guanzam sustentat et ecce,
> ecce repentinae sua brancant viscera doiae,
> namque novo partu miseram fiolare bisognat.
> Argutos meschina foras mandare cridores
> cogitur, ac ne sit compresa in pectore calcat
> spicula quae nondum natus tirat undique Baldus.
> Tantum invita fremit, nunc ve uno saepe fianco,
> nunc altro sese (visu miserabile) voltat.
> Non commater adest, solitum quae porgat aiuttum,
> ancillas, servasque vocat, quibus ante solebat
> commandare, velut commandat filia regis;
> et vocat indarnum, quia tantum gatta valebat
> respondere gnao sed non donare socorsum.

[Bardovina remains at home lonely; she cannot stop the tear from her eyes as her husband departs. Pensively she rests her face in her hands; but suddenly the pain of labor gripes her entrails, thus the unfortunate one must give birth to her first child. The miserable one thinks of letting out sharp screams, and in order not to be heard presses her chest against the kicks that the not yet born Baldus delivers from everywhere. So much did she involuntarily quiver, often turning to one side or to the other with her distressed face. No midwife is present, who ordinarily lends help; she calls the maids and the servants, to whom she used to impart orders as the daughter of the king; but she calls in vain, because her cries were of as much help as the cat's mewing.]

There is a gentle and compassionate participation and at the same time an observing with an air of indifferent curiosity, which mark every small detail, even the grotesque, of the spectacle before us: the attacks of labor pains, the repressed screams, the kicks of the child from within, the rolling of the suffering woman from side to side, the futility of her calling for help, attested to by the mewing of the cat, sole spectator, representing the final felicitous touch of the picture. This characterizes Folengo's art, to which dog Latin is intrinsic, for Latin as such and measured in hexameters confers solemnity of tone to the rather comical care with which he brings to the fore, and all on the same level, the material appearances of things, their corporeity, and, through dog Latin and dialectal forms, provides the vivid colors of his pictures. In my *Nuovi saggi sulla letteratura italiana del Seicento* (2d ed., 1949, pp. 78–85), I discussed the poor poetic inspiration running through the pedantic verses of Fidenzio, which were neglected by the Italian critics or con-

To describe the impression that poetry leaves in the human mind, the word "melancholy" was spontaneously born on man's lips. And indeed the conciliation of the opposites, in whose conflict alone life throbs; the vanishing of passion, which together with suffering bring an indefinable but voluptuous warmth; the detachment from the terrestrial surroundings, which render us brutal, even if they are the surroundings where we enjoy, suffer, and dream; this elevation of poetry to the heavens—all is like a looking back, with no regret, but at the same time not without tears. Poetry was placed beside love almost as a sister, and with love was united and fused as one creature, which partakes of both. But if the whole of reality is consumed in the passion of love, poetry is, then, the sunset of love—the sunset of love in the euthanasia of memory. A veil of sadness seems to envelop beauty, but it is not a veil: it is the very face of beauty.

sidered to be a frigid little game or, at best, documents concerning the sixteenth-century polemic against pedantry.[8]

Suffering in laughter and smiles. "Questo che par sorriso ed è dolore" [This which resembles a smile and is pain] (Giusti) has become almost a trite expression.[9] It is also found in Shelley's ode *To a Skylark:*

> Our sincerest laughter
> With some pain is fraught. . . .

From "comical" characters, who are at the same time poetic, from the Don Quixotes, the Falstaffs, the pedant Wagner, emanates something far different from the simple hilarity aroused by light buffoonery, something stronger and louder than they can evoke.

Melancholy. "Let me remind you that (how or why we know not) this certain taint of sadness is inseparably connected with all the higher manifestations of true Beauty" (E. A. Poe, *The Poetic Principle*). In a rather toilsome and confused manner, but with a strong sense of truth, Baudelaire wrote: "J'ai trouvé la définition du Beau, de mon Beau. C'est quelque chose d'ardent et de triste, quelque chose d'un peu vague . . ."; and, according to his idea, a beautiful feminine face "fait rêver à la fois, mais d'une manière confuse, de volupté et de tristesse" and contains "une idée de mélancolie, de lassitude, même de satiété—soit une idée contraire, c'est-à-dire une ardeur, un désir de vivre, associés avec une amertume refluante, comme venant de privation ou de désespérance. Le mystère, le regret sont aussi des caractères du Beau" (*Journal intime*, pp. 84–85, in *Oeuvres posthumes*, Paris, 1908). And [August] Platen expressed himself in these terms: "Wer die Schönneit angeschaut mit Augen,/ Ist dem Tode schon anheimgegeben" ("He who contemplates beauty with his eyes is already committed to death"). Even our Carducci said in his last days, that his poetry had been "a dream of furor, love, and sadness." Moreover, a certain melancholy colors the sweetness which Virgil celebrated in his poetry: "Tale tuum carmen nobis, divine poeta,/ quale sapor fessis in gramine, quale per aestum/ dulcis aquae saliente sitim restinguere rivo" [Your poetry is to us, O divine poet, like sleeping on the grass when we are tired, or quenching a hot weather thirst with a fresh draught from a tumbling brook] (*Bucolics* 5. 45–47).

---

8. See text, chap. 1, n. 10.

9. Giuseppe Giusti (1809–1850), satirical poet and patriot, very popular for his sarcasm against the Habsburgs and his staunch devotion to the cause of the Risorgimento.

3. Prose Expression

It is commonly understood that poetry belongs to the sphere of imagination, dream, unreality; but this idea requires revision and correction, for poetry must be more exactly defined as something preceding the distinction between the real and the unreal and, therefore, not subsumed under either of the two opposite categories. Poetry is the sphere of pure quality without the predicate of existence, that is, without thought and criticism, which distinguish and thus transform the world of imagination into that of reality. Prose expression distinguishes itself from poetic expression just as fancy does from thought, and poetizing from philosophizing. Any other distinction, based on physical differences among articulated sounds, their order and position, the sequence of rhythms and meters, is fruitless, whether it concerns poetic expression or any of the other forms of expression that we are examining. All these forms, viewed from outside, have the same sounds and manifest the same sequence, with only slight and illusory differences. The problem concerning the difference between poetic expression and prose expression, on the contrary, was, we may say, exhaustively resolved from the time Aristotle indicated its pointlessness by observing that there is philosophy in rhymed words and poems in prose.[11] In modern attempts to review the problem, there was no hope of reaching a better conclusion.

In the light of the relation we have recognized between poetry and philosophy, we notice with astonishment the great distortions contained in some theories which, though they stop short of identifying poetry with philosophy, subordinate poetry to philosophy, with philosophy giving poetry a goal and a rational structure. Not only has philosophy no power whatever

Poetry as mystery. To poetry, as to beauty in general, was attributed the character of mystery. And in fact poetry offers the mystery of reality, or reality as mystery not yet penetrated by that light which is criticism or thought—the eternal conqueror of mystery.

Physiological and physical definitions of poetry. These definitions are proposed from time to time, but they are apt merely to arouse a smile such as at an extravagant jest. So, recently, it was maintained that poetry is a "laryngobuccal gesture" or a "muscular pleasure," during which "the mouth palpates, tastes, touches, and weighs the words" (see the names of the authors of such theories in J. Cassou, *Pour la poésie*, Paris, 1935, pp. 15–18).

Attempts to differentiate prose from poetry in verbal form. The old essay by Manso, "Ueber die Begriffe von Prosa und Rhetorik," in *Charaktere d. vornehmsten Dichter* (Leipzig, 1796, vol. 5, pp. 229–40), in order to show the gradual passage from prose to poetry, points out these five forms of the same thought: (1) I was under a tree; (2) I was lying under a tree; (3) I was lying under a beechtree; (4) I was lying under a shady beechtree; (5) "Patulae recubans sub tegmine fagi" [I am lying under the cover of a spreading beechtree]. But, first of all, the passage from prose to poetry is not gradual; second, each of these ever more particular determinations can be prosaic or poetic according to the context, that is, according to the spirit moving it from within.

The language of poetry and the language of prose. If it is impossible to distinguish from the outside the poetic form from the forms of prose, it is equally impossible to distinguish poetic words from prose words. By designating from the outside certain words as poetic words or prose words, one simply makes a historical observation (like those found in grammars and dictionaries) concerning the recurrence of certain words, for a longer or shorter time, in poetry rather than in prose, or the other way around.

The efforts described by literary histories to form a "poetic language" or, rather, to extend to poetry the language of prose (Ronsard and the Pléiade in the first instance, Malherbe in the second), are tendencies which concern themselves sometimes with the production of poetry, sometimes with the production of prose works, and which only in appearance take the form of "questions of language."

Poetry as the work of "reason". It does not serve any purpose to recall the rejections of poetry uttered by philosophers, for such rejections are already dead and

---

11. *Poetics* 1.

over poetry ("Sorbonae nullum ius in Parnasso" [the Sorbonne has no authority in Parnassus]), which had its birth prior to and unaided by philosophy, but when philosophy approaches, instead of giving birth or vigor to poetry it brings death, for poetry comes to an end precisely when it enters the world of logical reasoning and reality. Nonetheless, that distortion, like all errors (providing that they do not become arid formulae mechanically repeated, as academicians and professors repeat them), also contains lively elements of truth. One of them is the legitimate exigency to assert, against the wild outburst of passion and sentimental and sensual overflow, the ideal and theoretical character of poetry and its theoretical operativeness.

Good observation and poor definition lead, in this regard, to the assertion that criticism must work (and does work) within the creative process of poetry; for without criticism perfection and beauty would be unattainable. But one should not forget that "criticism," in this case, is simply a metaphor; and when the metaphor is confused with the concept from which it is derived (in this instance the true concept of criticism), it is perverted into a play on words which discolors poetry and, as we said, brings about its death; for the function of true criticism is to distinguish between the real and the unreal. The criticism taken in the metaphorical sense, on the contrary, is nothing but poetry itself, which cannot realize itself without self-government, without inner restraint, "sibi imperiosa" [master of itself] (to use a Horatian expression), without taking and rejecting, trying and retrying, operating "tacito quodam sensu" [in a certain tacit sense] until it finds full satisfaction in the image expressed by sounds. In this, poetry is similar to every human act, which contains within itself the sense of what is useful and what is harmful. We may perhaps call "theory and criticism of economics" the movement of a person sitting on a chair and turning and moving his body until he finds a comfortable position, thus coming to rest. We may call "obstetrical criticism" the efforts and pauses and resumed efforts of a woman in labor. We use this latter comparison because the "birth pangs of genius" are commonly likened to those of childbirth. Certainly, true poets do not give birth without pain; in fact, painlessness is not a good sign: the easy transformation of everything into verse and "piget corrigere et longi ferre laboris onus" [annoyance to correct and to bear the burden of long labor], as Ovid confessed of himself, does not bring honor.

forgotten; so is that by Plato and so are those suggested by the Cartesian school. An indirect and unconscious rejection was in the reduction of poetry to "reason" ("Le goût n'est rien qu'un bon sens délicat,/ Et le génie est la raison sublime," wrote Marie-Joseph Chénier in developing a thought from Boileau).[10] To attenuate the enormity of this apparent mistake, one must consider that "reason" was understood in a very vague manner and could also include the dignity of the beautiful; as a result, the mistake did not ordinarily appear in its crudity.

The so-called unconscious choice in the composition of poetry. This is formulated in many poetics, such as, for instance, that of R. Lehmann (*Deutsche Poetik*, Munich, 1908, p. 36): "To say it briefly, the mysterious phenomenon of an unconscious choice is the very essence of artistic activity."

The name of criticism mentioned in vain. Poetry and classical poetry, if one reflects, are synonyms, equivalent to poetry and beautiful poetry (for poetry would not be poetry if it were not beautiful). But also in the case of "classic" a similar error was made when criticism was introduced in the creative-poetic process, since criticism can emerge only when this process is completed. "Classique est l'écrivain qui porte un critique en soi-même et l'associe intimement à ses travaux" (P. Valéry, *Variété*, Paris, 1930, vol. 2, p. 155).

The immediate sense of the beautiful and the ugly, and critical judgment. The immediate discernment of the beautiful from the ugly in the production and appreciation of art was already felt and distinguished from criticism by the writers of treatises in antiquity, as "sensus tacitus . . . sine ulla arte aut ratione" [tacit sense . . . without art or logic], common to the learned and the illiterate, or to the "vulgus," who "si quid claudicat, sensit" [if something is faulty feel it] (Cicero, *De Oratore* 3. 51). The nonlogical character of such discernment was effectively emphasized by Quintilian in reference to Cicero's sentence: "Neminem vestrum ignorare arbitror, iudices, hunc per hosce dies sermonem vulgi fuisse" [I suppose that not one of you, O judges, is unaware that this has been the talk of the common people for the past several days], on which he makes these comments: "Cur hosce potius quam hos? Neque enim erat asperum. Rationem fortasse non reddam, sentiam tamen esse melius. Cur non satis sit sermonem vulgi fuisse (compositio enim patiebatur)? Ig-

10. M.-J. Chénier, "La raison," in *Poésies* (Brussels, 1842), p. 81, ll. 13–14.

This does not mean that true critical judgments cannot intervene in the course, or rather in the suspensions and intervals, of poetic labor. But if they are reflections and judgments, however useful in dispelling theoretical prejudices, they are poetically sterile; for the generative virtue lies solely in the inner self-control, which is not at all unconscious and instinctive, as someone has defined it, but rather active and conscious, though not self-conscious, and capable of logical distinctions, as is the judgment of criticism. For this reason, by rejecting the foreign and ineffective intervention of criticism in poetic creation and by warning that "a thousand Athenses and Romes" will never be able to put the words of poetry on the lips of men if nature refuses to do so, we reject, on the other hand, the contradictory concept of genius deprived of taste (unless we take this concept to mean an uneven and intermittent genius) and, on the contrary, insist on the unity and identity of genius and taste.

One more element contributed to giving a semblance of truth to the false relationship between poetry and philosophy, and that was the conception of philosophy as the contemplation of pure ideas, which in passing from abstractness to imagination took on the form of deities setting up a sort of mythology, more subtle and popular than the earlier mythology, but substantially no less fanciful. In its fancifulness that superhuman world of ideal essences took on the aspect, too, of a world of human creatures with human attitudes and gestures, like a new Olympus akin to that of the Homeric gods. That world seemed therefore to be a natural reality to poetry, and indeed, as its contemplators and visionaries conceived it, it was the worthiest and highest subject matter. But serious thought and philosophy, unlike abstract or mythological contemplation, is judgment, that is, thinking of ideas, categories, and concepts, but only insofar as they apply to facts. And to judge implies to qualify by distinguishing the real from the unreal, which is what poetry does not and cannot do, and does not care to do, happy at being what it is. If someone knows any other definition of thought and philosophy, we beg him to communicate it to us so that we may correct and amplify our horizon, which is enclosed within insurmountable limits.[12] If no further help is offered, we hold that no other form of thought is possible outside the one identified with judgment and no other determination of judgment outside the one it acquires in its real and historical existence. Even when one thinks pure ideas, that is, the pure categories of the real (real and unreal, being and non-being, true and

norabo, sed ut audio hoc, animus accipit plenum sine hac geminatione non esse. Ad sensum igitur referenda sunt" [Why does he use hosce rather than hos, for hos was not harsh? I do not know the reason; I feel, however, that hosce is a better choice. Why would it not be sufficient simply to say sermonem vulgi fuisse, which would have been admitted by the structure of the phrase? I do not know; but when I hear the words, I feel that the period would be unsatisfactory without a clause to correspond to that which precedes. It is to the judgment, therefore, that such matter must be referred] (Institutionis oratoriae 9. 4. 119).

Poetry as an expression of ideas. Contemporary with Goethe's poetry, magnificent in its spontaneity, freedom of movement, and variety of inspiration, there were in Germany different kinds of works which had their origins in the philosophical speculations of the time and which designated as content of poetry the idea, or the concept; these were to be expressed in beautiful forms, following the Greek, Italian, and Spanish, or other models. "Intellect" and "technique," as it was called, that is, the formal external elaboration, were believed to be the two elements of poetry, forgetting or ignoring poetry's own unique element—creative fancy—which draws everything from within itself and is itself both content and form. Goethe, who observed and characterized such works, named the period in which they were produced the "age of forced talents" and, on the basis of evidence, could not avoid placing Schiller at the head of that group. He recognized, however, euphemistically speaking, that Schiller was "a truly poetic temperament, but also a spirit leaning heavily toward reflection, and that many things, which in the poet must arise in an unconscious and spontaneous manner, were in him constrained by the violence of reflection." This friendly euphemism and sympathetic attitude permitted the long duration among the Germans of the astounding Goethe-Schiller poetic dyad. Nor did the basic intellectualism, not only of Schiller, but also of the Schlegels and other romantics, escape Goethe's acumen (see *Werke*, ed. Goedeke, vol. 27, pp. 251–52, the piece "Epoche der forcierten Talente"). Recently, even in Italy, poetically impotent talents have tried, from necessity, to bring into fashion the formula of poetry as "expression of

---

12. This is one more "crack" at Gentile.

false, good and evil, and so on), one thinks them only as the process by which they are individualized in facts, as the positing and solving of problems historically raised by them; in themselves, however, pure ideas are nothing but thought, the subject, never the object of knowledge.

Now, if thought has the function only of distinguishing the images of the real from the images of the unreal, and it does not itself create these images which as such are the matter that poetic fancy prepares for thought, prose expression, unlike poetic expression, will not consist in the expression of affections and feelings, but in the definitions of thought. It will not, then, express images, but symbols or signs of concepts.

This character is evident in the prose of the abstract sciences, very much so in mathematics, a little less so in physics and chemistry and in the classifications of natural sciences, and also in the treatment of a specialized aspect of philosophy, which is separated, for purely didactic purposes, from the facts on which it is founded. The same character is certainly no less obvious in historical prose which constitutes the fundamental case in point, since it is the primary act of judgment in its concreteness and wholeness, and in which more than anywhere else the signs seem to be concealed behind a thick cluster of images. So much so that the ancient rhetoricians insisted that history be differentiated from both oratory and other forms of prose because "proxima poetis et quodammodo carmen solutum" [it borders on poetry but is free to some ex-

ideas"—poetry drawing its high vigor from the intellect—against ingenuous poetry; they were evidently unaware that they were saying something quite old, already properly refuted and placed in the museum of criticism under the label "Forcierte Talenten."

Lyrical intuition. The reader who expected to find in these pages dealing with the specific character of poetry a definition of "lyrical intuition," or "pure intuition," which I previously used to designate it, must note that these definitions say exactly the same thing as those employed here. "Pure" intuition means "aconceptual" and "ahistorical"; and this can only be "lyrical," that is, affection transformed into active contemplation [*teoresi*]. I find it convenient to vary the definition of a concept, so that its intrinsic quality may be understood and, as far as possible, the superstition of the words avoided and the easy tendency to psittacism prevented.

Historical judgment the sole form of thought. An ample and detailed demonstration of this point is found in my *Logic* (1909; 7th ed., 1945); but the thesis was exposed again and defended in my brief essay "Intorno all'intúito e al giudizio" (*Ultimi saggi*, pp. 259–65). One should not allow oneself to be misled by the abstract consideration of judgments: even philosophical "definitions" draw their meaning and strength from historical reference; and the "observations," which give a foundation to natural and physico-mathematical sciences, in the last analysis consist in what else if not in the judgments on particular facts, that is, historical judgments?

Poetry, philosophy, and history. If Aristotle considered poetry "more philosophical and rigorous" than history (*Poetics* 9), the ultimate reason for his thinking must be sought in his concept of history. He still considered history as no more than a chronicle of facts dealing with the individual per se—"what Alcibiades did or suffered," to mention the example he offers—without referring the particular to the necessary and the universal (cf. chap. 23). His concept of history was still confused and far removed from what is meant by "history" in modern thought.

Definition and opposition of poetry and prose. "The demands of Truth are severe; she has no sympathy with the myrtles. All *that* which is so indispensable in Song, is precisely all *that* with which *she* has nothing whatever to do. It is but making her a flaunting paradox, to wreathe her in gems and flowers. In enforcing a truth, we need severity rather than efflorescence of language. We must be simple, precise, terse. We must be cool, calm, unimpassioned. In a word, we must be in that mood which, as nearly as possible, is the exact converse of the poetical . . ." (E. A. Poe,

tent from the restraints of meter] and composed "verbis ferme poetarum" [in almost poetic words].[13]

If one takes a page from a novel and compares it with a page of history, one may in both note similar words, similar syntactical structure and rhythm, and the evocation of similar images, so that there seems to be no difference whatever between the two. But while in the former the images stand on their own in the unity of intuition, which gave form to a particular tone of feeling, in the latter they are moved by an invisible thread guided by thought, from which they draw their coherence and unity, not from intuition and imagination. They look like images, but they are concepts in their finished form, signs of the active categories incarnate in the characters and actions of history, and diversified and opposed dialectically in their development. In the first, there is a central warmth which spreads to all the parts; in the second, there is a coolness, ready to extinguish or mitigate any flame of poetry which may light up, and to keep immune or protected the mental threads, which are stretched, tied, and untied to achieve the purpose.

This, too, is in its way a drama, the drama of thought—dialectic; and its coolness hides a secret warmth, coolness being only an appearance for the purpose of defense against extrinsic warmth. An esthetician of the old school, one of those who dallied in building scales and systems for the various arts, could not decide whether to exclude Dialectic entirely from the sphere of Beauty that he was describing; and, like our own Tari, he placed it at the "frontier . . . like a sun which, after setting, leaves on the horizon a consoling afterglow, however pallid and dull."[14] The truth is that the soul of prose is entirely different from the soul of poetry; and in its formation it takes an opposite attitude, the ideal that the prose writers cultivate being diverse from and opposite to that of the poet, for it does not move toward the sensuousness of the image, but toward the purity of the sign. So much so that more than once on that ideal was woven the utopia of the reduction of every prose expression to mathematical symbols; not only did Spinoza and other philosophers write in a geometrical style or try the symbols of calculus, but some historians (no less a man than Vincenzo Cuoco among them)[15] dreamed of the

The Poetic Principle). *Nevertheless, by marking such physiognomic contrast, one does not arrive at the dominant and essential trait, which consists in the difference between the "word" of poetry and the "sign" of prose.*

Poetry as a "symbol". Poetry is never a "symbol," that is, a sign for something else. The universal is not symbolized in poetry, but is poetry itself as the individual-universal. The word "symbol," however, is sometimes used in the figurative sense to adumbrate the nonrealistic character of poetry.

Historical prose and poetry. Larsson (La logique de la poésie, Fr. trans., Paris, 1919, pp. 96–97) says that "si l'on compare le portrait d'un personnage dans une oeuvre littéraire et le portrait du même personnage dans un travail historique, scientifique, on trouvera généralement que ce dernier est moins juste et moins exact que l'autre. Que si un historien ou un critique veut dessiner d'une façon adéquate une individualité, il est obligé lui aussi d'écouter de plus près et de noter avec plus d'attention les sons accessoires que rendent les mots." It is to be noted here that the difference is not one of greater or lesser justness and exactness, but of the purpose for which each portrait was intended. In the words of the poet, that portrait is a living and concrete and pictorial and musical feeling of the poet; in the prose of the historian and of the scientist, it is a thought which analyzes the particulars of a fact.

Prose and images. That prose gives to images the character of signs can also be surmised from Aristotle's advice to Theophrastus, approved by the author of On the Sublime; such advice suggested that, in order to mitigate the boldness of the metaphors, it was well to insert "so to speak," "if I may use the figure," and "if I may be so bold as to say," and so forth (On the Sublime, chap. 32). Boileau rightly commented on that in the following terms (Réflexions critiques sur Longin, Réfl. 11): "Le conseil est excellent, mais n'a d'usage que dans la prose; car ces excuses sont rarement souffertes dans la poésie, où elles auraient quelque chose de sec et de languissant, parce que la poésie porte son excuse avec soi."

Poetry and prose. Just as the words in poetry are word-images, and not signs for concepts, so are the lines and the colors of the figurative arts. Wilhelm Humboldt, speaking of the art of two peoples far away from one another in time and space—the Egyptians and the Mexicans—and of the many resemblances between the works of the one and those of the other, attribute these resemblances to the fact that "both had to overcome the terrible stumbling block of every art,

---

13. Quintilian, *Institutionis oratoriae libri duodecim* 10. 1. 31 (Croce's note).

14. Antonio Tari (1809–1884), philosopher and esthetician, whose major work, *Estetica ideale* (1863), was a metaphysics of the Beautiful. His complete system included *Estetica esistenziale* (published partially after his death) and *Estetica reale* (never printed). His whole undertaking appeared as an attempt to reconcile the Hegelian with the Herbartian esthetics and was not altogether original.

15. Vincenzo Cuoco (1770–1823), author of *Saggio storico sulla rivolu-*

substitution, in historical narration, of the names of characters by letters of the alphabet. We have called it utopia because in that usage names, number and algebraic letters are no more than symbols, and there is neither a possibility nor a useful purpose in transferring to any discipline the signs proper to another discipline.

Prose expression, insofar as it is a symbol or sign, is not truly language any more than is the natural manifestation of feeling, for true language is only the poetic expression. This fact unveils the profound meaning of an ancient saying that poetry is "the maternal language of mankind" and of another that "the poets came into the world earlier than the prose writers." Poetry is language in its original freshness, and, when an exploration in depth was undertaken into the nature of the language (even by a semimythological approach which proposed the problem as an inquiry into the historical origin of language, as though language were a fact with origins in a given historical time), all superficial theories which explained it as originating from the interjection (passion or feeling), from onomatopoeia (the copying or imitation of things), from social conventions (the establishment of signs), from the activity of reflection (logical analysis) had to be discarded in favor of the explanatory principle offered by poetry. Thus Vico pointed out that "within the origins of poetry . . . we have found the origins of languages."[16] Others, such as Herder, described the creative process of poetry in order to represent dramatically the first man uttering the first word, which was not a word to be found in a dictionary, but an expression complete in itself and the bud of the first poem. It was surmised that the first language, poetic in its origin, corrupted itself and decayed to practical language for utilitarian usage and that only from time to time, by the miracle of genius, would it be rediscovered by a few chosen ones who would be able to bring out the bright stream again to shine in the light of the sun. But the language never corrupted itself and never lost its poetic character (this would have been against its nature); and that imaginary utilitarian language is nothing but the complex of nonpoetic expressions, that is, the emotional and the prose expressions, and

which consists in the use of the image as a sign of writing" (see the lecture *Ueber die Aufgabe des Geschichtsschreibers, 1821, p. 372, of my translation to be found in the appendix of Conversazioni critiche, 2d ed., vol. 4, pp. 365–83).*

Esthetics and philosophy of the language. The identification of the two philosophies was brought about by myself in my Tesi fondamentali (1900), in which I showed that the problems and concepts of the two sciences, held previously to be diverse, are the same (see Aesthetic, pp. 140–52, 325–33). This identification was very influential on philology and linguistics, particularly in Germany and Italy, the more so since there supervened, to validate it, the crisis of method which was also called "la faillite de l'étymologie phonétique." On this see my note "La crisi della linguistica," in Problemi d'estetica, 4th ed., 1949, pp. 205–10.

---

zione napoletana del 1799 (1800), which supposedly marks a turning point in Italian historiography. Cuoco, moving away from the historical conception of the Enlightenment, follows in the footsteps of Vico's theories, seeking the ideal causes which shaped historical events. In support of his own point in the text, Croce quotes in a note, from Cuoco's preface to the second edition of *Saggio storico* (1806), the following passage: "I am firmly convinced that if most of the histories were written with the letters of the alphabet replacing the names of persons, the instruction which we could draw from these histories would be exactly the same."

16. *The New Science*, par. 472.

finally the oratorical expression of which we shall speak in the following section. Even in daily expressions and conversations we can see, if we pay due attention, how words are in their lively flow constantly renewed and invented imaginatively and how poetry flourishes—a poetry in various keys, severe and sublime, tender, gracious, and smiling.

The poetry that surfaces in common conversation. This intervention of fancy which in common conversation transfigures and idealizes feeling, at times softening the expression and at times turning feeling into the comic or the humorous, is seen in action when one glances at some collection of phrases such as the old booklet by Luigi Morandi, *In quanti modi si possa morire in Italia* [The number of ways one can die in Italy] (2d ed., Turin, Paravia, 1883), or better still, the rich monograph by Spitzer (who was in charge of the censorship of letters from Italian war prisoners), *Die umschreibungen des Begriffes "Hunger" im Italienischen* (Halle, 1921). The monograph contains hundreds and hundreds of imaginative ways of saying more or less covertly and with varying emphasis "I am hungry." For instance: "Here, one is a little chaste about eating"; "the air is very appetizing"; "from the first day I arrived in Austria I made a friend named Hunger, who has developed a great affection for me and whom I will never be able to forget"; "I have become very thin and I plan to be a champion featherweight aviator"; "the doctors say that in order to live long one must get up from the table a little hungry: I am running the risk of living as long as Methuselah"; "excellent health and appetite in abundance"; "the fourth musical note makes itself strongly heard";[11] "I am undergoing full treatment for the prevention of gastritis"; "here we are highly conscious hygienists," and so forth.

4. Oratorical Expression

Practical activity avails itself of articulated sounds in order to arouse certain states of mind, and this is what we call oratorical expression. To put it in the simplest terms, we may say that emotional expression is characterized by exclamations while oratorical expression is characterized by imperatives such as "Come on!" "Quick!" "Go away!" "Down!" and the like. But orators use these words as sounds and not as language or conceptual signs, for they never bend or force poetic words and images to serve the end of oratory, even if people say the contrary, and continue to say so, without really meaning it.

It is important to note this fact because in the old

The practical nature of oratorical expression. Such practical nature is also implied in the definition by the ancient rhetoricians, according to which oratorical art consists "in augendo minuendoque" [increasing and decreasing]: during the seventeenth century in Italy, the oratorical manner of speaking was called, without the slightest intention of reprobation or irony, "exaggeration" (with a double *g*, to be in agreement with the etymology). For such a character also, a particular form of syllogistic—the enthymematic—was assigned to oratorical art.

11. *Fa(me), which means hunger.*

28

esthetics[17] and philosophies of art there was the category of "nonfree arts," which were really serving other than artistic ends. Among these arts, alongside those curiously termed "nonfree arts of perception" (that is, objects and utensils such as a house, a garden, a cup, a necklace—all good for practical usage and esthetic enjoyment as well), were placed the "nonfree arts of the imagination," those of speech or oratory, which were thought to bend the sequence of poetic images to practical use. But there was in this an unconscious and involuntary violation of the laws of the Spirit allowing and justifying philosophically a sort of enslavement of imagination and thought—two faculties that can neither be enslaved nor enslave themselves, nor silenced in their interior voice; at the most they can be led to give utterance to a false and deceptive voice, which, as such, renders the true voice more resounding and the pain of remorse more piercing.

Oratorical expression, which is practical in its essence, differs from any other form of practicality only outwardly, not in any substantial characteristic. It is somewhat amusing to observe Quintilian's embarrassment when he tries to establish a true differentiation and discovers it in its aim at "persuading"; but, at the same time, he realizes that persuasion can be brought about equally well by means other than articulated sounds: "verum et pecunia persuadet et gratia et auctoritas dicentis et dignitas, postremo aspectus etiam ipse sine voce, quo vel recordatio meritorum cuiusque vel facies aliqua miserabilis vel formae pulchritudo sententiam dictat" [but the money, the gracefulness, the authority, and the dignity of the speaker have the power of persuasion; even if silent, his very personal appearance, which recalls either the services rendered or some misfortune or the beauty of a person, draws forth an opinion];[18] he cites as an example Hyperides baring the beautiful breast of Phryne, and Antonius tearing away the clothing of Aquilius to discover the scars of his glorious wounds. But the definition of oratory as aiming at "persuasion" through "words" falls short of satisfying Quintilian because "persuadent dicendo . . . vel ducunt in id quod volunt, alii quoque, ut meretrices, adulatores, corruptores" [not only the orator but others, such as harlots, flatterers, and seducers, persuade with their speeches, or lead one where they wish][19]—an association not acceptable to the serious and dignified orator. Nor, in truth, can one distinguish intrinsically between persuading by words and gestures and influencing the will of others by

Its nonlogical nature. Aristotle (*De interpretatione* 4) had already discarded oratorical expression along with the poetical from the domain of logic because they were not "enunciative," did not utter the true or the false; they expressed, for instance, an entreaty, which is a request, not an affirmation. Aristotle assigned them to Rhetoric and to Poetics, without further distinction between them.

Persuasion. "Persuasion" had so much importance and prominence in the Greco-Roman world that it was raised to the level of a goddess. On this deity there is a dissertation by Otto Jahn, *Peitho: die Göttin der Ueberredung* (Greifswald, 1846). Gorgias, in his *Eulogy for Helen,* called the word "a great dominator, which in a very small and invisible body, is able to accomplish divine things, succeeding in fact in calming fear, in eliminating pain, in arousing joy, and in inspiring pity"; and he compared it to fascination and magic, for persuasion united with magic "is able to give to

17. See E. von Hartmann, *Philosophie des Schönen* (Leipzig, 1888), pp. 594–623 (Croce's note).
18. *Institutionis oratoriae* 2. 15. 6 (Croce's note).
19. Ibid., sec. 2.

forceful means. The two goddesses, Peitho and Anan-kaia, Persuasion and Force, whom Themistocles said he would take with him in order to make the men of Andros pay the tribute, were in substance one and the same goddess; and whether by words or by force, she could do no more than try to promote in the men of Andros only a state of mind, not persuasion and will, that is, an act of freedom which men accomplish freely. The idea itself of restricting the field of oratory to preparing and bringing about volition is arbitrary and untenable; oratorical expression encompasses a much broader domain which is that of inducing states of mind of every sort, as will be further demonstrated.

The ancient rhetoricians, in fact, attributed to the orator the function not only of "persuading" but also of "teaching" and "giving pleasure." The "teaching," however, was not really a theoretical and true teaching, but simply a "persuading" through practical allurements and the appeal to certain beliefs; similarly, the "pleasure giving" ("delectare"), though mostly aimed at "persuasion," sometimes was understood to have its own independent end—pleasure itself. And this is the correct way of understanding it, that is, by viewing it as another particular practical sphere alongside the sphere which is entirely concerned with promoting volitions. This new practical sphere, when correctly defined, has no other function than to arouse emotions for the purpose of entertainment—any kind of emotions, and not only those of pleasure (pleasure and delight are implied in the very fact that the emotions are aimed at entertainment). This activity satisfies a need of the human mind, which, (unlike nature) being unable to remain at rest, abhors remaining in a vacuum. Thus, when man tires at one kind of work, he turns to a different and easier one; or, in order to exercise his mind, he fancies the various situations of life and lives the accompanying emotions, which are also imaginary since they, too, spring from fancy and not from true action and reality.

Because of the enjoyment of emotion as such, regardless of its particular content, the pleasure of en-

the soul the mold it wants" (in I Sofisti, trans. Cardini, Bari, 1923, pp. 57–59).

"Delectation" for persuasion and "delectation" for its own sake. The passage by Cicero (*De optimo genere oratorum* 1) says exactly, "optimus est enim orator qui dicendo animos audientium et docet et delectat et permovet. Docere debitum est; delectare, honorarium; permovere, necessarium" [the orator is really excellent when his words teach, delight, and persuade the minds of his listeners; to teach is a duty; to give delight is a mark of honor; to persuade is necessary].

But "delectation" as an end in itself is better expressed in the prologue of Apuleius's novel, *Metamorphoseon* 1: "Ego tibi sermone isto Milesio varias fabulas conseram, auresque tuas benivolas lepido susurro permulceam. . . . Lector, intende: laetaberis" [In this Milesian conversation I shall tie together varied stories and delight your obliging ears with a lovely murmur. . . . Reader, pay attention, you will rejoice].

The need for emotions for their own sake. Goethe, in *Wilhelm Meisters theatralische Sendung*, describes such a need in regard to the theater; "As soon as the soul and the body are restored to a condition of well-being through sleep and rest, both feel again the need to move, to act, to be stimulated and excited, and thus to feel again their own existence. . . ." This explains the attraction of people to the spectacles of executions, to which the "executions invented by the poet" are certainly to be preferred. "Even the desire for cruel destruction, which is frighteningly noted in children and which one tries to expel by punishment, has secret ways and hiding places through which it mixes with the sweetest pleasures. All these inner meanderings are in the theatrical spectacles and are, particularly in tragedy, run through by electrical sparks, and man is

tertainment distinguishes itself from the pleasure of imagination; it also distinguishes itself, in other respects, from playing, with which it has often been confused (and art and poetry were, as a result, blasphemously confused with playing). For playing is a broader concept, not tied to any special activity, but expressing a change from one activity to another for relief from weariness caused by the first. This change is noticed in the choice of pastimes that laboring men make, so that they may draw from it some usefulness, following in this to some extent the maxim fully practiced by the hardworking Muratori,[20] when in a sonnet he prescribed for himself: "Non la quiete, ma il mutar fatica/ alla fatica sia solo ristoro" [not rest but change of task is the only relief to the weariness of toil]. This need for entertainment is hedonistic, utilitarian, economic in character, which moral conscience does not object to, limiting itself to intervening from time to time with reproaches when entertainment, from an indispensable relaxation, changes to pure waste of time which may become habitual; and the reproaches apply also when the switch from one task to an easier one implies the dereliction of urgent duty.

The extension of the field of oratory to include, in addition to the aim of persuading, also the aim of entertaining places the manipulators of emotions for entertainment on a level with the orators of parliaments and tribunals; thus oratory encompasses everything from the most tragic emotions to the lightest and gayest, from the sacred to the profane, from the loftiest to the lowliest, from the healthy to the unwholesome and morbid or even licentious and libidinous. These emotion-rousers, who include dramatists, novelists, actors, mimes, movie stars, histrions, buffoons, tightrope walkers, acrobats, athletes, runners, form a somewhat mixed company which must be considered no worse than that of courtesans and panderers of whom the good Quintilian could not logically know how to rid himself. They were among themselves companions and rivals, for often the nonwriters among the emotion-stirrers were able to triumph over the writers, as happened to Terence three times, when the theater where his beautiful comedy, *Hecyra*, was being performed, was deserted by the crowd which preferred the tightrope walkers, the boxers, and the gladiators performing at the same time. This shows that the preference of the crowd in our own day for the powerful attraction of sports over art and literature (a pref-

taken by frenzy, and the more obscure the tragedy is the greater pleasure it gives" (bk. 2, chap. 5).

The pleasures of imagination. See one of my essays on the subject in *The Conduct of Life*, pp. 113–23.[12]

The concept of "playing." The definition of the concept of "playing" given here, in opposition to the definitions by psychologists and by Schiller, is already in an article of mine, written in 1903. See *Conversazioni critiche*, 4th ed., vol. 1, pp. 5–6.

Morality in the emotions of imagination. One could answer the too harsh moralists, who judge and condemn the pleasure experienced in the emotions of imagination (as though they were intentions, volitions, and actions), in the way that Saint Justina, in Calderón's

---

20. Ludovico Antonio Muratori (1672–1750), an eminently erudite historian, author of several works in Italian and in Latin. He follows the trends of the historiography of the Enlightenment, characterized by a particular interest in documentation and erudition as an objective illustration of events.

12. The Italian title is *Frammenti di etica*, now a part of *Etica e politica* (part of which was translated as *Politics and Morals*).

erence which is distressing to those, in all parts of the world, who are used to a different set of values) could add luster to the memory of similar triumphs in past centuries, if sports were able to review their historical glories. The two-sided and conflicting attitude observed in poets and men of letters toward the theater—the distrust and dislike on the one hand and the attraction on the other—is caused by the fear of being overpowered by an unpoetic, antiliterary, and histrionic force and by the simultaneous wish to triumph in the theatrical field, that is, to find there also a victory for poetry and literature.

The ancient rhetoricians rightly maintained that oratorical art should not be judged "ab eventu," that is, by its success in achieving in a particular case the desired aim (which was persuasion); it must be judged, they said, in the same manner that doctors are judged, by their demonstrated ability and not by the recovery or death of their patients. Works of entertainment, similarly, ought to be judged solely by the use the authors make of the means available for their purpose, not by the effect produced. And if the work is done properly, the author should not be blamed when the audience is left unmoved or bored, or when, instead of seeking sheer entertainment, it passes from the emotions of fancy to physical violence, such as, for instance, stoning the actor playing the villain, as happened more than once in popular theaters and as Don Quixote himself did, thus revealing in that act his own generous impetuosity. But oratorical art, in its whole sphere, is practical and not esthetical in nature, and consequently its value must be assessed according to the quality of the persons for whom it is intended. The orator for the so-called masses (formerly called the plebes) may reasonably employ language and gestures which "l'onestate ad ogni atto dismagano" [are always offensive to dignity];[21] whereas a dignified and decorous orator, acting in that manner before a public of the same kind, would be a bad orator, an advocate who does not serve his purpose. Similarly, since there is a public which is attracted by roughly sketched and colored images and follows them with emotion, weeping and laughing, the best entertainers for this public would be Anne Radcliffe, Eugène Sue, Paul de Kock, Emile Gaboriau, Georges Ohnet, Xavier de Montépin, and the writers of cheerful tales, thrillers, dramas for open theaters, and the like. They are so well suited for the purpose that, it is said, Pope Gregory XVI, who was a passionate reader of Paul de Kock's novels, asked a French visitor, as a first question: "What is Mr. Paul de Kock doing now?"

drama *El mágico prodigioso,* answered the devil who thought her to be in his power because of the love dream for Ciprian in which she had lulled herself:

> Pues no lograrás tu intento;
> que esta pena, esta pasión,
> que afligió mi pensamiento,
> llevó la imaginatión,
> pero no el consentimiento. (jornada tercera)

[Certainly you will not succeed in your aim;/ because this suffering, this passion,/ which afflicted my mind,/ won my imagination, but not my consent.]

---

21. Dante, *Purgatorio* 3. 11.

Artless books, in fact, have exercised an attraction, not only on a pope, who was after all a simpleminded friar; but also, perhaps by contrast on highly cultivated minds such as Madame de Sévigné, who, while judging La Calprenède's novels to be "détestables," was irresistibly drawn to them. With the passing of centuries and the changing of public tastes, it is hard to understand how those books could arouse interest and fanaticism, and the *Colloandro fedele, Le Juif errant*,[22] and the like, run into many editions and be translated in all languages. And yet, if we consider the taste of the lower classes and of young people, we will observe that even today those works still find readers who take pleasure in them.

The practical character of oratorical art remained solidly in the mind of ancient rhetoricians, and we prefer to appeal to their authority; for in no other time was that art so accurately and splendidly studied and exposed. This practical character explains why they shunned the "quaestiones infinitae," that is, purely theoretical and scientific, and restricted their treatises only to "hypotheses" or "quaestiones finitae," to the

Madame de Sévigné and the novels. See her letters of July 5 and 12, 1671: "Je songe quelquefois d'où vient la folie que j'ai pour ces sottises-là: j'ai peine à le comprendre. Vous vous souvenez peut-être assez de moi pour savoir à quel point je suis blessée des méchants styles; j'ai quelque lumière pour les bons, et personne n'est plus touchée que moi des charmes de l'éloquence. Le style de La Calprenède est maudit en mille endroits; de grandes périodes de roman, de méchants mots; je sens tout cela. . . . Je trouve que celui *(le style)* de La Calprenède est détestable, et cependant je ne laisse pas de m'y prendre comme à de la glu: la beauté des sentiments, la violence des passions, la grandeur des événements et le succès miraculeux de leurs redoutables épées, tout cela m'entraîne comme une petite fille; j'entre dans leurs desseins; et si je n'avais M. de La Rochefoucauld et M. d'Hacqueville pour me consoler, je me pendrais de trouver encore en moi cette faiblesse."

Contrivers of works for entertainment. A typical portrait of such contrivers is that of Eugène Scribe as given by G. Lanson (*Histoire de la littérature française*, 8th ed. Paris, 1905, p. 974): "Scribe est un artiste: en ce sens que ses combinaisons dramatiques n'ont d'autre fin qu'elles-mêmes. Le théâtre pour lui est un art qui se suffit; il n'y a pas besoin de pensée ni de poésie ni de style; il suffit que la pièce soit bien construite. Le métier, la technique sont tout à ses yeux, et il y est maître. Les faits et les caractères ne sont pour lui que des rouages dont il compose sa machine: il ne cherche ni à représenter la vie ni à étudier les passions, ni à proposer une morale. Vraies ou fausses, invraisemblables ou banales, il prend indifféremment toutes données, il n'a souci que de les ajuster, de les emboîter, de les lier, de façon que, à point nommé, se décroche la grande scène du III, et que le dénoûment s'amène sans frottement. Il a le génie des préparations . . . les indications de faits qui doivent servir à faire basculer soudainement l'intrigue."

Poetic expression and oratorical expression. The ancients toiled a great deal on the distinction between the two expressions ("poetae quaestionem attulerunt, quidnam esset illud, quo ipsi differrent ab oratoribus" [the poets gave rise to the question of what made them different from the orators]; and it would be useful to trace the history of their attempts in that direction. Cicero saw in the poets a greater freedom in the formation and collocation of words, and sometimes a predominance of sound over things: "Ego autem, etiamsi quorundam grandis et ornata vox est poetarum, tamen

22. The first novel is by Giovanni Ambrosio Marini (1594–1650), published in 1642 as *Colloandro sconosciuto*, and later, in 1652, as *Colloandro fedele*. The second is the famous novel by Eugène Sue, published in 1845, one of the first great novels to be serialized.

"contentiones causarum," which had furnished the reason for composing those treatises and which constituted their most conspicuous as well as their primary object. While acknowledging some affinities between the orator and the poet, they often expressed a mistrust of reading and imitating the poets, who were arousing an interest foreign to practical concerns, for they used, as Cicero said, "aliam quandam linguam" [a different language];[23] poets and orators, as is confirmed by Quintilian, will hurt one another if they do not keep in mind that "sua cuique proposita est lex, suus cuique decor" [each genre has its own prescribed law; each its appropriate dress].[24] Because of this practical character, the theory of the form of speech or of elocution had a secondary position in the ancient treatises and only slowly succeeded in detaching itself as a discipline in its own right; this was achieved in modern times. By contrast, the ancient books of rhetoric dealt amply and in detail with human "customs" and "feelings," which the orator was expected to know well; and to this end, theory was called upon to help experience.

Just as the oratory of entertainment had its enemies, so did that of persuasion; the former was brought into question, not only on some of its aspects, but on its very right of existence; memorable in this respect are the persecutions against the theater by the church, which went so far as to deny Christian burial to dramatists and actors. The oratory of persuasion was disapproved from ancient times as "fallendi ars" [art of deceiving], inspired not by "bona conscientia" but only by the pursuit of the "victoria litigantis" [victory of the quarrelsome]. A great thinker such as Immanuel Kant expressed his total disapproval of it, labeling it an art which exploits man's weaknesses; and even if its aims and its results are good, it is always improper. He points out that the flourishing of oratory corresponds to the decadence of the state and the patriotic virtues of Athens and Rome.[25] To that art Kant contrasts the quite different pronouncements of the man who has a clear and sure knowledge of things, a warm and generous heart, and who speaks effectively without art. To justify the oratory of entertainment we have already used the argument symbolized by the apologue of the overstretched bow. We can perhaps observe that the church itself, while condemning the theater, was compelled at the same time to establish theaters or to allow their establishment in order to stage moving mystery plays, religious and edifying dramas, "autos" and lives of saints, all inevitably con-

in iis cum licentiam statuo maiorem esse quam in nobis, faciendorum iungendorumque verborum, tum etiam nonnulli aurium voluptati vocibus magis quam rebus inserviunt" [As for me, even though some poets use grand and figurative language, I recognize that they have a greater freedom in the formation and arrangement of words than we orators have, and also that, with the approval of some critics, they pay more attention to sound than to sense] (Orator 20). On the difference between poetic images and rhetorical images, one must bear in mind chap. 15 of On the Sublime.

Was Virgil an orator or a poet? This was the title of a dialogue by Annius Publius Florus [Vergilius orator an poeta], of which only an introductory-descriptive fragment is extant (see the appendix of Epitome, ed. Rosbach, Leipzig, 1896); but it must not be understood, even remotely, in the sense in which the same words sound in modern criticism concerning poetic and literary works. Macrobius dealt with the same question in his Saturnalia, reaching the conclusion, after producing a large selection of examples, that Virgil is to be considered "non minus oratorem quam poetam, in quo et tanta orandi disciplina, et tam diligens observatio rhetoricae artis ostenderetur" [no less an orator than a poet for exhibiting so much discipline in speech and such diligent observance of rhetorical art] as to show excellence in all the four kinds of expression, whereas Cicero excelled only in the "copiosum" (see particularly bk. 5, chap. 1). The above question, in short, arose from looking to Virgil's work for whatever it could offer for the teaching of eloquence.

The distinction between oratory and poetry. The distinction between poetry and oratory has been at times obliterated, holding both, as well as every other art, to be the "expression of the sensitive man," the word "expression" covering diverse spiritual attitudes. Toward the end of the eighteenth century, Platner (see E. Bergmann, Ernst Platner und die Kunstphilosophie des XVII Jahrh., Leipzig, 1913, p. 193), in emphasizing that poetry and oratory are one and the same thing and both perfect emotional orations, added: "Pope's Essay on Man is an oration, no less so than Rousseau's Discours sur l'inégalité parmi les hommes." And, in a certain respect, the observation was right, but it showed simply that the work by Pope was not a good example of genuine poetry.

Poetry mistaken for oratory. This mistake, which at any rate has a long tradition among the authors of poetics and philosophers, is noted by Giuseppe Mazzini for whom art was the "expression, by symbols, of the thought of an age, which becomes legislation in

23. De Oratore 2. 14. See also 1. 16 (Croce's note).
24. Institutionis oratoriae 10. 2. 21–22 (Croce's note).
25. Critique of Judgment, sec. 53 (Croce's note).

taining profane elements, which could not be excised from the whole. No need to say that the theater is closely related to the liturgical drama and to the holy mass by the single actor whose deuteragonist is the chorister serving and giving the responses. But for the oratory of persuasion, the moral obligations, "omnes animi virtutes" [all the virtues of the soul], required of its practitioner by Cicero and Quintilian,[26] were not enough to justify it. The justification for this oratory as well as for the other was expected to be elicited from within itself, from its own purpose, which is none other than that of usefulness, prudence, diplomacy; in short, a spiritual and practical form which Kant, as though from unyielding reluctance, constantly avoided and disregarded, thus leaving a serious gap in the "inventory of the human spirit," which he had set out to outline. Like Kant, many other philosophers preferred to ignore or declined to explore in depth this form of oratory, either for lack of experience or for lack of appropriate incentive. Like politics, the whole oratory of persuasion, which lies within the sphere of politics, can be rejected in words, but in fact it imposes itself upon those who reject it. The Christian writers, who at first showed abhorrence for the schools of rhetoric, ended by attending those schools, and soon they had their Basils, Gregory Nazianzens, John Chrysostoms. Tolstoy says in his *Diary* that "for women, language is only a means for achieving an end, and they strip it of its fundamental function, which is the expression of truth." But men, in this case, are like women; they all, when it is convenient, use language as oratorical expression; that is, they do not really utter words which express truth, but they emit articulate sounds and thereby perform actions; and in so doing they avoid becoming guilty of falsehood or lies. Maurice Barrès, who perhaps had never before reflected on the intrinsic nature of expressions, one day happened to become suddenly conscious of that nature while seeking in vain the logical meaning of a famous slogan by Gambetta. "But is it necessary that combinations of words like these," he wrote, "should have a meaning? Is it not enough that they succeeded in producing the impression they produced?"[27] Certainly, famous articulate sounds were uttered in the heat of wars and battles, not to express a logical or poetical meaning, but to produce a determinate impression. History records the answer of the

politics, reason in philosophy, synthesis and faith in religion"; thus the poet was conceived as "the apostle, the priest of that thought, the man who, by translating it into particularly attractive forms, images, and harmonies, moves the mass of believers to translate it into action" (Bini's preface to Mazzini's *Scritti*). From this one may logically deduce not only the aphorism of Lenin (which aroused so much scandal in our western countries), according to which "la chose littéraire" must be at the service of the proletarian cause, but also the practice in every type of absolutist government of constraining and directing art, even though by this practice one cannot in the end give life either to beautiful art or to the oratory springing from the heart.

Oratory and truth. About the oratorical moment in every communication of truth, see my essay, "Telling the Truth" (*The Conduct of Life*, pp. 52–61), in which I demonstrate that truth cannot be directly poured into the souls of others and that one can only be stimulated, by the voice and other means, to think it.

---

26. *Institutionis oratoriae*, proemium (Croce's note).

27. The phrase by Gambetta was "La question sociale n'existe pas." Croce's quote reproduces the sense of Barrès' text, but not the exact words: " . . . faut-il qu'elle ait un sens? Certaines formules d'orateurs prétendent moins exprimer une vérité qu'obtenir un effet immédiat sur l'auditoire" (*Les Déracinés* [Paris: Club de l'honnête homme, 1965], vol. 3, p. 200).

Greek captain to someone informing him of the enemy's superior forces, namely, that it was not important to know the number of the enemy but to know where they could be found and attacked; or the shout of Frederick II of Prussia asking his fleeing soldiers whether they really thought that they could be on earth forever—a shout that stopped them and made it possible to reorganize and lead them against the enemy; or the word which General Cambronne, having been accepted into high society and having married an English lady, would never openly admit to having uttered at Waterloo.[28]

5. *The Circularity of the Spirit*

Oratorical expression has led us to the very middle of the practical sphere, that of the will and action, to which we have arrived through a logical process beginning with feeling and its natural expression, then passing to intuition or fancy, which transforms feeling into image and correlative expression and gives it poetic form; and from there to thought, which existentializes and judges the world of images; and from thought to action, which from the world thus apprehended goes further to create a new world of reality.[29]

Having arrived at the creative act, can we proceed further? Which other spiritual form will follow this act?

The truth of the matter is that the movement of spiritual activity, upon reaching its completion, begins afresh as though returning to its point of departure; it becomes feeling again, and with feeling a new cycle begins, following the previous rhythm but constantly growing and increasingly becoming richer and more perfect. The life of the spirit cannot be conceived of as a series of separate compartments, once designated as "the faculties of the soul";[30] nor as a linear development from a minimum to a maximum, for, despite the appearance of motion, this is a stasis, that is, the abstract position of a single and therefore static form. It is strange that, while the "circulatio sanguinis" in the physiological organism is accepted and celebrated as a memorable discovery, there is strong

28. The words attributed to Cambronne when summoned to surrender are "La garde meurt et ne se rend pas." But the true word he shouted at the enemy was "Merde!"

29. Croce's title of this section is "Il 'Ricorso'" (The recourse), in the Vichean sense. I felt that "The Circularity of the Spirit" was a better characterization of the content.

30. Because of his conception of the spirit as having four forms, Croce himself was accused by Gentile of compartmentalizing the spirit.

opposition to the idea of spiritual circularity, which is among the first to be conceived by the human mind and which a great Italian philosopher[31] adopted as a basic principle for the explanation of the spirit and history as "course" and "recourse."

Now, how does action again become feeling? What is this feeling which we have postulated at the outset of our investigation as the necessary presupposition and the material of poetry and, as such, formless matter,[32] and to which we have attributed, nevertheless, a form and concreteness of its own before and outside its relationship to poetry?

Feeling, in its extrapoetic autonomy, is nothing but practical life itself which, being action, is by the same token suffering (according to the denominations of the two Aristotelian categories) and altogether action, the feeling of action, and action, pleasure, and suffering. Practical activity is called "feeling" only when it becomes the material of contemplation, "teoresi"; when, being no longer action, it is felt and regarded merely as passion.

This appearance of duality, which arises from the relationship just mentioned, is the cause of the constant use of the word *feeling* in connection with poetry, even by those who radically deny "feeling" as a third form of the spirit, placed at the beginning or between theory and practice—a form which the eighteenth-century philosophers were led to invent because of their failure to analyze thoroughly the two fundamental forms in all their modes and processes. Had they investigated the problem more thoroughly, they would have realized that the hypothetical third form was not needed.

The identification of the concept of feeling with that of practical life joins together the two ends of the spiritual circle; herein lies its importance for the general conception of reality. But a more particular im-

31. Vico.
32. This seems to correspond to "immediate expression" as described above, sec. 1.

The nonexistence of feeling as a category. About my criticism of the category "feeling," see *The Philosophy of the Practical,* pt. 1, sec. 1, chap. 2, and for the history of this category see, in the same work, pt. 1, sec. 1, chap. 9; cf. also *Ultimi saggi,* 2d ed., pp. 110–11, 121. We might also ask the reader at this point to consider (even though the request or recommendation, while unnecessary for the reader endowed with philosophical spirit, would be useless for those not so disposed) that the distinctions established above, and the others that we are gradually establishing, are not related to descriptive psychology; they refer to spiritual categories, that is, to necessary principles for the thinking of reality, and implicit in reality itself; and being "factors" or makers, they are for this very reason not materially or singularly perceptible "facts."

Feeling as the indeterminate. The feeling which is postulated here as the antecedent of poetic expression, insofar as it is understood as being mere passion, mere intertwining and clashing without solution between the infinite desires and their contraries, is the dialectic moment of the indeterminate, the unreal outside the relation with the determining act (in turn, the act or process, without that relation, would be equally unreal). If feeling were determinate in expression, it would already be poetry; if it were determinate in logical apprehension, it would already be historical knowing; if in the practical form, it would be a determinate impulse and action. It seems at times that poetic expression itself creates a feeling not yet possessed or existing. Nevertheless, it brings about and creates perennially the first transformation of raw and indeterminate feeling into esthetic vision. Hence we reaffirm the consequence that this transformation which is poetry does not presuppose judgments and concepts, nor volitions, nor already formed images, either, but that, on the contrary, it presupposes the complete dissolution of all these elements in the formless and indeterminate, from which new poetry springs as a new determination.

The vastness of poetic inspiration. Flaubert asserted the insensibility-sensibility of the poet. While the poet does not allow himself to be constrained within a particular and limited feeling (which, being limited and

portance must be attached to it in regard to poetry, for only through the resolution of feeling into practical life it is possible for the guardians of the dignity and honor of poetry (who consider feeling to be the most elementary fact of the spirit and, therefore, the lowest poetic matter) to do away with the fruitless preoccupation and the more fruitless labor of seeking a richer and more serious content for it in morality, in politics, in history, in religion, and in philosophy. These zealots of the usefulness of poetry become annoying, if for nothing else, for the inconsistency between their apostolic presumption and the actual and total unintelligence of the things they talk about.

The content of feeling does not need artificial attachments to big things for the very reason that the whole of practical life flows into it, from the most elementary, which is the very joy of living with its conflicts and suffering, to the dreams and toils of love, the affections for family and country, the political struggles and wars, the enthusiasm for ideals, the impulses of heroism, the devotion to sacrifice. What, then, are those bores talking about when they beg for the introduction of morality in poetry? Does the moral law not lie in feeling as the center of the whole of practical life? And what are they babbling about when they say that thought is not a part of poetry (as it ought to be), if practical life springs from thought, and all that man thinks in philosophy and the sciences, all that has become faith in him, is encompassed by poetry? Does not poetry encompass all the creations of human fancy together with thought and all the poetry which has already risen from the soul, all the art which has been created and which flows into feeling thus giving birth to new poetry? In short, in feeling there is immanent the past and the present, the history of humanity and its aspiration for the future; and if this were the place to push our inquiry further, we could demonstrate that poetry encompasses also the "reality" ("Wirklichkeit") of which Goethe spoke, and the "nature" of which people have always been speaking, when urging the poets and artists to "return" to nature; the hesitations and the fears that the poet or the artist may arbitrarily alter and falsify reality and nature were thus dispelled, for the poet and the artist bear reality and nature within themselves, in their blood and soul. Together with re-

particular, would be practical in nature), he nevertheless vibrates in the most varied feelings. "Il n'y a pas d'insensibilité à cela, seulement je sympathise tout aussi bien, peut-être mieux, aux misères disparues des peuples morts, auxquelles personne ne pense maintenant, à tous les cris qu'ils ont poussés, et qu'on n'entend plus . . . Je suis le frère en Dieu de tout ce qui vit, de la girafe et du crocodile comme de l'homme, et le concitoyen de tout ce qui habite le grand hôtel garni de l'Univers" (Corresp., vol. 1, pp. 37–38: letter of August 2, 1846).

Poetry as "moment" and poetry as "state of mind". If feeling is poetic during every minute in the life of the spirit, why is poetry considered to be a rare and great achievement? The difficulty can be solved by pointing out that the perpetually recurring "moment" is something other than the poetic "state," which is what is commonly called poetry. There is, in this respect, a fitting comparison in a German writer of esthetics: ". . . that psychic activity, which predominates in esthetic impression, did not, in ordinary consciousness, occupy the summit; thus it rather resembles a bridge on which busy daily life runs speedily along without interruption, with no other thought than that of reaching the opposite side; whereas, in order to stop on that bridge and enjoy the sight it offers, one would need a Sunday, a holiday disposition" (K. Groos, *Einleitung in die Aesthetik,* Giessen, 1892, p. 7).

The past, the present, and the future in the poet. Let us leave to the inquiries and conjectures of students of prehistory and of the customs of savage or barbaric populations the problem of the union, in the same person, of the functions of the poet, the exhorter or orator, the preserver of the past and the seer of the future; we may say that the concept of the poet-prophet makes no sense, even if some rhetorician of philosophy is to this day still pleased with it.[13] We remember with a smile Victor Hugo's declamation:

Oui, c'est vrai, le poète est puissant. Qui l'ignore?
L'esprit, force et clarté, sort de sa voix sonore.
Trophonius est seul dans son caveau divin:
L'homme lui dit: —Poète! —et l'abîme: —Devin![14]

Morality in poetry. To the proposition that morality always is present in poetry because it exists in the universe, we must link other propositions (in order to actualize them) from the various "kalokagathia" which unify the beautiful and the good, or find at the basis of every kind of beauty a spirit of goodness, or assert

13. The reference is clearly to Gentile, whose esthetics has romantic tendencies.

14. Hugo, *Dieu,* "Les Voix," *Oeuvres poétiques complètes* (Paris: Pauvert, 1961, p. 1208, ll. 969–72.

ality and nature there is in them culture, doctrine, and knowledge, to the extent and in the quality that circumstances require. And it is a conceited act of arrogance to assume that the poet must be provided with doctrine and knowledge or that he must be exhorted to acquire them by himself, in order to remedy an ignorance that actually never exists in him. Certainly, the poet or the artist does not possess the praxis, the thought, the culture, and the other things in the same manner as the warrior who has to fight, the politician who has to act, the hero who sacrifices himself, the philosopher who reflects; that is to say, he does not actually do these things, for in this case he would be warrior, politician, hero, philosopher, and not poet or artist. He possesses them in his own feeling, in a dormant state; his genius awakes them, and that submerged world emerges again, similar yet different, fresh and primitive, no longer thought out and actualized, and not yet resubmitted to the toils of thought nor pushed to the struggles of the world of action; but only contemplated. It is a "juventus mundi," which is the eternal youth or adolescence of the poet, a youth or adolescence which is metaphorical, not to be confused with the grimaces and the stuttering by which bad poets falsify real youth and adolescence. The poet, like Ulysses, like Aeneas, is "multa passus" {has gone through many things}; and, nevertheless, what did Friederich Schiller admire in Goethe, so experienced in so many passions, so intellectual, and of such a refined culture, if not precisely his ingenuousness *(der naive Genius)*?

with Kant that beauty "is the symbol of morality." It can be added that in the lack of morality, that is, of humanity, lies the reason for which the so-called impressionistic poetry, now so fashionable because of the deep spiritual poverty of our times, is inferior to poetry, for it is an effort to reach the sublime with an empty soul and mind.

Poetry as idiocy. *We are learning (not from literary gazettes alone, but from academic writings as well) that, as a result of the doctrine we are advocating, that is, that of poetry as the first theoretical form of the spirit—and therefore nonconceptual and noncritical— the poet ought to be all sense, bereft of moral conscience, lacking ideas and culture, and, in short, deficient, ignorant, and idiotic. It is, indeed, a great satisfaction to be so well understood!*

The poet and the young boy. *This is an image that arose spontaneously to express the primitive nature of poetry; Vico used it extensively (see secs. 37 and 52 of his New Science: "Fancy is vivid to excess in young boys"; "the men in the infancy of the world were by nature sublime poets"). But this is an image, and one must not interpret it literally. For the "poeta ut puer" [poet as a young boy], and the "puer ut poeta," see my criticism of Pascoli's Il fanciullino in La letteratura della nuova Italia, 5th ed., vol. 4, pp. 121–214.[15] All this, however, does not prevent the above-mentioned gazettes and academic writers from mistaking the author of criticism for the criticized author or from blaming the former for having reduced the poet to a "stammering young boy."*

---

15. Pascoli's "Il fanciullino" (The little boy) is found in *Pensieri e discorsi* (1807) and was meant to be an exposition of his theory of art. He voices the idea that the poet is a child and should address himself to the taste and interests of children, or of the child which is in all of us. These ideas are close to Vico's conception of poetry. Vico pointed out that primitive epochs produce spontaneous poetry, but are superseded by thought and philosophy, which represent the expression of the maturity of man and civilization.

6. Literary Expression

In the foregoing examination of the forms of spiritual life and their corresponding expressions, we have not met with literary expression, which is obviously neither the poetic nor the prosaical, nor the oratorical, nor the emotional.

Certainly it was not possible to meet with literary expression because it belongs to a different spiritual level rather than to those fundamental forms. It is in fact possible to know and to act without necessarily passing through literature, or "beautiful literature," as it was called in other times. Ancient rhetoricians admitted this when, with Cicero, they recognized that history can be written "sine ullis ornamentis" [without any ornaments],[33] as the annalists wrote it, for it was enough for them that "intelligatur quid dicant" [what they relate can be understood],[34] providing, of course, it be done "sine mendacio" [without deceiving];[35] they admitted, therefore, that historians, as pure historians, are "non exornatores sed tantummodo narratores" [not embellishers of facts, but simply narrators],[36] or that philosophy and science do not require "ornatus"; as we recalled, they concurred with Quintilian that the effectiveness of persuasion can be achieved even without speech.

Literary expression arises from a particular act of spiritual economy, which manifests itself in a specific disposition and institution. It must be pointed out that the moments of the spirit, its forms, while indivisible in their factual concreteness, take on a particular singleness in the individual, not by an abstract division, but by a kind of increased energy or prevalence, and by habit and virtue alike. This results in the specification of the oneness of man into a man of action, a man of contemplation, a poet, a philosopher, a naturalist, a mathematician, a politician, an apostle, and so on (there is no need to enumerate or exemplify the most particular specifications). This division is necessary for any work to be accomplished and is, therefore, allowed and demanded by the oneness of man, by humanity; but care must be taken that the specification is not perverted into a separation and unrelatedness (for that would mean disintegration of the spirit and of its specifications) and that specialists do not become "dimidiati viri" [halved men], that is, no longer integral men. Spiritual economy is intended to

Allegory. We have not mentioned allegory among the forms of expression discussed because it is not a direct manner of spiritual manifestation, but a sort of cryptography. See my essay "Sulla natura dell'allegoria," in *Nuovi saggi d'estetica,* 3d ed., pp. 329–38, in which I defined this essential point neglected by critics who have constant recourse (especially in regard to certain poets, and specifically to Dante) to that word without having first defined it thoroughly (cf. my *Poetry of Dante,* introduction, pp. 18–25).

"Poetry," "Art," "Literature." The first two words have become synonymous in modern esthetics, but a certain tendency to differentiate them is found in some critics, such as De Sanctis, who distinguish the "poet" from the "artist" and say, for instance, that Dante was "more poet than artist" and that Petrarch was "more artist than poet." The distinction, in reality, cannot be justified conceptually, having a somewhat impressionistic character. Flaubert also used it in writing that "Musset est plus poète qu'artiste, et maintenant beaucoup plus homme que poète" (*Correspondance,* vol. 2, p. 81). It would be more appropriate to reserve the name of "poetry" for every esthetic creation (in sounds, tones, colors, and so forth) and that of "art" for every literature (there is literature also in music and painting, and so forth). But although such use might prove very convenient, and one is strongly tempted to have recourse to it (one may do so, without sinning, even in ordinary speech), in scientific terminology it would be counter to the synonymy which we have been establishing and which presents some advantages, for it corrects all of that sentimental and passionally excited content, which, contrary to etymology, was infused in the word "poetry" (particularly in the romantic age), thus bringing it back to its original meaning of "making" and "shaping."

33. *De Oratore* 2. 12 (Croce's note).
34. Ibid.
35. Ibid. The Latin phrase is not exactly as quoted by Croce.
36. Ibid.

maintain a balance between particularizations so that they may be united, not only in society, but also in the individual himself, where they may all be somehow present and active. This is what, in the first instance, we call civilization; in the second, education—education in its harmonious and universal character, which is culture. And since the breaking forth, in the quiet and normal flow of civil life, of the great changes and progress and great deeds and works does not occur without causing some major or minor imbalance in the social forces or without causing inevitable destruction, these changes and events are to some extent always revolutionary, violent, or even barbaric in nature. The absorption of the individual into an idea, a mission, a dream of art brings about a similar imbalance and something resembling almost an obsession, a mania; hence the saying that "nullum grande ingenium est sine mixtura dementiae" [there is no great talent without a measure of madness], from which, later, during the times of naive positivism, the theory was drawn that "genius is madness," without avoiding the inverse conclusion that madmen are genial.

Now, literary expression is one of the parts of civilization and education similar to courtesy and good manners. It consists in the achieved harmony between the nonpoetic expressions, namely, the emotional, the prosaical, the oratorical or the exciting, and the poetic, so that the former, while retaining their own individual identity, do not offend the poetic and artistic consciousness. Consequently, if poetry is the maternal language of mankind, literature is mankind's teacher of civilization, or one of its teachers in that field. Even in barbarous and rustic times, the song of the poet continued to be heard, and indeed there was someone who declared,[37] not without exaggeration, that the most propitious social condition for poetry is barbarity. But literature does not flourish in a barbarous society, for if it did, such a society would have attained the civilized stage.

The balance between the two kinds of expression is obtained, not by sacrificing one to the other, in the sort of subjugation that we reject also here, but by taking both into account and by the right proportion of each in the new form of expression, which is practical or conceptual or emotional at times, poetic at others—but of a poetic character that accepts extrapoetic elements as its presuppositions, respecting their own nature. Thus a "love passion" creates "the talent" to speak beautifully about love ("ingenium nobis ipsa puella facit" [the girl herself creates in us the talent]), and the poem is the path to the heart of the beloved

The character of literary prose. Wilhelm Humboldt (Ueber die Verschiedenheit des menschlichen Sprachbaues, 1836; Berlin, 1935, chap. 17, pp. 222–28) treats the question of literary expression, which he calls the "ennobled discourse" ("die veredelte Rede") in contrast with mere prose to which he assigns, instead, the aim of communication and ordinary discourse. Of this literary expression, which he considers as the traveling companion of poetry in the intellectual journey of nations, he grasps the physiognomy (though he does not trace either the genesis or the diverse forms), as we have tried to do here. "The discerning intellect," he writes, "does not operate alone; the other forces cooperate with it and fashion the mode of conceiving which, by a loftier expression, is called spiritual ("geistvoll"). In this unified form the spirit also confers upon the language, besides the elaboration of the object, the character of its own feeling ("Stimmung"). Language, elevated by the power of thought, avails itself of its prerogatives, but subordinates them to the governing purpose. The ethical disposition of feeling is communicated to language and the soul radiates from the style. Prose reveals, in a way very peculiar to itself, through the subordination and coordination of the sentences, the logical eurhythmy corresponding to the development of thought, which, in the general elevation, is imparted to prosaic speech by its special purpose. If the poet is carried away by this elevation, he turns poetry into something similar to rhetorical

37. Reference to Vico.

("ad dominam faciles aditus per carmina quaero" [through poetry I seek to gain an easy access to the woman]), and an indignation ("indignatio") which burns in the heart against the evil in man and society "facit versus." We may call it beautiful and robust "verse," but not poetic intuition and contemplation and rapture and ecstasy; for, in this case, the extrapoetic elements would be transformed into something else. These verses and similar ways of saying things well and beautifully are forms which distinguish themselves from content, being only the "dress" of content.

Such dress is the Ciceronian "in ipsa oratione quasi quemdam numerum versumque conficere" [the speech produces, as it were, the rhythm of verses], the "dicere explicate, abundanter, illuminate, idest ornate" [to speak explicitly, copiously, luminously, that is what I call ornate];[38] and "ornatus," or χόσμος, was the definition given for the literary form, the "elegant" form, elegant being as appropriate to literature as it was foreign to poetry. But, of all the elements composing literature, the "ornatus" was the only one characterizing it, and it alone could exceed and become the whole, thus altering the tacit balance attained; added therefore was the "aptum," or πρέπον, as a restraining principle, that is, the "aptum" in regard to content, which should always be kept in mind in studying what is appropriate to it. If this principle is not observed, the expression falls into various affectations, preciosity, pedantry, pompousness, excessive polish; whereas, on the other hand, if the ornate is neglected, the expression falls again into the primitive crudeness. Only by avoiding both obstacles can one attain the aim of giving currency to the nonpoetic or realistic expressions without offending esthetic sensibility, but rather pleasing it.

In my first research and polemics about the science of Esthetics, I refuted and rejected from the sphere of this science the concept of form as "dress," of beauty as "ornament" added to "bare" expression, demonstrating the contradiction and absurdity. And to prove this absurdity, I pointed out the use of the dualistic expedient called the "convenient," which was invoked as a remedy, though not arising from within the form itself. And certainly I was very right on this, since the concept of a practical combination for the satisfaction of two different exigencies has been unduly transferred

(literary) prose; since all the elements mentioned individually work together in spirited prose, the full vivid origin of thought is reflected in it, the struggle of the spirit with its object. Where the object permits, thought shapes itself as a free and direct inspiration and imitates, in the domain of truth, the independent beauty of poetry."

History and criticism of the theory of rhetoric or literary form. The criticism of the theory of the "ornate form" is found in my Aesthetic, pt. 1, chap. 9; the history of rhetorical art in antiquity and modern times, in pt. 2, chap. 19, sec. 1.

---

38. *De Oratore* 3. 14. Following is the exact quote: "Qui distincte, qui explicate, qui abundanter, qui illuminate, et rebus, et verbis dicunt, et in ipsa oratione quasi quendam numerum versumque conficiunt; id est, quod dico, ornate" [(the orator is) he who speaks distinctly, explicitly, copiously, luminously, (as to subject as well as words, and who produces in his speech, as it were, the rhythm of verses; that is what I call ornate].

to and placed in the poetic sphere by the authors of rhetorics and poetics and by the estheticians and critics, altering and corrupting the nature of this sphere. But in my youthful radicalism I failed to ask whether that which was intolerable in poetry could be acceptable in another sphere—a sphere which must exist, otherwise the error itself could not have arisen, for the error always arises from the transfer of an order of concepts to a domain alien to their nature. By correcting my youthful radicalism, as I have always done in every field of my study and in life itself, I have now found the sphere I was looking for, which is none other than that of "literary expression."

Just as the concept of form is modified in the domain of literature, so is the meaning of the word "beauty," which is no longer the goddess filling man with a sweet and at the same time painful feeling, according to the Euripedean definition of love,[39] but rather a refined and decorous person who mitigates and tames people's impetuousness, expressing it in a calm and harmonious voice. And the concept of art changes, for art is no longer identical with the poetic elaboration of expression, but distinguishes itself from the latter, becoming an elaboration of literary expression. As a result, even "art" and "poetry" are sometimes in opposition to each other. The concept of taste is modified, too, for it is no longer consciousness of poetry, which controls its own creation, but something belonging to the practical sphere and to which the attribute of "reason," or "reasonableness," necessary to practical life, is better fitted; it is called "taste," but could also be called "tact," having a closer connection with practical life. In fact, it is with this oscillation between the poetic faculty and the practical faculty that the concept of taste first appeared in the seventeenth century in Italian critics and theorists and in the Spaniard Baltasar Gracián. The idea of "genius" is modified as well, taking the meaning of "ingenium," or ingeniousness, which had the same etymology and which suggests more directly practical skill. The complete yielding to inspiration which is the surest sign of poetry, the yielding to the universal, is not required for literature; on the contrary, writers are urged always to have a clear and pre-established end, never losing sight of it or of the people to whom the work is ad-

39. *Hippolytus*, 1. 348 (Croce's note).

The inseparability of content and form in poetry, and the separability of the same in literature. The division that rhetoric (insofar as it is theory of literature) made between content and form, bare thought and ornate thought, was, as we have mentioned, inadvertently carried into the doctrine of poetry, so that poetry was for a long time conceived from a rhetorical, that is, literary, point of view. It seems that in antiquity someone criticized such a division in poetry, because in the fragments of the book on the poems of the Epicurean Philodemus of Gadara (first century B.C.), Neoptolemus of Paros is blamed for having separated the form of speech from the subject matter (τὴν σύνθεσιν τῆς λέξεως τῶν διανοημάτων): *Philodemos über die Gedichte*, ed. Jensen, p. 29; see A. Rostagni, *Sulle tracce di un'estetica dell'intuizione presso gli antichi*, 1920 (cf. *Conversazioni critiche*, 2d ed., vol. 3, pp. 32–33). But the weight these words may have had is not possible to determine with certainty because of our limited knowledge on the matter. Certainly, the synthetic unity of content and form is tightly connected with modern philosophy, especially after Kant.

The twofold consideration in literature. It follows from this that the twofold examination of content and form is as inadmissible in poetry as it is pertinent in the criticism of literature, in which one deals, in reality, with the examination of two forms: one immediate or volitional or of mere signs, the other of culture. And the true origin of the esthetic dualism between content and form, which costs so much effort to overcome through the unification of the two terms, is not in the theory of poetry, but in that of literature, to which it belongs.

Taste in an esthetical-practical sense. For the history and concept of taste, see my *Aesthetic*, pt. 2, chap. 3, and *Storia dell'età barocca*, pp. 265–71.

Goethe noticed that the French word "goût" had not the same meaning as the German "Geschmack," the latter referring to the beauty of poetry and art, the former to the social "convenances" to be observed and whose observance was extended to the sphere of poetry (see a note entitled "Geschmack" added to his translation of Diderot's *Neveu de Rameau*). But one must admit, without going to the extremes reached by the old French society on this matter, that in literature, unlike poetry, taste is not only the discerner of beauty, but of practical propriety as well, and that the latter is predominant in literature.

dressed, the particular audience. The "sacred furor," the "divine madness," the "inspiration" of genius are alien to literature and would not do it any good. But there is one inspiration which is not alien to literature; it derives from the serious preoccupation with the things to be said, the love of thought, of action, of one's own feeling. And this inspiration, too, requires warmth, spontaneity, and "fluent writing." Although it is the opposite of poetry, it cannot reconcile itself with practicality, either; it can never become a skill, for if it loses conviction and sincerity, it becomes empty and cold, contrived, shrieking, bombastic, and, in short, bad literature. Professional literary men are sometimes paid more or less well, but they are always despised. Their convictions on the things to say which capture the soul are expressed by their "style," style being more properly a literary concept, for only in literature are there as many styles as there are individuals and things (hence the controversies on whether the style is the "man" or the "thing"); in poetry, however infinitely varied, the style is unique—the eternal and unmistakable accent of poetry, which resounds in the most diverse times and places and in the most diverse subjects.

Kant had a gleam of the nature of literature, or eloquence ("Beredsamkeit"), as it is also called; he said that it is the "art of carrying on a serious business of the understanding as if it were a free play of the imagination." But his definition is insufficient and is further made worse by the ensuing definition of poetry, which is analogical and antithetical: "The art of conducting a free play of the imagination as if it were a serious

Against empty literature. Against empty literature are addressed all the reiterated assertions, in antiquity, in the sixteenth, seventeenth, nineteenth centuries, that what makes good writing is the soul, mental power, the knowledge of things, and that words follow the inner impulse and that, if they do not follow it (as Montaigne said), they will be dragged by force. But the danger lies exactly in this "being dragged by force"; these assertions are, therefore, to be interpreted as an emphasis on one of the two elements of literary form against the prevalence of the other, in this case the prevalence of χόσμος [order] over πρέπον [propriety]. Equally justified, in the opposite case, that is, when the writing appears rough and clumsy, are the opposite assertions concerning the necessity of form or of χόσμος.

Style. In antiquity style was more usually classified according to the diversity of things, that is, the subject matter. Hence, among other things, Hermogenes' ιδέαι [figures, qualities of style] which gave little prominence to the character of personalities (see E. Norden, *Die antike Kunstprose*, Leipzig, 1923, pp. 11–12, 323). In modern times the concept that styles are to be differentiated according to individual temperaments has prevailed (see, concerning the origins of this modern conception, my *Storia dell'età barocca* 3d ed., pp. 172–74). In literature both elements are present, harmonized in the literary form. In poetry the relation is different (no longer one of distinction between content and form), and the individual style is enhanced to a universal one, to be called, therefore, individual-universal, of man and eternal poetry together.

Elegance. I marked (*Conversazioni critiche*, 2d ed., vol. 3, pp. 174–75) the difference between "selectness," which belongs to poetry and which separates poetry from the practical sphere, and "elegance," which belongs to oratory as a means among others for dominating the reader or listener and for keeping him in awe. This is the contrary of what Boileau said (letter to Maucroix, April 29, 1695): "Plus les choses sont

business of the understanding."[40] Baumgarten had more explicitly designated the "repraesentationes oratoriae" as "imperfectae" in comparison to poetry, which is "repraesentatio perfecta";[41] but he did not develop the positive elements contained in the negative characteristic of imperfection; he did not show the limit that literary expressions find in the realistic content which, in limiting them, is itself limited by them. This reciprocal limitation and inseparability of the two moments makes it impossible ever to take the literary form separately and enjoy it as poetry, because this form reveals in every word, in every position, in every rhythm, in every inflection the presence of the realistic content, and its fittingness lies in its relation to such content. One may read Cicero's page (second oration against Verres) in which he magnificently explains the many thoughts, affections, memories, and hopes that citizens of Segesta had placed in the artistically perfect statue of the goddess Diana, which was in their city and which the victorious Carthaginians had once taken away to Carthage and later, to the great joy of the Segestaeans, had returned it following Scipio's victory; he tells how they now installed on a high pedestal the virgin goddess with arrows on her shoulders and the bow on her left side and a torch on her right; and calls to their minds the heartbreaking suffering and weeping which accompanied her departure when Verres took her away from them. There is here all the material for a historical ballad in the manner of Platen; but Cicero did not write the ballad, and that page preserves in each part the imprint of the prosecuting lawyer composing it. One may reread another famous page by Cicero in the *Pro Archia*, in which with moving words he celebrates the incomparable benefit of study, the company it represents for man, the strength it gives to the soul to overcome the adversity of fate—a page which seems to have a lyrical movement and yet is not lyric. These expressions, however lofty, resemble the small bird in Goethe's ode, which, having broken the thread, flies through the fields, but is no longer the bird of yesteryear, because it carried a piece of thread on its leg, the sign that it once belonged to someone. It is said about beautiful books of literature, history, philosophy, and autobiography that they read "like a novel," that they sound "like a poem," that they move "like a drama"; but these are emphatic expressions, muted by the qualifications "like" and "as."

sèches et malaisées à dire en vers, plus elles frappent quand elles sont dites noblement et avec cette élégance, qui fait proprement la poésie."

"Negligence" in prose. What is called "negligence" in prose works is also a part of literary skill. "Her negligences are tricks," as Tasso says of Sophronia. And Leopardi writes (Pensieri vol. 5, pp. 155–56): "An appearance of carelessness, neglect, unconcern, almost indifference is very beautiful in writings. It is one of the forms of simplicity. . . . But such a form never arises from real negligence; on the contrary, it arises from a great deal of skill and constant care and study. When negligence is real, the feeling experienced in reading the work is one of difficulty, fatigue, craft, affectation, hardship. For the ease that must be felt in writings is the most difficult quality to transmit to them; nor can the habit or the act of transmitting it be achieved without a great effort." This is, then, among other things, a way of mistrusting conventional formulas and complicated literary phrases, to which immediate expression has recourse in its awkward fury.

Poetry, literature, and form. The current sayings that poetry is not content but form, that it is not a thing but a way of saying a thing are true; but the first is too generic, for any spiritual act consists in the form appropriate to it, not in the content; and the second, though more specific, does not at all distinguish poetry from literature. Housman, who repeats this ("poetry is not the thing said but a way of saying it": The Name and Nature of Poetry, p. 35), cancels the distinction between the two and goes, certainly unintentionally, against his whole line of reasoning.

Excellent prose, but not poetry. I cited two examples in Cicero, but I could as well have taken two from famous pages of Tacitus, who, animated by a multitude of strong feelings and his own particular desire to do justice, represents with great vigor sublime, moving, or horrible spectacles, maintaining an elevated and austere rhythm, disdainful of easy and vulgar attitudes, but nevertheless always resolving into the tone of historical thought the poetic motifs which seem to surface. Thus, in presenting the figure of Arminius' wife, brought as a prisoner with other women before Germanicus (Annales 1. 57): "Inerant feminae nobiles: inter quas uxor Arminii, eademque filia Segestis, mariti magis quam parentis animo, neque victa in lacrimas, neque voce supplex, compressis entra sinum manibus, gravidum uterum intuens" [Among them

---

40. *Critique of Judgment*, sec. 51 (Croce's note).

41. *Meditationes philosophicae de nonnullis ad poema pertinentibus* [Philosophical meditations on the subject of poetry] (1735), secs. 97, 11 (Croce's note).

Literature, no less than oratory, has had and still has its detractors. They are found, first of all, among practical men who aim straight for their goal, with no concern for esthetic needs or for "little literary flowers," as the derisory word goes; then, among the sorrowful, the loving, the passionate, and the agitated, who do not know how to free themselves from the grip of their passion and who sometimes feel that they would profane their sincerity if they dwelt on searching for fine words to express it; and finally, among the thinkers and scientists—especially the shaggy and unsociable ones—enemies of the Graces. Still others among the detractors are the readers who prefer the extraliterary expressions to the literary, namely, the convulsive oratory, the disorderly utterances, the scientific sketches, the unadorned page, finding in these an easier contact with the experience of reality; the researchers of historical documents, for whom the superimposed literary elaboration is naturally only a

were noble women, including Arminius' wife, daughter of Segestes. She was by temperament closer to her husband than to her father. She made no appeals and shed no submissive tears; she stood still, her hands clasped inside her robe, staring down at her pregnant body]. Similar is another scene, that of Nero after the killing of his mother. Upset and fearful, the emperor pretends grief in the midst of courtiers who feign to thank the gods for his narrow escape in the attempt against his life that his mother is said to have plotted; but, at the same time, among so many imitative expressions of grief, the surrounding nature, which does not change its aspect and which stands as a severe witness, makes his stay there intolerable and drives him away: "Amici dehinc adire templa, et, coepto exemplo, proxima Campaniae municipia victimis et legationibus laetitiam testari: ipse, diversa simulatione, maestus, et quasi incolumitati suae infensus, ac morti parentis illacrimans. Quia tamen non, ut hominum vultus, ita locorum facies mutantur, obversabaturque maris illius et litorum gravis aspectus (et erant, qui crederent sonitum tubae collibus circum editis planctusque tumulo matris audiri), Neapolim concessit" [His friends then went to the temples, and the example was followed by the Campanian towns nearby, which expressed their joy by sacrifices and deputations. His insincerity took a different form. He adopted a gloomy appearance as though, sorry to be safe, he was mourning his mother's death. But the aspect of the countryside does not change like those men; and his gaze could not escape the dreadful view of that sea and shore. Besides, the coast echoed (some believed) with trumpet blasts from the neighboring hills and wails from his mother's grave. So he departed for Naples] (Annales 14. 10).

Philosophical prose never equatable to poetry. Only upon superficial consideration can the splendidly imaginative prose of a philosopher appear to be poetry—more rightly than a truly poetic work which is composed in a language similar in appearance to conversation. It seemed so to some critics mentioned by Cicero: "Video visum esse nonnullis Platonis et Democriti locutionem, etsi absit a versu, tamen quod clarissimis verborum luminibus utatur, potius poema putandum quam comicorum poetarum, apud quos, nisi quod versiculi sunt, nihil est aliud quotidiani dissimile sermonis" [Some, I know, have held that the language which, though not in verse, has a vigorous movement and uses striking stylistic ornaments has more right to be considered poetry than the language of comedy, which differs from ordinary conversation only because it is in a sort of verse form] (Orator 20). But the diction of philosophers, however sublime and imaginative,

hindrance to clear sight. This pleasure in the document sometimes is such as to be mistaken for esthetic pleasure, for it is difficult to distinguish the one from the other when they are mixed together. For instance, in the general admiration for Cellini's autobiography, one ends by admiring not only the geniality of his artistic spirit in the movement of his lively narration, but even the badly constructed sentences in which he often entangled himself and from which he could have extricated himself if he had possessed a better literary skill. Certainly Varchi behaved properly when he refused to touch Cellini's writing, not because the correction of Cellini's bad style would not have been desirable, but simply because the working together of two such different minds would have resulted in falling into the mediocre and the colorless.[42]

Whatever the case may be, literature can defend itself by the mere fact that it is cultivated in every part of the civilized world; in Europe, since the time the Sicilian Corax, Tisias, and Gorgias opened schools and began to formulate precepts and doctrines on it, the tradition has never been broken, not even during the Middle Ages; in fact, the Middle Ages showed, in their scattered cultural centers, more interest in literature and rhetoric than in poetry. But the great age of literature and literati was that of Renaissance and post-Renaissance humanism. Even in the last centuries, despite rationalism and enlightenment, which demanded things and not words, and romanticism, which demanded groans and shrieks and frenzy and not studied and well-composed expressions (which gave a bad reputation to "rhetorical art"), the virtue of

certainly is not poetry, as the apparently modest or humble discourse in a comedy or in a so-called domestic drama can sometimes be.

On the conception of the relation between content and form in eloquence. G. A. Borgese attempted (in "Pensieri sull'eloquenza" in the volume *Poetica dell'unitá*, Milan, 1934) to solve the problem of the relation between poetry and literature, calling the latter "eloquence" without distinguishing it sufficiently from oratory, which is only one of its particular forms; and he arrived at the erroneous conclusion that the practical aim is extrinsic in eloquence (as are the practical aims of the poets in regard to their poems) and that, therefore, one can disregard it and enjoy only poetry, or that such aim is transient in relation to poetry, which will continue to exist, being in due time cleansed of it. "The particular style of eloquence consists in a 'lyrical reason.' Insofar as the oration tends to an end, it is conceived and constructed as prose and science; insofar as one feels the immediacy, the definitiveness, the urgency (what we called transiency) of such an end, 'desinit in carmen' [it ends in song], it is fused into tragic beauty" (Borgese, *Poetica dell'unità*, p. 58). But the practical end is in eloquence or literature, like that of prose and that of emotional effusion, intrinsic to and constitutive of the literary form of which it governs every movement and every accent. One cannot be a poet without abandoning the tone of eloquence and injecting in its movement a very different tone, which is in disharmony with its nature and could even lead to laughter. And when one wishes to detach from an oration some page to enjoy as if it were poetry, the poetry must be added through a process of purification and fanciful accentuation, that is, created on one's own.

The end in literature. Dumas-fils, in protesting the doctrine of the autonomy of art, cried aloud: "*Toute littérature qui n'a pas en vue la perfectibilité, la moralisation, l'idéal, l'utile en un mot, est une littérature rachitique et malsaine, née morte.*" "Literature" perhaps yes; but never poetry, which is poetry precisely because it has nothing "en vue."

---

42. Benedetto Varchi (1503–1565), a Florentine historian and humanist, author of *Storia fiorentina* 1527–1538), published only in 1721. His other works include poems and theatrical works. He was Cellini's contemporary.

literary propriety is still alive and active, even if not widely; it contributes whatever it can to preserving the forms of civilization, despite the lack of delicacy and urbanity in the times closer to our own.

But poetry is not among the adversaries of literature, for the latter places itself at the side of poetry as a friend of a smaller stature, which does not rise to the level of poetry and does not even try, because in doing so it would become an equal and this would mark its end. What other proximity is better or more fitting to literature? Spontaneously, in books entitled "arts of writing" or "literary institutions," the theory of poetry and that of literature have always been treated together; under the name of "history of poetry and literature" or "history of poetry and eloquence," their stories have been narrated in an intermingled fashion. Aristotle noticed the lack of a name common to both;[43] but that name can never exist, because poetry and literature, though on the one hand touching each other, still remain two different things.

7. The Domains of Literature

The works of literature, according to the genesis which we have explained, are grouped into four categories, the first of which is the literary elaboration of feeling.[44] This elaboration is achieved through the mediation of reflection, which unties a certain feeling from the fancy that enveloped and idealized it and reestablishes it in its own reality—an individual reality which we want to keep in our memory exactly as it is and thus portray it "realistically." This process has taken us completely outside the immediacy of feeling, outside the excitement of joy or pain, outside the voluptuousness of weeping and the sweetness of moaning (so dear to sensitive and sentimental souls), and we are in the domain of the artistic elaboration of literary expression. If, in some parts of this expression, immediate and untamed elements still persist and resist or if the expression allows itself to be somehow contaminated in order to heighten its effect through the artificial and semiconscious histrionism which is often observed to varying degrees in public manifestations of feeling, all is immediately perceived by our taste as being inappropriate and ugly, like a spot or spots that must be removed from literary expression through fur-

43. *Poetics* 1. (Croce's note).
44. Keeping in mind the distinction between *works of literature* and *works of poetry*, it is clear that feeling can receive a poetic or a literary elaboration.

ther work. There are famous writers, such as Byron, Lamartine, Musset (to recall just a few), whose works belong for the most part to the effusive-literary kind in which women succeeded better than men; for women perhaps have no vigorous genius for other things; in fact, the only woman who in ancient times rose to the sphere of poetry was called "manly," "mascula Sappho."[45] Sainte-Beuve, writing about Marceline Desbordes-Valmore, said that women know how "envelopper de mélodies leur souffrance"; the same can be said of a woman with a perspicuous and strong mind, Madame de Staël, who in her novels remained within her own personal and passional experiences.

Such, in substance, is the whole nature and sweep of the rich literature of lyricism ("lyricism," not the true "lyric"), which manifests itself in effusive works, in confessions, verses, epistles, diaries and memoirs, or, somewhat disguised, in novels and plays and poems; and it is even infused into parts of histories and philosophies or embodied in pseudohistories and pseudophilosophies. This "lyrical" literature cannot be identified with autobiography, for in autobiography one subjects one's own feelings and actions, or tries to subject them, to moral and historical judgment, whereas in "lyrical" literature these feelings and actions are represented without being judged, are only clad in beautiful words. A conspicuous part of the so-called religious poetry belongs to this lyricism, when it does not remain within the sphere of immediate feeling; for, contrary to what some people like to assert, not only is it not poetry (obviously because it is religion), but also it does not lend itself easily to poetry; in order to become poetry, it must humanize itself, that is, spread and lose itself. Ascetic souls are not wrong in exorcizing poetry, painting, and any other kind of beauty as temptations of the devil. Religion, on the other hand, in its practical manifestations, lends a subject matter to the literature of effusion and to the various forms of oratorical expression (among which there are beautiful things, such as *De imitatione Christi*,[46] the writings by St. Catherine of Siena, and by St. Therese, the sermons by Bossuet), and also, being a doctrinal and theological system, to didacticism. Despite the pious unctions and the artificial exaltations, the poetry which reigns in our memory and which lives in our conscience did not start with the Bible (in which one cannot deny that there are shining passages), but with the Homeric poems, with that Homer who was as little religious as

45. Horace *Epistles* 1. 19. 28 (Croce's note).

46. A book of Christian devotion, written between 1390 and 1440, attributed to the German mystic writer Thomas à Kempis (Hemerken), 1380–1471.

Lyricism and lyric. The confusion between "lyricism" and "lyricity," that is, poetry, occurs frequently. And it was lyricism, mistaken for poetry, not lyricity, that by contrast brought about impersonal, objective poetry and the like: lyricism, "le moi haïssable," not only in morality but also in esthetics.

Lamartine. In the poetry of Lamartine, so loved at one time in Europe and now alien to our souls, there is a great deal of eloquent expression of feeling and thought with interrogative and exclamatory sentences. His lyrics are in fact woven with such sentences. The complacency of the author, his cult of his own feelings, take away the immediacy of his sentiment and prevent him from creating original forms, which he always replaces with facile oratorical or melodramatic ones. Acting on behalf of himself, he theatricalizes his feelings: "Who is he?" "Where does he go?" "Silence!" "But there it is!" and other similar devices. He is a sublime, doleful, melancholic, and noble type of poet. His rhythmic period is pleasing, but extrinsic: "arrangé" with gracefulness, but "arrangé" nonetheless. This can be observed even in some of his famous lyrics, such as "Le Lac":

> *Temps jaloux, se peut-il que ces moments d'ivresse*
> *Où l'amour à longs flots nous verse le bonheur,*
> *S'envolent loin de nous de la même vitesse*
>   *Que les jours de malheur?*
> *Eh quoi! n'en pourrons-nous fixer au moins la trace?*
> *Quoi! passés pour jamais? Quoi! tout entiers perdus?*
> *Ce temps qui les donna, ce temps qui les efface,*
>   *Ne nous les rendra plus?*
> *Éternité, néant, passé, sombres abîmes,*
> *Que faites-vous des jours que vous engloutissez?*
> *Parlez: nous rendrez-vous ces extases sublimes*
>   *Que vous nous ravissez? . . .*[16]

One may also see *Le Souvenir*, in which a similar feeling is superficialized. Poetic eloquence, as it appears in Vigny, is passionate and innocent, and speaks to itself; the other, eloquence proper, has its eye on the public and is therefore attuned to the public. The historians of French literature give Lamartine credit for having revived poetry (which, after Corneille and Racine, had been trifling with amatory, "badin," and sa-

16. The poem is found in *Les méditations poétiques* (1820).

William Shakespeare. However, the literature of effusion is divided into bad, mediocre, good, and excellent; but even in the excellent—the most restrained, decorous, fine, and gentle—man speaks of himself as an individual, tenaciously tied to the exigencies of his concrete individuality; therefore, even in the best effusive literature one does not feel the trepidation of the individual's sense of modesty vis-à-vis humanity, which elevates and transcends him. There is a lack of decency—the decency of which the Roman Sulpicia already felt no need, even defying it ("peccasse iuvat, vultus componere famae taedet" [it is good to have sinned; I am weary of putting on a face of respectability]),[47] and which in feminine literature is more gravely violated than in the masculine. We mean decency not only in this particular sense, but also in general, as restraint from exhibiting one's own sentimental affairs. This is not so much a vice of the literature of effusion; it is rather its very character; and this fact must be kept in mind, in order to avoid expecting from it what it cannot, does not, and must not give.

tirical tones) and for having elevated it again to a loftier level of inspiration—the soul, religion, freedom; and there is truth in this, at least as far as French poetry is concerned. However, he retains a great deal of the old unpoetic style of eighteenth-century poetry and the poetry of the Napoleonic age, a style at times ratiocinative, at times declamatory.

Art and religion. The effusive, oratorical, or didactic character of religious expression reveals the baselessness of the theories which identify religion with art or place both at the same level. Such identification or link appeared plausible to Hegel and to others from his school or similar schools because they all conceived of art as a sort of mythology and thus a sort of religion. But, among the thinkers of the same period, Schleiermacher did not fall into this error; he acutely discerned the intrinsic quality of both art and religion. The contrast which has many times been noticed between religion and beauty applies in general to oratory when the latter is directed to uncultivated minds. In religion these minds allow themselves to be impressed by monstrous idols or ugly images of saints rather than by artistic figures and images; in oratory they are impressed by gorgeous constructions in bad taste rather than by elegant and precise architectural lines and beautiful decorations. The priest, insofar as he is the caretaker of souls, not of imagination and emotions, is therefore the natural enemy of the beautiful works of art which are found in places of worship. Experience attests to that. I still keep a painful memory of forty years ago, when, having gone to Brindisi to see the famous twelfth-century pavement on which characters and scenes of Carolingian epics were portrayed, I found instead a memorial stone in honor of the archbishop who had taken care of the cleaning away of that old stuff and of the replacement of it with a new and shiny pavement.

Religion that dies in poetry. It is so in all true poets, and primarily in Dante, in whose poetry, even where the content is more particularly religious, there is, strictly speaking, no religion, but a human heart. In the very Inni Sacri by Manzoni (as De Sanctis has already noted), the poetic is precisely that which goes beyond dogma, devotion, and worship.

Poetry and religious asceticism. I find in the memoirs of De Tilly (Paris, 1828, vol. 1, p. 13) an amusing anecdote to show the terrestrial and the human in poetry, when he speaks of his grandmother and her strict religiosity: "Je me souviens qu'elle nommait Corneille et Racine des empoisonneurs d'âmes: le premier, disait-elle, est un déclamateur profane, et le second, un enchanteur suscité par le démon."

Recent effusive forms. The difficult resolution of lyri-

---

47. Sulpicia was a talented and beautiful young woman whose love for Cerinthus was sung by Tibullus in his *Elegies* 4. 2–6. She herself supposedly wrote six short compositions addressed to her lover, which have become a part of Tibullus' *Elegies* 4. 7–12. The quote is taken from poem 7, ll. 9–10.

Richer and more varied perhaps is oratorical literature which, even more than effusive literature, assumes a variety of forms, borrowing the whole terminology of the literary genres and their subdivisions. Only a small part of it is constituted by the so-called speeches delivered by lawyers, parliamentarians, preachers or even printed by newspaper columnists; the rest is to be found in poems celebrating the glories of nations, cities, and states, and exhorting youth to preserve and further the work of their ancestors; in political poems, in national and patriotic anthems ("Allons, enfants de la patrie . . ."), political party hymns (the "workers hymn"); in violent or playful, ironical and derisive satires; in invectives, such as the iambs by André Chénier and Auguste Barbier; in tragedies, such as Voltaire's *Mahomet*, Schiller's *William Tell*, Niccolini's *Arnaldo*;[48] in comedies, especially in the so-called character comedies (according to Baudelaire, *Tartuffe* is not a comedy but a "lampoon"),[49] and in other works which openly show their theses; in novels in the manner of George Sand, Victor Hugo, Guerrazzi,[50] and Zola's later works; in exhortative odes, such as the many by Horace; in fables and in epigrams; and here again in many history books, which are history only in appearance, being in fact more than history. The first composers of verses in our literature felt the great difference between high poetry and trifling oratorical expression or sheer emotional effusions, and they modestly called themselves "speakers in rhyme." Many works, large and small, of oratorical literature attain excellence; but it would be out of place to ask of any of them what Flaubert was asking of *Uncle Tom's Cabin* (war instrument against slavery in

cism into serene poetry, which only genius can accomplish, ought to be the guiding principle in interpreting and contemplating many works of contemporary literature, such as those by Proust, where one feels that what dominates the soul of the author is a sensual and somewhat perverse eroticism, an eroticism which is already diffused in the longing for reliving the sensations of a time past. But this state of mind does not express itself in a lyrical motif and poetic form, as it does, for example, in the better works of Maupassant, who is less complicated and more creative, while feeling a similar state of mind.

Ironic poetry. A great deal of it has been written in past years in all literatures; but, even if at times it is not lacking in a certain gracefulness, basically it is literature, not poetry. See, for example, the poetry of Jules Laforgue, called "désenchantée," a quality that cannot be that of poetry, which is always "enchantement." It seems that Laforgue himself was somewhat conscious of it: "Pour un coeur authentique,/ Me ferais-je des blessures!/ Et ma littérature/ Fermerait boutique" (*Les complaintes*, in *Poésies*, Paris, 1913, p. 195). Irony had already appeared to Vico to be a non-poetic form (see my essay on the theory of laughter and irony in G. B. Vico, in *Saggio sullo Hegel, seguito da altri scritti di storia della filosofia*, 4th ed., 1948, p. 283;[17] and cf. *Nuovi saggi d'estetica*, 3d ed., pp. 135–39).

Oratorical literature. Lucan belongs to those orators who write in verse, "ardens et concitatus, et sententiis clarissimus, et, ut dicam quod sentio, magis oratoribus quam poetis imitandus" [fiery and spirited, and sublime in sentiment, and, to say what I think, deserving to be numbered rather with orators than poets], according to Quintilian's judgment (*Institutionis oratoriae* 10. 1. 90), which, though contested, was uncontestable. Pichon says in his *Histoire de la littérature latine* (Paris, 1903, p. 570): "Nous pour qui la poésie consiste surtout dans l'intervention personnelle de l'écrivain, nous la retrouverons chez Lucain autant et plus peut-être que chez Virgile; rarement un auteur s'est exprimé plus fortement, plus violemment dans son oeuvre," and so on. The error here lies exactly in the "nous pour qui," in the mistaken conception of poetry, for the other qualities had already been recognized by Quintilian with the "ardens et concitatus." Lucan has the constant awareness of the orator who stands before a public to whom his speech is ad-

48. Giambattista Niccolini (1782–1861), poet and historian, author of tragedies. His *Arnaldo da Brescia* (1843), expressed his ideal of political freedom embodied by Arnaldo (d. 1155), a rebellious priest, strong opponent of the temporal power of the popes, and outspoken critic of the wealth and corruption of the clergy.

49. *Oeuvres posthumes* (Paris: Conard, 1952), vol. 2, p. 114: "Mon opinion sur *Tartuffe* est que ce n'est pas une comédie, mais un pamphlet."

50. Francesco Domenico Guerrazzi (1804–1873), patriot and novelist in the historical genre. His major historical novels are *La battaglia di Benevento* (1828) and *L'assedio di Firenze* (1836), both colored by political and moral considerations and not strictly historical. He was strongly influenced by Byron (whom he met at Pisa in 1821) both in mood and style, typical of the gloomy and desperate romanticism of the English poet.

17. Only the original essay was translated as *What Is Living and What Is Dead in the Philosophy of Hegel* (literal translation of the Italian title). The extensive appendix (pp. 144–206) and "Scritti vari di storia della filosofia" (pp. 207–432) added to the 2d edition (1913) were never translated into English.

America), namely, that the book should not have been composed from the "point de vue moral et religieux," but from the "point de vue humain" and that it should have gone beyond the "présent" and transcended the passions of the time;[51] for it is obvious that, if the novel had been thus conceived and developed, it would have been not a battle cry, but a work of serene poetry, which would not have served the purpose. At best, one could have expected that, in conceiving and developing it as a polemical novel, the author might have used more skill in composition, representation, and style; but it is not always possible to possess in this kind of literature the exquisite taste of Manzoni, who wrote *The Betrothed*, a tale of moral exhortation which, though conducted from the beginning to the end with the eyes fixed to this purpose, seems nevertheless so spontaneous and natural that the critics still insist in analyzing and discussing it as a novel poetic in inspiration and expression; they do not realize that they are falling into inextricable contradictions, thus obscuring a work which in itself is so clear.

dressed. *Sometimes he is very effective, as in the magnificent commemoration of Pompey, or in the epicedium of liberty; however, one can be very effective in speech, without speaking poetically. At other times he is declamatory, rhetorical, monotonous; but this is attributable to his shortcomings, not to his character.*

Political poetry. A well-known Austrian political and politically liberal poet, Anastasius Grün (A. Auersperg) extolled in verse the power of political poetry thus:

> Politisch Lied, du Donner, der Felsenherzen spaltet,
> Du heil'ge Oriflamme, zum Siegeszug entfaltet,
> Du Feuersäule, dem Volke aus Knechtschaftswüsten hellend,
> Du Jerichoposaun, der Zwingsherrn Bollwerk allzerschellend.
> Sieghafter Sparterfeldherr, der Freiheit Türmer du,
> Du Todeslawine Murtens, Bastillenstürmer du. . . .

[*Political song, you thunder splitting the hearts of rocks, you holy Oriflame, unfolded for triumphal progress, you fiery column enlightening the people out of the desert of slavery, you trumpet of Jericho smashing into pieces the bulwork of despots, you victorious Spartan general, liberty's watchtower, you deadly avalanche of Murten, assailant of fortresses, you. . . .] These lines, rather than refuting Goethe's words, seem to confirm them. Political poetry is usually ugly, for the very reason that it is written for soldiers and for crowds and does not concern itself with literary refinements.*

Treitschke, speaking of the year 1813 and of the large number of political poems composed during that time, and of Goethe who kept away from it, wrote: "What politically mature peoples express in the press, in speeches, and in dissertations for publicity purposes, in this generation for which poetry was always the crown of life, took poetic form immediately, and the most beautiful political poetry that a nation can ever boast was born; it was a sequel of poems of a heroic age, and we would be at fault if we looked at them only with esthetic eyes" (Deutsche Geschichte, vol. 1, p. 433). But there is a certain contradiction in defining that poetry as "the most beautiful political poetry that a nation can ever boast" while at the same time preventing us from looking at it only with "esthetic eyes."

In any event, a great distance runs between one kind of political poetry and another, as, for instance, between the Marseillaise and Ca ira.[18] The Iambs of André Chénier are still sharp and cutting, and it is a

---

51. *Correspondance* (Paris: Conard, 1927), vol. 3, p. 60: letter to Louise Colet, December 9, 1852.

18. *A series of twelve sonnets by Carducci (Rime nuove 7), devoted to moments or events of the French Revolution.*

pleasure to repeat them on the unfortunate occasion of similar political situations:

On vit: on vit infâme. Eh bien! Il fallut l'être.
L'infâme, après tout, mange et dort.
Ici, même, en ces parcs où la mort nous fait paître,
Où la hache nous tire au sort,
Beaux poulets sont écrits; maris, amants sont dupes;
Caquetage, intrigues de sots.
On y chante; on y joue; on y lève des jupes;
On y fait chansons et bons mots. . . .
Le pourvoyeur paraît. Quelle sera la proie
Que la hache appelle aujourd'hui?
Chacun frisonne, écoute; et chacun avec joie
Voit que ce n'est pas encor lui.
Ce sera toi demain, insensible imbécile!

And read again also *L'Idole* by Barbier, against the legend and the worship of Napoleon instituted after 1830:

Napoléon n'est plus ce voleur de couronne,
    Cet usurpateur effronté,
Qui serra sans pitié, sous les coussins du trône,
    la gorge de la Liberté;
Ce triste et vieux forçat de la Sainte Alliance
    Qui mourut sur un noir rocher,
Traînant comme un boulet l'image de la France,
    Sous le bâton de l'étranger;
Non, non, Napoléon n'est plus souillé de fanges;
    Grâce aux flatteurs mélodieux,
Aux poètes menteurs, aux sonneurs de louanges,
    César est mis au rang des dieux. . . .

Certainly, the flow of this composition is that of a harangue, divided into several points, so that the thesis may be made more persuasive through demonstration; passion, of course, is not transfigured, but tightened and directed to an end; the images are strong and violent, but none of them is dreamed of and cherished for its own sake; the verse has no inner musicality. However, this does not prevent it from being good literature, and the nonpoetic verse from being, in its own way, necessary.

Against the summary condemnation of the political poetry of our Risorgimento as nonpoetry, I demonstrated elsewhere the extent to which in authors such as Berchet, Poerio, and Aleardi (but not in Prati) poetry was a dream of heroism, trepidation for cherished things, virile sentiment for life and thus pure and simple poetry.[19] Also, the oratorical iambs and epodes

---

19. *Giovanni Berchet (1783–1851), Alessandro Poerio (1802–1848), Aleardo Aleardi (1812–1878), Giovanni Prati (1814–1884) were poets and patriots. Most of their works are related to their political activities and aspirations, with the exception of Prati, whose best-known pieces are of a different nature. All of them belong to the romantic movement, with the last two marking the beginning of the decadence of romanticism.*

of young Carducci possess here and there certain traits that foreshadow his Rime nuove *[1861–1887].*

Mahomet by Voltaire. Voltaire's tragedy was conceived as a battle against the imposture which founds religions and avails itself of fanaticism, as a sort of higher Tartuffe, *and was entitled* Le fanatisme ou Mahomet le prophète. *But the play was not as successful as that of Molière, which Voltaire took as his model, for the idea is disturbed by the usual conventional lovers' parts; as a result, the young man who should be carried away by fanaticism is, at the same time, a lover on whose passion blackmail has a great sway and who, like all other "jeunes premiers" of that theater, is full of generous and human sentiment. The same can be said of the remaining characters who, for theatrical rather than poetic reasons, are all inconsistent with the idea they represent, including Mohammed. Pope Benedict XIV, to whom Voltaire dedicated the tragedy and who answered the author with a letter which is a masterpiece of hypocritical condescension, must have thought that Mohammed, who was a criminal in private life, did not damage much the idea of religion, nor that of religious fanaticism, and that he could do no more than contribute to reinforcing the popular conception of the Moslem faith. That Goethe wasted his time translating that unpleasant tragedy was explained (and it could not have been explained otherwise) by his needs as an impresario under pressure to furnish "interesting" plays for the Weimar theater and by his complacency as a courtier who followed in that choice the indication of his master.*[20]

The character of The Betrothed. *See my essays on the subject in* European Literature of the Nineteenth Century, *pp. 145–56, and in* Conversazioni critiche *(2d ed., vol. 3, pp. 247–50; they are now collected in the volume* Alessandro Manzoni, saggi e discussioni, *4th ed., 1952).*

Really, I have nothing to add to what I wrote in those essays, being unconvinced that the objections raised against them had any foundation. Since De Sanctis' interpretation of Manzoni was contrasted to mine, I only transcribe here a passage of his concerning the tone of The Betrothed: *"There are in the theater of the world two temperature levels: one is that of the spectators, the other that of the actors. The latter are in a well-determined situation in relation to the cold and indifferent public; thus if they warm up too much and raise their tone too high and place themselves in a highly heated atmosphere, a dissonance between them and the public is quickly perceived. The public may, at the most, admire certain art effects; but it will*

---

20. *Duke Karl August.*

The third category is that of the works for entertainment, which range from emotions of horror to emotions of hilarity. At one extreme there are the so-called horror tragedies developed by the Italians in the sixteenth century (taking the lead from Seneca) and subsequently imitated extensively by all of the other European nations; these tragedies resembled the horrifying performances of the Grand Guignol and certain hair-raising novels which provided the kind of emotions sought by those who enjoyed the sight of public capital executions. At the other extreme there are works producing merriment and laughter—laughter which at times rises to its highest summit, at times spreads through the plains and the low lands. Between the two extremes there stand the representations of prowess and the representations of love (the "matière de France" and the "matière de Bretagne," as they are designated), which constitute a large literary body. Prowess and love are embodied by poems and short stories and dramas and melodramas and epinician odes and sirventes and sonnets and madrigals and canzones and eclogues and idylls and odes and anacreontic short odes and other small forms, which fill books of verses and of prose and provide work every day for printing shops. Their reading and theatrical recitations occupy people's leisure time, as they occupied that of the Romans and the Greeks, of the feudal and chivalric societies, of the common people in the communal repub-

never take part in the play wholly and completely. It may shout a 'bravo!' but there is in its customary atmosphere something that refuses to yield, and if you insist and apply pressure, you are faced with protests and rebellion. This happens if you keep too close to ideas and create an artificial world, and refuse to take into account the moderate temperature level in which men live. Common sense, in this case, resorts to vengeance by answering through irony. Now the singularity of our poet is that, while he lives in the midst of the dearest and noblest ideals of life, and displays them to you and tries to draw you to them, he identifies himself with the public and reflects its impressions and its good sense; and by using a little irony, he prevents your irony and brings you always back from very extraordinary situations to the average level of things." This explains, adds De Sanctis, the great popularity of this book {The Betrothed}. And I dare ask whether this is not exactly an excellent analysis of an oratorical way of persuading. Poetry—as I have written in other instances—is a conversation with God; but oratory is a conversation with men.

Italian criticism about The Betrothed, so abundant and detailed during the past years, has been lacking in broad historical outlook; and if I have already reminded the authors of this criticism of the threads by which their work is linked to Voltaire's novels, I think also that it is time to insist on the ties it has with the English novels of the eighteenth century (for instance, with Fielding's Tom Jones). From that mode of narration accompanied by psychological and moral commentaries emerged the very form of the novels by Walter Scott, who added to the moral interest (inspired in him by the Goethe of Goetz von Berlichingen) that of the evocation of history and old customs. Manzoni, on the contrary, remained completely alien to the new type of novel, having no extrinsic aim, all passional and poetic—the novel that was anticipated by Werther and, to some extent, by Manon Lescaut, and widely cultivated in the nineteenth century, when it produced its masterpieces.

Tales of battles and prowess. From the great epic poets one draws much more than the delight deriving from the description of battles and great master strokes, which are typical of the epic for entertainment. In the heart of Homer's heroes there is the nostalgia for home, for spouse, for family, as Helen knew too well when, roaming around the great horse brought into Troy, she kept calling for her compatriots.

lics, of the gentlemen of the courts, and of the active bourgeois; they were the pastime of the ladies and young ladies and ordinary women of all times, who took pleasure in what, thanks to them, was called "amusing literature."

Here again, alongside and against clumsy works (though very effective in their aim to entertain readers of a certain level) stand refined works (for instance, opposite Georges Ohnet's love novels stand those by Jules Sandeau and Octave Feuillet) as well as pleasing and moving works which reach a high degree of gracefulness and perfection of style, as in some of the mystery stories by Edgar Allen Poe. However, even the works which are perfect for their purpose show the sign diversifying them from poetry; for unlike poetry, which is individuality and universality in one, they tend toward the "typical" of the various modes of emotion. Thus the tragedies (contrary to those by Sophocles or Shakespeare) are patterned according to a "tragic type," novels according to the "novelistic type," comedies according to the "comic type" or even to the "masks" of the "commedia dell'arte." And in this sphere, not in that of poetry, one can justify certain controversies, such as whether it is necessary in dramas and novels that virtue prevail over vice and be rewarded by good fortune or divine justice; or whether dramas and novels end well only when concluding happily. There is a conflict between the lovers of emotion as such (as mere emotion of whatever character and degree) and others who inject into that entertainment the varied hedonistic or eudaemonic needs for the pleasure of imagination and, therefore, expect the moral and the happy ending; and also, in order to avoid returning home with the unhappy ending of the tragedy on their mind and consequently failing to sleep during the night, they have imposed the theatrical practice of an all-weeping tragedy, followed by an all-laughing farce.

Elegant literature for entertainment. One would read with pleasure this page by Jules Lemaître (*Les contemporains,* vol. 3, pp. 5–6) in reference to the novels of Octave Feuillet: "*Rien ne me semblait plus beau, plus passionné et plus élégant que ces histoires d'amour. Ces sveltes amazones rencontrées dans les bois, si capricieuses et si énigmatiques; ces jeunes hommes si beaux, si tristes et si prompts aux actes héroïques; ces vieilles châtelaines et ces vieux gentilshommes si dignes, si polis et si fiers; tout ce monde supérieurement distingué de ducs, de comtes et de marquis, cette vie de château et cette vie parisienne, ces conversations soignées où tout le monde a de l'esprit; et, sous la politesse raffinée des manières, sous l'appareil convenu des habitudes mondaines, ces drames de passion folle, ces amours qui brûlent et qui tuent, ces morts romantiques de jeunes femmes inconsolées . . . amour, héroïsme, Amadis, Corysandre, et quelquefois Didon en plein faubourg Saint-Germain, tout cela me remplissait de l'admiration la plus naïve et la plus fervente, et m'induisait en vagues rêveries et me donnait un grand désir de pleurer.*"

Literature for entertainment drawn from history. The works which avail themselves of historical narrations for the purpose of arousing emotions (and enhance them by historical references) contribute a great deal to the literature for entertainment. The method is the inverse of that used by poets (who, as Goethe said, do not know historical characters, but sometimes honor them by taking their names in order to express their own feelings), and it is a literary, not a poetic, method. Schiller, without realizing it, confessed that his talent was that of a man of letters and not a poet when he wrote to Goethe: "I would like to be told to choose nothing but historical subjects; those of free invention would be stumbling blocks for me. Idealizing the realistic is quite a different operation from that of realizing the ideal; the latter is the case of free fiction. I have the power to revive a given and limited material, and, so to speak, to put warmth into it and dilate it; for, the objective determinateness of such material keeps a brake on my fancy and opposes my arbitrariness" (letter of January 1, 1798).

Pseudohistories for emotion and entertainment. A great contribution to such literature comes from the many volumes of so-called anecdotal histories which sometimes resemble detective novels and sometimes erotic stories. They can be, and often are, the kinds of books that are perfectly documented and developed with critical discernment; yet they are not histories, because history is qualified by the moral and intellectual interest which inspires it; in those novels, on the other

All this is very simple to understand and explain; but the process that takes place in the last of the four categories of literary works—the didactic—is a little less simple. Here literature accompanies and controls thought and science which express themselves, as we have shown, by signs or images-signs. Now, why does rigorous science not keep to itself and operate through its own signs; why does it agree to collaborate with literature? There are, in fact, among the scientists and philosophers, those who do not accept this collaboration and who defend themselves strenuously. And whenever they are forced to accept it, they limit themselves to the minimum, to something invisible which looks like nothing; they are the "monastic" philosophers who, according to circumstances and moods, are usually either admired or pitied or ridiculed. But there are others who seek it, and they are the ones who belong not only to the history of philosophy and of science, but also to the history of literature, and they often acquire in it a prominent place. And in which

hand, the only concern is the search for varied emotions.

Pleasing works. It very often happens that works which are well composed from a literary point of view and which have a pleasing content are mistaken for poetry; among such works are those narrating and dramatizing heroism and vague love stories, which are praised as a token of gratitude for the pleasure they have offered. But, writes E. A. Poe (*The Poetic Principle*): "He who shall simply sing, with however glowing enthusiasm, or with however vivid a truth of description, of the sights, and sounds, and odors, and colors, and sentiments, which greet him in common with all mankind—he, I say, has yet failed to prove his divine title."

Tendency toward the typical. The tendency toward the typical, first noted in Menander's comedy, was interpreted by Vico, Nietzsche, and other critics as the outcome of the development of Socratic philosophy. But this tendency arose spontaneously, in all times and places, in comic representations; and, if anything, the Greek philosophers, rather than producing it, availed themselves of it. It seems that Theophrastus, in his *Characters*, depicted comedic types. The passages of Plautus, Horace, Apuleius, in which the comedic types are surveyed, are well known. But the same typology, as we have said, could be drawn from other theatrical dramas and from novels.

The deceit of appearances. All this is, as we said, very simple, but only in theory. Many works of effusive, oratorical, and emotional literature present themselves under such a guise as to deceive concerning their real nature. Notwithstanding, they do not deceive the sharpness of your hearing, that is, the true esthetic consciousness, and consequently not the discernment and judgment, either. Everything in such works seems to be poetry; but the ultimate touch is missing, the touch of beauty.

The tight fist and the open hand. The relation between merely scientific prose and literary prose is explained more particularly by the comparison the stoics (namely, Zeno) used to make between dialectic and rhetoric: the tight fist and the open hand, the "more compressed" or "contracted" speech characterizing the former, the "more extended" speech characterizing the latter.

The technical "jargon." The opposition between anti-literary and literary prose also manifests itself in the two conflicting demands of a "technical" and a "non-technical" language, more accurately a literary one. The right answer is the aversion to the so-called technical jargon which is in the end an accusation of a lack of sociality.

Colorless writing. Most of those who, in treating

way, in adopting literature, can they associate it with the images-signs, which are the proper and adequate expressions of thought? The way becomes clear when one considers that the thinker is not an abstract thinker, but a man who in the toil of his thought puts the whole of his being, commits the whole of his feeling and dreams and hopes and despair, and becomes disheartened or encouraged, and cries in triumph, even though he never runs naked like Archimedes through the streets of Syracuse. And such human drama, within which the drama of his thought unfolds, is indeed the subject matter of literature. Living with himself and in society with other men, he not only feels, but he also receives the impulse to act on his own mind and on the minds of others in order to open and to keep open the avenues of his own thought. He combats prejudices, revives the power of invention, exhorts, inflames, satirizes: and all this is matter for literature, too, for it is oratorical expression. Thus, from the philosopher, the historian, and the scientist, grows the writer—the writer who speaks to his time and to his people, as well as to the people and the times to come; he speaks also to the people of different languages who must acquire the means to read his pages. This is the writer who in antiquity was named Plato or Cicero, Thucydides or Livy, and in modern times Petrarch and Erasmus (who put an end to scholastic jargon and dealt humanistically with morality and religion), and Galileo (who presented his great discoveries in noble prose and witty dialogues), and Voltaire (who battled susperstition and defended reason all over the world with his light sentences and his graceful maliciousness). Everyone knows the great and just glory that belongs to France, the country of medieval scholasticism and of the mathematical rationalism of modern times, for its literary prose. The Germans, who felt the lack of such prose for a long time, gave a sigh of satisfaction and they applauded when Lessing appeared. One ought not to pay attention to the disdain that thinkers continue to express toward "literature," because they usually refer to false and ugly literature, or sometimes to poetic dreams. Jean Calvin may have been unfair toward poetry when he said that language was not given to man "pour faire rêver les auditeurs et pour les laisser en tel état"; but he added that he liked to write "avec rondeur et naïveté," and in so doing he was one of the creators of French literary prose. Didactic literature, like other forms of literature, is not represented only by the so-called prose, that is, the "oratio soluta" [free from the fetters of meter], through all of its gradations, from works for the high and restricted society of philosophers and scientists to works of vulgarization and even

philosophical, historical, and scientific subjects, put in writing whatever comes to their minds rather than composing properly, are not found among "writers," nor are they found among austere scientists (who prefer to express themselves by means of symbols and to write as little literary prose as possible). They are people in whom the vulgarity of form is usually united to that of thought. Strong thinkers are almost always strong writers, although uneven at times. Greco-Roman antiquity, which created the concept of eloquence or literature, demanded that works of thought be in perfect literary form.

Scientific prose and literary prose. Literary affectation is disagreeable everywhere, without any doubt, and therefore also in scientific things. But it is not understood why the opposite, that is, awkwardness, should not be equally disagreeable. Lessing showed surprise in 1755 concerning the books of Mendelssohn: because they were well written, the seriousness of their content was overlooked. "Are abstract thoughts in beautiful dress, then, such a new thing among us that, because of the charm of the appearance, the solidity of the substance must be disregarded? If these thoughts were presented in barbarous expressions of a language resembling Latin, they would be meditated and discussed. Why do we not consider both [content and form]? Simply because they are well written? Is perhaps the German, with a solid head, dull and inimical to all gracefulness to such an extent? Or, when knowledgeable in literature, is he so superficial that he is unwilling to think and incapable of writing well? It is a great misfortune for one to be both a solid thinker and a man of taste! One must be divided into two in order to find competent judges: when he thinks, he must forget that he can write well; and, when he writes well, he must forget that he can think."

Prose in verse. There is didactic prose which needs verse, not, certainly (as in memorial verse), to recall more easily some ideas and information, nor (which is the same thing) to divulgate them, but because the tone of that prose requires verse; not poetic but prosaic verse. Voltaire offers very beautiful examples of it; one example is the vivacious defense that he, the apostle of "reason," makes of the incomparable pleasure of fancies and beliefs:

> O l'heureux temps que celui de ces fables
> Des bons démons, des esprits familiers,
> Des farfadets aux mortels secourables!
> On écoutait, tous ces faits admirables,
> Dans un château près d'un large foyer;
> Le père et l'oncle, et la mère et la fille,
> Et les voisins et toute la famille
> Ouvrait l'oreille à monsieur l'aumônier,

works for ladies and children. In fact, books of geometry and physics for ladies, and endearing little books of philosophy, and various children's stories were often composed; such literature also includes novels (historical, social, scientific, philosophical), comedies and other dramas, apologues and epigrams, and versified poems which are definitely "didactic," not poetic works.

Qui leur faisait des contes de sorcier.
On a banni les démons et les fées;
Sous la raison les grâces étouffées
Livrent nos coeurs à l'insipidité;
Le raisonneur tristement s'accrédite.
On court, hélas! après la vérité;
Ah! croyez-moi, l'erreur a son mérite![21]

Not less perfect prose, in which the meter is, as in the previous lines, very natural, is his letter to Madame Lullin:

> *"Je veux dans mes derniers adieux,*
> *Disait Tibulle à son amante,*
> *Attacher mes yeux sur tes yeux,*
> *Te presser de ma main mourante."*
>   *Mais quand on sent qu'on va passer,*
> *Quand l'âme fuit avec la vie,*
> *A-t-on des yeux pour voir Délie,*
> *Et des mains pour la caresser?*
>   *Dans ce moment chacun oublie*
> *Tout ce qu'il a fait en santé.*
> *Quel mortel s'est jamais flatté*
> *D'un rendez-vous à l'agonie?*
>   *Délie elle-même, à son tour,*
> *S'en va dans la nuit éternelle,*
> *En oubliant qu'elle fut belle,*
> *Et qu'elle a vécu pour l'amour.*
>   *Nous naissons, nous vivons, bergère,*
> *Nous mourons sans savoir comment;*
> *Chacun est parti du néant:*
> *Où va-t-il? . . . Dieu le sait, ma chère.[22]*

Prose and, generally, literature in verse can achieve admirable perfection, which can be enjoyed and admired, providing that one does not make the mistake of comparing it to poetry, for it is not poetry, nor is it meant to be.

Poetry in verse and poetry in prose. The old Aristotelian assertion concerning a novel in a kind of prose to be called poetry reappears in a graceful scene of Lope de Vega's La dama boba (act 1, sc. 4):

Celia

En fin, es poeta en prosa.

Nise

Y de una historia amorosa,
digna de aplauso y teatro.
Hay dos prosas diferentes,
poética y historial:
la historial, lisa y leal,
cuenta verdades patentes,
    con frase y términos claros;
la poética es hermosa,
varia, culta, licenciosa,
y oscura aun a ingenios raros;

21. "Ce qui plaît aux dames," *Oeuvres complètes*, ed. L. Moland (Paris: Garnier, 1877–82), vol. 10, p. 19.
22. "Madame Lullin," *ibid.*, vol. 8, p. 540.

> tiene mil exornaciones
> y retóricas figuras.
>
> *Celia*
>
> Pues de cosas tan escuras
> juzgan tantos?
>
> *Nise*
>
> No le pones,
> Celia, pequeña objectión;
> pero así corre el engaño
> del mundo.

[*Celia*: In short, he is a poet in prose. *Nise*: And of a love story worthy of applause and the theater. There are two different forms of prose: the poetical and the historical; the historical, smooth and faithful, narrates evident truths in clear phrases and words; the poetic is beautiful, varied, elegant, free, and yet obscure even to uncommon talents; it contains thousands of ornaments and rhetorical figures. *Celia:* Well, do so many people pass judgment on such obscure things? *Nise:* You are not raising a trivial objection; but this is the way deceit lives in the world.]

Juvenal. When one thinks of the incisive images, the robust verses that Juvenal coined (which are constantly repeated—without knowing that they are his—because it would be impossible to say things better), one rejects categorically the current judgment that he was one of those stump orators who flourished abundantly under the Empire. But one cannot consider him a great wise man either, or a man of high moral judgment, "rigide, austère, éclatant, violent, grave, juste," as Victor Hugo described him,[23] placing him among his "hommes océans"; for, in truth, it did not seem to be a sign of wisdom on his part to inveigh against women, marriage, old age, and other immutable realities or circumstances of life. In a sermonizing or satirical tone, he gives literary form, at times excellent, to his violent irritation, to his "indignatio," whether reasonable or not.

Lucretius. The definitions of the various types of literature can seldom become, individually, definitions of single personalities, who often unite in themselves poetry and nonpoetry—and more than one kind of nonpoetry. Is Lucretius, for instance, as we have stated, didactic, that is, a prose writer in the solemn form of the verse? There is didacticism in him, undoubtedly, but there is something more and of greater importance—the passional element and, more precisely, the passional-religious element, and along with this a sorrowful and perhaps desperately amorous, disenchanted, bitter, yet compassionate soul, which seeks

---

23. *William Shakespeare*, pt. 1, bk. 2, chap. 7 ("Les génies").

appeasement *in a faith, in a doctrine of redemption, and in a redeemer, in this case Epicurus, who is for him what Christ is for Christians. Lucretius' description, for instance, of the insatiability of love is not simply that of a psychologist and naturalist, but the description of one who suffers or has suffered from that passion. And in the description there is the poet, at times permeated by that pathos, at other times dominating it.*

Pindar. Another *instance of the difficulty of thoroughly understanding an author is offered by Pindar. There is now a tendency to eliminate from his odes, as being foreign elements, both the parts celebrating the games' winners and the moral sentences accompanying such celebration, seeing the poetry of the odes only in the picturesque and musical representation of myths. But these commemorations of myths would lose vigor, or rather would not arise at all, if they were not supported by the ethical, religious, and social sentiment. In the most recent literature on Pindar, that at least which came to my attention, I do not see any reference to the old book by Villemain,* Essai sur le génie de Pindare *(Paris, 1859), in which a very fruitful comparison is made between Pindar and Bossuet: "Bossuet, le plus grand lettré comme le plus grand inspiré des siècles nouveaux de l'Eglise, et le moderne du génie le plus antique, touchait intimement, sans le vouloir, à cette poésie lyrique et gnomique, dont Pindare fut l'Homère. . . . Il était en intelligence, en harmonie de l'âme avec cette poésie morale venue de Pythagore et déclarée sainte par Platon, toute pleine d'éclatantes peintures et de graves pensées, et souvent si chaste et si haute que les premiers pères de l'Eglise l'accusaient d'avoir dérobé la parole à Dieu. . . . Une autre disposition encore rapprochait naturellement le language de l'évêque moderne et celui du chantre thébain. C'était un instinct de la grandeur sous toutes les formes, un goût pour les choses éclatantes, depuis les phénomènes de la nature jusqu'aux pompes de la puissance et de la richesse humaines; c'était aussi ce ferme jugement en contraste avec l'imagination éblouie, ce retour sévère et triste qui abat ce qu'elle avait d'abord admiré et se donne le spectacle de deux grandeurs également senties, celle du monument et celle de la ruine. . . . C'est ainsi, c'est avec un semblable regard mélancolique et vaste, que souvent, à l'occasion d'une prouesse vulgaire et d'un nom sans souvenir, le poète thébain suscite une émotion profonde par quelque leçon sévère sur la faiblesse de l'homme et les jeux accablants du sort. Car ce poète, ce musicien, est un sage, un disciple immédiat de l'école philosophique la plus pure avant Socrate et Platon . . ."* [pp. 16–20].

8. "Art for Art's Sake"

Poetic expression, which gave birth to literary expression by fusing itself with extrapoetic elements in a particular and practical combination, can on the other hand become directly an object of love and of worship, and be no longer treated as an expression, but as something sought for itself, thus leading to what is called "art for art's sake."

Like every love this too is founded on a real need; and the need here is poetic expression. But like every love, this develops beyond and even against the satisfaction of the original need. Thus one loves horses, dogs, guns, and books, even without riding, hunting, fighting in battles, reading books, and being in fact unwilling to do any of these things; likewise, the miser loves the shiny gold, a means for every comfort, without even thinking of converting it into an object of comfort; similarly, one seriously loves women without any desire to possess them, fearing that the possession would destroy the best or the whole of that love and that the spell would thus be broken.

Certainly even love, in going beyond the immediate need, responds to the desire for an ideal shelter which offers a voluptuousness superior to any other and leaving no wish for any other—the voluptuousness of blissful rest. And since life is kindled by desires which press on one another relentlessly, thus rejecting in its movement this blissful rest, the feeling of voluptuous stillness is at the same time the feeling of disintegration and death. This explains the link between love and death and the poet's lines according to which, when a deep love is born in the heart for the first time, "languido e stanco insiem con esso in petto/ un desiderio di morir si sente" [(the lover) languid and weary, with this love in his heart, feels the desire to die].[52] And none the less that dream recurs tenaciously and becomes the fabric of life, one of its necessary moments. For the real torment, the infernal torment, is lack of love, aridity of the heart; this is said in the verse of another but lesser poet who laments such desolation: "Ahi, grave, amanti, è la sventura mia! Pietà di me, non amo!" [Ah! Lovers, great is my misfortune! Pity me, I do not love!].[53] In a jesting mood, but with a serious intention, Lawrence Sterne confessed that he always had a Dulcinea in his mind, because by this his soul "harmonized itself"; and that he always had been in love at times with one princess, at times with another, and that he hoped to live in this

Art for art's sake. This formula is in the title of Albert Cassagne's book, *La théorie de l'art pour l'art en France chez les premiers romantiques et les premiers réalistes* (Paris, 1906), and in the recent one by Louise Rosenblatt, *L'idée de l'art pour l'art dans la littérature anglaise pendant la période victorienne* (Paris, 1931). Neither of the books, however, has any relation to the concept we deal with here, for both take that formula to be an assertion or vindication of the autonomy of art, as was understood by many of those who dealt with the problem; and taken in that sense would have been unchallengeable and indeed a "truism" or a tautology, if the proponents of it had known how to stick to the concept they had enunciated and to prevent contaminations and to reason it out adequately.

"Art for art's sake," which is the object of our discussion, is, instead, a particular spiritual attitude, of which we have tried to give the theory, without following that vague, unstable formula—a theory mentioned here and there by critics and authors, but only accidentally and in an aphoristic and contradictory manner. A scholar of good will should, indeed, undertake the writing of a particular history of that attitude and also of the theoretical awareness or semiawareness of it. But, to do it properly, it is necessary first of all to determine clearly the concept which must serve as a starting point: and this is, in reality, what is missing in the two works mentioned above.

52. Leopardi, "Amore e morte," ll. 30–31.
53. Lorenzo Stecchetti, *Postuma* 41, "Scritto sopra un sasso."

manner until the moment he had to commit his soul to God.

But, without going further into the theory of love, let us dwell on the love for poetic expression. Like every other love, it seeks the presence of and the contact with the object of its desires, and therefore turns into a cult and a practice of those expressions for their own sake, having nothing in particular to transform into beauty and lacking solicitation from any of the extrapoetic contents which we have found in effusive, oratorical, entertaining, and didactic literature. Something analogous is noticed in the sphere of thought, in which sometimes one plays with thought for the pleasure of playing, for the sake of logic, as in the case of riddles; it is a game in subtlety with the development of long, precise, and superfluous argumentations, which one takes pleasure in multiplying and carrying to their ultimate possibilities, enjoying one's own virtuosity in something that really deserves no more than passing mention.

To love and seek poetic expressions as objects or (which is here the same thing) persons mean to seek the images out of their context, detached and abstract, and to admire, caress, and fix them in articulated sounds, striving for the perfection of each image. And this is what is found in the pages of the "art for art's sake" virtuosi, so perfect in every detail as to arouse the impatience and the annoyance of the poetic spirit, which is ready to throw away all these perfect pages in order to express itself "without perfection" (that is, with a different perfection) by first eliminating from each page the too conspicuous and heavy images and words so that the page may flow swiftly and smoothly. For this form of art, which gives so much relief to each image, lacks the ground that unifies all the images together and mitigates them, the ground that alone could generate their poetic life and give them measure and proportion. And not only is the poetic content lacking, but so are the elements on which literature is founded, that is, the various extrapoetic contents already familiar to us. Those single images stand like idols which the artist molds and worships.

Neither poetry nor prose. There is, without doubt, prose (and good prose) in good verse; but rightly Gosse rejects the judgment on Dryden and Pope as *"classics not of English poetry but prose,"* although he is not right in the dilemma he presents: "Pope n'était pas un classique de la prose; il écrivait presque exclusivement en vers artistiques d'une technique achevée, qui peuvent éluder les formules romantiques, mais qui doivent être de la poésie ou rien. Le meilleur moyen d'en sortir, c'est d'admettre que c'est de la poésie et d'en donner la définition." The best way to solve the problem is to admit that it is properly neither poetry nor prose, but art for art's sake. In fact, Gosse adds: "Ils voulurent exprimer ces pensées et ces émotions communes avec une exactitude parfaite, faire de leur forme et de leur substance un amalgame intensément solide, capable de supporter leur soigneux travail" (*Histoire de la littérature anglaise,* trans. from the German, p. 225). If poetry were merely an amalgam made possible by accurate and subtle work, neither Homer nor Dante nor Shakespeare would be poets.

Forms and the form. De Sanctis would say that in works of art for art's sake one sees "the forms but not the Form," with a capital letter, as his old disciple, A. C. de Meis, used to say. Among other things, De Sanctis, being a great advocate of the autonomy of art, judged the theories of Victor Hugo and of all the ro-

And since images are refinished and enjoyed like *things*, the articulate sounds expressing them can be detached and can become things too, and be loved and sought after for their own sake, not for their direct expressive function. Thus, the virtuosi of beautiful images are joined by the virtuosi of beautiful sounds—beautiful by association with images and remembrances—which have already resounded in great poems (and are loved as one loves the gloves and the ribbon belonging to the cherished woman), in archaic poetry, in poetry in foreign languages, in those which combine new rhythms and sounds, and so on. The great creator of images is often united in the same person with the lover, the seeker, and the inventor of words, as in Victor Hugo and even more in D'Annunzio. At this point one understands how a certain theory of "art for art's sake" is being constructed for those critics who pretend to find and explain the beauty of a line (which is spiritual beauty) in sounds for sounds' sake, in accents, rhythms, "music," as they generally call it, thus showing little esteem, not only for poetry, but also for music itself.

mantics to be "exaggerations," for they had drawn, from the principle of autonomy, "the excessive formula: art for art's sake" (essay on *Settembrini e i suoi critici*). In other words, De Sanctis had noted that at the bottom of the formula there was something particular and diverse, though he was unable to determine what it was.

Impeccable poets. Praised as "impeccable" are the artisans of art for art's sake (remember the dedication of Baudelaire to Gautier: "Au poète impeccable, au parfait magicien ès lettres françaises"); but one would not dare praise in like terms any true poet. Of such craftsmen one would better say what Ovid said of the learned and exquisite Callimachus: "Quamvis ingenio non valet, arte valet" [although he has no merit for his talent, he has for his art] (*Amores* 1. 15). The true poet is aware of being a sinner and, as it is said in the text [page 104 of this book], begs indulgence. Who has not met at times, in the so-called literary world, those who kept saying that the only ambition they had was to leave ten "impeccable," "perfect," "marmoreal" verses, and so on? These souls were bereft of affections and thoughts, and equally lacking in ideals.

The overwrought form. To the art for art's sake theory are linked somehow those writers whose form is noted as being "overelaborated," such as Courier in France or Tommaseo in Italy. The latter very seldom (only in a few short poems) was in possession of the fundamental motif strongly enough to be able to develop from it the particulars or to connect the particulars to the fundamental motif. As a result, he quite often worked out the particulars away from the focus; hence the impression of admirable fragments given by his best pages of prose and his best verses (see my *Letteratura della nuova Italia*, 5th ed., vol. 1, pp. 67–71).

The poet and language. The love of the poet for language is different from that of the virtuoso and the lover of art for art's sake: in language the poet loves the feeling which has become an image and has thus acquired a body, a living corporeal existence. But a poet will never feel as D'Annunzio said he felt: "Divina è la Parola:/ ne la pura Bellezza il ciel ripose/ ogni nostra letizia; e il Verso è tutto [Divine is the word:/ in pure Beauty heaven placed/ our every joy/ and Verse is all" (*L'Isottèo*, last lines)], which is the lust of an esthete. In another respect, it was wittily observed that poets fall in love, not with natural things, but rather with the names of these things, which, "enriched by many associations, saturated with many colours, . . . acquired a life of their own, moving on another plane than that of things" (Havelock Ellis, *The Dance of Life*, London, 1923, p. 169). This, though it seems to be a contradiction, is cross-evidence of what we have just noted. In fact, those names of things have filled themselves, in the poet, with feeling and have assumed the character of fancy, which fully satisfies him and in some way renders him indifferent to "things," that is, to the concepts and facts of which the names are intellectual signs. This clarifies the inanity of Pascoli's censure of certain poets because they showed no knowledge of plants, flowers, birds, and often mistook one species for the other or imagined them different from what they really were (cf. *La Letteratura della nuova Italia*, 5th ed., vol. 4, pp. 123–24, where, in reference to birds, I pointed out that, in the final analysis, a poet is not a hunter).

Coinage of new words. The pleasure of coining new words or the search for rare ones is, too, typical of the artists of "art for art's sake" and not of poets, who renovate the words constantly without being aware of it; therefore, they seem satisfied with the words existing in common speech, since they can, by a new arrangement, draw from them whatever they need. So said Maupassant, who did not want to hear about "écriture artiste" or rare and rich language, being satisfied with a limited number of words which he placed in the right spot in phrases variedly constructed and musically rhythmized. Prior to Maupassant, the same thought, in which there is as much truth as there is illusion, is found in the important *Discours sur la poésie naturelle et sur le langage poétique* of Louis Racine, who was a very good judge of poetry: "La glorie d'inventer des mots, gloire frivole et facile, n'est pas celle que cherchent les bons écrivains; ils n'ambitionnent que celle d'inventer des tours nouveaux. C'est à quoi nos grands poètes se sont principalement attachés, et c'est par là qu'ennoblissant notre style poétique, ils ont en même temps perfectionné notre langue. L'art de mettre les mots à leur place, qui est l'art de bien écrire, ne s'apprend point dans les grammaires: c'est le génie qui le donne" (Boileau, *l'Art poétique*, Paris, 1804, appendix, pp. 58–59).

Modern Latin poetry. Primarily, if not exclusively, in relation to the art for art's sake theory, we must view the Latin poetry of the Renaissance and the following centuries, when Latin had become "a sort of sacred language, sacred from the lay and profane point of view, surrounded with love and reverence, an aristocratic language in which thoughts were heightened and loftily expressed." Especially in idyllic and erotic compositions, there is "a love for the pleasing things together with a love for the dress of the things, a dress which was itself the object of pleasure: this was a double enjoyment, a double voluptuousness of men and of literati, which, though very often coinciding, can be distinguished through its different origins"

This is not to say that "stylists," "esthetes," "Parnassians," "Alexandrinians," "decadents," or whatever the artists of "art for art's sake" were called, are completely lacking every poetic content serving as a support and a subject for their works; there is sometimes the semblance of a poetic motif, sometimes there is one of the extrapoetic elements that we already know. But they are like coatracks on which one hangs splendid robes and precious furs. The poetic motif is weak and incapable of dominating the spirit, and the conceptual, moral, or other content becomes obvious, common and uninteresting, and does not engage the intellect and the passions; to do so would be a hindrance to the display of virtuosity and art for art's sake. A case in point is the famous French stylist, Boileau, who, lacking imagination and experience of life and history, had in substance nothing to say except to criticize bad writers. Another case in point is the "English Boileau," Alexander Pope, who also had no original ideas and who collected the concepts of his *Essay on Criticism* from common sense and from generally known books of poetics and rhetoric, and picked up from the moralists or from current observations the elements for his other essay, *An Essay on Man*. The real aim of both writers was to hammer out perfect verses. Boileau wrote satires; but what did he care about the weaknesses, the errors, and the vices afflicting individuals and society? The truth perhaps came out of his mouth unwittingly, when he answered those who urged him to stop satirizing: "Et sur quoi donc faut-il que s'exercent mes vers?"[54] The reprobation of human vices was for him a "pretext"; and this is exactly the word we find in a recent esthete or stylist, Jean Moréas, for whom the world exists only "pour servir de prétexte à ses chants." These men were allowed to enter the city of poetry through the door of another art—painting, sculpture, music. Théophile Gautier was defined a "painter in verse," and D'Annunzio, an "author of symphonies," and José-Maria de Heredia, a "medalist" or a "carver of cameos"; but for this defensive argument to be acceptable it would be necessary to prove that these other arts are not poetry, that is, that they have no soul; for the question here concerns the lack of soul. With these virtuosi the worst happens when, forgetting their own being, they attempt to transform their array of images into real poetry; and in so doing they become wrapped up in sensuality and hedonism. By this we do not mean that some of these writers, and more than one of those mentioned, possessed no flashes of poetry or that they did not at times write perfect poems. Certainly their ancestor, the

("Poesia latina del Rinascimento," in my *Poesia popolare e poesia d'arte*, 2d ed., pp. 443–48).

The decadents. This term, it seems, was first used in France to designate the young poets after 1870 and then adopted as a school motto by those who attached to the term a positive meaning and took pride in it. The well-known sonnet by Verlaine ("Je suis l'Empire à la fin de la décadence") was printed in 1883, and three years later a review and a weekly entitled *La Décadence* were founded (see Verlaine, *Poésies complètes*, ed. de la Pléiade, p. 945, notes).

---

54. Satire IX, "A son Esprit," l. 250.

"classic" of the genre, the sixteenth-century Góngora, was a poet, both in his early beautiful romances ("Servía en Orán al Rey," or "Amarrado a un duro banco," or "La más bella niña") and in his later and more characteristic work, *Soledades*, in which, while indulging in deliberate obscurities and riddles, he refined and subtilized, as a stylist and cultivator of art for art's sake, the traditional poetic and humanistic phraseology, revitalizing it with magnificent and warm visions of aspects of nature. In others of these lovers of the form for its own sake, the process at times becomes somewhat intimate, developing a particular feeling—"a vain desire for ancient beauty," Carducci would say—by which their art warms up in a sort of "poetry of poetry." It is clear that, in art for art's sake, as in the other forms considered here, we are establishing the character of each form on the basis of its own principles and method, without giving a thorough judgment of the writers representing it, for they are always something more or something less than the concept that they are meant to exemplify.

Góngora and other stylists. The best esthetic interpretation that I know on Góngora is that by Dámaso Alonso (introduction to his edition of *Soledades*, Madrid, 1927); see also the introduction by H. Brunn to the German translation of the same *Soledades* (Munich, 1934). "In Góngora's poetry," writes Alonso, "flowers, trees, earth animals, birds, fish, the varieties of foods . . . march off before the eyes of the reader in a sumptuous parade. The most faithful symbol of this poetry is the horn of plenty. What were they thinking about, those who said that *Soledades* was empty? The work is so nourished that it hardly can encompass in so little space such a variety of forms. It is so full of life—too full" (pp. 30–31). "From all this poetry, therefore, comes a constant caress to our senses. There is nothing more sensual; and of all sensual touches, the most extreme—those of sound and color" (p. 21) [quoted in Spanish]. An example of these qualities can be found in the following lines (*Soledades*, 1st Soledad, ll. 725–31), in which a young bride is depicted:

> . . . la que en sí bella se esconde
> con ceño dulce, y con silencio afable,
> beldad parlera, gracia muda ostenta:
> cual del rizado verde botón donde
> abrevia su hermosura virgen rosa,
>   las cisuras cairela
> un color que la púrpura que cela
> por brújula concede vergonzosa.

[. . . of her who with sweet pride in her loveliness retires, and with affable silence shows her talkative beauty and mute grace: as the crinkled green bud in which the virgin rose immures its loveliness, a color adorns the gashes and allows one to pry into the purple therein blushingly hiding.]

This mode of expression by Góngora certainly does not suggest a "mystery," but rather "makes mysterious what in itself is clear; and working this way it creates not simply a poetic work but also the 'drama,' that is, the effort of poetic creation itself, as Leo Spitzer acutely observed ("Zu Góngoras Soledades," in *Romanische Stil-und Literaturstudien*, Marburg, 1931, vol. 2, pp. 126–40): this brings out in Góngora not a new and profound poetic character, but the baroque or nonpoetic element which coexisted with his exquisite poetic fancy; the union of geniality and artifice that resulted in the mixed feelings of reprobation and attraction aroused by his later mode of poetic composition.

In the Italian baroque writers, too (except in Marino, who was, in substance, a luxuriant rhetorician, but in such as Achillini, Artale, Lubrano, and others), one easily finds similar traits, as can be seen by leafing through the collection entitled *Lirici marinisti* (ed. Benedetto Croce, Bari, 1911). But of a quite different strength was one Italian "stylist," Giovanni della Casa, who, highly regarded for about two centuries (by Vico, by Foscolo), was later unjustly neglected or not understood. I have tried to make readers understand his work and thus feel the poetic breath circulating in it (see *Poesia popolare e poesia d'arte*, 2d ed., pp. 375–84).

Poets of art for art's sake. One must not, after all, extol to the summit of poetic beauty—as is common today—the overwrought works of the tormented seekers of art for art's sake and stylistic refinements. Even in the best of them the longing for, the voluptuousness of, mere sensuousness prevails over the moral and religious drama of humanity; as a result, the pleasure offered by those verses and images is too narrow, and this is immediately felt when one turns again to the great poets—Homer, Dante, Shakespeare, Goethe. It is like the change from breathing in a closed room (or perhaps a room where the cool air is generated by mechanical fans!) to breathing in the open and brisk air of the fields and mountains.

The literature, as they call it, of "exception" usually provides the lover of poetry (and the seeker of the history of poetry) the tickle or the delight resulting from something *curious*, rather than genuine and true poetic emotion.

Poetry on poetry. I had occasion to study it in one of its Italian practitioners, Vincenzo Monti (*European Literature in the Nineteenth Century*, pp. 18–29; but see also for other instances *La Letterature della nuova Italia*, 5th ed., vol. 2, pp. 292–93). Platen saw under that guise (and judged it accordingly) the art of Canova (a sort of Monti of sculpture), by contrasting it to the direct art of Donatello:

> Sehnsucht nach den Antiken erregte der weiche Canova
> doch dein männlicher Ernst trifft, o Donato, das Herz!

(The mellow Canova aroused nostalgia for the ancients; but your virile seriousness, O Donatello, goes straight to the heart!)

D'Annunzio's poetry, for example, is not a poetry of poetry, which is a form of love, but flatly a libido applied to the words of others' poems—a libido that caused the compilation of the ample catalogues of his so-called plagiarisms. Strictly speaking, his appropriations were not plagiarisms, that is, they were not prompted so much by the desire to usurp the praises due others as by the pleasure of bringing into his "harem" and possessing in their carnality certain images and certain words, among them at times the most venerable ones because of their ethical and religious origins.

The art for art's sake category itself has its own merit, which is not exactly poetic or even literary, but is a merit nonetheless. This is so true that among its cultivators one discerns those capable and those incapable, the correct and the incorrect, the serious and the nonserious. Art for art's sake may become a tiresome craft, as shown by the works of the Provençal poets of the "trobar clus," and "escur," "subtil"; it may become an acrobatic exercise, as in the Italian and foreign baroque writers; or an insipid pastime, as in the little games of "echoes," "acrostics," "equivocal rhymes," "identical rhymes," and "imitative" harmonies, "correlative" verses, "leporiambs," and even verses which in the written form take the shape of utensils and animals. This can be cold imitation and a hodgepodge of poetic forms, and it can be a clumsy effort at figurative expression. In all of these instances love is lacking; and the lack of love is accompanied by the incapacity to give the works the truth and the beauty which they could attain within the limits marked above; that is, the truth and beauty of garlands and of laces of images which a string ties together, always somewhat extrinsically. Who is not pleased at times to repeat to himself detached words and lines and hemistichs, with sensual pleasure, or to sing trifles, "nugas canoras" [melodious trifles], which are nevertheless "canorae"? St. Augustine remembered his great delight in listening to an orator at whose words "verbis eius" (he says) "suspendebar intentus, rerum autem incuriosus et contemptor astabam, et delectabar suavitate sermonis" [my attention was captured by his words, and I stood there careless and scornful of the matter, only delighted by the sweetness of his speech].[55] Art for art's sake, too, accomplishes therefore a particular function; it satisfies a particular need. It is a love among other loves, a slavery for love among other slaveries for love.

Little lexical and metric games and oddities. In the old treatises of poetics, such as the *Dizionario della poesia volgare* by Affò (Parma, 1777), one finds descriptions and examples of them; but a larger number than anywhere else is found in *Rythmica* by Father Caramuel (2d ed., *duplo auctior*, Campaniae, 1678). On the "cento" there are two volumes by O. Delepierre, *Tableau de la littérature du centon* (London, 1874–1875). A little collection of "literary difficulties and oddities" (poetic compositions in the form of a bagpipe, axe, cross, and so forth, acrostics, anacyclic, sotadic or recurrent, ophidian or serpentine, correlative verses, and so forth), can be seen in "Letteratura delle nazioni" (in Cesare Cantù, *Storia universale*, 10th ed., appendix, pp. 230–38).

Eloquence and poetry. Only in a country like France, where eloquence, that is, literature, has been so great and powerful, even so powerful as to encumber poetry (remember Buffon who, to praise a poem, called it "as beautiful as beautiful prose," and D'Alembert, similarly: "Voici, ce qui me semble la loi rigoureuse, mais juste, que notre siècle impose aux poètes: il ne reconnait plus pour bon en vers que ce qu'il trouverait excellent en prose";[24] and, in the preceding century, the futile efforts of Mademoiselle de Gournay to defend Ronsard's work against the prosaic writers of the school of Malherbe); only in such a tradition can one understand the violent rebellion against eloquence and literature, which breaks out in certain "schools" there ("prends l'éloquence et tords-lui le cou!").[25] In Italy, on the contrary, that extreme power being lacking, there was congeniality and reciprocal respect between poetry and eloquence, as can be seen in our last great poet, Carducci. Even De Sanctis in his criticism did not oppose the two, but requested that each of them be lively and genuine.

9. *"Pure Poetry"*

The so-called pure poetry comes preceded by a long theoretical prologue, which, in truth, is the only thing related to our inquiry, since the practical production issuing from such a prologue, whatever its character and originality, remains outside the contemplative and theoretical sphere.

55. *Confessiones* 5. 13.

24. D'Alembert, "Réflexions sur la poésie," *Oeuvres compètes* (Geneva: Slatkine Reprints, 1967), vol. 4, p. 294.
25. Verlaine, "Art poétique," *Jadis et naguère* (1884).

In the above-mentioned theoretical prologue, every conception of poetry as the expression of an emotional, a conceptual, an oratorical, or a moving content is rejected: thus a protest is raised against the confusion between poetry and literature. The expediency and emphasis of the protest can be understood and justified when one considers that this protest took place first in a country such as France, which, more than any other country, and much more than Italy, has been the land of literature—the literature that even today, as at the time of Brunetto Latini,[56] shows itself to be "plus délitable" in the French language.

And if that protest had developed the negative concepts implicit in it, with logical coherence, with philosophical depth, and knowledge of the history of doctrines (which it did not, its authors being far removed from these things), one would have obtained a criticism of all false esthetics, which derive from the confusion between poetry and literature, that is, between true expression, which is the poetic, and other expressions, which are called "expressions" but are not so, as we have seen. In fact, there exist false esthetics—materialistic, positivistic, psychological, utilitarian, and the like—but they are a part of erroneous philosophies and gnoseologies which bear those names and are refuted through the general criticism of materialism, psychologism, utilitarianism, and so on. In a more specific sense, false esthetics are the intellectualistic or conceptualistic, which mistakes literary prose for poetry; the emotional, which mistakes feeling or the literary expression of feeling for poetry; the practical, which confuses poetry with the literary expression of oratory; the hedonistic, which confuses poetry with literature for amusement; and, finally, the formalistic, which mistakes poetry for the delectations of art for art's sake. These are false esthetics which sometimes combine into two or three, as in the "miscere utile dulci, delectando pariterque monendo" {blending pleasure and profit by delight and skillful instruction},[57] and sometimes add one to another and regard the sum thus formed as the true and whole idea of poetry. The determination of the character proper of poetry has a long and laborious history, and few are the philosophers who have been able to grasp that character. Poetics reached maturity later than rhetoric and for a long time remained under its dependence.

Symbolism. "Symbolism" is connected to the particular conditions of French poetry; it represents another intellectualistic attempt to liberate poetry from oratory and prose. But the concept of "symbol" was mentioned earlier and we have demonstrated how it is alien to the theory of poetry.

The late and difficult foundation of a science of poetry. The origin of the true (philosophical) science of poetry and art lies in the new conception of the spirit as ideal history, asserted by Vico and, with less depth and emphasis the Leibnizian school; hence, in the sphere of knowledge, three distinct stages were recognized: that of "feeling without perceiving" (which corresponds to our emotion), that of "perceiving with a troubled and agitated mind" (which corresponds to our lyrical intuition or poetry), and that of "reflecting with a clear mind" (which is the equivalent of philosophy, criticism, history, and so forth): see the "Axioms" [103] in [Vico's] *The New Science.* Similarly, see in the Leibnizians and in Baumgarten: "obscuritas, claritas, distinctio"; and the determination of "claritas" as "pulcritudo" and thus the principle of poetry and art. All this had to pass through varied travail before acquiring the richness and neatness of present-day esthetic thought; but this present-day thought must acknowledge its religious origins in those first distinctions.

Didactic poetry. One of the tangible signs of the profound change which was taking place from the late eighteenth century onward in the concept of poetry was the disappearnace of the category of didactic poems from treatises on poetics and from criticism. See a little note by Goethe ("Ueber das Lehrgedcht," in 1825, in *Werke,* ed. Geodeke, vol. 27, pp. 138–39), in which he declares it improper to place next to the three genres—lyric, epic, and dramatic—the didactic genre, which differentiates itself from the others, not in form (as the others do between themselves), but in content; the didactic genre, unlike poetry, does not teach by hints, as does life itself, but in the manner of schools.

"Descriptivism," tightly connected with didacti-

---

56. Brunetto Latini (1220–1294), a Florentine scholar, regarded as a man of great learning. He was a friend and perhaps a teacher of Dante. His reputation rests on an encyclopedic work, *Li Livre dou Trésor,* written in French between 1262 and 1266 while he was exiled in France. He later composed an abridged version of it in Italian verse, *Tesoretto.*

57. Horace, *De arte poetica,* ll. 343–44. The two lines are not quoted in their entirety.

cism, also fell into scornful discredit. By depicting objects through the eye of the naturalist, "descriptivism" concerned itself with giving prominence to all their characteristics, without transfiguring these objects into images of feeling.

The case of Horace. Many dissertations have been written on the fortune of Horace, but I do not believe that any essay was ever written to illustrate his reputation as a poet in light of the old and the new ideas of poetry and the fluctuating interest between poetry and literature. As long as poetry was thought to consist principally in the elegance of expression with which one adorned political celebrations, in the wisdom of thoughts and admonitions on the one hand and in the eroticism of little dramas and comedies and the delights of country life on the other, Horace was greatly appreciated. He reigned as a poet during the eighteenth century, which found in him an affinity of tendencies; and he was the favorite of Abbot Galiani, who all his life never tired of reading him; he was the poet of Immanuel Kant, who was not much gifted for poetry. Some voices containing admiration for Horace were certainly heard; they sounded clearer and more distinct later with Goethe and Hegel. In the nineteenth century Horace lost the place he had once occupied in people's minds; and this is mentioned as a significant fact, not as a deserved rejection. Alfred de Vigny, one of the great poets of the century, associated Horace with Voltaire, and in their manner of creation he sensed the extinction of the poetic tone:

> *Tu chantas en buvant dans les banquets d'Horace*
> *Et Voltaire à la cour te traîna devant nous,*
> *Vestale aux feux éteints! . . . [Maison du berger]*

"If the so-called 'lyrical cry' be of the essence of a true lyric," writes an excellent critic who is carried away by the indefinable charm of the Horatian odes, "they [the odes] are not true lyrics at all" (J. W. Mackail, Latin Literature, London, 1919, pp. 112–13). But it is not the "cry" of "lyricism" that matters here; it is rather the inner accent, which in the odes is not substantially different from that of the previous satires and the subsequent epistles. This was in fact recognized by the same critic, who continues: "Few of them are free from a marked artificiality, an almost rigid adherence to canon. Their range of feeling is studiously narrow. Beside the air and fire of a lyric of Catullus, an ode of Horace for the moment grows pale and heavy, 'cineris specie decoloratur' [discolors to appear like ash]. Beside one of the pathetic half-lines of Virgil, with their broken gleams and murmurs as of another world, a Horatian phrase loses lustre and sound." Moreover, all this is followed, perhaps uncon-

sciously, by the observation: "Yet Horace appeals to a tenfold larger audience than Catullus—to a larger audience, it may even be said, than Virgil." In fact, the situations of Horace are always morally and psychologically rethought and expressed after this inner conceptualization; and this makes them accessible to a larger public, which is not, after all, the public that seeks and discerns the particular form of poetic emotion. Our ancestors could express all their reflections on life, sententiously using verses from Horace, much as grandmothers and great-grandmothers recited little arias by Metastasio. Voltaire, in his *Epître à Horace*, tells how much the Latin poet offered him:

> Tes vers en tout pays sont cités d'âge en âge. . . .
> Avec toi l'homme apprend à souffrir l'indigence,
> A jouir sagement d'une honnête opulence,
> A vivre avec soi-même, à servir ses amis,
> A se moquer un peu de ses sots ennemis,
> A sortir d'une vie ou triste ou fortunée,
> En rendant grâce à Dieu de nous l'avoir donnée![26]

The comparison now usually made between Horace and Goethe is groundless, for even when Goethe had become a wise man and the poet of wisdom, he nevertheless remained so powerfully lyrical as to permeate with lyrical accent also his new moral attitude.

But, by insisting on this characteristic of Horace's odes and by taking them as a symbol of a concept of poetry (which modern esthetics does not consider to be the original one), we do not mean to deny their "indefinable charm" of which the English critic speaks and which continues to exercise itself on the readers, though it should be explained in another way, through the concepts of a gnomic and paraenetic literature, very fine and exquisite because espoused to the cult of forms. Once the intimate character of Horace's work is understood, one goes back to love and enjoy it with renewed pleasure.

German romanticism. The antecedents of "pure poetry" are noticed in the theories and efforts, or the vague aspirations, of some romantics—those of Tieck toward the arabesque insofar as it is the expression of the pure movement of the spirit or those of Novalis toward a poetry the words of which have no meaning, their value consisting in their musical sounds. German romanticism, unwholesome in many of its aspects, contained within itself the seeds of subsequent decadentism.

Poetry and words. There is a "famous assertion" by Mallarmé, often cited with admiration: "On ne fait pas de la poésie avec des idées, mais avec des mots."[27]

The error, however, is not so much in the fact that the above-mentioned criticism contained in that theoretical prologue is not cast within a philosophical or historical context; it is rather in the fact that there is a persistence in interpreting genuine poetry (the poetry which has appeared in the world from Homer to Goethe, Ibsen, Tolstoy, and all historically existing poetry) as being a literary form shaping a practical content—emotional or conceptual. These rebels against the French literary tradition reaffirm, on the contrary, by the very emphasis of their negation, the tradition itself, which is rationalistic and intellectualistic, and which in the Descartes and Malebranches had already shown itself to be inimical to and incapable of understanding poetry and fancy.

---

26. *Oeuvres complètes*, vol. 10, p. 446 (first line, p. 444).

27. The exact quotation is "Ce n'est point avec des idées que l'on fait des vers. . . . C'est avec des mots." This pronouncement was made by Mal-

This assertion must be countered by simply saying that poetry is not made with "mots" (vocables) or "idées" (concepts), but with poetry itself, with that creation of the imagination that becomes, through its self-creative act, the living word.

Against all poetry that has appeared in the world. This adverse attitude and ensuing judgment exist also in some contemporary schools related to that of "pure poetry." Of the "dadaist" group (to which Gide belonged for some time) one reads that "ils se livraient à une surenchère forcenée: Tzara, leur meilleur chef de publicité, organisait la réclame-dada; Aragon, en casquette et en ceinture rouge, invectivait les puissances du jour; André Breton, avec une politesse exquise, annonçait la fin de cette immense farce qui a nom l'art" (L. Pierre-Quint, *André Gide*, Paris, 1932, p. 86).

"Pure poetry" and amusement. "Je vais faire à présent un aveu. . . . Il ne faut pas craindre de dire que le domaine des lettres n'est qu'une province du vaste empire des divertissements. . . . Mais il y a cependant plusieurs publics: parmi lesquels il n'est pas impossible d'en trouver quelqu'un qui ne conçoive pas le plaisir sans peine, qui n'aime point de jouer sans payer, et même qui ne se trouve pas heureux si son bonheur n'est en partie son oeuvre propre dont il veut ressentir ce qu'elle lui coûte" (P. Valéry, *Variété*, vol. 2, pp. 222–23). Mallarmé also said that, by naming an object, one would take away three fourths of the enjoyment of the poem, "qui est fait du bonheur de deviner peu à peu."[28]

An Italian, who wanted to try this "amusement" for himself, describes the procedure and offers a justification in these terms: "The starting point was the discovery of the esthetic value of a mere sequence of words: images and sounds create a sensible form, which can be complicated at will, enriched with inner agreements, harmonies, rhythms, that is, with inner correspondences; and the use of these for the expression of a state of mind, even if the logical connection disappears and the whole has no precise meaning. The point of arrival is the conception of pure poetry as a sort of tapestry or a verbal arabesque; a music of ideas, in sum, which develops under the dual control of the ears and the imagination; a four-dimensional kind of music. All poetry has always had, as a substratum, an arabesque. What else are the rhythm and rhyme, if not the squaring of the spoken form—a means for subdividing the discourse into more or less regular units,

---

larmé in a conversation with the painter Edgar Degas, and is reported by Paul Valéry in *Oeuvres*, (Paris: Gallimard, 1960), vol. 2, p. 1208; see also Mallarmé, *Correspondance* (Paris: Gallimard, 1959), vol. 3, p. 254, n. 1.

28. "Réponses à des enquêtes sur l'évolution littéraire," *Oeuvres complètes* (Paris: Gallimard, 1945), p. 864.

Thus the poetry they speak of (which would be none other than that beginning with themselves), though not meant to be literature, is not poetry either; it is not the identity of content and form, the expression of the full humanity, the vision of the particular in the universal, as was set forth at the beginning of this inquiry, to which I furnished the directive principle. On the contrary, it is the negation of poetry as expression and the substitution of this concept with another—that of poetry as "suggestion," the suggestion which exercises itself through articulate sounds that have no meaning or (which is the same thing) express nothing determinate, but that stimulate the reader to understand them as he pleases and invite him to form, by and for himself, the images he likes and those which correspond to his own feeling.

Now, since all things which surround us at every moment are occasions and stimuli for our images and thoughts, and also for our desires and actions (and, therefore, all of them "suggest"), we have in this the proof of the complete vacuity of that concept of suggestion which would determine the goal of a work of pure poetry. Such a work, whether the result of a spasmodic or skillful effort (always inexpressive), does not belong to either the sphere of inspiration or to any contemplative and cognitive process, but only to the will which, by reflection and calculation, shapes sounds and rhythms and thus constructs the object which pleases the author, offering the readers, as we have seen, merely a blind and accidental stimulation for their affections. There is in this an amusement for one's own exclusive benefit or for the purpose of propagating such an amusement around oneself. This idea that art is nothing but "amusement" was expounded by one of the theorists of pure poetry, thus giving encouragement to the strangest practices and programs on that area. Their titles and battle cries today run through brigades of proponents and literary journals which we do not need to mention here because it is hoped that they will soon be forgotten.

into symmetrical intervals, in the same manner as the musician does with beats? But only during the last years has poetry attempted to become a pure form; on the one hand by divesting itself of every intellectualistic content and yielding to prose the function of expressing drama; on the other by emphasizing the artifice that is peculiar to it, and pushing its manner of expression farther away from the common language" (M. Viscardini, in *Gazzetta del popolo*, Turin, November 4, 1931).

But in regard to "tapestry," which is a comparison (also applied to music) much used in dealing with works of "pure poetry," it would be after all a respectful and prudent act to ask an artist producing "tapestries" whether he really works in that manner or whether he, too, starts from a feeling of joy, splendor, majesty, severity, and so on, that is, from an "intuition" which he expresses through the lines and colors he weaves.

Intense poetry and pure poetry. Intense poetry is a very rare work, characteristic of poetic genius. "Pure poets" try to realize it artificially, moving with light heart straight toward it, without burdening themselves with all that genius musters, dominates, and transfigures within itself.

Deliberate obscurity. This perversion, which, as we have seen, plays a large part today in the so-called hermetic poetry, is something old; Quintilian, in fact, in describing it, observed that it was already old in his own times because Titus Livy had talked about it. The passage from Quintilian is worth reading: "*Neque id novum vitium est, cum iam apud Titum Livium inveniam, fuisse praeceptorem aliquem, qui discipulos obscurare, quae dicerent, iuberet, greco verbo utens σκότισον. Unde illa scilicet egregia laudatio: 'tanto melior: ne ego quidem intellexi.' . . . Pervasitque iam multos ista persuasio, ut id iam demum eleganter atque exquisite dictum putent, quod interpretandum sit: sed auditoribus etiam nonnullis grata sunt haec, quae cum intellexerunt, acumine suo delectantur et gaudent, non quasi audierint, sed quasi invenerint*" [This fault is by no means of recent date, as I find in Livy that there was a teacher in his day who exhorted his pupils to obscure what they said, using the Greek word *skotison* [darkness]: hence, I suppose, that extraordinary praise: "so much the better; even I myself was unable to understand it." . . . And there is an opinion now prevalent with many, that they ought to think that only what is elegantly and exquisitely expressed needs to be interpreted. But it is also pleasing to certain listeners, who, when they find out the meaning of it, are delighted with their own acumen, and applaud themselves as if they had not merely *heard it but invented it]* (*Institutionis oratoriae*, bk. 8, chap. 2, pp. 18, 19).

The obscure and the difficult. From the "obscure"—be it artificial like the above mentioned, that is, variedly quackish, or be it natural, the result of confused thinking or imagining—one must obviously distinguish the "difficult," the obscurity of which lies not in the work but in the reader who does not accomplish the necessary effort to overcome it. Rightly Góngora protested: "I do not present *Soledades* as something obscure, but people, being afflicted by deliberate maliciousness, find obscurity in the very language of the work." If the verses of *Soledades* are first interpreted with patient care, they become clear and beautiful, like those quoted earlier as an example. Góngora said also: "While bringing me honor, it caused me to become obscure to ignorant people, for it is the distinction of learned men to speak in a way that sounds like Greek to the ignorant; so that pearls may not be cast before swine" (*Obras completas*, ed. Gimenez, 3d ed., Madrid, 1951, pp. 896, 897) [quoted in Spanish]. The fault, if any, of Góngora lies in his intention to be difficult—an intention which preoccupies him, as can be easily seen in his disdainful and haughty attitude.

The struggle against the ineffable. Among the blind impulses that drive toward so-called pure poetry, one finds at times the well-known torment of the inadequacy of the expression to feeling, for feeling in itself remains always inexpressible in its realistic existence and, therefore, appears distorted in the expression. Poetry, which expresses everything, has many times expressed also this torment of the inexpressible, as in the two celebrated lines by Manzoni: "Ch'io sento come il più divin s'invola,/ Né può il giogo patir de la parola" [What I feel to be most divine flies away,/ For it cannot suffer the yoke of the word] (poem left unpublished by the author and of which some octaves have recently been found and printed by D. Bulferetti in *La Fiera Letteraria*, Milan, November 20, 1927). Philosophy has demonstrated the genesis of this illusion; and I began (as was recalled above) my youthful treatise, *Aesthetic*, with a similar demonstration. It is clear that poetry is always supercession of feeling and elevation of it to the sphere of contemplation [*teoresi*].

A feeling cannot but be felt, that is, suffered; and it cannot be expressed while remaining in its realistic suffering. Practically, the authors of such pure poetry either repeat, often prosaically, the assertion of their inability to express, by scorning and cursing the language (which appears to them as collapse or treason); or, in their torment, in their desperate struggle against the ineffable, in their infirmity and folly, they break out in some dazzling images and thus burn up,

But others among these theorists are not satisfied with this kind of pastime and want to go deeper within themselves to reach the universal soul and lose themselves in it, like oriental rather than European mystics, renouncing action, which seems to them to be dualistic because it breaks the static unity into distincts. And in participating in this superrealism and mysticism and orientalism and occultism and magic, the pure poet becomes serious and grave, and thus he shows himself to the beholders; his personality, as a result, appears shrouded in mystery, his head is crowned by a nimbus, his word sounds like that of one who promises, in obscure utterances or in well-distributed silence, portentous innovations in the world or, at the very least, a novel way of perceiving the world and of behaving in it. The faithfuls of Mallarmé regarded him almost as the high priest of an inaccessible deity; and if one reads what was written on Stephan George by his disciples, one will end by wondering whether they are speaking of a poet or the founder of a religion, for they attribute to him the idea of the "whole" man, the man who asserts himself in resisting progress, who encloses himself within his own ego, and who finds within himself his own fulfillment. By this, according to his disciples, he initiated a new historical era with its appropriate symbol—no longer the "disc," the symbol of antiquity; not the "cupola," under which the Middle Ages took shelter; nor the "straight line," the symbol of a progressive age: but the symbol of the "radiating sphere of forces." Arthur Rimbaud in his own way would also have been a seer, having attempted to realize the new vision and the new ethics of the world by denying logic and morality and giving himself up to the wild and disorderly impulses of all the senses and realizing the perfect "voyou" or the perfect rogue in order to grasp, through such experiences, the ultimate meaning of reality. The truth is, however, that from the faithful survivors of the churches formed around the new saints we have curious information and strange judgments; for instance, of the revered Mallarmé, whom they surrounded with great expectations, avidly absorbing every word he deigned to utter, they said that the secret of his behavior lay in his painful condition of impotent creator and of "raté," or failure; this, somehow, was suspected in an unbiased reading of his pages.

For these reasons, as we have said, what is typical and original in the creation of pure poetry is outside the theoretical and contemplative sphere, and does not add any new expressive category to those which we have discussed, even if this sphere were expanded into others, far removed from us, such as that of magic and that of thaumaturgy.

What, on the other hand, is neither typical nor original in pure poetry are single lines, stanzas, some short compositions which one understands, admires, learns by heart in the Mallarmés, the Georges, the Valérys. These belong neither to pure poetry nor to its theories, but to the hidden work of the old, expressive, and impure poetry, or, better, to the perennial poetry without adjectives, which in the finite grasps the infinite.

in a narrow sphere of expression, all the poetic power of which they are capable.

"Pure poetry" and silence. Another tendency of pure poets, besides that of not expressing but vaguely suggesting, is the tendency toward silence, which is accomplished in the mystic annihilation of desire and thought: "There are three modes of silence. The first is of speech, the second of desire, and the third of thought. Through the first one acquires virtue, through the second quiet, through the third an inner shelter. By not speaking, desiring, and thinking, one reaches the true and perfect mystic silence, in which God speaks to the soul, communicates to it, and teaches it, in its most intimate depths, the most perfect and highest wisdom" (Molinos, *Guía espiritual,* bk. 1, chap. 17) [quoted in Spanish].

The program of a pure poet. In the *Anthologie des poètes français contemporains,* edited by G. Walch (Paris-Leyde, 1907), I happened to notice the name of one of the most celebrated pure poets of our day—Paul Valéry—at the origin of contemporary French poetry. In this anthology there are some verses of his preceded by some judgments on his art; one of these judgments (by P. Léautaud) says: "M. Paul Valéry s'adonne depuis quelques années à des recherches extra-littéraires et qu'il est malaisé de définir, car elles semblent se fonder sur une confusion préméditée des méthodes des sciences exactes et des instincts artistiques." The other (by Paul Souchon) reads: "M. Valéry est représentant d'un art d'exception, d'une poésie restrainte à une élite et à l'expression de beautés mystérieuses. . . . Il est le joailler des princes. Sa poésie restera comme un beau danger, attirant et souvent fatal" (vol. 3, pp. 53–54). At the end, Valéry himself intervenes in the anthology to declare his own doctrine: "Un poème est une durée pendant laquelle, lecteur, je respire suivant une loi qui fut préparée. Je donne mon souffle et les machines de ma voix; ou seulement leur pouvoir, qui se concilie avec le silence. Je m'abandonne à l'adorable allure: lire, vivre où mènent les mots. . . . Leur apparition est écrite. Leur sonorité fut écoutée. Leur ébranlement se compose d'après une méditation antérieure, et ils se précipiteront, en groupes magnifiques, dans la résonance. Même mes étonnements sont assurés: ils sont cachés d'avance et font partie du nombre" (vol. 3, p. 57).

"Pure poetry" and kindred schools. Of the many volumes written on the subject, one of the most learned and best composed is that of M. Raymond, *De Baudelaire au surréalisme: Essai sur le mouvement poétique contemporain* (Paris, 1934). Of particular interest is the thesis of B. Archer Morrissette, *Les aspects fondamentaux de l'esthétique symboliste* (Clermont-Ferrand, 1933),

for it seeks points of contact between my esthetic doctrine and those of today's French schools; but these points of contact are not found, except in some negations whose spirit is completely different from the two cases considered. Concerning Mallarmé and his theories and those of his disciples, see one of my essays in Poesia e non poesia, 5th ed., 1950, pp. 314–25.[29]

Pure poetry and impotence. For this judgment, which was given in regard to Mallarmé, see, besides the essay just mentioned, my book review in La critica 40 (1942): 112. Since Mallarmé has reigned and still reigns in the poetic schools not only in France but also in Germany, England, Italy, and Spain, and more or less all over, the astonishing thing is that his impotence has had so much generating power as to fill the world with his homogeneous children. The truth of it is that bad examples, those which in one way or another substitute the mechanical for the creative, prove extensive, and more effective than good ones.

10. Poetry, Nonpoetry, Antipoetry

The above-described literary forms, as well as the virtuosity of art for art's sake, are not forms of antipoetry, of ugliness, of disvalue; they are not negative, but positive forms, for each of them, as we have always pointed out, dialecticizes itself in its peculiar positive and negative, beauty and ugliness. We must insist on this point because often the recognition of the fact that literature is not poetry is thoughtlessly taken to be an indication of disvalue—a disvalue which fosters the mental disposition of those who, either because of excessive love for poetry or because of love of such love, show, as we have already noted, little esteem for that great and noble part of human culture and civilization which is literature.[58] The result of this kind of prejudice is that when criticism demonstrates a certain work to be oratorical or didactic in inspiration and therefore not fundamentally poetic, such work is to be condemned or undermined. But what could one ever undermine (to go back to an example already cited) in the novel *The Betrothed* by pointing out the moral preoccupation which generated it and which animates it in each of its parts?[59] The work remains what it has

Each thing is beautiful in its own place. Goethe, speaking about didactic poems and similar genres, such as the descriptive and the satirical ("scheltende"), excluded them from the sphere of true poetry, defining them "intermediate creatures between poetry and rhetoric"; he rightly insisted, nevertheless, on their right to exist. "The intrinsic merit of didactic poetry, that is, an instructive work of art, adorned with

58. Actually Croce himself had been the most radical scorner of "literature" or the "literary form"; and he had been harshly criticized for his negative judgment about nonpoetic expression. Here he finally came to recognize the positive value of literature and the discipline governing it.

59. Toward the end of his life, Croce had a change of heart concerning Manzoni's masterpiece and admitted that *The Betrothed* is a genuine work of art (see *Terze pagine sparse*, vol. 1 [1955], pp. 128–30).

29. *Unfortunately the essay on Mallarmé does not appear in the English translation of the book, European Literature of the Nineteenth Century, which was made from an earlier edition.*

always been for those who felt it and loved it; and it will continue to be appreciated ever more deeply. If anything is to be undermined, it is the judgments of the interpreters and the critics, and never Manzoni's work. One must always retain intact the admiration for beautiful literary works, even if they are nonpoetic or poetic only in their own particular way, that is, as a mixture of poetry and something else. Such works are not only the orations by Demosthenes, the histories by Tacitus and Machiavelli, the *Essais* by Montaigne, the *Discours de la méthode* by Descartes, the *Provinciales* by Pascal, but also the letters, the sermons, and the odes by Horace, the jesting, satirical, and admonishing comedies by Aristophanes, the epic of the "Homère bouffon" that was Rabelais, the comedies by the great Molière and those by the lesser Goldoni, the novels by Fielding and those by Walter Scott, certain parts of the gnomic writings by Goethe, the satires by Alfieri, and so on—all of them beautiful things, but things which could not, properly speaking, be called poetry if (as De Sanctis, who greatly loved and appreciated Goldoni, ended by saying in regard to the latter's comedies) the "divine sadness" does not reign in them. As for myself, I do not feel the blush which would inundate someone else's face when I say that I like Alexandre Dumas' *Trois Mousquetaires*, which I judged to be written with sprightliness and ease. It is still read and enjoyed by many, with no offense to poetry, though they hide their enjoyment as if it were an illicit delight; and they should be encouraged to set aside their false shame and the concomitant embarrassment.

rhythmical euphony and with embellishments of the imagination, written in a graceful and articulate manner, has not yet in any way diminished. From the rhymed chronicles, the memorial verses of the ancient pedagogues, up to the best works of the kind that can be remembered, everything can be accepted; but everything in its own place and with the dignity that it deserves" (Werke, vol. 27, p. 138).

Molière and Goldoni. The greatness of Molière lies in his admirable moral observation which nourishes a no less admirable comicality and gaiety. But nobody has found in him, among so many other delightful things, the poetic dream. In *Le Misanthrope* there is bitterness, which produces a discordant effect; in *Le Tartuffe* there is a harsh satire, which by certain traits joins hands with *Les Provinciales*; this is why those two comedies have been judged by some as superior and by others as inferior to the comedies completely comical in character, and as a departure of Molière from his own natural and inborn tone. A different and poetic interpretation can only come from the reader's injection of some of his own personal feelings and reflections into the works. It seems that Goethe was subject to illusions of this kind when he felt Molière's comedies to be skirting the tragic, and judged *L'Avare* to be among the greatest and most tragic, in which, however, there was nothing but moral typology, caricature, and hilarity. Everyone remembers, in the ending, the self-caricature of the character who addresses himself to the spectators: *"Quel bruit fait-on là-haut est-ce mon voleur qu'y est? De grâce, si l'on sait des nouvelles de mon voleur, je supplie que l'on m'en dise. N'est-il point caché là parmi vous? Ils me regardent tous et se mettent à rire. Vous verrez qu'ils ont part, sans doute, au vol que l'on m'a fait. Allons vite, des commissaires, des archers, des prévôts, des juges, des gênes, des potences et des bourreaux. Je veux faire pendre tout le monde; et, si je ne retrouve mon argent, je me pendrai moi-même après."*

Goldoni is inferior to Molière in moral observation. Because of a lesser intellect, moving within a simpler sphere of experience, Goldoni's talent consists entirely in this capacity to view the hilarious aspect of men, their little passions, faults and vices, and thoughtlessness, of which they almost always repent and correct themselves. He was a good-natured man, with honest intentions, meekness, compassion, and indulgence; but his vein was that and no more. "He lacks (we quote De Sanctis) that divine sadness which is the ideal of the comic poet and which keeps him above his own world, as though it were his creature, which he caresses with his eyes and does not leave until he has *given it the last finishing touch" (History of Italian Literature, vol. 2, p. 872).*

Nevertheless, recently it was discovered that Goldoni was a "lyric" poet and a "musician," and it was asserted that "the lyricism of the Goldonian tone lies in the joy of the high-sounding dialogical architecture: a continuous melopoeia through the comedy, which at times lulls itself in charming ariette, at other times rests in elegant rhythms of recitative; but more often the melopoeia harmonizes with the state of mind in a playful manner or, breaking any fixed form with the impetuous flowing of its vein, becomes a melodic recitative, tied above all to the needs of the expression, without renouncing, however, the pure, beautiful, and sensual singing of our race" (E. Rho, "Il tono goldoniano," *Nuova antologia*, June 1, 1933). The essay shows how far the so-called criticism of the "Pure," that is, abstract, "Form" can go, when transferred from the figurative arts to music and poetry, from which it should be, instead, driven out (as in fact we are now doing).

Aristophanes. With the Schlegels and the other romantics, the misunderstanding of Aristophanes' comedies begins; these comedies are elevated to the level of poetry, powerful poetry, set opposite tragedy yet differentiated from Menander's new comedy, which would be prose entirely. This was a Vichean interpretation (see my *Philosophy of Giambattista Vico*, p. 193) which the romantics, and the romantic Nietzsche, adopted and exaggerated, but which must be accepted with caution by those who have present in their mind the poetry in the known fragments by Meander, already felt in the so-called halved Menander—Terence. (Since Terence was at times so warmhearted and poetic, one may ask, with due respect to Julius Caesar, why he was referred to as the "halved Menander"). The same caution must be used by those who are aware of the tight connections brought to light between the new comedy and the Roman amorous elegy. About Terence see my study in *La critica* 34 (1936): now in *Poesia antica e moderna*, 3d ed., 1950. "Ancient comedy," wrote A. W. Schlegel, "is a poetic genre as independent and original as is tragedy, and is at the same height as the latter, that is, it rises above a limited reality to the domain of free creative imagination" (*Vorlesungen über dramatische Poesie*, chap. 6); such an interpretation will serve also to open the way to romantic humor and irony and to the somewhat frigid Aristophanic comedies which were attempted at that time. But, on this aspect, it is well to stick to the characterization that Aristophanes himself gives (*Ecclesiazousai* 1054–56) of his art, wherein he requests that

Antipoetry and the ugly are something else. They consist in the interference of the will which pursues its practical ends within the process of artistic creation; a similar interference is produced in the process of thought by error or falsehood. It is a dialectical moment, which cannot be specifically illustrated here, for it would be necessary to start from the consideration of contrariness and of the general theory of evil, of the reality and, at the same time, the unreality of the negative, of the reality and the unreality of death in life. Thus, on the one hand, the ugly is what the poetic work, in its relentless process of formation, constantly rejects, preventing it from realizing itself; but, on the other hand, it is what realizes itself in works negatively called ugly, though in fact they are not negative, because they always serve the practical and personal purpose of their author, and are therefore positive. The arbitrary interference of the will in the poetic process concretizes itself only through nonpoetic expressions, precisely the literary, which are substituted for the absent poetic expression; something similar happens in literary works, through the introduction of nonmediated and nonfused poetic expressions, or through the use of didactic and pathetic expressions when the oratorical are required, or vice versa (the use of "nervos et aculeos" [vigor and sting]—in Cicero's words—when instead one's writing is "docendi causa, non capiendi" [for the purpose of instructing, not captivating]).[60] All this does not mean antipoeticality per se, either in the nonpoetic or in the literary expressions; there are (it is said and said well) no words beautiful or ugly in themselves, but all of them are beautiful or ugly depending on whether they are or are not in their right place. Nonpoetry is not antipoetry, that is, the poetically ugly; and, similarly, poetry is the nonliterary but not the antiliterary, for literature has its own beauty as well as its own ugliness or "antiliterature."

One should consider, more appropriately, the relation of poetry to literature from another angle—that of the relative scarcity of true poetry (poetry springing only from a "state of grace") and the relative abundance of literature (which requires a more ordinary aptitude and serves a more common purpose). Is it perhaps not the case to recognize that great poetry, like great philosophy, is almost entirely European? This

"the wise ones among the spectators judge him by remembering the wise things he said, and those who love to laugh by remembering the mirthful things, so that he may receive a double approbation." For certainly he says serious things (and, since we deal here with literary criticism, we confine ourselves to noting the austere sense of poetry and artistic form he showed even if under the guise of ethical formulas); but all of the serious things, alternating with laughter, are clothed in the generally happy tone of his comedies. Those who, by holding to the idea that poetry is fragmentary in nature, wish to separate in Aristophanes the comical from the lyrical parts, and place the latter, for instance, in the choruses of The Clouds and of The Birds, forget that these are aspects of the same playful imagination, like the lines of tragic authors which Aristophanes willingly inserted in his dialogical repartees.

The "Homère bouffon." This designation, which in its precise form goes back to Charles Nodier, prompts the observation that the work for laughter may reach, within its own genre, even colossal proportions, but may not surpass the limits implicit in its own nature. Though always a narrator of something enormous, Rabelais does not go beyond these limits; he does not stretch and relax and delight the imagination in the same manner as did in antiquity the author of the Satyricon, who was a narrator of the sensual, bestial, and plebeian in forms which are out of proportion ("novae simplicitatis opus . . . quodque facit populus, candida lingua refert" [work of an unusual ingenuousness . . . telling in frank language, what people do]);[30] and in this he also reached colossality. The astonishing richness of images and the power of expression of these works make them appear as dealing with a very serious subject; the labor of form confers in fact seriousness upon the subject, for the writer puts into it all the care and the scruple of the artist. Readers and critics of such works are thus led to musings, to the search for allegorical meanings, and to attempts to discover mysterious poetic veins. One can say that the greatest triumph of the clownish spirit of works of this kind is achieved when they succeed in carrying away and inebriating the readers to the point of disconcerting them and making them see double.

Despite the evidence, and because of the vague usage of the term "poetry," one can read in Faguet: "Rabelais est un grand poète en prose. Celui qui l'a appelé l'Homère bouffon, lui a trouvé son nom. Il raconte merveilleusement, avec une verve étonnante, un mouvement extraordinaire, une ampleur de poète

---

60. Orator 19.

30. Chap. 132, last poetic passage.

fact seems apparent if we consider the various peoples and historical epochs and restrain the strong cosmopolitan inclinations and the exaggerated exaltation of things oriental, an exaltation simply due to their novelty and the difficulty of their discovery. As poetry is rare, so are the readers who understand it; they are in fact rarer than those who understand literature. And since no one allows himself, judging by the large number of bad poets, to be led to the conclusion that poetry is easy (for the opposite is true), so one must not allow oneself to be deceived by the great number of readers who cry for poetry while they have the same mentality as bad poets and are driven by the same ambitions; nor by the many others who pretend to observe and study it, while in fact they look for the historical allusions, the biographical references, the concepts and the tendencies encompassed by its content. They do not study the form; they study the words, the metaphors and schemes, which grammarians, rhetoricians, and vocabularians are interested in extracting from poetry.

If one observes the crowd running, or made to run, toward works of poetry, one realizes that in order to entertain this crowd it is necessary to feed it either anecdotes about these works and their authors or extravagant connections between the works and the passions and interests of the day. Even when poetry seems to be the object of the crowd's attention and enjoyment, very often the truth is that poetry is not read in the simple yet difficult key of poetry, but is interpreted as oratory, didacticism, lyricism, autobiography and thus brought close to the spirit of the unpoetic readers. And if it does not lend itself to this, because it is poetry pure and simple, one hears the observation that "there is no substance" to it. It would seem ironical to credit the "general consensus," the "popular judgment" with discerning and upholding truly poetic works and drawing attention to them, if for "popular judgment" and "general consensus" were not meant, in reality, the ideal judgment and the consensus formed in elite minds—the minds which transmit them to their peers, who are the only ones worthy and in a position to receive them and impose them upon the "communis opinio," that is, upon the lips of the people. We say upon the lips, not the soul; for how could people really attend to their own business with so much devotion, how could they conduct with so much perfection and capability the industry and commerce indispensable to their practical life, if they were haunted and agitated by the spirits of Dante and Shakespeare? It is, then, providential that poetry, like philosophy in its specific form, that is, its intense form, is cultivated and worshiped only by a few.

épique: personne n'a raconté comme Rabelais; de plus il peint tout puissamment" (*Petite histoire de la littérature française*, Paris, n.d., pp. 41–42). *But Voltaire in a letter to Madame du Deffand had written, instead, with his usual good sense: "Rabelais, quand il est bon, est le premier des bons bouffons. Il ne faut pas qu'il y ait deux hommes de ce métier dans une nation, mais il faut qu'il y en ait un" (quoted by Faguet himself, ibid.).*

The assertion of the general comprehension of poetry and the incomprehension of philosophy. *The aversion to and derision of philosophy on the part of common people seem to be in contrast with their admiration and love for poetry and art. It only seems so; for, if from that apparent affection one subtracts all their interest in the subject matter, the incidents, and the circumstances of art, one realizes that of admiration for art as such very little will survive—perhaps no more than that expressed for philosophy, whenever philosophy provides or seems to provide some maxims for use in life and in social and political affairs.*

The "popularity" of poetry and literature. *The question of whether poetry or literature is popular in this or in that country makes no sense and can receive only arbitrary and conjectural answers. It was raised in our country by Ruggiero Bonghi, who denied that Italian literature was as popular in Italy as was French literature in France (see his Lettere critiche, 1856). But three years earlier Hippolyte Taine maintained, in a long analysis (La Fontaine et ses fables, Paris, 1853, pt. 1, chap. 4), that "il est rare en France de rencontrer un grand écrivain qui soit populaire: ordinairement ceux qui sont populaires ne sont point grands, et ceux qui sont grands ne sont point populaires," and, by contrast, asserted that German literature was popular in Germany. It is possible that some writer I do not know has maintained in turn that German literature is not really popular in Germany. These questions, however, are meaningless because of their lack of conceptual clarity concerning the things under discussion.*

Taking pleasure in the nonpoetic in poetry. *Housman himself also remarks that one can be insensible to poetry and yet find pleasure in poems: "Poems very seldom consist of poetry and nothing else; and pleasure can be derived also from their other ingredients. I am convinced that most readers, when they think that they are admiring poetry, are deceived by their inability to analyze their sensations, and that they are really admiring, not the poetry of the passage before them, but something else in it, which they like better than the poetry" (The Name and Nature of Poetry, pp. 33–34).*

The rarity of love and the intelligence of poetry. *F. Th.*

One observes similar events also in the life of the individual. If children possess more imagination than fancy, and youths more passions and curiosity and therefore prefer passional, moving, exciting or even sententious and paradoxical works (which they often mistake for poetry), they can, but only through experience and the maturity of taste, finally acquire the delicate and severe sense of poetry. This progress could symbolically be perceived in the transition from Dante's *Inferno*, where passions burn in darkness, to the "dolce color d'oriental zaffiro" [sweet color of oriental sapphire] of *Purgatorio*.[61]

Vischer writes in Auch Einer (Berlin, n.d., p. 467): "The majority of men expect poetry to offer them, pleasingly, their own ordinary images, embellished with silver tinsel and gilded paper. But since poetry overturns, rather, the ordinary conception of the world, no great poet would have ever become famous if the few who know what imagination is had not little by little created a following, which gradually became larger. By throwing stone after stone into the stagnant water of public opinion, they finally succeeded in putting into motion the circle of waves of the entire surface. If this had not happened, Iffland and even Kotzebue would even today be at the summit of public favor, and Goethe and Schiller would be considered as extravagant minds." With a similar or greater pessimism, the following was noted about Dante's poem: "What readers has the Divine Comedy now? A few poets, a few lovers of poetry, a few strayed cross-word puzzlers, for the rest, a diminishing band of culture-fans and erudition-snobs. These last feel as triumphantly superior in their exclusive learning as would the social snob if, alone of all his acquaintances, he had met the Prince of Wales, or could speak of Mr. Michael Arlen by his pet name" (Aldous Huxley, Music at Night and Other Essays, Leipzig, 1933, p. 44).

The sense of poetry. One could try to write a history of the sense of poetry in various ages and peoples. In Italy it persisted vigorously in many a mind even through the baroque age (see my Storia dell'età barocca in Italia, 3d ed., 1953, passim); and, at the end of that age, it burst forth into a powerful self-assertion such as that found in Vico's New Science, which celebrates Homer and Dante and genuine poetry, even if rudimentary. In the eighteenth century, when that sense was lowered generally all over Europe because of the prevalence of rationalistic and polemical interests, in Italy it was not completely extinguished, and the ideas of the Enlightenment affected it only superficially. It is certain, in other respects, that toward the end of that century and the beginning of the following, Germany gave or awakened a truer sense of poetry. It is well, in that respect, to see as a contrast the discoverer of spiritual and intellectual Germany, Madame de Staël, with her German friends. Schiller wrote: "Madame de Staël has no sense of what we call poetry: from poetic works she appropriates only what is passional, oratorical, or else the general ideas they contain . . ." (letter to Goethe, December 21, 1803): that was the truth. On the contrary, her friend, Benjamin Constant, remarked in his diary: "Je voyage avec Madame Necker (the cousin of Madame de Staël), qui m'a rejoint. Je lui lis quelques poésies fugitives (the Lieder) de Goethe. Mais quelle difficulté de faire entrer

61. *Purgatorio* 1. 13.

la poésie allemande dans une tête accoutumée à la poésie française. La poésie française a toujours un but autre que les beautés poétiques. C'est de la morale, ou de l'utilité, ou de l'expérience, de la finesse ou du persiflage, en un mot toujours de la réflexion. En somme, la poésie n'y existe jamais que comme véhicule ou comme moyen. Il n'y a pas ce vague, cet abandon à des sensations non réfléchies, ces descriptions si naturelles, tellement commandées par l'impression, que l'auteur ne paraît pas s'apercevoir qu'il décrit. Voilà ce qui fait le caractère de la poésie allemande, et ce qui (depuis que je la connais) me paraît être le caractère essentiel de la véritable poésie" (*Journal intime*, ed. Melegari, p. 40).

Youth and poetry. How receptive are the young (I refer to the time when I, too, was young) to the works of the Schillers, the Byrons, the Hugos, and the Mussets, and with how much difficulty do they succeed, in their early years, in enjoying the poetry of a Petrarch! Propertius, who, after all, knew how to be a true and great poet, was counting on the young for his amorous, passional, and sorrowful poems; and thinking of his grave, he said: "Nec poterunt iuvenes nostro reticere sepulcro: —Ardoris nostri magne poeta, iaces" [The young could not help coming to my grave and saying: O great poet of our passion, you lie here] (*Elegies* 1. 7). Thus we the young used to go and bring flowers to the "sepulcrum" of the poet of our passion, to the grave of Alfred de Musset at the Père Lachaise cemetery, shaded by the weeping willow.

The taste for poetry according to age. Montaigne said of himself: "Dès ma première enfance, la poésie a eu cela, de me transpercer et transporter; mais ce ressentiment bien vif qui est naturellement en moi, a été diversement manié par diversité de formes, non tant plus hautes et plus basses (car c'étaient toujours des plus hautes en chaque espèce) comme différentes en couleur: premièrement une fluidité gaie et ingénieuse; depuis une subtilité aiguë relevée; enfin, une force mûre et constante. L'exemple le dira mieux: Ovide, Lucain, Virgile" (*Essais*, bk. 1, chap. 37).

II

The Life of Poetry

1. The Re-Evocation of Poetry, the Means of Interpretation

Once the poetic expression is formed, the poet repeats it mentally or rereads it in the written form, some years or months or days or hours later, when, through the changing of conditions and times, he has become other than he was. Now, if this expression lives again within his changed self, it similarly lives again in others who are, as it were, himself, because they are united to him by a common humanity; they are his contemporaries or his posterity for ever and ever. This is the eternal rebirth, that is, the re-evocation of poetry.

The re-evocation cannot be effectuated except as a retracing of the creative process of the poetic expression, and this is generally a role assigned to taste. But since taste and genius are, as we know, inseparable, that is, not two but one act in its self-creation (which is feeling becoming conscious of itself and, in so doing, creating itself), the re-evocation is to be attributed more exactly to taste-genius, or simply to genius, which, having created that expression, re-creates it perpetually.

It is genius which created that expression—not the genius of such and such an individual, naturalistically conceived and limited, but the genius of humanity, which grew through the assimilation of that spiritual creation and possesses it now within itself as an indestructible force. Even if it never returned to the lips of anyone in the world, it would live nevertheless. It would be like the solitary lamp which, in the words of Mörike, was hanging from a light chain in a room once a nest of pleasure and now deserted, and on its

The genius of humanity. The joy which everyone feels in a poem (as though the poem were the reader's own work, his own creation) proves that the creator of poetry is not the single individual as such, but the genius of humanity, which lies in everyone. The author of *On the Sublime* notes that "our spirit, when rising high to true sublimity, is filled with a sense of happy and joyful accomplishment, as if it had itself produced

84

white cup, bordered by acanthus leaves, a joyful band of dancing youths is pictured; but no human eye turns now toward that charming form, still resplendent but enjoying its own beauty in solitude. How many poems remained like that lamp for many centuries, with no one to sing them again! How many of them still remain so! How many will perhaps never return from the kingdom of shadows to the light! And yet, even in the kingdom of shadows they live and act: gentle feelings and strong thoughts and generous urges, which arise in us without our knowing how, come from them. They come from those ideal creatures, whose faces we do not always see and which are put into the world by the fancy of poets, the minds of philosophers, benevolent souls—all immortal children of mortal men.

But for the very reason that humanity is engaged in diverse activities rather than only in works of poetry and even less in this or that particular poetry, the process of re-evocation, though intrinsically universal, is not always realized or is realized with varying degrees of difficulty. Men are not all and always poets, and often, taken by their practical activities or by the toil of meditation, appear to be even intolerant and scornful toward any form of poetry. The necessary variety of human feelings and actions, on the one hand, interposes obstacles to poetic re-evocation, which strives to unfold freely and is hindered and stopped by prejudices crowding the mind, by the soul distracted from and oblivious to poetry, thus being turned to other goals by powerful passions. And the course of events itself interposes to the mind obstacles of another nature, called accidental, such as the failure to find again the written page which would help the memory, or to find it still readable. All these are hindrances often observed in the very person who had formed the original expression—the author of the poem. Taken by other activities for the satisfaction of other needs, he becomes incapable, on going back to poetry, of reviving it within himself fully, because he now lacks, totally or partially, the subjective and objective conditions possessed at the moment of creation.

what it hears" (chap. 7). On the contrary, when this feeling is not experienced, and we say of a poem "that we would not like to have been the author," we mean that poetry itself is lacking, and that what stands before us belongs to the sphere of the individual's practical life and, therefore, not of the human *that is found in all of us.*

Immortality. Immortality belongs to the individual insofar as he actualizes the universal in his work, and not to an abstract and inconceivable individual outside and beyond the work: ". . . My Trésor, *in which I still live," said the soul of Brunetto Latini to Dante; and this was Brunetto's immortality. Hence his sense of responsibility was not toward the laws of men, but toward the eternal of which we are the artisans: "non sibi, sed toti genitum se credere mundo" [believing to have generated not himself but the whole world.]*

Changes within ourselves. It is commonly pointed out that the feeling toward poetry varies from one individual to another, and one easily forgets that, as Montaigne said, "il se trouve autant de différences de nous à nous-mêmes que de nous à autrui." One forgets, because it is unpleasant to draw the conclusion that individuals are incorrigibly incoherent; this would mean that we ourselves are incorrigibly incoherent and that, in substance, our spirit is in a state of disintegration and decay. And we pay no attention to the fact that our vital effort is a constant re-establishment of coherence within ourselves, which corresponds to a similar effort in human society.

He tries then, if that be the case, to find the lost sheet and to revive and decipher the signs in it, or to drive away his boiling passions, shake off his distraction, and concentrate upon himself, look into his memory, excite his fancy; and with skill and effort he finally begins to recapture and re-create the poetry already created. In this toil he is brought sometimes to form conjectures; sometimes he realizes that, whenever he believes that he has re-evoked this or that word of the original poem, he has in fact replaced the words with others. So, if his memory becomes clearer or if he interprets his writing better or finds a more readable copy, he notices the changes which have taken place—changes which sometimes can weaken the original words, sometimes turn out to be, by chance, a happy correction and an improvement.

What are these efforts that the author carries out in order to recapture his own work? What are they, in their limited scope, if not parts of that broad human activity generally called "philology"? Such efforts are like shoots and small plants; philology is like trees and woods and gardens and cultivated fields: but both are of the same quality.

In philology the loss or dispersion of documents of poetry gives impulsion to heuristic, to the research and the findings which are laudably accomplished by men well suited for and disciplined in this kind of work. Such is the work which constitutes the glory of the Italian humanists, who undertook long trips in the East and to other European countries, searching every corner of old abbeys to bring back Greek and Latin codices and to "free," as they said, "the ancestors from slavery by the barbarians"; these are the endeavors in which scholars in every part of the world are still competing; and if they do not always, or if they do rarely, free the ancestors from the slavery of the barbarians, often they free them from the macabre contact with the sheets of papyrus wrapping the Egyptian mummies, and bring into the light and the warmth of the sun Sappho and Bacchylides and Menander and Herondas. And the art of rendering writings legible is the technique of restoration, which is aided by physics and chemistry in removing the superimposed writing without destroying the underlying one, and in rendering visible, by means of decolorants and photography, the underlying without obliterating the superimposed in the palimpsest and in fixing the charred Herculaneum papyri without splintering or pulverizing them at the touch. And the other art, that of reading old orthography, is paleography, and there are as many paleographies as there are alphabets and letter forms. The restitution of the original phoneme or articulated sound, by choosing

Historical interpretation of poetry. There is no need for new proofs to support the assertion that this interpretation is not a method invented by someone at a certain time, but a necessary and perpetual process of the human mind. I called attention (*Promblemi d'estetica*, 4th ed., pp. 36–37) to an example from the ancients: the interpretation given by Socrates in *Protagoras* (342–48) of a song by Simonides.

The necessity of philology for the re-creation of poetry. Among the number of stupidities or ridiculous pronouncements which we heard and still hear from time to time from conceited esthetes is the assertion that poetry, to be enjoyed, does not need the help of philology or historical knowledge. To one of these, who cited the *Orlando Furioso* as a perfectly comprehensible work even to those with no culture whatever, I answered many years ago that the understanding of only the first line of that poem would require a great deal of historical erudition: one must know, for instance, that the "knights" mentioned there are not the knights of the crown of Italy and that the "arms" are not those seen in armories (like those in the poem by Regaldi),[31] but are the battles, and so on. Certainly, it is possible, instead of learning the words or the images of the poet, to replace them with others of one's own invention; but this procedure amounts not only to not reading the poem, but also to a lack of respect, or one would say, of good breeding, toward the poet. One may believe, as was the case, that by "femmine da conio" (*Inferno* 28. 66) Dante means women used for pecuniary gain; but philology has come to instruct us that, according to the language of the time, and with a better concordance of images, "conio" more appropriately meant "deceit," and therefore "women to be deceived." One may misunderstand, as commonly happens, the "peregrin che tornar vuole" (*Paradiso* 1. 5) to mean the traveler who, arriving at the end of his journey, is taken by the desire to return to his homeland; but here, too, philology warns us that the

---

31. *Giuseppe Regaldi (1809–1883), extemporaneous poet much admired in his times; he did not produce anything of great poetic value and is now completely forgotten.*

from the various readings offered by the various copies of one text, and the introduction of corrections and the filling of lacunae constitute the critique of the text; and it requires that the families of manuscripts and printings and their geneologies be constructed to this end. This is followed by glossaries of sounds and forms for the individual words and authors; by the lexicons of the language of a people, or of more languages together, in which the words are arranged in correspondence with their meaning; by morphologies and syntaxes, metrics and similar instruments; by literary and historical commentaries, in which the meaning of words and phrases is determined by putting them in relation to information about things, facts, and ideas. We set aside the typographers and the publishers, who take care of the clear printing of the texts and put them into circulation; and the librarians, who watch over the conservation of printed materials and manuscripts; and the bibliographers, who catalogue the editions. All these persons are usually not mentioned among the philologists, but they deserve to be for their part in rendering possible or easier the communication of poetry.

In view of this enormous amount of philological work, the dilettanti of poetry and literature, fearing that they are expected to do some of it, cry out that there is no need for so much bustling around because poetry "speaks for itself." This is, undoubtedly, very true; but, in order to listen to poetry's voice, it is necessary to get close to it, and philology prepares the way. Philology does not give, they repeat, the capacity to feel poetry, and philologists in this respect are inferior to ignorant and simple minds and, generally, indifferent, unmindful, and almost hostile toward that form of spiritual expression on which they spend their lives; for they remain around it without going inside and content themselves with the calm joys of external research, lacking the desire to experience stronger excitement and more intense joy. But the aim of philology is not to provide sensitivity toward poetry, nor to substitute its own work for that sensitivity; its only goal is rather to develop in man, through the removal of difficulties and obstacles, the modest ability to reach the threshold of poetry. And if it is, unfortunately, a fact of experience that philologists, by the ordinary form of their talent or as a result of their exclusive specialization, generally do not feel poetry, it is to be hoped that they (those who can at least and to the extent they can), may remedy this deficiency, not only to avoid being in the grotesque situation of the "asinus portans mysteria" [ass bearing mysteries] (though this would concern the perfecting of the philologist and not that of philology), but also

"peregrino" is one of the seven varieties of falcons, that is, the "pilgrim falcon," thus clarifying and explaining the image. The phrase of Cacciaguida "Moronto fu mio frate ed Eliseo" (*Paradiso* 15. 136) could well be understood, as the majority of commentators understand it, to mean that he reveals that he had two brothers by those names; but philology, pointing out that the information is given in an awkward and not entirely correct grammatical form (and in that form is out of context and useless), interprets the phrase more accurately on the basis of the knowledge available concerning the Florentine families of that time, that is, that Cacciaguida meant to say, instead, that he had a brother, Moronto, who kept the family name of Eliseo, while the branch originated by Cacciaguida himself took the family name of his wife, Alighieri, who came from Val di Pado. And so on.

The dislike for philology. Often this dislike, which assumes the form of aversion for philology in its universality, is no more than a particular aversion for what is also usually called "hypercriticism," that is, arbitrary and capricious philology, which mistakes imagination for legitimate conjectures, and conjectures for established realities, and of which we have the worse proofs in classical philology with its corrupting of texts and its arbitrary corrections. Against this a return to the "acritical" tradition is invoked, which, not being guilty of that systematic arbitrariness, promises or seems to promise, by comparison, a greater genuineness. It is more or less like passing from excessive use of drugs, which damage the organism, to the temporary refusal of any drug whatever, or to the extreme reduction of medication in homeopathy (and, as a result, sometimes health reflourishes!). But often the aversion is aroused by the philologist's unawareness of the ends which philology serves; hence research for the sake of research, which deforms the body of philology into a sort of elephantiasis.

for the better conduct of philology itself, which must be prevented from falling into the complex, the useless, and the inappropriate and made to become more properly "philology," a friend of the "logos" or rather of poetic "language."

However, as we have noted, the obstacles are created not only by the lack, or the damages and the obscurity of the texts of poetry, but also by the soul torn by passions, which tend to drag within their orbit the sounds of poetry, interpreting and treating them as manifestations of what is loved or abhorred, and by the mind wrestling with false and confused doctrines, which lead it to seek in those sounds, under the name of poetry, expressions of an entirely different quality—prose, oratory, effusions, emotions. These are the same obstacles which poetry encounters in its self-creation and which return here under changed circumstances; and the remedies are substantially the same, with appropriate adjustments. As for passions and external interests, there is nothing else to do but wait for their appeasement or try to subdue them, in order to reach in oneself the serenity of mind needed for listening to poetry; as for the confusing and false doctrines and the theoretical prejudices and the bad philosophies, they must be defeated through criticism and a sound doctrine, through setting the superior against the inferior philosophy. Here, too, the usual dilettanti raise their voices to protest that philosophy is completely alien to the case and that one must avoid encumbering the mind with it, for the mind must remain open only to poetry. And again they bring forward an indisputable truth. But this truth must be taken rigorously, that is, that the mind must not be encumbered with bad philosophy, either; and that, when there is the intrusion of bad philosophy (as there always is, more or less), the exhortation to drive it out and forget it is not enough, for it cannot be forgotten by order. It then becomes necessary to put good philosophy to work. The latter, however, never intervenes to stand tediously, with its argumentations and problems, before poetry or to try to enter its sphere; on the contrary, having driven out the intruder and thus accomplished its function of policing and housecleaning, it discreetly takes its leave in obedience to its own principles. As a result, the spirit is left in an aphilosophical condition, that of "docta ignorantia," and, as it is said, disposed to receive the "pure impression" of poetry.

Such an "impression," which De Sanctis considered to be the sacred moment of the critic and advised that it not be lost or allowed to cool (for in that case the very consciousness of the work would be lost in the darkness of uncertainty), is in no way an ordinary im-

The learned and the ignorant in regard to poetry. One may ask how it happens that learned philologists in a position to explain every word and every historical reference in a poem are completely obtuse about understanding it and feeling it as poetry, whereas simple and naive minds, ignorant of history, understand and feel it, even if some particulars are obscure to them, or are, with little damage, misunderstood by them. The explanation can be given by pointing out that the words "ignorant of history" mean, in this case, simply those who lack "some historical information," but are not, as a consequence, bereft of that historical consciousness which accompanies life itself and which can be very strong and sure (by natural intuition, as we say) in the nonprofessional philologists. If to that historical sense, which life carries with itself, a natural opening toward poetry is united, one may clearly perceive the reason for the existence of a superior intelligence among simple people as compared to the barrenness of learned men.

pression as understood by vulgar impressionism, but it is an esthetic impression; it is no more and no less than the capacity to stay with poetry, to live with it, to trace back its creative process. And this capacity as such is always acquired even when, as in the happiest of cases, it seems to be completely natural and unrelated to any cultural preparation; for nothing in the universe is merely natural and unhistorical, and there is always a need for a major or minor degree of preparation in order to resume and continue life's work.

2. Skeptical Objections to the Possibility of Re-Evocation

Cultural or historical preparation, however, is not the act by which poetry is re-evoked and re-created; if such preparation purifies and predisposes the mind, it does not confer upon it the poetic warmth which must be self-generated; and, if it gives materially, or nearly so, the articulate sounds just as the author expressed and wrote them, it does not by doing so give his living word, his poetry.

And here we face a difficulty which seems at first insurmountable, because in order to relive the poet's words those sounds must be connected to their meaning and filled with the feeling and the reality which had already been their content. But, on the other hand, this feeling and this reality can only be found again in the transfiguration made by the poet, in the content-form, and therefore in the sounds in which he expressed them, and in no others.

To seek the content of poetic feeling in outer reality, as some try to do, is, if one reflects carefully, the puerile illusion of those who do not perceive the difference between philology and the interpretative-esthetic process, which is subsequent to philology; and they engage in compiling the inventory of the world of the poet in order to reach his poetry. It would be like undertaking the inventory of the universe; for the whole universe is contracted and condensed in the feeling and intuition of the poet. This would amount to opening a vicious progress to the infinite. And, in fact, even when the execution of the inventory is arbitrarily restricted to what seems to be most closely related to the personality of the poet, such as the political events of his time and his people, his loves and his hates, his failures and accomplishments in public and private life, his fortunes and misfortunes, his personal associations, the books he read and loved, and so on, all this can always prove too much and too little at the same time. Everybody knows and can verify the inconclu-

The act of the apprehension of poetry. In order to feel a poem, one must accomplish an act of interiorization without which the sounds in which the poem was expressed will be hollow. One looks without seeing, hears without understanding. To those who are in this situation, Goethe addresses an impatient exhortation in the epigram *Die Gedichte,* which we translate here:

Poems are like stained-glass windows:
windows that, looked at from the square,
show on the walls a line of bare, dark holes;
and this is the way common people look at them,
and then declare that they see nothing. But please enter
the temple once through the door and look! There
they are, figures and scenes, and sky and sea, all
appearing luminous in the glass.
Creatures of God, simple and happy, give
joy to your eyes and nourishment to your soul!

siveness and the spontaneous irony of such inquiries which pose as interpretations of poetry in numberless volumes—volumes that, after wandering outside the sphere of poetry and in domains having nothing to do with it, declare with satisfaction at the end of their excursions that this is the way to "explain" poetry. But, in truth, poetry (if we are allowed to personify it), in hearing the recitation of a long series of information—alien and indifferent to it and digressing from it—remains silent and astonished, or assumes the face of a sphinx.

Only those who believe poetry to be something practical among practical things and a logical illation among logical illations can be satisfied with such explanations; and, acting accordingly, consider the *Divine Comedy* to be a simple continuation of Dante's activities as a political partisan; the *Canzoniere* of Petrarch, a series of love notes to solicit the grace of Madonna Laura; the *Orlando Furioso*, an amusement like any other, by virtue of which Mr. Ludovico avoided the heavy duties as a courtier and administrator imposed upon him by his masters, the D'Estes; and the *Sabato del villaggio* and the ode *A Silvia* as symptomatic manifestations of the dropsy and the other ills afflicting Giacomo Leopardi. These interpretations, or similar ones, are read in the learned "literature" of the critics who called themselves "positivists."

But if one cannot depart from those sounds (although their spiritual meaning is only in the feeling and reality that the poet's fancy transfigured), is this not a desperate and vicious circle which is to be thrown out together with the presupposition from which it originated—the re-evocability of poetry? There are in fact simplistic and fundamentally unrefined intellects which do hesitate to cling mindlessly to this point of view and to maintain that every re-creation is really a new and different poem;[1] every reading of poetry is a fantastic writing and printing of another poem which flourished from that act in the spirit of the reader and which resounds in his own new words. But, by holding this view, one does not only deny the re-evocability, but even the essence itself of poetry, which is lowered to a practical act, always new and different because the course of things is always new and different; the hands cannot be wet twice in the same water of a river.

This is, in short, the nature of every esthetic skepticism, that is, confusion of poetry with practical action and practical-passional pleasure. This skepticism is the continuation of the traditional, which was en-

"Explanatio verborum" and the understanding of poetry. The German philologist Dübner—the one who worked a great deal for the editions of the Greek classics of Didot—and the French academician Désiré Nisard read together some passages from Homer. Nisard says of Dübner: "Pour l'exactitude, l'explication verbale, la notion de chaque mot, c'était merveilleux. Mais, pour le sentiment, il me sembla qu'il n'eût pas expliqué d'une autre façon un morceau d'Apollonius de Rhodes. Je me mis à commenter le passage à la manière française. Quand j'eus fini, Dübner me dit: —Pour que le grec ait tout son prix, il y faut l'explication philologique allemande et le commentaire français. —Je ne poussai pas la modestie jusqu'à n'être pas de son avis" (D. Nisard, *Souvenirs*, Paris, 1888, vol. 2, p. 7).

Indifference toward the beautiful and the ugly, and the negation of poetry. A philosophy which enjoyed some currency in the past years in Italian schools (cf. *Conversazioni critiche*, 2d ed., vol. 4, pp. 297–341) after denying, through the actuality of the act, the difference between true and false, and good and evil, finally turned its solemn attention to the sphere of poetry to negate the difference between beautiful and ugly.[32] Thus it has fully accomplished its program, and it can rest in peace in the tranquil awareness of having liberated mankind from its own whim.

---

1. Criticism of Gentile's theory concerning translation. See Gentile's *Philosophy of Art*, trans. G. Gullace (Ithaca and London: Cornell University Press, 1972), pp. lv–lvi, 216–219.

32. Gentile's philosophy.

trenched in the aphorism that "about taste (that is, pleasure) there is no ground for discussion." Immanuel Kant brought the aphorism to an end by demonstrating that in the human spirit there is a special quality of pleasure which must be discussed because it has a universal and absolute character and is bereft of practical interest, although it is distinct from the approbation which is given to conceptual thinking according to truth. The assertion of the "relativity of taste," which by this formula lowered poetry and beauty to a hedonistic phenomenon, is nowadays no longer the object of attack and defense, of acceptance or rejection, for it has completely ended the historical function which it exercised in the eighteenth century of making it imperative for philosophy to inquire into the problems of poetry and art. This inquiry showed the untenability of the "relativity of taste." Thus, after Kant, when the idea was resumed by some positivists, associationists, utilitarians, and evolutionists, it appeared to be no longer a theory, but a proof of their lack of culture. It reappeared at times in the pages of men of letters such as Jules Lemaître; but this proves simply that men of letters are not always reflective and that they do not delve deeply; in fact, Lemaître, who was a connoisseur and keen judge of poetry, shattered his skeptical theory with his own judgments while pretending on the other hand to shatter his judgments with his own theory. He was acting as one who coquettishly does too much while saying that he does nothing, and gives too much while saying that he gave nothing of worth.

Like skepticism in general, esthetic skepticism is the result of imagining that things are on one side and that men are on the other with their constantly varying feelings; thus the skeptics deceive themselves into believing that feeling is thinking and judging things; as a result, they are unable to get out of the sphere of their own feelings and they never reach the truth of things. Reality is not, however, made up of things and feelings, but only of acts; such is thought and fancy, and there are acts which do not realize themselves and their own end according to their own nature. The alleged disagreement among men about their conceptions and judgments, their moral ideals, the perception of the beautiful and the ugly—the disagreement that is the war horse happily ridden by the skeptics—may have a semblance of reality and may be allowed as a way of reciprocal understanding in ordinary conversation, but in actual reality the disagreement does not exist. Looking closely at the disagreements we are now considering in the sphere of poetry, we discover through the analysis of it, not disagreements, but diversity of acts which do not conflict

Criticism reduced to the narration of the adventures of the soul. Concerning Jules Lemaître, see my Nuovi saggi d'estetica, 3d ed., pp. 203–08. Far inferior to him as an expert in poetry is Anatole France, who proposed a theory according to which the critic must not distinguish the beautiful from the ugly and characterize them, but must do the only thing he can, that is, "raconter les aventures de son âme," through the reading of works of art. A witty and well-thought-out answer to this bad way of reasoning is found in a book which perhaps did not receive the attention it deserves: "Pour être franc, le critique devrait dire: — Messieurs, je vais parler de moi à propos de Shakespeare, à propos de Racine, ou de Pascal, ou de Goethe. C'est une assez belle occasion. —Mais pourquoi l'occasion est-elle si belle? Serait-elle donc moins belle s'il devait raconter les aventures de son âme au milieu des oeuvres de Paul de Kock, de Ponson du Terrail, de Xavier de Montépin ou de Zola?" (A. Wolkoff-Mouromtzoff, L'à peu près dans la critique et le vrai sens de l'imitation dans l'art, Bergamo, 1913, p. 3).

The various meanings of the word "beautiful." It is not worth dwelling on those judgments whose nonesthetic character is evident, though they avail themselves of the word "beautiful." Even in some positivistic esthetics, I think that I have read, as proof of the existence of a "visceral beauty," that peasants, after eating well and drinking better, say: I feel beautiful! But the times of that positivism are over for good, at least ideally, for those who, like myself, are no longer able to

against one another. Let us consider a short poem by Catullus: "Vivamus, mea Lesbia, atque amemus" [let us live and love, O my Lesbia],[2] presented to a crowd of people, some of whom judge it as beautiful, others as ugly. A first distinction must somehow be made concerning the crowd, because some or many of its components have not felt the poem to be either good or bad, but repeat the words heard from others or utter words without thinking in order to show that they are intelligent and learned and to present an appearance of enthusiasm or disdain. They do not, therefore, represent disagreements in their feelings; they are simply repeating what they heard. It is known through daily experience how great their contribution is in the domain of gossip, in which everyone displays his own vanity in regard to poetry, the other arts, philosophy, politics, and everything else. One would bestow upon them too much honor by raising them to the rank of opponents; in actuality this is not done and they are left to chat, no one paying attention to their admiration or vituperation, but rather smiling at their utterances. There remain the other two cases: the case of those who have really experienced a feeling of consent and pleasure and the case of those who have had a feeling of dissent and displeasure. But if that poem is beautiful it is impossible that the soul which has entered into relation with beauty has not experienced its joy and does not praise its beauty. Thus, for those who have experienced an opposite feeling, there is no other possible explanation except that in fact they have not entered into contact with poetry as such, but only with its subject matter, mistaking it (to continue the example of Catullus' poem) for the utterance of a moral act; and, judging this to be blameworthy, they call the poem ugly because it is the celebration of sensual joy and an invitation to forget in the storm of kisses to meditate on the trumpets of the final judgment and thus be prevented from sinning. This is confirmed by the fact that, whenever we recall the asserters of ugliness to the beauty of the poem they vituperated, and we recite it in such a way that they can feel it and their esthetic fiber is touched by it, we hear them repeat: "Yes, as form, it is beautiful, but as poetry it is ugly," or similar expressions. And those who feel, reason, and react thus, are legion and we shall not raise them to the rank of opponents, either. We shall call them moralists, incapable of breaking the wall of their exclusive passion, and arid in their heart and imagination. There remains, then, as a residue of our analysis, only the case of those who feel the beauty of what is beautiful, and for whom the specta-

2. *Poems (Catulli Veronensis Liber)* 5. 1.

take an interest, even a negative one, in such nonsense. If the metaphors and consequent conceptual confusions could be prevented by the etymology, a major help could be offered not by the word "bello" (if it is true that it derives from a "ben' lus"), but the German "schön" (if it is true that it derives from "schauen"—to contemplate): I say *if*, for etymology is, very often, a science more uncertain than metereology.

Apparent discordances in judgment. It is very difficult to be seriously in disagreement, in the matter of esthetic judgment, when one reads, for instance, the admiration of the German critics for Lessing's *Minna von Barnhelm* and for that work's dominant character, Major Tellheim, the "true incarnation of the rigid morality of the Prussian officer"; or for *Kabale und Liebe* by Schiller and for the character, young Ferdinand, who calls himself the "deutsche Jüngling," "the Young German"; or the admiration for *Die Räuber*, which was held as the "best poem of youth in all literatures" and as the anticipation and incarnation of "the French Revolution," thus joining hands with "Dostoevski's characters," and so on. As for me, I maintain that those critics greatly admire the Prussian military man, the "young German," the youthful inexperience and rebellion, and that they give no thought to what poetry is; and such being the case, I can understand them and be in sympathetic agreement with them. If they had their minds on poetry, if they had truly given attention to it, certainly they would have spoken very differently about those works; and in this case there would also be agreement.

Similarly, when one reads of the admiration of Huysmans and similar "delicate spirits" for Lucan, Prudentius, Sidonius, Paulinus of Pella, and so on, in preference to the "monotonous" Virgil and Horace, I can well applaud Lemaître, who counters: "Et vous avez tort . . . car c'est justement la versification de Lucain qui est monotone; et c'est la langue de Lucain qui est abstraite et sèche. Et quant à vos admirations pour les écrivains de l'extrême décadence, si elles sont sincères, grand bien vous fasse! Ils peuvent amuser un quart d'heure par leurs enfantillages séniles: mais ce sont eux qui sont des radoteurs et des crétins: lisez-les plutôt" (*Les contemporains*, vol. 1, p. 327). But, at the same time, I have the feeling that in this case we are again outside the judgment on poetry, and that the "thing" with which we are concerned here is the pleasure that a man with a nervous disorder may derive from things relating to his sickly condition, and the delight that a morally decadent person may derive from what "bene olet" [pleases] his sense of smell in times of decadence, or, perhaps even the pleasure of a

cle of conflicting feelings about the works of poetry disappears like a bad dream.

But to make it appear as daydreaming the "auctoritas humani generis" [authority of mankind] would be enough, even without a methodical demonstration. The constant and lively disputations about beauty and poetry, the relentless meditation on the principles governing them, or if nothing else the immense bulk of philological work called to their aid—a work which has been increasing and perfecting itself constantly: from the Alexandrian grammarians or the "ordinators" of the age of Pisistratus (just to take a starting point in time) to the Italian school of the Renaissance, to the French, Dutch, English, German, and the present-day European and American schools—reflect a widespread activity which poets such as Angelo Poliziano, the author of *Miscellanee*, did not disdain to participate in and to promote. It seems certain that such extensive, manifold, and serious labor would not have been undertaken and pursued by mankind (which on the whole is not in the habit of wasting time) if it were simply for the futile attempt to produce pleasures having a practical value—that is, giving men a palate and a stomach capable of enjoying and digesting the acorns and the raw meat which nourished and delighted their remote ancestors, or even the Spartan "black broth"; and making them taste with pleasure, alternating it with that of today, the cuisine of the Middle Ages or even that of the sixteenth and seventeenth centuries, which almost frightens us only from reading the recipes found in treatises; and God alone knows what would happen if these experiences were repeated. Certainly there is no better example than what the guests of Madame Dacier felt, when, according to an anecdote or a legend, she served precisely the "black broth."[3] It seems that the learned lady had found, through her philological knowledge, the ingredients for that dish and the way of preparing it; but she forgot to change the stomachs of the academicians she had invited to those of the ancient Spartans.

lazy man who amuses himself with the strange sensations he stimulates within himself. And here, too, I am not in disagreement.

I remember that one day, several decades ago, walking in the company of Salvatore di Giacomo, whom I had met in the street, we stopped to look at the shop window of an antiquarian, where an eighteenth-century portrait was exhibited.[33] This threw my poet friend into ecstasy, due to his tender sensitivity for whatever reminded him of the age of face powder and the minuet. And after he had warmly expressed to me his feeling in the presence of that work, suddenly, as though dropping a secondary observation, he said to me: "And yet this portrait is ugly, badly designed, and poorly painted!" Enchanting, therefore, as a reminder of the eighteenth century, but ugly as a painting. And here again, I did not feel any reason for disagreement, and did not engage in any controversy with him.

3. Madame Dacier (1654–1720), an enthusiastic admirer of ancient literature, particularly Homer, translated into French prose the *Iliad* (1699) and the *Odyssey* (1708) and other classical works, and played an important part in the controversy about the "ancients and the moderns" (La Querelle des anciens et des modernes), which was triggered by Boileau and Charles Perrault in 1687 and resumed later by others, until a sort of conciliation was reached in 1716.

33. *Salvatore di Giacomo, Neapolitan dialectal poet (1860–1934) whose work was highly admired by Croce.*

3. The Historical-Esthetical Interpretation

Since it is impossible to eliminate that vicious circle without eliminating the very idea of poetry, there is nothing more to do except look into the matter more carefully. If we do so, we will finally realize that that circle is not at all vicious, but rather (if you prefer) magic—the very magic by which in every moment we deeply understand one another, live and think because others live and think with us and in so doing are personal and social, individual and universal, single men and humanity.

By this magic we accomplish daily the miracle of understanding and comprehending the languages which we call foreign; and this is not achieved by having before our senses and intellect the objects, the customs, the events, the persons referred to in those languages, or by knowing the approximate and abstract correspondences of meaning of their articulated sounds with the abstract articulated sounds drawn from the manner of speaking that is familiar to us. All the knowledge furnished us by philology, certainly very useful, would remain disintegrated and inert without the fundamental and essential condition that we are speaking beings and that our interlocutor in a foreign language is a speaking being and that our intonations and his are homogeneous—both being the accent of our common humanity and, therefore, felt reciprocally by all through consensus or sympathy.

And new and foreign for us are not only the languages which we customarily so designate, but (to hold to the reality of the thing and to the rigor of the concept) every word we listen to is a new and foreign language because it was never spoken before and is not identified with any spoken before; in hearing it for the first time, we understand it only by means of one of those acts of consensus and sympathy which we have recognized as fundamental and essential. These acts of consensus are always the result of efforts, of "philological preparation," major or minor, apparent or hidden and almost invisible, drawn from books or from one's own memory, sometimes laboriously and slowly, other times easily and rapidly—so easily and rapidly and obviously that we cannot help feeling a certain astonishment in hearing it now designated by the solemn name of "philology." And every poem which is created and which we re-create in ourselves is nothing but the expression of a new language, since the illusion that the poets, and generally all speaking men, use articulated sounds as ready-made labels which they have only to arrange in a new order is a myth created by lexicographers and grammarians; and we shall not

Mutual understanding based on the foundation of our common humanity. The attempts to explain the reciprocal understanding among men speaking through imitations, associations, conversations, inferences, and the like, are so insufficient and powerless that, by comparison, it is preferable to accept the doctrine of the *"communicatio idiomatum"* through God's work, which even in its mythological form contains a truth within itself: men understand one another because they all exist, live, and die in God.

The difficulty for the new poetry to make itself understood. How difficult it is to understand the language of a truly new and original work! "Ce qui est cause qu'une oeuvre de génie est difficilement admirée tout de suite, c'est que celui qui l'a écrite est extraordinaire, que peu de gens lui ressemblent. C'est son oeuvre elle-même qui, en fécondant les rares esprits capables de la comprendre, les fera croître et multiplier. . . . Ce qu'on appelle la postérité, c'est la postérité de l'oeuvre. Il faut que l'oeuvre . . . crée elle-même sa postérité" (M. Proust, A l'ombre des jeunes filles en fleurs, vol. 1, pp. 144–45). Prior to Proust the same image had been used by Landor: "Until we find the door and the clue the new writer remains obscure. Therein lies the truth of Landor's saying that the poet must himself create the beings who are to enjoy his Paradise" (Havelock Ellis, The Dance of Life, p. 172). Proust also observes (A l'ombre, pp. 172–73): "D'ailleurs, toute nouveauté ayant pour condition

waste time here in refuting it again. Moreover, the dictum that every poem is a new language belongs to common experience and reflection; and beware when a poem is an old language, that is, a mechanical combination of already fixed forms, of words already spoken! For it simply becomes a little game (sometimes even sleight of hand) or mere accident similar to the legendary sponge of Apelle.[4] And this happens when the language—the sum of expressions already produced—poetizes instead of the poet, that is, without the intervention of the creative poetic spirit.

In this way, through articulated sound, the image which found expression in, and actually was, that sound enters at the same time the soul of the listener and the reader. And if there is still some obscurity and lacuna in the apprehension and understanding of it, it will be necessary to request and wait for new aid from "philology" (in the broad and also narrow sense in which this term is taken)—an aid that will dispel the obscurity and fill the lacuna, without the interference of our personal fancies. The feeling accompanying the re-creation of a poem is one of repugnance to such contamination and an act of reverence toward poetry, in the presence of which one must behave, according to a known simile, as though in the presence of a worthy man, with hat in hand, listening to what he says without interrupting him.

l'élimination préalable du poncif auquel nous étions habitués, et qui nous semblait la réalité même, toute conversation neuve, aussi bien que toute peinture, toute musique originale, paraîtra toujours alambiquée et fatigante. Elle repose sur des figures auxquelles nous ne sommes pas accoutumés, le causeur nous paraît ne parler que par métaphores, ce qui lasse et donne l'impression d'un manque de vérité. Au fond, les anciennes formes de langage avaient été elles aussi autrefois des images difficiles à suivre quand l'auditeur ne connaissait pas encore l'univers qu'elles peignaient; mais depuis longtemps on se figure que c'était l'univers réel, on se repose sur lui."

Poetry and the nation. It is an error to think that poetry can be felt only by the nation which produces it and in whose language it is written. Some estheticians, Schleiermacher among them, have fallen into this error (see my Ultimi saggi, 2d ed., pp. 164–65). But the mistake can be refuted with the simple observation that, since there are in the nation itself those who understand a poem in the national language and those who do not, clearly the comprehension is attained through something other than nationality. On the other hand, one must not ignore the fact that the comprehension of the poetry of a nation is enriched and deepened also through the experience and the observations of the readers and critics of other nations.

The language which is poetic in itself. It is said in the well-known epigram of Goethe:

*Weil es ein Vers dir gelingt in einer gebildenten Sprache
Die für dich dichtet und denkt, glaubst du schon Dichter
zu sein.*

(Since you wrote a successful verse in a cultured language which poetises and thinks for you, you already believe that you are a poet.)

Jules Lemaître noted that something similar often happened to Hugo: "Il a été le roi des mots. Mais les mots, après tant de siècles de littérature, sont tout imprégnés de sentiments et de pensée: ils devaient donc par la vertu de leurs assemblages le forcer à penser et à sentir. A cause de cela, ce songeur si peu philosophe a quelquefois des vers profonds; et ce poète, de beaucoup d'imagination que de tendresse, a des vers délicats et tendres" (Les contemporains, vol. 4, p. 138).

The slow acceptance of the new poetry. Poetic works may have a quick success for sentimental, conceptual, and practical reasons. But their poetry is always slow to penetrate, as can be proved by historical exposition of the fortune of poets. Of our nineteenth-century poets, Leopardi owed his European reputation to his avowed pessimism; his poetic enchantment only began to be felt in 1842 through the work of the young De

---

4. A sponge, soaked with a variety of colors, that Apelle, according to legend, threw against the mouth of the horse, he had painted, in order to give the magnificent effect of foam coming from the horse in battle.

The interpretation thus accomplished is historical; but not in the sense of a historiographical judgment, or this would take us outside poetry into the higher sphere of reflection; and not in the philological sense, either, for philology in itself is not history and has here simply an instrumental function. The interpretation is historical in the sense that it is not creation, but re-creation, and is done on an already existing (historically existing) poem, since nothing exists outside history. Such a historical interpretation has always been done and no other could have been possible; but to fix clearly this theoretical point and draw from it a detailed methodology, a more profound concept of history was necessary, a concept which began to develop toward maturity in the eighteenth century and continued to do so, in the midst of many controversies and interruptions, through the nineteenth century and which is still struggling toward its goal. Its adversaries are the relativists, the "contingentists,"[5] the phenomenologists, the actualists, who in the particular domain of poetry and art become hedonists.

But, in positing the historical character of the interpretation of poetry, one determines a moment it has in common with the interpretation of all other so-called expressions which have been analyzed and defined: prose, oratory, literature of entertainment, effusive literature—no work of which is understandable if it is not, with the aid of philology, felt and understood in its historical existence. Even immediate expression or nonexpression requires this historical interpretation, since as we know it is a "sign" which must not be integrated with imagination, but with the observation and the thinking of the reality for which it stands, in the same manner that the physician conducts his diagnosis. Poetry is a historical fact, but a historical fact having its own quality, diverse from the quality of

Sanctis; Foscolo owed his reputation to *Jacopo Ortis* rather than to the "smoky enigma" (as Giordani called it) of *I Sepolcri*,[34] to say nothing of *Le Grazie*, which in the long run appeared simply as material for an unfinished poem; Carducci was thought of for a long time as an Alexandrian, an indefatigable collector of historical erudition and, therefore, obscure. The fortune of poets is also interrupted by long periods of obscuration of their glory, of incomprehension or negation: ups and downs to which Homer and Dante and Shakespeare and all other great poets were subject.

On the theory of the historical interpretation of the beautiful. I have traced back the origin of this theory to the highest concept of history and its central importance in the life of the spirit. The concept had its beginning in some eighteenth-century thinkers and was exemplified by the peculiar contrast between Herder and the contingentist and phenomenalist Riedel (see one of my essays ["La teoria del guidizio estetico come guidizio storico"] in *Ultimi saggi*, 2d ed., pp. 135–46).

Fancies on fancies. By rejecting, as we must, criticism based on the principles of estheticism, we do not reject, nor could we, the natural flourishing of fancies on fancies through which the characters and the verses

---

5. "Contingentism" designates a nineteenth-century philosophical movement in France against materialism and positivism and the idea of *necessity* characterizing the laws of nature. The major representative of the movement, Emile Boutroux (1845–1921), gave it a complete formulation in his *De la contingence des lois de la nature* (1874).

34. *Foscolo's best and most widely known poem.*

other historical facts; and if, like the other facts, it originates from existing reality and like them goes beyond this determined reality, its "going beyond and creating" consist in the intuitive union and fusion of the particular with the universal, the individual with the cosmos; its point of departure (as Goethe once said about art in general) is the "characteristic," but its goal is "beauty."[6] Thus the historical interpretation of art is nothing but esthetic interpretation, which is not the negation of historicity nor an addition to historicity, but its true historicity. So one may as well call that interpretation "historical," meaning "historical interpretation of poetry," or "esthetic," signifying the interpretation "of poetry existing historically"; and only for didactic clarity, and not for eclectic combination, can it be called "historical-esthetical," since we are unwilling to coin a compound word of our own expressing more energetically the fusion of two elements, which are two in the abstract analysis, but one act alone in reality.

This allows us to understand the reason, and the unreason, of the two schools which compete in the domain of the interpretation of poetry and which battled much in Italy, especially during the first years of this century, which were so full of intellectual life. And the fight was not in vain, for these schools exhausted themselves in that senseless struggle (they could not exhaust themselves in any other way) and abandoned the field to their common adversary—the historical-esthetic interpretation which has been explained above and which is the only legitimate and true one. Of the two schools one assumed the title "historical" and should have been called at the most "historicistic" (marking it with a derogatory stigma), because its purpose was to interpret poetry, not as poetry, but as prose, oratory, and so on—elements which sometimes were found in poetry as added nonpoetic parts and which sometimes were not found at all, but were introduced, that is, imagined, thus misunderstanding and altering the very poetic parts. More often the school treated them only as documents of extrapoetic history in order to construct the biographies of the authors and the backgrounds of the lives of other peoples in other times.

The other school pompously called itself "esthetical," but, in its turn, it deserved the name "esthetizing" [*estetizzante*] with its derogatory stigma, because it set against the falsification of the historical interpretation of poetry a similar falsification of the esthetic interpretation—it set a caricature against another caricature. And appearing as caricatural characters were

of the poets acquire new meaning, sometimes more profound and more beautiful than the original. Certainly, "c'est beau, mais ce n'est pas la guerre": this is not criticism and history, the only things with which we are dealing here; and yet at times these fancies are not to be scorned. I, for instance, am unable to share the disdainful and compassionate smile of the experts in Latin phraseology, when they hear someone repeat the Virgilian "sunt lacrimae rerum" [Aeneid 1. 462], mistaking it for "the tears of things." Do you think that the thought of pain lying in things themselves and of things being filled with tears is laughable? Every quotation of a verse or image from a poet in reference to a concept (as is usually done with the prose of philosophers) acquires a diverse meaning from the one the poet originally intended—a meaning, if nothing else, richer in references. Who could or would prevent this?

The historical school and the esthetic school. It was the author of this book who, in the course of the discussions and polemics of the time, divested the two schools of the names by which they masked themselves illegitimately and rebaptized them as the "historicistic" school and the "estheticistic" school, respectively, with the result we mentioned. For other information, see my Letteratura della nuova Italia, 5th ed., vol. 2, pp. 97–102; and Problemi d'estetica, 4th ed., pp. 33–35.

---

6. *Der Sammler und die Seinigen*, letter 5 (Croce's note).

the pensive and grave yet naive interpreters of poetry as nonpoetry, as well as the happy but less naive and somewhat quackish ones who substituted the poetry of poets for their own semipoetry or the exhibitions of sham poetry. Now, this battling, as we said, is forgotten in Italy, where, if the number of the followers of the first school has shrunk and their importance has decreased, the followers of the second have almost disappeared. In this respect, some light made its way into the mind. But it seems that the same cannot be said of other cultured countries where the debate did not run its course or did not run it in a similar intense and radical manner; consequently, the benefits drawn from it have been much inferior and less solid. Nonetheless, if the historicistic and "estheticistic" theories as such can be declared outgrown and are discussed now as historical facts rather than questions open to controversy, one must be alerted to the tendency they represented—the tendency to historicize poetry badly, and the tendency to replace it with new and personal fancies—for these are perpetual sources of errors or dangers which mislead even those who reason theoretically and profess the right theory and have the good will to abide by it in their judgments.

A couple of examples may suffice to demonstrate these active dangers and the errors they generate. One of them is offered by the controversy on the manner of understanding ancient poetry, that is, the Greco-Roman, although by the expression "ancient poetry" one should mean all poetry which belongs more or less to the past and is detached and yet linked to us, that is, poetry which is not in the making, but which has already been produced and so can be interpreted. Whatever the case may be, it is well to insist on the necessity of avoiding the interpretation of poetry through contemporary and modern concepts and feelings, for this would lead, indeed, not to an interpretation but to a new fancy of ours, not unlike that of Cesarotti, who portrayed Homer with a wig and pigtail, flowery suit and sword—even if, rather than the eighteenth-century gentleman, one would today see in Cesarotti's portrayal more likely the nineteenth-century decadent.[7] In other words, we would in this way return to the manner of the estheticism already criticized. But when this estheticism is rejected with the idea that Greco-Roman poetry is to be interpreted by Greco-Roman feelings, we fall into the opposite error of historicism because the concepts and feelings and the

7. Melchiorre Cesarotti (1730–1808), a man of great learning and a professor of Greek and Hebrew in Padua. He believed that in order to enjoy the masterpieces of antiquity it was necessary to modernize them according to the taste of his time; to this end he translated, among other ancient works, the *Iliad* under the title *The Death of Hector*.

whole reality of which they were a part have been transfigured by poetry and have lost the historical and unilateral character in order to receive the human and all-inclusive character. The episode of Hector and Andromache and that of Nausicaa and the Island of the Phaeacians are not taking place in Greece or in any other part of the earth, not in a particular moment in time, but in an ideal place and in time eternal. The Greek language, the knowledge of historical events and customs and all the other necessary things provided by philology for our understanding, are no more than ladders to climb to a sphere in which those ladders no longer have any use, to a heaven from where one has lost sight of the earth. If we want to have a direct experience of this truth, we need only take a look in reading Homer at the figures that in some editions accompany the various cantos and which are derived from vases and gems and paintings and sculptures of warriors on chariots, of archaic deities, of priests with miters, of people crossing the seas on ships belonging to a previous era, and the like; and one will feel disgust and nausea rather than uneasiness. What is the purpose of these little men, these barbaric idols, these representations of battles and seafaring in the midst of Achilles and Ajax, of Athena and Aphrodite, of the battles being fought in the *Iliad* and the seas being crossed in the *Odyssey*? And if we want to remember another experience, we may think of the aversion of the true poets (unlike the poetasters) to setting their pictures on the front page of their books, and of the disappointment of the readers who do not find their poets in realistic pictures. This originally prompted the idea of the "ideal picture" of the poet (so much so that even the aforementioned poetasters often have themselves portrayed with thick hair and eyes turned heavenward as they await inspiration). Moreover, the care the poets take in hiding information concerning persons and facts which served as a pretext and subject are well known, as are the stupid and odious revelations of this nature by which scholars believe they are throwing light on poetry, and the indignation of Goethe when he was subjected to this kind of torture, in anticipation of the glory of his name. What advantage could one obtain, what consolation could one enjoy in making the personal acquaintance of Lesbia, Cynthia, Beatrice, Laura, Charlotte, Fanny, Aspasia, Nerina, and Silvia, of the "brown woman," the "veiled woman," if not that of measuring once again the well-known distance between the imaginary human love and factual reality, and the bigger distance between love and poetry?[8] At

8. Some of these names, such as Beatrice and Laura, are well known.

The nonhistorical nature of poetic characters and scenes. The invective that Henri Becque levels at Taine on this subject is very amusing in reference to Hamlet: "Laissez-moi donc tranquille avec votre homme du XVIᵉ siècle! Nous n'admettons qu'un personnage retrouve tout à coup son siècle," and so on (see it, reported at length and commented on, in my *Conversazioni critiche*, 2d ed., vol. 3, pp. 390–94).

Improper historical determinations given to poetry. "These images must be looked at from a distance. If you get too close, you destroy them. You discuss whether Nerina was the daughter of a coachman or of a hatmaker. Alas! You have destroyed Nerina" (De Sanctis, in the essay "La Nerina di Giacomo Leopardi").[35] This is an old but not yet abandoned vice of criticism in Germany, a criticism which engages in similar research on the precise and documented reality of the persons and the events reflected in poetry, as though poetry were a mirror. It Italy, for about seventy years, such a distortion by German criticism was proved and denounced by Vittorio Imbriani (cf. my book *Goethe*, 4th ed., vol. 2, pp. 118–20).[36]

At this very moment I happen to see, in a methodological dissertation, the first two lines of *Le balcon*, by Baudelaire, which were presented as a proof of the tight connection between biography and poetry and of the necessity to refer to the former in order to understand the latter:

Mère des souvenirs, maîtresse des maîtresses,
Ô toi, tous mes plaisirs! ô toi, tous mes devoirs! . . .

The last hemistich, the critic remarks, would mean nothing, or very little, "pour un lecteur, même attentif, mais ignorant la destinée affreuse de la mulâtresse alcoolique que Baudelaire protégea fidèlement, même

35. Nerina, the name of a young girl, loved by the poet, who died in her youth. She appears in Leopardi's poem "Le ricordance" (Remembrances).

36. The work by Imbriani (1840–1886) referred to here is *Un capolavoro sbagliato* (Goethe's *Faust*). The 1st ed. of Croce's *Goethe* was published in 1919. The 4th ed. (1946) is in 2 vols., vol. 2 containing a selection of poems in the Italian translation. Only vol. 1 is available in English.

99

most this may help verify what was suspected by a writer, whose name now escapes me, that all those women were ugly and, in their feelings, words, and gestures, little different from servants.

pendant ses années de noire misère." Now those words, for the reader who is ignorant of Baudelaire's erotic-sentimental affairs, mean fully as much as they ought to mean, by telling of a woman toward whom are directed all of the thoughts, the intentions, the efforts, and the industriousness of the man who loves her ("*tous mes devoirs*"), because she is the source of all the delights that he has on earth ("*tous mes plaisirs*"). The knowledge of biographical events not only fails to add anything necessary, but also brings in something superfluous (the "mulatto," the "alcoholic," and so on), which distracts the reader from the vision of the lyric—among the most beautiful by Baudelaire—and may even arouse in him a sort of disgust similar to that of Manzoni vis-à-vis an erotic-celebrative ode by Parini, which made him ponder on the obscene and coarse Venetian lady who had inspired the eighteenth-century abbot. While the lyric has purified the troubled waters of reality, we are trying to throw the sediments into the pure and filtered water again and then stir it. In still another lyric by Baudelaire [*Les Fleurs du mal*, c]: "*La servante au grand coeur dont vous étiez jalouse. . . ."* Who is "*vous*"? The text does not say. And it does not matter, for everybody feels in this accent a rivalry among different forms of affection, be it the rivalry of the mother, the sister, the wife, or the mistress toward the humble woman who has raised the poet and whom she loves with pure devotion—the woman he always seeks because of her constant affection; and, if she is alive, he seeks her in life; if she is dead, in his memory. But the knowledge of Baudelaire's biography, observes the same critic, adds something which is lacking because of the indeterminateness of the "*vous*": the bighearted servant's name was "Mariette"; and "*c'est avec une émotion réelle que l'on revoit l'enfance tragique du poète: Madame Aupick, remariée, mère médiocre mais non insensible, désespérée quelquefois de voir son fils lui échapper, grande dame luttant contre la femme du peuple à laquelle l'enfant se cramponne. A qui devons-nous, cette image troublante? Au texte, qui nous laisse ignorer l'identité du 'vous'? Ou bien aux historiens Crépet?"* (H. K. Brugmans, "*Défense de la dialectique," Neophilologus* 21 [1935], offprint, p. 8). But this "*émotion réelle*" is well defined as "*une image troublante*," because it, in fact, muddles and disturbs the reading of the poem, recalling the particular circumstances of one of the many cases of children who, being neglected in their infancy by their mothers, were loved and protected by the servant.

The historical meaning of a poem. The tenacity with which critics persist in seeking the historical meaning of a poem, that is, the event, the action, or the ethico-

---

For the benefit of those who are unfamiliar with the other names, we shall identify them, even at the risk of redundancy: for Lesbia, see above, n. 2; Cynthia was the woman to whom Propertius devoted the first two books of his *Elegies*; Charlotte is the feminine character in Goethe's *Sorrows of Young Werther*; Fanny is possibly Fanny Brawne, the woman loved by John Keats; Silvia, Aspasia, Nerina appear in Leopardi's poems—the first two in the poems bearing these fictional names as titles, the third in the poem entitled *Le Ricordanze* (The remembrances).

Another example is the obstinacy with which the aims of the poets and their concepts continue to be investigated by asserting that the knowledge of these is indispensable for the understanding of their poetry. And it would be pertinent here to ask, in a preliminary and methodic way, how one could in this case go about understanding the poetry of those poets who did not propose any "aim" and did not have any "concept" of the very feeling that they truly represented, since it is certainly impossible to maintain that the poet needs an aim or a concept, that is, that he must also be an orator or a philosopher.

But the truth is that even those among them who are orators and philosophers and have aims and concepts cannot, as poets, express them because aims and concepts are expressed only in oratory and prose. Therefore, in the creative process of their works, they set aims and concepts aside or detach them or keep them only as particular rhythms of their feelings, stripped of their cold conceptuality and stark practicality. Only an optical illusion can make us see in the Greek tragedy the idea of fate, or in the work of a Christian poet that of providence, for both "fate" and "providence" are concepts and therefore thinkable and not representable; and what is represented will always and only be a feeling of terror and resignation under the name of fate, and a feeling of confidence and hope under the name of providence; they are lights and shadows, not concepts. The poets, when asked about fate, providence, justice and injustice, the laws of the gods and those of men, and when they are accused of impiety in such matters, should answer as Paolo Veronese did when called before the tribunal of the Inquisition for having introduced in one of his paintings

political tendency expressed in it, shows basically a deficiency of poetic sense or, at least, of the idea of what exactly poetry is. To awaken from such hard dogmatic slumber, one would do well to reflect that historical meaning, sought in poetry, is always found in antipoetry or bad poetry (needless to say that it is perfectly in its proper place in nonpoetry or literature); and that there is no sadder funeral for a poet than to say that he already "belongs to history," and no longer to the eternal human soul. Béranger was greatly acclaimed and exalted for about thirty years in France and outside France; but when no one wanted to hear of him any more and he was compared to "une étoile filante," a French poet said, in disagreement and praise: "Si elle tombait du ciel de la poésie, elle s'arrêterait non moins brillante dans le firmament de l'histoire." To which was rightly added the gloss: "Suprême consacration aux yeux des historiens, chute dernière aux yeux des poètes" (P. Moreau, "Le mystère Béranger," Revue d'histoire littéraire de la France 40 [1933]: 208). See also one of my short notices concerning Pascoli's saying that poetry needs the "patina of time": a poet that consoles himself in such thoughts, I said, would resemble those who, because of the scarce interest they arouse while alive among their contemporaries, console themselves in the thought that one day glory will come and their cadavers will attract the eyes of the curious as do the mummies in a museum (Conversazioni critiche, 4th ed., vol. 1, pp. 73–75).

Objections concerning the impossibility of reliving the past. It has been noted that we moderns cannot "have an adequate idea of the importance that the Greeks attached to their gymnastic games in general and to the four national competitions in particular," nor can we, above all, "get interested, to any degree, in their way of feeling"; hence "the major difficulty in understanding and enjoying Pindar's poetry" (see the development of this objection in the introduction of Fraccaroli to his translation of Pindar, 2d ed., Milan, 1913, I, pp. 58–64). But, insofar as Pindar was a poet, he was transcending that idea and that feeling, and we, by transcending them too, do understand and feel what in his work is poetry. Not only the gymnastic games of the Greeks, but also all the particularity of the customs and the feelings of men in history are felt by us, not directly, like those who lived the experience, but only as they resound in our actual feeling, with a greater or smaller participation or indifference, or in a similar and diverse manner at the same time. As a result of this, it has been said that history itself, every history, is always "contemporary history."

Italian literary criticism. May I be permitted to add

a figure which conflicted with the sacred history from which he had drawn the subject.[9] He said that he was painting "with the consideration that his intellect was able to understand"; that the figure of which he was accused was added "as an ornament" because he needed a certain color or shade of color whether it was in the "story" or not; and that, finally, painters "take the license that poets and madmen take."

here that in the strong emphasis given on the "lyricity" of every kind of poetry and art and, therefore, on the nonhistorical character of their images, lies perhaps one of the principal and most substantial reforms introduced in Italian criticism after De Sanctis, which carries with it a reform in the construction of the history of poetry, distinguished, in this respect, from the history of literature.

4. The Hatred for the Ugly, the Indulgence toward Imperfections, and the Indifference for the Structural Elements

The reader of a poem, by identifying himself with the author and by expanding his soul into the soul of the author, rises like him above individual interests and affections in a given situation and cleanses himself through a catharsis similar to that of the author and like him opens his soul to the joy of beauty.

But the opposite happens to him in the presence of sham poems, of things presenting themselves with a semblance of poetry in which he discovers, when trying to re-create and enjoy them, none but practical things—things called "ugly" because of their deceptiveness. In this discovery he suffers disappointment and displeasure, whereas he who produced them experienced great enjoyment. And it could not be otherwise, for he who constructs things which are ugly for others entertains the belief and the illusion that he is constructing works of beauty and that he is satisfying his own ambition, flattering his own vanity and proving to himself and to others that he is a man of genius, an artist and a creator. The bad poet "gaudet in se et se ipse miratur," [is happy with himself and full of self-admiration], and for this contentment of his he very often presents himself in social life as courteous and agreeable, "venustus et dicax et urbanus" [charming, witty, and urbane], exactly as did the Suffenus depicted by Catullus[10]—the Suffenus who, in writing verse: "unus caprimulgus aut fossor videtur" [gives the impression of being a goat milker or a digger]. When he writes verse he is a butcher, a torturer of the ear and the imagination; and, consequently, cultivated people of taste keep clear of him. He instead seeks them out, cajoles, courts, and flatters them, alluring them in order to nourish his illusion with praise and to increase the pleasure of his vanity. Satire and comedy provide the means to deflate bad poets;

The contentment of the bad poet. To the satirical portrait, given by Catullus, one may add the verses of Horace (Epistles 2. 2. 106–08):

> Ridentur mala qui componunt carmina: verum
> gaudent scribentes et se venerantur et ultro,
> si taceas, laudant quidquid scripsere beati.

[Bad poets are ridiculed: yet they rejoice in writing and they worship themselves, and, if you remain silent, will even praise their senseless writings.]

The situation turns to a tragic one in Shakespeare's Julius Caesar (act 3, sc. 3), in the encounter of the poet Cinna with the furious plebeians:

Third pleb.: Your name, Sir, truly.
Cinna: Truly, my name is Cinna.
First pleb.: Tear him to pieces; he is a conspirator.
Cinna: I am Cinna the poet, I am Cinna the poet.
Fourth pleb.: Tear him for his bad verses, tear him for his bad verses.

But, except in the wild imagination of Shakespeare, society does not punish bad poets; it leaves them in their illusions and pleasures. A case, perhaps unique, of disciplinary punishment inflicted upon one of them is found in Diario politico, by Margherita di Collegno (Milan, 1926), in the entry of June 1, 1852: "We have seen something new in these days. The Minister of Public Education inflicted a punishment on a professor

9. See L. Venturi, *Storia dell'arte italiana* 9. 4. 752–54 (Croce's note).
10. *Poems* 22 (Croce's note).

but perhaps no vengeance equals the torture they inflict on others, in which they show themselves to be more annoying and persistent than any troublesome buzzing and stinging mosquito.

And if the worst poets are less hated than either the mediocre or the merely bad ones, it is because the worst ones are less dreadful and more easily singled out and ostracized by everyone. If our hate does not strike at the open and frank manufacturers and merchants of ugly things, it is because these people do not bother anyone who does not look for them. Ordinarily, well aware of the worthlessness of their works, they modestly and intelligently will tell you: "Don't read my novel, it is not for you"; or they even imitate the just zeal of Nana's impresario who, when someone would talk to him about his "theater," would interrupt with annoyance and anger: "Do not call it my theater; call it my whorehouse." [11]

Nevertheless, not even the horror of ugliness should push one to such an extreme as to change this horror to an *odium auctoris* and the accompanying prejudices, thus presenting one's enjoyment of poetry wherever one finds it; for, as it sometimes flourishes solitarily on arid intellectual rocks and in other inhospitable places, so may it also flourish among ugly things. "Malgré son fatras obscur,/ souvent Brébeuf étincelle," said Boileau; [12] and in a different sense Petrarch said: "Ma tarde non fur mai grazie divine" [but divine gifts were never tardy] [13] And there are those who, after years and years of bad literature, finally produce, when least expected, a short story or a drama genially conceived; and there are, as we know, one-sonnet poets.

If Suffenus is satisfied with himself, Virgil is not, because he constantly feels the imperfections of his own work, thinks about them, tries to correct them without always succeeding. His dissatisfaction goes as far as ordering, while dying, that the papers containing the *Aeneid* be burned. The imperfections of a work do not make it an ugly one; an ugly work is a non-poetic work, which lives on (if it does) for reasons other than poetic; whereas the work born as poetry leaves on earth, like a celestial creature, the mark of its passing. The poet (like the moral man who in his acts is never free of certain defects) suffers from the defects he perceives in his work, and he would like to

of literature of Grenoble for having written bad verses." Sometimes, even bureaucracy is witty.

Anecdote about composers of verses. To scatter with a few brief laughs these historical-critical postscripts— to render pleasant ("amenizar," as the Spaniards say) the discourse—I beg permission to point out that I have had personal experience with the great bravery, the imperturbable courage with which poetic vanity (and perhaps every kind of vanity) infuses the mind. For, by coincidences which do not call for mention here, I happened to be deserted in my own town not only by legions of so-called friends (Rutebeuf knew and qualified them well: "Ce sont amis que vent emporte,/ Et il ventait devant ma porte"),[37] but also by men of letters and by scholars, who would have liked to continue or to engage in intellectual relations with me, but did not dare. Well, the only ones who remained faithful to me and in fact increased in number, the only ones who showed themselves to possess courageous determination at all costs are the composers of verses, who keep on sending me their products, printed or in manuscripts or typescripts, with very kind and courteous letters requesting my judgment. Bad poetry, then, much more firmly than the "mens solida," challenges that "ardor" and that "vultus," which have become famous, and in certain times and countries have even become proverbial of one of the major odes by Horace (3. 3: ["Strength of the Righteous"]).

Sporadic poetry. "Un homme de goût, longtemps en contact avec son poète, peut rendre ainsi l'étincelle une fois, sans que cela tire à conséquence" (Saint-Beuve, *Tableau de la littérature française au seizième siècle*, Paris, II, p. 376). Among those who succeeded or whose one poem alone survived is the French Félix Arvers, with the sonnet: "Mon âme a son secret, ma vie a son mystère. . . ."

Poetry wherever it is found. I would like to go on pointing out, as examples, the poetry which emerges where one would expect it the least. There was at one time in San Vitale of Ravenna the epitaph (preserved by Paolo Diacono) of one Alemannian, Droctulft, who had abandoned the Lombards in order to defend that city against them. The versified epitaph contained an attestation of gratitude for that man who had sacri-

---

11. Nana, main character in Zola's novel by the same title. She is a vaudeville actress who attracts the spectators with her beauty and nudity, and is exploited by her avid impresari, who push her impudence to counterbalance her poor voice.

12. The two lines appear in an epigram by Boileau. See *Oeuvres poétiques* (Paris: Firmin Didot, 1859), p. 403 (epigram 27). Brébeuf (1617–1661), a greatly admired poet of his times, became one of Boileau's victims (see *Art poétique*, chant 1, *Epître* 8, and *Le Lutrin* 5).

13. *Trionfi: Il Trionfo dell'Eternità*, 1. 13.

37. "La complainte Rutebeuf," ll. 122–23, *Oeuvres complètes* (Paris: Picard, 1969), vol. 1, p. 557.

remove them all, even the least trace. He always dreams of sending it throughout the world as (according to the image that Iacopone found for the Soul)[14] the king of France sent his beloved daughter and only heiress, "dressed in a white stole," and resplendent in her candor to the eyes of the beholders of "all countries." But poetry visits the mind with the flash of lightning and the human work follows, attracted and fascinated by it and grasping from it as much as it can; in vain does one ask it to stop and allow itself to be looked at more closely; but at other times it does not come back at all; and the poet remains with his words, both the luminous and the opaque, which wait and beseech and may or may not obtain the ray that enlightens them. So Virgil, in order not to lose the whole for the part or the particle, the maximum for the minimum, thus allowing the happy moment to flee, resigned himself, according to his biographer, to writing some imperfect lines or composing them in a tentative manner (". . . ne quid impetum moraretur, quaedam imperfecta transmisit, alia laevissimis versibus veluti fulsit") [so that nothing might delay the impulse of inspiration, he wrote down certain things imperfectly, certain others he marked as though in tentative verses],[15] consoling himself and joking with his friends by calling those verses "supports" ("tibicines"), which served to support the building until he could replace them with solid columns. And the poet suffers for those imperfections and would like to remedy them; yet, as though because of a sacred reverence toward the mystery which acted in him, he hesitates to touch them with a cold mind for fear of damage; for a cool mind is not warm fancy, and the file is a dangerous instrument, which can "refine" but can also ."exterere," as Quintilian said, that is, take away the best.[16] The poet, then, can only ask for indulgence, as implicitly as did Dante, admitting that many times the form does not conform to the intention of art, "perchè a risponder la materia è sorda" [the matter being deaf to summoning;][17] as Goethe did explicitly, begging not to overuse a correcting or cautioning hand and not to stop the poet's mill while it is turning because "those who understand us know also how to forgive us."

14. Iacopone da Todi (ca 1230–1306), mystic poet, born in Todi (Umbria), author of *Laudi spirituali*. Croce's reference here is to "Laude 25."

15. Aelius Donatus, *Vita Vergiliana*, sec. 24. Croce's quotation was corrected because inaccurate.

16. *Institutionis oratoriae* 10. 4. 3. The phrase reads: " . . . that the file polish our work, and not wear it down to nothing."

17. *Paradiso* 1. 129.

ficed his affection for his dear ones to the new homeland ("contempsit caros, dum nos amat ille, parentes/ hanc patriam reputans esse, Ravenna, suam" [he scorned his own dear parents to love us, considering Ravenna to be his fatherland]). But in dictating these distichs, the unknown author is taken by a lyric-epic vision of Droctulft, and in a few lines sculpts him in his physical strength and in his majesty and humanity of barbarian: "Terribilis visu facies, sed mente benignus,/ Longaque robusto pectore barba fuit!" [Dreadful he looks on sight, but kindly is his spirit./ And with his long beard falling upon his robust chest].

From the day I read *Rerum langobardicarum scriptores*, this Droctulft entered the legion of poetic figures that live in my memory.

The flashing of poetic inspiration. Shelley dwells on this point: "A man cannot say: 'I will compose poetry.' Even the greatest poet cannot say it; for the mind in creation is as a fading coal, which some invisible influence, like an inconstant wind, awakens to transitory brightness; this power arises from within, like the colour of a flower which fades and changes as it is developed, and the conscious portions of our natures are unprophetic either of its approach or its departure. Could this influence be durable in its original purity and force, it is impossible to predict the greatness of the results; but when composition begins, inspiration is already on the decline, and the most glorious poetry that has ever been communicated to the world is probably a feeble shadow of the original conceptions of the poet. I appeal to the greatest poets of the present day, whether it be not an error to assert that the finest passages of poetry are produced by labor and study" (*A Defence of Poetry*).

The unity of inspiration. In a letter by Clausewitz there is an acute observation by Madame de Staël: "Madame de Staël," wrote Clausewitz from Lausanne on August 16, 1807, "complained about the long sentences in German prose. I remarked that this length has nevertheless a certain energy: she struck back by saying that this advantage, providing it does not cost too much, is unquestionable: 'car il serait à désirer de pouvoir rendre tout un livre par un seul souffle.' Certain persons in society would have estimated that I uttered a gross stupidity, if the beautiful observation of Madame de Staël had not surpassed what I said" (K. Schwartz, *Leben des Generals Carl von Clausewitz*, Berlin, 1878, vol. 1, pp. 286–87).

The indulgence poets demand. Racine in his first preface to *Britannicus* wrote: "Ceux qui voient le mieux nos défauts sont ceux qui les dissimulent le plus volontiers: ils nous pardonnent les endroits qui leur ont déplu en faveur de ceux qui leur ont donné du plaisir."

Poetic minds, men of serious taste, great minds, and generous hearts promptly grant this forgiveness, in poetry as well as in morality, looking at the substance of a work as well as the substance of an action and a life; whereas the Zoïluses of all times behave in a peevish and inexorable manner (which is found in the area of morality in those "servants" for whom there are no "great men" and who notice every single hair on the master's suit): the Zoïluses who write the detailed catalogue of the poet's imperfections, of his oversights, his errors and who, when they want to praise him, put next to these the catalogue of merits and beautiful things; but they are unable to understand that the defects can exist by virtue of the merits, the particular uncertainties and blunders because of the impetuosity of the power pervading the whole, and that one must always start from the center and not dwell on the periphery. Alfieri presents a great deal of harshness and intellectualistic abstractness, but despite that he is a poet, greater than the smooth Metastasio,[18] always perfect in his own way. *Il cinque maggio* by Manzoni has many times been censured line by line and phrase by phrase, and not always without reason; despite that, it is a great lyric. In the presence of interpreters who boast of being "exquisite" and "subtle" and are praised for supposedly being so and who point out and underline the imperfections and the weak points of poets as though they have made glorious discoveries through their sensibility and acumen, the poetic reader and the man of serious taste feel a surge of impatience and uneasiness, as though they want to say: "Why, yes! We had seen these things, too, and before you; only we did not want to point them out and underline them, because we did not have to."

And Rabelais humorously said: "*Bon soir, messieurs, perdonatemi, et ne pensez tant à mes fautes que ne pensez bien es vostres*" (bk. 2, chap. 34).

The interpretation dear to the poet. Pascoli, who praised imperfection, quoted willingly the distich of Martial: "*Omnia vis belle, Matho, dicere. Dic aliquando/ Et bene: dic neutrum; dic aliquando male*" [You want to say everything well, Matho. Speak sometimes well, sometimes neither well nor badly, sometimes even badly] (*Epigrams*, bk. 10, 46). In any event, we must keep in mind that this epigram is not really addressed to a poet, but to a legist who was fastidious about his constantly flowery speech. In reality, the poet does not like the extrinsic perfection of art: he seeks perfection indefatigably and resigns himself to imperfection only when nothing else can be done for fear of the worst.

The balance sheet of merits and demerits. Perhaps there is no form for the judgment of poetry more stupid than that which, instead of saying the only thing of interest, that is, if a poem is or is not poetry, says that it has such and such defects, but is redeemed by such and such merits; and among the redeemable faults may happen to be the lack of inspiration or of originality, that is, the lack of poetry! I take at random one of these judgments which is at hand: "*Sans doute, on a toujours reproché à J.-B. Rousseau la stérilité de son imagination, mais qui se trouve compensée par le choix judicieux de celle des anciens, soit sacrés soit profanes, qu'il a revêtu d'un éclat de style,*" and so on. This type of judgment corresponds to many others found in books, particularly those written by professors who are accustomed to giving marks of merit and demerit to their students in the various subjects and then drawing an average for the purpose of passing or failing them; and these professors carry this mental habit (dangerous even in education) into the judgment of poetry.

A famous sonnet by Ronsard.

> *Quand vous serez bien vieille, au soir à la chandelle,*
> *Assise au près du feu dévidant et filant,*
> *Direz chantant mes vers, en vous esmerveillant:*
> *—Ronsard me célébroit du temps que je estois belle.*
>
> *Lors vous n'aurez servant oyant telle nouvelle,*
> *Déjà sur le labeur à demy sommeillant,*
> *Qui au bruit de mon nom ne s'aille resveillant,*
> *Bénissant vostre nom de louange immortelle.*[38]

Poetry is all here. The two tercets are allowed to be with the rest because without them the sonnet would not be complete; but, whether Ronsard started with the thought contained in them to arrive later at the

---

18. Pietro Metastasio (1698–1782), Italian poet, very popular and greatly admired in his own times for his many melodramas, a genre which he brought to technical perfection.

38. *Les amours*, bk. 3: "Sonnets pour Hélène."

In poetry we encounter not only imperfections which by definition are corrigible and in fact are, most of them, corrected in the course of the work or by a return of the creative moment; but we encounter also unpoetic things which are not corrigible and which do not arouse in the reader, as they did not in the author, either displeasure or reprobation, but are regarded with a certain indifference. These are the conventional or structural parts existing in every poetic work, sometimes hardly visible and at other times very prominent, especially in works of great extension and complexity. A typical case of these conventional and structural parts is that in which they are added as fillers interposed between poetic parts, and which were called "chevilles" in French and "zeppe" in Italian,[19] and which Galileo designated as "intarsiature," and Gino Capponi as "arithmetical parts."[20] This is a vice (said Foscolo) that no poetic talent "can avoid," a "defect" that cannot "humanly be escaped."[21] With these words one comes to recognize that they are not, properly speaking, defects and vices, otherwise they could be avoided. Where do they really originate? From the necessity of retaining the rhythmical unity of the expression even with the sacrifice, in some parts, of the coherence of an image to a sound which is itself an image corresponding to the poetic motif. We may re-

19. Fillers, paddings, expletives.

20. Gino Capponi (1792–1876), Italian historian, pedagogist, patriot, born in Florence of an ancient noble family.

21. Ugo Foscolo (1778–1827), one of the major Italian poets of the nineteenth century. His poetic masterpiece is *I Sepolcri* (1807). Translated into Italian Sterne's *Sentimental Journey* (1813). Died in London, where he spent the last eleven years of his life in self-imposed exile. Wrote in English a number of critical essays. See his *Saggi di letteratura italiana*, ed. Cesare Foligno (Firenze: Le Monnier, 1958), 2 vols.

poetic quatrains or whether he added the tercets to the quatrains, born first in his imagination, they [the tercets] remain like a frame alien to the poetic element:

> Je seroys sous la terre et, fantôme sans os,
> Par les ombres myrteux je prendray mon repos.
> Vous serez au foyer une vieille accroupie,
>
> Regrettant mon amour et votre fier desdain.
> Vivez, si m'en croyez, n'attendez à demain.
> Cueillez dès aujourd'hui les roses de la vie.

In these, as happens with things that do not flow naturally, the author forces his hand on his own images and spoils them. He does so with that "vieille accroupie," so unkind as compared to "bien vieille" in the first quatrain, and with a return not only to the same image, but also to "foyer," where the old lady would be crouching.

I have analyzed an analogous case of poetry, which flourishes in the midst of an artificial thought or of a theme foreign to it, particularly in connection with Petrarch's sonnet: "Movesi il vecchierel canuto e bianco" [Slowly walks the little old white-haired man]. (See *Conversazioni critiche*, 2d ed., vol. 3, pp. 215–26).

Mediocre but flawless poetry. The ancients already reproached those who preferred mediocre but flawless poetry to great but faulty poetry, that is, those who preferred Apollonius to Homer, Bacchylides to Pindar, Ion to Sophocles, and so forth: see *On the Sublime*, chap. 33 and following, where it is explained why inaccuracies and negligences are found in great works, while faults are easily avoided in humble and mediocre ones.

Inevitable padding. "There is no poetic talent that in rhyme, and more often in the octave, can avoid the vice that Galileo, very clearly and philosophically, calls 'intarsia,' accusing Tasso of it and contrasting Tasso's padding with the roundness and fullness of Ariosto's poetry. I shall not excuse Tasso for it, but I shall blame the meter and dare accuse of illiberality and partisan furor the censor, since Tasso's padding shows at least that he tried to cover it ingeniously and decorously as though he was conscious of a defect which could not humanly be avoided; whereas Ariosto inserts his padding intrusively, almost as though he were making fools of his readers" (Ugo Foscolo, *D'Omero, del vero modo di tradurlo e di poetare*, in *Opere*, Florence, vol. 9, pp. 325–26). And citing a case of "padding" in Ariosto, Foscolo continues: "But out of one hundred thousand readers few will not be angry with the poet, and very few, rather than blaming the poet, will blame the weakness of the human intellect, which, though partaking of the divine nature, must

call the four admirable lines by which Ariosto expresses the bewilderment and anguish of Fiordiligi when the two barons, companions of Brandimarte, appeared alone and speechless before her after combat:

> Tosto che entrâro, ed ella loro il viso
> vide di gaudio in tal vittoria privo
> senz'altro annunzio sa, senz'altro avviso,
> che Brandimarte suo non è più vivo! . . . .[22]

[As soon as they entered and she saw no joy in their faces, after such a victory, she knew without other announcement, without other notice, that her Brandimarte was no longer alive.] One may note that in the third line "announcement" [*annunzio*] and "notice" [*avviso*] are two words saying the same thing and perhaps neither with complete appropriateness, and that "avviso" was chosen for the rhyme. But the accelerated rhythm obtained by the sequence of the two words, separated and yet linked by a caesura, is like the precipitous throbbing of Fiordiligi's heart and creates a superior poetic image; and the rhyme at the end of the line links the throbbing to the composure and bewilderment in the presence of the two men appearing with no light of joy in their faces.

nevertheless always avail *itself of ineffective instruments and means for the purpose. Homer, more than any other poet, employs such padding especially where the verse does not allow him to express his whole concept. Therefore, if he has to mention Agamemnon in half a line, he will fill the space with the epithets 'shepherd of peoples,' 'emperor of the braves,' 'son of the bellicose Athreus,' and so forth. As a result, very many other verses, often in succession, end with the words 'well-haired Achaeans,' or 'well-buskined Achaeans'; and the gods, for the most, are called by all of their attributes; but when the rest of the thought can be grafted onto the same verse, then Homer puts aside gods and people, and runs directly, without epithets, and more energetically to the goal"* (p. 326).

The "chevilles" [padding]. "Dès que le poète a appris son art et s'est habitué à se rendre compte de ses visions, il entend à la fois, vite, de façon à le briser, non pas seulement une rime jumelle, mais toutes les rimes d'une strophe ou d'un morceau, et après les rimes tous les mots caractéristiques et saillants qui feront image, et, après ces mots, tous ceux qui leur sont corrélatifs, longs si les premiers sont courts, sourds, brillants, muets, colorés de telle ou telle façon, tels enfin qu'ils doivent être pour compléter le sens et l'harmonie des premiers et pour former avec eux un tout énergique, gracieux, vivant et solide. Le reste, ce qui n'a pas été révélé, trouvé ainsi, les soudures, ce que le poète doit rajouter pour boucher les trous avec sa main d'artiste et d'ouvrier, est ce qu'on appelle les CHEVILLES. . . . Ceux qui nous conseillent d'éviter les chevilles, me feraient plaisir d'attacher deux planches l'une à l'autre au moyen de la pensée, ou de lier ensemble deux barres de fer en remplaçant les vis par la conciliation. . . . Bien plus, il y a autant de chevilles dans un bon poème que dans un mauvais, et quand nous en serons là, je ferai toucher du doigt à mes lecteurs! Toute la différence c'est que les chevilles des mauvais poètes sont placées bêtement, tandis que celles des bons poètes sont des miracles d'invention et d'ingéniosité" (Th. de Banville, *Petit traité de poésie française*, Paris, 1891, pp. 66–67).

The rhyme that takes away freedom. The well-known essay by D. Gnoli, "La rima e la poesia italiana" (*Nuova Antologia*, December 1876, pp. 705–35) is dominated by the concept that in a poem there is first an inner poetry and then an outer one which is meant to reproduce faithfully the former, and that the verse and the rhyme are added because of a need for something delightful, and that this need is satisfied to the detriment of faithfulness. "Do you want to render your poetry delightful, effective, elegant, through musical elements, clothing your thought with verses? You

---

22. *Orlando Furioso* 43. 157.

Of these would-be shortcomings one sometimes accuses the "rhyme," the great seducer and corruptor, and, to avoid exposure to that temptation and the risk of succumbing, unrhymed verse is suggested—the "blank verse" with rhymes appearing at random, without any predetermined place; and, sometimes, the shortcomings are attributed to the metric pattern itself and the closed stanza, and to remedy this the use of the so-called free verse (uneven in lines and stanzas) is proposed. But if those blank verses, those open stanzas, those free verses are moved by poetic inspiration and have their exigencies and laws, they will always be brought to the point of having to accept some fillers, wedges, and inlays. If instead they are, as ordinarily is the case (especially in compositions in blank verse), cold intellectualistic excogitations, one may expect also in this case that they need wedges, the only difference being that these are ugly wedges for ugly things. Nobody will smile at them with indulgence and acceptance, as one does at those of the poets which are defined as "lively defects." But, in truth, those of the poets required by the harmony of the expression are not in themselves either good or bad, for they are only supports for the poetic effect.

Touching upon these very delicate arguments brings to mind a word from a master, Eckhart, who, after saying that God's eye is the eye with which man sees God and that if God did not exist man would not exist either, nor would God without the existence of man, is frightened by the profound but almost heretical words he said and he hurried to admonish: "However, it is not necessary to know these things, because they are easily misunderstood and can be understood only in their concepts."[23] It is indeed necessary that our affairs be known to the philosopher, the interpreter, the critic; the poets do well to ignore them or not to dwell on them, and to remain in their holy simplicity of eternally dissatisfied, tireless perfectionists and humble inlayers at the service of this perfection when they cannot avoid doing so. And the interpreters and critics, they too, will do well to treat our things in a manner reflecting their good upbringing which forbids the insistence on knowing why a man, who is

must pay for it, you must yield a part of the freedom of expressing your own thought in words. Would you also like the rhyme? You must yield a little more of that primitive freedom. Do you also want proportion and measure in the strophe? Music is disposed to lend its help to poetry, but it must be paid for the service. And it demands to be paid well!" (p. 707). By continuing our reasoning from this premise, we would do well to conclude that the words themselves take away our freedom and "require to be paid"; and this seems to be true at times: hence the so-called ineffable and the idea that the "word" is a tyrannical "yoke" and that, in order to preserve the fidelity of the inner image, the "nonexpression" (strange to say) is necessary (silence would not even be enough, for in it one speaks with oneself). Gnoli, like others, did not realize that inner poetry, indeterminate in regard to rhythm, verse, rhyme, musicality, and the like, does not exist, for the poetic seed, like other seeds, contains within itself the branches, leaves, flowers, and fruits; and poetry cannot be judged by comparison to a nonexistent model, but only by comparison within itself, that is, by seeking the coherence of the forms in which it unfolded and actualized itself. Only by this may one discern the cases in which poetry sounds perfectly harmonious, from those in which the verse and the rhyme are forced, or from those in which poetry reaches harmony through the expediency of "padding" or "cheville," as we say.

Poetry and structural passages. "The toil and the delay recommended by critics can be justly interpreted to mean no more than careful observation of the inspired moments and an artificial connection of the spaces between their suggestions by the intertexture of conventional expressions—a necessity imposed only by the limitedness of the poetical faculty itself; for Milton conceived *Paradise Lost* as a whole before he executed it in portions" (Shelley, *A Defence of Poetry*).

---

23. As quoted by Hegel in *Philosophie der Religion*, ed. Lasson, vol. 1, p. 257 (Croce's note).

alive and moves, wears glasses in order to see well or carries a stick to lean on in walking.

One more analogous case of conventional or structural expedients is encountered when two pieces of poetry are linked in like manner; and to give a small example of this, too, after quoting the most beautiful stanza by Ariosto, I can quote from one of the most poetic episodes of Dante's *Divine Comedy*, that of Francesca da Rimini. After Francesca had narrated her love and the tragedy which led her and her lover to a common death (ending the narration with a word of hate against the murderer and fratricide), the pilgrim going through the dark places, deeply moved by her story, asks her:

> Ma dimmi: al tempo de' dolci sospiri,
> a che e come concedette amore
> che conosceste i dubbiosi desiri?[24]

[Tell me: in that time of sighing-sweet desires,/ How, and by what, did love his power disclose/ And grant you knowledge of your hidden fires]. Why this question? Perhaps for pure curiosity? Or for the unwholesome pleasure of gossip? Certainly not. The question is there exclusively to link the first to the second piece of poetry in which Francesca will reminisce, rapidly and painfully, the moment in which she and her lover were overcome and carried away by passion. Those lines are a small wooden bridge to cross from one green band to the other, and no one pays attention to the little bridge; everyone, after contemplating the first spectacle, immerses himself wholly in the contemplation of the second. Here again the conventional or structural piece serves for giving, in its entirety, the poetry of Francesca, which Dante could not otherwise give because of the very pattern of the poem, woven with meetings of souls and with questions and answers.

Of the same nature as these lines are the informative and glossarial parts of poems, dramas, and novels and, usually the expositions of the antecedent facts by one of the characters, and the reports of unseen events, assigned to a "messenger," and sometimes the reflections and commentaries of the choruses of a Greek tragedy, the reviews and the genealogies in the epic, the psychological explanations in the novels, and the introduction, in all of these forms of poetic works, of characters whose function it is to permit the progress of the action and who therefore cannot and must not reach poetic intensity. For if the Virgilian "pius Aeneas" (just to mention one) is not taken away by the fancy and the heart, as was Dido, whom he forsook, it is not because he is "pious" and morally and reli-

Poetic license. As is known, Banville, in the *Petit traité* cited earlier, disposes of poetic license in the chapter bearing that title by the cutting sentence: "Il n'y en a pas" [There is none] (p. 68). Strictly speaking he is right, for in poetry, as in morality, the concept of "licit" is excluded or, to put it another way, there is no "licit" other than that demanded by esthetic consciousness. The so-called licenses are arbitrary departures, due to haste or laziness, from the historical forms of expression we have already treated, and as such they are esthetically inadmissible.

Structure and poetry. Critics at times happened to note, almost in jest, the hindrances that the presence of the chorus in Greek tragedy creates or should create for the development of the action. In the poem of Dante hindrances of the same nature have also been

---

24. *Inferno* 5. 118–20.

giously conceived, as is believed, or because the traitors of love do not speak to the poetic heart (since the contrary could be proved), but more truly because he was conceived with the aim of representing and celebrating Rome's history; and, merely in order to introduce into the poem the origin of the long enmity and the war against Carthage, he was forced to abandon the passionate Carthaginian queen. The Godfrey of *Jerusalem Delivered* is pious and yet poetic, or certainly more poetic than Aeneas, who is more "contrived." There is no need to multiply the examples of these links and constructions, which are obvious; we must also repeat, in regard to them, that, though poetically unimportant, they are used awkwardly by bad poets and gracefully and tastefully by good poets.

Therefore, as in the other case, this sort of expedient is adopted in order to allow the river of poetry to flow in its plenitude and richness, and at the same time not lose the superior harmony of its whole and the wholeness of its parts, which would be lost if that river were dispersed into rivulets and ponds and little streams. It is not a question, as Chateaubriand thought, of tiredness on the part of the poet who from time to time, in certain instances, would rest and allow the reader to rest, since the latter, too, would be tired of the excessively intense enjoyment of poetry and be grateful for the respite. Chateaubriand added that, as far as he was concerned, he never would have wished the beautiful passages of *Le Cid* and *Horace* to be held together "par des harmonies élégantes et travaillées," but rather by weak and unpretentious links.[25] On the other hand, the anthologies of "good pieces," though useful or indispensable for certain didactic ends, do not satisfy fully the lovers of poetry, precisely because they offer those pieces in isolation and as though out of tune, bereft of the "structural parts" which kept them tied to one another.

But the just acceptance of these "structural parts" must not be perverted to mean the acceptance of them as poetry; this would be unfair, and is in fact the error committed by interpreters with little understanding, either because they are dominated by a sort of superstitious reverence toward the famous poets (whom they do not honor by equating their poetry with their technical skill) or for a serious lack of intelligence and esthetic sensibility. Elsewhere I compared their behavior to that of the Trojans who, having eaten the bread on the tables and being still hungry, began to eat the tables. But bread is bread and tables are tables, and the hooks and other supports of a painting are not the

noticed: "*The poet must also contend with repetition of similar situations, and we find him trying hard to vary them, without being altogether able to overcome their monotony. As an instance of this, we may select the astonishment of the souls in Purgatory when they perceive that Dante throws a shadow and the explanations that Virgil is obliged to supply from time to time. At a certain point, Virgil himself appears to become impatient with it and to act like the man in the old story who had a stain of oil upon his clothes and was so informed by everyone he saw. Finally, whenever he met anyone, he said at once: 'Yes, I know, I have an oil stain.' So, too, Virgil says, 'Without your asking, I confess to you that what you behold is a human body, by which the light of the sun upon earth is broken'*" (*The Poetry of Dante*, pp. 94–95).

The system of tragedy. For Corneille's system see my essay on him in *Ariosto, Shakespeare and Cornielle,* chap. 15.

25. Chateaubriand, *Essai sur la littérature anglaise, Oeuvres complètes* (Paris: Garnier, 1861), vol. 11, p. 681.

painting. Such confusion led to the praising of Corneille, Calderón, Apostolo Zeno,[26] and others, for having found for the French tragedy, the Spanish comedy, the Italian melodrama, and for other genres a structure and a mechanism which was passed on to their successors, both poets and nonpoets; it led also to the celebration of Aeschylus for adding the second actor in the Greek tragedy, and to the attribution of great merit to the inventor of the eight-line stanza and the sonnet, and to the introducer of these schemes to other peoples. The consequence is that, because of the misunderstood quality of the structural elements, poetry is considered to be a sequence of conventions and artifices, and poets the inventors of them; and the "inventions," the "skillfulness," and almost the astuteness and shrewdness that they employ are the object of particular studies full of wonder and admiration.

It is all the more necessary to condemn and repress such voraciously indiscriminate swallowing of things digestible and indigestible, since it gave birth, by reaction, to the opposite and no less fallacious theory which does not admit in a work of poetry anything but "poetic parts." This theory took two forms: one maintaining that only short poems are poetic—those read at one sitting, in a quarter of an hour at the most—not the tragedies which require several hours, or long poems and novels which demand many days of reading; the other holding that poetry exists in "spots" or "fragments" and that the rest is an inert mass, in which the "fragments" are inlaid and from which they must be removed. The first form introduces, by a serious and logical mistake, the concept of time in an ideal process, as though the composition of a poem and the reading of it, whether lasting a clocked minute or years, do not take place in an ideal rhythm which seizes both author and reader and casts them out of time. The erroneousness of such a theory is proven by the facts, because the poetry of a poem, drama, novel, poetically inspired, does not lie only in single passages, but circulates throughout the whole; and there are works from which no passage can be detached and placed in an anthology as a beautiful piece; and yet one feels in these works the poetry thoroughly pervading them. This consideration is also valid for the refutation of the second form of the theory. Perhaps it is not worth noting that this second form has generated the school of the so-called fragmentists,

---

26. Apostolo Zeno (1668–1750), poet and author of melodramas. Tried, before Metastasio, to bring about the reform of the melodramatic genre in order to give it the dignity of classical tragedy through the regularization of its technique. But, though a man of lucid understanding concerning the problem, he was not highly gifted as a poet, and his melodramas have no merits other than those of technical skill. The reform he envisioned was to be accomplished by Metastasio.

Poetry and brevity. The theory of poetic brevity belongs to Poe: "I hold that a long poem does not exist. I maintain that the phrase 'a long poem' is simply a flat contradiction in terms. I need scarcely observe that a poem deserves its title only inasmuch as it excites by elevating the soul. The value of the poem is in the ratio of this elevating excitement. But all excitements are, because of a psychic necessity, transient. That degree of excitement which would entitle a poem to be so called at all cannot be sustained throughout a composition of any great length. After the lapse of half an hour, at the very utmost, it flags—fails—a revulsion ensues—and then the poem is, in effect, and in fact, no longer such" (The Poetic Principle [The Complete Tales and Poems of E. A. Poe, New York, 1938, p. 889]). An echo of this is in Baudelaire's preface to Nouvelles histoires extraordinaires: "Voilà évidemment le poème épique condamné. Car un ouvrage de cette dimension ne peut être considéré comme poétique qu'en tant qu'on sacrifie la condition vitale de toute oeuvre d'art, l'Unité; je ne veux pas parler de l'unité dans la conception, mais de l'unité dans l'impression, de la totalité de l'effet, comme je l'ai déjà dit quand j'ai eu à comparer le roman avec la nouvelle. Le poème épique nous apparaît donc, esthétiquement parlant, comme un paradoxe. Il est possible que les anciens âges aient produit des séries de poèmes lyriques, reliées postérieurement par les compilateurs en poèmes épiques, mais toute 'intention épique' résulte évidemment d'un sens imparfait de l'art. Le temps de ces anomalies artistiques est passé" [pp. xviii–xix]. Coleridge also observed that "a poem of any length neither can be, nor

who deliberately write fragments in order to be sure that they produce solely unadulterated poetry; and one can imagine what insipidities come out of their endeavors.

A third case worth remembering, concerning the relation between structure and poetry, is the one in which the poet takes a fable, whether traditional or invented by himself, not to blend with his poetry and transfigure it into the image of his feeling, but because it is pleasing to him or to his readers who are fond of this sort of action and passion, this kind of story, these characters and names; and, taking the fable as a framework, the poet embroiders his poetry, which sometimes covers and hides the framework totally and thus abolishes it, but sometimes does not cover it entirely and lets it remain there by itself to a varying extent. Also in this case, the attitude of the poetry interpreter must be one of indifference toward the framework and of exclusive interest in the poetic embroidery on it. But in this instance, too, the unintelligent and inadequate poetry readers mistake the framework for the embroidery and take to considering the former in itself as substantial poetry or as a poetic motif; hence all the dissertations on the way in which the themes of Prometheus and Orestes, of Lucretia and Sophonisba, of Faust and Don Giovanni, and so on, must be treated, and on the various ways in which they have been treated by indifferent authors; whereas it ought to be clear that the poet is never to be found in those events and characters, but only in what he is capable of infusing into or adding to them of his own and of universal nature. Since the frameworks, taken in that manner, are also found in Shakespeare, who many a time took his high flight touching only lightly upon the tales of popular fables, an insistent criticism was leveled against the Shakespearean inconsistencies and contradictions and puerilities; one of the last expounders of such criticism was Leo Tolstoy, who mistook the plot of *King Lear* for the poetry of *King Lear*.

One last case, which is a variation of the third, deserves not only to be remembered, but also to be given particular attention because it involves at least two of the greatest poets of Europe: not Homer or Shakespeare, but Dante and Goethe, both being not only extraordinary poetic temperaments ("Natur," as Goethe said of Dante), but equally strong in their thought, and both being spirits with warm religious and moral affections, deeply concerned with human destiny and the human conduct of life. Together with their poetic images, they developed in their minds concepts and

ought to be, all poetry" (Biographia Literaria [London, 1885, p. 149]).

These assertions, though theoretically not well founded, were, nevertheless, justified by the fact that they opposed the huge historical-philosophical poems envisioned and executed during the romantic age and which aimed at usurping the function of the philosophical systems, the religious writings, and the encyclopedias.

The theory of poetry as a fragment. Gino Capponi supported this theory in his letters to Tommaseo in 1833: "The only poetry for us mortals is the lyric, but in the lyric itself one cannot weave a series of ideas without adding to five poetic parts ten arithmetical ones; and arithmetic is the filler of the space left by the poetic fragments." The theory reappeared later in Pascoli: see, for both, my Conversazioni critiche, 4th ed., vol. 1, pp. 63–67.

Histories of themes. A criticism of histories of esthetics dealing with poetic themes can be found, with specific examples, in my Problemi d'estetica, 4th ed., pp. 77–90. In Germany a special branch of philology is the "Stoff und Motivgeschichte."

The unity of poetry. The unity of poetry is nothing more than poetry itself in its effectiveness as poetry, in its synthetic nature and not (as the old writers of treatises imagined and the unaware followers of their doctrines, who still exist today, repeat) something which unifies poems: a something that is found to be, if one really asks what it is, no more than the book, or rather the volume, in which a poem is materially inserted and is in the company not only of other and different poems, but also of poetry and antipoetry. What importance could it ever have for a man sensitive to poetry that a poetic creation, whose beauty ravishes him, corresponds or not to the design of the book or volume? Just as little as the concern that a man in love with a woman has about her social relations; the lover's imagination separates her from these relations and transfers her to the society of his own heart and fancy. This, which is the only proper way of treating poetry, has been erroneously called "fragmentist criticism"; but what "fragmentism" and its mistake really are have been shown above [reference to the text]. For the same reasons one should label as fragmentistic the philosopher's act that separates the true thought of another philosopher (that is, that which alone has effective logical unity) from contradictory concepts, mythological or passional elements, and the like, which frequently become united. But neither the discerning intelligence of philosophy nor that of poetry

affections which they poured into their poems in an attempt to transform everything into poetry. But, in reality, they were able to transform only what had become feeling in them, not what had taken a conceptual form (science and philosophy) or a practical form (oratory, satire, and so on) in their minds. So Dante and Goethe in the *Divine Comedy* and in *Faust*, respectively (and not only in these works), gathered their doctrinal convictions, their exhortations and admonitions and the song of their own feelings. They gave birth to two very complex works, powerfully unharmonious in their interior; one almost geometrized in its external appearance (being the narration of a journey through the three kingdoms of the world beyond, to which was devoted a canticle of thirty-three cantos in terza rima, all preceded by an introductory canto completing the round figure of one hundred); the other unconcerned even with this external order. In the two works the diverse elements are at times intertwined, at times separated, at other times conflicting with each other, but nonetheless they are among the most impressive that the human mind has ever produced. The interpreters of the two works raised the so-called problem of "unity," that is, whether the unity is to lie in one element or the other, or in their synthesis; and because of the already mentioned genesis of the poems, it was perfectly natural that this problem would be raised; but, stated in these terms, it was equally natural that it would show itself to be insoluble. In order to state the problem properly and thus be able to solve it, the critics should have taken that genesis into account and kept in mind the concept of poetry and that of nonpoetry and distinguished in both works the structure from the poetry; the only caution that should have been used was to realize that, for such energetic spirits as Dante and Goethe, structure was not, either poetically or intellectually and morally, the indifferent framework that we have seen in other poets who were simply poets; but it was a vital part of their soul, it was distinct and, at the same time, conjoined with poetry, which is fostered by it in a unity not static but dialectic. For us, in order to understand their soul and even the shape of their poetry, the structure cannot be indifferent. Like all other structures, it must be indifferent only insofar as within it their poetry does not really sing.

is fragmentism; in like manner, the delicate shadings of mental refinement are not the sign of weakness as they appear to some who compare this refinement to their own impetuosity, but a sign of strength, the weakness being their impetuosity. The efforts to unify the complicated spiritual-esthetic process are acts of crude force carried out by people with little understanding of the matter.

The problem of unity in the poems of Dante and of Goethe. See in regard to Dante my Poetry of Dante and Conversazioni critiche (2d ed., vol. 3, pp. 197–207) and the two recent essays by S. Breglia, Poesia e struttura nella Divina commedia (Genoa, 1935) and by W. Vetterl, Die Aesthetische Deutung und das Problem der Einheit der Göttlichen Komödie (Strasbourg, 1935). On these works see Conversazioni critiche, 2d ed., vol. 5, pp. 99–104; concerning Goethe, see my book Goethe (in the 4th ed., 1946, I have collected several other writings on the subject). As for Dante, we have arrived in Italy at the clear distinction between quaestio structurae and quaestio poëseos, thanks to a lively and serious sentiment of poetic concreteness which is in our tradition; and critical judgment, by confirming the spontaneous impressions of taste, has removed the obstacle interposed by the confusion of the two very different orders of problems (which can always be interposed) between intuition and the enjoyment of Dante's poetic inspiration. See, among the most recent works, the one by M. Rossi, Gusto filologico e gusto poetico (Bari, 1942). But in Germany, where Faust was more than once under erratic religious, moral, and nationalistic accusations, it is believed even today that the Goethean masterpiece was redeemed through interpretations which, founded on the same confused premise, give the illusion of reaching justifiable conclusions—conclusions which supposedly (it is said) touched the summit and received the laurel in the book by Rickert, a philosopher completely inexperienced in poetry, that is, in esthetics. See this hardly acceptable eureka in the essay by E. Beutler, "Der Kampf um die Faustdichtung," in Essays um Goethe (Leipzig, 1941, pp. 300–18), in which, among other things, one can read a juicy and instructive history of the fortune, or rather the misfortune, of Faust during the one-and-a-half century of German criticism.

5. The Untranslatability of Poetic Re-Evocation

The historical-esthetic interpretation, by re-evoking poetry, revives the images of the poet in the articulated sounds in which they were first expressed and in their original concreteness, which is poetry itself. And all the effort of the manifold work of interpretation is aimed at this sole and supreme goal.

To ask whether poetry is translatable into other articulate sounds or other kinds of expressions, such as the musical tones, the colors and lines of painting and sculpture, is a question that one can hardly formulate, because it already implies a negative answer that precludes the question. The impossibility of translation is the very reality of poetry in its creation and re-creation.

The problems to be raised on this point are of a different character and are neither included in that question nor otherwise formulated, even if they are obscurely felt. They concern the origin of the concept of "translation," which does not exist within the sphere of poetry, and the true nature of what we call "translations of poetic works," which are necessary and which have always been done.

There is no doubt that the sphere in which translation takes place is that of prose expression, which is accomplished with symbols and signs. These signs, not only those used in mathematics, physics, and the other sciences, but also those used in philosophy and history, are interchangeable according to need. We may say that what the Germans call "Begriff," we shall call "concept"; what they call "Pflicht," we shall call "duty"; and through these words we shall think the same spiritual categories that they think through theirs. Similarly, within the area of one national language, for instance, what Vico called "the certainty of the law," we shall call in modern terms "the moment of power or of political force," and what he called "the certainty of knowing" as distinguished from and opposed to "truth," we shall call "intuition," distinguishing it from "concept," and thus we make ourselves more easily understood. This alone is true "translation," and it consists in establishing the equivalence of the signs for reciprocal comprehension and understanding; this equivalence is used in order to avoid the misunderstandings due to the variety of signs, which in this case certainly does not help the saving of energy nor the smoother progress of inquiry and learning. The tendency of science and philosophy points toward the unification of signs, or, as it is said, of terminology, and to a sort of international language (a learned

The untranslatability of poetry. "Hence the vanity of translation; it were as wise to cast a violet into a crucible that you might discover the formal principles of its color and odor as to seek to transfuse from one language to another the creations of a poet. The plant must spring again from its seed, or it will bear no flower. . . ." (Shelley, A Defence of Poetry). Such a recognition of intrinsic impossibility was very often for-

"lingua franca"), it being impossible now to go back to the centuries when the members of the "republic of letters" availed themselves of the venerable Latin language. While the proposal for unification had some practical results in the abstract sciences, the natural sciences found help in Latin and Greek; and although, to some extent, the interpenetration of cultures gives the national languages themselves an international usage and makes the need for artificial unification less urgently felt, the variety of signs and the consequent necessity of translations will always persist because new concepts emerge constantly, not only in the diversity of nations and their languages, but also in the individuals who, together with the new concepts, create new signs.

Prose, then, can be translated, but translation must be limited to the prose which is merely prose, to the prosaism of prose; for, if translation is extended to literary prose, as was thoughtlessly done by someone,[27] it would no longer be valid. Literary prose, like any other form of literature, is elaborated so as to give it an esthetic character. And this presents an insurmountable obstacle to translation similar to that of translating poetry. Plato and Augustine, Herodotus and Tacitus, Giordano Bruno and Montaigne are not, strictly speaking, translatable, for no other language can render the color and the harmony, the sound and rhythm of the original. They, too, because of their qualities as writers, require a re-creation, as do the poets—a re-creation which revives them in their untranslatable personal tone.

What, then, are the translations of poetic and literary works, whose right has been implicitly admitted above? They are, first of all, two diverse things according to whether they are means to a different end or complete works in themselves. In the first instance, they are simply instruments for the apprehension of the original works—instruments by which these works are actually analyzed and clarified in their verbal elements, thus preparing the further synthesis, which is to be sought only in the original expression. One can lament and exorcise, by exaggerating esthetic sensibility, the massacre which is or was usually done in schools to the poets when translating them into prose; but the fact is that it is impossible to learn how to read Horace and Pindar without going through those literal prose translations, which from time to time become useful even for the comprehension of the poets, and perhaps for some passages by Foscolo, Leopardi, Carducci, who belong to the nineteenth century. Those literal and prose translations, even if rhythmical

27. See above, n. 1.

and imitating well the original without efforts and contortions, demand to be integrated with the original; and when this is not done, either because of unwillingness or inability to learn the original language (as often happens with translations of works from Far Eastern languages), they can serve to give a vague feeling of those works, but not the true knowledge of their individual character. Hence the saying that true poetry persists even in literal and prose translations. It persists, indeed, and transmits its power; but like Adam's soul, invisible in the rays enveloping him, or, rather, like the animal to which Dante at that point compares him—the animal which "snorts" and shakes in the cloth in which it is wrapped: "Sì che l'affetto convien che si paia,/ per lo seguir, che face a lui, la 'nvoglia" [So that its feeling must be revealed by the response that its covering makes to it].[28]

Poetic translations are a different matter because they re-create the original poetry combining it with the feelings of the reader who, owing to his diverse historical conditioning and diverse individual personality, is unlike the author. And from this new sentimental situation springs that so-called translating through which an ancient soul poetizes in a modern soul. If this were the poetic activity of the original poet, it could express itself only in the same sounds in which it already expressed itself; and the poetic translation would not take place. Thus Vincenzo Monti translated the *Iliad*, and made of it a masterpiece;[29] thus other (but not many) poetically inspired translators produced beautiful works having artistic value of their own which are unfairly placed in literary history together with unpoetic or prosaic translations, or with the many others which mix the two different approaches, making translations objectionable and giving translators in general a bad name. With a graceful and significant image, we Italians call the translations of the first kind the "ugly-faithful," and those of the second kind the "beautiful-unfaithful"; but those made by mediocre translators belong to an intolerable third kind, that of the "ugly-unfaithful."

mulated, and one may say that it has become a general conviction.

On this topic, as well as on translating as a new creation, one must read the book by R. Borchardt, *Das Gespräch über Formen und Platons Lysis deutsch* (Leipzig, 1905).

Poetic translations and new poems on ancient motifs. Poets in the past willingly took pleasure in treating in their own way situations already treated by other poets: like the foray of Diomedes and Ulysses in the Trojan camp, which in the *Aeneid* becomes that of Euryalus and Nisus, and in the *Orlando Furioso* that of Cloridan and Medor. Here the situation, that is, the material fact, is more or less the same; but the tone or poetic motif is new each time. In poetic translations, on the other hand, what one tries to retain is more or less the fundamental poetic motif.

Works that lose and works that gain. In beautiful poetic translations one cannot say that poetry is improved or impaired, because translation gives poetic variations that present advantages on the one hand and disadvantages on the other. But those works which are not poetry and are, for instance, literature for emotion and entertainment can definitely gain by being put into a better literary form than the original. This was noted by the English critics, Swinburne among them, in the works of Byron with respect to their fortune on the Continent; it was pointed out, in this connection, that Byron was not a poet, a creator of poetic forms, but "a scene painter."

The beautiful infidèles. When one compares word by word artistic translations with the original, none of them can be said to be satisfactory. But it is not in this way that they must be judged; on the contrary, one must first of all determine whether, in their inevitable

---

28. *Paradiso* 26. 98–99.

29. Vincenzo Monti (1754–1828), Italian poet of volatile political feelings, but not without poetic merits. His fame rests mainly on his translation of the *Iliad* into Italian in hendecasyllabic blank verses, which are a masterpiece of neoclassical taste.

Artistic translations, aspiring to the unfaithfulness of beauty, are not only those from one language into another, which we have so far envisioned, nor those which try to translate works of poetry into musical, pictorial, and sculptural variations and into graphic "illustrations" which adorn or deface the editions of the poets; but also those which seem to render the expression more vivid and concrete: the representation of dramas composed by poets. The authors of these translations are not, to be more exact, William Shakespeare, but Garrick and Salvini; not Alfieri, but Gustavo Modena; not Dumas-fils or Sardou, but Eleonora Duse.[30] The poetry of dramas is not enjoyed unless one reads the drama in solitude, which drama can be artistically superior, sometimes inferior, to the stage presentation, but is unquestionably different from it. The declamation itself or the recitation of a poem is not that poem, but something else, beautiful or ugly, which must be judged within its own sphere. Poets tolerate badly the declaimers of their verses, and they themselves do not recite them willingly (in this also, they are the opposite of the Suffenuses, who, because of their character, are always ready, even anxious to do so); and, when they decide to read them, they do not mime or dramatize them; they do not thunder or sing them; they prefer to recite them in a soft voice, with a certain monotony, being careful only to articulate well and to make the rhythm felt because they know that their poetry is an inner voice to which no human voice is equal, it being a "cantar che nell'anima si sente" [a singing felt in the soul.][31]

This rational and radical negation of the translatability of poetry, which applies to the author himself when he tries to render his poetry into spoken words, proves the inanity of a theory (followed by more than one in Italy nowadays) according to which translations are so effective that we never read a poem without translating it into our own language; nor do we understand and speak a foreign language without, by this very act, translating it into our own.[32] But the facts attest to the contrary; for reading a poem, truly reading it (not performing an exercise in scansion for the purpose of reading the poem later), means grasp-

variations, they have rendered the general character of the original motif and structure; second, even if this has not been achieved, whether they can stand on their own as new poems or at least as literary works.

Various questions on translating. I deal with this problem in particular in an essay collected in my *Goethe* (4th ed., vol. 2, pp. 148–62) and in another, "Il giudizio della poesia su traduzioni," collected in *Discorsi di varia filosofia* (1945, vol. 2, pp. 90–94).

Graphic illustrations of poetic works. See on the subject some observations in my *Problemi d'estetica*, 4th ed., pp. 267–69.

Reading of poems. Fine observations on this are found in Albert Verwey, *Europäische Aufsätze* (trans. from the Dutch, Leipzig, 1919, pp. 282–96); and valuable research on the differences between written and oral poetry are found in P. Servien, *Principes d'esthétique, problèmes d'art et langage des sciences* (Paris, 1935); see on this book my *Conversazioni critiche*, 2d ed., vol. 5, pp. 51–52.

There are somewhat naive complaints that verses have been, for centuries, "vers pour les yeux du lecteur, ensuite compris et sentis, et non pas entendus d'abord; ils sont images visuelles et non impressions sonores, . . . allongés sur du papier blanc," and that "bien rares sont les privilégiés qui peuvent recréer instantanément dans leur cerveau des harmonies de sons avec la portée de la musique" (P. Martino, *Verlaine*, Paris, 1924, p. 165). Verses are not learned through the eyes, but through all the senses and with the entire soul, and the "privileged few" are those who feel poetry.

On the closeness of the actor and the translator, see *Conversazioni critiche*, 2d ed., vol. 3, pp. 71–72. The work of the musical performer has no relation to that of the translator, nor to that of the actor and declaimer; it is rather to be compared to that of the poet who is again finding and repeating within himself one of his own early poems: see on this the chapter "Il problema dell'interpretazione" in A. Parente, *La musica e le arti* (Bari, 1936, pp. 212–29).

---

30. Tommaso Salvini (1829–1915), tragic actor who performed all over Europe and in America; his vast repertory included many Shakespearean plays. Gustavo Modena (1803–1861), tragic actor who encouraged the beginnings of Salvini; Alfieri's plays constituted a large part of his repertory. Victorien Sardou (1831–1908), one of the most prolific French dramatists of the nineteenth century, contemporary of Dumas-fils.

31. Petrarch, *Canzoniere* 213. 6.

32. See above, n. 1.

not allow this if for no other reason than because no one would be in a position to avail himself of the permission. All poets and lovers of poetry pass judgment on what they and others do, and all have some concepts on this matter and they use them in their judgments. For if some people appear to have found an inexhaustible source of pleasure and contentment in vituperating criticism, in defining it as "the force of impotents," and in referring to critics (as Victor Hugo used to do) as "eunuchs" who ought to be wiped out of the world as useless and disgusting elements, these enemies of criticism are in this respect not unlike the people who vituperate and scorn medicine and who would like equally to abolish it, but who then run to consult the physician as soon as they hurt their finger.

So impossible is it to do without criticism that the pretension to drive it out of the world often changes to another pretension, that is, to retain it, but to make it a privilege of the poets themselves, since they are the only judges of what they produce. This request would have on its side (although those who make it are unaware of it) the true and profound gnoseological doctrine that one knows only what he does ("verum et factum reciprocantur").[1] Since poetry is created by the poet, but re-created by all other men, that is, by the genius of humanity, and since the poet himself does not behave differently from other men in the presence of poetry already created, it is impossible to grant to the poets by vocation or profession the exclusivity of a privilege which belongs to all men, who in a universal sense are all poets. Moreover, since in order to convert the "fact" into "truth" the fact must be elaborated mentally, the poets succeed in this no better and no worse than anybody else, though sometimes miserably; for if other men have in some instances the obtuseness of disinterest toward poetry, poets have very often another obtuseness which springs from personal interest; they consider to be poetry only their own or that which is similar to their own.

We need not describe what would happen if there were no criticism in the world, because things would occur no differently than if any of the other necessary forms of the spirit were missing: in other words, nothing at all would change; thus hypotheses of this sort are pointless. But we could think of what would happen, or to put it more clearly observe what happens when, relatively speaking, the minds are distracted and when, as a result, criticism becomes weak or does not exercise its function freely. Beautiful things re-

fait de la critique quand on ne peut pas faire de l'art, de même qu'on se met mouchard quand on ne peut pas être soldat" (*Correspondance*, vol. 1, p. 182: letter of October 2, 1846). Despite this, Flaubert outlined his program for a criticism which was really a criticism of artistic form (see *Correspondance*, vol. 2, pp. 315, 331–32, 338; vol. 3, p. 386).

The scarcity of good criticism. Here, too, it is interesting to cite Montaigne, who went as far as to consider good criticism more scarce than poetry: "Voici merveille: nous avons bien plus de poètes que de juges et interprètes de poésie: il est plus aisé de la faire que de la connaître. A certaine mesure basse, on la peut juger par les préceptes et par art: mais la bonne, la suprême, la divine, est au-dessus des règles et de la raison. Quiconque en discerne la beauté d'une vue ferme et rassise, il ne la voit pas, non plus que la splendeur d'un éclair: elle ne pratique point notre jugement; elle le ravit et ravage. La fureur qui stimule celui qui la sait pénétrer frappe encores un troisième à la lui ouir traiter et réciter; comme l'aimant non seulement attire une aiguille, mais infond encores en celle-ci sa faculté d'en attirer d'autres. . . ." (*Essais*, bk. 1, chap. 37).

---

1. Vichean theory of the identity of "truth" and "fact." See Vico's *De antiquissima italorum sapientia*, chap. 1.

main, then, without praise and recognition of their value, the ugly ones without condemnation, and the temple of poetry becomes filled with *vendentes et ementes* [people selling and buying], and there is no one to drive them out. Minds will feel the beautiful and the ugly and will suffer for one and the other just as they suffer when the good and evil, the justice and injustice they feel are unsupported by the moral and juridical sanction of the judgment or the sentence. Esthetic consciousness, like moral consciousness, is disarmed and cannot fight: only criticism is armed and combative. The feeling of taste or distaste, however strong, could bring about anything except that unique act which is accomplished by judgment and which is simply to give a name to things and thus point to the way of behaving toward them.

To name things is the ultimate end of a hard labor; and literary criticism was considered in antiquity extremely hard labor by the strongest critic—the unknown author of *On the Sublime*.[2] It presupposes, in the first place, the necessary and often slow and painful philological preparation and the subsequent interpretation of poetry which, if it really exists, is absorbed and made joyfully one's own through the contemplative mind; if, instead, it proves to be a lie and nonexistent, its ugly face disappoints and irritates the critic. In this lies the so-called sensibility which is required in the critic and without which his criticism would not only prove defective, but would even lack the content on which to exercise itself. In fact, on which poetry would the critic reflect, if he did not feel any and therefore did not possess any? There are critics more sensitive to certain poems than to others, critics of limited taste or of ample and varied taste (and however ample and varied their taste, they cannot expect to be sensitive to all poems or to every single poem in every moment of their lives); there are those endowed with little sensitivity, who are proportionately lacking as well in the gift of criticism. No judgment, not even the simplest, is conceivable without a basic sensitivity. And the critic must consider the mind as the only witness to be interrogated in the presence of the image that the re-evocation offers him. The mind alone furnishes the elements for his judgment; for the mind is that witness which, if allowed to escape, cannot be replaced. It is like the voice of moral conscience, which alone can give direction with certainty, and which must always be kept vigilant and active, never allowing the dispersion of one of its words or accents. As temptations and snares from all over contribute to divert us from moral conscience, so do temptations

The "sensitive" critic. Sensibility is an essential moment of criticism, but is not criticism; and, therefore, when to the philosophers-critics the "sensitive" critics are opposed, or rather superposed, one commits the error of placing a minus over a plus, the partial over the total, for a philosopher cannot be a critic of poetry unless he has sensibility to begin with, and therefore combines within himself the sensitive critic. It is a fact that there are critics who are sensible and scarcely philosophical; but it is also a fact that, because of this deficiency in theoretical discipline, they do not properly reason out their correct esthetic impressions; nor are they capable of keeping them always free, in their exposition, from the mixture of feelings and their completely personal tendencies, of whose nature they are not aware. Thus it is not surprising that they are not too judicious in their pronouncements about beautiful works which do not affect their sensibility or to which their sensibility has not yet been extended. When the question is raised as to whether a purely sensitive critic is better than a purely philosophical one, it is clear that the former must be preferred to the latter, who is in fact a bad philosopher-critic; for the former stands on the first step of criticism from which one can climb to the second; whereas the other has not even reached the first step and gropes among

2. Chap. 6 (Croce's note).

and snares likewise try to hinder the voice of taste, of that proper way of judging which is (to quote Molière's words in *Critique de l'école des femmes*) "de se laisser prendre aux choses et de n'avoir ni prévention aveugle ni complaisance affectée ni délicatesse ridicule."[3] These temptations and snares are, for instance, the invitation (accompanied by threat) not to depart from opinions, beliefs, the judgments of the majority, from the scruples and the hypocrisy of moralists, from the tendencies of the fashion, from the enthusiasm of the vulgar, the respect for an external authority, the propensity to see as beautiful all things produced by someone who once produced something beautiful or, contrarily, to consider ugly the works of those who once committed the human sin of ugliness, even if they have now redeemed themselves; the fear of compromising yourself by being the first to assert or deny (above all to assert) the beauty of beautiful things; the false shame by which one is led to accept things that have no real merit but that others cunningly hint are so constructed that only privileged souls can feel and understand them; the generous but imprudent impulse to find in others the realization of our own best ideals—which leads to seeing wrongly and to exaggerating (as happened to the old Goethe in regard to the young Byron) the diffidence toward the new because of excessive fondness for the old, or the scorn for the ancient because of the excessive fondness for the modern; the attraction for the images which correspond to our dear and gentle feelings—to say nothing of the vulgar motives which derive from personal or political or religious love or hate, because we would certainly not like to report here the two obvious suggestions and advice on honesty made to the critic by Alexander Pope in his already cited *Essay*.[4]

---

3. Scene V.
4. See pt. 3 of Pope's poem.

hollow formulas, without ever touching art. As a result, from these bad and mediocre ratiocinating critics we turn with great eagerness to listen to the simple lovers of art, the simple sensitive critics, whose insufficient theoretical principles we are ready to forgive, as easily as we are ready to forgive their eventual whims.

Moralistic reluctancies and hypocrisies. It is well to recall those which still persist in the more or less unfair official or academic judgments expounded by French criticism about Flaubert, Baudelaire, Henry Becque, Maupassant, and others.

The fear of being the first to assert the beauty of a work of art. Sainte-Beuve, speaking of Henri de Latouche, who was the first to publish the poems of André Chénier and to uphold their beauty, wrote: "En un mot, M. de Latouche, en cette occasion, fit un acte de goût original et courageux, ce qui est aussi rare et plus rare encore qu'un acte de courage dans l'ordre civil" (*Causeries du lundi*, vol. 3, pp. 481–82).

Poe also wrote that a sure sign from which one can discover that a critic has neither taste nor doctrine is when he rarely dares to praise a passage by an author who has not already been received and applauded by the public; in other instances, such a critic dwells entirely on small errors. Poe recalled a satirical fancy from *Ragguagli di Parnaso* [Advertisements from Parnassus] by our seventeenth-century Traiano Boccalini: "Zoilus once presented Apollo a very caustic criticism upon a very admirable book—whereupon the god asked him for the beauties of the work. He replied that he only busied himself about the errors. On hearing this, Apollo, handing him a sack of unwinnowed wheat, bade him pick out *all the chaff* for his reward" [*The Poetic Principle, The Complete Tales and Poems of E. A. Poe*, p. 899].

In some cases the real problem is a lack of courage, due to human considerations; but in the majority of the cases it reflects a lack of confidence in one's own intuition. Professors and academicians particularly are very good in idle judgments on works consecrated by the reputation of many centuries; but they get lost in the presence of new works and do not know what to think of them or what attitude they ought to take, and they look around trying to act in accordance with general opinion. When they finally decide to judge, they often let themselves be fooled by the weakest and most artificial writers, who would not fool either a naive reader or an experienced "journalist."

On the other hand, grimacing and disapproving seem to be the safest courses of action, because they can always point out as a pretext the faults of which no work is exempt; and, in all cases, their dissatisfaction, which is due to incapacity, can be disguised in a hard-to-please attitude deriving from a pretended refinement of taste and high ideals.

Praise for the old and scorn for the new. Read in this regard Horace's epistle 1 in bk. 2: "*Ingeniis non ille favet plauditque sepultis,/ nostra sed impugnat, nos nostraque lividus odit*" [He does not favor and praise the departed geniuses, but takes ours to task and hates us and our works with spitefulness].

On the admiration for ancient things, one must note the manner in which Quintilian marks the difference between veneration, "*religio*," and the sentiment of beauty, "*species*," in regard to Ennius: "*Ennium sicut sacros vetustate lucos adoremus, in quibus grandia et antiqua robora iam non tantam habent speciem quantam religionem*" [Ennius we may worship, as we worship groves sacred from their antiquity; groves in which gigantic and aged oaks affect us not so much by their beauty as by the religious awe they inspire in us] (*Institutionis oratoriae* 10. 1. 88).

Poetry of more or less difficult access, exotic in general, or removed from us because of the diversity of customs, history, and the strangeness of the language, also leads us to an overevaluation of it; this has happened with Indian and Persian poetry, when we had first knowledge of it in Europe. Hegel said, in reference to the conventional admiration, fashionable in his times, for the moral maxims of Confucius, that we Europeans have something better in *De officiis* of Cicero; we should have repeated so in regard to some poems and dramas from the Far East, which were not above the average pastoral poems, melodramas, and novel of chivalry and gallantry existing abundantly in our literatures.

The narrow and exclusive recognition of only the poetry which was closer and more familiar to the reader used to be more common in other times than ours; and the scorn for the old in favor of the new belongs to times of little historical consciousness, such as, for instance, our Italian seventeenth century and the French eighteenth century.

Feigned feeling and understanding. Horace in *Epistles*, bk. 2, 1, writes: "*Laudat et illud,/ quod mecum ignorat, solus vult scire videri*" [He praises the song (of Numa), of whom he is as ignorant as I am, and pretends that he alone knows it]. In this respect one can take, as an apologue, the delightful little story which is also found among the children's stories by Andersen: *The Emperor's New Clothes.*

Camoëns. In the past, certain judgments, though now no longer frequent, have produced errors which have been perpetuated by tradition and convention. A case in point is Camoëns and his poem. By way of warning against such judgments (and certainly not be-

But other and diverse traps arise from the works themselves to be examined, for not only do they not bear the label indicating the category to which they belong, but they very often also bear a deceptive and misleading label. A didactic poem: what is more discredited than a didactic poem? But that poem may be Virgil's *Georgics*, which is poetry. A comedy: in what can it differ from prose? And when it lacks "*acer spiritus ac vis*" [biting spirit and vigor] in words and deeds, is it not perhaps "*sermo merus*" [plain talk], even when it is in metric form ("*pede certo*")[5] and obeys the rules of verse? But that comedy may be the *Mariage de Figaro*, which is poetry, or is full of poetry. A fable exemplifies a maxim of morality or prudence; but La Fontaine's fables often go beyond Aesop and Phaedrus and are little dramas perfect in themselves, or even acute notations of the author's feelings and reflections. A scholastic-theological tercet from Dante's *Paradiso* lifts you to the sublime and a Goethean "*Spruch*" smiles at you with graceful beauty. On the contrary, epics in agile and elegant octaves, such as the *Lusíadas*, are political panegyrics of a people and their history; others in barbaric rhythms, such as the *Nibelungenlied*, seem to promise a fiery and yet human

5. Horace, *Satires* 1. 4. 46–48.

song, and in fact a nation or a race claims it as its epic song; but in reality the poem does not detach itself from the material intricacy of marvelous or atrocious events, it does not rise above them. Still others expound neither more nor less than the history of God and man, and though they glow with the great names of their authors and the admiration of many centuries, nonetheless (as in the case of *Paradise Lost*) they show themselves to be only words of noble humanism in exquisite and sometimes poetic lines. And novels, which are disguised in poetry, reveal themselves to be historical monographs for the divulgation of history, essays in social typology, inflamed diatribes, magic lanterns for amusement, confessions of afflicted souls, essays in artistic style.

cause of an aversion for a poet and a poem that exercise a strong attraction on us), it is well to point out that the high praises of Frederick Schlegel for the *Lusíadas* ("Geschichte der alten und neuen Literatur," lecture 11, in *Werke*, vol. 1, Vienna, 1846) were based on completely arbitrary and extra-poetic concepts. For Schlegel the epic poem was supposed to be "national"; and, therefore, the greatest epic poem in ancient and modern times was the *Lusíadas*. This idea, if we reflect, is bereft of any sense. And it is difficult to attribute any sense to the comparison he makes between the *Lusíadas* and the *Orlando Furioso*, arriving at the inferiority of the latter; or to the other comparison between the *Lusíadas* and *Jerusalem Delivered*, with a similar conclusion, because Tasso, unlike Camoëns, had not utilized thoroughly the epic theme of the Crusades; thus he is supposedly one of those poets who, instead of conceiving a world and disappearing in it (which means simply writing history), represent "only themselves and their best sentiment." In other words, Tasso's fault lay in being a poet and in having created Rinaldo and Armida and Erminia and Tancredi. Almost all the other works on the *Lusíadas* followed the example offered by Schlegel's judgment; they could be thus summarized: the *Lusíadas* "as for poetic power really are of little value; but they are the greatest heroic poem of modern and of all times!"

The Nibelungenlied and the Chanson de Roland. It is about time, perhaps, that we find a middle point between the scornful and disdainful judgment of Frederick II of Prussia and the exaltations of the romantic critics and philologists who have made the *Nibelungenlied* the "great national poem of Germany" and even (it is hard to understand why) "the book of the German families." And one might calmly recognize that the song is truly neither poetic nor epic, that it is rough in its composition, that it lacks ethos, and that its very pathos lies not so much in its tragicalness as in an accumulation of horrors. I do not understand why Germany (which has a Goethe) also must absolutely possess a great national epic poem: these are fixations of the advocates of literary genres and of nationalists with no common sense. Do people really believe that the Homeric poems are the expression or the program of Greek history, the *Aeneid* of Roman history, *La Chanson de Roland* of the history of France, and the *Divine Comedy* of the history of Italy? When will these minds free themselves of such nonsense?

La Chanson de Roland is something else from the poetic point of view; it is the poetry of the austere and tragic character of a faith for which men fight and die without rest or joy, with the vision of reward in the after life. Its form, elementary and popular, is com-

pletely coherent with this inspiration, even in what may appear to be dry and unpleasant. The monotony of which it is accused because of the narration of so many battles is natural in the readers who cannot transfer fully into a narration destined for an audience of princes, barons, warriors, and knights, who had never enough of those stories and followed them with a passion which constitutes the fundamental motif of the poem. The repetition, or better, the correspondence of certain acts or words is in the poem like so many internal rhymes of the tale.

Also popular and genuine in character is the very elementary Spanish poem of El Cid, full of admiration for the brave man who earns his living by his sword and who also has recourse to cunning, but retains his generosity and honor. Here is the hero who shows to his wife and his daughters the city of Valencia, which he had seized:

> *Adeliñó mio Cid con ellas al alcaçer,*
> *Allá las subie en el más alto logar.*
> *Ojos vellidos catan a todas partes,*
> *Miran Valencia como yaze la çibdad,*
> *E del otra parte a ojo han el mar,*
> *Miran la huerta, espessa es e grand,*
> *Alçan las manos para Dios rogar*
> *Desta ganançia cómmo es buena e grand. . . .*

[My Cid brings them to the citadel, to the very highest place, and they gaze about them with their lovely eyes. They see Valencia, how it spreads before them, and beyond it the sea, and there the Garden of Valencia, vast and thickly planted, and all things to delight them, and they raise their hands and give thanks to God for this gift, so rich and great] [canto 2]. And he wants his women to witness the siege laid to him by the king, and the battle:

En estas tierras agenas verán, las moradas cómmo se fazen,
Afarto verán por los ojos cómmo se gana el pan!

[. . . they shall learn how we make our living in this foreign land! With their own eyes they shall see how we earn our bread!] [canto 2].

Milton. *With the passing of time Milton, once very highly praised by critics and the writers of literary treatises for reasons alien to poetry, has been losing his hold on the European soul; this may be explained by the fact that the admiration for him was mainly inspired by his great daring in conceiving an epic poem, not on the siege of Troy, nor on the foundation of Rome, nor on Jerusalem delivered from the heathens, nor on any other particular historical event, but on no less than the very creation of the world and man. Goethe greatly admired him—"an excellent and in every sense interesting man"—but he was unable to enjoy Paradise Lost, on which he expressed an almost* totally negative judgment. And this appeal to the character of the man recurs in nearly all the critics. Treitschke sees, or thinks he sees, in that respect something more: "The true magic of the poem lies in the character of the poet, in his profoundly sad spirit, his disdain toward the world which throws its shadow on everything" (*Historische und politische Aufsätze*, vol. 1, p. 45). Other judgments on the poem, such as those made famous by Addison and by Macaulay, are founded on somewhat rhetorical concepts; and as far as Macaulay is concerned, it comes to mind that he considered as a very great lyric poet, "the greatest of modern times," our dry and boring declaimer Vincenzo Filicaia (see on this judgment by Macaulay my *Nuovi saggi sulla letteratura italiana del Seicento*, 2d ed., pp. 326–28).

In the poetic work of Milton there are certainly some very beautiful passages in *Comus* and, in a different tone, in *Samson Agonistes*, and in the very lyrics and verses of *Paradise Lost*; but, in order to understand their character, we must link them mainly to the Italian humanistic refinement, of which Milton was a disciple and an admirer (he even loved the ultrahumanist Giambattista Marino, the "dulciloquens," as Milton called him). The line by which he announces the argument of the poem, "Things unattempted yet in prose or rhyme," is a translation from Ariosto: "Cose non dette in prosa mai né in rima"; and, moreover, it is not even accurate to say that his subject was new and never attempted, for Italian literature had a long series of dramas and poems on the creation of the world and the fall of Adam (not to mention the singular poem of the French Du Bartas): hence the many discussions which took place at the time concerning the "Italian sources" of Milton. But this is not important. The rapture that one feels for some of his beautiful verses is similar to what we are accustomed to feeling for some verses of our own poets, also minor, of the sixteenth century, in Latin or Italian.

One can read between the lines the sentiment of respect and devotion that the critics have for him: his poem "can show a sustained magnificence of poetic conception, and of poetic treatment in the solemn and serious way, which has practically never been denied by any competent critic"; "It has been pronounced not delightful by persons not incompetent: it can never, by any such, be pronounced not great"; "As regards form, it practically endowed English with a new medium for great nondramatic poetry . . . " (G. Saintsbury, *Cambridge History of English Literature*, vol. 7, p. 119).

Achilleis by Goethe. Since this fragment by Goethe has been the object of study also in Italy (see T. Tosi,

And while unadorned stanzas, of a modest development, are pure lyrics which carry you away in the realm of dreams, others richly adorned, superb and resounding, like those by the Italian, French, English, and German "Pindarics" of the seventeenth and eighteenth centuries, leave you extremely cold. Sometimes in one of these authors multiple attitudes are intertwined—reflective and lyrical, critical and poetical, pathetic and tragic; this leads to changing judgments and to a varying history of his renown, now extolled to the heavens, now blamed or suspected and therefore the object of renewed controversies, as is, more or less, the case of Euripides. One must be cautious about what the creators of beautiful works say of themselves, for they are often mistaken; and they are led to deceive the reader concerning the ends they propose to attain because their belief in these ends turns out to be contradicted by facts. We must keep our eyes fixed only on the fact that poetry has no other end than itself. Sometimes the poets insist on putting into relief the worst parts of their talent and their weakest and most faulty works, and they even feel hurt if someone praises the beautiful ones; at other times they take pleasure in disparaging themselves and in hiding their true face, as Baudelaire did, thus making it difficult for him to be rightfully recognized as one of the greatest poets of the nineteenth century.

Sensibility never errs; taste, that is, the joy of the beautiful, is either present or absent; the joy of the ugly does not err either, in its own way, because it is the joy of something which pleases though ugly in itself; but the judgment which gives things a name, which tells the truth about them, may be led to error. And if it errs, if it asserts the false, it fails in its duty to discern reality from unreality and the quality of diverse and varying realities and, in this case, poetry from antipoetry, and poetry from literature, which has its own beauty but is not poetry; and in failing in its function, judgment does not serve justice, but favors injustice. The authors of erroneous judgments do not ruin or torture poetic geniuses (who do not allow themselves to be ruined and if they allow themselves to be tortured it is because they are predisposed to it, like Torquato Tasso), but they certainly preclude the knowledge of beauty for a length of time or to some social and national groups. Therefore, the analogy between the judgment and the moral conscience becomes, in the unity of the mind, a relation of identity between the two. The formulation of judgments on works of poetry implies thus a scrupulous conscience.

Atene e Roma, vol. 5, 1902, and *L'Achilleide, trans. and notes L. Bianchi, Bologna, 1930)* and the judgment of German critics has been controversial, I shall take as a small example some difficulties which must be overcome in order to "bring into focus" (as one might say) a work of art. The first difficulties were prepared by Goethe himself, who for some time played with the idea of continuing the* Iliad *with a lyrical poem up to the death of Achilles and the fall of Troy; he spoke a great deal of this project of his and left many notes about possible schemes among his papers; but then, in fact, he did not go beyond the 650 verses which are extant and which are what they are, regardless of Goethe's intentions and illusions, and which we must set aside and forget. But forgetting, though necessary, has not been easy and prompt, so much so that most critics, led by Bernays, took as a basis for judgment none other than the so-called Homeric character, or, more generally, the Greek character, and, finding this character lacking in those verses, condemned them and the very project of the work, on the assumption that it would have been carried out to completion in the same tone. Another group of critics, Germanophiles or German-crazy, at the head of whom was Vischer, followed suit, though for opposite reasons; they held that Goethe, by adopting the "Greek" style, had betrayed the "Germanic" style, and failed in his duty to continue to bring* Faust *to completion in Germanic style. A third group, more timid and less capable of making decisions, expressed the opinion that the* Achilleis, *amounting simply to a "fragment," could not be judged equitably. But here is finally Wilhelm Scherer rebelling against such assessments on the basis of extrinsic patterns and asserting that the fragment, as it stands, is a splendid piece of poetry; in this he claimed to be supported by his poet friends such as Geibel and others. In this way, and not without error and toil, the correct point of view is reached, which is to look at the work itself, simply letting taste be the judge, for taste is free of prejudices and finds with joy in those verses neither the Homeric nor the classic but the Goethean soul and mind. But what, in the end, is the character of these verses? What is the source of the "enthusiasm" that Scherer believed came from them, an enthusiasm that, in this case, is lyrical enthusiasm and therefore expression? A more perceptive reflection, with more attention to the impressions of taste, cannot fail to lead to the recognition that in the verses of the* Achilleis *Goethe did not achieve the pathos of a subsequent fragment on Helen, but maintained a style (at that time customary with him) which viewed humanity with a mixture of serenity and emotion, indulgence and loftiness, serious comprehension of the* painful and the tragic, and the exhortation to wisdom. Poetry serves at times as decoration (as in the initial lights of dawn, "the rose-fingered goddess" who, while the burning pyre is about to extinguish itself on the ashes of Hector, "adorns the earth and the sea so that the horror of the flames grows pale"); at times it is dominated by the calmness of the great knower of the human heart (as in the case of Thetis, who, begging for the life of her son and being sternly rejected by Hera after impetuously pouring out her grief, sits beside Leto, who had a maternal heart greater than the other Uranians and "enjoys there the plenitude of her affliction"). The assembly of the gods, which occupies the greatest part of the fragment, is certainly not presented in burlesque style, as was often done (beginning with the poems by Tassoni and Bracciolini),[39] because Goethe did not write to make people laugh; nevertheless, he mischievously and merrily underlines, in the figure of Aphrodite, the "ogling goddess," who unwillingly detaches herself from her lover and, "charmingly exhausted as though the night had not given her enough rest, abandons herself to the arms of her throne." One might compare the passage on Achilles' grave, dug on the top of the hill, and on the glory that radiates from there to the eyes of the seafarers to the closing lines of *I Sepolcri* to notice the difference in tone. Whoever carries out a project of this nature will establish historically what Goethe really felt and what he gave form to in the *Achilleis*; and those who, as a result, will read these verses will be prevented from going around and hitting their heads against the wall of the "Homeric character," the "Germanic character," "lyrical enthusiasm," and the like, and will be shown the way toward a comprehension and enjoyment of poetry.

The double meaning of "taste". Taste in the poetic sense and taste in the literary sense, although related to each other, are essentially distinct concepts, and at times they also conflict and generate perplexity and contrary judgments; a general example is offered by the strong opposition and the long resistance of the French literary and social taste to the poetry of Homer, Dante, and, most particularly, Shakespeare. In the abundant literature which illustrates this subject, one should see the book by L. Morandi, *Voltaire contro Shakespeare, Baretti contro Voltaire* (Città di Castello, 1884).

The intentions and the aims of the poets. At one time, inquiry into the aim of a poet's work was a common endeavor; and critics tried to deduce this aim not only

39. Alessandro Tassoni (1565–1635), author of *La secchia rapita* (The rape of the pail), a heroicomic poem, in twelve cantos in octaves, which was imitated by Pope. Bracciolini, see text, chap. 4, n. 9.

from what they found in the work, but also from the statements and confessions of the author, from testimony by contemporaries and from other documents. De Sanctis' greatest merit is perhaps in having recognized and said in his methodology of literary criticism (which is the most salutary lesson imparted by him about eighty years ago) that the intentions and the aims of the poets remain of necessity alien to their poetry and that it does not matter what the poet proposes or wishes to do or believes himself to be doing, but rather what he actually has done, even if unaware and in conflict with his professed aim. As a result, that inquiry is now, at least in Italy, no longer undertaken and is transferred outside the field of poetry. The intentions and the aims of the poet belong to his critical and moral convictions and can be realized only in the eventually nonpoetic parts of his work.

To exemplify this maxim one need only note what the best critics have always said about Tolstoy: "The images that he has created have a life of their own, independent of the intentions of the author; they come directly into relation with the reader, speaking for themselves, and irrevocably leading the reader to thoughts and consequences, which had never been in the mind of the author and which he would never have approved of" (P. Krapotkin, *Ideali e realtà nella letteratura russa*, trans. from the Russian, Naples, 1921, p. 120). This, after all, is true not only of poetry, but also of literature and every kind of work in which the real intention, so to speak, is always that of the work itself and not a velleity, a mental reservation, or a reflection of those who undertake to compose it.

The fundamental philosophy of criticism. Concerning this subject, I refer the reader to my essay "La critica come filosofia" in *Nuovi saggi d'estetica* (3d ed., pp. 199–215). It is understood that the philosophy whose necessity is asserted here is not that indigestive heap of abstractions and badly founded questions which go under the name of "philosophy" in the schools,[40] but that which is capable, in any form whatever, to penetrate history, that is, the facts of humanity; the "home philosophy" of which Shaftesbury spoke, and not the "mock philosophy," which he rightly spurned.

The shakiness of the concept of poetry. This shakiness is noted very frequently in critics, particularly in the hesitancy of their judgments. For instance, Lanson writes concerning Boileau: "Si l'on ne recherche dans les vers de Boileau que des 'impressions,' on lui rendra justice. Il a fait, sans se douter qu'il en faisait, des transpositions d'art étonnantes pour le temps: il a rendu par des mots, dans des vers, des effets qu'on

The scrupulousness of conscience, which demands careful listening to sensibility and taste, also demands the most rigorous thinking of the categories, which is the other element of judgment, the element which is intrinsic and essential to it. And the thinking of the categories can be carried out only through philosophy, and not through a part of it, such as the philosophy of art or esthetics, for this is not really comprehensible and thinkable outside the whole of which it is a part, that is, outside its relation to the philosophy of all the other forms of the spirit. This might seem too much of a burden to be carried by the critic of poetry; doubtless one would say that the critic must not have distorted ideas, must know what poetry is, what its contrary is, and what is distinct from poetry; but this should not imply that he must become a philosopher, since for his purpose he needs only a clear mind or common sense, as can be proved by so many excellent judgments given by wise men who were, nevertheless, incapable of carrying on a philosophical discussion.

---

40. *The reference is again to Gentile's philosophy.*

Certainly, common sense is sufficient in many cases, and it is a blessing that this is so; but what, after all, is common sense—the adoption of just criteria—if not the historical result of philosophizing, the philosophical conclusions which are expressed in sentences and which have become well-established presuppositions of judgment? These conclusions and sentences, however, are not always enough, for from time to time one stumbles upon difficulties concerning their meaning and their exact limits; at other times it is impossible with their help alone to defeat the re-emergence of brand-new sophisms, and we are confused and we try to analyze the theory in all its breadth, without success; and then it becomes necessary to go to their source—philosophy. In Italy the criticism of poetry and literature took the direction which, after many conflicts and delays, brought it by virtue of the impulse given by De Sanctis to a form generally more mature than that seen elsewhere; although De Sanctis was not a disciplined philosopher, he had a speculative mind and was educated in the Neapolitan cultural environment, strongly speculative and dialectical by close and remote traditions—opposed to the abstractions of intellectualism and faithful to the concreteness of history and the ideality and, at the same time, the sensuousness of poetry. And the perfecting of criticism is preceded in Italy by the perfecting of esthetics and of all of the philosophical methodology moving at the same pace; or, to put it in a way closer to the truth, criticism and esthetics, like history and philosophy, perfected themselves through reciprocal help, exchanging problems and solutions, which are not intelligible without the experience of poetry and art. Outside Italy one notices more frequently the want of balance, now toward mere sensibility, which is easily perverted into impressionism and psychologism, now toward the abstract intellect, which theorizes rationalistically and positivistically, while ignoring or forgetting the reality of poetry.

demande d'ordinaire au burin ou au pinceau. Et il a une précision, une vigueur, parfois une finesse de rendu qui sont d'un maître. . . . Est-ce de la poésie? Je ne sais: car qui décidera s'il y a, s'il peut y avoir une poésie vraiment, absolument réaliste? Mais c'est de l'art à coup sûr, et du grand art, par la probité de la facture solide et serrée, par le respect profond du modèle, par le large et le sûr emploi du métier" (Histoire de la littérature française, p. 489). Or even in regard to Lamartine: "Pourtant, c'est un grand poète, le plus naturel des poètes, 'le plus poète' si la poésie est essentiellement le sentiment. . . . Il ne se sentait pas sollicité à faire ce dur labeur de gratte-papier, à enlever patiemment, douloureusement, les négligences, incorrections, longueurs, répétitions, monotonie, prosaïsme: toutes les inégalités de l'oeuvre n'étaient-elles pas, elles aussi, des produits spontanés de son âme?" (p. 936). This would be the time to repeat the saying: one must decide.

Distinguishing the various qualities of pleasure. If there were only one kind of pleasure, that of beauty, the critical distinction would be easy, and Molière would be perfectly right (*Critique de l'école des femmes*, scene 6):

Uranie: Pour moi, quand je vois une comédie, je regarde seulement si les choses me touchent; et, lorsque je m'y suis bien divertie, je ne vais point demander si j'ai eu tort, et si les règles d'Aristote me défendaient de rire.
Dorante: C'est justement comme un homme qui aurait trouvé une sauce excellente, et qui voudrait examiner si elle est bonne sur les préceptes du Cuisinier français.
Uranie: Il est vrai, et j'admire les raffinements de certaines gens sur des choses que nous devons sentir par nous-mêmes.

But a pleasure may be effective, and yet of a non-esthetic but sensual and practical nature; it may even be of esthetic quality in a certain respect, but not of a purely poetic quality; such esthetic quality may derive, as we know, from literary beauty. Thus the experience of pleasure is not the proof of the existence of poetry. Brunetière, confusedly feeling that not every pleasure is poetic in nature, comically took to task pleasure itself: "Quelle cruelle destinée est celle du critique! Tous les autres hommes suivent les impulsions de leur goût. Lui seul passe son temps à combattre le sien! S'il s'abandonne à son plaisir, une voix lui crie:—Malheureux, que fais-tu? Quoi! Tu pleures aux *Deux gosses* et tu ris au *Plus heureux des trois!* Labiche t'amuse, et Dennery t'émeut! Tu frédonnes du Béranger! Tu lis peut-être de l'Alexandre Dumas en cachette et du Soulié! Où sont tes principes, ta mission, ton sacerdoce?" (*Revue d'histoire littéraire de la France* 40 [1933]: p. 197).

French criticism and German criticism. We must keep in mind the character which De Sanctis, eighty years ago, attributed to the two diverse methods of criticism, the French and the German (see his essay on Lamartine's *Cours de littérature*).[41] *In general, things today stand as they stood then, except that German criticism no longer has, as it did at that time, the philosophy of the glorious age (1780–1830) as its foundation, but other philosophies too inept and uncertain, and it is now much more contaminated by biography, psychologism, and racism than it was during the romantic age.*

The present condition of esthetics in France. *We refer here to the esthetics contained in "treatises," which could be more or less symbolized by concepts like the ones we read in one of the latest issues of the* Revue philosophique 59 (1905): 312: "L'art est une activité complexe qui comporte au moins deux jugements, l'un de précision, l'autre de qualité, et trois catégories de plaisir: un plaisir physique (tel, je suppose, que celui donné en musique par le son pur, et que j'ai essayé de faire ressortir dans la sensibilité musicale), une délectation intellectuelle qui touche parfois à l'ordre sportif, et le plaisir esthétique pur, fruit de la présence simultanée en nous du sentiment et de l'image. Ce serait, si je comprends bien, une volupté de création et de re-création. En ce sens, le plaisir esthétique tient plus de l'action que de l'entendement ou de la sensibilité; la matière en est peut-être l'émotion en soi," *and so on. At this point I feel compelled to repeat what I have already had occasion to say many times, namely, that in France the true theorists of art are not found among professors of philosophy and writers of treatises—almost all of them very mediocre—but among the great artists: Flaubert, Baudelaire, Becque, who, indeed, openly showed signs of intolerance against the nonsense of the* "universitaires qui se mêlent de l'art."

2. *Beauty, the Sole Category of Esthetic Judgment*

Great and varied, then, is the labor, the effort, and the thought of the man who wants to "give names to things,"[6] to the things pertaining to poetry and literature; we have many times pronounced these names in reference to their chief exponents with whom we have dealt in the course of this work. The judgment of poetry has a single indivisible category, that of beauty;

---

6. Cf. Cicero, *Tusculanae disputationes* 1. 25: "Does that man seem to be compounded of this earthly, mortal, and perishing nature, who first invented names for everything, which, if you believe Pythagoras, is the highest pitch of wisdom?"

41. *Saggi critici*, ed. P. Arcari, vol. 2, pp. 1–24 (first published in *Rivista contemporanea* [1857]).

and, on the basis of this category, it designates the works re-evoked by the imagination as "beautiful" or "ugly" and distinguishes the "fully or poetically beautiful" from the "literarily beautiful," dividing these last into works of emotional effusion, of prose or instruction, of oratory, of entertaining literature, and of art for art's sake (according to the varied content—sentimental, intellectual, or volitional—that they clothe with beautiful form). These delicate differentiations cannot be mechanical or easy, for the theoretical distinctions provided by philosophy and imposed upon them, while on the one hand offering necessary instruments, on the other constitute a more serious burden—the obligation to use them properly, that is, not to abuse them. The abuse or the foolish use of these instruments by the indiscreet and the inexpert causes unreasonable complaints which are damaging to the instruments themselves. The complainers forget the words of Jacobi on a similar occasion, namely, that what cannot be abused is of no use.[7]

Thus the category of beauty is one and indivisible, although its single manifestations are infinite and can be grouped into completely empirical classes (as classes always are) having nothing in common with the speculative distinctions determined by a rational concept. When one examines the various forms believed to be speculatively distinguishable within beauty, namely, those which at one time the esthetiticians called "variations of the beautiful," such as the "sublime," the "tragic," the "comic," the "humorous," the "graceful," and so on, one finds no more than abstractions formed from single groups of beautiful works and referable to their content, not to their form, which alone constitutes beauty. If some of these empirical concepts were refined and sharpened into a speculative form, purifying them of their particular matter, as was done with the concept of the "humorous" (thought by certain theorists to be a sort of synthesis of the tragic and the sublime and the comic and the graceful and so on),[8] one gets close to a synonym for beauty, which encompasses all of the aspects of the spirit and is, therefore, the resolution of the contrasts into the unity and of the unilateral visions into the fullness of humanity.

The same conclusion is reached through the examination of another system of groups, also at first formed empirically by abstracting certain elements and forms

Mechanical use of the method. Whoever sets certain definitions and concepts, tracing their correlative methodologies, certainly finds it very painful when his formulas, which he wishes to keep alive and flexible in constant development toward further determinations, are stiffened at the hands of people who use them as though they were sledgehammers, picks, axes, and similar large and heavy instruments for cutting and tearing down. Such occurrences help to understand Marx's feeling of annoyance when, after hearing at a congress the constant superstitious references to the principles of "Marxism," began his own speech by saying smilingly: "Moi, je ne suis pas marxiste!" This is the attitude which the discoverer and explainer of truths is led to take in the presence of the mechanical use others make of the truths he found; such use also prompts him to reject any adjective drawn from his name or the reduction of his name to an abstract ending in "ism." But, in so doing, he only manifests his dissatisfaction and performs his duty of discouraging the mechanization of his principles; he cannot, however, prevent it. The need for articles of faith and for catechisms at every step of life is one among other constant human needs, which can be qualified and treated for what they are, can be repressed, but never permanently uprooted.

---

7. Croce's reference here is probably to F. H. Jacobi (1743–1819), German antirationalist philosopher and a leading advocate of the philosophy of feeling and belief. But since there is a J. G. Jacobi (1740–1814), elder brother of the former and an anacreontic poet, the reference is not clear.

8. See Croce's *Aesthetic*, pp. 90–91, for the explanation of the concept of "humorous."

from individual works; this system is that of the three supreme and fundamental genres—the lyric, the epic, the dramatic—which were then raised to the position of eternal categories of poetry. According to this theory, the poet either sings his personal feelings or narrates the deeds of other men; or he arranges matters in such a way as to have the actions of others represented by a third person, without his own intervention as narrator; and he must take one of these three paths and move along it without encroaching upon the others. But the three paths, when closely considered, do not seem to be really three; there are some people who cast doubt on the second, that of the narrator, and they either combine it with the first or they abolish it because mere narration is not the expression of feelings or dramatic presentation; some others make the first and the second into byways leading to the third great road—the drama—which, from the Greeks to the romantics, was often idolized as the only form close to the ideal of poetry.[9] But the truth is that the lyric poet dramatizes his feelings and that the dramatic poet lyricizes his actions; and if the lyric poet fails to do this, he will be emotional, but not lyrical, and, if the dramatic poet fails in this, he will be an author of plays, not a poet. Reducing then the trinity of the three necessary forms to the duality of lyric and drama, and this duality to distinction and opposition, what else is found at the bottom if not the relation of content to poetic expression, of feeling to intuition?

The primacy of dramatic poetry. This primacy, which had among the Athenians nothing more than a practical importance in theatrical representations of social life (and this brought about a corresponding doctrinal interest in Aristotle's *Poetics*: see Rostagni's introduction to his edition of the *Poetics* [Turin, 1927], particularly p. lxxvii) went as far as to be formulated in metaphysical terms by German estheticians. For instance, in Vischer's *Aesthetik* (Stuttgart, 1857, vol. 3, p. 2, par. 895–903), we read that art in general creates, in identical manner, a world of objects in plastic art and a purely subjective life in music and poetry by repeating the philogenesis in the ontogenesis; it re-creates the objective moment in the epic, the subjective in the lyric, and the synthesis of the two in the drama, thus reaching the summit not only of itself, but of all art. These are not so much clever combinations and little games with concepts as they are troubled dreams caused by the obsession with literary genres, with the arts, and the struggle among them for primacy, hegemony, and domination.

The impossibility of distinguishing lyric, epic, and dramatic genres. Even subtle talents failed in such an enterprise: see Humboldt's essay on *Hermann und Dorothee*, in which he maintains that there are two dispositions of esthetic states, that aimed at arousing in the listener or spectator a general contemplation from which the epos derives and that aimed at arousing a particular sensation from which the lyric and the drama come: the first disposition—the epic—elevates us above the object, confers upon it objectivity, impartiality, and totality, thus transporting us outside ourselves, and so on (par. 64, 65). Goethe, recognizing that "the epic poet and the dramatic poet are subject to the same general poetic laws, especially those concerning unity and development, and that, in ad-

---

9. See Aristotle, *Poetics* 26. This is in part also the theory of Victor Hugo ("Préface de Cromwell") when he placed the "dramatic age" at the summit of the historical process of the human mind, that is, after the "lyrical age" and the "epic age."

dition, both treat similar objects and can use every kind of motif," established the great and essential difference between them as follows: "the epic poet exposes the event as completely past, and the dramatic poet as completely present"; as a result, the former is symbolized by the rhapsodist, surrounded by calm listeners, the latter by the mime, surrounded by people who listen impatiently (Ueber epische und dramatische Dichtung, 1797: Werke, vol. 27, pp. 119–41). But this is an extrinsic difference which may suggest only vague empirical rules concerning composition in particular cases.

Identity between lyric, epic, and dramatic poetry. This identity asserts itself in the very words of those who deny it and wish to keep the distinction; the following passage proves it: "Objective poetry, like lyric poetry, also springs from the inner experiences of the poet. But these experiences do not remain, as in lyric poets, within the sphere of feeling and thought: the imagination of the epic and the dramatic poet creates figures and characters that, though nourished by the blood from his heart, detach themselves from him and, plastically shaped, bear the traits of their own independent existence. The poet takes part in their actions and destiny as he takes part in those of his children and his closest friends; but he himself remains outside the world of his own creation: he disappears behind that world, or better, vanishes into it; and his personality, which in the lyric is the central light to which converge the beams of both the sentiment and the idea, here appears to be extinguished" (Lehmann, Poetik, p. 139). In this, one must note among other things that the author, in order to make possible the impossible differentiation he wants to put forth, supposes that the lyric poet deals with "feeling" and "thought" and not at all with "imagination," as does every other poet.

The origin of the distinction between classic and romantic. Goethe says (Conversations with Eckermann, March 21, 1830) that he "laid down the maxim of objective poetry, and would allow no other; but Schiller, who worked quite in the subjective way, deemed his own fashion the right one, and, to defend himself against me, wrote the essay on Naïve and Sentimental Poetry: the two kinds of poetry were then called 'classic' and 'romantic.'" Thus, in the last analysis, the origin of the famous distinction would have been occasioned by a poetic deficiency noticed in Schiller and by his "subjective" disposition, that is, the disposition toward the excitement of passion, the intentional and the intellectualistic; and, rightly, that category of the sentimental and romantic, both in its origin and in its historical development, has always been used to indicate weak

The same relation is found in the famous division of poetry into classic and romantic. This division has had an empirical and lexicographical value by designating with the first adjective the ancient poetry of Greece and Rome, and with the second the Christian and modern; but unfortunately it has also had a speculative value by distinguishing two different categories of poetry. The accidental originator of the second meaning was Goethe,[10] who later repented of the dichotomy he had created, which was taken over by Schiller and exaggerated and made rigid by the romantics. The scission introduced into the concept of the wholeness of poetry—the wholeness of beauty—became the more insufferable since the romantics were led to reject the poetry of "classicism" as "cold" and unpoetic, and the classicists to reject that of "romanticism" as "formless," unartistic and unpoetic; the fact is that the only thinkable division in this case is not a division but an antinomy—the contrast between the beautiful and the ugly. For the two terms, romanticism and classicism, when thoroughly analyzed and speculatively developed, lead us to the relationship between "dramati-

---

10. *Conversations with Eckermann*, April 2, 1828.

cism" and "lyricism," intuition and feeling, form and content, that is, between two terms whose truth lies only in their synthesis; this synthesis cannot be achieved by one abstract term rejecting the other, but by the resolution of the one into the other, a resolution which preserves and transcends both.[11] Thus against classicism and romanticism there was set "classicality," a word to which was attributed the demerit (which is, on the contrary, its very merit) of "meaning nothing," and which in fact does not posit any determination of abstract content, because "classicality" simply means the excellent expression, the perfect expression—beauty.

poetic talents. In the face of the growing and pressing manifestations of such would-be poetry, Goethe changed the preceding dichotomy to an antinomy, maintaining that "the classic is the healthy and the romantic the sickly" ("das Klassische ist das Gesunde, und das Romantische das Kranke," April 2, 1829). As for the talent of Schiller, not very poetic, one may say that the author himself, who had a certain philsophical talent, defines it in a letter to Goethe (January 2, 1798): "Your method of alternating production and reflection is really enviable and admirable. The two operations are truly separate in you and thus are both executed with so much purity. You, as long as you work, are really in the dark, and the light is solely within yourself; and, when you begin to reflect, this inner light comes forth and irradiates the objects for you and for others. In me the two modes of activity are mixed and with little advantage for the creative process." But Schiller was a beautiful mind and an honest soul: poets far weaker than he said later: "We are unable to create images; therefore, true poetry is that which rhymes concepts"; or "We are unable to create harmonious verses; therefore, true poetry is that which is made by screaming, sobbing, and imprecating."

Classicality. Classicality is to be understood in a completely ideal sense as synonymous with perfect poetry and, mainly, in its original meaning (of something of "the first order"). Against this stands the historiographic sense of that word in reference to the Greco-Roman world, in which case one speaks of classicality not only in poetry and the arts, but also in philosophy, in politics, and so on. Already Madame de Staël knew and distinguished the two meanings: "On prend quelquefois le mot 'classique' comme synonime de 'perfection.' Je m'en sers ici dans une autre acception, en considérant la poésie classique comme celle des anciens et la poésie romantique comme celle qui tient de quelque manière aux traditions chevaleresques" (De l'Allemagne, vol. 2, p. 11). See the essays collected in the volume *Das Problem des Klassischen und die Antike,* eighth lecture, ed. W. Jaeger (Leipzig-Berlin, 1931). But, in this second and historiographic sense, the concept loses every determinateness, changes to vague representations and fancies. In its ideal sense itself, the word "classicality" has above all the function of negating such a hybrid conceptual-historical sense; and, therefore, it is a merit if, as a French critic noted, the word "ne signifie rien." The tautology in this case stands guard at the door to forbid the introduction of false distinctions and arbitrary characteristics. From "classicality" it is customary to distinguish "classicism," which means school and imitation.

"Greekness" as a symbol. "The clarity of vision, the

11. The reference is clearly to Gentile's dialectic of opposites. But Gentile's opposites are also resolved into the synthesis!

One could continue with other divisions less famous than, or varying from, the preceding, such as that of art and primitive poetry, and that of art and learned poetry,[12] with preference given sometimes to the first and sometimes to the second, though both are parts of the whole art which is at one and the same time primitiveness and culture. But the danger of scission introduced into the concept of beauty, which was the real spiritual heresy of Germany (reference is made here to the esthetic field and not to the religious field which, instead, helped the progress of the European mind), does not lie in the wearisome conflict of two empty concepts—abstract classicism and abstract romanticism, abstract primitivism and abstract learning—and the logomachy and the waste of time resulting from it, but in the conversion of those pseudoesthetic concepts into practical attitudes, considering such practical determinations to be forms of poetry; thus poetry was given a practical meaning, the practical meaning that hedonists, utilitarians, and materialists gave to their philosophies. Noteworthy in this respect is the present rise in Germany of a new ideal form—the baroque—which is added to the previous two.[13] This ideal form derives from an esthetically negative concept, which was nevertheless applied to determine a particular attitude of poetry and literature; therefore, it would be well to wait until, by another step forward, one more form will be concocted, that of poetic and literary ugliness, and it, too, will be declared a particular spiritual attitude. And such it undoubtedly is; but a spiritual attitude brought about by false appearances which are accepted through vanity and greed is by its own nature the negation of poetry.

---

12. See Croce, *Poesia antica e moderna* (1940).

13. For Croce's negative concept of "baroque," see particularly his *Storia dell'età barocca in Italia* (1929).

facility of communication, is what ravishes us; and if we now assert that we find all this in works which are genuinely Greek, which contain the noblest subject matter and the worthiest content, and an accomplished and sure execution, it will be well understood why we invariably begin from Greekness and always aim at it. Let everyone be Greek in his own way; but he must be really so!" These words of Goethe (*Antik und Modern,* in *Werke,* vol. 30, p. 122) meant: let everyone, in his own way, elevate himself to beauty.

Romanticism in its esthetically negative sense. Having established above the meanings in which the word "classicality" is used, the word "romanticism" can have, in the theory of poetic form, only a negative sense, suggesting imperfections of various nature and, specifically, as we noticed, sentimentalism or sentimental rhetoric or any other unpoetic emphasis. That romantic works are inferior because of this has been noticed many times. Schérer wrote in *Etudes sur la littérature contemporaine* (Paris, 1876, vol. 5, p. 226): "Le romantisme a fait de l'originalité avec de l'imitation, et de la naïveté avec des efforts."

Romanticism in the material sense. Romanticism was also viewed as the passional element of art in itself; in such a case, the relation to be brought out is that of matter and form:

> Der Gehalt in deinem Busen,
> Und die Form in deinem Geist;

"the matter in your bosom and the form in your mind," as Goethe put it (see *Conversazioni critiche,* 2d ed., vol. 3, p. 65).

Romanticism. About romanticism in all of its aspects—intellectual, moral, and esthetic—see the succinct analysis that I gave, the result of long reflections and research, in my *History of Europe in the Nineteenth Century,* chap. 3.

The Attic, the Asiatic, and the Rhodian styles. One must read in chap. 10 of bk. 12 of Quintilian [*Institutionis oratoriae*] his excellent criticism about the distinction of styles in Attic, Asiatic, and Rhodian, and against the conception of a style as the touchstone of artistic values. He defends the variety of styles according to orators and situations, and concludes that, if one chooses a priori only one style—the Attic, for instance—as a yardstick, the word "Attic" becomes the equivalent of excellent, despite the fact that the Attic orators themselves were different from one another.

Different ideas about poetry according to various peoples and times. It is worth pointing out an erroneous saying, whose bad effects are reflected in criticism; it consists in the idea that the concept of poetry changes *according to various times and peoples and that it must be judged in accordance with the different conceptions, that is, the lyric of the "stil nuovo" according to the theory of the "stil nuovo," that of the sixteenth century according to the poetics of that century, and so on. However, what changes at best is the meaning of the word "poetry," but never the "poetry" in itself or in its concept, which always stands as a perpetual precondition, expressed or implied, of every esthetic judgment. On this subject I offered some observations in an essay of mine on the sixteenth-century poet Angelo di Costanzo (see Uomini e cose della vecchia Italia, 2d ed., vol. 1, pp. 88–90).*

Sometimes, that saying is in contradiction to the erroneous judgment of poetry according to the narrow sentiment or fashion at a particular time, as, for instance, that in which we live; but since in this case, instead of rising to the ideal criterion, we go back to another time, to the fourteenth or the sixteenth century, we remain caught in the error we meant to avoid.

"The primitive". In Italy this concept, with its antithesis of "scientific," or "learned," or "classical" art, has in the last years been given prominence by L. Venturi (*Il gusto dei primitivi*, Bologna, 1926: cf. *Conversazioni critiche*, 2d ed., vol. 3, pp. 124–28); and some of his students have managed to extend it to the criticism of poetry, pointing out, for instance, on the basis of that criterion, the time when the "primitivity," that is, the "genuineness," of Italian poetry came to an end; this would have occurred at the end of the fifteenth century with Poliziano and Boiardo (that is, precisely with the two humanists versed in Greek and Latin literature!), who would be "primitive," while in the following generation Ariosto would already be a scientific and learned poet. In fact, both Poliziano and Boiardo appear as primitive when looked at from the point of view of the art of Ariosto, because always, in every age, one looks at the preceding age as more naive, simpler, less complicated and less rich, and, therefore, to a certain extent, primitive by comparison to the subsequent age (I pointed this out in *Poesia popolare e poesia d'arte*, 2d ed., p. 237: cf. *Conversazioni critiche*, 2d ed., vol. 5, pp. 62–65). In conclusion, in this manner of thinking "on est toujours primitif pour quelqu'un"—primitive in the same way that a technical instrument is called so in comparison to the more perfected one; and the one which at present is more perfected will in its turn become primitive.*

Realism and idealism in poetry. This division of the wholeness of poetry into two diverse or contrasting poetic forms is also to be thrown into a corner with others of the kind; after all, for one who observes carefully, such division substantially is the equivalent of*

This conversion of poetry into something practical prepared it for political and social divisions. And the very pseudoesthetic forms, while tending on the one hand to remain purely ideal and to affirm themselves as generally human (hence the rediscovery of a "romanticism" not only "modern" but also "Greek" or "Roman," of a "baroque" not only of seventeenth-century Europe but also of the "Hellenistic" or "late Roman" period, of a "classicism" not only of the golden age of Greece and of Rome but also "French" and "German," and the like), tended on the other hand to fix themselves as typical of particular peoples and races. Classical poetry has been identified with the poetic mode of the Latin and neo-Latin peoples; romantic poetry with that of the Germanic peoples (despite the terminology of the word, which seems to imply the opposite), even if now its place seems to have been taken over by the "baroque," which for certain German theorists sounds like a greater and more vigorous and virile attribute of the Germans from earliest times. But now, without passing through the intermediary of those ideal forms, peoples, races, and social classes have been endowed with forms of poetry appropriate to each, deeply separated from one another, unknown to one another, fighting against one another, as those peoples and races and classes did in the sphere of practical reality. Thus there seems to be now, among others, a "Germanic" poetry created by pure Germans which only Germans can feel and judge; and a "proletarian" poetry (namely in Russia) that only the proletarians are in a position to produce and understand and about which the bourgeois have no right to open their mouths, not even to admire it. Not only is beauty no longer whole and indivisible, but its subdivisions, though arbitrary, are not those intentionally and universally human, namely, dramatic and lyric, ingenuous and sentimental, classical and romantic. Its divisions are now the peoples themselves and the classes with whose activities the works of poetry are identified; the category of judgment is therefore, by turns "Germany," "France," "England," "Russia," "Italy"; or "bourgeoisie," "democracy," "hammer and sickle," "swastika," and so on.

It is, then, the more urgent to reaffirm the indivisibility of beauty, the only category of judgment, since the divisions which are nowadays made not only break, as did the ancient divisions, the esthetic unity of mankind, but they destroy humanity itself, enclosing it into circles foreign to each other and irreconcilably and perpetually inimical.

the preceding one between classicism and romanticism. What is displeasing in so-called realistic poetry are the immediate and rudimentary impressions of reality which are not in harmony with and resolved into a poetic motif; and, conversely, what displeases in so-called idealistic poetry is the lack of relation to passion, which is replaced by conventional schemes; thus the remedy for the one and the other is the image, both corporeal and ideal, which is the whole of true poetry. The advocates of the one and the other of these unilateral tendencies are ordinarily the intellectualists such as were, or soon became, the romanticists.

The "baroque" as an art form. See my analysis of the three positive meanings which critics recently have tried to give to the "baroque": as a "form of art," as an "artistic age," as a "moral attitude." The demonstration of the lack of foundation of these three meanings is found in my Storia dell'età barocca, 3d ed. (particularly in a final note, pp. 491–96). Information about newer, but not wiser, German literature on the argument is found in L. Vincenti, "Interpretazioni del barocco tedesco" (Studi germanici [Florence], fasc. 1, 1935, pp. 39–72). In the German criticism of poetry and the arts, that concept continues to be used arbitrarily and confusedly, as can be observed in the recent Geschichte der Kunst by R. Hamann (Berlin, 1935), in which Raphael is presented as the expression of a "baroque-classicistic primitivism," Rubens as the expression of the second "sensualistic baroque," and the rococo as a third baroque: the three forms are explained as reactions to three previous "naturalisms" (see the above-mentioned Studi germanici, fasc. 3, 1935, pp. 422–28). Moreover, I noticed that in a recent history of Roman literature (cf. Deutsche Literaturzeitung, January 12, 1936, column 58) Plautus is defined as "master of the baroque" and Terence as "representative of the classic," and the like. All that false ideology has not penetrated Italy, or else has penetrated very weakly, because of the defense that I rushed to build up against it at the first threats, thus re-establishing the original negative concept of baroque, which is the only one having scientific value and usefulness.

3. The Characterization of Poetry and the Completion of the Hermeneutical-Critical Process

If taste in poetry attracts the beautiful and repels the ugly, esthetic judgment points to the quality of both. It has often been a cause for wonder that esthetic judgment has been so poor in distinctive terminology applying to beauty and so rich in words applying to the ugly. This was attributed to natural wickedness, which has one hundred eyes open for evil and only one, half-closed, for good. This is the natural result of what we have just demonstrated, namely, that the beautiful insofar as it is beautiful allows no divisions and distinctions. The terminology of the beautiful should not be considered to be poor, but rather monotonous because it is a continual series of synonyms which, by the words "harmony," "truth," "simplicity," "unity in variety," "naturalness," "sincerity," "imaginative vigor," "lyrical intensity," "delicacy," "serenity," "sublimity," and the like, repeat the same concept of "beautiful expression." On the other hand, since the ugly arises from the breaking of esthetic coherence for a practical end or for convenience, its concept is specified in all the ways in which that incoherence manifests itself according to various circumstances. These ways are numerous and give rise to a terminology that continually enriches itself with new words: "incorrect," "redundant," "negligent," "awkward," "miserable," "swelling," "declamatory," "charlatanesque," "affected," "buffoonish," "baroque," "sentimental," "sensual," "frivolous," "obscene," "rude," "crude," "violent," "abortive," "vulgar," "plebeian," "languid," "pedestrian," "conventional," "mechanical," "banal," "hard," "heavy," "precious," "distorted," "overdone," and so on, ad infinitum.

But esthetic judgment, in defining the attractions and repugnances of taste, remains bound to it and inseparable from it, in accordance with the nature of all true and concrete judgments, which is identity of intuition and category, of intuitive subject and conceptual predicate, and not an abstract relation among concepts, for it is never so, except outwardly or on the surface. The didactic form, in which the critic sets forth his judgment, shows this clearly, since, like the critic of figurative arts (who, by presupposing always the vision of the original painting or sculpture or architecture, helps the formulation of his judgments through drawings or photographic reproductions of the originals), the critic of poetry uses paraphrases or quotations from the poem he examines. His discourse is empty for the reader who does not enter into relation with the poem and becomes empty for the critic himself when he loses sight of it and is led to wander about in generalities or to lose himself in subtleties.

However, the work of the critic does not consist wholly in showing the beautiful and the ugly at the very moment he feels them as such. We are justifiably dissatisfied when the critic limits himself to pointing at or naming the parts that are beautiful and those

The meager terminology of the beautiful and the rich terminology of the ugly. This observation has been made many times; but the first to make it, to my knowledge, was Goethe in an essay written in 1817–1819: *Urteilsworte französischer Kritiker,* in which he shows, through examples drawn mostly from Grimm's *Correspondence,* the "richness of expressions for distaste and the scarcity of expressions for praise," used by the French in the matter of art (see *Werke,* ed. Goedeke, 27, pp. 148–52). But Goethe did not concern himself with the esthetic problem he was encountering, and considered the quantitative unevenness as reflecting the particular character of the French and their literature.

The moment of impression. Following are some admonitions and exhortations left by De Sanctis on the subject: "Criticism is founded on the truth and freshness of first impressions, which one must have in order to re-evoke and examine diligently. Just as poetics cannot replace genius, criticism cannot replace taste, and taste is the genius of the critic. It is said that the poetic talent is inborn; critical talent is also inborn, for there is in the critic a power given to him by nature. . . . Do you want, O critic, to judge well? Preserve this previous faculty, remain a man and beware, above all, of your theories which, separated from your sentiment, are empty and dead abstractions (*Saggio sopra un dramma di G. Gattinelli*). "Discussions suited to idle minds, fond of riddles and obtuse to the pure and direct impressions of art. . . . Trust to your own impressions, especially the first, which are the best. Later you can elucidate them, you can educate your taste; but your path must not be encumbered at the outset by preconceived judgments and artificial methods" (*Saggio sulla Francesca da Rimini*).[42]

42. The essay can now be found in English in *De Sanctis on Dante,* trans. Joseph Rossi and Alfred Galpin (Madison: University of Wisconsin Press, 1957), chap. 3; quotation from p. 35.

that are not; we say in this case that rather than being a critic he is a man of taste and can give only half a critical judgment, to which we must add the other half in order to complete it.

The missing half, whose lack is felt, will not be that which some theories required the critic to provide, that is, besides his esthetic judgment, a redoing or a re-expression of the poet's work by acting almost as *artifex additus artifici* [artist added to artist][14] for, if such redoing and re-expression are not the deprecated orgies of estheticism which improperly undertake to celebrate the work of art (a celebration amounting to an intrusive singing on one's own, often forced and out of tune, accompanying or mixing with that of the poet), they are a "translation" in the sense and within the limits we have already described. But the translation if analytical and prosaic pertains at best to the philological preparation for reading and not to the criticism of poetry; and if synthetic and artistic it does not belong to criticism, either, because it is a variation of the work of poetry, whereas criticism remains attached to the individual reality of it and cannot detach itself without ceasing to be criticism.

Nor does it consist in furnishing the intuitive equivalent of poetry, for this is impossible; some maintain, however, that it must furnish the "rational" equivalent. But if this were possible, poetry would not have come into the world or it would soon have been ejected as superfluous, for we would have been able to obtain its "equivalent," moreover in a rational form. This would have been like obtaining a sum of money, not in paper, but in minted gold. Although this confutation is offered somewhat in jest, it contains at the bottom the serious answer that a rational equivalent of intuition is contrary to the logical nature of judgment, because it cancels one of the terms of the relation which is the source of its very life.

In completing his judgment, the critic offers neither intuitive re-creations nor logical equivalents of poetry; but he gives a characterization, which is something different. And this characterization cannot concern itself, for the reasons indicated above, with the form of poetry which is whole, indivisible, and identical in all poets, that being the form of beauty; so whenever we say that a poem pleases for this or that particular character, either we fall into a naive illusion by attributing to an abstract and dead particularity what is wholly concrete and living, or we repeat, as we said, tautologically (even if in diverse verbal forms), that beauty is beauty. Still less can the char-

14. Croce's formula would be, instead, "Philosopher added to artist" (*philosophus additus artifici*).

Singing with the poet. When I reminded the critic to keep in mind the obligation of singing with the poet, but not competing with him in singing, an esthete replied that I did not understand the sacred furor of a possessed critic because I had not experienced it. I retorted in jest by recalling that in German concert halls there is a sign: "Das Mitsingen ist verboten" (Singing with the singer is forbidden). See *Nuovi saggi di estetica*, 3d ed., pp. 221–25.

The titles of poems. When the titles which the poets usually attach to their poems are not a mere label, they are already a first attempt to qualify the content and thus furnish an indication of it to the reader: so much does this operation of qualifying correspond to a need of the mind!

Nonexistence of particular characteristics attributable to beauty. I wrote in my *Nuovi saggi d'estetica* 3d ed., p. 284): "But of the beautiful, insofar as it is beautiful, there is nothing else to say. In the presence of it the connoisseur of art, the man who has a thorough knowledge of it, 'obstupescit' [is stupefied], and even 'obticet' [remains silent]. Certainly, one may say: It is beautiful because these lines are arranged in such and such a manner, these lights are distributed in such and such a way, and so on. —But how many other works

acterization consist in the hybrid labor halfway between esthetical and grammatical, rhetorical and lexical, such as is practiced by some positivistic philologists and which, like all hybrids, is completely sterile. By breaking the forms of poetry into words and metaphors, comparisons, figures, syntactic connections, rhythmic schemes, and so forth, we do not grasp the character of poetry, which is revived and contemplated only in the total intuition of its oneness; but we end up by putting together a pitiful heap of lifeless fragments, which can be discarded as worthless.

have, generally, the same arrangement of lines and distribution of lights, yet are ugly! In this way of judging 'il più divin s'invola' [the element most divine vanishes]. One may also say: I am in love with that woman because she is kind, because she has black eyes, because she has delicate hands, and so forth. — But how many other women are kind, have delicate hands and black eyes, and so forth, with whom we are not in love? One loves because one loves, say the theorists of love; and a work of art is beautiful because it is beautiful, the critic must say."

Works on style. There are hundreds of works on style or, rather, statistics of metaphors, similes, and so forth, customary in German universities and in those universities which imitate the German methods; and it is no exaggeration to say that they serve no purpose. They prove as little as does a dissertation that I just happened to review (see *Conversazioni critiche,* 2d ed., vol. 5, pp. 86–87) on "the way the characters in the dramas of Grillparzer, Hebbel, and Ludwig die" (thirty-seven on the stage by mortal wounds, forty-four backstage, this many in battle, that many by execution, this number directly, and that number murdered indirectly, and so forth).

In Germany "stylistics" has been given a more serious orientation thanks to Vossler and Spitzer and others, who constitute a new philological school, in which the so-called stylistic consideration has the function of a mere didactic point of departure for the comprehension of the individual poet or poem. In this case, there is no difference whatever between stylistic and esthetic criticism, as I have already pointed out (*Conversazioni critiche,* 2d ed., vol. 3, pp. 101–05), and as Spitzer himself confirms (*Romanische Stil-und Literaturstudien,* vol. 1, pp. 29–30, note).

Many and sometimes valuable works which now are also frequently coming out in Italy on the "language of the writers," prompt two observations, however. The first is precisely that of the intrinsic identity of the study of poetry with the study of language, for the language is not the "medium" or the "instrument" of poetry, but is poetry itself; therefore, it can never be detached from the movement and the life of poetry, except in certain empirical divisions—divisions which soon prove to be of bad use or no use at all, when the words and the other forms of language are not, in the analysis of the critic, constantly linked to the one soul which dictated them. The second observation is that one should not forget, as often happens, that the sole aim of criticism is to promote and direct the comprehension of the poetic and the literary work in the readers, who must not be overburdened with the excessive fragmentation of that which their intuition grasps in

The characterization refers properly to the content of poetry, to the feeling expressed by poetry and by the same expressive act, amplified and transferred within its own sphere. By abstracting from this idealization, we must now reconsider poetry in its own features, in that "characteristic" which, according to the already mentioned words of Goethe,[15] is like the starting point of the "beautiful." All that which has not become the content of poetry and remains outside it, linked to the work materially or pertaining to the person of the poet, is excluded from the process whose aim is to grasp and define the generating motif of poetry which shapes and animates all parts of the poem.

But the object of this further investigation is human reality in its wholeness, in all its infinite forms, all of which by turn emerge as regenerating motifs of poetic expression. As a result, the critic is required to know the human heart and critics are esteemed, not only for their expertise concerning the beauty of form, but also for their knowledge "delli vizî umani e del valore" [of the human vices and virtues];[16] this by reaction leads to our impatience with those who discuss poetry without having ever loved and dreamed and experienced the tempest of the various passions and endured their assaults, or without having sought and

15. See above, chap. 2, n. 6.
16. Dante, *Inferno* 26. 99.

a flash; the critic must not lose sight of his true purpose by displaying his own diligence and scholarly subtlety.

On the other hand, those who misunderstand the legitimate purpose of esthetic criticism, which is to study only the "language of the artists," refer to the critics who aim at determining the inspirational motifs of works of art as "psychologists" or "moralists"; they do not realize, because of a certain mental naiveté, that the apparent psychological or moral determination is no more than the determination of what is poetic in the work, as distinguished from the non-poetic elements which could have been mingled in it by the author or introduced by the critics who misinterpreted what had become a living poetic language; and they are also unjust toward themselves because they are not aware that, through the metaphors of words, of syntactical, metrical, and stylistic forms, or of light and shade, design, color, chiaroscuro, nuances, and the like, they are doing no more than determining and distinguishing (when they have a real perception and enjoyment of poetry or painting) the inspirational motifs of the works before them, which, of necessity, are always spiritual or moral acts (whatever you may please to call them) and never material things.

The limit of characterization. May I say that, in my long career as a literary critic, I have always been aware of this limit (which is after all not a limit, but the very nature and function of criticism) in my characterization of poets; and I have therefore always observed the necessary moderation. For instance, my essay on Ariosto, after explaining that the character of the poetry of the *Orlando Furioso* lies in the emphasis on the moment of "harmony," that is, on the movement of things in their emerging, conflicting, and coming again to a peaceful agreement, I added the following reservation: "But we shall not allow ourselves to be taken in by the foolish belief, which characterizes many present-day critics, that in our esthetic formulas we have provided an equivalent of Ariosto's poetry. . . . Also our new determinations must be posited and dismantled, retaining only the new results, through which we shall discard other false concepts enunciated by the critics concerning Ariosto, and shall point out the outstanding traits of the subject matter that he chose to fashion, and the manner and the tone of his song. The poetry of the *Orlando Furioso*, like all poetry, is an *individuum ineffabile*; and Ariosto, the Poet of Harmony, never completely coincides with the broader Ariosto, who is more than the Poet of Harmony, as we have defined him explicitly or implicitly. This concrete and living Ariosto we

enlarged their experience in that matter through intelligence and sympathy—the impatience, we mean, with the "normaliens," as they are called in France by poets and artists, and the "professors," as we say in Italy. For these reasons, it is also said with the right intention but the wrong concept, that the true critic of poetry must also be "a moralist." The critic must not contain within himself the moralist, but the philosopher who has meditated on the human spirit in its distinctions and oppositions and in its dialectic. He must not be the philosopher applying his concepts to the formulation of philosophical, scientific, political, moral judgments or judgments in classes or types corresponding to the varying feelings and activities of the mind, thus changing himself to a psychologist. The characterization of poetry implies the determination of its content or fundamental motif and the assigning of it to a psychological class or type by approximation. And in so doing the critic shows his acumen and delicacy and finesse; in this labor he is satisfied only when, by reading and rereading and considering, he succeeds in grasping that fundamental trait and in defining it with a formula announcing the successful inclusion of the feeling of the single work of poetry in the most suitable class which he knows or has thought out for the occasion.

The most suitable class is always simply a class, that is, a general concept, while poetry is, instead, not the general, but the individual-universal, the finite-infinite; as a result, the formula, however close to the poetic re-evocation, never coincides with it; indeed, between the two there is always an abyss. The formula which characterizes poetry, when compared to it, always appears more or less rigid and harsh. Hence, after the momentary satisfaction, our discontent even with the most elaborated critical formulae, including our own, which have been produced through so much mental tension, brain work, scrupulous delicacy; hence, too, the impulse to turn our back to the formula or to immerse ourselves again in the individual and living poetry. So Goethe said that it was not at all possible to talk of Shakespeare, for every discussion would be insufficient, and that he had tried to discuss him in his *Meister*, but with no results;[17] and similarly Wilhelm Humboldt, speaking precisely of Goethe and describing some of his characteristics, interrupted himself to say that he "had only mentioned these things, because to speak or write about a poet is nothing but wandering around the ineffable" ("als ein Herumgehen um das Unaussprechliche").[18] But the critic

do not propose to exhaust and replace; on the contrary, being present in the reader's imagination and in ours, he is our constant point of reference in our critical elucidations, which, without such presupposition, would turn out to be unintelligible" (*Ariosto, Shakespeare and Corneille*, pp. 46–47). Likewise, my essay *The Poetry of Dante* closes with these words: "Such, in rapid strokes, is the portrait of Dante, the authentic portrait, which emerges from his own writings. But it must never be forgotten that this picture, which serves to differentiate Dante from other poets and helps to achieve an intelligent understanding of his works, becomes, in common with all characterization, narrow and, so to speak, prosaic, if it be not set in the fullness of poetry—poetry alone—which never imprisons itself in any one thing or group of things, but spreads itself throughout the cosmos. . . . This is the essential, which cannot be described otherwise than as universal poetry. From this point of view Dante is no longer Dante as a definite individual, but that marveling and impassioned voice which the human soul transmits from age to age in the ever-recurring creation of the world. Here, all differences vanish; the eternal and sublime burden of the song alone resounds—which has the same fundamental quality in all great poets and artists, always new, always old, received by us with ever-renewed excitement and joy" (p. 254).

17. *Conversations with Eckermann*, December 25, 1825 (Croce's note).
18. W. v. Humboldt in his essay on Goethe's *Italienischen Reise*, in *Ausgewählte Philosophische Schriften*, ed. J. Schubert (Leipzig: Dür, 1910).

who is experienced in his job and who understands the underlying theory knows very well how things work, and he himself feels that the formula does not coincide with poetry and that one cannot express in general terms what has already expressed itself in intuitive terms, and that "effable" in itself becomes "ineffable" in the new relation. All the same he labors tirelessly because he knows that in so doing he accomplishes a necessary function; and he strives to think out classes always closer to the original poetry, though always separated from it by a distance that can only be crossed by a leap. The thing which makes him indignant is to observe that other critics, rather than resuming the work where he left off and trying to carry it further, apply classes either too heterogeneous or too general, which he had discarded and replaced with more appropriate ones. What annoys and torments him is to find his formulae in the mouths of people who have stiffened and dogmatized them, not accepted them with the wise skepticism which the matter requires. If he discusses them with someone (and certainly he always does), this someone will be another critic, and not poetry, because he also knows that criticism, reaching its summit—characterization—is by its own nature "criticism of criticism." What is changing through this labor toward a greater subtlety is not poetry, which is "definite," but the form of characterization, which is always "indefinite": indefinite because the movement of the human spirit proposes ever-new difficulties and arouses ever-new problems. The critic has formed an instrument which is better than those existing previously, and he wants to perfect it further or have others perfect it, for he knows its value and use.

Whatever its value may be is shown when one reflects that in the final product, in that formula, is contained the long process one has gone through in the grasping of poetry, from the philological preparation to the intuitive re-evocation, and from this to the judgment which characterized it. Therefore, though it is no longer the living process, it is the most effective means for facilitating its repetition without undergoing the labor already done, taking advantage of past efforts and sparing the strength for new labor. The function of the critic, when he has before him a poetic expression to interpret and judge, is to indicate to the readers (after studying it with the help of the particular disposition of his natural talent which he cultivates through special knowledge and submission

Criticism and the history of criticism. For the reasons we have mentioned, critical monographs always contain, by general indications or in full detail, the history of previous characterizations, of which the new and more precise determination or elucidation is a step forward. This is unavoidable. Incompetent critics, however, showed astonishment at the fact that my monographs on Dante, Ariosto, Shakespeare, Corneille (to recall the most important) dwell lengthily in most parts on the reconstruction of the history of Dante, Ariosto, Shakespeare, and Corneille criticism, and so on. Those who presume, without this reconstruction, to exercise the function of critics and say that they study the work of poetry directly, heedless of what has already been babbled concerning it, utter a half-truth, that is, an error; for the direct and "unprejudiced" intuition of a work of art is, beyond a doubt, indispensable and essential, but the act of characterization is always "prejudiced," that is, faced by other judgments which motivate it and to which it is opposed; therefore, it requires criticism in order to realize itself, that is, the history of previous judgments, so that these, as they are, may not, from the progressive steps of scientific labor, turn into obstacles and "prejudices." In fact, the slaves of prejudices are exactly those who think they have freed themselves from such prejudices by disregarding them.

The possession of poetry. The critical formula is fashioned not only for the benefit of the readers, but also, and primarily, for the benefit of the critic himself who fashions it and who, through it, continues to possess the poem which he once possessed in the re-creation studiously achieved. This possession certainly does not eliminate the necessity of further acts of consolidation and strengthening, that is, of new determinations which accomplish or test the formula he coined.

to a special discipline) the point of view from which poetic expression must be considered, that is, to communicate to them the characterization he has worked out. In so doing, he shakes their inertness and their pondering about where to begin—a situation in which they often find themselves in the presence of a new expression; he also spares them the long wandering around among other inferior formulae about classes far removed and different, or too general in relation to that which is closest to poetry. Doubtless he offers by this action a great benefit, although he cannot offer the benefit of causing poetry to be felt and enjoyed because this act can be accomplished only by ourselves. And if we do not accomplish that act despite his help, and if we remain in a state of passivity, it is our own fault. The benefit the critic offers is the one alluded to by Sainte-Beuve when, in a famous statement of his, much deeper than he perhaps realized, he said that "criticism is the art of teaching how to read";[19] this is what we owe to all the great critics who have taught us how to read the poets. What a confused and bewildered world we would find ourselves in if we were suddenly thrown into the middle of the songs of the poets, or amidst the words sung in their own way by nonpoets, or among the false songs of bad poets, without criticism having in advance ordered this world in our mind by separating the diverse voices—the poetic from the nonpoetic and both from the falsely poetic, the major voices worthy of being listened to from the minor voices—and determining thus the meaning of each of them, without having familiarized us with that world as if it were our own house, the house of our heart, of our fancy! This is what criticism has done with its labor throughout the centuries, and we are enjoying the fruits of it, though as usual we are often thankless and ungrateful toward the donors of this gift.

The characterization of poetry and the historiographical in general. It is not superfluous to note that the formation and the function of the characterization which we have exposed in relation to poetry takes place in every other field of historiography, which always supposes that the facts of which one writes are alive in one's conscience or vivified through documents; and after speculatively determining their quality (after having judged them), they are characterized with the help of psychological and empirical concepts. When the live consciousness of the fact is suppressed, every historical characterization disappears into the generic and becomes bereft of history, whereas it is full and effective in that relation precisely because it serves to keep firm and clear, before the mind, the individual fact which was intuited and thought.

The praise of criticism. I had intended to add at this point a "Eulogy of Criticism" similar to those which, at one time, were composed about "Prudence," "Fortitude," "Justice," "Temperance," "Courage," and other virtues. In this eulogy I would have shown, as in a painting, to those who are ignorant or forgetful, the battles fought and the victories won by criticism for the glory of true poets and for the defeat of the "false and deceitful gods." And such an "opus oratorium" would be of some usefulness; but I lost interest in writing it, thinking of the academic tradition of such eulogies and of how they provoked, by reaction, the "chapters" [burlesque poems in terza rima] of Francesco Berni and the "babblings" in praise of lying, excommunication, plague, French disease, bad night, and so on.[43] The "Eulogy of Criticism" remains, therefore, among the things not written; but not, however, inexistent.

---

19. *Portraits littéraires* (Paris: Garnier, 1862), vol. 3, p. 546; see also *Causeries du Lundi*, vol. 1. p. 278.

43. Francesco Berni (1498–1535), Italian poet famous for his burlesque poems, most of them dealing with trivial or obscene subjects.

4. Esthetic Judgment As the History of Poetry

Let us now take up again the examination of the esthetic judgment of poetry in order to see its relation to historical statement or affirmation—which is the generating cell of a more complex history that can be thought or written. The examination and comparison lead us to recognize that that judgment is nothing but a perfect historical statement. It says in fact that at a certain moment an A, which is a work of poetry characterized in a certain way, appeared and inserted itself in the sequence of events. The construction of any other history cannot be attained otherwise, even if A, instead of being a work of poetry, is a philosopheme, an institution, a military operation, a religious belief, and so forth. There is nothing to be added in order to conclude with certainty that the esthetic judgment of a poem contains its history or, to be more precise, that the judgment is the history of the poem.[20]

The self-evidence of this truth is obscured by the conception of reality as divided into "facts" and "values," for which there could be history without values and values without history; consequently, one must first ascertain the reality of a fact and then determine whether it has value or not, whether its "being" corresponds to its "ought-to-be." This is a metaphysical conception which sublimates in philosophical terminology the superficial and commonplace manner of representing dualistically the relation of fact to value; and, since it is superficial and commonplace, it is no wonder that it is found also outside the rigorously reasoned systematizations (such as, for instance, that of Herbart),[21] in positivism and psychologism, and that it is commonly accepted in the schools. In these schools, or in many of them, there still exists the distinction between "le développement," or the historical unfolding of poetry, which is a matter of science, and "le jugement," which should be a personal and subjective reaction. Science must not concern itself with this judgment, allowing it only as a pardonable release of feelings or a delight of fancy or a somewhat desperate and vain attempt at a judgment, at the conclusion of careful and solid research on the historical development. But in the work of poetry fact and value are one and the same thing, as they are in every other human work. The same is true of thought to which no value is added; for, if it is thought and not fiction of

20. See Croce, "La riforma della storia artistica e letteraria," in *Nuovi saggi d'estetica*, 4th ed. (1958), pp. 157–97.
21. Although early in his career Croce was influenced by Herbart, in his *Aesthetic* (pt. 2, chap. 10) he censures him.

thought, it is itself the value. The same is true of action if it is action and not velleity of action. Consequently, the judgment of value is the very judgment of fact; and since a fact is not thinkable except as a process of self-creation and therefore as history, it is a historical judgment. In the judgment of poetry the whole genesis of the work is made present and living in thought through the re-evocation and the process of interpretation inherent in the judgment.

It may seem that the identification of the judgment of poetry with its history breaks up history into a multiplicity of single histories, placed one beside the other, thus destroying the order of succession which is indispensable to historical thought. But the judgment of poetry not only does not deny this order; it does not even remotely prescind from it. On the contrary, it presupposes and reaffirms this order continually. Who could ever seriously understand and think of the *Divine Comedy* if it were placed earlier than, or at the same time as, the *Iliad*; the *Orlando Furioso*, earlier than, or at the same time as, *La Chanson de Roland*. Every work is properly interpreted and re-evoked only in its historical position, in which all preceding works converge in it together with all preceding history of which they are a part.

This reply, however fitting, does not fully satisfy those who tenaciously hold to obsolete conceptions, because in the back of their mind there is a history of poetry which not only considers the single works in their succession, but also establishes among them a direct connection, making each of them come forth from the preceding to generate the next; compared to this connection, the succession we have here admitted appears as a discontinuous and extrinsic series. Now, if the works of poetry are generated from other works of poetry, they would ultimately form a single process and there would be only a single work of poetry; but this work would in fact never be accomplished because it would always be in the process of elaboration; it could never, therefore, be re-evoked and comprehended in its wholeness as a single work. Yet in our experience every work is an object of enjoyment and intelligence only when grasped as a whole. One can only love and embrace individual women; how could we love and embrace the single woman if she were in a perpetual process of formation, if her womanliness were in the process of infinite becoming? This suffices to demonstrate the impossibility of that supposed history, which in the end is clarified by the origin of its own error, if we consider that the connection between the single works certainly cannot be lacking, but that such connection is in history as a whole and not in the direct links among facts of a certain quality, as though

The reform of the history of poetry and literature in the sense of individualization. See my essay of 1917, "La riforma della storia artistica e letteraria," in *Nuovi saggi d'estetica* (3d ed., pp. 157–97). The necessity of extending such reform to the history of figurative arts is demonstrated by J. Schlosser, *Sull'antica storiografia italiana dell'arte* (trans. from the German, Palermo, 1932); see also another volume by the same author, recently translated into Italian, *La storia delle arti figurative nelle esperienze e nei ricordi di un suo cultore* (Bari, 1936, pp. 47–57).

The "unitarians." Both in the discussions aroused by this thesis of mine in reference to the individualizing history of poetry and in other theses on the distinction of the poetic from the non-poetic element in Dante and Goethe, as well as in those on my rejection of the so-called unitarian national histories (beginning with the history of Italy), I had occasion to notice among my opponents a strange type of "extreme unitarian."[44] He imagines that he has to defend, with his call for unity, the exigency of strong and synthetic art against disintegrated and fragmentary art, of strong and synthetic thought against thought which gets lost in distinctions; and he does not even remotely suspect that the unity is never in things, but in the spirit of the poet who creates the poetic image, and in the mind of

44. Gentile.

147

they arose and grew outside the relation with facts of a different quality. Poetry does not generate poetry, just as philosophy does not generate philosophy, nor does action generate action, unless each of them passes through all the other forms of the spirit; the new action has as its necessary condition new fancies and concepts; the fancy demands a new philosophy, new facts, and new actions; the new poetry, new thoughts and new actions and thus new feelings. The history of poetry, which unfolds within its own limits is, in the last analysis, the imagination of philologists. In noting the abstract resemblance and kinships among poetic works, they arrange them in a chain that they construct and imagine that they have breathed into the chain thus constructed a "vis generativa," which has transformed it into a biblical order of generations.

Nevertheless, some still object that, in conceiving the history of poetry as the very judgment of single poems, one loses an essential concept of history, which is that of progress, because every individual work of poetry would have within itself its own perfection and would have its own progress only in the very labor of its self-creation. But the same is true of every other human work, because every truth we think of, every good action we accomplish, has in itself its own perfection. General historical progress is not progress of the categories and spiritual forms; these are its causes and they would not be such if they had not constancy and did not always generate definite and concrete beauties, truths, and moral acts. General historical progress is the movement of the spirit in the dialectic of all its forms. And this progress, this perpetual enrichment, this perpetual growth do not escape any intelligent reader of poetry as he moves from Homer to Dante, from Dante to Shakespeare, from Shakespeare to Goethe; for he would see clearly that Shakespeare would not have understood Goethe, nor Dante Shakespeare, nor Homer Dante, while Dante contained Homer, hailing him as "supreme poet,"[22] and Goethe contained Shakespeare, whose work he kept before him as the "enormous volume of destiny."[23] Yet the poetic work of each of them is beautiful and perfect in itself and was not, insofar as being poetry, perfected by the poetry of any successor.

the thinker who, by distinguishing, qualifies and unites; as a result, the unity sought in the external world ends by being no more than the unity of imagination. He who thinks of poetry according to the nature of poetry thinks of it, by the same token, in a unitarian manner; but he who, to unify it, comes to consider it according to an extrinsic criterion can never unify it, for he does not think of it. We must point out that the extreme unitarians are nearly all either superficial journalists or rhetoricians holding academic chairs—people who are hardly believed to possess in abundance the "strong and synthetic thought" of which they boast.

Poets generating from one another. The historians of poetry present nothing more frequently than such "families": the children, grandchildren, and great-grandchildren of Rousseau, Chateaubriand, Balzac, and so on. But one must speak of this with great caution, because in the historical consideration, unlike the vulgar physiological consideration, each poet is the child of all the poets who preceded him and of none of them in particular: he is, therefore, the child of himself. See on this the protest by Tolstoy against the filiation Stendhal-Balzac-Flaubert, which he labeled the "invention of critics": "Geniuses do not follow one another: they are always independent" (cf. my *Nuovi saggi d' estetica*, 3d ed., p. 268).

On the meaning of nonprogress in poetry. As further clarification of what was said about the false idea of progress—an idea that was transferred from the total movement of history to the single act so as to imagine progress in the quality of this act and, consequently, progress in the spiritual category—I must point out that the general consciousness of truth has reacted against such an idea, not only as far as concerns art, but also as far as concerns moral life. The result has been a renewed recognition of the fact that "in art there is no progress," just as there is "no progress in morality," and that everyone, in both spheres, must resume his own effort with his own strength, because good and evil, beautiful and ugly, stand before us today just as they stood yesterday or some thousand years back. It is true that people generally feel (remember the paradox of the now-forgotten Buckle)[45] that this is not the case with science, in which knowledge is always accrued and added; but, in so saying, one takes a logical leap, because the problem does not concern at all the ever-growing range of information

---

22. Dante, *Inferno* 4. 88.
23. Goethe, *Lehejahre des Meister*, bk. 3, chap. 2 (Croce's note).

45. *Henry Thomas Buckle (1821–1862), English historian, author of* History of Civilization in England *(1856–1861). Croce sharply criticised Buckle's positivistic approach to history, which he likened to that of Comte and Taine—expression of a paradoxical determinism (see particularly Croce,* History: Its Theory and Practice, *index).*

This reaffirmed perfection of each work in itself seems to shake another principle of historical construction, to wit, the level of importance of each work in relation to others, the hierarchy among works; but certainly, if this hierarchy could be established only by a criterion extraneous and repugnant to the works (philosophical, moral, utilitarian, or whatever else it may be), it should be resolutely renounced. But without the arbitrary use of extraneous criteria, the importance of each work is determined in a spontaneous manner, and the hierarchy establishes itself spontaneously by the very character of each work, which in the mind of its reader takes a certain place and no other. And, in general, since each man establishes among these the hierarchy which best suits him, works of poetry are distinguished from those of literature through the growing consciousness that literature is one thing and poetry another. Within the very sphere of poetry, a vague line separates elementary or popular poetry from the complex poetry called "art poetry";[24] and a similar line divides "art poetry," in which there persists a certain leaning toward virtuosity, from the poetry in which the fusion of content and form is perfect and, through the most exquisite elaboration, the supreme simplicity is reached; and the works which are variations of the same fundamental motif and those which are creations of new fundamental motifs are grouped in various classes—minor and major, according to the increasing degree of complexity. Every nation raises one or more poets above the others; and Italy, at the close of that period of its literature running from the thirteenth to the eighteenth century, gave prominence to four—the "four poets."[25] And in further selection Europe decided on four or five as the major poets among all those born of all of its peoples. No reason can be seen for denying or diminishing the beauty of beautiful things, or for distorting their nature by measuring them with an extraneous

or its ever-growing historical complexity (as it does not concern the ever-growing number of works of art or moral acts), but concerns the very act of knowing, in which it is evident that our mind each time starts from the beginning, each time falls again into darkness and re-emerges to light, and that true and false stand against each other as in the past, and shall stand against each other in the future. Some German esthetician called this character of the work of art which begins and ends with itself "Inselhaftigkeit," its "insularity." But such an image, which does not represent well the living self-generation of the work of art, has also the additional fault of attributing, as properly belonging to art, what, in reality, belongs to every spiritual act.

Folk poetry and "art" poetry. This problem is dealt with in all of its aspects in the book already mentioned: *Poesia popolare e poesia d'arte*, in which I demonstrated and exemplified the principle that "popular poetry is in the esthetic sphere the analogue of common sense in the intellectual sphere, and candidness or innocence in the moral sphere. It expresses emotions not aroused directly by great efforts of thought or by passion; it portrays simple feelings in correspondingly simple forms. High poetry stirs in us large masses of remembrances, experiences, thoughts, multiple feelings and degrees and shades of feelings; popular poetry does not expand in circles so wide and deliberately aimed at a purpose, but it reaches the purpose through a rapid and short route. The words and rhythms in which it embodies itself are perfectly adequate to its motifs, just as the words and rhythms suited to 'art' poetry are adequate to this kind of poetry with their complex allusions, which are lacking in popular poetry" (2d ed., pp. 5–6).

The hierarchy of the works of art. This exigency does not lend itself to scientific systematizations. Taine skirts the comic when, in a book serious in its aim and in the effort to attain it, he tried to set on a scientific basis the hierarchy of the works of art (*De l'idéal dans l'art:*[46] see on it my *Nuovi saggi d'estetica*, 3d ed., pp. 140–42). Everyone satisfies this hierarchical exigency by himself as a personal matter, changing his preferences according to varying circumstances; however, because of a likeness of average artistic interests among people, there is always a certain approximative general consent in this matter.

Small poetry and great poetry. I talked on this in relation to some sonnets and one ode by Ronsard (see *Poesia antica e moderna*, 3d ed., pp. 257–64), pointing

---

24. See Croce *Poesia popolare e poesia d'arte* (1933).
25. Dante, Petrarch, Ariosto, Tasso.

46. This work (1867) constitutes pt. 5 of his *La philosophie de l'art* in the edition of 1880.

Renaissance or the origin and development of the Risorgimento; one can notice here the way in which poems and comedies, short stories, novels which are anything but poetry, and verses which are not verses, being faulty in their meter and ungrammatical in their syntax, were utilized because of their forceful assertion of the needs, the desires, the intentions, the volitions, and the actions of the times. We are not going to dwell on the case of literary works (not even with a single example), because the political harangues, the forensic summations, the satires, the various forms of emotions at which the literature of entertainment aims, the apologies, the autobiographical confessions, and so forth, are the most conspicuous materials of political and moral history; on the other hand, works of literary prose, which the history of literature considers in their literary character, are comprised, because of their content, in the histories of philosophy and of science: to be precise, in all the above-mentioned cases it would be more appropriate to speak of practical facts and thoughts which belong, by their own nature, to those histories, rather than of poetic and literary documents for extrapoetic histories. And here is the explanation of the meaning and the particular demonstration of a truth which this writer has many times enunciated in his historical works and which has aroused dismay in those who prefer to be irrationally scandalized rather than undergo the labor of reflection and comprehension; this truth is that "ugly and nonpoetic works are much more documentary than poetic works"; if something is to be questioned in this statement, it is its mildness: it should have read, in an absolute manner, that only nonpoetic works are documentary, not the others.

When we write the history of certain thoughts or moral tendencies, whether we present them as a history of poetry and literature of the various states of mind characterized by the words "classicism" and "romanticism" or whether we present them as a history of the conditions of Greek civilization in the third and second centuries B.C. as revealed by the antinomy between the "Asiatic" and the "Attic" styles, or as a history of the idea of passional love which developed in ancient literature from Euripides' Phaedra and Apollonius of Rhodes' Medea to Virgil's Dido: there is no need to quarrel on the working of the titles, when the works, whatever their designation, are in themselves perfectly logical and deal with themes, having a raison d'être and being treated suitably. Nor, certainly, can one quibble about the title when in opening a book of the history of the French or German language one finds instead the history of French or German feelings, customs, and civilization insofar as they are expressed, in a literary or nonliterary fashion, in articulated sounds. Such a thing is not really a history of the language—history of the "living word"—for the "living word" does not live concretely outside poetry and beautiful eloquence; but it is, nevertheless, a history of no mean importance and instruction. Doubtless it would be well to avoid the misunderstanding about titles; but the intelligent man does not allow himself to be confused and always knows what to make out of titles.

The misunderstanding is more dangerous when these histories alternate with the history of poetry in a single didactic treatise as though they were histories of the same object. This would occur when, in a history of French poetry, a history of the French language in the sense explained above, is interpolated or when in a history of German poetry and literature another history, even in a synthetic form (for instance, that of philosophy from Leibniz to Hegel) is intercalated. But here, in any case, the two different histories run parallel, despite their involutions; and if they contain a literary incongruity in the treatment (which, on the other hand, can be a divulgatory and didactic congruity), still they are not, strictly speaking, a false history of poetry.

The false history of poetry, on the contrary, arises when the extrapoetic history—political, moral, or philosophical—becomes the criterion for the judgment of the history of poetry, reducing poetry to a spokesman for peoples and parties, to the expression of polemics, of revolt and war, of cleverness and astuteness; to a weapon for fighting, and even to an exposition of ideas and systems of beliefs. Poets are thus likened to philosophers, politicians, warriors, apostles, preachers, assigning them to functions alien to their nature, lending them a face inflamed by passion or shrunk by the effort of reflection, which no poet ever had: they are no longer like Ludovico Ariosto, who, "nell'ampia fronte e nel fiso occhio e tardo/ lo stupor dei gran sogni anco ritiene" [in the broad forehead and in the attentive and weary eye/ he still retains the fascination of great dreams].[29] A typical example of such clumsy histories is found in those written according to the above-mentioned criteria (nationalistic or variedly classicistic) and in those dictated by religious beliefs. There is no doubt that such patchworks enjoy the favor of those who find themselves in these accomplishments, that is, those who find their incapacity to understand and comprehend poetry and the capacity to take political sides, to agitate themselves fanatically, and to absolve and condemn ecclesi-

The history of the language as a history of culture. I refer the reader for this part to a series of book reviews and discussions collected in *Conversazioni critiche,* 4th ed., vol. 1, pp. 87–105; vol. 3, pp. 95–106.

Histories of languages as moral and political histories. Since we do not yet have a history of the Italian language, we shall refer to the many which already exist of the French language: that by Brunot (*Histoire de la langue française,* Paris, 1913–), that by Vossler (*Frankreichs Kultur und Sprache,* 2d ed., Heidelberg, 1929), and the most recent one by W. von Wartburg (*Evolution et structure de la langue française,* Leipzig, 1934). This last (to restrict ourselves to it alone) contains the history of the various populations mixing on French soil from prehistoric ages to the present and of their institutions, customs, and thought, and the related forms of language. This whole history is narrated on the following scheme: "Nous avons vu la société féodale se transformer insensiblement. Nous avons rappelé les événements qui ont changé l'ancienne France et en ont fait l'état moderne. Des changements si profonds doivent être accompagnés de changements analogues de la langue. En effet . . . " (p. 110). Or: "Nous venons de voir par où le XVIIIᵉ siècle continue le XVIIᵉ, et par où il s'oppose à celui-ci. Or, l'histoire de la langue est tout à fait analogue à ce développement," and so on (p. 183). A history of the language, abstracted from the concreteness and individuality of the poetic works and becoming the history of practical life, must be written in this manner and no other; and this and no other is its logical and scientific form.

The history of literature as political, social, and moral history. The author of this book, who had dealt in special essays with the European poets of the nineteenth century from the only possible point of view—that of poetry (see *European Literature in the Nineteenth Century, La letteratura della nuova Italia,* and so forth)—had again to treat the same period from a different perspective and for a different purpose (using the documentation that poets can offer to ethical-political

---

29. Carducci, "Dietro un ritratto dell'Ariosto," *Rime Nuove* 20.

astically. It could also be, as it seemed and as it was said, that their manner of presenting poets and poetry becomes more dramatic than that of the art critic with his "cold eye of connoisseur"; but for passionate spectacles there are theaters and there is no need to transfer these spectacles to the "templa serena" [quiet temples] of thought.

Without falling into such violence and inhuman partisanship, and holding also to a sort of eclecticism which allows the consideration of pure poetic values, the historiography that subjects poetry to an extra-poetic criterion re-emerged, but in a form more human and esthetic, in the idea of literature "as an expression of society" and of literary history as a mirror of civil, moral, religious, and intellectual life. This was the type of historiography formed between the eighteenth and nineteenth centuries in the wake of the increasing general interest in historical studies; and this type itself represented a step forward in comparison with the purely extrinsic historiography—biographical and bibliographical—and with that which used to judge poetry and literature according to fixed models without interpreting them historically. But this historiography is now clearly old, being unable to hold its own either in the presence of more precise and mature concepts concerning the nature of poetry and of literature or in the presence of the much more advanced methodology of historiography. The error, which lies in its presupposition, shows itself to be more insidious and thus more difficult to drive out or correct, especially because it is found in a work which had a healthy influence on the new Italian criticism, but which, having been conceived in the middle of the nineteenth century in the Hegelian and romantic circles, substantially accepted their tenets. The work alluded to is the *History of Italian Literature* by De Sanctis. The strong concept of the originality of poetry, the freshness of impressions that we gathered from it, the vivid sense of the individuality of the poetic work, were not always to him a sure and sufficient defense against the consequences of his presuppositions. As a result, it appeared to him that the *Decameron* was the moral antithesis of the *Divine Comedy*; the *Orlando Furioso*, the expression of the exhaustion of every ideal in Italy, except that of art for art's sake; the music of the seventeenth and eighteenth centuries, the disintegration of thought and feeling in the vacuousness of sounds; Carlo Goldoni, the initiator of modern realism; Giuseppe Parini, the first apparition of the new Italian of the Risorgimento; Vincenzo Monti, the surviving Italian of the political and moral decadence; the literature of the nineteenth century, the conflict between the liberal and the democratic schools. And

history), just as he did in *History of Europe in the Nineteenth Century* and *A History of Italy, 1871–1915*. But, in completing two different works on the same subject, he did not feel in himself any conflict (which would have arisen if he had mixed and falsely unified the two diverse exigencies); on the contrary, he felt that in this manner he had confirmed, through examples, the agreement which is, after all, that of *hoc facere et alterum non omittere* [doing this without omitting that].

Sociological and nationalistic histories of literature. For the criticism of the histories by Brandes, Meyer, and Bartel, see my *Nuovi saggi d'estetica*, 3d ed., pp. 181–97). Why do not nations (this is the question being asked today) flatly assume names of animals, as do the primitive tribes in their "totem," considering themselves descendants of this or that animal? The truth is that even those primitive conceptions had an ethical and religious character which is lacking in today's stupid nationalism.

Outline of a recent history of German literature. The *Abriss der deutschen Literaturgeschichte*, written by about ten learned Germans (Leipzig, 1930; 3d ed., 1932), "proposes to go back to the spiritual essentiality and put into relief the fundamental trait of the modern conception of literature, presenting the history of literature in its living sense and as progressive attestation of the unfolding of the German spirit. . . . The methodological foundation of the book is the conviction that the history of literature is to be exposed both as a history of the conception of life and as a history of artistic taste. In its broadest sense, it is the history of the German man as the object of poetic representation; in its narrower meaning, it is a history of poetic art as the shaping of this object." Thus, starting from the chivalric ideal all the way up to the modernism of the "neue Sachlichkeit," of the new positivity, great and mediocre poets or poetasters and their works are put together indiscriminately and treated collectively in relation to the various determinations of the epochs that they are supposed to represent; what *Werther*, *Faust*, *Iphigenie*, the *Lieder* are in themselves, from the poetic point of view, does not seem to constitute the subject matter of poetry for the authors of the work.

Also some recent anthologies of the German lyric (for instance, *Die Schönsten deutschen Gedichte*, ed. Goldscheider) are organized according to this criterion: that is, as a sample-book of "flowery Gothic," full Renaissance," "first baroque," "full baroque," "late baroque," and so forth, up to "romantic expressionism," and "twentieth-century romantic."

he treated likewise other authors and works. Although such interpretations were in him incidental and superficial and more than anything else represented scraps of a thought already superseded and in some instances the sign of the pressure exercised on the critic by the function of the political educator that De Sanctis performed so well, we are convinced of the necessity and urgency to correct the error originating from such interpretations.

Literature as an expression of society. Against this formula (on the origin of which see *Problemi d'estetica*, 4th ed., pp. 56–59) attempts were made to demonstrate the lack of coincidence between the events in political and social history and the works of poetry and literature, thus showing the independence of the two histories (for instance, in a recent essay by Fernand Baldensperger, on which see *Conversazioni critiche*, 2d ed., vol. 3, pp. 93–95). But every act of whatever quality has its origins in all other acts, and, in this respect, no act is independent, that is, born out of nothing. Sole and true independence lies in the quality of the act, in its originality, which is irreducible to the quality of other acts. That formula could be of value against the idea of poetry as a sort of academic exercise in beautiful writing, calling attention to the historical conditionality of poetry and thus to its seriousness. But outside this sense and this usage, it can have no other meaning or (which is the same thing) may have many, true or false, according to whichever way the words "society" and "expression" are defined.

The History of Italian Literature by De Sanctis. This book by De Sanctis was considered (and the consideration was the equivalent of a censure) to be a mere series of critical essays on single writers, whereas it is exactly the opposite, that is, a history of the Italian people as reflected in poets and writers; and both the praise and the blame must be reversed. For the disputable aspect of that "history of poetry" is its "social" approach; and the emphasis placed on the personality of the authors is its great merit: the accent springing from the artistic sense prevented De Sanctis from submerging and dispersing in the thread of social history the individual physiognomy of poetic works. Those who, for the sake of saying something, are today preaching a "return to De Sanctis," should be asked (if it is worth asking) to which De Sanctis they would like "to return": the old-fashioned De Sanctis still unconsciously entangled here and there in the old esthetics of content; or the new De Sanctis, who formulated the concept of poetry as form and gave prominence to poetic individuality? One must not return to the first, and one cannot return to the second, for the simple reason that we have already returned—we live with him and in him.

The Strength and the limits of De Sanctis' criticism and historiography. See what I have said in the essay "De Sanctis e l'hegelismo," in *Saggio sullo Hegel e altri scritti*, 4th ed., 1948, pp. 369–95,[47] and in a note on the "Fortuna del De Sanctis," in the volume *Una famiglia di patrioti ed altri saggi*, 3d ed., 1949, pp.

47. *See above, n. 17.*

299–304; on some particular points see *Poesia popolare e poesia d'arte,* 2d ed., pp. 83–84, 94.

Vico's Homer. Even Vico's interpretation of Homer, though new and revolutionary and in contrast with the anti-Homerism and neoclassicism of the sixteenth and seventeenth centuries (which put Homer back in his place of honor as a great poet), is colored by the historicistic and sociological characterization which Vico had in mind. This explains his portrayal of Homer as violent and ferocious and barbarous and uneducated and popular, in every way identical with the society of which he was supposedly the expression. In the criticism after Vico's as well as in today's criticism the portrait has been softened a great deal, not only by demonstrating that in Homer there is discipline and schooling, but also by pointing out his smiling and gentle and ironical traits. Already in the eighteenth century Fielding, in his *Tom Jones* (bk. 8, chap. 1), observed that the way in which Homer treated the gods "must have shocked the credulity of the pious and sagacious heathen; and . . . could never have been defended, unless by agreeing with a supposition to which I [Fielding] have been sometimes almost inclined, that this most glorious poet, as he certainly was, had an intent to burlesque the superstitious faith of his own age and country."

The history of poetry as ethical and social development. The passage from the history of poetry to the history of the ethical and social spirit is also found in the introduction of Dilthey to his much-praised book *Das Erlebnis und die Dichtung* (Leipzig, 1910), in which he broadly outlines the history of poetry from the Middle Ages to the nineteenth century. It suffices to read a few lines to understand that the consideration made carries us outside the sphere of poetry: "We find poetry determined first by the common spirit of the small political military societies, and it expresses in the lyrical mood the spirit of these societies, . . . and embodies its ideals in actions and in epic characters"; and here are the last lines: "In ever-new relations these forces of enlightenment manifested themselves, from Voltaire to Marivaux, from *Minna {von Bernhelm}* of Lessing to the *Barbier de Séville* and to the *Mariage de Figaro* of Beaumarchais, as accomplished creations of a society that wished to see and enjoy its equivocal life in serene gaiety" [pp. 1, 10]. Dilthey, who was able to grasp with great keenness moral, religious, and philosophical developments, does not seem to have had an equal disposition in poetic things per se.

Poetry and the poet of the future. Toward the end of the literary history of a people and of an age, or in special inquiries, it was at times customary, and perhaps still is, to inquire about the probable character of

Another type of research which equally conflicts with the nature of the subject dealt with is that concerning the character of the poetry of this or that nation, of this or that period. The general or class representations obtained by working abstractly on the various poetic works of a given nation or period (even when some common traits are established) do not serve, as do the characterizations of single works, as an instrument of conservation and reproduction of the results of interpretation and of historical-esthetic criticism for the purpose of the re-evocation. In fact, passing to the single work, which is the only object of the history of poetry, those traits either are not found or, if they are, have a varying importance from a maximum to a minimum, and often an importance by opposition, since the determinate feeling of the work opposes and rejects such traits; this means that one must go back, of necessity, to the characteristic of the individual work. Those common traits may be useful (at least when they are determined with prudence and are not lost in empty generalizations or in fanciful constructions) to political, civil, and moral history to the same extent as the characterizations formulated on the basis of other kinds of documents concerning the life of that nation or that period, which are, when considered closely, nothing but abstract schemes of concrete histories. The same can easily be seen in regard to general characteristics, usually established with a negative or limitative emphasis by distinguishing ages of progress from ages of decadence or of progress in some respects and decadence in some others (as when one speaks of "rationalistic but unpoetic" ages, or of "warlike but uncivilized" ages), or even by labeling peoples "philosophical but not artistic," "religious but not political," "superior," or "inferior." Poetry, in its intense expression, can arise in each or in none of these ages and peoples, just as the consciousness and the affirmation of freedom can become strong and concrete during periods of servitude and deeper than it was during periods of freedom; and, in any case, also these negative and limitative characteristics serve for moral

the "poetry of the future" and of the "great poet of the future." These inquiries are connected indirectly with the political-social conception of the history of poetry, for the political-social histories, always generated by political and social problems, are followed as a natural course by the delineations and the prospects of the action, which sometimes in fanciful men take on the appearance of horoscopes and prophesies. But in poetry what is the value of intentions and orientations abstractly outlined? If inspiration and poetic execution are lacking, that program and that prophesy will have no power either to arouse or to prepare them. And, if the inspiration is kindled, poetry will be a new accent that no one can predict as a factual reality or predetermine for the formulation of a program.

The character of national literatures. See in this respect my criticism of the "character" which has been, in various theorizations, attributed to Italian literature (*Conversazioni critiche*, 2d ed., vol. 3, pp. 257–66). A Portuguese critic who defends the legitimacy of such characterology and does the utmost to establish the character of Spanish literature, candidly writes: "*Uma litteratura è um grande camposanto, e ninguem dirá che seja impossivel descrever objectivamente um camposanto, especie de paisagem immobilisada pela varinha magica dalguma fada. O predominio dalguns generos, a carencia doutros, a acceitação publica preferente doutros, a porfiada continuidade de themas e de formas, estâo a desenhar uma physionomia e a revelar-nos a essencia intima duma imaginação nacional, com suas aptidôes, preferencias e negações*" [Literature is a big cemetery, and no one will say that it is impossible to describe a cemetery objectively, which is a sort of landscape immobilized by the magic wand of some witch. The predominance of some genres, the scarcity of others, the preferential public acceptance of others, the obstinate continuance of themes and forms are there to depict a physiognomy and to reveal to us the intimate essence of a national imagination, with its aptitudes, preferences, and negations] (Fid. De Figueiredo, *Caracteristicas da litteratura hespanhola*, Santiago, 1935, p. 8). In these words one should retain especially the comparison of literature, thus viewed, to a cemetery, in which the life of poetry is extinguished.

The characteristics of peoples as reflected in their poetry. It is difficult, in generalizing such characteristics, not to get into the fanciful and thus bounce from one characteristic to another or one in opposition to the first. All remember the ill-famed characteristic that Mommsen, in his *Roman History*, sketched concerning Roman and Italian poetry, to which he denied any virtue in the serious and tragic genre, attributed the ten-

and political history and not for the history of poetry. "Revolutions in poetry" are often pointed out; but every poem is in itself a little revolution and the creation of a "novus ordo"; what we call revolution in this context reflects always a practical attitude and has more correctly been called "revolution of taste" (in accordance with the sense that the word carries here), of the predilections which determine fashion. Philippides of *The Clouds*, a young man obsessed by "the new," rejected the old Aeschylus, so unrefined, incoherent, noisy, and the old Simonides, a bad poet; and with them and the old poetry he rejected so many other things, which Aristophanes enumerates, since they did not agree with new customs. The error generated by such inquiries consists, as in the case of pseudopoetic histories, in transferring the categories thus formed from the field of political and moral history (where they can be of some use) to the field of poetry (where they can lend themselves to nothing but abuse).

Finally, a third form of false histories of poetry corresponds to a perversion of historiography in general, that is, to the audacious as well as thoughtless transcending of concrete history in order to write another which would be real only in appearance and actualized by forces unknown to experience and consciousness, but familar to metaphysical invention. As a metaphysics, this transcending historiography assumed varying attitudes according to the origins (materialistic or idealistic) of its inventions: in the first case, it took the name of "science of history" or "of the laws of history"; in the second, "philosophy of history." In the

dency toward the rhetorical, and recognized the capacity for the satirical and burlesque; nevertheless, I am reading now an essay by Norden on the Virgilian episode of Orpheus and Eurydice (in *Sitzungsberichte der preussischen Akademie der Wissenschaften*, 1934, p. 663), in which it is said in regard to Virgil's style that in this "new form of style speaks a nationality that has a prominent character of its own, the Italian, with accentuated solemnity, 'maiestas et pompa,' 'religio,' and 'sanctitas,' a nationality that, as Horace says (*Epistles* 2. 1. 166), 'spirat tragicum'; and that opens its path leading later to Dante and Michelangelo." As we can see, the characteristic sketched by Mommsen seems here to be reversed.

The character of Spanish literature. I also was led to research of this nature, that is, to establish the character of Spanish literature (in my *Uomini e cose della vecchia Italia*, 2d ed., vol. 1, pp. 214–22), in order to try to explain the reasons it had not exercised in Europe the influence that was in turn exercised by Italian, French, English, and German literatures; and I attributed such reasons to its persistent medieval and popular character, which prevented it from contributing anything relevant to the formation of the modern European spirit. My research was, in that case, not on poetry and literature, but on philosophy and ethics; and it was legitimate and necessary for the purpose, because the part played by Spain in the life of modern Europe has been ill-determined by recent historians, who have lost sight of the fact that to the power of Spain is owed particularly the salvation of the Catholic church, threatened by the spreading of the Reformation, and that the Spanish people were prepared for this (and no other) task by the struggle sustained for centuries on their own soil and, so to speak, in their very bosom, against the Moors. As for poetry, such demonstration implies the reading of almost all of the Spanish poetry, from the *Poema de mio Cid* and the *Romances* to the dramas of Lope de Vega and Tirso de Molina, in a simple and popular tone, without seeking in them that which is not and cannot be there, and enjoying that which is there and its marvelous spontaneousness and freshness.

National characterization of poets. These characterizations should be forbidden as are unbecoming words, for it is unbecoming to characterize a poet in that way, restricting him to the particular function of representative of a country; those who do this, because of their misguided affection toward their native land, instead of honoring their national poets, deprive them of their universally human character and undermine them as poets. It is not enough to drive the devil away through Beelzebub, recalling, as was done many times in such history of poetry the sham explanations by means of entities naturalistic in appearance but metaphysical and therefore imaginary in substance (such as the "race," the "geographical environment," the "moment," or the "event") are derived from a materialistic attitude; from an idealistic attitude are derived the explanations by means of metaphysical entities called ideas (such as the idea of the "finite," the "infinite," "God," the "State," "love," "romanity," "germanity," and so forth), which would inspire the poets, speak through their mouths, and make out of the poets' works their own "allegories." Sometimes one attitude, sometimes the other, and often both together (because the two metaphysical conceptions combine themselves) are responsible for little prejudices and bad habits in judgment, according to which one hears that such a poem is "truly French" or "truly German," that another poem could not have been written except in the "fogs of the north" or under the "bright sky of Italy," that still another would not have sprung so vigorously without the repercussions of a determinate revolutionary movement or military triumph, that such and such a poem has a hidden meaning, which the author was not aware of and which the clear-sighted interpreter reveals as theophany of that recondite idea. In both instances—that of the "science of history," which employs the concept of cause, as well as that of the "philosophy of history," which uses the concept of "end" or rather "external finality" (for here again the two combine themselves)—there emerges the outline of a sort of development or "evolution" which is nothing but the imaginative hypostasis or the mythology of the ideal and historical development of the real world. So the circularity of the spirit, its "course and recourse," is mythologized in the eternal succession of historical epochs which run from barbarity to civilization and from civilization to barbarity; and the eternal passage from one degree of the spirit to another is mythologized in the temporal succession of epochs, each representing and completing a degree of the spirit. These are the two mythologies to which Vico and Hegel directed their powerful speculations on the "eternal ideal history" and on the "dialectic"—imperishable acquisitions for philosophical thought. As for the history of poetry, as well as for other histories, the theory of the historical cycles hinders the understanding of the perpetual growth of the spirit on itself and therefore the converging of the "courses and recourses" (which are eternal and yet of every instant) in the single course of history,[30] and the enrichment of poetry with the enrichment of human consciousness.

polemics (see, for instance, the book by Baldensperger, *La littérature*, Paris, 1913), that Dante was of German origin, Boccaccio was French through his mother and his place of birth, Corneille was Norman, and Foscolo Greek, and so on; but it is necessary to deny radically the very foundation of the relation which one intends to establish between the concept of poetry and that of nation.

The epochs of poetry. The great dissimilarity between the characteristics of historical epochs and poetry acquires prominence in the delineation which Goethe one day gave, as though in jest, of the "Epochs of German literature from 1750 to 1820." From 1770 to 1790: "Restless. Foolhardy. Overflowing. Honest and frivolous. Scorning and heedless of any respect. English culture. Arbitrary in destroying form and reflective in restoring it." From 1790 to 1810: "Appeased. Tender. Setting limits to itself. Seriously religious. Patriotically active. Meddling. Spanish culture. Neglecting form." And so on for the other periods (*Werke*, vol. 27, pp. 250–51). But, considered from the poetic point of view, the two twenty-year periods whose characteristics have been mentioned are truly characterized only by works such as *Werther*, *Faust*, *Prometheus*, *Mahomet*, *The Wandering Jew*, *Iphigenie*, *Tasso*, *Wilhelm Meister*, *Achilleis*, songs, odes, ballads, elegies, epigrams, and so forth, that is, individual creations by Goethe and some by minor poets: each work constitutes in itself an *epoch*, a true poetic epoch in the development of history.

The "decadence" of poetry. Since the concept of decadence has its use, though restricted, in cultural, moral, and political history, the term is badly used when one speaks of the "decadence" of poetry to mean that in one's own times or for longer or shorter periods no poets or great poets have appeared. But great poetry is a gift from the gods, who give it when they please. Italy, after Tasso and until Alfieri and Foscolo, had no great poets; nor did France after Racine and until Vigny; nor did Germany for several centuries before Goethe and for a century after him; the same can be said for all other countries. The conception of the great poet is an industrial conception of poetry, as though the great poet opens a factory and those who are around him or follow him have the obligation to continue and improve it, for the good of the company. When the facts reveal otherwise, people are led to declare the firm bankrupt.

Courses and recourses in literary history. Attempts to fashion literary history according to this rhythm reappear from time to time.[48] See, for instance, among the

---

30. Vichean conception of history; see *The New Science*, bks. 4, 5.

48. "Course and recourse" are two terms used by Vico to express the

And the other theory of historical epochs, according to which each epoch carries out one part of the work and all together bring the whole to completion, is likewise difficult to comprehend, for it marks the end of political and ethical life and of philosophy itself, as they reach their ideal end; it marks also the end of poetry, as it has accomplished its function: Hegel, in fact, coherent with his premises, did not hesitate to assert and, indeed, declare the death of poetry as something which had already occurred. Current prejudices and judgments, even if unaware of their own origins, are to be attributed to similar doctrines. The idea, for instance, that literary histories develop by necessary cycles, or that in rationalistic epochs poetry cannot arise, or that in the modern era, which is one of action and practice, poetry no longer has function, being forever contaminated by men who cannot even hope to find it in heaven (for in heaven there would be no place for something so sensitive and sensible) is the result of these prejudices.

All the false histories that we have reviewed have little currency in Italy for the reason already mentioned, although scattered manifestations, as is natural, are noted: they are survivals due to habits or weak attempts toward renovation. The best historical and critical work is now carried out in Italy in historical-esthetic monographs on single authors, leaving to school manuals the general exposition of literary works. In France the naturalistic and deterministic metaphysics in the manner of Taine ("race, milieu, moment") did not make a school and it is now almost forgotten: the literary histories written there have the great merit of giving a lively prominence to the personality of the authors, even if they scarcely distinguish between esthetic and biographical problems. But in Germany, where at the end of the eighteenth century esthetics and the history of poetry received a vigorous impulse and were profoundly renewed, a great confusion reigns today in this area, so that the expression "corruptio optimi pessima" [the corruption of the best man is the worst kind of corruption] comes spontaneously to our lips. Now, the Germans are cultivating at times, as history of poetry, a "Geistesgeschichte," that is, a history of spiritual problems, drawn from the works of poetry; at times a "Stilgeschichte," consisting in the history of the "classical" spirit, of the "romantic" spirit, of the "baroque" spirit, or of other such spirits, succeeding one another on the world scene; at times a "Generationslehre," which seeks to explain the changes in literature by the succession of generations and the personalities that each of them would produce; at other times a "history of the countries and the races, that is, of poetry insofar

most recent, *"La notion de retour périodique dans l'histoire littéraire"* by L. Cazamian (*Annales de l'université de Paris*, March, 1926) as applied to English literature, which would include periods of intellectualism or classicism, and periods of sensibility, passionality, and imagination, that is, romanticism. But this amounts, at most, to vague general tendencies, which do not alter in their intrinsic nature genuine poetic creations.

The death of poetry. On the genesis of the Hegelian theory concerning the death of poetry, a death which has already occurred in the modern age, see my detailed essay in *Ultimi saggi*, 2d ed., pp. 147–60.

Present day conditions of literary criticism and historiography. As far as Italy in particular is concerned, see my essay, reprinted in the appendix in *Storia della storiografia italiana nel secolo decimonono*, 3d ed., 1947, vol. 2, pp. 179–209, where I discuss the orientation taken by these studies and the problems solved and those debated in present times.

---

movement of human history. For a more detailed explanation, see Vico, *The New Science*, trans. Thomas Bergin and Max Fisch (Ithaca: Cornell University Press, 1968), pp. xlii–xliii.

as it reflects these things; and very often they resort to the ravings of nationalism, racism, and antisemitism, dragging poetry into it, claiming that for the Germans the only measure of poetry must be the "deutsche Dichtung" and the "deutsche Kunst" and that they do not seek the "beautiful," as do the corrupt and sluggish Latins, but the "titanic" (that titanic which often prompts the temptation of a word game: "tetanic"!). The concept of the history of poetry coinciding with the judgment of poetry is far removed from them; and one of the practitioners of literary history, according to the forms catalogued above, declares with the haughtiness of a scientist that he knows only historical tasks and that he is not interested in knowing which poets have written beautiful poems. This statement leads to the conclusion that a poem as such is not a historical event and, by closely following this logic, that it does not exist. This is the implicit conception in all of the false histories of poetry.

6. *The History of Poetry and the Personality of the Poet*

What must the critic and historian of poetry do when he has in front of him a mass of documents concerning the poet? If he knows what he is about, he discards the information and documents related solely to the poet's private life (his economic endeavors, his habits, his likes and dislikes, his relations with his parents, his wife, his children, and so forth), and those related solely to his public life (important offices he may have held as a party leader, agitator, deputy, minister, administrator of his town, of his province, and so forth), and, in addition (in the event he had worked in the scientific field), all that which concerns his studies in botany, or in anatomy, philosophy, or history; he shall consider only the documents and information related to poetry. The materials set aside will be all together taken into consideration by the historians of the other aspects of his life. For instance, those who narrate the events of the republic of Florence will deal also with the battle of Campaldino and with Dante, who was one of the combatants; or those who commemorate the splendors of the Grand Duchy of Weimar will speak of Goethe, who was even war minister or something of the kind; those who write the history of anatomy, botany, and physics will deal with the anatomic discoveries of Goethe himself, with his ideas on plants and his controversy over Newtonian optics. But the historian of poetry has no reason to concern himself with these things. It is useless to deny

Criticism and the man. It is a commonplace in France that criticism must, through the work, reveal the man. But the contrary is true, that is, that criticism must reveal the man in the work, since he coincides with his poetic work and is the man-poet. All the rest may arouse curiosity and invite psychological and moral considerations, as when we know a poet personally and take a walk with him or go to dinner with him and then report our impression that he is a good natured man, very amiable or, on the contrary, that he is disagreeable, suspicious, and hard to please, all qualities about which we like to gossip in our conversations; but these things have no positive relation with the knowledge and criticism of poetry.

Practical life and passional life as the subject matter of poetry. Naturally, the passional life of the poet, which offers him the subject matter for his poetry, does not elicit an equivalent response in his practical life, in the sense that what concerns him deeply in practical life, that on which he toils the hardest, may of necessity become a subject—the most important one—of his poetry. A fleeting moment of his practical life, an incident, so to speak, can put into motion the whole world that he carries within himself; and then, as Pro-that every event in a man's life, every experience, every thought, every emotion, is reflected somehow in his poetry because, having already admitted that poetry reflects not only the personal life of the author but the life of all men, and indeed of the whole universe,[31] that denial or generic consideration does not take us far; the question is to see, case by case, which of those facts must be properly referred to in the interpretation of poetry.

When we say "documents and information related to poetry," we mean precisely the necessary or at least the useful elements to be collected for the philological preparation required in the interpretation of a determinate poem. So, in order to understand the obscure mention, in the tenth canto of the *Inferno*, of the reason that the "first" friend and near brother of Dante, Guido Cavalcanti, was not at the side of the Poet in the great journey, it may not be idle to remember that Dante was one of the Priors who exiled Cavalcanti and that, upon return from exile, Cavalcanti died. Likewise, it will not be fruitless to learn that Goethe did not hesitate to reshape one of his own works according to an idea different from that which he had in conceiving and writing it originally—such as the discovery of the *Ur-Meister* revealed in regard to the composition of *Wilhelm Meisters Leherjahre*;[32] and that he felt a certain indifference toward questions of composition to the point of ordering the obsequious Eckermann to take from a drawer a notebook of diverse thoughts and to insert them in *Wanderjahre* in order to increase the size of the volume. This information concerning his way of manipulating the external form of his works could alert us against being too obstinate in seeking homogeneity between the second and the first *Faust* and the coherence among their various parts.

The hope of broadening philology by such means and of understanding better and more easily certain aspects of poetry prompts serious minds to inquire into the practical life of the poets; and it is not the poets' fault if frivolous minds, eager to amuse themselves or hoping to acquire reputation by busying themselves somehow, use this as a pretext for collecting and throwing onto the works of poets heaps of erudite rubbish—a fact that everybody deplores but nobody can prevent, the more so because it is mixed with the superstitious cult of genius. Certainly it causes much distraction from poetry and a great deal of gossip and anecdotes and controversies about these anecdotes, which disrupt and suffocate the voice of poetry. So one reaches the point of rejoicing that little or

pertius sang, "*maxima de nihilo nascitur historia*" [a great history comes out of nothing] (*Elegies 2. 1*). When we read about the vicissitudes of the practical life of poets as a premise for the explanation of their poetry, we are immediately struck by the irrelevance of all or most of the facts narrated about them; for among such facts we do not find, or we find somehow scattered, that moment, that occasion which provoked the inner agitation appeased in poetry. The authors of these narrations seem to forget that the person of the poet is the Aeolian harp which vibrates at a breathing of the universe.

Biography and poetry. The lack of coincidence between poetry and biography (the latter understood as the narration of relevant events from the practical point of view) can be demonstrated by the following example. When Gaston Paris (so one of his students says) was working on a book on Villon, a question confronted him, "*dont l'obscurité arrêtait tout net son élan*": the question of whether Villon, when he was composing his *Grand Testament*, had or had not already been condemned to death, and, consequently, "*si le poète, quand il parle de la mort avec un réalisme si terrible, faisait oeuvre de littérature pure ou traduisait en vers les souvenirs personnels de son existence.*" But the question really was an idle one, from the poetic point of view. The student we have mentioned was Marcel Schwob (see his *Mélanges d'histoire littéraire*, Paris, 1928, p. 284), who later was able, through research in the archives, to establish that Villon's sentencing occurred after the publication of that poem; thus, the poet "*avait été, en parlant de la mort, non son propre biographe, mais l'interprète de l'humanité.*" This is always true with the poet, even when he seems to be writing his autobiography.

31. See Croce, "Il carattere di totalità dell'espressione artistica," in *Nuovi saggi d'estetica*, pp. 117–34.
32. See Croce, *Goethe*, trans. Ainslie, pp. 86–94.

almost nothing is known about Shakespeare and his practical life or that there are beautiful works to which it was forgotten to put the name of the author, such as the little masterpiece *Lazarillo de Tormes*, which served as a model for innumerable picaresque novels. The advantages that the knowledge of the author's practical life offers to poetry do not amount to much, nor are they irreplaceable or incomprehensible.

The poet is, therefore, nothing but his poetry. This assertion is not paradoxical if we consider that the philosopher is also nothing but his philosophy, and the statesman nothing but his action and political creation, and that these are the things we learn from the historians of philosophy and of politics and not the instances of Bacon's barratry or the deeds attributed to Caesar by his soldiers during the time he was at King Nicodeme's.

And if a poet has composed only one poem or if only one of his poems is extant, his own characteristics coincide perfectly with those of his only poem. But, since a poet usually composes many poems, all or a large number of which are extant, the mind of the critic constructs not only the characteristics of every single poem but also that of the author, of his poetic personality. To this end the critic eliminates from consideration first of all the unsuccessful or ugly works, the works that the poet composed, for instance, in order to satisfy his eagerness or to compete with poets very different from himself, or his ambition to try themes alien to his own genius; these works, being negative in nature, would not furnish any characteristic traits. The literary works which the poet may have composed are reserved by the critic for subsequent and complementary consideration (almost every poet has composed many literary works, and customarily in greater number than poems, with which he mixed them indiscriminately, holding them to be equally sincere expressions of his feelings). Finally, after accomplishing this, the mind of the critic concentrates solely on the beautiful poems, seeking in them the author's fundamental state of mind—a difficult endeavor, which requires more mental tension and observation than do single poems.

In relation to the author's fundamental state of mind, single works of poetry may be seen as consecutive attempts and approximations aiming at grasping this state of mind, with only one or a few of them expressing it fully, the others being sketches and anticipations; but the poet, upon reaching the full expression of his fundamental state of mind, may remain silent or may unhappily repeat himself and work artificially. Single works, on the other hand, may also be seen as irradiations of the same motif or state of

The poetic personality. I pointed out in Conversazioni critiche (2d ed., vol. 5, p. 82) that the problem of the poetic personality is not to be mistaken, as it has been, for the antiquated one of the so-called substantiality of the individual soul; my remarks were occasioned by a book of J. Tielrooy, Déterminisme et personnalité en histoire littéraire (Haarlem, 1934), from which I learned, not without astonishment, that this mistake has been made by some recent writers, and even as a result of some writings of mine.

mind, in diverse situations and circumstances, with each poem having its own autonomy and beauty. Torquato Tasso is more or less an example of the first case; and Petrarch or Leopardi (setting aside the latter's early poems), of the second.

But it may also happen that in his work of characterization the critic discovers two or more fundamental states of mind, which succeed one another in the poet, as, in the case of Dante, the passage from the lyric of the "stil nuovo"[33] to the *Divine Comedy*; in the case of Goethe, the passage from *Werther* and *Faust* to *Iphigenis*; or they may even alternate, as the happy and the tragic dramas in Shakespeare, the first appearing among his early works and reappearing among the last. The critic in this instance seeks to discover a deeper state of mind, susceptible to great developments or even revolutionary reversals, and he thus unifies these diverse states of mind by dialecticizing them. And, if after that single works still resist this constructive process and no link whatever is discovered between them and the others, he must consider this work an "exception," that is, something sporadic, born in that field out of seeds blown there by the wind, unless he himself or others, through deeper research, succeed in tying the exception to the rule and in finding the link which at first had escaped the mind's eye.

The aim of this constructive work—which is the highest that the critic is called upon to accomplish and in which good critics of single poems sometimes show themselves to be inadequate or even uninterested—is the forging of an instrument analogous to that used for the interpretation of a single poem, an interpretation which serves to give an orientation concerning the character of the whole work of a poet. That this ulterior work of characterization was said to be impossible and abstract is no surprise, and it is useless to speak about it and repeat previous explanations and refutations. Essays or monographs on poets attain their goal when they are not only collections of scattered observations and esthetic commentaries about single poems, but when they succeed also in giving the characteristic of the fundamental motif or state of mind of the poet, thus correcting or enriching with new elements what we possessed on the same subject.[34]

The various personalities of a poet. One may see how this research already took shape in antiquity in regard to Homer, whose two poems seemed to be of such different tones as to be attributed to two different moods: the *Iliad*, all action and exploits, sung in the vigor of his youthful age; the *Odyssey*, all narrations such as old men like to tell, resembles the setting sun, as is said in *On the Sublime* (chap. 9).

33. The expression "dolce stil nuovo" was used to indicate a new poetic school to which Dante belonged at the time of *La vita nuova*. The expression is found in *Purgatorio* 26. 57, where Dante characterizes himself as one who " . . . when love inspires me, I note and write just as it dictates." The "stil nuovo" school stripped love of all earthly elements and gave it an elevated, mystic meaning. The poets upheld, together with the delicacy and aristocratic refinements of expression, the cult of woman conceived as a means of ascending to the understanding of God.

34. It would be interesting to compare this statement with Sainte-

The relation between the poetic personality and the practical life of the man-poet is the same as that between poetry in general and practical life, that is, it is not a relation of identity nor of independence, and if ordinarily only one practical individual coincides with a poetic personality—physically distinct—there are cases in which the physical individuals coinciding with the same poetic personality number two or more. It is not unusual that two individuals collaborate in theatrical works (for instance, Meilhac-Havély) or in stories (Erckmann-Chatrian), but there are also examples of collaboration in works more properly of poetic creation, such as that of the Goncourt Brothers; although one of them (as the survivor of the two said) was more capable in construction and plot, and the other in writing and style, it is clear that this plus or minus in the two was fused in a single creative activity, in a manner not dissimilar to that of conflicting tendencies and attitudes battling in the head of a single individual. To those who were asking for curiosity's sake or those who set out resolutely to discover which of the distichs of *Xenia*, published with the names of both Goethe and Schiller, belonged to one and which to the other, Goethe answered with annoyance: "As though this had any value and brought any profit! As though it was not enough that these distichs are there! . . . We have composed many distichs together. Often I gave the thought, Schiller the verse; often it happened the other way around; often Schiller wrote a line and I the other. How can we now discuss the mine and the thine?"[35]

But we find cases in which many works express the same fundamental state of mind yet belong to distinct individual authors. This creates the difficulty of determining the authorship, especially when it is not proved by unquestionable documentation; and what a surprise when newly discovered documents prove with certainty that the works, which had previously been attributed to an already known author on the basis of internal evidence such as intonation and style, belong to some other author or authors! Although this has happened rarely in the literature of the last five centuries, by virtue of the art of printing and the copyright laws, it happened frequently, as we know, in the literature of the thirteenth and fourteenth centuries, in which there exist a great number of verses without the name of the author or attributed to more than one author. We must admit, however, that what is perhaps unconsciously sought through the research concerning

Beuve, "Qu'est-ce qu'un classique?" in *Causeries du Lundi* (Paris: Garnier, n. d.), vol. 3, pp. 38–55.

35. *Conversations with Eckermann*, December 10, 1826 (Croce's note).

authorship is not the name put on a poem, but the merit and the characterization of the poem itself, which is the only thing having importance for the history of poetry.

It is necessary to hold jealously to the distinction between the poetic and the practical personalities and between the two different lives of the man-poet, and to exclude rigorously any deduction of the one from the other, so that one may avoid the sequel of erroneous judgments resulting from the confusion of the two personalities and the two lives. The image of the poet's practical personality superimposed on that of his poetry falsifies poetry and, conversely, the image of his poetry falsifies that of his practical life, for in the one case the dreams of the poet are attributed, as a practical reality, to the practical man, and in the other the affections and emotions of the practical man are attributed, as a poetic reality, to the poet. Thus the protests of the poets sound as "lasciva est nobis pagina, vita proba" [my writings are licentious, my life is virtuous].[36] Sometimes it happens that a poem is enriched by bringing into it the splendor of the practical life of the man-poet, which may have been very noble and heroic; at other times the condemnation and scorn that the author deserved for his weaknesses and culpability may throw a shadow over his poem. The accusation of insincerity against poets is widespread and commonplace, and it is substantiated by comparing the feelings they sang in their poems with those they actually nourished as the source of their actions. Such comparison shows that the virtue of the women they exalted in their poems was contested and denied in their private correspondence; the civil and military courage by which they seemd to be inflamed in their poems which inflamed others conflicted with the little courage they demonstrated in real life; the men and deeds they exalted in their poetry were disesteemed and abhorred or not tolerated by them in reality. We can quote, in this respect, the subtle answer by which the poet Waller in a courtly manner was able to get out of trouble with King Charles II, who pointed out to him the great inferiority of the songs Waller was composing for him in comparison with those he had composed for Cromwell: "Sir, we poets are more successful in fictions!" Whoever knows not only poetry but also the human heart judges that it is natural for man to sing of what he desires to possess, of what he wants but does not have the means and strength to attain; and that sometimes, from the contrast between an impure and sinful life and the ideal that goads and reproaches, a much purer and nobler poem is drawn,

36. Martial, *Epigrams* 1. 4. 8.

because poetry, as we have said, springs from the "unsatisfied desire" and not from the satisfied desire, from which nothing is generated. And so much the more is it necessary to retain the boundaries between the two distinct personalities, since the mediocre poets, that is, the bad poets, and even some with a certain talent but with a mind that is little refined try with exhibitions of singular, bizarre, or scandalous acts to strike the imagination and lend their verses an interest that is lacking in or is different from the one they ought to arouse.

"Ideal" is the name for the poetic personality in contrast to the practical personality, which alone would be "real"; but the poetic personality is no less real than the other for those who assert the reality of the poets as the apostle asserts the reality of Christ while denying the "Christ of the flesh." Poets are ethereal persons who do not live in a superworld, but in our world, lively and active in their pure humanity, and who are asked and from whom is obtained the sweetness of consolation. Giosuè Carducci (allow me to remember these words from one of his lyrics because I am always moved whenever they come to mind) asked the poets for fortitude and resignation in facing and accepting the supreme instant of death, which he sublimated and sweetened in his mind as the " . . . passo che Omero ellenico/ e il cristiano Dante passarono" [the crossing that the Hellenic Homer/ and the Christian Dante crossed].[37]

Poetry and unsatisfied desire. On this subject, interesting considerations are read in the book by A. Kingsley Porter, *Beyond Architecture* (Boston, 1928), pp. 58, 83: see *Conversazioni critiche*, 2d ed., vol. 3, p. 147. Gino Capponi wrote in a letter of 1833: "I am hungry for verses, that is, for the desire to desire" (*Carteggio col Tommaseo*, vol. 1, p. 40).

The unity of the writer and the citizen. This is the lesson that we have received from our writers of the Risorgimento, and it resounds in the whole of the *History of Italian Literature* by De Sanctis. Those who once learned it have not forgotten it. Unfortunately, recent experiences prove that many of the people who spoke of it so much had not learned it well, for from their lips it had not descended into their hearts. But the unity of the moral man and the writer, asserted in that manner, the unity from which the writer himself derives his strength ("pectus est quod disertum facit" [the heart makes one eloquent]), does not take place in the case of the poet, who, unlike the writer, does not express but transcends every practical interest, and yet is united also to the moral man, but on another level, that is, in his very transcending of practical interest, which is his vocation and his duty as well. It is clear that on the basis of this we cannot make an exception for the man-poet as far as the duties of practical life are concerned; but we can arrive at a sort of comprehension of and indulgence toward the true poets for their usually somewhat fanciful judgments and for their indifference toward political problems. What can we do? A French writer (Gautier, if my memory does not fail me) wrote that the genius is "borné"; he does not understand some things; he pays no attention to other things; and he does not possess certain capabilities. It is said of Lully that one day, while at dinner with a nobleman, he expressed so many extravagant views that the host, turning to the other guests, said: "Ne l'écoutez pas, cet homme n'a pas le sens commun: il est tout génie." One must be much more severe and pitiless toward those who (we find them among the romantics and now among the decadents), though lacking genius, claim for themselves the aristocratic limits and obtusity to which they are not entitled, and on the basis of their poetic pretensions assign to themselves the right to a foolish and depraved life.

Also senseless is the aim to actualize in reality the

---

37. *Odi barbare* 47, last stanza.

This elevated sentiment, this true intelligence of the poetic personality, leads us to look with a certain disgust at what the poetic personality has become in the feelings and the mind of a large part of contemporary literature and contemporary criticism and history. It has become a morbid convulsion of excited nerves, the object of an equally morbid attraction, not dissimilar to the troubled emotion that the Flaubertian St. Anthony expressed at the sight of the enormous Catoblépas unconsciously devouring its own limbs for nourishment ("sa stupidité m'attire").[38] In that blind convulsion of nervous substance everything becomes identical, everything is transformed into quivers and spasms and voluptuous, painful, and libidinous ticklings. The personality is no longer defined by the work but, rather, the work by the animal content of the individuality, in which the personality is submerged and lost. And poetry (when we hear about poetry), the noblest poetry, becomes contaminated, exhaling a nauseating odor of sex and predatory instinct. This idea, truly decadent, of personality which explicitly or implicitly is noted all over in the contemporary world, has given in Germany the principle and directives ("Persönlichkeit") to a school of political and literary history which, notwithstanding the particular merits of individual works it produced, also promotes and outlines a false history of poetry to be added to the many histories mentioned above—a false history that, in its principle, is something pathological and behaves pathologically in many of its interpretations and representations.

dreams of art, to construct an esthetic and poetic life by posing as wandering knights, robbers, oriental despots, supermen, or the like. Applying to our case the saying of Alphonse Karr in regard to rod fishing, we must say here that, if at one end of this dream there may sometimes be a poet, at the other there is certainly an imbecile.[49]

Practical and poetic values. The tendency to elevate the value of a poet by means of considerations extraneous to poetry led, in Germany, to taking sides with Schiller, the poet of freedom and of the rebellion against foreign domination, and to the slighting of Goethe; this tendency is now revived among many German critics who have come to rediscover the sublimity and solemnity of Schiller's dramas. But in poetry a little *Lied* by Goethe is far superior to any pompous *Don Carlos* or *Wallenstein* or *Jungfrau von Orleans*; and there is no dithyrambic eloquence or apology capable of persuading of the contrary the naively pure and sure consciousness of beauty.

Decadentistic theory of personality. I became aware of its real nature about twenty years ago when I was able to obtain, from Switzerland, the book on Goethe by Gundolf (it was during the war). I read the work, and, going beyond the glaring and persuasive appearances, I grasped the intimate thought or the mental bent of the author. So, since then, in that mystically unitary conception which converted itself into naturalism and portrayed great men in the guise of animals, "be it (I said) a powerful and admirable animal or a sacred animal," I detected "sensual and naturalistic decadentism" which has among its characteristics "monstrous traits and morbid colors" (*Goethe*, 4th ed., vol. 1, pp. 142–43). I add, for the sake of truth, that Gundolf, in his posthumously published book on Shakespeare, accepted my distinction between practical and poetic personality, though he did not take advantage of it for the substantial correction of his ideology.

This perverse idea of personality, which is built on strayed consciousness of ideal values, corrupts every form of healthy esthetic life as well as political and social life; for the circles of these esthetes have fostered the aversion for liberty (that is, for true individuality and personality), and envisioned the reduction of Europe to a sort of jesuitic state like Paraguay, on whose pinnacle there would be the sacred animal, the personality of the dictator. The relations of the school of Gundolf with Stephan George are known; also known,

---

38. Flaubert, *La tentation de Saint Antoine* (Paris: Conard, 1902), p. 196. The Catoblépas is a fantastic animal with horns and a thin neck which allows the head to drag on the ground.

49. The reference here seems to be to Karr, *Les guêpes*, vol. 6 (1883), pp. 102–05. Alphonse Karr (1808–1890), French journalist and novelist, wrote his "wasps" monthly between 1839 and 1849. The one to which Croce alludes is "La pêche aux électeurs: les divers modes de cette pêche" (June 1846).

and illustrated in various books, is the relation between George's ideas and those of antiliberalism and
the German dictatorship of today. That after the advent of the dictatorship George kept out of it is something which does honor to a man of dignity, but does
not change the nature of his ethical ideal.

I would be out of place, and outside the context of
this book, to expose in detail the genesis of the theory
of the *persönlichkeit*. It suffices to mention that, by abstracting from the ideal values which alone, in individualizing themselves, compose the true personality,
what is left is the brutal biological individual which,
abandoned to itself, appears to be monstrous and morbid. Modern decadentism, in descending to and reaching this lowest degree, pretends to have touched the
mysterious bottom, the "roots" of humanity (as Barrès
called them), but it only reaches the exact zone from
which humanity elevated itself, rising above it by permeating it with human values. Burn the human body
(as a Neapolitan philosopher whom I knew in the
beautiful years used to say) and its ashes will always be
the ashes of a man and not the ashes of an animal.

Concurrent with this theory of personality, rather
than parallel with it, is the so-called psychoanalysis,
whose fortune is, like that of the other, a proof of the
misguided or perverted consciousness of the spirituality of man. For psychoanalysis the poetic image is the
hidden or disguised means of satisfying certain appe-
tites of eroticism or violence, which are hindered, in
ordinary life, by the restraint of the moral conscience.
See in this regard Guido De Ruggiero, *Filosofi del novecento* (Bari, 1934), pp. 271–92; and Francesco Flora,
Civiltà del novecento (Bari, 1934), pp. 145–234.

Personality and poetry. An example of the unfortunately frequent manner in which the personality in
general and the poetic personality in particular are
now understood is found in these words of a writer
who, surprisingly enough, is a neo-Catholic: "Ecrire,
surtout des poèmes, égale transpirer. L'oeuvre est une
sueur. Il serait malsain de courir, de jouer, de se pro-
mener, d'être un athlète sans sueur. Seuls la prome-
nade d'un homme et l'homme lui-même m'intéressent.
C'est pourquoi peu d'oeuvres de vivants me touchent.
Dans l'oeuvre d'un mort, dans le parfum de sa sueur,
je cherche un témoignage d'activité. Le Louvre est une
Morgue: on y va reconnaître ses amis . . ." (Jean Coc-
teau, *Le secret professionnel*, Paris, 1922, p. 21).

7. The Empirical Poetics

Esthetic judgment, which is formed by virtue of mental categories, that is, pure concepts, is essentially philosophical and not empirical; likewise esthetics is philosophical and not empirical insofar as it is methodology of that judgment or science of the category of the beautiful. Those who dream of an esthetics proceeding empirically by inductions and generalizations, by the setting up of laws similar to those of physics or even by the applying of mathematical formulae in an attempt to modify the nature of the esthetic judgment, show little understanding of it. On the whole, attempts of this kind have always failed miserably; in fact, they have attracted so little attention that almost no one cared to show how simplistic their purpose was; nor did anyone stop to look (with amusement) at the laughable ways these attempts were carried out, even when they were the work of men with some merit in other respects, as was the case with Fechner.[39]

This does not prevent us, however, from admitting the legitimate existence of both the empirical judgment of the beautiful and an esthetics or empirical poetics, composed of empirical concepts whose function is classificatory and not cognitive and judicial. But this esthetics, with the corresponding judgments, is not only unable to replace speculative esthetics, but, when well conceived, on the contrary, presupposes it as its own foundation, if it is true that psychology (psychology and not psychologism, which is a bad philosophy and a metaphysics) presupposes philosophy.

And these empirical or representative judgments and concepts are known and familiar to us who have already seen them at work in the double function they accomplish in things related to poetry. They are used by the esthetic judgment to recognize the ugly and to point out its multiple forms; they serve to facilitate, through this esthetic-historical judgment, the interpretation and re-evocation of poetry by virtue of the characterization.

An empirical poetics simply consists of a series of these two orders of representative concepts which grows continually by progressive specifications; the first concept can be called one of evaluation or, rather, of reprobation; the second of qualification or, rather, of characterization.

As such, they are constructed with universally hu-

Positivistic and inductive esthetics. On the esthetics "from below" of Fechner, see my *Aesthetic* (historical part, chap. 17, pp. 394–97); here I also collected a selection of the laughable attempts of the same kind, which, at that time, thirty-five years ago, it was necessary to criticize; but now one could even avoid mentioning them, if there were no risk of the ever-present possibility of "multa nascentur" [many things being born].

The empirical concepts of poetry. See a brief essay of mine written in 1924: "Per una poetica moderna" (now in *Nuovi saggi d'estetica,* 3d ed., pp. 315–28), where I outlined these two orders of empirical concepts.

The classification of masterpieces. In a book, unknown in Italy, by the Rumanian M. Dragomirescu, *La science de la littérature* (Paris, 1928–1929), through a curious naturalistic doctrine, it is energetically maintained that the study of poetry is none but the study of "masterpieces," in their purely ideal and poetic value. The author asserts that "de même que la Minéralogie, la Zoologie, la Botanique, la Science de la Littérature doit aboutir à la classification naturelle des chefs-d'oeuvre"; it must, therefore, bring together, over the centuries and the geographical distances, in one same category "les chefs-d'oeuvre qui ont le même type, ont la même forme littéraire et sont du même genre"; for instance, a drama by Aeschylus and one by Rostand, an ode by Pindar and one by Victor Hugo. In this way, one can give "un conspectus général de la littérature universelle, ainsi que la Zoologie le fait pour tous les

39. G. Th. Fechner (1801–1887), German scientist and philosopher, pioneer of psychophysics, author of an experimental esthetics, *Vorschule der Aesthetik* (1876).

man elements, related to the human spirit. This must be pointed out because there are among them some that at times assume historical names, such as "alexandrinism," "secentismo," "arcadism," as an obvious metaphor for the historical periods in which certain esthetic forms or deformations seem to have been prevalent; but they have ever since, either mentally or in verbal utterances, been defined according to their pure human characteristics, psychologically and not historically. Contrarily, it also happens that some of those concepts are employed, always by the metaphorical procedure, to characterize historical epochs; for instance, the concept of that particular form of ugliness called baroque, which has come to designate, for Italy and a great part of Europe, the literature and art (and also the customs) of the period from about the last quarter of the sixteenth century to the third quarter of the seventeenth. Now, it is certain that that century did not produce only things with a negative value, that is, ugly, but also produced works noteworthy in various ways for their literary effectiveness and even works of imaginative and poetic merits. Nowadays these merits have come to be vindicated against too narrow criteria of judgment in the art of language as well as in the figurative and architectural arts. But this has also led to the ill-founded objections against those who restore and retain the original negative meaning of that term, which is the only correct meaning, expressing a form of ugliness.[40] These objections are summarized in the assertion that there exist "baroque works which are beautiful," and that, consequently, the baroque is "a form of art": such assertion implies a thoughtless shifting from the scientific and proper use to the historical metaphor employed to designate a complex and a sequel of works which from the esthetic point of view must be considered and judged, each in its own individuality.

The available didactic elaborations of empirical poetics are not satisfying by the very reason of their lack of self-consciousness. As a result, instead of remaining, as they should, rigorously in the empirical sphere, they involve themselves with the philosophical problems and concepts of esthetics and poetics; thus an abundance of monstrous theories, arbitrary and confusing definitions concerning beauty, poetry, and the poetic forms. But, moreover, even in their merely empirical parts by which they could be of great service, they appear terribly old.

They are still founded almost entirely on the ancient tripartition of poetry into lyric, epic, and dramatic, and on the ancient divisions of rhetoric, imprudently

animaux en dehors des conditions de temps, d'espace et de causalité où ils vivent et disparaissent" (vol. 1, p. 58). Dragomirescu does not realize that, if the systematics of zoology serves a purpose, the systematics which he proposes of the masterpieces would serve none, for as far as animals are concerned it is enough for us to know in general their external conformation and habits in order to be able to use these animals for our own purposes or to protect ourselves against them; but the only aim of literary criticism is the re-evocation and the comprehension of individual poetic works; to know whether an ode by Pindar and an ode by Victor Hugo belong to the same genre and subject matter and have the same external form and thus have been placed on the same shelf by the classifier or the librarian does not help us to re-evoke and comprehend either the ode by Pindar or the ode by Victor Hugo. Sometimes, certain comparisons of similar or opposite works by different and far-removed authors and peoples may be of some value for giving a more conspicuous relief to the intrinsic character of each work, but this will serve only a didactic and pedagogical purpose.

40. See above, n. 13.

transferred to poetry; they bring about little change in the ancient catalogues of the vices into which the literary form falls. They did realize that criticism of poetry, especially in the past one hundred and fifty years, has developed for its own needs a rich series of empirical concepts which almost entirely replace the ancient, but grasp distinctions which neither antiquity nor the Middle Ages nor the Renaissance nor neoclassicism were able to grasp or even to suspect. As for the negative or reprobative concepts, the ones we possess now are of a completely different nature as compared with the "pleonasm," "tautology," "topeinosis," "macrology," "cacozelon," "cacosyntheton," "aschematon," catalogued by the Greek and Roman rhetoricians. Our perception and characterization of the ugly has become much deeper and more acute, and more differentiated; our casuistry (in the positive sense of the word) has become extraordinarily rich. We have analyzed and pointed out the most diverse and complicated and often fleeting and concealed modes of deviation from poetic genuineness, as well as the most skillful and glittering intellectualisms, the most subtle departures of the rhythm of intuition from the rhythm of sounds, the most astute pretensions of new intuitions through extrinsic repetitions or combinations made up of already existing expressions; and we know even the so-called morbid forms of expression, the vice of which is moral in origin and therefore very serious because it attacks the roots of the soul; but such a vice is not vulgar, and the works which it affects often appear under the aspect of "sick beauty." Our research on the activity of feelings is more profound and acute, more delicate and exquisite, with Christianity and the knowledge of sin and the introspection of the modern conscience which aims at knowing man in his full reality and which searches every corner of his soul, so that the modern characterizations and the modern forms of poetry would astonish the ancients and would give us the measure of the immense progress accomplished by thought. In light of these considerations, it would be well to make a collection of the new classificatory concepts, arranging them either in the form of a dictionary of the terminology of poetic and literary criticism or (and it would be better) in the form of an empirical systematics which groups them by affinity. But in this second form one would have to be very careful to avoid the temptation of tightening too much the threads of the empirical systematics when tying them to their philosophical principles, for by so doing the empirical poetics would waver, become confused, and finally vanish.

We limit ourselves to this warning because it does not seem necessary to explain again and refute those

Old and new poetics. My essay, mentioned above, *"Per una poetica moderna"* [*Nuovi saggi d'estetica*], was meant to point out the obsolescence of the constructive schemes of the poetics which are still being published today and of the necessity for renovating and modernizing them.

Sickly beauty. As an example of sickly beauty, it was noted in regard to Platen, and, in another sense, to Flaubert (specifically in *Salammbô* and *La tentation*) that the belabored, perfect, crystal-clear form of their works does not always resolve itself into a turbid content, but often compresses and binds it through an effort of the will which is not a genuine way of liberation and appeasement in the poetic image, of which Goethe spoke. See concerning Platen the book by Ermatinger, *Die deutsche Lyrik seit Herder* (Leipzig-Berlin, 1925), vol. 2, p. 247; and concerning Flaubert, my essay in *European Literature in the Nineteenth Century*, pp. 297–311.

Empirical poetics is not to be rendered philosophical. For this part one should keep in mind the analogous methodological considerations that Clausewitz made concerning the doctrines on the art of war in his book *Vom*

speculative and dialectical essays being written until recently, especially in the German esthetics. These essays gave to the catalogue of psychological "categories" (drawn from individual poems) the pompous name, indicated earlier, of "Doctrine of the modifications of the beautiful," and to the catalogue of the negative concepts the name of "Phenomenology of the ugly." These philosophers took to heart their thankless task and endured infernal tortures with a heroic pedantry worthy of Sisyphus, Ixion, and the Danaides; they persisted in deducing speculatively and developing dialectically empirical concepts which are nominal and which cannot be developed, but simply juxtaposed, thereby escaping the philosophers' constant and renewed efforts. But one must add that the very concepts they used were gathered not from the criticism of poetry and art, but from the commonplace confusions between the beautiful in art and all other things upon which the name of beautiful is metaphorically conferred. Thus they treated philosophically and dialecticized not only what was not philosophical, but also a medley of notions, intolerable even in an empirical poetics, which never lacks a certain principle of order. So for Rosenkranz the categories of the ugly were not only the "incorrect," the "disharmonic," the "formless," and the other, similar formal deviations, but also the "horrible," the "criminal," the "malignant," the "repugnant," the "diabolic," and every other word which aroused a feeling of reprobation and horror.[41]

Empirical poetics have a direct practical aim; they are a handy instrument for grasping in the concrete the principles which they contain and for employing properly the terminology thus far established for the negative judgments of the ugly and for the psychological characterizations of poems; it would be well, therefore, to have the nominalistic definitions of the concepts in these treatises accompanied by appropriate examples which would show at the same time their use and their limits, the degree of comprehension of single poems which is achieved through these concepts, the need to increase, always through discernment, the distinctions and, at the same time, the distance which always exist between the characterization and the individuality of a poem. To accomplish this task one must be endowed with many gifts of talent and culture, not easy to find together. A good work of empirical nature is, in a certain sense, more difficult and complicated than a purely philosophical work or one of concrete criticism and history of poetry because

Kriege (see my essay on Clausewitz in Ultimi saggi, 2d ed., pp. 266–79).

Modifications of the beautiful and the phenomenology of the ugly. For the exposition and criticism as well as the satire of this German doctrine, see my Aesthetic, especially pt. 2, chap. 13, pp. 343–49. The most characteristic book on this subject, and the one which has a very promising title, is that mentioned in the text, Aesthetik des Hässlichen by K. Rosenkranz (Königsberg, 1853). "I tried," writes the author in the introduction (pp. iv–v), "to develop the concept of Ugly as a middle term between that of the Beautiful and that of the Comic, from its beginnings up to that completeness which is given in the portrayal of the Satanic, and to expose the world of the Ugly from the first chaotic nebula, which is the Amorphic and the Asymetric, up to its more intense formations and the infinite variety of the disorganization of the Beautiful through caricature. The Formless, the Incorrect, and the Deformed constitute the different degrees of this series of successive metamorphoses. An attempt was made to show how the Ugly has its positive presupposition in the Beautiful, which it destroys producing, instead of the Sublime, the Trivial; instead of the Pleasing, the Repugnant; instead of the Ideal, the Caricature. All the arts and all the artistic ages among the most diverse peoples are here called upon to illuminate with appropriate examples the development of concepts."

---

41. Karl Rosenkranz 1805–1879), author of *Aesthetics of Ugliness* (*Aesthetik des Hässlichen* [1853]). See Croce, *Aesthetic*, pp. 347–48.

it presupposes all these works, and not in the brain of somebody else, but in the brain—active by exercise and experience—of him who undertakes such a work. For this is not only a work of conceptual creation and intellectual acumen, but also one of practical balance and wisdom, of a wisdom which does not always arise from great mental effort.

IV

The Formation of the Poet and the Precepts

1. *Spontaneity and Discipline*

If the feeling of the poet encloses within itself history and if in that feeling lives, together with thought, the poetry of centuries which is fused and transfigured in the new expression, then one understands why the poet is impelled by the impulse to create originally and, at the same time, by the necessity to be attuned to the voice of the poetry which resounded before his own and to respond to it as in a chorus. Tacitly, before listening to the exhortations by others, he seems to say to himself: "Be thyself!" "Follow thine own nature!" "Imitate the great models!"

These exhortations may seem contradictory, but they are, on the contrary, concurrent and convergent, leading up to the single act which is altogether one of freedom and necessity, spontaneity and discipline, two terms so indivisible that by eliminating one the other would vanish completely. What does "imitation of nature" by itself mean? Perhaps those "copies" or duplicates of facts and natural objects which do not belong either to art or to knowledge and are made for trifling with or for displaying virtuosity? What does "imitation of a poem" mean? Perhaps the repetition of the poem, the multiplication of the scripts and printings containing it, or perhaps the plagiarism which is

Poetry and the new way of poetising. This very beautiful epigram by Goethe, who recalls one of his visits to Mantua, may well express how ancient poetry involves the new poet and attracts him to its sphere and frees his heart for singing:

*Kaum an dem blaueren Himmel erblickt'ich die glänzende
    Sonne,
Reich, vom Felsen herab, Epheu zu Kränzen geschmückt,
Sah den emsingen Winzer die Rebe der Pappel verbin-
    den,
Ueber die Wiege Virgil's kam mir ein laulicher Wind;
Da gesellten die Musen sich gleich zum Freunde; wir
    pflogen
Abgerissnes Gespräch, wie es den Wanderer freut.*

(As soon as I had looked at the fulgent sun in the blue sky and the ivy which was hanging ever-richer from the cliffs, interwoven in crowns, and had perceived the industrious vine grower tying the vine twig to the poplar, a tepid breeze came to me in Virgil's cradle; and then immediately the Muses rejoined their friend, and we resumed an interrupted discourse, such as the wayfarer delights to hear.)

175

something alien and indifferent to art? What is the absolute or abstract "originality" in its isolation? Perhaps the absolute beginning of the world by the advent of a new poet? And, for mercy's sake, at what moment of the new poet's life would such a cataclysm take place which would open a gap between himself and the surrounding and preceding reality? Really, such extravagances have never been in the minds even of those who seem, in words, to hold to one of these exigencies to the exclusion of the other. When questioned, in fact, they say that they mean a "relative" originality, a "nonmaterial" imitation of nature, a "nonservile" imitation of the poetic models. And, when we inquire about the motives of their exhortations, we find always a concrete reference to one or more works blamed for lacking inspiration and, therefore, for not being original, for having no roots in life and reality, that is, for being incorrect, out of tune, arbitrary, in which images are incoherent and the elaboration of form is inadequate. Also the ancient poetics, after proposing and debating at length the question of whether nature or art is needed to form the poet, ended in the conclusion that one cannot do anything without the other—study would be fruitless without a rich vein and so would be the natural talent without the refinement of discipline—and that the two forces conspire to achieve the same end (coniurant amice [join together amicably]).

It is possible that the only ones who have somehow believed and still believe seriously that the poets do nothing but imitate, that is, secretly plagiarize one another (the successor the predecessor, and so on, through the chain of times up to the point where robber and robbed are lost in the darkness of prehistory) have been the so-called seekers of sources. They are, in fact, the philologists who, having noticed some traces of the earlier poetry in the later, at a certain moment imagined, because of their lack of poetic sense, that poems are never original, that is, that in the last analysis they do not exist as poetry, and that it is the privilege of the philologist's acumen and cleverness to open the eyes of the public, demonstrating with unchallengeable factual proofs that poets generally sell stolen merchandise as their own and that they take a cow for a bull. But with this imprudent conclusion they passed from the observation of external resemblances to an internal esthetic judgment, with the result that the research on sources was discredited and ridiculed; the more so since the affection of those philologists for the discoveries they imagined they would make changed to blind fanaticism and led them to find borrowings and thefts even in the most natural encounters. The search for the resonances and reminis-

Plagiarism. That the concept of plagiarism is completely alien to art is something that I explained in *Problemi d'estetica*, 4th ed., pp. 67–70.

Originality. "People are always talking about originality; but what do they mean? As soon as we are born, the world begins to work upon us, and this goes on to the end. And, after all, what can we call our own except energy, strength, and will? If I could give an account of all that I owe to great predecessors and contemporaries, there would be only a small balance in my favor" (Goethe, *Conversations with Eckermann,* May 12, 1825).

No ideal importance is to be recognized in the so-called rebellions against everything ancient and existent, or, as they are called, in the "youth movements," from which nothing ever comes, or could come. At most, they can serve to give free rein to a physiological or pathological need, whatever it may be, for excitement, shouting, and noise. In true and productive talents, opposition never takes that broad and generic form, but is specific and never without the moment of union, from which recognition and reconciliation subsequently follow.

Imitation. On the doctrine of "imitation" during the Renaissance, see *Poesia popolare e poesia d'arte,* 2d ed., pp. 350–52.

Imitation and emulation. Goethe, Moritz, Platner, and other German theorists at the end of the eighteenth century replaced the word "to imitate" ("nachahmen") with the word "to emulate" ("nacheifern"), which seemed to them to be more appropriate.

Research on "sources". For a criticism of what was called so, see *Problemi d'estetica*, 4th ed., pp. 487–502.

Seventy years ago in Italy and elsewhere, research on sources had become an obsession; it seemed to be the most beautiful and the rarest flower of literary studies: he who was able to discover the so-called sources of a poem earned a medal for bravery, a gold medal.

Here is one more remembrance of my youth: a philologist who was a friend of mine and, I would say, a colleague in our visits to archives and libraries, a zealous searcher of sources, one day whispered to me, with a bitter grimace and a look of sincere disgust on his lips, his conclusive aphorism: poets are all thieves! To reinforce his conviction, I answered with a saying attributed to Voltaire: that true poets do worse, for they not only steal, but they kill those whom they have robbed.

The "scientist" of literature. The investigation of the

cences which are fused and somehow sensed in the new work, when contained within rational limits, may have its usefulness, as does any other philological inquiry; but it would be well to put aside, together with its extravagant ideology, the title given to it, "research on the sources." The "source" of a poem is always the soul of the poet and never the things, the words, the verses born in other souls.

sources and the biography of the author, carried out with the mental disposition of a police officer or a district attorney, or even, if you prefer, of a pathologist or alienist, were considered fifty years ago the very object of the critic and historian of literature, upon whom alone was conferred the title of "scientist." Biography, however, overwhelmed poetry and dissolved it into practical elements, and the research on sources demonstrated it to be a re-presentation, with a more or less new varnish, of things already existing. This kind of mistrust, aversion, and cruelty in regard to poetry seemed to be a guarantee of incorruptible scientific rigorousness, against which the allurement of beauty proved to be ineffective. Love for beauty and hate for ugliness were left to the weak-minded, the ignorant, the dilettante, and to sentimental young ladies, as an object for entertainment and diversion in places such as drawing rooms or, rather, coffeehouses. And when the "scientist" deigned to consider the form of poetry, he indicated the list of words, syntactic modes, metaphors, and so forth, which go under the name of stylistics, and of which we talked earlier. Thus, in this respect also, he remained strictly scientific. And what self-sufficiency, what scorn toward those who were unable to act with equal rigorousness! Those scientists of literature were annoying at that time; later they appeared to be ridiculous; and now, with the changing of the times, they are remembered now and then with a certain tenderness, because, in substance, they believed in their "science," and, in order to serve it well, they renounced feeling and thinking and for it they stood in a condition (to use Bruno's words) of "holy stupidity."

The sources and the poets. *In order to demonstrate how research on sources is in itself inept at determining the judgment of poetry, it would be enough to study extreme cases of exquisite poets who (like Sannazaro in reference to his* De Partu Virginis*) boasted of having used no other words or modes than those found in Virgil and other ancients, and to contrast their works to those of the mechanical composers of patchworks. André Chénier also vaunted his constant use of the forms from the ancients:*

Dévot adorateur de ces maîtres antiques,
Je veux m'envelopper de leurs saintes reliques.

But he also said:

Tantôt chez un auteur j'adopte une pensée,
Mais qui revêt chez moi, souvent entrelacée,
Mes images, mes tours, jeune et frais ornement;
Tantôt je ne retiens que les mots seulement;
J'en détourne le sens, et l'art sait les contraindre
Vers des objets nouveaux qu'ils s'étonnent de peindre . . .
                                                    (Epître 3, à Le Brun)

The poet achieves his formation through hard work aimed at a double yet unique goal; on the one hand he seeks to link himself to the tradition of poetry by resuming in his own voice the eternal motif of poetic song, on the other to dig within himself and discover his own originality, his own personality, his own mission, and to make his own voice resound purely. Even the poet who seems to be the most uncultivated, if he is a true poet, seeks and works out this union often in the most singular and unexpected ways, through desultory and accidental readings, words rapidly grasped in a conversation, vibrations perceived in the air. More often the intermediary is another poet, who is for him the synthesis of all others, another poet for whom he feels a growing attachment and with whom he becomes familiar; this rule of the single poet-model was established by the Italian rhetoricians of the sixteenth century who wrote about poetic imitation, and the compliance with it was considered to be the sign of a serious formation, more so than the shifting interest in many and diverse poets. But the intimate dialogue between the old and the new poet remains a mystery, a secret of two souls, for what the one teaches and what the other learns is a mystery. Certainly, the subject of the intimate dialogue concerns not only the roads to follow but also the roads to avoid, not only doing something dissimilar to that which the earlier poet did but also doing something dissimilar and contrary to it—something contrary which finds its strength in its very contrariness. To what extent was Virgil a master and an author to Dante? What is the "beautiful style" which Dante borrowed from him? No one knows and no one has ever known, but no one has dared to have a doubt about Dante's expression of gratitude.[1] And how many poets whose early works were imitated and most warmly but superficially loved were later abandoned and often looked at with an unfair, though not unjustified, abhorrence!

The blame on those who borrow from previous works. *It is usually noted with disfavor that such and such a part of a work is derived from a previous work; but the disfavor, in this case, is not brought about by seeing the previous work live again in the later one, that is, the past in the present, but rather by "not seeing it live again," by noticing the inner poverty that the borrowing uncovers, the cock feathers with which impotence awkwardly adorns itself. No one ever thinks of either blaming Torquato Tasso or esteeming him less because he had borrowed the admirable scene in which Erminia, looking at the crusaders' camp where her beloved is, feels the presence and the unattainable joy of love, and sings:*

> *Poi, rimirando il campo, ella dicea:*
> *—O belle agli occhi miei tende latine!*
> *Aura spira da voi che mi ricrea*
> *e mi conforta pur che m'avvicine . . . [canto 6,*
> *lines 104–08].*

[Beholding then the camp, she said: O Latin tents, beautiful to my eyes! An aura comes from you that relieves and comforts me as I approach you.] These lines would not have come into existence if Propertius' Tarpeia (Elegies, bk. 4, pt. 4), looking from the fortress of the Capitol at the fires and pavilions of the Sabine camp, where Tatius was with whom she had fallen in love, had not similarly desired and sighed:

> *Ignes castrorum et Tatiae praetoria turmae*
> *et famosa oculis arma Sabina meis,*
> *o utinam ad vestros sedeam captiva Penates,*
> *dum captiva mei conspicer esse Tati!*

[O campfires, lordly tents of Tatius and his men and you, Sabine arms, famous in my eyes, Oh might I even as a captive sit at your Penates, and as a captive be within sight of my Tatius.] But if there is similarity in the two passages, there is also dissimilarity, and no one because of the existence of Propertius' verses will hold those of Tasso to be superfluous, as borrowed works are.

Original literatures and literatures of imitation. *An extension of the erroneous criticism of the sources is found in the judgments on the poems and literatures of the various peoples, some of which are declared to be "original" and others to be "derived" (that is, "imitations"), as is Roman literature in relation to Greek literature, or the Italian in relation to the Latin, or certain ages of single literatures, such as the French during its age of Italianism and Hispanicism, the Spanish and the Germans during their ages of gallicism, and so on. But all literatures have their antecedents, and the point to be considered is not that obvious relation, but the way in which they have reacted*

---

1. *Inferno* 1. 86–87.

The process by which man reaches his deep self—of which he had a vague notion (the consciousness of having a word of his own to say to the world), but not yet the knowledge and the actual possession—is just as complicated and varying. Some grasp it quickly, others spend long years, and only in late life does their soul reach fruition. There are those who for a long time dwell on a false self which they present to others and to the literary world; but then they become aware of the illusion into which they have fallen and been trapped, and they drive out the intruder. There is also talk about things that poets supposedly write "for exercise"; but this is only a manner of speaking, for nobody can write just for exercise, with a cold mind, not even school children in their compositions. One cannot even consider art for art's sake to be pure exercise; for, as we have seen, such an exercise is the effect of love. The works which appear as exercises were composed with a serious intent, even though they turned out to be faulty or to be failures; and when later the original and living works are published, the preceding ones appear as the necessary roads leading to them. And it is in retrospect and by interpreting this necessity as a conscious intention that one can call the early works "exercises." Likewise, it is said of certain authors that, rather than poets, they were teachers of poets, having taught their successors words, rhythms, meters, breaks, and other modes and forms out of which they constructed poetic expressions. But in reality they did not mean to be and were not teachers; they were poets, more or less intense, more or less accomplished, and were able to light up the genius of others only with their poetic sparks. The poet thus forms himself by constant work, groping and toiling, seeking the beautiful and falling into the ugly, amidst remorse and embarrassment. Which poet is not ashamed and would not, if he could, destroy (while trying to hide them and hoping they are forgotten or by rejecting them) many of his compositions, which, indeed, when written, had taken all of the strength he possessed? The poet learns his trade, as does everybody else, at his own expense, that is to say, not gratuitously, delightfully, easily; his apprenticeship cannot

to previous literatures, what they originally produced through their original authors, those worthy of the name.

The only teacher. The same advice from our critics and treatise writers of the sixteenth century is reiterated by Banville: "Fermez tous les autres et ne lisez plus que celui-là. Lisez-le sans cesse, sans repos, sans trêve, comme un luthérien lit sa Bible ou comme un bon Anglais lettré lit son Shakespeare et, croyez-moi, cette fréquentation obstinée d'un maître vous vaudra mieux que tous les enseignements possibles (*Petit traité*, p. 76, mentioned earlier).

The sympathy and hostility of others. If predictable or prophetic criticism is to be denied every consistency (see above, p. 156, "Poetry and the poet of the future"), and if the poet forms himself only through his own powers and the critic has no part either in the conception or in the gestation, but enters the picture only when the work has come to light, one cannot ignore or censure the action accomplished by some of them in being the companions of the artist in his hopes and toils, in consoling him in his moments of discouragement, in recalling him from his straying, in advising him modestly and discreetly. This action, though, even when exercised with the pen, is not criticism, but the action of a friend, morally effective, esthetically of no value. Artists, in asking for criticism, usually expect nothing more than this proof of sympathy, this warmth which is sweet as well as beneficial to them (though the opposite—poverty and hostility—is also beneficial). All depends upon what they are able to draw from endearments and lampoons, whether they are able to convert them into the stimulation of energy. As is known, friends are often harmful, and enemies useful, both without intention.

Poets-institutors. Words and attitudes, which passed from minor to major poets or from superficial works to poems that made those words and attitudes profound, were noted, for example, in Victor Hugo in relation to Baudelaire. An essay on what passed from Vincenzo Monti to Foscolo, Leopardi, and Carducci is found in *La critica* 33 (1936):484–87.

How the poet learns. I wish to quote once more the old alienist and (exceptional case) fine literary man, Havelock Ellis: "The great writer can only learn out of himself. He learns to write as a child learns to walk. For the laws of the logic of thought are none other than those of physical movement. There is stumbling, awkwardness, hesitation, experiment—before at last the learner attains the perfect command of that divine rhythm and perilous poise in which he asserts his supreme human privilege. But the process of his learning rests ultimately on his own structure and function

be accomplished through safe exercises, for this would be like learning how to swim without ever jumping into the sea and swallowing salty water.

The autodidacticism of the poet cannot be reduced to school discipline, nor can it be helped and complemented by that discipline. Schools are for literature, not for poetry; and in literature itself they cannot form the writer, who forms himself only when a thought or a passion moves him and gives him a style; but they teach what can be taught, which amounts to subduing and refining the immediate expression and giving it an orderly and correct form. There were, in the past, schools of poetry; there must still be in the conservative English universities the chair of "poetry"; but this is, like those of the past, a school of versification, dictated by the social customs, by their ceremonials, their solemnities, their games, which demanded that one knew how to compose verses; and there was almost no one with any culture who was unable to put together a sonnet or rhyme a madrigal. The philosopher Vico, who was teaching rhetoric at the University of Naples and who was perhaps the first to think out the sublime concept of poetry, which is that of modern times, was compelled by his duties not only to instruct his students in writing verses, but himself to compose, on demand or on order and for the most diverse occasions, hundreds of sonnets in Italian and elegies and other poems in Latin. At the bottom of the complaint about the nonhumanistic character of

and not on others' example. . . . For the style that is founded on a model is the negation of style" (*The Dance of Life*, p. 188).

One must keep in mind that, for the poet, as well as for the critical and scientific talent, and for the morally superior man, the sign of what he will be cannot be derived from the first manifestations, which may be deceptive, as deceptive as those of the so-called promising talent or of the easy kindness and goodness of those who have not undergone the test of life and, later facing this test, soon set aside their superficial virtues and replace them with the opposite ones—selfishness and rudeness. The only criterion for assessing the value of talents and minds lies in their capacity of development and progress; on the basis of this criterion, initial errors and faults and mediocre and ugly works of art can constitute degrees of ascension; it may often happen conversely that the first proofs are laudable and lauded, but not followed by others equally successful; or that no progress is made thereon and they remain as an insurmountable "mode"; or simply that the further development is nothing but an entanglement in the ugly, ignoble, insipid, or quackish.

The complete editions of the poets. To be considered in bad taste are the editions, even called "national," which have now been made of Leopardi, Manzoni, or Carducci, adding to their poems all the youthful and mediocre productions and all the sketches and first drafts of their works. One may understand the historical-biographical interest (on the other hand, very limited and of little fruitfulness) leading to such publications. One may understand also the zeal of salvaging everything written by a great man by printing it; but why not call such publications "archives" of such and such a poet instead of calling them "works" and putting them together with the true poetic works? This is not only an insult to the memory of the poet, but an insult to the poetic sense of the readers.

The art of versification and poetry. "*Je sais bien que je me suis placé entre les deux cornes d'un dilemme terrible. Si la Rime, va-t-on me dire, est tout le vers, et si la Rime est révélée au seul poète, qu'avez-vous donc à enseigner comme versification à celui qui n'est pas poète? —En d'autres termes, peut-on, sans être poète, faire des vers supportables, et quel moyen y a-t-il à employer pour cela? Hélas! oui, la chose se peut; nous sommes assez singes de notre nature pour tout imiter, même la beauté et même le génie, et je suis homme à donner, comme un autre, cette consultation empirique*" (Banville, *Petit traité*, p. 67).

the literary teaching in today's schools there is regret for the loss of the customs of the good old times. But, although a certain instruction in verse making would perhaps still have something positive (both in relation to prose writing and as a means for measuring by personal experience the distance between verses ably but mechanically contrived, and the winged verses of true poets), the method by which poems are read in schools is the only legitimate one, for it conforms to the principle that they can be interpreted, re-evoked, and judged only historically, that is, esthetically. If this in the end is not always achieved in schools, it is the fault of the teachers who are learned in philology but who have little taste. Schools of poetry seem now to have been opened in Russia; and this is a natural thing because poetry is conceived there as the manifestation of the needs of the proletarian class and as its instrument for propaganda; and for the expression of these needs and the spreading of propaganda one can provide very well through methodic training. But what cannot be taught is the spontaneity and freedom of genius, which, just because it is genius, knows how to find its deepest self by its own labor, and how to join itself to the genius of humanity through discipline.

Discipline implies will; and poetic genius is volitional, tenacious, patient; it wins over all resistance, overcomes every obstacle. It is volitional not as understood by the poets of "pure poetry" who, with will and without inspiration, construct playthings and other little objects for their own amusement or for producing an impression on others. The volition of genius, one could say, is like a mother who considers her whole organism sacred to the seed she carries in her womb, a mother who would spare no labor to raise her offspring to be strong and beautiful. And in this act the poet is moral, not through a morality imposed upon him from the outside (by forcing on him the theme and the feelings to be expressed in his work and by restricting the work through this vain tyranny, thus corrupting morality itself, which turns into insincerity), but because of that morality, which is submission to a supraindividual duty of which the individual is aware and feels that he is no more than an instrument. Therefore, he sustains many battles with himself before fighting the world; he renounces many comforts and many ambitions and is very attentive to the dignity of his poetry, which he preserves jealously uncontaminated, "vergine di servo encomio e di codardo oltraggio" [unsullied by servile admiration and cowardly insult].[2] He may be guilty in other aspects

The morality of the poet. "The young poets always think that poetizing well is more honorable than living morally; but poetizing well is nothing but an aspect of moral life" (Albert Verwey, *Europäische Aufsätze*, Ital. trans., p. 240). Heinrich Heine left a saying (*Lutetia*, letter 42) which the famous dancer Vestris used to repeat: "A dancer must be a virtuous man" ("tugendhaft").

The poet and egoism. Although there is often talk about the selfishness of the poet, and Gozzano portrays it in certain verses of his at the moment when, being advised of the sickness and agony of his mother, he answers with annoyance: "Let me dream, let me dream!"; although even a certain writer of philosophical problems has theorized on this egoism of the artist

2. Manzoni, *Il cinque maggio*, ll. 19–20 (poem on the death of Napoleon).

181

written in verse; that comedy must be written in verse, but in muted tone or in prose, and must end happily; that history, unlike chronicle, adorns its narration with reflections and expounds in it the events, the passions, the thoughts of the historical characters in the form of orations and harangues.

Observations of this kind abound in the treatises that divide and subdivide metaphors, verses, strophic forms, and the forms of composition. But they, too, do all this on the basis of existing poems and literary works to which they implicitly or explicitly refer, always keeping them in mind. In our times these treatises are composed in ever-smaller number and size than in the past and they are consulted less than the grammars themselves. This is in part due to a better concept of art, which shifted the preference to the direct reading of the writers, and in part to the fact, as we have already mentioned, that the schools of rhetoric and versification have been vanishing with the corresponding social customs. But the old treatises have not completely fallen into oblivion, nor has the function they performed become altogether superfluous, although sometimes it is not executed in the grave form of the treatise, but in a light, varied, and aphoristic manner. The romantics, who denied the precepts, actually denied the ancient ones; but they formulated new ones, on the whole less estimable because less accurate and subtle. There is no writer who from time to time does not turn his attention to the relations between those abstract forms and abstract contents without learning something. One would learn something even by reopening the books of Aristotle, the pseudo-Longinus, Cicero, and Quintilian or, just to mention one of the modern Italians, that great lexicographer, grammarian, rhetorician, and, in sum, preceptist who was Niccolò Tommaseo.[3] What would one learn? To pay attention, in the work that occupies one's mind, to this or that form of expression existing

ings and concepts of meters is evident in every study of this kind. The best one can do is to smile about it, as did Carducci in *Ragioni metriche* [*Odi barbare* 2. 34], written to celebrate the shapeliness of a Roman lady:

> Scarso, o nipote di Rea, l'endecasillabo ha il passo,
> a misurare i clivi de le bellezze vostre:
> solo col pié trïonfale l'eroico esametro puote
> scander la vïa sacra de le lunate spalle. . . .
> Batta l'alcaica strofe trepidando l'ali, e si scaldi
> ai forti amori; indietro tu, settenario vile.
> Oh, su la chioma ondosa che simile a notte discende
> pel crepuscolo pario de le doriche forme
> (lasciate a le serve, nipote di Rea, gli ottonari),
> corona aurea di stelle fulga l'asclepiadea.

[*O granddaughter of Rhea, the hendecasyllable moves too slowly / to measure the declivities of your beautiful form: / only the heroic hexameter can, in triumphal step, / scan the sacred path of your crescent-shaped shoulders. . . . / That the alcaic strophe in trepidation may flap its wings, and warm / the strong love; step back, you, vile septenary. / Oh, that upon your wavy hair that falls like night / through the Parian twilight of your Doric forms / (leave to the servants, O granddaughter of Rhea, the octosyllables) / may shine the asclepiads like a golden crown of stars.*]

In this passage, though the verse has a facetious tone, there is the imagination and the accent of a poet, who, in his admiration for feminine beauty, summons up and chooses the historical meters familiar to him (which are for him living creatures), those which seem to be best suited to follow the line of the beautiful woman and to crown her forehead.

The necessity for a course in rhetoric. "Les talents les plus libres et les plus originaux ne deviennent parfaits que s'ils ont eu une discipline première, s'ils ont fait une bonne rhétorique; madame de Sévigné fit la sienne sous Ménage et sous Chapelain" (Sainte-Beuve, in an essay of 1829, reprinted as a preface to Madame de Sévigné's *Lettres choisies*, Paris, n.d.). Likewise, whatever the insufficency of scholastic and formalistic logic, it is usually recommended that one submit to its discipline in order to be able to define concepts well, to maintain a distinction among them, to set the premises, and to draw the consequences logically. Those who have not had such training are recognizable in inquiries and discussions, from the facility with which they use concepts not yet analyzed, or deform them in dealing with them, or, in reasoning, fall into passionate inconsequences.

---

3. Niccolò Tommaseo (1802–1874), Italian writer and philologist whose renown is linked to his *Dizionario dei sinonimi* (1830) and particularly to his *Dizionario della lingua italiana* (1856).

historically. To reproduce them? Certainly not; the ap-
ing which is ordinarily done is not what we have in
mind. To allow them to operate in one's mind and
predispose it in a certain way? Of course! The lack of
this practice and discipline is usually noticeable in the
works of some writers, just as, on the other hand, one
recognizes in the most free and original writers that,
at some point in the past, they had their course of
"rhétorique," as the French still say.

These "precepts" are what many refer to as "technique" and which they reccommend as necessary and
certainly useful to the writer and the artist in general.
And there would be no cause here to quarrel about
names, if in this as in other cases the choice of them
did not hide confusion and consequent false deductions and conclusions. Precepts are not techniques, for
the latter term applies more properly to the practical
modifications, the manipulations, so to speak, of matters and natural bodies in view of certain ends, such as
fixing, for preservation and communication, expressions already formed and, in our case, certain articulate sounds; in this regard we may say that we speak
of the varied "techniques of the arts." As for poetry,
"technique" will be the writing, the printing, even
the recording. All these things are of no little importance and may even rise to their particular beauty, as
when Bodoni gives a typographical dress to Greek,
Latin, Italian, and French poets.[4] The precepts, on the
contrary, not only are different from technique, but
they are not even analogous to it because they do not
furnish, as technique does, formulae to be put into
practice or prescriptions, such as when one says: "Mix
these materials and you will have oil paints, or these
and those and you will have watercolors." Since the
usefulness of precepts has been contested, or, rather,
the precepts have been repressed in their exaggerations
precisely because they pretended to formulate new
prescriptions or to become technique (which was the
legitimate reason for the exaggerated and ill-inten-
tioned romantic rebellion against them), discussion
arose as to whether technique is necessary to the poet.
Certainly, the poet has no need for technique in the
creative act of his image and expression: technique is
completely alien to this act;[5] but, on the other hand,

*The ancients and rhetoric. J. J. Burckhardt wrote in
Die Zeit Constantin's des Grossen (Leipzig, 1880, pp.
279–80): "Has not antiquity, by chance, overes-
teemed the elaboration of speaking and writing?
Would it not have done better to fill the heads of the
youths with useful knowledge? The answer is that we
do not have the right to express a judgment on the
matter as long as we ourselves are everywhere at the
mercy of the lack of form (Formlösigkeit), as long as at
least one of our writers has an inkling of the true art
of the period. Rhetoric, with its subsidiary sciences,
was for the ancients the indispensable accomplishment
of their ways of beautiful and free life, regulated by
the laws of their arts and their poetry. Life in our times
has, in some respects, higher principles and aims, but
it is uneven and in disharmony: the most beautiful
and the most delicate principle in it stands beside the
rude barbarity: the multiplicity of our affairs does not
allow us even to be scandalized about it."*

---

4. Giambattista Bodoni (1740–1813), Italian printer and typeface de-
signer, famous for the splendid editions of Greek, Latin, Italian, and
French classics. He is considered to be the father of the "modern" style of
type.
5. Croce's conception of technique met with sharp criticism, especially from the practitioners and critics of the fine arts who held opposite
views. While Croce maintains that technique (the expressive means) is
extrinsic to the creative process, they consider technique to be indispensable to artistic creation. Technique, in other words, does not intervene
after the act of creation, as Croce would have it, merely to externalize the

to ask whether the poet needs technique amounts to asking whether the painter needs coloring material and brushes, and the sculptor marble and a chisel. Even during the times of illiteracy, when poetry was transmitted orally, a technique was necessary—this was mnemonics.

The effectiveness of precepts is different from that of the esthetic law or a set of technical rules; it is the effectiveness of the historically existent, from which one must go further but without leaping over it. Such an effectiveness exercises itself not only by means of theoretical formulae, but also through men, those men of prominent character, those writers and original poets who are called masters or school leaders. No books of instructions had so many fervid readers and disciples as those of Petrarch, Boccaccio, Tasso, Manzoni, or Leopardi. The romantics themselves, individualistic only in words, followed in the footsteps of the masters, who for them were Shakespeare or Goethe, and often much lesser men—Schiller or Walter Scott or Victor Hugo; romanticism, in fact, exalted as school leaders not only the great poets but also those who mixed little poetry with much literature, or even the charlatans of some character, such as Marino.[6] But, if we consider only the school leaders, the truly poetic geniuses, such precepts (which are learned through personalities, "per exempla," and through "poetic schools" freely constituted, rather than by classroom teaching) do not operate except as reminders and exhortations that existing expressions must be superseded by new expressions. Thus the mere listeners to these reminders and exhortations contribute nothing to the living history of poetry, if for lack of personal and genial dispositions they repeat and combine mechanically or vary artifically the original words of the school founders. The stagnation resulting from this is broken, in poetry as well as in philosophy, only by the so-called unfaithful disciple, the very faithfully unfaithful pupil, the one who has something of his own to say, the only one worthy of his teacher whose power was meant to arouse power and not to promote stag-

Technique in the sense of historical tradition. Certain demands or strange pretensions can be understood only by reference to technique as "historical tradition"; such is the demand by some critics that it is necessary "to free ourselves from techniques" and that we must "be again virgin or primitive." Now, to "free oneself from technique," that is, in this sense, from history, is not possible; nor is the return to "virginity and primitivity" in contradiction to the observance of technique; this return in fact takes place with every new inspiration and creation, and is one of the two inseparable moments of the same act.

The "technical analyses". The so-called technical analyses of poetic works, which are the favorite exercise in German doctoral dissertations, accomplish nothing except to lower the poetic work to the level of an industrial product, of a mechanical object which can be disassembled, and the wheels and springs taken out to show how it is built: the introduction, the disposition, the connections, the digressions, the expedients to lengthen or to shorten, the final effect, and so on, in all the details. This procedure falsifies, in the work of calculation, the nature of poetic expression; at most one may grasp the mechanical part of the work, when there is one, but its soul always escapes. Undertaking to discover by this means the secret of beauty, these analyzers report at the end of their wearisome work information that has nothing to do with either beauty or ugliness, and is in truth completely insipid.

Founders of schools. Marino was not the only founder of a school of poetry in that century, but there were others who seemed more receptive to the growing need for "novelty," such as Giuseppe Battista and Giuseppe Artale; the former was the leader, the latter the second in command of that sort of "baroque of the baroque" which flourished in the second half of the seventeenth century: "Our captain was Battista, / our lieutenant was Artale, / against them what bravery could stand?" So said one who in his youth had shared that fanaticism (see *Saggi sulla letteratura italiana del Seicento*, 3d ed., p. 401).

---

image of the poet for practical reasons, but it is the instrument by which the artist's imagination shapes its fictional world. For a criticism of Croce's theory, see especially Alfredo Gargiulo, *Scritti d'estetica* (Florence: Le Monnier, 1952), and Gentile, *The Philosophy of Art*, pp. xlix–liv, 185–94.

6. Giambattista Marino (1569–1625), Italian poet whose *Adone* (1623) strongly impressed his contemporaries for the brilliance and consummate mastery of technique, the extravagances of its conceits and the artificial splendor of its style. The word "Marinism," which was used to characterize the epoch, has for Croce a negative meaning in art. It is for him an epoch of decadence expressed by the search for the astonishing, the exaggerated, the subtle and complicated, but which lacks real poetic feeling. The tendency took also the name of *seicentismo* and baroque; see above, chap. 3, n. 13; see also *Lirici marinisti*, ed. Croce (1910).

nation. The schools, on the other hand, led by non-poets, by persons lacking even the particular brilliant flippancy of the charlatans, rely on programs, on precepts; but they reveal their nonentity in the complete absence of any new poet, that is, of any new poetic work. Nowadays there are a great many of these sham schools, with titles, passwords, programs, special journals, and many people who stir themselves up and make a big noise. One can get rid of them with the modest request: "Show me, among the works you produced, a single poem, a beautiful poem, which flies from mouth to mouth and which I can enjoy and learn by heart, as is done with beautiful poems." But in their answer they are lavish with programs and promises for the future, "inania verba" [empty words] being unable to do anything else.

Recent poetic schools. In a work on the poetic schools in France, from symbolism to about 1910 (Florian-Parmentier, *Toute la lyre: Anthologie critique*, Paris, 1911), the author surveys about thirty: "verlibrisme," "décadisme," "magnificisme," "magisme," "paroxisme," "ésotérisme," "naturisme," "somptuarisme," "intégralisme," "robinsonisme," "néo-romantisme," "unanimisme," "primitivisme," "subjectivisme," "sincérisme," "intensisme," "futurisme" (imported from Italy), and so on. A list of this sort is enough to bring into evidence the ridiculousness of the whole thing: the ridiculousness of the schools, not only larger in number than individual poets, but also with empty programs, without a single poet.

3. The Stiffening of Literary Genres and Their Disintegration

The error of a statement, the evil of an act do not derive from what these things are in themselves, but from their presuming to be what they are not. Just as moral precepts and logical precepts were perverted—the first into juridical casuistry and the second into scholasticism, thus arousing Pascal and Galileo to rebellion—so the literary and poetic precepts degenerated into the doctrine of literary genres. The perversion consists in stiffening the historical "reminders," contained in the entries and definitions offered by dictionaries and in the schemes of grammars, books of rhetoric and poetic and literary instructions, into philosophical definitions and categories; and turning the rules, which embodied the precepts and which had by no means power of law, into absolute orders and laws. The prudent Quintilian, becoming aware of the danger, protested against "praecepta" which "plerique scriptores artium" [most of the writers on rhetoric] used to administer "quasi quasdam leges immutabili necessitate constrictas" [as though they were immutable laws by which one is by necessity circumscribed]—against what he called precepts "universalia vel perpetualia" [universal and absolute] ("katholiká"), since "raro reperitur hoc genus, ut non labefactari parte aliqua aut subrui possit" [seldom is there any kind which cannot be weakened somehow or completely shattered].[7]

The impossibility of determining the genres philosophically. A good way to touch by hand this impossibility is to examine the efforts made by Lessing for two little genres, the fable and the epigram,[51] in dissertations certainly valuable for the particular observations and judgments contained in them. The only research that can be conducted on a genre is historical in nature, dealing with the social and cultural needs which led to certain customs and usages, from which, by abstraction, the so-called genre was derived. But these are things that, strictly speaking, have nothing to do with poetry.

7. *Institutionis oratoriae* 2. 13, 14 (Croce's note).

51. The reference here is to Lessing, *Zerstreute Anmerkungen über das Epigramm* (1771).

And now because of disregard for this wise precept concerning precepts, lexicographers and grammarians elevated themselves haughtily but imprudently to the function of legislators of language as to words and connections between words to be used, and the authors of rhetorics and poetics to that of legislators of prose and poetry. And since the content of their precepts was, as we have seen, historical and since history moves and changes and does not stop on anyone's orders, they engage in litigations (armed with their absolute precepts) with the living language and free poetic creation; and they busy themselves with screaming from every corner: "Do not trespass!" "It cannot be done!" "It is forbidden!"

Such a spectacle is somewhat comical and has often been regarded as so. Those lexicographers and rhetoricians and defenders of the genres, always saying "you can and cannot," have been ridiculed as being pedants, maniacs, laughable tyrants, on whom reality always turns its back, continuing to go on its own way and ignoring their prohibitions. But the laughter and mockery only point out that something is wrong, though the error is not disposed of as long as the principle itself, which gives rise and persistence to the error, remains untouched. And errors are not only ridiculous but also troublesome, painful, and even tragic because the onlooker laughs, but he who commits them acts seriously, does badly, and causes damage. So it is in every aspect of life; and so it has happened, keeping in mind due proportions and diversity, in literature and poetry as a result of the erroneous doctrine of the literary genres.[8]

The history of poetry and the history of philosophy by genres. The history of philosophy is also dominated (often unconsciously) by the serious error of "history by genre": so, instead of studying the thought of a philosopher (if it is that of a philosopher and not of a rehearser or a compiler), ever new because born under new historical conditions which have aroused new problems, it is classified either according to genre ("spiritualism," "materialism," "idealism," "realism," "dualism," "contingentism," "positivism," and so on, or according to school (the "Platonic," the "Aristotelian," the "Cartesian," the "Kantian," the "Hegelian," and so on); and, as a result, one believes that everything has been said when a thought is given one of those nicknames which do not designate anything in particular, not even a precise historical relation, because a truly philosophical thought comprises within itself all previous thoughts (and not those of a single author) and supersedes all of them. On the subject see one of my essays in Discorsi de varia filosofia, vol. 1, pp. 107–15. But if it proved to be practically difficult and time-consuming to make people understand that only single poems, and not the poetic genres, are real, it

---

8. See Croce, *Aesthetic* (pp. 436–49), "History of the Artistic and Literary Kinds." For another point of view, see Gentile, *The Philosophy of Art*, pp. lii–liii, 197–202.

It suffices here to mention as an example the constant hindrance this doctrine has been for poets and writers to whom it forbade the use of certain words because they were foreign, dialectal, new, and in summary not recorded by the dictionaries; of certain word flexions not yet accepted by morphologies and syntaxes; of certain forms of drama or comedy or lyric conflicting with the accepted genres and the forms assigned to them. This not only undermined and discredited beautiful works, but it also afflicted the conscience of the writers and poets themselves who gave importance to those founders of rules and believed in those rules, although their direct experience ought to have convinced them otherwise (but this is one of the many cases in which having a fact before your eyes does not mean that you see or perceive it). The illusory fear of faults which they would be responsible for prompted the writers and poets, for the sake of being at peace with those implacable censors and with their own weakness of conscience, to accept their commandments, to purge their personal vocabulary of colorful elements, to reword their phrases, thus lowering their vivaciousness and mutilating or stretching the natural developments of their fancies and thoughts, in the attempt to make them coincide with the fixed schemes of the epic, the tragedy, the novel, and history. Almost all of the corrections and alterations made when *Jerusalem Delivered* was changed to *Jerusalem Conquered* and those of the same kind made by Manzoni in the second edition of *The Betrothed* in obedience to the theory, or rather the whim, of the single norm of the living Florentine language show the extrinsic character, the signs of servitude, even if this servitude is voluntary. And if, by way of speaking, one could show in the form of a graph (as is done for showing the process of fever in an organism or the movements of the earth), the preoccupations, the scruples, the remorse, the anguish, the desperation, the vain efforts, the unfair sacrifices that the literary rules have cost the poets and the writers, one would be stupefied once again at how men allow themselves to be tortured by other men over trifles and even further lend themselves with docility to self-flagellation, becoming "heautontimoroumenoi" or, as Alfieri translated it, "their own executioners." It is customary to say, in defense of this fierce pedantry, that a great deal of the strength and fineness shining in works of prose and verse are the result of it and that these qualities are not found wherever that

will be an almost desperate undertaking to persuade them that in philosophy also what really exists are the thinkers and their well-determined thoughts and that the classifications do not help either the intelligence or the judgment. It is comfortable to believe, or to pretend to believe, that one knows, when one knows nothing; and it is equally comfortable to fight and to tear down a castle built by the imagination of idle people, rather than to wrestle with the asperity of a new and true thought.

Criticism of the doctrine of literary genres. My radical rejection of the literary genres is found in my *Aesthetic* (pt. 1, chap. 4, pp. 35–38; pt. 2, chap. 19, pp. 436–49; see also *Nuovi saggi d'estetica*, 2d ed., pp. 46–49).

J. Petersen ("Zur Lehre von den Dichtungsgattungen," in *Festschrift für August Sauer*, Stuttgart, 1920, pp. 72–116) has undertaken the defense of that doctrine, maintaining its importance against me and Gundolf, who had accepted my conclusions. The reading of Petersen's apology is advised for those who feel the need to be reassured in their adverse conclusions. One may see also by the same Petersen, who is a diligent philologist and editor, the book which was called "the harvest of his scientific life," *Die Wissenschaft von der Dichtkunst* (Berlin, 1939, vol. 1), in order to assess what he had learned about poetry during his entire life as a philologist.

tyranny was not exercised and wherever the writing of prose and verse was allowed to go on at one's own pleasure. But that good result is not due to pedantry, because wickedness and stupidity as such never produced positive benefits, but rather to that bit of good esthetic criticism which combines with such pedantry sometimes in the same person. Thus, in certain cases, an archaic or exotic or dialectal word or a neologism is rejected, not really because it is archaic, exotic, dialectal, and new (if it were so there would be no work of poetry which could withstand criticism), but because the words have sounds mechanically repeated or awkwardly and improperly combined for no expressive necessity. Or a departure from customary rules is criticized, not because it is a departure (for any new prose or poetry is a departure), but because in that case it is no more than an intellectualistic prejudice against novelty for novelty's sake or an extravagance or an act of thoughtlessness. There is no reason, however, for resorting to nonsensical reasoning in order to inflict a just punishment. Moreover, after that pedantry was in a large part swept away, the same good results, and perhaps better ones, were obtained and are being obtained by virtue of the rigor of criticism, which concerns itself with individual cases; for the really exemplary punishments are always individualized.

The damage from the stiffening of the preceptual schemes has been much more visible especially in the criticism of literature, in which these schemes constituted the basis for expressions of praise and blame for a long time (at least in the general and official opinion of cultivated readers as well as in books), though they have never been able to influence the actual esthetic pleasure and displeasure, taste and distaste—which continued to manifest themselves freely, according to instances and persons, sometimes covertly, sometimes heretically. The Homeric poems, Dante's poem, the plays of Shakespeare—all of them were singled out for their major or minor sins against the rules or for ignoring the rules; and, conversely, the mediocre rhymes of so many Petrarchists and the regular epic poems by Bracciolini, Graziani, Caraccio, and the like, were approved and eulogized.[9] While the readers were carried away by irregular works and refused to read the regular ones or were yawning at them, criticism, firm in its criterion of genres, stopped its ears to the bewitching songs of the siren and attended to its high function as executor of justice in obedience to reason, unwittingly parodying Plato, who, dolefully but inflexibly

Production by genres. [Vronsky] *"had a talent for understanding art and probably, with his gift for copying, he imagined he possessed the creative powers essential for an artist. After hesitating for some time as to which style of painting to take up—religious, historical, 'genre,' or realistic—he set to work. He appreciated all the different styles and could not find inspiration in any of them, but he could not conceive that it was possible to be ignorant of the different schools of painting and to be inspired by what is within the soul, regardless of whether what is painted will belong to any recognized school. Since he did not know this, and drew his inspiration not directly from life but indirectly from other painters' interpretations of life, he found inspiration very readily and easily; and equally readily and easily produced paintings very similar to the particular style he was trying to imitate"* (*Anna Karenina*, pt. 5, chap. 8).

9. Francesco Bracciolini (1566–1645), author of *La Croce Racquistata* (1611); Girolamo Graziani (1604–1675), author of *Conquisto di Granata* (1650); Antonio Caraccio (1630–1703), author of *L'Impero vendicato* (1690).

(because this was the command of the "logos"), drove the poets out of his republic.

But, since the criticism of poetry is the history of poetry, a last consequence to be drawn—and which was drawn—from the stiffening of the genres is that the protagonist of the history of poetry is not the poetry, but the genre, and more precisely the genres. This consequence was wholly logical, because, by conceiving of them as esthetic categories, the genres become the actual creators of poetry, the real makers of its history. Thus, the history of poetry began to be expounded by genre, breaking poetic personalities and assigning the "disiecta membra" [scattered parts] to the genre to which they would belong, judging the poet on the basis of whether he had, well or badly, cultivated the genre and observed its laws. A piece of Dante or Ariosto, of Tasso or Alfieri belonged to the history of the lyric genre, another to that of satire, a third one to the epic, a fourth to that of tragedy, a fifth to that of comedy, and their whole belonged nowhere; and in these compartments each was in the company not only of other great men but also of many mediocre ones, who were perhaps more honored than the great men, because the latter, when carried away by their fancy, had dared to violate the genre, whereas the mediocre ones espoused the genre and chastely cohabited in the compartment, under the tutelage of the law and the doctrine. Subsequently, the historical exigency, which became stronger in the nineteenth century, affected also this kind of history of poetry and demanded that it conform to the concept of development, that is, of historicity. But since this request met with the strong and vigorous presence of the literary genres, which it was impossible to eject from literary histories (in which, on the contrary, they were highly respected), the concept of development was construed not as the development of poetry, but as that of the genre; and histories of the lyric and of the epic poems, of the tragedy and the comedy, of the novel were written not only of the lyric in general, but also of the ode, the elegy, the sonnet, the canzone, the madrigal, the "Lied," and so forth; and not only of the dramatic in its two fundamental forms, but of the tragicomedy, the farce, the eclogue, the pastoral, the piscatorial, the sacred representations, the lives of saints, the "autos," the melodrama, the weepy comedy, the social comedy, the thesis comedy, and so on—these histories, the genres, the subgenres, the sub-subgenres appear, rise, grow, reach the point of perfection and maturity, and then, alas, begin to get old and finally die. Just as in the sky there seem to be extinguished stars, so among the eternal categories of poetry there seem to be the "dead genre," such as the epic, which was said to have

The evolution of the genres and esthetic enjoyment. Jules Lemaître took pleasure in making fun of Brunetière, who is the advocate—as we hinted—of the history of poetry and literature treated as "evolution of genres"; Brunetière was convinced that it was impossible to judge until all the magnificent evolutionary history, which he was putting together with great pain, was properly constructed. And here are Lemaître's remarks: "*Oui, cela est beau. Mais en voici le rachat. Quelle tristesse ce doit être de ne plus pouvoir ouvrir un livre sans se souvenir de tous les autres et sans l'y comparer! . . . Cette critique-là, qui n'est qu'une idéologie, exclut presque entièrement la volupté qui naît du contact plein, naïf, et comme abandonné, avec l'oeuvre d'art*" (*Les contemporains,* vol. 6, preface).

Histories of the genres. The "history of the poetic and literary genres" is that which mostly fosters the conceitedness of the "scientists" of literature, upon whom we touched earlier; for it is evident that this history can be written by abstracting from the taste, intelli-

lost its conditions for living in modern times, and the tragedy, which was uprooted by the drama. And when there were single works irreducible to and above or outside the rules of the genres, they were considered to be heteroclitic and historically insignificant; and a work of genius which had no place in the development of the genre seemed to be a fruit out of season and therefore not to be taken into account in the great course of the history of the genre. Moreover, the perversion of idealistic philosophy into evolutionary positivism prompted a critic to apply to poetry Darwin's theory on the evolution of species;[10] being a logician, this critic imagined and carried out as far as he could a literary history in which the genres proliferated and multiplied themselves without a need for the opposite sex and fought among themselves and overpowered one another, and some of them were obliterated while some others survived the struggle for existence. All this happened, so to speak, in city streets, so that, if works composed in the seventeenth century (for instance, the letters of Madame de Sévigné, which remained unpublished for a long time) were not able to participate in the great struggle of their times, they were consequently disregarded in those histories or were transferred to the following century; this was precisely the case with the letters of Madame de Sévigné, which were published in the eighteenth century and thence began their struggle and their superior life as a genre.[11] The history "by genre" is the last among the "false histories," which we had to mention and characterize.

The criticism of this sort of historiography and of the rigid preceptive schemes and, therefore, of the literary genres (which were systematized and dialecticized and raised to the level of esthetic categories and corresponding realities), as well as the criticism of the empirical grammars elevated to the rank of philosophical grammars, and of the Academy's dictionaries claiming themselves alone to contain the words from sound stock has been too long and slow because for many centuries it limited itself to a simple criticism of the too narrow and too rigid boundaries imposed by the genres. This is noticed, as a typical case, in the criticism of Lessing, who, from the French classicistic poetics, decided to go back to the broader one of Aristotle. The battle raged, for instance, against the

gence, and judgment of poetry. It also fosters the belief we have brought into evidence that the proper object of science is the "development" (of the genre) and not the "judgment." But if modest qualities of heart and mind are required to treat the history of the "evolution of tragedy," "comedy," the "epic poem," the "chivalric poem," the "liturgical drama," the "novel," the "pastoral," the "satire," and so forth, others less common are necessary in order to understand what the poetry of a single creator of poetry consists of and to interpret it well. The same learned authors of histories of the evolution of the genres often prove very inept when they must speak of works of genius that they encounter along the way. Of this fact I cited examples, on other occasions, drawn from books by Rajna, who was celebrated for his histories of the French epic and the sources of the *Orlando Furioso*, and although rigorous, accurate, and zealous in this, he was equally superficial and puerile in his judgments on the *Orlando Furioso* and on the *Morgante*.[52]

Distorted reasoning resulting from the presupposition of the genres. One of the many examples which could be cited is the following: "Boileau a séparé les genres avec trop de précision. On est revenu aujourd'hui de leur confusion, et l'on reconnaît que leur distinction est fondée en raison. Mais il faut que ce soit la nature même qui les distingue et les maintienne, comme elle maintient à peu près les espèces animales. C'est affaire à l'expérience de montrer s'il y a des formes mixtes qui soient légitimes, c'est-à-dire viables et permanentes, etc." (Lanson, *Histoire de la littérature française*, p. 494). *This passage asserts (1) that the genres are "a natural fact": in which case they would be alien to poetry which is a spiritual act; (2) that they are founded "on reason," that is, they are logical distinctions: in which case they would not be a natural fact, nor would they have anything to do with poetry; (3) that experience shall decide whether mixed forms are legitimate, liv-*

---

10. The reference is clearly to Ferdinand Brunetière's theory of the evolution of literary genres, which applies the Darwinian doctrine to literary phenomena; see Bruntière *L'Evolution des genres*, vol. 1, *L'Evolution de la critique* (1890), and *L'Evolution de la poésie lyrique au XIXᵉ siècle* (1894).

11. Madame de Sévigné's correspondence covers the years 1671–1696. It was published in 1726, but to my knowledge no literary history treats it among the works of the eighteenth century.

52. Pio Rajna (1847–1930), Italian philologist and practioner of the "historical method" aimed at the study of sources as the best way for ascertaining literary facts. His *Le origini dell'epopea francese* (1884) gave him a European renown. In most of his works he dealt with the history of themes. The work to which Croce refers here is *Le fonti dell'Orlando Furioso* (1876).

three unities in the tragedy (of time, place, and action) in an attempt to reduce them to one, that of action; or against the rule prohibiting the run-on line in poetry in order to allow it in some cases; or against the grammatical rules derived only from very few authors and, finally, against the dictionaries founded on the so-called texts of language. Seldom is the error discovered in its principle; and, even when this was vaguely perceived, the question was not studied in depth, so deeply were the minds entrapped in the presupposition that poetry was divisible and consisted in the so-called genres. In Italy esthetics and the criticism of poetry are now completely liberated, and one can presume that there will be no new fall into that trap, except for some little stumbling because of inexperience or not enough caution. But, in the esthetics and poetics composed elsewhere, the genres still reign with almost uncontrolled power, and, in the actual criticism of poetry, if they do not have the authority of other times, their presence is strongly felt because very often the judgment to be expressed concerning the essence of a work of poetry is, by turns, replaced by the judgment and the reflection on the judgment conducted with reference to the peculiar nature of the "novel," or the "short story," or the "historical drama," or the "symbolist drama."

The other method of abstract criticism which took as a point of reference not the genre but the work of a master and judged not according to poetry but according to Virgil or Petrarch can now be considered almost completely abandoned. The only traces of it which still remain are found in the imprudent use of "literary parallels" in which, by placing two authors side by side (rather than using this approach only to bring out, through differentiation, the individuality of each), the critic ends up by looking at one from the point of view of the other and thus by distorting the one or the other, or both.

Certainly, by the flat rejection of the doctrine of literary genres, we do not reject those discreet precepts whose nature we have described and which were the foundation of the genres; and, by the flat refusal to use them in the history of poetry, we do not refuse to consider them in cultural, moral, and social history, since their rules, though esthetically arbitrary and baseless, were the expression of needs of a different nature. This explains, for instance, the restoration of the ancient genres during the Renaissance, which were meant to end the rudimentariness and rawness of the Middle Ages; this explains also, by another example, the conception of the "drame bourgeois" against the courtly tragedy, the "drame bourgeois" representing one of the aspects of the social transformation taking place dur-

ing, and permanent: this last observation would bring in, though obscurely and only by implication, the concrete work of the artist, who would combine the various genres into mixed forms. And, certainly, the artist feels and transcends his own feeling in the beautiful form which is always (so to speak) a "mixed genre," for it can be related to all genres together; in other words, it is not a genre, but an individual form, which, if it is beautiful, is thereby "legitimate," "living," and "permanent": it is the individual form itself, not the "genre."

The use of literary genres in the history of culture and moral life. On this subject I wrote an essay (see my book Poesia popolare e poesia d'arte) where I established the meaning which the proposed and defended "tragic genre" (imitated from the Greek), "comic genre" (imitated from the Greco-Roman type), "lyric genre" (imitated from Petrarch), and so on, had at the beginning of the sixteenth century and to what cultural and mental needs those genres answered, to what new poetic works they corresponded, and in what way all of them represented a real cultural, intellectual, and moral growth.

ing the eighteenth century. And the doctrine of the genres itself, insofar as it was an effort to transform them into esthetic categories, did mark a progress because it was a first effort, though badly directed, to understand poetry scientifically and philosophically; nor did the poetics in this respect precede the esthetics without reason, nor the philosophical grammars the philosophy of language.

This justice was to be done also to the doctrine of literary genres because in the whole course of this exposition we have managed always to be vigilant in order to avoid being drawn, by the necessity of our criticism and polemic, to violent, paradoxical, and unilateral conclusions; and, even where our negation was most radical, we sought to avoid, as it is said, "throwing the baby out with the bathwater." We have pointed out the dangers of philology in the re-evocation of poetry; but we have vindicated the rights of philology to the hermeneutic preparation of poetry. We have pointed out the error of the historical interpretations (in a materialistic sense) of ideal poetry; but we have also demonstrated that the esthetic interpretation is, and cannot but be, in its very act, historical. We have rejected the intervention of philosophy in the creation and re-evocation of poetry; but we have also affirmed its necessity in criticism and its usefulness, though indirect, in making it possible for genius and taste to be left free, straight, and sound. We have brought in as much as we could for a better understanding of poetry; but we have always realized that we could contribute nothing to genius and taste, which have to operate on their own. Thus, to the poet and the lover of poetry we would wish to say, at the end of these elucidations, what Virgil said to Dante:

> . . . e se' venuto in parte
> Dov'io per me più oltre non discerno.
> Tratto t'ho qui con ingegno e con arte;
> Lo tuo piacere omai prendi per duce!
> Fuor sei de l'erte vie, fuor sei de l'arte.[12]

[. . . you have come to a place/ where I can discern nothing further./ I have led you here with reason and art;/ henceforth let your pleasure be your guide!/ The steep and narrow ways are now behind you.]

12. *Purgatorio* 27. 128–32.

4. *Poetry and the Other Arts*

Out of the steep and narrow ways, then! That Virgil (that is, human Reason), who acted as a guide in the journey, was not Poetics but Esthetics, with the whole of philosophy of which it is a part. There is no problem that we have treated, no statement that we have made in this matter, which is not a general esthetic pronouncement. It is so for poetry and it is so for the other arts. The theory of individual arts with particular rules of their own (which raises the merely physical distinctions of "techniques" to the level of esthetic distinctions)[13] has been shattered with a peremptory argumentation against which no valid refutation has been so far produced. That which is fundamental in poetry and distinguishes it from the arhythmic, immediate expression and through poetry transmits it to literature is rhythm, the soul of poetic expression, and therefore the poetic expression itself, the intuition or the rhythmization of the universe, whereas thought is its systematization. And rhythm is the characteristic of each art, and it takes in each of them this or that name and in each of them follows its own roads (which are not the five defined by the theorists of the five arts, but are numberless, as numberless as the varieties of conditions in which art is produced), according to the dispositions and preparation it finds in the individual—dispositions that are sometimes for articulate sounds, sometimes for colors, or for relief, or architectonic lines, and not for an articulate sound in the abstract, but for unrhymed or rhymed discourse, for this or that mode according to the infinite possibilites of articulate sounds (there are poets who can write only in one meter and not in others, only in their dialect and not in the national language, and so on); and the same can be said of the infinite contrasts of light and shade and of the infinite shades of colors, and so on. But, when the expression is completed, when one has gone through its totality, living in it and for it, forgetting the external circumstances of one's ears, eyes, all the so-called senses, one can no longer say that it is sound or tone or color or relief or odor or taste or anything else, because it is all of these things together and none of them in particular; this explains the reason for the spontaneous disposition, in speaking of one art, to apply to it terms used in reference to other arts—the "pictorial," the "sculptural," and "architectonic," the "musical" in poetry, and conversely. Even at the moment that poetry dawns on the soul, a sort

The rhythm. Here is another definition of poetry ("poetry is rhythm") which is resolved into previous ones, but which is also apt to baffle the rehearsers of formulas. The lack and weakness of rhythm is a lack of poetry. Ermatinger (*Das dichterische Kunstwerk*, Leipzig-Berlin, 1921, p. 263) notes that "there are many lyric poets who can write splendid verses for content, language, and meter, and lack the rhythm as an inner intuitive motivation"; this means that such splendor is a false glare. I had to express some reservations concerning Pascoli's poetry (see *La Letteratura della nuova Italia*, 5th ed., vol. 4, p. 118) because of the almost constant lack of rhythm.

Occasionally one happens to observe with astonishment that few and simple words, which in themselves seem to have a prosaic and practical character, sometimes sound like very great, sometimes like very sweet, poetry, as a result of their arrangement, that is, the rhythm which links them or rather generates them.

That there is, besides the rhythm of poetry, a rhythm of prose or, rather, of literature, is something implying that literature alone, according to the theory that we have given, partakes of poetry and its spiritual law, in a way dissimilar to that of the immediate expression. Anyway, in order to mark such a difference, Goethe said that poetry must not only be "rhythmic," but also "melodic" (Annalen, on the date of 1805).

The interiority of rhythm and its universality in all the arts. The author of *On the Sublime* (chap. 39) brings close to music and the power of musical harmony the order of words, which he considers natural to man, to the soul of man, and not to man's hearing, music

---

13. See Croce, *Aesthetic* (pp. 449–58), "The Theory of the Limits of the Arts."

of initial oscillation and perplexity of the rhythm toward tone, color, figure, and speech has been felt by some poet who has analyzed himself introspectively. Whatever it may be (and illusion and fancy easily enter these very delicate analyses of the transient), that which concerns us here is the formed image and its esthetic character, which always transcends the characteristics physically determined and separated by the abstractionists of the so-called single arts.

being such as to put into motion facts, thoughts, beauty, harmonies which are within ourselves, and to transport them into others. Diderot certainly remembered this chapter when he spoke highly of the nature of rhythm: "Qu'est-ce donc que le rhythme? . . . C'est l'image même de l'âme. Le sentiment se plie de lui-même à l'infinie variété du rhythme. Ce n'est pas à l'oreille seulement, c'est à l'âme, d'où elle est émanée, que la véritable harmonie s'adresse. Ne dites pas d'un poète sec, dur et barbare, qu'il n'a pas d'oreille. Dites qu'il n'a pas d'âme" (Oeuvres, vol. 14, p. 429).

Also futile, therefore, is every effort to determine in a particular way the various rhythms, which, once detached from poetry and rendered abstract, no longer have any relation to "poeticality." And futile, strictly on the basis of theory, is the distinction itself between rhythm and rhyme; for rhythmizing is a constant rhyming, even when the rhymes are not considered to be such by the grammarians, who, on the other hand, often accept rhymes which, in reality, do not rhyme.

The germination of poetic intuition. The dramatist and critic Otto Ludwig, in a work entitled *Mein Verfassen beim poetischen Schaffen* (My way of composing in poetic creation) narrates how a drama developed in his mind: "At the outset there is a mental disposition musical in nature, which soon becomes color, then I see figures, one or more, with their own attitudes and gestures; each figure is seen for itself or in relation to another; and this is like an impression in copper of that color on paper or, to put it more exactly, like a statue of marble or a plastic group on which the sun spreads a veil of that color. This apparition of color emerges in my mind also when I read a poetic work which has struck me; if I transfer myself in a situation like that of Goethe's poetry, I have a heavy yellow-gold color which turns to brown-gold; when I read Schiller I have a radiant crimson; when I read Shakespeare, each scene is a nuance of the particular color of the whole drama. Strangely enough, that figure or that group is not ordinarily the figure of a catastrophe; often it is only a characteristic figure in some pathetic situation; but an entire series is soon linked to it, and I do not perceive at once the fable of the drama (the plot of the story), for, before and after the first perception of the situation, ever-new figures and plastico-mimetic groups emerge, until the entire drama, with all its scenes, is present in my mind" (*Werke,* ed. Schweizer, Leipzig-Vienna, vol. 3, pp. 370–73). But what should be considered impossible is the fact that a poem may be born as a result of a series of calculations and choices, as Poe tells us in regard to *The Raven* in his *Philosophy of Composition.* At most, there may be some intellective and ratiocinative interpositions as the toiling of the critic

But, if for each of the single arts (and here we can accept, to facilitate the discussion, the grouping of the arts in the five principal and traditional ones) the esthetic problems and concepts are the same, they often appear in forms and words which do not allow one to recognize their sameness at first, or they appear with a scope, an importance and an urgency greater in some than in others. What is the distinction, which has been quite fruitfully introduced in discussing painting, between the "illustrative element" and the "decorative element," if not the one in poetry between the "fable" and the "lyric," or between "structure" and "poetry"? What is the polemical assertion in disputes about music, such as that in music there are no "definite" sentiments, but only "indefinite" ones, if not the same as that about poetry—that poetry does not give images of a "historical" reality, but gives merely ideal or "human" images? What is the other controversy about "ideas" in painting or in music, if not the corresponding controversy about the ideas and "concepts" in poetry? What are the various "manners" noticed in a painter, if not the various personalities succeeding each other or alternating in the poet? (Guercino used to ask his customers whether they wanted the painting of his "first" or of his "second" manner).[14] What is the "Friend of Sandro," brilliantly excogitated by B. Berenson and whose existence is not attested to by any historian or historical document, if not the myth of that "state of mind," of that "fundamental poetic motif" of which we have already spoken and which can be expressed also by means of a number of characters physically distinct?[15] And are not the hitherto disputed pretensions of a "pure painting," without subject, without feelings, without expression, with signs which would be furnished by an unknown magic power, the very same as those we hear from the inventors of "pure poetry"? On the other hand, in the figurative and architectonic arts, the questions concerning authorship arise incomparably more frequently and in larger number than in poetry and literature (which are always helped by a tentative distribution of the works according to the physical persons of the authors); however, in the figurative and architectonic

against himself; but this serves as a preparation or liberation for the spontaneous resumption of the imaginative and creative process. Ludwig (chap. 1) also describes a fervid intellectual process, but he recognizes it to be poetically impotent. The material that we possess concerning confessions and declarations by poets in regard to the construction of their works and the mode of their poetic creation would deserve to be collected, coordinated, and subjected to examination, both critical and reconstructive, which would require, on the other hand, a great deal of wisely skeptical caution.

Illustration and decoration. It happens that one may experience in poetry the same astonishment of revelation as in painting, when, not having gone beyond the knowledge of the subject represented, all of a sudden the intimate vision of lines and colors opens before one's eyes. One may read and understand a poem without suspecting its poetic character, as though one read historical information or a newspaper article. Vittorio Alfieri, recalling a visit by Abbott Caluso in Florence and the benefit he drew from the conversation with him, expressed to the abbot "an eternal gratitude" for having "taught him how to enjoy and feel and discern the beautiful and immense variety of Virgil's verses," which "until then he had only read and understood; which meant nothing when compared with the benefit one must derive from reading a poet of such magnitude" (*Vita*, pt. 4, chap. 7). And in regard to Caluso, I find in his little-known book *Della poesia* (Turin, 1806, pp. 185–86), this anecdote in support of the difficulty of grasping poeticality beyond the materiality of things: "I remember," he writes, "a great talent who, greatest in the study of physics and little less in that of mathematics, was also, in the study of poetry, of no mean sense of value; and yet I heard him criticize the words of the sonnet 159 by Petrarch as being empty of credible feeling:

> *L'erbetta verde, e i fior di color mille*
> *sparsi sotto quell'elce antica e negra,*
> *pregan pur che il bel pié li prema o tocchi.*

[The young green grass, and the flowers in thousands of colors scattered under that old and dark holm oak, pray that the beautiful foot may press or touch them.] He asked me: 'Speaking in a nonfigurative form, what does he mean by this?' I answered: 'He says that Love at times makes a gentle soul suffer sweetly; and the poet, by expressing such an enchanting and sweet suffering, manifests the delight and power of his own love. It is true that lovers also know well that it is useless to have the grass crushed by a beautiful foot; but precisely because from the pleasure, from the de-

14. Guercino is the name given to G. F. Barbieri (1591–1666), an Italian painter whose works were greatly appreciated in his own times for their originality and particularly for their sharp contrast of light. In reference to his paintings, critics speak of his "first," "second," and "third" manner.

15. "L'amico di Sandro" is the title of an essay by Bernard Berenson (1865–1959), published in the *Gazette des Beaux-Arts* (1899); in the essay he tries to reconstruct an artistic personality from works attributed to Florentine masters.

arts, too, the search for the name of the physical person of the artist yields the way to the search for the merit and the character of the work, irrespective of the hands from which it may have come. And, in those arts, the intolerance for "schools" and "disciples" is much less noticeable than in poetry, in which the imitators were since early times scorned as "servum pecus" [servile herd][16] and mediocre poets were not tolerated and were denied every right to existence. This is mainly explained by the fact that everyone may have in his possession the printed volumes of poetic masterpieces, but, in order to adorn houses and churches and public buildings with works of the other arts, it is often necessary to settle for what the disciples and the mediocre artists can furnish. This does not mean that it would not be a good idea to prune somehow the histories of figurative and architectonic arts (which still occupy much space in the museum catalogues and in the descriptions of cities) and make more room for masterpieces and original and beautiful works, as rare in those arts as they are in poetry. But we stop here in our enumeration and demonstration of encounters and resemblances and differences, which could be very abundant and would require a special study.

sire that man feels every time he thinks of contact with his beloved, one goes on to suppose, through a great process of imagination, the same feeling, the same desire in the grass. I, therefore, consider the tercet to be wonderful.'"

More on illustration and decoration. Not so much for the sake of mentioning a precedent of today's theory but more for the sake of reasserting its justness, it is well to transcribe this passage from Madame de Staël's *De l'Allemagne* (vol. 2, chap. 32), in which the distinction is lucidly expressed: "Ceux qui n'aiment pas beaucoup la peinture en elle-même attachent une grande importance aux sujets des tableaux; ils voudraient y retrouver les impressions que produisent les scenes dramatiques; il en est de même en musique: quand on la sent faiblement, on exige qu'elle se conforme avec fidélité aux moindres nuances des paroles; mais quand elle émeut jusqu'au fond de l'âme, toute attention donnée à ce qui n'est pas elle ne serait qu'une distraction importune; et pourvu qu'il n'y ait pas d'opposition entre le poème et la musique, on s'abandonne à l'art qui doit toujours l'emporter sur tous les autres. Car la rêverie délicieuse dans laquelle il nous plonge, anéantit les pensées que les mots peuvent exprimer, et la musique réveillant en nous le sentiment de l'infini, tout ce qui tend à particulariser l'objet de la mélodie doit en diminuer l'effet" (written in 1809).

Research on authorships. See *Nuovi saggi d'estetica*, 3d ed., pp. 228–32, and what I said on the subject in *Conversazioni critiche*, 2d ed., vol. 3, pp. 180–81: "If the effort to assign the works to their legitimate authors, on which the historian of art insists so much, were to be taken, as is commonly believed, as research of a biographical nature, the reference to the real author of the work would be not only of a mediocre importance, but also of little hope. The skepsis is directed, and for good reasons, against the validity of the documents, against that of the voluntary or involuntary signs which ought to reassure the hand of the artist against so-called stylistic determinations, against the criterion of the high or low value and of the nonvalue, and so on; for, as a result of these, often a work is attributed to an author on the basis of intuition alone. But in those efforts for the determination of authorships, and in the inquiries to which sometimes they lead, and in the characteristics which along the way are brought to light, there is often something more profound involved: the search for ideal attributions, that is, for the value and quality which is characteristic of this or that artistic form in relation to the others; in other words, for the only problem of true art criticism and history."

16. Horace, *Epistles* 1. 19. 19.

I call to memory here the conversations and discussions between Friedrich Wolf and his "Friends of Art" of Weimar, in 1805, in which Wolf supported the point of view of the philologist who bases himself on documents, and Goethe and the others, though firm in their conviction that "historicity is the foundation of every judgment as well as every practical emulation," maintained that only through the contemplation of art was it possible to discern "time and place, teacher and pupil, originality and imitation, the precursors and the epigones" (Goethe, Annalen, on the date of 1805). In this there was the seed of the opposition between extrinsic historicism and intrinsic historicity, which coincides with esthetic judgment.

Authorships and falsifications. *The question of falsifications, that is, of works written in a way that leads to the belief that they belong to an author other than the real one, also takes on, in the figurative arts, an importance that it does not have in poetry and literature because it presents, in addition, the problem of the technique of imitation, more or less perfect, of the objects which serve for the inner reproduction of the esthetic image. If, by a miracle of technique, one succeeds in reproducing in a perfect manner, with all the feeling of the original touch, a beautiful painting or a statue, the original object would be left with the sentimental value of historical objects, but not a real superiority over the reproduction, which, in this case, would serve the same purpose perfectly. As for the falsifications which are variations or combinations of original works, the dilemma which arises is of a completely esthetic nature, that is, whether they are permeated by a new motif which will make new beautiful works out of them, or whether this new motif is lacking and the variation and combination is simply mechanical. This double consideration also takes place concerning works considered authentic, that is, composed without intent of false authorship. In poetry examples of falsifications, although of little importance, can be seen in the rhyme of the incunabula of our literature, in the codices of Arborea,[53] in Dantesque lyrics, and so on, or also in poems by Tasso, such as those edited by Alberti (let alone the long poems in octaves dictated in seances by the spirit of Ariosto, to among others the painter Scaramuccia,[54] in the preface of one of which it is opportunely explained that the form is mediocre because of the long obsolescence of Ariosto's*

---

53. "Codici di Arborea" were manuscripts found in Sardinia containing relics of Sardinian literature and history in antiquity and the Middle Ages. They were published in 1863, but their authenticity was questioned and a long debate ensued.

54. Luigi P. Scaramuccia (1616–1680), second-rate painter, more important for some of his writings about art and his contribution to art criticism.

spirit, which for over three centuries had ceased to versify!). In short, in figurative arts as well as in poetry, there is always the question of esthetic discernment and nothing else. If for the figurative arts the question takes a broader importance than for the other arts, it is due to the fact that the productions of figurative arts are salable, but cannot be multiplied or produced in series, and are furthermore looked after by people who know little or nothing about art, being satisfied with the assurance that the works are "authentic."

History of poetry and history of the figurative arts. "People believe that the character of the historical knowledge of poetry is to survey the works by series of schools and genres or by geographical and chronological localization. Thus there are those who believe that knowing the history of figurative arts is viewing the works grouped by schools; this is the naive belief of travelers and excursionists, holding the 'guide' in their hands and having their eyes more on the guide than on the works. But that so-called artistic knowledge is a knowledge of indexes, intermingled with many yawns, though repressed. The intelligent person knows how to isolate the work and immerse himself in it alone; the man with a true artistic sense usually goes to a museum or to a church to contemplate once more his favorite work, and in that contemplation he lives again and understands its history, the only true history which is its own. And he leaves the rest to professors who classify, to archeologists who quarrel, to guides who accompany those travelers and excursionists" (*Conversazioni critiche*, 2d ed., vol. 3, pp. 176–77).

Usefulness of special books on the single arts. Here, too, Goethe, though under the influence of the erroneous theories of Lessing, expressed a just exigency when, in noting that philosophers had subsumed the arts under the supreme concept of Art, admonished that "it was time again to take them out of the common pot and to reassign to each art, particularly painting and sculpture, its own principles." Not "its own principles," we would say, because they do not exist; but the "specific method" whose need is legitimate. His words are to be highly approved, the more so since he added: "But to do this, truly, one needs a psychology still to be invented, which accrues perhaps every year only a fraction of experience" (*Werke*, vol. 27, pp. 16–17), that is, of the real experience of art, of intimate knowledge of beautiful works, which is really what gives solidity to endeavors of this sort.

What has been said suffices to illustrate the advisability of composing theoretical books on the single arts, not for discussing particular esthetic concepts in each of them, but, on the contrary, for emphasizing in each the very concepts of esthetics ("quasi cynosura quaedam artium specialium" [as guiding stars for the various subsidiary arts], as Baumgarten put it)[17], through the diversity of terminologies, mental habits, importance and urgency, and the exemplifying material. The consideration that the lovers of poetry and its critics and historians are to a certain extent specialized and have more experience with things concerning poetry and the difficulties which it presents than with things pertaining to the other arts has led to the writing of this book by an author who has already dealt with esthetics in relation to all of the arts and who also has a great familiarity with poetry and literature, through his long and (he would hope) uncommon experience as a critic and a historian.

17. *Aesthetica*, sec. 71.

Bibliography
Index

Bibliography

The following bibliographical list contains only titles appearing in English and does not pretend to be either exhaustive or selective. For a complete bibliography since 1960, the reader may refer to L. M. Palmer and H. S. Harris, eds., *Thought, Action and Intuition* (Hildesheim-New York: Georg Olms, 1975), pp. 330–63. For bibliographical information relative to the period before 1960, the reader may consult Gian N. G. Orsini, *Benedetto Croce: Philosopher of Art and Literary Critic* (Carbondale: Southern Illinois University Press, 1961), pp. 299–367.

Ainslie, Douglas. "The Philosopher of Aesthetics." *Fortnightly Review* 92 (1909):679–788.

———. "Shakespeare and Croce." *English Review* 26 (1918):117–21.

Bergel, Lienhard. "Croce as a Critic of Goethe." *Comparative Literature* 1 (1949):349–59.

———. "Benedetto Croce (1866–1952)." *Books Abroad* 31 (1957):349–52.

———. "Benedetto Croce, Poe, and American Criticism." *Comparative Literature* 12 (1960):507 16.

———. "Vico for Our Time." *Rivista di studi crociani* 9 (1972):135–42.

Bertocci, P. A. "Croce's Aesthetics in Context." *Personalist* 38 (1957):248–59.

———. "The Development of Croce's Aesthetic." *Boston University Graduate Journal* 10 (1962):86–95, 127–39.

Biondi, Raymond. "Philology and History: A Note on Croce's Hispanism." *Rivista di studi crociani* 6 (1969): 447–50.

Blocker, H. Gene. "Another Look at Aesthetic Imagination." *Journal of Aesthetics and Art Criticism* 30 (1972):529–36.

Bosanquet, B. *Three Lectures on Aesthetic*. London: Macmillan, 1915.

———. "The Philosophy of Benedetto Croce." *Quarterly Review* 231 (1919):359–77.

———. "Croce's Aesthetics." In *Proceedings of the British Academy* 9 (1919–1920):1–28.

Brancaforte, Benito. "Benedetto Croce as Critic of Spanish Literature: Theory and Practice." *Dissertation Abstracts* 26 (1965):2744.

———. "Benedetto Croce's Changing Attitude toward the Relevance of Spanish Influence in Italy." *Italica* 44 (1967):326–43.

———. "Croce on Lope and Calderon: The Application of an Aesthetic Theory." *Symposium* 23 (1969):101–15.

———. "Benedetto Croce and the Theory of Popularism in Spanish Literature." *Hispanic Review* 38 (1970):69–79.

Brown, Merle. "Croce's Early Aesthetics: 1894–1912." *Journal of Aesthetics and Art Criticism* 22 (1963):29–41.

———. *Neo-Idealistic Aesthetics: Croce, Gentile, Collingwood*. Detroit: Wayne State University Press, 1966.

———. "The Philosopher-Critic." In *Poetic Theory/Poetic Practice*. Papers of the Midwest Modern Language Association. Edited by R. Scholes. Iowa City: Midwest Modern Language Association, 1969.

Caponigri, A. R. *History and Liberty: The Historical Writings of Benedetto Croce*. London: Routledge & Paul, 1955.

Carr, H. Wildon. *The Philosophy of Benedetto Croce*. London: Macmillan, 1917; and New York: Russell & Russell, 1969.

———. *"Time" and "History" in Contemporary Philosophy, with Special Reference to Bergson and Croce*. Reprint from *Proceedings of the British Academy*, vol. 8, 1918. 19 p.

Carritt, E. F. *The Theory of Beauty*. London: Methuen, 1914.

———. "Croce and His Aesthetic." *Mind* 62 (1953):452–64.

———. "A Reply to Dr. Patankar on 'Expression'." *British Journal of Aesthetics* 2 (1962):126–32.

Carsaniga, Giovanni. "Benedetto Croce and His Influence on Italian Thought." *Alta: University of Birmingham Review* (1967):94–102.

Carus, P. "Croce's Use of the Word 'Intuition'." *Monist* 26 (1916):312–15.

Cock, A. A. "The Aesthetics of Benedetto Croce." *Aristotelian Society*, n.s. 15 (1914–1915):164–98.

Crespi, Angelo. *Contemporary Thought of Italy*. New York: Knopf, 1926.

Croce, Benedetto. *Aesthetic as Science of Expression and General Linguistic*. Translated by D. Ainslie. London: Macmillan, 1909; and Gloucester: P. Smith, 1960.

————. *The Breviary of Aesthetics*. Translated by D. Ainslie. In *The Book of the Opening of the Rice Institute*, vol. 2 (Houston, 1912) and *Rice Institute Pamphlets* 47 (1961):1–88. Under the title *Essence of Aesthetics*, London: Heinemann, 1921; and Derby, Pa.: Arden Library, 1978.

————. *The Philosophy of Giambattista Vico*. Translated by R. G. Collingwood. London: Latimer, 1913; and New York: Russell & Russell, 1964.

————. *Historical Materialism and the Economics of Karl Marx*. Translated by C. M. Meredith. London: Latimer, 1914; and New York: Russell & Russell, 1966.

————. *What is Living and What is Dead of the Philosophy of Hegel*. Translated by D. Ainslie. London: Macmillan, 1915.

————. "Aesthetic Education." *Pitman's Encyclopaedia of Education*. London, 1915.

————. *Philosophy of the Practical: Economic and Ethic*. Translated by D. Ainslie. London: Macmillan, 1915; and New York: Biblo and Tannen, 1967.

————. *Logic as the Science of the Pure Concept*. Translated by D. Ainslie. London: Macmillan, 1917.

————. "The Character of Totality of Artistic Expression." Translated by D. Ainslie. *English Review* 26 (1918):475–86.

————. *Ariosto, Shakespeare and Corneille*. Translated by D. Ainslie. New York: Holt & Co., 1920.

————. "Literary Criticism as Philosophy." Translated by D. Ainslie. *Contemporary Review* 118 (1920):531–41.

————. *Theory and History of Historiography*. Translated by D. Ainslie. London, 1921. Published in the U.S. under the title *History, Its Theory and Practice*. New York: Harcourt, Brace & Co., 1921.

————. *The Poetry of Dante*. Translated by D. Ainslie. London: G. Allen & Unwin, 1922.

————. *Goethe*. Translated and with an Introduction by D. Ainslie. London: Methuen, 1923.

————. "The Nature of Architecture." *Architecture* 16 (1923):273–78.

————. *European Literature of the Nineteenth Century*. Translated by D. Ainslie. London: Chapman & Hall, 1924.

————. "On the Nature of Allegory." *Criterion* 3 (1925):405–12.

————. "Nationalism and Literature." *Menorah Journal* 10 (1925):428–35.

————. *An Autobiography*. Translated by R. G. Collingwood. Oxford: The Clarendon Press, 1927.

————. "The Poetry of Racine." *Dial* 84 (1928):483–88.

————. "Aesthetics." Translated by R. G. Collingwood. *Encyclopaedia Britannica*, 14th ed., 1929.

————. *A History of Italy, 1871–1915*. Translated by Cecilia M. Ady. Oxford: The Clarendon Press, 1929.

————. *The Defense of Poetry*. Translated by E. F. Carritt. Oxford: The Clarendon Press, 1933.

————. "Commedia dell'Arte." *Theatre Arts Monthly* 17 (1933):929–39.

————. "Introduction to Eighteenth-Century Aesthetics." Translated by R. G. Collingwood. *Philosophy* 9 (1934):157–67.

————. *History as the Story of Liberty*. Translated by Sylvia Sprigge. New York: Norton & Co., 1941.

————. *Politics and Morals*. Translated by S. Castiglione. New York: Philosophical Library, 1945.

————. "On the Aesthetics of Dewey." Translated by K. Gilbert. *Journal of Aesthetics and Art Criticism* 6 (1948):203–07.

————. *My Philosophy and Other Essays on the Moral and Political Problems of Our Times*. Selected by R. Klibansky and translated by E. F. Carritt. London: G. Allen & Unwin, 1949.

————. "The Condition of Criticism in Italy." Translated by F. J. Thompson. In *Johns Hopkins University: Lectures in Criticism*. New York: Pantheon Books, 1949.

————. *Croce, the King and the Allies*. Extracts from a Diary by B. C.: July 1943–June 1944. Translated by Sylvia Sprigge. New York: Norton & Co., 1950.

————. "Goethe and Germany." In *Goethe: Hommage*. New York: UNESCO, 1950.

————. "Dewey's Aesthetics and Theory of Knowledge." Translated by F. S. Simoni, *Journal of Aesthetics and Art Criticism* 11 (1952):1–6.

————. "Intuition and Expression." In *A Modern Book of Esthetics*. Edited by B. Rader. New York: Holt, Rinehart & Winston, 1960.

————. *History of Europe in the Nineteenth Century*. Translated by Henry Furst. New York: Harcourt, Brace & World, 1963.

————. "An Unknown Page from the Last Month of Hegel's Life." Translated by J. W. Hellesheim and E. Caserta. *Personalist* 45 (1964):329–353.

————. *Guide to Aesthetics*. Translated with an Introduction by Patrick Romanell. New York: Bobbs-Merrill, 1965.

————. *Philosophy, Poetry, History: An Anthology of Essays*. Translated and with an Introduction by Cecil Sprigge. London: Oxford University Press, 1966.

————. *Essays on Marx and Russia*. Selected and translated with an Introduction by A. A. de Gennaro. New York: Frederick Ungar Publishing Co., 1966.

————. *The Conduct of Life*. Translated by A. Livingston. Freeport, N.Y.: Books for Libraries, 1968.

————. *History of the Kingdom of Naples*. Edited with an Introduction by H. Stuart Hughes. Translated by Frances Frenaye. Chicago: University of Chicago Press, 1970.

De Gennaro, Angelo. "The Drama of the Aesthetics of Benedetto Croce." *The Journal of Aesthetics and Art Criticism* 15 (1956):117–21.

————. "An Approach to Benedetto Croce." *Personalist* 42 (1961):21–27.

————. *The Philosophy of Benedetto Croce: An Introduction.* New York: Philosophical Library, 1961.

————. "Croce and Marx." *Personalist* 43 (1962):466–72.

————. "Croce and Vico." *Journal of Aesthetics and Art Criticism.* 22 (1963):43–46.

————. "Croce and Hegel." *Personalist* 44 (1963):302–06.

————. "Croce and De Sanctis." *Journal of Aesthetics and Art Criticism* 23 (1964–1965):228–31.

————. "Croce and Collingwood." *Personalist* 46 (1965):193–202.

————. "Benedetto Croce and Herbert Read." *Journal of Aesthetics and Art Criticism* 26 (1968):307–10.

————. "Vico and Croce: The Genesis of Croce's Aesthetics." *Personalist* 50 (1969):508–25.

Destler, Chester McArthur. "The Crocean Origin of Becker's Historical Relativism." *History and Theory: Studies in the Philosophy of History* 9 (1970):335–42.

Dimler, G. Richard, S. J. "Creative Intuition in the Aesthetic Theories of Croce and Maritain." *New Scholasticism* 37 (1963):472–92.

Donagan, A. "The Croce-Collingwood Theory of Art." *Philosophy* 33 (1958):162–67.

————. "Collingwood's Debt to Croce." *Mind* 81 (1972):265–66.

Douglas, George. "A Reconsideration of the Dewey-Croce Exchange." *Journal of Aesthetics and Art Criticism* 28 (1970):497–504.

————. "Croce's Early Aesthetic and American Critical Theory." *Comparative Literature Studies* 7 (1970):204–15.

————. "Croce's Expression Theory of Art Revisited." *Personalist* 54 (1973):204–15.

Ducasse, C. J. *The Philosophy of Art.* New York: The Dial Press, 1929.

Ehrenpreis, Irvin. *The "Types Approach" to Literature.* New York: King's Crown Press, 1945.

Errante, Guido. "Croce's Aesthetics as Related to the Whole of His Philosophical Thought." In *Italian Culture in the Twentieth Century.* New York: Columbia University, Casa Italiana, 1952.

Gilbert, Allan. "Benedetto Croce's Poetic." *Italica* 41 (1964):150–57.

Grassi, Joseph. "Croce's Attitude Toward Present Day Political Ideologies." *Rivista di studi crociani* 8 (1971):411–24.

Gullace, Giovanni. "Gentile versus Croce: A Comparison of Two Rival Esthetic Systems." *Symposium* 11 (1957):75–91.

————. "Poetry and Literature in Croce's *La Poesia.*" *Journal of Aesthetics and Art Criticism* 19 (1961):453–61.

————. "An American Symposium on Benedetto Croce." *International Studies in Philosophy* 9 (1977):127–34.

Hall, Robert. "Sapir and Croce on Language." *American Anthropologist* 71 (1969):498–99.

Harrington, David. "Benedetto Croce's Dante Criticism: A Review." *Western Humanities Review* 19 (1965):3–17.

Harris, H. S. "Benedetto Croce." In *Encyclopedia of Philosophy*, vol. 2. New York: Macmillan and the Free Press, 1967.

————. "What is Living and What is Dead in the Philosophy of Croce?" *Dialogue* 6 (1967):399–405.

Hospers, J. "The Croce-Collingwood Theory of Art." *Philosophy* 31 (1956):291–300.

Hughes, Serge. "The Role of French Culture in the Development of Croce's Thought." Ph.D. dissertation, Princeton University, 1955.

Hughes, H. Stuart. "Benedetto Croce on the *History of the Kingdom of Naples.*" *Midway* 9 (1968):107–16.

Krieger, M. "Benedetto Croce and the Recent Poetics of Organicism." *Comparative Literature* 7 (1955):252–58.

Mastrangelo, Aida. "Benedetto Croce and the New Critics." *Studi Americani* 9 (1964):455–65.

Milburn, Myra. "Benedetto Croce's Theory of Truth: A Critical Evaluation." *Filosofia* 19 (1968):725–34.

Momigliano, Arnaldo. "Reconsidering B. Croce (1866–1952)," *Durham University Journal* 49 (1966):1–12.

Montale, Eugenio. "Lesson on Croce: Esthetics and Criticism." *Italian Quarterly* 7 (1963):48–65.

Montano, Rocco. "Crocean Influence and Historicism in Italy." *Comparative Literature Studies* 1 (1964):273–86.

Mure, G. R. "The Economic and the Moral in the Philosophy of Croce." *Rivista di studi crociani* 4 (1967):166–72.

Nahm, C. M. "The Philosophy of Artistic Expression: The Crocean Hypothesis." *Journal of Aesthetics and Art Criticism* 13 (1955):300–13.

Nardo, G. J. *The Aesthetics of Benedetto Croce: A Critical Evaluation of its Terminology and Internal Consistency.* Ann Arbor, Mich.: University Microfilms, 1957.

Newbolt, H. "The Poet and His Audience." *English Review* 25 (1917):198–214.

Ogden, Morris H. "Croce's *Aesthetic.*" *Philosophical Review* 15 (1906):653–57.

Orsini, Gian N. G. *Benedetto Croce: Philosopher of Art and Literary Critic.* Carbondale: Southern Illinois University Press, 1961.

————. "Croce as a Comparatist." In *Yearbook of Comparative and General Literature.* University of North Carolina Studies in Comparative Literature, vol. 10, 1961.

————. "Recent Accounts of Croce." *Italian Quarterly* 5 (1961):61–64.

————. "Feuerbach's Supposed Objection to Hegel." *Journal of the History of Ideas* 30 (1969):85–90.

————. "The Friends of Croce." *Italian Quarterly* 49 (1969):77–80.

Palmer, L. M., and Harris, H. S., eds. *Thought, Action and Intuition: A Symposium on the Philosophy of Benedetto Croce.* Hildesheim-New York: Georg Olms, 1975.

Patankar, R. B. "What does Croce Mean by 'Expression'?" *British Journal of Aesthetics* 2 (1962):112–25.

Pesce, Domenico. "A Note on Croce's Distinction between Poetry and Literature." *Journal of Aesthetics and Art Criticism* 13 (1953):314–15.

Piccoli, Raffaello. "Benedetto Croce's *Aesthetic.*" *Monist* 26 (1916):161–81.

————. *Benedetto Croce: An Introduction to His Philosophy.* New York: Harcourt, Brace & Co., 1922.

Pois, Robert. "Two Poles within Historicism: Croce and Meinecke." *Journal of the History of Ideas* 31 (1970):253–72.

Porter, N. "An Interpretation of Croce's Aesthetic." *Austra-*

lasian Journal of Psychology and Philosophy 7 (1929):19–36.

Potter, Stephen. "The Development of Contextualistic Aesthetics." *Antioch Review* 38 (1968):169–85.

Powell, A. E. [Mrs. E. Dodds]. *The Romantic Theory of Poetry: An Examination in the Light of Croce's Aesthetic*. London: E. Arnold & Co., 1926.

Prezzolini, Giuseppe. "Benedetto Croce: The Man and the Educator." *Cesare Barbieri Courier* 8 (1966):10–13.

Read, Sir Herbert. "The Essence of Beauty." *John O'London's Weekly*, 6 July 1961, p. 3.

Reynolds, Barbara. "Benedetto Croce." *Times* (London), 3 October 1963, p. 15.

Robertson, John Mackinnon. *Croce as Shakespearean Critic*. New York: Haskell House, 1974.

Roditi, E. "The Growth and Structure of Croce's Philosophy." *Journal of Aesthetics and Art Criticism* 2 (1942):14–29.

Romanell, P. *Croce versus Gentile: A Dialogue on Contemporary Italian Philosophy*. New York: Vanni, 1946.

———. "A Comment on Croce's and Dewey's Aesthetics." *Journal of Aesthetics and Art Criticism* 8 (1949):125–28.

———. "Romanticism and Croce's Conception of Science." *Review of Metaphysics* 9 (1956):505–14.

———. Introduction to *Guide to Aesthetics*, by Benedetto Croce. Translated by Patrick Romanell. New York: Bobbs-Merrill, 1965.

Saragat, Giuseppe. *On the Centenary of the Birth of Benedetto Croce*. New York: Istituto Italiano di Cultura, 1966.

Scaglione, Aldo. "Croce's Definition of Literary Criticism." *Journal of Aesthetics and Art Criticism* 17 (1959):447–56.

———. "Croce as a Cosmopolitan Critic." In A. Bugliani, ed., *The Two Hesperias*. Madrid: José Porrúa Turanzas, 1977.

Seerveld, Calvin G. *Benedetto Croce's Earlier Aesthetic Theories and Literary Criticism: A Critical Philosophical Look at the Development during His Rationalistic Years*. Kampen, Netherlands: J. H. Kok, 1958.

Simoni, F. S. "Benedetto Croce: A Case of International Misunderstanding." *Journal of Aesthetics and Art Criticism* 11 (1952):7–14.

Smith, J. A. *The Nature of Art*. Oxford: The Clarendon Press, 1924.

Spingarn, J. E. *Creative Criticism: Essays on the Unity of Genius and Taste*. New York: Holt & Co., 1917.

———. "The Rich Storehouse of Croce's Thought." *Dial* 64 (1918):485–86.

Sprigge, Cecil. *Benedetto Croce: The Man and the Thinker*. New Haven: Yale University Press, 1952.

———. "Benedetto Croce: Man and Thinker." In B. Croce, *Philosophy, Poetry, History: An Anthology of Essays*. Translated and with an Introduction by Cecil Sprigge. London: Oxford University Press, 1966.

Steinman, James. "Santayana and Croce: An Aesthetic Reconciliation." *Journal of Aesthetics and Art Criticism* 30 (1971):251–53.

Stenberg, T. G. "Croce and American Literary Criticism." *Sewanee Review* 33 (1925):219–23.

Struckmeyer, O. K. *Croce and Literary Criticism*. Cambridge, Eng.: R. I. Severs, 1921.

Tagliacozzo, Giorgio. "Economic Vichianism: Vico, Galiani, Croce—Economics, Economic Liberalism." In *Giambattista Vico: An International Symposium*. Edited by G. Tagliacozzo and H. V. White. Baltimore: Johns Hopkins University Press, 1969.

Tholfsen, Trygve. "What is Living in Croce's Theory of History?" *Historian* 23 (1961):288–302.

Thompson, F. S. "The Passion of His Life Was Beauty." *Roanoke Times*, 1 October 1961.

Walkley, A. B. *Pastiche and Prejudice*. London: Heinemann, 1921.

———. *Still More Prejudice*. London: Heinemann, 1925.

Wasiolek, E. "Croce and Contextualist Criticism." *Modern Philology* 57 (1959):44–54.

Wellek, René. "Benedetto Croce: Literary Critic and Historian." *Comparative Literature* 5 (1953):75–82.

White, Hayden. "The Abiding Relevance of Croce's Idea of History." *Journal of Modern History* 35 (1963):109–24.

———. "What Is Living and What Is Dead in Croce's Criticism of Vico." In *Giambattista Vico: An International Symposium*. Edited by G. Tagliacozzo and H. V. White. Baltimore: Johns Hopkins University Press, 1969.

———. "Croce and Becker: A Note on the Evidence of Influence." *History and Theory: Studies in the Philosophy of History* 10 (1971):222–27.

Wimsatt, W. K. "Croce and Art for Art's Sake." *Essays in Criticism* 6 (1956):358–60.

Wimsatt, W. K., and Brooks, C. E. *Literary Criticism: A Short History*. New York: Knopf, 1957.

Zink, Sidney. "Intuition and Externalization in Croce's *Aesthetic*." *Journal of Philosophy* 47 (1950):210–16.

Index